Politics and International Law

Making, Breaking, and Upholding Global Rules

International law shapes nearly every aspect of our lives. It affects the food we eat, the products we buy, the rights we hold, and the wars we fight. Yet international law is often believed to be the exclusive domain of well-heeled professionals with years of legal training. This text uses clear, accessible writing and contemporary political examples to explain where international law comes from, how actors decide whether to follow international law, and how international law is upheld using legal and political tools. Suitable for undergraduate and graduate students, this book is accessible to a wide audience and is written for anyone who wants to understand how global rules shape and transform international politics.

Each chapter is framed by a case study that examines a current political issue, such as the bombing of Yemen or the use of chemical weapons in Syria, encouraging students to draw connections between theoretical concepts and real-world situations. The chapters are modular and self-contained, and each is paired with multiple Supplemental Cases: edited and annotated judicial opinions. They are accompanied by ready-to-use PowerPoint slides and a testbank for instructors.

Leslie Johns is Professor of Political Science and Law at UCLA. She has published numerous scholarly articles in top peer-reviewed journals, including the *American Political Science Review, International Organization*, and *The Journal of Politics*. This book is based on over a decade of teaching undergraduate and graduate political science students at UCLA.

Politics and International Law

Making, Breaking, and Upholding Global Rules

Leslie Johns

University of California, Los Angeles

CAMBRIDGE
UNIVERSITY PRESS

CAMBRIDGE
UNIVERSITY PRESS

University Printing House, Cambridge CB2 8BS, United Kingdom

One Liberty Plaza, 20th Floor, New York, NY 10006, USA

477 Williamstown Road, Port Melbourne, VIC 3207, Australia

314–321, 3rd Floor, Plot 3, Splendor Forum, Jasola District Centre, New Delhi – 110025, India

103 Penang Road, #05–06/07, Visioncrest Commercial, Singapore 238467

Cambridge University Press is part of the University of Cambridge.

It furthers the University's mission by disseminating knowledge in the pursuit of education, learning, and research at the highest international levels of excellence.

www.cambridge.org
Information on this title: www.cambridge.org/highereducation/isbn/9781108833707
DOI: 10.1017/9781108981149

First published 2022

Printed in the United Kingdom by TJ Books Limited, Padstow Cornwall

A catalogue record for this publication is available from the British Library.

Library of Congress Cataloging-in-Publication Data
Names: Johns, Leslie Nicole, 1979- author.
Title: Politics and international law / Leslie Johns, University of California, Los Angeles
Description: Cambridge, United Kingdom ; New York, NY : Cambridge University Press, 2022. | Includes index.
Identifiers: LCCN 2021053662 (print) | LCCN 2021053663 (ebook) | ISBN 9781108833707 (hardback) | ISBN 9781108986656 (paperback) | ISBN 9781108981149 (ebook)
Subjects: LCSH: International law—Political aspects.
Classification: LCC KZ1250 .J64 2022 (print) | LCC KZ1250 (ebook) | DDC 341—dc23/eng/20211109
LC record available at https://lccn.loc.gov/2021053662
LC ebook record available at https://lccn.loc.gov/2021053663

ISBN 978-1-108-83370-7 Hardback
ISBN 978-1-108-98665-6 Paperback

Additional resources for this publication at www.cambridge.org/johns

Contents

Detailed Contents

Figures

Tables

Preface

We live in and by the law. It makes us what we are. ... We are subjects of law's empire, liegemen to its methods and ideals, bound in spirit while we debate what we must therefore do.
—Ronald Dworkin, 1986, *Law's Empire*, Harvard University Press, p. vii

International law shapes nearly every aspect of our lives.

It affects the food we eat, the products we buy, the rights we hold, and the wars we fight. Turn on the television news, browse an Internet news site, listen to talk radio—you cannot escape international law. The British Parliament votes (yet again) on how to exit the European Union. US politicians debate the rights of migrants at the US–Mexico border, and whether they should get asylum from violence in Central America. The US president orders a military strike against Iran after the downing of a US drone, then cancels it because he believes it is not a proportionate response. A heat wave in Europe prompts debates about global warming. A German company is publicly chastised for delivering chemicals to Syria that can be used to make nerve gas. Governments worldwide restrict civil rights to protect public health during a global pandemic. On any given day, the list goes on and on ...

This wasn't always so. Throughout history, political leaders crafted rules to manage their relationships. These rules appeared in both formal written agreements and informal norms about state behavior. They created order and meaning within international communities. Since rules were generally made and upheld by the most powerful states, observers often concluded that powerful states do what they please, while weak states suffer what they must. Yet in the modern era—particularly after World War II—the "international community" became truly global, and international law began to touch the everyday lives of average individuals. Today, we are all part of international law's empire, whether we want to be or not. To paraphrase philosopher Ronald Dworkin, we are bound by international law's spirit, even when we are unsure what we must do.

The broad scope and power of international law often escapes the notice of even the most educated and well-informed observer of international politics because international law is different from domestic law. It is made using different processes than domestic law, it is broken for different reasons, and it is upheld using different tools. Yet these differences between international and domestic law do not render international law meaningless. Rather, these differences require us to develop a nuanced understanding of how states and other actors make, break, and uphold international law.

This book seeks to explain and understand the ways in which international law affects our daily lives. It provides a comprehensive framework for understanding where international law comes from, how actors decide whether to follow international law, and how international law is upheld using various legal and political tools. It then introduces eight major subject areas of international law, balancing legal explanations of how law works against political understandings of why it is used. The text is supplemented throughout by real-world cases and disputes that show international law in practice.

***

On a personal note, three of my earliest memories involve international law.

One memory is buying canned tuna fish at the grocery store. As a precocious child, I chided my mother for purchasing the discount brand of canned tuna. I wanted her to buy the more expensive brands, whose packaging showed a cartoon image of a happy dolphin. In the 1980s, these images indicated that the tuna was caught with dolphin-friendly nets. I celebrated when the US passed laws to make dolphin-safe nets mandatory, then was dismayed when those laws were struck down by an international trade tribunal. As a college student, I saw photographs of people dressed in dolphin costumes, protesting the newly formed World Trade Organization at the infamous 1999 "Battle in Seattle." While I didn't fully understand the politics of what I watched, I was happy to see the dolphins get some attention.

A second memory is that international law destroyed my hair. Like most girls in the US in the 1980s, I wore my hair with feathered bangs, which were puffed-up and held in place by a generous mist of aerosol hairspray. I learned in school that chlorofluorocarbons emissions from aerosol hairspray and other consumer products were destroying the ozone layer of the atmosphere. But I still felt sad when the US joined and ratified the Montreal Protocol of 1987, taking away my beloved aerosol hairspray cans and replacing them with pump bottles that spat out wet clumps of goo. Good-bye, feathered bangs!

One final memory comes from 1990. As a child in San Antonio, Texas, almost all my classmates had close family members in the military. When Iraq invaded Kuwait in August 1990, every military family knew that its world had changed dramatically. Within days, massive numbers of troops were deployed to Saudi Arabia to begin preparing for combat. Every day in school, children arrived crying because their parents had been sent away. Weekly school drills taught us how to behave during a bombing, to lie crouched over our knees along the linoleum-tiled hallways, with our fingers interlaced around our necks. And then we waited. And we waited. And we waited. Throughout fall 1990, we were told that our troops in Saudi Arabia had to wait for permission to fight from the United Nations. And we saw US generals on television, saying that our parents would die because UN delays were allowing Saddam Hussein to better prepare his defenses for war.

Now that I am a political science professor in the US, I am often confronted by undergraduate and graduate students who believe that international law doesn't matter. When I hear such opinions, I remember the smiling dolphins, feathered bangs, and the smell of linoleum as I crouched over my knees. These are my personal reminders that international law matters, in ways that are both mundane and deeply profound. My hope is that this book causes you to reflect on the ways that international law has touched your own life, as well as how you would like it to shape your future.

Leslie Johns
July 2021

Acronyms

AB	Appellate Body
ABM	antiballistic missile
AP/I	Additional Protocol I
AP/II	Additional Protocol II
BWC	Biological Weapons Convention
CAT	Convention against Torture
CESCR	Committee on Economic, Social and Cultural Rights
CIL	customary international law
CITES	Convention on International Trade in Endangered Species
CPA	Coalition Provisional Authority
CPW	circumstance precluding wrongfulness
CTBT	Comprehensive Nuclear-Test-Ban Treaty
CVD	countervailing duty
CWC	Chemical Weapons Convention
DRC	Democratic Republic of the Congo
DSS	dispute settlement system
ECHR	European Court of Human Rights
ECOWAS	Economic Community of West African States
EEC	European Economic Community
EEZ	exclusive economic zone
EU	European Union
FDI	foreign direct investment
G7	Group of Seven
G8	Group of Eight
GATT	General Agreement on Tariffs and Trade
GCC	Gulf Cooperation Council
HRC	Human Rights Committee
IACHR	Inter-American Court of Human Rights
IC	indigenous communities
ICC	International Criminal Court
ICCPR	International Covenant on Civil and Political Rights
ICESCR	International Covenant on Economic, Social and Cultural Rights
ICJ	International Court of Justice
ICRW	International Convention for the Regulation of Whaling
ICSID	International Center for the Settlement of Investment Disputes
ICTR	International Criminal Tribunal for Rwanda

ICTY	International Criminal Tribunal for the former Yugoslavia
ILC	International Law Commission
ILO	International Labour Organization
IO	international organization
ISDS	investor–state dispute settlement
ISI	import substitution industrialization
ISIL	Islamic State of Iraq and the Levant (also called ISIS, Islamic State in Iraq and Syria, Islamic State, Daesh)
ITLOS	International Tribunal for the Law of the Sea
LRTAP	Long-Range Transboundary Air Pollution Convention
MFN	most-favored nation
MLC	*Mouvement de libération du Congo*
MNC	multinational corporation
MRM	marine resource management
NAFTA	North American Free Trade Agreement
NATO	North Atlantic Treaty Organization
NGO	non-governmental organization
NIAC	non-international armed conflict
NPT	Non-Proliferation Treaty
PCA	Permanent Court of Arbitration
PCIJ	Permanent Court of International Justice
PLO	Palestinian Liberation Organization
POW	prisoner of war
PTA	preferential trade agreements
ROPME	Regional Organization for the Protection of Marine Environment
RTS	Radio Television of Serbia
SPR	single presentation requirement
TIP	trafficking in persons
UCLA	unilaterally controlled Latino assets
UN	United Nations
UNCLOS	UN Convention on the Law of the Sea
UNFCCC	UN Framework Convention on Climate Change
UNGA	UN General Assembly
UNSC	UN Security Council
UPC	*Union des Patriotes Congolais*
VCCR	Vienna Convention on Consular Relations
VCLT	Vienna Convention on the Law of Treaties
VER	voluntary export restraint
WHO	World Health Organization
WWI	World War I
WWII	World War II

PART I
Fundamentals

1 Competing Perspectives on International Law and Politics

1.1 Case Study: Fighting Climate Change

In late 2015, almost every state in the world pledged its support for the Paris Climate Agreement. This environmental agreement declares that "climate change is a common concern of humankind" and calls upon its member states "to undertake … ambitious efforts" to limit greenhouse gas emissions.[1] The path to Paris

Figure 1.1 The Eiffel Tower shows France's support for the Paris Climate Agreement in December 2015.

wasn't easy. Environmental advocacy in the United Nations began in the 1960s and 1970s. This advocacy eventually pushed states, in 1992, to begin attending annual UN negotiations on climate change. These negotiations eventually yielded the Paris Climate Agreement.

Despite its broad aspirations, the Paris Climate Agreement imposes few constraints on states. It asks each state to make a voluntary "nationally determined contribution" to cutting emissions, acknowledging that states face "different national circumstances."[2] For example, the European Union pledged to cut its greenhouse gas emissions by at least 40 percent from its 1990 levels.[3] In contrast, New Zealand pledged to cut its emissions by only 11 percent, reflecting the fact that its 1990 levels were far lower than those of the EU. Regardless of their size, these voluntary contributions are not binding under international law.[4] These non-binding pledges allowed many politicians (including US President Barack Obama) to sign the agreement without seeking approval from their domestic legislature. Finally, the agreement does not punish member states that fall short on their voluntary contributions. States face no tangible consequences for failing to abide by their pledges.

Within developed states, the Paris Climate Agreement was hailed as a landmark achievement. Malcolm Turnbull, Prime Minister of Australia, proclaimed in 2015: "We do not doubt the implications of the science, or the scale of the challenge. But above all, we do not doubt the capacity of humanity to meet it."[5] However, many developing states were less enthusiastic, noting that the problem of climate change had been caused by other states. For example, Narendra Modi, Prime Minister of India, noted: "The prosperous still have a strong carbon footprint. And the world's billions at the bottom of the development ladder are seeking space to grow ... Climate justice demands that, with the littler carbon space we still have, developing countries should have enough room to grow."[6] While all states are affected by climate change, many developing states resent being asked to solve a problem created by powerful and rich states.

Why did diverse actors invest so much time and effort in creating an agreement that requires so little of states? Does the Paris Climate Agreement reflect the broad consensus of the entire international community, or merely the narrow preferences of powerful and rich states? Finally, will the agreement be effective in limiting greenhouse gas emissions and curbing climate change?

Answering these questions requires that we understand and address the following issues:

- *How did we get here?* How did we arrive at our modern conceptions of the international law? What major ideas and thinkers shaped the evolution of international law, and why do they still matter?
- *Who matters under international law?* Are states the only important actors in modern international law? Or can other actors—like advocacy groups, international organizations, and multinational corporations—also shape international law?
- *How does international law influence politics?* Does international law actually change political behavior? If so, how and why does law matter?

Each of these questions reflects differing conceptions about how we should study and understand international law. Scholars who focus on the historical and philosophical foundations of international law often ask: "How did we get here?" They tend to study key historical events and philosophical texts to help them understand contemporary international law. In contrast, scholars who focus on contemporary advocacy and lawmaking usually ask: "Who matters under international law?" This question is usually grounded in the belief that more actors should have access to international advocacy and lawmaking. Finally, scholars who study political science from an analytical perspective tend to ask: "How does international law influence politics?" They seek to understand when and why law matters (and when it does not). This chapter does not take a position on what is the best way to study international law. Rather it introduces different conceptual lenses that you may find useful as you learn about international law.

The chapter is organized as follows. Section 1.2 provides a historical overview of international law, emphasizing intellectual debates that affect contemporary law and politics. Section 1.3 then discusses various actors in modern international law, including states, international organizations, peoples (groups), individuals, and non-governmental organizations. Then section 1.4 focuses on competing perspectives about how international law influences politics. Finally, section 1.5 returns to the case of climate change and international law.

1.2   How Did We Get Here?

Histories of international law are driven by assumptions about who makes law and how it is upheld. They are also often culturally biased, reflecting the views of powerful states. As a result, there are a number of competing theories about where international law comes from and when in history it began. Here, we survey the competing narratives about the origins of modern international law.

Ancient Societies

Some scholars argue that international law existed at the dawn of recorded history. Ancient societies in China, Egypt, Greece, India, and Mesopotamia wrote agreements about conflict and diplomacy.[7] For example, during the Warring States Era of 481–221 B.C.E., Chinese societies created military and political alliances.[8] In ancient times, communication and travel were limited, so most legal rules were decentralized and local. They governed neighboring societies rather than a global community. Rules between Asian states were not the same as those between European states. Scholarship on ancient law documents a global history in which non-European societies made international rules.

Scholars who examine ancient sources view international law as a tool for managing routine interactions between societies. These societies were not modern states. For example, they often lacked well-defined territory over which they had effective control. Additionally, no rules governed who could make law, and who could not. It is therefore difficult to apply modern concepts—like the distinction between domestic and international law—to these ancient societies.

Accounts of ancient societies usually suggest that law was upheld by the self-interest of leaders, rather than through inherent normative force. Ancient societies were not bound by common normative structures. Agreements were therefore driven by political expediency, such as alliances against a common enemy.[9] When agreements stopped being useful, leaders had little reason to comply with them.

Middle Ages (500–1500)

Alternatively, some scholars trace the origins of international law to Western Europe in the Middle Ages. At that time, Western Europe was divided into feudal societies under the spiritual jurisdiction of the Roman Catholic Church. Many of these societies also fell under the secular jurisdiction of the Holy Roman Empire, beginning in 800. Political authority and legal obligations were based on personal pledges of loyalty by individuals (to lords, kings, etc.), which often overlapped for a piece of territory. A common challenge was therefore conflict over the allocation of economic and political power amongst multiple leaders with overlapping authority.

These overlapping economic and political claims were managed in part by **natural law**, a legal theory that claims that universal laws bind all human beings, regardless of their social context or whether they have explicitly consented. For example, many natural law theorists claim that cannibalism violates natural law because it is inherently unnatural to eat other human beings. A natural law scholar would therefore argue that cannibalism is legally prohibited everywhere in the world.

The concept of natural law comes from the writings of Aristotle, which were revived in the Middle Ages by Thomas Aquinas, a Dominican friar. Aquinas sought to reconcile Aristotle with Christian theology by arguing that natural law could be inferred by human reason. Aquinas began with assumptions about the basic needs and desires of all humans, and then applied logical reasoning to infer how natural law applied to social problems. For example, Aquinas developed theories of just war, which constrained when leaders could start wars, while other scholars wrote about conduct during war.

Other kinds of law existed during the European Middle Ages. Individuals with feudal authority often wrote agreements that were spiritually binding pledges between individuals.[10] Because these agreements were between individuals, the agreement ended when a signatory died. Additionally, economic groups developed legal rules in the Middle Ages. Traders developed commercial rules to govern transactions across communities, while seafarers in the Mediterranean and the Baltic Sea developed maritime codes.

Because modern-day states did not exist in the Middle Ages in Europe, diverse actors made international law. The lack of clear hierarchical political structures created ambiguity about who could make law and how to resolve legal disputes. For example, papal edicts in the late 1400s gave the Portuguese and Spanish Empires exclusive rights to explore the Americas. While many experts believed that these edicts were legally binding, others argued that they violated natural law and were not legally valid.[11]

How was law upheld in the Middle Ages? The common religion of Christianity gave normative force to European law. Natural law and agreements between leaders were viewed as individual commitments to God. Political leaders who broke such rules could face financial and spiritual punishment by the Roman Catholic Church. Popes also often frequently intervened in political disputes between leaders. Religion ensured that law constrained political leaders.

However, this legal system was limited: it only applied to Western Europe. Legal theorists, like the Italian scholar Bartolus, often asserted that the Holy Roman Emperor (a secular leader anointed by the Church) was the ruler of the entire world. Yet in practice, the Roman Catholic Church only controlled a small portion of the globe. For example, in other regions, the Orthodox Church and Muslim leaders had similar influence, but scholars have largely ignored their legal practices. Scholars who focus on Western Europe in the Middle Ages therefore cannot provide a global account of law, only a regional one. Additionally, some scholars object to locating the origins of international law in the European Middle Ages precisely because this law derived its normative force from religion. Such scholars argue that European rules in the Middle Ages were a moral or ethical system, rather than a legal system.

Classical Era (1500–1815)

Many accounts of international law begin with classical international law, which was developed in Western Europe in 1500–1815. The first half of the classical era was characterized by two major events. First, Portugal and Spain, the predominant naval powers, competed over territories in the Americas and Asia. This competition raised complicated legal, moral, and religious questions about the ownership of American and Asian territories, and the legal obligations of Portugal and Spain towards native peoples. Second, the Protestant Reformation eroded the political power of the Roman Catholic Church, generating religious conflicts seen in the Thirty Years War of 1618–1648.

These events shaped political authority. The Church's decline prompted new arguments that states had legal personality, duties, and rights, independent of the individuals who governed them. For example, the Italian diplomat Niccolò Machiavelli argued in his 1513 masterpiece, *The Prince*, that princes—as political leaders—were not subject to the same morality as ordinary individuals. He believed that behavior that would be unacceptable in private life, like deception, could be beneficial when it advanced state interests. Similarly, scholars such as Frenchman Jean Bodin and Englishman Thomas Hobbes argued that political leaders had legitimacy and power, independent of religious authority. Naval exploration and religious warfare also fueled growing state capacity in Western Europe: states asserted authority and developed tax bureaucracies to fund exploration and warfare.

Figure 1.2 A 1598 etching from a Spanish manuscript depicts the torture of native Americans by a Spanish man. While some Spanish scholars used religious law to justify Spain's conquest of the Americas, others used natural law to condemn Spain's treatment of native American populations.

These long-running trends in political authority are apparent in the 1648 Treaty of Westphalia, which ended religious warfare in Western Europe. As part of the peace agreement, participants agreed that each leader could choose the religion of his own territory, but could not interfere in the religion of other territories. The principle of **sovereignty** thus stipulated that political leaders have both (1) authority over the internal policies of their own territory, and (2) an obligation not to interfere in the internal policies of other territories. Since sovereignty and state capacity are key attributes of modern states, many political scientists identify the Treaty of Westphalia as the beginning of the modern international system.

During the second half of the classical era, European states developed more powerful domestic governments, allowing them to better control, tax, and regulate territory. They also used international agreements to clearly map their borders, further consolidating their sovereignty.[12] States began to claim control over maritime regions adjacent to their land, which became known as the territorial sea.[13] Finally, growing commerce expanded diplomatic contacts and agreements between European states and the Ottoman Empire, which was a Muslim society spanning southeast Europe, the Middle East, and North Africa.

As domestic government grew more powerful, many philosophers emphasized individual autonomy in a movement called the **Enlightenment**. Some of these thinkers (like John Locke and Adam Smith) focused on economic rights, while others (like Montesquieu) focused on political rights. These ideas triggered the 1789 French Revolution, in which rebels overthrew their monarch while invoking individual rights and freedom. This revolutionary zeal quickly degenerated into mass internal slaughter and conflicts with neighboring states in the guise of spreading Enlightenment ideals. The chaos of the French Revolution ultimately allowed the rise of Napoleon Bonaparte and his recurring attempts to conquer Europe, which lasted until 1815.

Throughout the classical era, international law scholars varied along an intellectual continuum.[14] Some scholars emphasized natural law, as shown in Table 1.1. Like their Middle Ages predecessors, these scholars believed that law could be inferred through human reason. Accordingly, their writings usually begin with assumptions about human desires and political authority, then make logical arguments about behavior, and finally draw conclusions about how leaders should behave. For example, the Spanish monk Francisco de Vitoria lectured in the 1530s about Spain's obligations under natural law towards native Americans. Subsequent German legal scholars, like Samuel Pufendorf and Christian Wolff, developed more comprehensive natural law theories at the international level. These writings frame international law as eternal and universal principles that apply across all states, regardless of whether states have consented to them.

Table 1.1 Competing Perspectives on International Law

Conceptual Issues	Natural Law	Voluntary Law	Communitarian Law
Who makes law?	Nature	States/humans	International community
How is law identified?	Assumptions and reasoning about human nature	States consent to rules	Common values
How is law upheld?	Normative claims	Instrumental force	Community activism
Attributes	• Universal • Eternal	• Local/regional (can vary across states) • Changeable over time	• Universal • Evolutionary
Time periods	Middle Ages; classical era	Classical era; positivist era; modern era	Modern era

Note: This table compares natural, voluntary, and communitarian law based on conceptual issues.

Other classical scholars emphasized **voluntary law**, which is man-made rules to which political leaders have consented, either explicitly or implicitly.[15] These writings describe how leaders actually behaved. For example, English scholar Richard Zouche and Dutch jurist Cornelius van Bynkershoek both catalogued state behavior on legal issues. By emphasizing agreements and state practice, they acknowledged that law can vary across states and change over time, as shown in Table 1.1.

In between these two positions, some scholars jointly invoked natural and voluntary law, including Dutchman Hugo Grotius. He was hired early in his career by the Dutch East India Company to defend its merchants after they seized a Portuguese ship. The result was a classic text in which Grotius asserted the freedom to navigate the sea under natural law, and catalogued Portuguese restrictions of this freedom. His later writings focused on the laws of war, including the claim that private actors (like the Dutch East India Company) could fight wars to remedy legal wrongs. Later scholars who balanced natural and voluntary law include Swiss scholar Emer de Vattel and German professor Georg Friedrich von Martens.

Overall, the formation of modern states—as abstract entities with legal duties and rights, and as powerful actors with territorial control—changed who made international law. Natural law scholars continued to believe that law inherently existed and was identifiable by reason. But voluntary law scholars gave states greater authority to make legal rules.

Classical scholars had competing views about why and how international law was upheld. For natural law scholars, the binding power of international law came from its normative force, although religious arguments declined over time. For voluntary law scholars, international law was a political tool that was upheld through instrumental force, including economic, military, and political power.

Given the abundance of important texts from this time, the classical era played a key role in the development of international law. Yet some critics dismiss these texts as overly focused on Western Europe. Natural law is a product of Western political thought, and scholars of voluntary law largely ignored non-European states. Interactions between European states and the Ottoman Empire, for example, had little influence on classical international law, and even less attention was paid to the interactions between non-European states.

Positivist Era (1815–1919)

International law scholars usually describe 1815–1919 as the positivist era. The term **positivism** describes modes of knowledge that emphasize observation and direct experience, as opposed to theoretical supposition. Most international law experts during the positivist era renounced natural law, focused on voluntary law, and emphasized written agreements.

In 1815, a European alliance defeated Napoleon Bonaparte and removed him from power. Afterwards, powerful states (including Austria, France, Prussia, Russia, and the UK) carefully balanced power to ensure that no state became too powerful within Europe. This balancing led to several major conflicts, including the Crimean War and the Franco-Prussian War, which were well-publicized to domestic publics.

Latin American societies began to declare and fight for their independence from European rule. These wars and subsequent economic development enticed many Europeans to invest in newly independent states like Argentina, Brazil, and Peru. Meanwhile, European states competed in Africa and Asia to build up empires in the mid- and late nineteenth century. In Africa, this process usually involved outright conquest and colonization, with European states displacing local governance. In parts of Asia—including China, Japan, and Siam (modern-day Thailand)—European states deferred somewhat to existing governments. Yet they also threatened force to coerce these governments into opening their states to European commerce and culture.[16]

These historical events were reflected in political theories of the time. Many European politicians feared the Enlightenment. A conservative backlash spread through many European states—including Austria, Prussia, and Russia—with absolutist governments asserting greater control over their subjects.[17] These governments associated Enlightenment ideals—like individual autonomy and self-determination—with rebellion against monarchy. Many political thinkers responded by reinforcing state power over individuals, and emphasizing nationalism over universalism. For example, Prussian philosopher Gottfried von Herder emphasized mankind's inherent differences, writing that "nature has not established her borders between remote lands in vain."[18] He believed that these differences implied that states should protect national values. Other scholars in the nineteenth century argued that racial and ethnic groups differed in their basic biology and intellectual capacities. These racist theories were often invoked to justify European political domination over Africa and Asia.

Historical events also influenced legal theory. One influential positivist thinker was Englishman John Austin. Austin defined law as a system of rules that were created and enforced by a supreme sovereign using sanctions. He considered other kinds of rules to be morals, rather than laws. Austin accordingly believed in voluntary law. He viewed natural law as a destructive force that threatened the stability of man-made law.[19] While Austin focused mainly on domestic law, he argued that international rules were not upheld by a central political authority, but were instead "enforced by moral sanctions: by fear on the part of nations ... of provoking general hostility, and incurring its probable evils."[20] Accordingly, Austin believed that international rules were not actually law, but rather "general opinion" about how states should behave.[21]

Many scholars disagreed with Austin's extreme positions. They believed that international law was a coherent concept, even without centralized political authority. However, these scholars mostly adhered to voluntary law, dismissing natural law's claims of universalism.[22] International law became primarily a profession, rather than an area of scholarship. Experts focused on writing treaties and representing states, rather than writing philosophical treatises about the international system.[23] Positivist texts, which summarized existing rules, were written by experts from all over the world and circulated widely in many languages.[24]

A few international law theorists argued for the primacy of nations (which are groups of individuals with a shared cultural or historical identity) over states (which are units of political governance). For example, Friedrich Carl von Savigny—part of the German historical school—argued that societies had unique historical experiences that led to differing cultural and legal values. Similarly, Giuseppe Mazzini of Genoa believed that international law bound nations with unique identities. Both scholars provided an intellectual framework for the creation of Germany and Italy as states with national identities.

While most positivist scholars emphasized that states make international law, not all states were included in this process.[25] Empire-building generated a discourse of "civilization" in which states that departed from European norms and values were viewed as lacking autonomy and equality in the international system.[26] For example, international lawyers often argued that African and Asian societies did not qualify as "states" within the international system because they were "uncivilized." Accordingly, African and Asian political leaders were routinely excluded from international conferences and denied influence over international law. As discussed in Chapter 2, this historical exclusion of Africans and Asians animated later debates in the twentieth century about how international law is made.

International lawyers in the positivist era focused on writing agreements to solve many important political problems. First, they negotiated commercial treaties that protected international trade and investment. These commercial treaties opened new ports to trade and specified the rights of foreigners who were living or traveling in foreign states. These rights were often upheld using **consular jurisdiction**, which was a separate legal system for foreigners, overseen by consular officials from the individual's home state. For example, UK nationals living in China in the late nineteenth century were subject to British (rather than Chinese) judicial institutions. These nationals usually lived in small enclaves in Chinese port cities with their own police and courts.[27] Consular jurisdiction reflected the prejudiced European belief that Chinese institutions should not have authority over "civilized" Europeans.

Second, the expansion of international commerce and travel fueled international law. International lawyers developed copyright and patent rules to protect

Figure 1.3 The cover of the French publication, *Le Petit Journal*, from November 19, 1911 reads: "France will be able to freely bring civilization, wealth, and peace to Morocco." The cover image shows an allegorical figure of France bringing books and gold coins to natives. In the upper right corner, a European soldier provides military instruction to a native. This image represents the discourse of "civilization" that motivated many Europeans to promote international law in the nineteenth and early twentieth century.

intellectual property. They also wrote rules for international mail delivery, telegraph communication, and railway services, and created international organizations like the International Telegraph Union. Growth in international commerce and travel also led to the development of **private international law**, which governs private relationships across states, including business contracts, marriages, and wills.[28]

Third, international lawyers wrote rules for armed conflicts. States in the positivist era believed that they could fight wars for any reason. Yet public awareness of destructive wars grew throughout the nineteenth century. Humanitarians, like Clara Barton, Henry Dunant, and Florence Nightingale, channeled this awareness into public activism.[29] Numerous international agreements from the positivist era limit the means and methods of fighting wars.

Finally, international lawyers promoted **arbitration**, which is a process in which one or more individuals decide a dispute based on evidence and arguments.[30] Arbitrators were sometimes political leaders who were not required to decide disputes based upon law or to provide reasoned explanations for their decisions. However, international arbitration became an increasingly legalized process during the positivist era.[31] States agreed in 1899 to create an international organization called the Permanent Court of Arbitration. Despite its name, this organization is not actually a court because it does not have a sitting body of judges who decide legal questions. Instead, it provides resources for arbitration and continues to oversee modern international disputes.

Modern Era (1919–present)

World War I generated massive deaths and economic costs for its participants. The 1919 victory of the Allied Powers (including France, Japan, Russia, the UK, and the US) over the Central Powers (including Austria-Hungary, Germany, and the Ottoman Empire) marked a transformation in the international system. WWI peace agreements required huge reparations and territorial transfers. Allied Powers demanded that Central Powers surrender their colonies to Allied control. They also created a new international organization called the **League of Nations** in 1920, to promote "international peace and security … by the firm establishment of … international law."[32] To achieve this goal, the League included rules and institutions to limit future international wars. It also monitored the treatment of minority populations under the WWI peace agreements and oversaw the colonial administration of former Central Powers territories, planting the seed for future decolonization.[33] Finally, it established the first international court to adjudicate international disputes: the Permanent Court of International Justice.[34] This court heard dozens of important cases in the 1920s and 1930s, shaping the development of international law.

The League ultimately failed to achieve international peace. The US refused to join, depriving the League of important political support. Meanwhile, many states launched expansionist wars, like Japan's 1931 invasion of Manchuria and Italy's 1935 invasion of Ethiopia. Observers criticized the League for failing to prevent these wars and punish the states that initiated them. Additionally, the rise of European fascism allowed the persecution of minority groups, particularly Jews. While some minority groups were under League protection, the broader persecution of

Jews challenged the League's legitimacy in protecting minorities and refugees.[35] By the late 1930s, the League had become politically irrelevant.

World War II prompted states to renew their support for an international organization devoted to peace and security. In 1945, states created the **United Nations**, whose main objective was "to maintain international peace and security."[36] Like the League, the UN limits war and created rules and institutions for the "progressive development towards self-government" of colonial territories.[37] Finally, the UN system includes the International Court of Justice (ICJ), the successor to the Permanent Court of International Justice. The ICJ remains an important modern-day court that adjudicates international disputes.[38] Outside of the UN, states created other international organizations to promote economic development.

After WWII, European states turned inward and rebuilt their domestic economies and societies. They slowly gave up colonial territories in the 1950s to 1970s, leading to an influx of new states from Africa and Asia into the UN. Meanwhile, the US and USSR became dominant rival powers. The US was a democracy with a capitalist economy, while the USSR was an autocracy with a state-controlled economy. Yet both tried to impose their values on other states, and each viewed the other as a threat to their own security. Accordingly, most states fell into one of three groups:

- First World: states that supported the US, which were mostly in North America, Western Europe, and East Asia;
- Second World: states that supported the USSR, which were mostly in Eastern Europe and North and Central Asia; and
- Third World: states that refused to consistently support either side, which were mostly in Africa, South Asia, and Latin America.

The US and USSR never directly fought against each other, leading historians to characterize the period 1945–1989 as the **Cold War**. Yet the US and USSR faced periodic crises in places like Berlin, Cuba, Czechoslovakia, and Hungary. They also frequently fueled internal conflicts in Third World states, like Angola and Nicaragua. Overall, Cold War tensions influenced important debates over international law.

After the collapse of the USSR in 1989, international law and politics changed dramatically. Russia took over the USSR's position in the UN and initially cooperated with the US in many areas, including election monitoring and peacekeeping. Broad support for democracy and individual rights suggested to many observers that states in 1989 had reached "the end-point of mankind's ideological evolution and the universalization of Western liberal democracy."[39] Additionally, broad support for **globalization**—the increased movement of goods, investment, and people across borders—triggered a new era of economic cooperation.

However, this optimism about democratic and economic convergence ultimately faded. Russia slowly transitioned back to autocratic rule, and the end of the Cold War allowed local tensions to rise, causing mass violence in places like Rwanda and Yugoslavia. The 1990s also saw a surge in transnational terrorism, which rose to public attention with the 2001 attacks in the US and subsequent attacks worldwide. Many states responded to these attacks by fighting wars in Afghanistan and Iraq, assisting civil conflicts in Libya and Syria, and restricting individual rights at home.

In the economic realm, globalization created new challenges for states. For example, China's entry into the World Trade Organization triggered many trade disputes, in part because its economic and political systems do not match those of the states that designed the international trade regime.[40] Additionally, the 2008 global financial crisis, which spread through economic connections across states, caused a domestic backlash against globalization.[41] The rise of Donald Trump in the US reflects a broader resurgence of nationalism in many parts of the world.

Political events after 1919 were reflected in political theory. The rise of fascism and the brutality of the Holocaust caused many political theorists to examine the survival of democracy. For example, Jewish philosopher Hannah Arendt was born in Germany, but fled to France and the US to escape anti-Semitism. She later worked as a journalist during Israel's 1961 trial of Adolf Eichmann, a Nazi official who facilitated the Holocaust. In some of her writings, Arendt examined how politicians used law and bureaucracy to suppress individual freedom.[42] She argued that evil acts were often driven by a desire for legal order and social belonging, rather than individual malice, and believed that an unthinking adherence to law could lead to immorality.[43]

Similarly, many intellectuals in the mid-twentieth century questioned whether democracy was consistent with justice. Fascism and the Holocaust suggested that democracy allowed majority populations to commit profound injustice toward minorities. Philosopher John Rawls suggested that principles of justice should be chosen from behind a theoretical "veil of ignorance"—that is, basic rights should be decided before individuals know their particular circumstances and preferences.[44] Rawls believed that legal principles should come not from the acts of self-interested individuals, but rather through abstract reasoning about how a state should be designed to promote liberty for all.

Relatedly, German philosopher Jürgen Habermas wrote extensively on deliberation and communication in politics. He believed that law was only legitimate when individuals had autonomy to preserve their own varying interests, and when they believed themselves to be creators of law.[45] While Habermas focused primarily on domestic deliberation, he believed that individual freedoms required a global order that enabled deliberation by individuals and non-governmental organizations.[46]

Figure 1.4 A photograph from April 1945 shows prisoners in the Buchenwald Concentration Camp shortly after their liberation by the Allies. Images like these caused many activists and scholars to argue that community values should trump man-made laws, such as the German laws that enabled the persecution of Jews and other minorities in the 1930s and 1940s.

Political events after 1919 also affected legal theory. Many legal theorists agreed with John Austin's conception of law as rules backed by sanctions. However, they disagreed with Austin's claim that legal authority came from an absolute sovereign. Instead, they identified alternative sources of legal authority. Austrian Hans Kelsen—who founded the Vienna School of jurisprudence—argued that law's authority came from a basic norm that "we ought to behave in the way that our fellow men usually behave and during a certain period of time used to behave."[47] Similarly, US scholar H.L.A. Hart argued that legal authority comes from social custom.[48] Unlike Austin, who provided a top-down argument in which law is created by sovereigns, Kelsen and Hart suggested a bottom-up account of lawmaking, in which societies determine what is law. Their arguments imply that legislative acts or executive decrees can be invalid if they contradict society's understanding of law.

Most international law experts continued to emphasize voluntary law in the early modern era. Voluntary law was particularly compelling to the USSR and newly independent states.[49] These states tried to preserve their sovereignty by emphasizing state consent in making international law. However, a growing number of experts began to challenge voluntary law. They sought "to sever the law from the state ideologically, with the higher dignity in the law. The role of the state in the formation of the law came therefore to be belittled in one way or another."[50]

The dominant challenge to voluntary law came from legal experts who argue that states belong to an **international community**, which is a group of global actors with legal interests and personality, independent of its members. This community includes individuals, international organizations, states, and other diverse actors. Experts from diverse global backgrounds have examined how the international community affects international law.[51] Some experts argue that the international community generates social relationships and understandings that shape international law. Others believe that the international community has a collective conscience or "general sense of justice" that mimics the role of natural law.[52] Still others believe that the international community determines the content of an unwritten constitution, which has higher authority than contractual agreements between states.

These arguments suggest an alternative to voluntary law, which we call **communitarian law**.[53] Communitarian scholars usually argue that the international community's "general collective interest takes precedence over the myriad parochial individual concerns."[54] Generally, these interests are expressed as abstract values like consensus, fairness, and justice.[55] These values are universal (because they apply to all states) and evolutionary (because they can change over time). Supporters of communitarian law believe that these values can override state consent and create legal obligations. Unlike voluntary law, which emphasizes state consent, communitarian law can be shaped by individuals, international organizations, and other non-state actors.

1.3 Who Matters in International Law?

International law creates both **duties**—which are obligations to behave in certain ways—and **rights**—which are entitlements to behave or be treated in certain ways. But who exactly has duties and rights under international law? The answer to this question has changed over time, based on evolving approaches to international law. Some important actors in contemporary international law include states, international organizations, peoples (groups), individuals, and non-governmental organizations. We discuss each of these actors in turn.

States

As modern states developed, political philosophers created theories of government in which states are autonomous entities with legal personalities. By the time of the positivist era, experts believed that international law only created duties and rights for states.[56] Yet not all states were equal under international law during the positivist era. European states in the nineteenth century generally excluded "uncivilized" societies, usually in Africa and Asia, from lawmaking. They believed that societies had to accept European norms and values to qualify as states under international law.

In the modern era, the criteria for statehood gradually evolved. Under contemporary international law, a **state** is an entity with:

a. a permanent population;
b. a defined territory;
c. government; and
d. capacity to enter into relations with the other states.[57]

Despite these clear criteria, experts sometimes still disagree about what qualifies as a state.

Consider the modern Palestinian Authority.[58] This organization was created in 1994, after the Oslo Accords between Israel and the Palestinian Liberation Organization, a political movement that represents the Palestinian people. The Palestinian Authority claims authority over the West Bank and Gaza Strip in the Middle East. While Israel and the Palestinian Authority do not agree on their precise borders, the Palestinian Authority has maintained control over a permanent population and territory since 1994. It also has a government that can enter into relationships with other states.

In 1994, the Palestinian Authority began an ambitious program to be recognized as a state under international law. It sought and received formal recognition from many UN members, including most states in Africa, Asia, the Middle East, and South America. It also joined many international treaties and organizations, including the Arab League and the Organization of Islamic Cooperation. However, many states—including Israel, France, the UK, and the US—refuse to recognize the Palestinian Authority as a state and oppose its membership in the United Nations, an important symbol of statehood. They believe that Palestine must negotiate a peace agreement that resolves its border dispute with Israel before it can become a state. Ambiguity about Palestinian statehood has led to ambiguity about its legal duties and rights. For example, legal experts debate whether the International Criminal Court can prosecute war crimes allegedly committed on Palestinian territory.

The Palestinian Authority's situation is relatively rare. Numerous states joined the UN in the early 1990s after the fall of the Soviet Union, including Armenia, Estonia, and Turkmenistan. Similarly, the breakup of Yugoslavia in the 1990s led to the admission of new states like Croatia, Serbia, and Slovenia. Other recent UN members include Timor-Leste and South Sudan, which secured independence from Indonesia and Sudan, respectively.

International Organizations

In the modern era, states use institutions—like the African Union and the United Nations—to make and uphold international law. But do these institutions have legal duties and rights, independent of their member states? Under modern international law, an **international organization** (IO) is "an organization established by a treaty or other instrument governed by international law and possessing its own international legal personality."[59] Ideally, an institution's founding treaty will specify whether the institution has legal personality as an IO.[60] However, sometimes these treaties are unclear.

For example, after the United Nations was created, states were initially uncertain about the legal status of UN employees because the UN Charter did not articulate the duties and rights of the UN itself. One specific question was: could the UN sue a state that harmed a UN employee? When asked this question, the ICJ argued that the UN should have duties and rights that are necessary to achieve its purpose. It wrote:

> Whereas a state possesses the totality of international rights and duties recognized by international law, the rights and duties of an entity such as the organization must depend upon its purposes and functions as specified or implied in its constituent documents and developed in practice.[61]

This reasoning suggests that experts should use a functionalist lens to analyze the duties and rights of international organizations. Namely, they should ask: what functions did states give to the organization? Then they should ask: what duties and rights would help the organization to achieve its functions?

The duties and rights of IOs is an important contemporary issue because of UN peacekeeping operations in places like Bosnia, Haiti, and Liberia. States often provide troops and equipment to operations that are approved by the UN Security Council. However, these troops remain under the command of states; they do not receive direct orders from the UN. It is therefore unclear whether the UN is legally responsible for misconduct by these troops. During the 1990s conflict in Bosnia, investigators revealed widespread involvement by UN peacekeepers in sex trafficking.[62] More recently, investigators documented sexual abuse of children and women by UN peacekeepers, who demanded sex in exchange for food, jobs, and money.[63]

Because the UN is not a state, it initially argued that it is not governed by the laws of armed conflict. This position softened with time, and the UN agreed in 1999 to special rules for armed conflict, which continue to evolve.[64] However, states that host and provide peacekeeping troops are often unable or unwilling to prosecute UN peacekeeping troops for sexual abuse.[65] Should the UN be responsible for such violations? Under the ICJ's reasoning, legal responsibility for sexual abuse by UN peacekeepers is unlikely to help the UN achieve its functions.

But should other criteria create UN responsibility? International law continues to evolve as states develop new frameworks for the legal responsibility of IOs.[66]

Peoples (Groups)

One important debate in modern international law is: do people (or groups) have duties and rights, independently of individuals? International law does not define the term "people," but many experts use the term **people** to describe individuals who live in a common cultural, ethnic, national, or racial community, including minority and indigenous groups. Recall that during the positivist era, some scholars believed that international law applied to nations, which are groups with a shared cultural or historical identity, rather than states. Similarly, after World War I, many peace agreements required the protection of minority groups, like Jews, in Germany and Poland. These agreements suggested that groups could have rights. Yet after World War II, most human rights discourse focused on individuals. The exception to this pattern was the right of self-determination, which was included in human rights agreements from the mid-1960s.[67]

At that time, self-determination was related to decolonization. States believed "that it was obligatory to bring forward dependent peoples to independence if they so chose."[68] Since these dependent peoples were not yet states, the obligation to grant independence suggested that international law included group rights. However, after these territories became independent, many newly independent states feared that claims to self-determination by minority groups would lead to "fragmentation of new nation states, with ethnic groups in one country seeking to secede or to join with the same ethnic groups in another country."[69] This political threat continues today. For example, do the people of Catalonia and Scotland have an international right to become independent from Spain and the UK, respectively? Are separatist movements in Azerbaijan, China, India, and Indonesia legitimate attempts to claim group rights? These disputes raise tensions between claims of self-determination and the territorial integrity of states.

Most treaties manage this tension by emphasizing individuals, rather than groups. Sometimes the difference between individuals and groups does not matter. For example, an individual right to practice a religion or speak a language also protects the related religious and linguistic groups. However, when a possible legal violation involves only a group (and not an individual), individual rights may not protect groups. For example, the Lubicon Lake Band, an indigenous people in Canada, argued in the 1980s that the Alberta government violated international law when it seized their land.[70] Because the Band held property collectively, the group argued that its right to self-determination had been violated. The Band accordingly filed a complaint against Canada at the UN's Human Rights Committee. However, the Committee refused to consider the issue of self-determination because it reasoned that it could only consider individual rights.[71]

The African human rights system provides an alternative approach by explicitly protecting groups. The African Charter on Human and Peoples' Rights (1981) says:

> All peoples ... shall freely determine their political status ...[72]
>
> All peoples shall freely dispose of their wealth and natural resources. This right shall be exercised in the exclusive interest of the people ...[73]
>
> All peoples shall have the right to their economic, social and cultural development with due regard to their freedom and identity ...[74]

These legal provisions create group rights, although the Charter does not define how a group of individuals can qualify as a "people."

One perspective is that "peoples" refers to the entire population of a state, rather than distinct subpopulations. For example, the Nigerian government agreed to hold a presidential election in 1993. The election was closely monitored by neutral observers to ensure that it was free and fair. When the government was displeased by the outcome, it annulled the election and prohibited Nigerian domestic courts from intervening. Human rights organizations quickly complained to the African Commission on Human and Peoples' Rights, arguing that Nigeria violated the collective right of all Nigerian citizens to "freely determine their political status."[75] The African Commission agreed, writing:

> The right of a people to determine their "political status" can be interpreted as involving the right of Nigerians to be able to choose freely those persons or party that will govern them ...
>
> The election at issue here ... was an exercise of the right of Nigerians to freely determine this political status. The subsequent annulment of the results by the authority in power is a violation of this right of the Nigerian people.[76]

This decision suggests that "peoples" refers to all citizens.

An alternative perspective is that "peoples" refers to subpopulations with unique identities. For example, the Endorois people lived near Lake Bogoria (in modern-day Kenya) for centuries.[77] Their land was held collectively, rather than owned by individual members of the tribe. In the 1970s, Kenya evicted the Endorois people to build a national game reserve. Kenya later leased mining rights and resold part of this land to third parties.[78] After decades of trying to secure compensation, the Endorois people filed a complaint at the African Commission on Human and Peoples' Rights. They alleged numerous violations of group rights, including the right to "freely dispose of their wealth and natural resources" and the right to "development."[79] In its written decision, the African Commission supported the Endorois's claim to be a legally protected "people," and found that Kenya had violated group human rights.[80]

Individuals

Modern international law clearly applies to individuals. However, this was not always true. During the classical and positivist eras, states often wrote agreements with treatment standards for nationals in foreign states, like the right to practice Christianity or seek consular assistance. These agreements were usually demanded by European states that wanted to protect their nationals in societies with different norms, like China, Japan, and the Ottoman Empire. However, these treatment standards were considered the rights of states, rather than of individuals.[81] If individuals believed that they had been mistreated by a foreign state, they had to seek diplomatic protection from their home state. For example, foreign investors who gave loans to newly independent Latin American states in the 1800s often asked their home states to intervene if the loans were not repaid.

The human rights movement after World War II fundamentally changed the status of individuals under international law. Multilateral and regional human rights treaties outlined numerous individual rights under international law. Additionally, these treaties created legal remedies for individuals who believed their rights were violated. At the multilateral level, individuals can file complaints at UN bodies that oversee treaty compliance. At the regional level, individuals can file lawsuits at the African Court on Human and Peoples' Rights, the European Court of Human Rights, and the Inter-American Court of Human Rights.

Similarly, states have expanded individual rights under international investment law. Modern investment treaties create extensive rights that protect investors from expropriation and other ill-treatment. If individuals believe that their rights have been violated by a foreign state, they can usually initiate international arbitration. Such arbitration cases are filed at numerous venues, including the Permanent Court of Arbitration and the International Center for the Settlement of Investment Disputes.

Even areas of international law that have traditionally applied only to states have sometimes been interpreted as creating individual rights. From 1998 to 2004, many states sued the US for violating the Vienna Convention on Consular Relations. This treaty allows states to create consulates so that their nationals can seek assistance while living or traveling abroad. US authorities had arrested numerous foreign nationals for committing serious crimes in the US. These individuals were imprisoned, prosecuted, and sentenced to death. Throughout this process, they were not informed by US authorities that they could contact their consulate to seek assistance. Numerous states argued that the US had violated Article 36 of the Convention, which required the US to "inform a [foreign] national ... without delay of his or her right to inform the consular post of his home state of his arrest or detention."[82]

The US acknowledged that it had broken international law, but argued that it had only violated state rights because it believed that the Convention did not create individual rights.[83] The US highlighted the Convention's preamble, which says that "the purpose of [consular] privileges and immunities is not to benefit individuals but to ensure the efficient performance of functions by consular posts on behalf of their respective states." Nonetheless, the ICJ ruled that Article 36's reference to "his or her right" meant that the treaty created individual rights.[84]

Non-Governmental Organizations

Finally, modern international law is often shaped by **non-governmental organizations** (NGOs), which are organizations that operate independently of states to achieve political objectives. These NGOs are conscious creations of individuals who share common preferences over political outcomes. Many NGOs in international politics are **advocacy groups**. These non-profit groups promote aspirational collective values, like human rights and environmental protection. Examples include:

- Amnesty International: a human rights group based in the UK;
- Committee to Protect Journalists: a human rights group based in the US;
- Greenpeace: an environmental group based in the Netherlands; and
- International Committee of the Red Cross: a humanitarian group based in Switzerland.

All of these advocacy groups influence international politics by helping to make and uphold international law. For example, Amnesty International and the Committee to Protect Journalists monitor state compliance with human rights agreements and provide legal assistance when these agreements are violated. Similarly, Greenpeace pressured states to join the Paris Climate Agreement. Finally, the International Committee of the Red Cross helped write many treaties that regulate armed conflict.

Other NGOs include **multinational corporations** (MNCs), which are profit-seeking groups that conduct business in multiple states. MNCs often lobby governments for more favorable international investment and trade agreements. They can also file arbitration cases against foreign governments if they believe that their investment rights have been violated. MNCs often use industry associations—like the International Chamber of Commerce, the International Tobacco Growers' Association, and the World Coal Association—to represent them at venues like the World Health Organization and the United Nations.[85]

In international trade, only states can file disputes with the World Trade Organization. Yet MNCs and industry associations often pressure governments to enforce international trade rules. For example, industry associations in Canada, the EU, and the US coordinated litigation in the 1990s against Korean alcohol tariffs.[86] Similarly, Nike, a shoe manufacturer, pressured the US to sue Argentina when it restricted footwear imports in 1997.[87] MNCs and industry associations can provide economic information and financial resources for litigation.[88]

Finally, NGOs can include **armed opposition groups**, which are non-state actors that fight to achieve political goals. Most modern wars take place within states, rather than between states. While international law clearly constrains states during interstate wars, few treaties explicitly address internal conflicts. Experts often debate which rules apply to internal conflicts between government forces and armed opposition groups. These armed opposition groups cannot join treaties because they are not states, but they often voluntarily pledge to comply with international law to gain support from domestic and international audiences.[89] Should these armed opposition groups be allowed to participate in the future development of international law? Participation would grant them legitimacy that is traditionally reserved for states, but excluding them limits the legitimacy of international law.

1.4   How Does International Law Influence Politics?

This book describes how states make, break, and uphold international law. But this subject is only worthy of study if we first believe that international law actually matters. And any attempt to assess *whether* law matters requires that we have a theory about *why* law matters. Theories of international law posit many different ways in which law may (or may not) influence politics. We classify these diverse theories into three groups: the critical, contractual, and sociological perspectives.

Critical Perspective

Scholars who adopt a critical perspective doubt whether international law has an independent causal impact on politics. Some critical scholars argue that states routinely violate international law, suggesting that law has no impact on state behavior. Yet it is a truism that "almost all nations observe almost all principles of international law and almost all of their obligations almost all of the time."[90] International law violations draw scrutiny and condemnation; routine compliance does not.

More sophisticated critiques of international law posit that any impact of law on politics is caused by selection effects. First, they argue that because states negotiate agreements, states can write rules that impose minimal or no constraints.[91] Second, they argue that if a state joins an agreement, this indicates that it supports the treaty and may have followed the treaty's rules, even if the agreement did not exist. Finally, they argue that even when rules aren't written in an agreement, international norms may be caused by coinciding interests, rather than legal obligations.[92]

For example, most states belong to the Non-Proliferation Treaty, which aims to prevent the spread of nuclear weapons. Some experts believe that this treaty is very important and successful because few states possess nuclear weapons. Yet many critics believe that states joined the treaty because they did not want nuclear weapons, which are expensive and dangerous. Therefore, the treaty may simply reflect how states would have behaved in the absence of law—compliance with the treaty does not imply that it has changed state behavior.

The critical perspective also emphasizes that international law is often ambiguous, making it vulnerable to manipulation. International law can often justify multiple different outcomes.[93] States may therefore use law to justify actions that serve their interests. Rather than constraining states, law may enable states by allowing them to cloak political decisions in legal rhetoric.[94]

For example, the 1945 UN Charter prohibits "the threat or use of force."[95] The UN Charter only allows force in self-defense or with UN Security Council authorization. Throughout the 1990s, multiple conflicts tore apart Yugoslavia, a multiethnic state in southeastern Europe. Kosovo was a small territory that was part of Serbia, a Yugoslavian region, but Kosovo's population was mostly ethnic Albanian (not Serbian). By 1998, military intelligence suggested that Serbia was planning an ethnic cleansing of Kosovo, but the UN Security Council refused to authorize conflict. Members of the North Atlantic Treaty Organization (NATO) ultimately acted independently by bombing Kosovo in 1999 to prevent the ethnic cleansing. No provision of the UN Charter says that humanitarian intervention is legal, but supporters of the intervention argued that international law includes an unwritten responsibility to protect, and that severe human rights violations (like ethnic cleansing) can make force legal.

One final critical perspective views law as a reflection of economic and political power. Powerful states may be able to use rewards and/or threats to coerce weak states into accepting and complying with their preferred rules.[96] International law may therefore be based on economic and military power, rather than genuine consent between states.

For example, recall that Portugal and Spain were the dominant maritime powers in the fifteenth century. They divided the world's oceans between themselves and declared that international law mandated a *mare clausum* (or "closed sea")—other states were not permitted to travel through the world's oceans without Portuguese or Spanish permission. When the Netherlands became a naval power, it argued that international law required a *mare liberum* (or "open sea"), in which all states could sail through the high seas. Changing legal doctrines were thus caused by changes in military power.[97]

Contractual Perspective

The contractual perspective views international law as a result of mutually beneficial cooperation between states. This perspective assumes that states have well-defined preferences over international cooperation, and that states act instrumentally to achieve their goals, given their preferences and beliefs about the behavior of others.[98] The contractual perspective hence matches the voluntarist assumption that states make laws by consenting to rules. This perspective does not mean that international law *always* benefits states; sometimes states may face situations in which international rules are costly. For example, a state that normally wants to protect human rights may be tempted to violate these rights in extreme scenarios, like a terrorist attack. Additionally, more powerful states may receive greater rewards from international law than less powerful states because they can write rules that are more beneficial to their interests. For example, states that develop new technologies have insisted that modern trade agreements include intellectual property rights, thereby disadvantaging states that do not develop new technologies. Nonetheless, the contractual perspective is based on the view that, *on average* and *in expectation*, international law improves outcomes for all states. Otherwise, a contractual scholar would argue, states would not consent to these rules.

One common challenge that states face is a **coordination problem**.[99] In a coordination problem, all states have a shared incentive to use a common rule, but states disagree or are uncertain about what that rule should be. Once states agree on the common rule, they have no incentive to unilaterally deviate from this rule. In this sense, the rule is self-enforcing—if a state believes that others will follow the rule, then it, too, wants to follow the rule.

For example, when states developed civil aviation in the early twentieth century, they crafted rules for international flights. Imagine an airplane that departs from New York City, stops to refuel in Paris, and then travels to Istanbul. To depart and land in each city safely, airline pilots must communicate with ground control stations in different states (the US, France, and Turkey). How should these individuals communicate? States agreed that international civil aviation needed a common language to ease communication, but they were initially uncertain about which language to choose. Some states argued that all pilots and ground control crew members should be required to speak French. Other states argued that English should be the language of civil aviation. States ultimately agreed on English as the universal standard, thereby preventing accidents on international flights.

A second important challenge is a **collaboration problem**.[100] In a collaboration problem, states jointly benefit from choosing the same action, but each state is tempted to unilaterally deviate to a different action. These incentives ensure that all states are worse off than if they jointly cooperate. Collaboration problems are thus characterized by a mismatch between individual and group incentives. International law can help states overcome collaboration problems by creating rules and institutions that monitor and punish deviations.

For example, consider international trade. Each state has control over whether to allow or restrict the entry of foreign goods into its domestic market. Trade has complex effects on domestic economies, but most economists argue that the optimal economic outcome is for all states to adopt free trade, thereby ensuring the efficient production of goods. Yet the politics of trade policy is heavily affected by import-competing firms, which usually pressure their governments to protect them from foreign competition by restricting trade. Absent international law, states will likely protect their markets by restricting trade. Yet all states would be better-off if they could jointly agree to free trade. International trade law facilitates free trade by creating rules and institutions that identify and punish trade violations.

Collaboration problems also hinder the provision of public goods, like a clean environment. For example, while all individuals benefit from clean air and water, they also all enjoy consuming products and services that generate pollution, like travel and video games. By satisfying their own desires, an individual doesn't fully internalize the collective costs of their decisions, leading to excessive environmental damage. Environmental treaties like the Paris Climate Agreement seek to restrict pollution to create a global benefit for all.

Contractual theories of international law also identify a third type of challenge: a **commitment problem**.[101] A commitment problem is characterized by sequential decision-making in which the plan of action that is initially optimal becomes suboptimal as time passes. This change in optimal behavior comes about because of the actions of others, and not because an actor has learned new information that allows them to make better decisions. Time-inconsistent preferences often result in pledges that initially appear beneficial to all, but are later broken after another party acts. International law can help to solve commitment problems if it imposes *ex post* costs on broken promises—that is, costs that are paid only if a promise is broken.

For example, resource-rich states in Africa, Asia, and Latin America often rely on multinational firms based in Europe and the US to provide the capital for oil and gas exploration. Before these states receive foreign investment, they are often willing to promise favorable terms—such as high returns, low tax rates, and weak regulation—to lure foreign investors. However, after a foreign investor has sunk their capital by drilling an oil well or developing a gas field, the host state has an incentive to break its prior promises, by keeping a larger share of the revenue, raising taxes, or increasing regulation. Of course, sophisticated investors are aware of time-inconsistent preferences, and they avoid investing in states that can easily break their promises. If host states cannot credibly commit to their promises, they will not be able to access foreign capital and grow their economies. International investment law attempts to solve such commitment problems by creating enforceable property rights for foreign investors. These rights both constrain and benefit capital-seeking states by making credible promises to foreign investors.

Finally, a state faces a **screening problem** when it has difficulty in credibly communicating its preferences to others. Unlike a commitment problem, a state's optimal course of action does not change over time in a screening problem. Rather, a state cannot find a way to credibly reveal its true preferences to others because some states have an incentive to deceive others to gain a strategic advantage. International law can help to resolve screening problems if joining an international agreement imposes *ex ante* costs—that is, if costs are paid before states join an agreement. This is usually most effective if the cost of joining the agreement varies based on the true preferences of states.

For example, imagine that a new government is elected in a state that has been fighting a war with an opponent. This opponent may be uncertain about whether the new government is dovish—and wants to resolve the war—or hawkish—and simply wants to continue the war. Suppose that hawkish governments have an incentive to pretend that they are dovish, thereby tricking their opponent into concessions. Then dovish governments will find it difficult to signal their true preferences to their opponents, generating two possible types of strategic errors. First, the opponent may continue fighting a dovish government that wants to compromise. Second, the opponent may stop fighting a hawkish government that will not compromise.

Now imagine that the new government drafts a non-binding ceasefire agreement, meaning that the government will not face any significant punishment for breaking the agreement. Suppose that a dovish government faces fewer *ex ante* costs from joining the agreement than a hawkish government. For example, perhaps the dovish government is supported by elite actors who favor compromise, while the hawkish government is supported by elite actors who oppose compromise. Under such assumptions, the dovish government will pay an *ex ante* cost to sign the non-binding ceasefire, the opposition will back down, and peace will resume. In contrast, the hawkish government will not pay the *ex ante* cost of a ceasefire, the opposition will not back down, and war will continue. In this scenario, a non-binding agreement can help dovish governments to credibly reveal their true preferences by paying an *ex ante* cost. Additionally, the screening mechanism helps the opposition to avoid suboptimal outcomes, like fighting a dovish government or disarming for a hawkish government.

Of course, real-world outcomes don't match these simplified scenarios precisely. Nonetheless, contractual theories seek to illustrate the precise causal pathways by which international law can solve strategic problems. These mechanisms can give us insight into when international law is—and is not—likely to be useful to states.

Sociological Perspective

Finally, some experts analyze international law from a sociological perspective. This perspective assumes that state preferences are malleable and that international law can help to change these preferences over time. One variant of this perspective emphasizes persuasion and socialization as important causal pathways for changing individual preferences.[102] At the elite level, international law may change policy-maker preferences by exposing them to new ideas. At the domestic level, international law may influence public opinion about foreign policy decisions. Both of these causal pathways can allow international law to influence international politics.

For example, one priority of the international community in the 1990s and 2000s was reducing human trafficking, which is the use of force, fraud, or coercion to secure labor. In 2001, the US government began monitoring and reporting on whether states followed international standards to combat human trafficking. These reports were backed by threats to cut foreign aid if states with poor reports did not reform their laws and policies. Yet the reporting system also often changed elite and public opinion about human trafficking.[103] US reports were widely publicized in local media, leading to public pressure for reform in states like Argentina, Indonesia, Israel, and Mozambique.[104]

A second variant of the sociological perspective emphasizes that states are not unitary actors—they are collectives of individuals with diverse preferences. International law can change political outcomes if it influences the relative power of individuals within a state, which in turn affects whose preferences shape outcomes. International law may empower particular groups by giving them access to international or transnational support.[105] Alternatively, it may allow groups to pressure their governments by invoking international standards.[106] Finally, it can give advocacy groups information and expertise about policy choices that these groups can leverage into policy changes.[107]

For example, European states cooperated in the 1980s to reduce acid rain, which is precipitation with dangerous chemicals from atmospheric pollution. The 1985 Sulphur Protocol required its members to dramatically cut sulfur emissions into the atmosphere. Environmental activists throughout Europe used the treaty negotiations and subsequent monitoring reports to publicize the importance of acid rain to the general public.[108] Increasing public awareness translated into growing support for pro-environment political parties in many states.[109]

1.5   Case Study Revisited: Will International Law Stop Climate Change?

We began this chapter by describing the 2015 Paris Climate Agreement. Recall that this agreement requires each state to choose a "nationally determined contribution" to reducing greenhouse gas emissions.[110] These voluntary contributions are not legally binding under international law and no international institution can punish states that fall short of their pledges. Yet despite these weaknesses, most environmental advocacy groups view the Paris Climate Agreement as an important achievement.

This case study connects to the three different conceptions about how we should study and understand international law.

- *How did we get here?* The road to Paris was very long, beginning with environmental advocacy in the United Nations in the 1960s and 1970s. This advocacy was grounded in the Enlightenment belief that humans possess the capacity to change the natural environment for both bad and good. The drafting of the Paris Climate Agreement reflects the rise of written agreements in the nineteenth century and the creation of the modern international community in the twentieth century. The Paris Climate Agreement reflects a delicate compromise between competing voluntary and communitarian perspectives on international law. Individual states set their own voluntary contributions, yet the agreement repeatedly invokes conceptions of the international community and the common value of environmental protection.
- *Who matters under international law?* The Paris Climate Agreement is the product of decades of interactions between diverse actors. Only states can actually join the Paris Climate Agreement. Yet the driving force behind this agreement was environmental advocacy groups that used the UN to promote their political agenda. Perhaps surprisingly, these groups were supported by many multinational corporations that believed that climate change advocacy would appeal to individual consumers and perhaps even boost their profits.[111]
- *How does international law influence politics?* Scholars have proposed many different ways in which law may (or may not) influence politics. The critical perspective would suggest that the Paris Climate Agreement reflects existing domestic political pressure to fight climate change. Because national contributions are voluntary, states can simply pledge what they would have done anyways in the absence of international law. In contrast, a contractual scholar would probably argue that climate change is fundamentally a collaboration problem—states collectively benefit by limiting their greenhouse gas emissions, but each state wants others to bear the cost of a clean environment, which is a public good. Finally, the sociological perspective suggests that international law can change political preferences either through persuasion or by altering the domestic political power of relevant actors.

We can now return to the big questions from the introduction. First, we asked: why did diverse actors invest so much time and effort in creating an agreement that requires so little of states? Different people will likely offer different explanations. A critical scholar would likely argue that the Paris Climate Agreement is just political theater designed to please domestic and international audiences, rather than a tangible attempt to change incentives or preferences. In contrast, a contractualist would argue that the Paris Climate Agreement can succeed as long as states face domestic or international political pressure to make significant

Figure 1.5 Students in New Delhi, India participate in a school strike in November 2019. These students were part of a worldwide movement called "Fridays for the Future" that tried to pressure leaders to implement the 2015 Paris Climate Agreement. Protests like these support the sociological view that international law helps to mobilize domestic pressure groups and to challenge the narrative that environmental agreements only reflect the preferences of rich and powerful states.

pledges and comply with them.[112] Finally, a supporter of the sociological perspective would probably argue that publicity about the Paris Climate Agreement informed elites and voters about the long-term costs of climate change, thereby affecting their preferred domestic policies.

Our second question was: does the Paris Climate Agreement reflect the broad consensus of the entire international community, or merely the narrow preferences of powerful and rich states? Your perspective on this question will probably be shaped by your viewpoint on state responsibility for climate change. On the one hand, climate change is a truly global problem that requires global cooperation. Even if developed states dramatically reduce their greenhouse gas emissions, progress will be impossible if developing states dramatically increase their own emissions. On the other hand, many observers view climate diplomacy as "organized hypocrisy."[113] Developed states—like EU members and the US—spent centuries building their wealth through pollution. Yet they now use the rhetoric of environmentalism to chastise states like China and India that want to grow their own economies.

Finally, we asked: will the Paris Climate Agreement be effective in limiting greenhouse gas emissions and curbing climate change? It is too early to know whether greenhouse gas emissions will continue to climb higher or decline. Additionally, even when we know actual emission levels, experts will likely argue about what emission levels would have been in the absence of the agreement. We thus do not know—and perhaps can never truly know—whether the Paris Climate Agreement is an effective agreement based on empirical evidence alone. Rather, our understanding of whether international law matters will depend on our theoretical perspective. None of the three major perspectives—critical, contractual, and sociological—is inherently true or false. Rather, each perspective is based on different assumptions and causal logic, which can be more or less useful for understanding international law and politics. Which perspective seems most useful to you for understanding the Paris Climate Agreement? Like the most important debates in politics, this question lacks clear answers. But the very process of discussing and debating such questions tells us who we are, as individuals and as a society.

2 | Making International Law

2.1 Case Study: North Korea Goes Nuclear

After decades of pressuring states to end nuclear tests, victory seemed apparent to anti-nuclear activists by 1996. All of the states with known nuclear weapons—China, France, Russia, the UK, and the US—had agreed via unilateral declarations to halt nuclear tests.[1] The international community then prohibited all nuclear tests in an agreement called the Comprehensive Nuclear-Test-Ban Treaty (CTBT). In September 1996, the UN General Assembly voted to support the CTBT, and the treaty opened for signature.[2]

The anti-nuclear movement faced a few setbacks in subsequent years. In 1998, India and Pakistan conducted nuclear tests after tensions grew between them. The

Figure 2.1 People in Seoul, South Korea watch a news broadcast in January 2016 showing evidence that North Korea had recently conducted a nuclear test. Such tests have prompted important debates about whether international law prohibits such nuclear tests.

nuclear weapons club thus expanded from five states with known nuclear weapons to seven. After intense pressure from the international community, the tension was slowly defused and both states vowed to stop nuclear tests. Then, in 1999, the US Senate refused to approve the CTBT, leaving it in a legal limbo since the treaty could not become binding international law until the US and forty-three other states ratified it. Nonetheless, many observers thought that US opposition to the CTBT would be overcome with time, and the US continued to pledge not to conduct future nuclear tests.

Progress unraveled in 2006, when the Korean Peninsula shook from a blast of magnitude 4.1—North Korea had tested its first nuclear device. Reactions to the test were intense. UK Prime Minister, Tony Blair, described the test as a "completely irresponsible act."[3] The US White House called it "a provocative act in defiance of the will of the international community."[4] States in the Asia-Pacific region—including Australia, Japan, and South Korea—were particularly concerned about regional stability.[5] Radioactive debris was detected in Canada, prompting global fears about the test's health effects.[6]

Despite condemnation, North Korea continued its tests. International monitors detected further tests in 2009, 2013, 2016, and 2017.[7] In 2016, UN Secretary-General Ban Ki-moon described North Korea's actions as "a grave contravention of the international norm against nuclear testing."[8] But was the prohibition on nuclear tests just a "norm," or was it something more? Did international law prohibit North Korea from conducting nuclear tests?

To answer these questions, we must understand how states make international law. Several methods are possible:

- *Treaties*: was North Korea a member of a legally binding written agreement that prohibited nuclear tests?
- *Customary international law*: did unwritten law prohibit nuclear tests? Was North Korea bound by the behavior and beliefs of other states, which refused to test nuclear weapons and believed such tests should be illegal?
- *Other important factors*: was North Korea's behavior illegal on any other basis?

This chapter examines how states make international law. We ask: "How do we know what is, and what is not, law, and how did this or that rule come to have that status?"[9] The international system lacks a central government with a written constitution. Yet states nonetheless make international law using tools that they recognize as appropriate methods. What are these tools and how do they work? How does politics affect the making of international law?

We begin in section 2.2 with treaties, which are written agreements that create binding legal commitments. We first discuss how states enter into treaties. We then discuss reservations, which states use to exclude or modify treaty provisions. We next proceed to debates about how treaties are interpreted. We conclude section 2.2 by describing how states exit from treaties. Section 2.3 focuses on customary international law, which is unwritten law that is built up over time. We describe how this process unfolds through both state practice and acceptance of law. We then examine many of the conceptual issues that affect customary international law. Section 2.4 discusses other important factors that states sometimes use to make international law. These include: general principles of law, unilateral declarations, and peremptory norms. Finally, we return in section 2.5 to the case of North Korea. We apply various ideas from this chapter—about treaties, customary international law, and other important factors—to assess North Korea's nuclear tests.

2.2 Treaties

One way that states can make international law is using treaties. The Vienna Convention on the Law of Treaties (VCLT) defines a **treaty** as:

> an international agreement concluded between states in written form and governed by international law, whether embodied in a single instrument or in two or more related instruments and whatever its particular designation.[10]

Despite its brevity, this definition contains many important elements.

First, the definition specifies which actors can write treaties. Historically, treaties have been agreements between states. Private actors—like individuals, companies, and non-governmental organizations—can help states to negotiate and uphold treaties, but they cannot join treaties. For example, anti-nuclear organizations cannot join the CTBT because they are not states. This distinction is important for groups that aspire to statehood. Being allowed to sign a treaty is an implicit recognition of statehood, and hence of political independence. Under modern international law, international organizations can also join treaties with states. Such treaties usually address the powers of international organizations.

Second, states must intend for an agreement to be legally binding ("governed by international law"). Not all international agreements pass this test. The Helsinki Declaration of 1975, which promoted stable borders and human rights in Eastern Europe, was politically important, but not legally binding. Such agreements are sometimes called **soft law**. While soft law may generate moral commitments, these are considered distinct from legal commitments.[11]

Finally, this definition describes the form of a treaty. A treaty must be a written document—it cannot be a verbal promise. A treaty may consist of a single document or multiple documents. For example, many treaties consist of a main text that is binding for all members, with optional add-on texts that create additional obligations. For example, many multilateral treaties include optional texts in which members accept the jurisdiction of the International Court of Justice (ICJ) to hear disputes about the treaty. A treaty's particular name ("whatever its designation") does not affect its legal status—treaties are sometimes called agreements, conventions, covenants, and so on.

The principle that underlies all treaties is ***pacta sunt servanda***, which translates from Latin to "agreements must be kept." This legal principle requires that "Every treaty in force is binding upon the parties to it and must be performed by them in good faith."[12] States have also developed other rules that govern treaties, which are written in the VCLT. Almost every state is a VCLT member, and almost all VCLT rules are accepted by non-members.

We examine how states make and use treaties in four sections, which correspond to the life-cycle of a treaty. First, we examine how states enter into treaties. Second, we examine reservations that states can use to exclude or modify treaty provisions. Third, we examine treaty interpretation, which consists of understanding and applying treaty rules. Finally, we examine how states can sometimes exit from treaties.

Entry into Treaties

The process of creating new treaties involves multiple time-consuming phases. We begin by describing how states negotiate and consent to treaty rules. Next, we discuss how states can create legal commitments during this process using interim obligations. We then discuss limits on the kinds of treaties that states can write.

Negotiations and Consent

How do states create and join treaties? For simple bilateral agreements, like aviation agreements, negotiating a treaty is relatively straightforward. Usually, after discussions between government officials, one state will draft a treaty text. This state often copies and adjusts text from prior agreements on similar issues. This state will then share and discuss the text with the other state. States then take turns revising the text until they agree to a final version.

Multilateral agreements require more complex negotiations, particularly if states are negotiating a regional agreement with many neighbors or a universal agreement that all states can join. Multilateral negotiations often begin with a study group made up of policy-makers, practitioners, and scholars. After meetings and discussions, the study group will usually write a report that assesses relevant legal issues and makes recommendations. After considering these recommendations (and perhaps commissioning further studies), states will organize a multilateral conference to negotiate a treaty text. Each state that is involved in a treaty's negotiation will send an official delegation, which is usually made up of government lawyers, private practitioners, and scholars. For contentious negotiations, states sometimes include politicians who will influence the domestic political decision about whether to join a treaty. Each delegation operates based on instructions from and consultations with its government.

While states are usually the main actors in treaty negotiations, sometimes non-governmental organizations and other private actors also participate. For example, the International Committee of the Red Cross helped to write early treaties on the law of armed conflict. Similarly, the Maritime Labour Convention of 2006, which created international labor rights for maritime workers, was written in tripartite conferences. Delegates to these conferences represented states, employers, and workers, and each of these groups had equal votes during negotiations. States agreed to this tripartite structure because they wanted a treaty that was supported by employers and workers.

Multilateral negotiations are usually coordinated and supervised by an international organization.[13] For example, when states negotiate universal treaties, they often work through the United Nations and the **International Law Commission** (ILC). The ILC was created by the UN General Assembly in 1947 to study legal issues and make recommendations about the codification and development of international law. The General Assembly elects ILC representatives, who are usually international law practitioners and scholars. The ILC works with the UN General Assembly to create a list of projects, and then files annual reports and asks states for feedback. Over time, the ILC progresses from writing studies to issuing recommendations, and then to drafting treaty texts. Once a text has garnered broad support, the UN organizes a conference to negotiate a final treaty. This process is difficult, and projects are often delayed by state disagreements. For example, the General Assembly asked the ILC in 1948 to "to study the desirability and possibility of establishing an international judicial organ for the trials of persons charged with genocide."[14] Fifty years later, this process resulted in the Rome Statute of 1998, which created the International Criminal Court (ICC).

An important product of any treaty negotiation is the preparatory work, which is commonly called by its French name: the **travaux préparatoires**. This work consists of the written documents, including study group reports and recommendations, draft treaty texts, written summaries of discussions, and negotiation memos. These documents help later readers to understand why states reached the final version of the text, and they are often used to interpret a treaty's meaning. Accordingly, states usually want to participate in treaty negotiations and document their views in the *travaux préparatoires*, even if they are unlikely to join the treaty.

After states have completed negotiations, they can begin the process of joining the treaty. Every treaty includes its own rules about how it will become legally binding. The details of these rules are usually affected by the domestic laws of participating states. For simple bilateral agreements, like aviation agreements, governments may have domestic authority to create international law by jointly signing the treaty. However, for most multilateral agreements, states create legal obligations using a multi-step process. As an extended example of this process, consider the Rome Statute.

The first step in joining a treaty is usually **signature** of the treaty text. When a state signs a treaty, it indicates its support and intent to join the treaty. After the Rome Statute was completed, states were allowed to sign it from July 1998 to the end of 2000. During this period, 138 states signed the treaty, including the United States, which signed the treaty on the last possible day.

Signature comes with benefits and responsibilities. For treaties that create institutions, a state must normally sign the treaty to participate in future activities. One key component in creating the ICC was rule-making—namely, writing court procedures and definitions of crimes that would be prosecuted by the Court. For a state to participate in these ongoing activities, it had to sign the Rome Statute. Many states that were unlikely to ever join the ICC—including Iran, Israel, Russia, Sudan, and the United States—rushed to sign the Rome Statute at the end of 2000 so that they could participate in ICC rule-making. Additionally, while signature alone does not fully bind a state to the treaty, it can create interim legal obligations, which are discussed below.

After a state signs a treaty, it is expected to follow its domestic laws to finalize its consent. Most states allow their executive or head of state to sign treaties, but require a legislative vote to fully consent to a treaty. While states often refer to such domestic legislative votes as ratification, the Vienna Convention on the

Law of Treaties defines **ratification** as "the international act ... whereby a state establishes on the international plane its consent to be bound by a treaty."[15] Under international law, ratification consists of two steps. First, the proper government official under domestic law (who is usually the executive or head of state) must sign a document called an instrument of ratification, which indicates that the state formally consents to be bound by the treaty. Second, the instrument of ratification must be sent to an official recipient. If the treaty is a bilateral agreement, the instrument is usually sent to the other state as verification of consent. If the treaty is a multilateral agreement, the instrument is sent to the treaty depository, which manages the treaty's paperwork. For most multilateral agreements, including the Rome Statute, the treaty depository is the UN Secretary-General.

Third, once a sufficient number of states have completed ratification, there is a process that leads to **entry into force**, which is when a treaty becomes legally binding for states that have ratified it. For a bilateral agreement, the treaty usually enters into force after both states have exchanged their instruments of ratification. In contrast, multilateral agreements specify how many or which states must submit their instruments of ratification to the treaty depository. Additionally, most multilateral agreements impose a waiting period. The Rome Statute specifies that the treaty enters into force "the first day of the month after the 60th day following the date of the deposit of the 60th instrument of ratification" with the UN Secretary-General.[16] The Rome Statute received its sixtieth ratification in mid-April 2002, so it entered into force on 1 July 2002. Occasionally, treaties require that specific states ratify before entry into force. For example, the CTBT includes a list of forty-four states that must ratify before the treaty enters into force.[17] All of these forty-four states possessed nuclear reactors when the treaty was being negotiated, and thus were perceived as possible nuclear threats.[18] Because many of these forty-four states have either not ratified (China, Egypt, Iran, Israel, and the US) or not even signed the treaty (India, North Korea, and Pakistan), it has not entered into force. The CTBT's long delay after signature is actually quite common. Because of the difficulty of ratifying treaties at the domestic level, treaties often take decades to enter into force.[19]

Finally, some treaties allow states to join even if they did not sign them. This process is called **accession**. The precise rules regarding accession vary across treaties. However, once a state has acceded, it is bound by the same obligations as all other treaty members. For example, Afghanistan, Japan, and Palestine have all acceded to the Rome Statute. Palestine's accession was particularly controversial, since some governments do not recognize Palestine as a state, and hence do not believe that Palestine should be allowed to join any treaties.

A state is usually bound by a treaty only when the treaty has entered into force, and the state has either ratified or acceded to the treaty. For example, in the

North Sea case at the ICJ in 1969, Denmark and the Netherlands tried to invoke the Geneva Convention on the Continental Shelf in their dispute with West Germany, which had signed, but not ratified, the treaty. Denmark and the Netherlands agreed that "in these circumstances the Convention cannot, as such, be binding."[20] Yet they argued that "by conduct, by public statements and proclamations, and in other ways, [West Germany] has unilaterally assumed the obligations of the Convention."[21] The ICJ disagreed with this argument, writing that West Germany's failure to ratify the Convention clearly indicated that it was not bound by the Convention.[22] The ICJ's reasoning reflected the traditional view that a state must ratify or accede to a treaty to be bound by it. Yet states have begun to challenge this view in recent decades by arguing that signature alone can create some legal obligations.

Interim Obligations

During the early development of international law, the gap between treaty signature and entry into force was relatively small.[23] Most European states had absolute monarchs with authority to ratify via signature. Also, most treaties were bilateral, so only two states needed to ratify them. Modern treaties usually involve significant delays. Most modern states must ratify via legislative votes. Additionally, multilateral treaties that aspire to universal membership, like the CTBT and the Rome Statute, require more ratifications to create law than bilateral treaties. Many modern treaties therefore live in a twilight period, in which states have negotiated and signed the treaty, but it has not yet entered into force. To offset this delay, states allow treaties to create some legal obligations for signatories prior to entry into force via interim obligations.

When the International Law Commission was drafting the Vienna Convention on the Law of Treaties in the 1950s and 1960s, it discussed the growing twilight period between signature and entry into force.[24] States agreed to allow treaty signature to create interim obligations, even absent ratification and entry into force. The VCLT says: "A state is obliged to refrain from acts which would defeat the object and purpose of a treaty when ... it has signed the treaty ... subject to ratification."[25] A state may escape from this interim obligation if it makes "its intention clear not to become a party to the treaty."[26] The VCLT does not define "object and purpose," creating confusion about what states must do during this twilight period. At a minimum, experts believe that states may not render "subsequent performance of the treaty ... impossible or 'meaningless.'"[27] For example, if an arms control agreement requires states to destroy half of their missiles, a signatory state may not produce more missiles to wipe out the effect of the treaty.[28]

Some experts find interim obligations meaningless because "object and purpose often means whatever states say it means."[29] Others argue that treaty signature creates moral obligations to follow treaty rules, even if these rules are not legally enforceable.[30] A few cases have tried to uphold interim obligations in domestic and European Union courts.[31]

One suggestive example of interim obligations involves the US and the Rome Statute. US President Clinton signed the Rome Statute, but knew that the US Senate would not approve it. He apparently believed that the cost of interim obligation was outweighed by the benefit of shaping the ICC's rules. However, US President Bush announced in 2001 that he was withdrawing the US signature. The move prompted surprise, and even some mockery, from international lawyers. One expert on treaties wrote "signature ... cannot be nullified even by the careful use of erasing fluid ... once it has been done, it has been done."[32]

Bush did not explain why he wanted to withdraw Clinton's signature, and the initial significance of the policy was unclear. The US then began pressuring other states to sign bilateral agreements refusing to surrender US citizens to the ICC.[33] Many experts believe these agreements violate the object and purpose of the Rome Statute. The Bush Administration did not "unsign" all of the treaties that it disliked. For example, the US remained a signatory of the Kyoto Protocol, even though Bush did not support it.[34] Therefore, the Bush Administration may have believed that "unsigning" the Rome Statute was necessary for its future policies.

Bush's action was later mimicked by other states. In 2016, the ICC Prosecutor revealed that she was investigating over 800 incidents in which Russia allegedly committed international crimes in Ukraine after its 2014 intervention.[35] A few days later, Russia declared that it, too, was "unsigning" the Rome Statute. Clearly, states do not believe that signature is meaningless.

Limits on Validity

Can states negotiate and join a treaty that is nonetheless without legal effect? The VCLT contains rules that limit the ability of states to write binding agreements. Any agreement that violates these rules is invalid, meaning that it is not a legally binding agreement. We can organize these rules into two categories—rules about process and rules about content. The VCLT also clarifies when states may not argue that a treaty is invalid.

First, the VCLT establishes that treaties can be invalid because of the negotiation process. When the VCLT was drafted in the 1950s and 1960s, many developing and newly independent states were concerned about the influence of economic and political power on international law. They argued that rich states had abused their power in the past by imposing treaties under threats of war. For example, both the US and the UK used military force to threaten China and Japan into signing trade agreements in the nineteenth century. Additionally, many developing states believed that economic power allowed some states to extract treaty concessions that were fundamentally unfair and unjust.[36] Developing states would often refer to an ancient Roman fable told by Phaedrus, in which a lion entered into a contract to hunt a stag with other animals. After jointly hunting the stag, the lion took the whole stag for himself, prompting Phaedrus to reflect that "Partnership with the mighty is never trustworthy."[37] This fable reflected the Roman law concept of a *leonina societas* (a "lion's partnership"), which is a contract in which one party bears all the risk, while another receives all the gain. Newly independent states and states under the influence of the Soviet Union often denounced treaties between powerful and weak states as fundamentally "leonine"—that is, biased in favor of the powerful and against the weak.[38]

While the VCLT text does not denounce leonine treaties, it does specify that a treaty is invalid if it is based on fraud, corruption, or coercion, including the threat or use of force.[39] Additionally, under some very limited circumstances, a treaty can be invalid if it relies on a significant error.[40] These rules were based on little to no previous state practice.[41] At the time, no state had successfully argued in an international venue that a treaty was invalid due to error, fraud, corruption, or coercion. Even now, it is unclear how an international court would apply these rules in a dispute.

Nonetheless, some domestic courts have ruled treaties invalid because of these factors. For example, Germany signed the Munich Agreement in 1938 with France, Italy, and the UK. These states allowed Germany to invade the Sudetenland, which belonged to Czechoslovakia, to appease Hitler and prevent a European war. After the invasion, Czechoslovakia signed a treaty with Germany recognizing its new border. After World War II, Dutch courts had to rule on whether individuals in the Sudetenland were Dutch allies or enemies (i.e. whether they were "German"). Numerous Dutch courts ruled that these individuals were not enemies because the Munich Agreement and Germany's subsequent treaty with Czechoslovakia were based on coercion, and hence were invalid.[42]

Second, the VCLT specifies that some treaties are invalid because of their content. These content-based rules are based on domestic contract law. In the US, domestic laws distinguish between **default rules**, which can be changed by individuals using contracts, and **mandatory rules**, which cannot be changed.[43] For example, the US has default rules for who inherits property when an individual dies, but an individual can opt out of these rules by writing a will. In contrast, minimum wage laws are mandatory: individuals cannot sign valid employment contracts that pay less than the minimum wage. A similar distinction exists in states with civil law systems, like France and Germany. Rules that are part of *jus dispositivum* ("law adopted by consent") can be changed by individuals via contracts, while rules that are part of *jus cogens* ("mandatory law") cannot be changed. In international law, a rule that is part of *jus cogens* is referred to as a **peremptory norm**.

Peremptory norms limit the kinds of treaties that states can write. Not surprisingly, the suggestion that international law has peremptory norms was extremely controversial during the VCLT negotiations.[44] The final VCLT text defines a peremptory norm as:

> a norm accepted and recognized by the international community of states as a whole as a norm from which no derogation is permitted and which can be modified only by a subsequent norm ... having the same character.[45]

Accordingly, the VCLT stipulates that: "A treaty is void if ... it conflicts with a peremptory norm."[46] However, the VCLT does not provide any examples of peremptory norms because states could not agree on a list of possible examples. Since the completion of the VCLT, states have used peremptory norms to challenge not only treaties, but also customary international law, UN Security Council resolutions, and other international acts. This topic is discussed in detail in section 2.4 (under "Peremptory Norms (*Jus Cogens*)").

Finally, the VCLT specifies when states cannot invalidate treaties. These rules eliminate possible excuses or justifications that a state might use to avoid treaty obligations. States vary in their domestic laws about who has authority to create treaty obligations. Prior to the VCLT, experts often disagreed about whether these domestic laws had an international effect.[47] For example, if a president or prime minister exceeded their domestic authority, was their state still bound under international law? The VCLT clarifies that such agreements are valid unless other states are notified in advance that the representative of the state has restricted authority.[48] Additionally, a state cannot avoid international legal obligations by arguing that these obligations conflict with its domestic laws unless all other states know of the conflict and the domestic law is "of fundamental importance."[49]

Reservations

States often limit their membership in treaties using reservations. When the US ratified the International Covenant on Civil and Political Rights (ICCPR), a core human rights treaty, it was concerned about Article 7, which requires that: "No one shall be subjected to torture or to cruel, inhuman or degrading treatment or punishment." The US worried that Article 7 might restrict its use of the death penalty. When the US Senate ratified the ICCPR, it put several limits on the US's membership, including the statement that "the United States reserves the right ... to impose capital punishment" and "considers itself bound by Article 7 ... to the extent that 'cruel, inhuman or degrading treatment or punishment' means the cruel and unusual treatment or punishment prohibited by the ... [US] Constitution."[50]

The Vienna Convention on the Law of Treaties defines a **reservation** as "a unilateral statement ... made by a state [that] purports to exclude or to modify the legal effect of certain provisions of the treaty in their application to that state."[51] Reservations are an important tool for multilateral treaties with broad and diverse members because it is difficult to reach an agreement that every state will completely accept. Some treaties prohibit reservations, so a state can only join if it accepts all of the treaty's terms. Other treaties allow some specified reservations and prohibit all others. However, most treaties are silent about whether states can impose reservations.

Three important legal questions dominate the law of treaty reservations:

- *Validity*: What criteria should be used to decide whether a reservation is allowed? Can a state exclude or modify any provision of a treaty, or are there inherent limits on reservations?
- *Authority*: Who has the authority to assess whether a reservation is valid? Do other states that are members of the treaty decide? Can international courts or bureaucracies decide?
- *Effect*: What happens if a reservation is not valid? Is the state still bound by the treaty, or is it no longer a member?

International law on these questions has changed dramatically over time.[52] After World War II, states began to create multilateral treaties with universal membership. The horrors of the Holocaust prompted the international community to prohibit genocide. However, not every state could agree on every provision of the Genocide Convention of 1948. Several states sought to join the treaty with reservations, which generated disagreement within the international community about the validity of reservations. The UN General Assembly asked the ICJ to clarify the legal status of reservations to the Genocide Convention.

In 1951, the ICJ issued its *Genocide* Advisory Opinion, which argued that states were limited in their reservations to the Genocide Convention. Namely, the Court established an **object and purpose test** for evaluating the validity of a treaty reservation. The Court argued:

> it is the compatibility of a reservation with the object and purpose of the Convention that must furnish the criterion for the attitude of a state in making the reservation ... as well as for the appraisal by a state in objecting to the reservation.[53]

The ICJ also argued that states had authority to decide whether to accept or oppose a reservation, reasoning that "in its treaty relations a state cannot be bound without its consent, and ... consequently no reservation can be effective against any state without its agreement."[54] However, the Court wrote that the only criterion for deciding whether to accept or oppose a reservation was whether the reservation was consistent with the object and purpose of the Convention.

Finally, the ICJ clarified the effect of opposition to a reservation. If one treaty-member opposed another state's reservation, then the treaty would not be in force between that particular pair of states. However, the treaty would be in force between the reserving state and all other treaty members that did not oppose the reservation. The Court argued:

As no state can be bound by a reservation to which it has not consented, it necessarily follows that each state objecting to it will or will not ... consider the reserving state to be a party to the Convention. In the ordinary course of events, such a decision will only affect the relationship between the state making the reservation and the objecting state.[55]

The practical consequence of this distinction was that it was possible to have a multilateral treaty that was not in force between all of the various pairs of treaty members. For example, suppose that three states—A, B, and C—negotiate an international treaty, and states A and B both ratify the treaty without any reservations, thereby creating treaty rights and obligations with respect to each other. This relationship is represented in Figure 2.2 by the solid arrow between states A and B. Now suppose that state C wishes to join the treaty with a reservation that modifies its obligations. If state A accepts the reservation, but state B opposes it, then the modified treaty is in effect between states A and C, as shown by the dashed line in Figure 2.2. However, states B and C have no legal rights or obligations towards one another. All three states—A, B, and C—are treaty members because they have ratified the treaty and created legal rights and obligations. But they do not have the same rights and obligations with respect to all other treaty members.

Despite its broad rhetoric and historical importance, two factors should keep us from overgeneralizing from the ICJ's 1951 Advisory Opinion. First, the ICJ noted that its findings only applied to the Genocide Convention of 1948 and were based on the Convention's "special characteristics."[56] In particular, the Court noted "the universal character both of the condemnation of genocide and of the co-operation required" to eliminate genocide.[57] It also noted: "In such a convention the contracting states

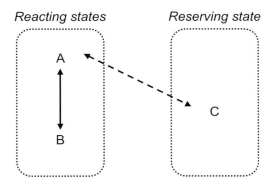

← → original treaty rights and obligations

← - → modified treaty rights and obligations

Figure 2.2 Treaty reservations under the ICJ's 1951 Advisory Opinion.
Note: States A and B have ratified the treaty without a reservation. State C has ratified with a reservation that state A accepts and state B opposes.

do not have any interests of their own; they merely have, one and all, a common interest."[58] The implication of these characteristics, in the Court's view, was that states should make the Genocide Convention as inclusive as possible. We don't know how the Court would have ruled if it had been asked to consider reservations to a trade agreement, for example. Second, the ICJ's advisory opinions are not legally binding. As their name suggests, advisory opinions are merely meant to advise the international community. They are not legally binding rulings. Nevertheless, the ICJ's reasoning influenced subsequent debate about the law of treaty reservations.

In the aftermath of the ICJ's advisory opinion, states disagreed about how the law of treaty reservations should operate. This debate played out in negotiations over the Vienna Convention on the Law of Treaties.[59] The VCLT partially adopts the ICJ's object and purpose test for most multilateral treaties. The VCLT notes that a treaty may contain its own rules on what kinds of reservations (if any) are allowed. In the absence of treaty-specific rules, the VCLT allows a state to make a reservation unless it "is incompatible with the object and purpose of the treaty."[60] However, the VCLT is unclear whether states can oppose a reservation for any reason or whether they can only oppose a reservation if they believe that it conflicts with the treaty's object and purpose.[61] Additionally, the VCLT gives international organizations the authority to accept or oppose treaty reservations in some very narrow circumstances, but it does not address the role of international courts or bureaucracies in assessing reservations more broadly.

Finally, the VCLT takes a mixed position on the issue of the effect of opposition to reservations. For most multilateral treaties, the VCLT applies a modified form of the ICJ approach. If a reacting state accepts a reservation, then the modified treaty goes into effect between the reserving and reacting states. And if a reacting state opposes a reservation, it must then decide whether or not the treaty is in effect between it and the reserving state. However, the VCLT does not specify which legal rights and obligations operate in this scenario: the original treaty terms, or the terms as modified by the reserving state.[62] This ambiguity became a key point of contention in contemporary international law.

Much of the contemporary debate over reservations has occurred in human rights law, in which states create legal obligations about how they treat individuals, rather than how they treat other states. In 1982, the Inter-American Court of Human Rights argued that this distinction was key for interpreting the legality of treaty reservations:

> modern human rights treaties ... are not multilateral treaties [that] accomplish the reciprocal exchange of rights for the mutual benefit of the contracting states. Their object and purpose is the protection of the basic rights of individual human beings ... In concluding these human rights treaties, the states ... submit themselves to a legal order within which they, for the common good, assume various obligations, not in relation to other states, but towards all individuals within their jurisdiction.[63]

Additionally, modern human rights treaties are overseen by international courts and bureaucracies that can hear individual complaints about alleged violations rights. It is therefore unclear how the logic of the ICJ advisory opinion and the VCLT apply in many human rights disputes. If a state attempts to exclude or modify part of a human rights treaty, can an international court and/or bureaucracy oversee compliance with that part of the treaty? What rules bind a state in its treatment of individuals if some states accept a reservation, while others oppose it? Should the opinion of these states even matter, given that the treaty creates legal rights for individuals, not states?

When the US joined the ICCPR with numerous reservations, the Human Rights Committee—an international bureaucracy that oversees compliance with the ICCPR—issued a document called General Comment No. 24. In this Comment, the Committee wrote that:

> The object and purpose of the Covenant is to create legally binding standards for human rights by defining certain civil and political rights and placing them in a framework of obligations which are legally binding for those states which ratify; and to provide an efficacious supervisory machinery for the obligations undertaken.[64]

The Human Rights Committee outlined numerous reservations that it believed did not meet the object and purpose test. While General Comment No. 24 did not mention the US specifically, it stated that "a state may not reserve the right ... to subject persons to cruel, inhuman or degrading treatment or punishment," which was a clear reference to the US reservations.[65] Additionally, the Committee wrote: "Of particular concern are widely formulated reservations which essentially render ineffective all Covenant rights which would require any change in national law ... No real international rights or obligations have thus been accepted."[66] This statement was a thinly veiled reference to the US reservations.

The Human Rights Committee went on to assert its own authority in overseeing ICCPR reservations. It argued that because the ICCPR creates rights for individuals, states could not be the sole authority in determining whether a reservation was valid. After all, states had little reason to oppose treaty reservations that did not actually affect them. Instead, it wrote: "It necessarily falls to the Committee to determine whether a specific reservation is compatible with the object and purpose of the Covenant."[67] Even though the Human Rights Committee lacked the authority to issue legally binding rulings in human rights disputes, it asserted the authority to assess the legality of ICCPR reservations.

Finally, the Human Rights Committee clarified the effect of invalid reservations:

> The normal consequence of an unacceptable reservation is not that the Covenant will not be in effect at all for a reserving party. Rather, such a reservation will generally be severable, in the sense that the Covenant will be operative for the reserving party without benefit of the reservation.[68]

The idea that reservations could be **severable**, or cut away from a state's ratification, was immensely controversial. It directly contradicted the ICJ's 1951 Advisory Opinion, and implied that states could be bound against their consent. Contemporary scholars recognized this as "a bold step towards the articulation of a new and separate reservations regime in respect of human rights treaties."[69]

Several states—including France, the UK, and the US—opposed General Comment No. 24. The US reiterated its traditional view that reservations were an important component in building support for multilateral agreements. Most importantly, the US strongly disagreed with the Committee's claims that reservations are severable. The US argued:

> The reservations contained in the United States instrument of ratification are integral parts of its consent to be bound by the Covenant and are not severable. If it were to be determined that any one or more of them were ineffective, the ratification as a whole could thereby be nullified.[70]

France echoed the US arguments, and added that the Human Rights Committee had overstepped its authority in claiming the power to assess reservations.[71] The UK was more moderate, but it wrote that: "The United Kingdom regards it as hardly feasible to try to hold a state to obligations under the Covenant which it ... has indicated its express unwillingness to accept."[72] The end result of the debate was a standoff: no consensus was reached on the Committee's authority or on severability of ICCPR reservations.

Around this same time, the European Court of Human Rights (ECHR) was hearing an important case. In the *Loizidou* case, the ECHR was asked to rule on alleged human rights violations that occurred in a Turkish-controlled portion of Cyprus. When it joined the Court in 1990, Turkey included a reservation that the Court had jurisdiction over "all matters ... performed within the boundaries of the national territory of the Republic of Turkey."[73] Turkey argued that the Court could not hear a case involving acts in Cyprus, which was not part of official Turkish territory. The Court argued in 1995 that it had the legal authority to rule on the reservation, and that the reservation was inconsistent with the object and purpose of the European Convention on Human Rights. Turkey argued that its reservation was not severable. It had joined the Court with conditions attached, and if the Court was not willing to abide by these conditions, then Turkey was not a member of the Court. However, the Court argued that Turkey's reservation was severable because this outcome would be more likely to promote human rights.[74] The Court went on to hear the merits of the case, and ruled that Turkey had indeed violated the European Convention on Human Rights.

What is the current status of the international law on treaty reservations? In 2011, the International Law Commission (ILC) issued a Guide to Practice on Reservations to Treaties. While this report is not considered a binding source of law, it is the most comprehensive assessment of the ways in which international law had evolved since the VCLT. The ILC Report reasserted the object and purpose test that was first proposed by the ICJ in 1951. However, it also said that when considering a treaty reservation, "states ... are free to object for any reason whatsoever," and "The objecting state may ... exclude all treaty relations between itself and the reserving state for any reason."[75]

The ILC also considered who has the authority to assess treaty reservations. The *Loizidou* case is just one example of many in which an international body has asserted the authority to assess reservations.[76] The ILC described this practice as "a relatively new phenomenon which was not taken into account by the [VCLT]."[77] Yet the subsequent development of international law indicated that international bodies, like the ECHR and Human Rights Committee, had the authority to assess treaty reservations. The ILC noted, however, that an assessment by an international body would have "neither more nor less authority" than its other findings, meaning that it would not necessarily be legally binding.[78]

Finally, the ILC addressed the effect of invalid treaty reservations: are treaty reservations severable? The ILC stated that the answer to this question "depends on the intention expressed by the reserving state ... on whether it intends to be bound by the treaty without the benefit of the reservation or whether it considers that it is not bound by the treaty."[79] That is, states should clearly indicate whether their reservations are severable. If a state does not indicate that its reservation is not severable, then it will be presumed to be severable.

While the ILC Report clarifies how states should behave in the future, it is unlikely to resolve disputes about past reservations. It also opens the door to potential new disputes because the ILC indicated that it does not view human rights law as inherently different from other areas of international law.[80] Treaty reservations will likely remain an intensely political area of international law.

Interpretation

After states have negotiated and joined a treaty, they often disagree about what the treaty requires. We use the term **interpretation** to describe the process of understanding a treaty's meaning and applying it to a factual situation.[81] Treaty interpretation is thus the key link between a written text and political decision-making. Interpretation usually hinges on state intent—what did states intend for the law to be when they wrote the treaty? Determining this intent can be difficult for many reasons. First, states may not have agreed about what the law should be. Treaties often reflect delicate compromises between states with competing interests and desires. Additionally, lawyers and policy-makers often encounter situations that were unanticipated by states that wrote a treaty. How can we know the intent of states if they never contemplated certain possibilities? Finally, the meaning of terms can change over time. Should such changes affect how law is interpreted? Experts vary dramatically in their approaches to these challenges, generating complex debates about treaty interpretation.

Basic Process

We can begin with a simple question: who interprets treaties? Any actor whose conduct is affected by international law is part of the interpretive process. At the international level, states frequently debate the meaning of international treaties, especially when they get involved in international disputes. At the domestic level, states employ international lawyers in their foreign ministries and other government bodies to assess the impact of international law on their policy choices. Domestic courts also interpret international treaties.

Private actors also interpret treaties that affect their own rights. Multinational corporations, which conduct business activities in multiple states, rely upon international lawyers to interpret international trade and investment law. Similarly, individuals who believe that they have been mistreated by governments must understand relevant human rights laws. Non-governmental organizations (NGOs) are also part of the interpretive process. Numerous human rights organizations assist individuals in assessing and litigating legal claims. Similarly, the International Committee of the Red Cross provides legal education to both governments and rebels that are fighting, helping these groups to understand the international law of armed conflict.

International organizations also interpret treaties.[82] For example, the World Trade Organization often discusses international trade law. These discussions are sometimes used to interpret laws during trade disputes. Similarly, the Human Rights Committee oversees and interprets the International Covenant on Civil and Political Rights. Neither of these organizations has authority to make international law independently of states. However, their expertise gives them influence over treaty interpretation. Finally, international courts—including standing courts, ad hoc arbitration bodies, and dispute settlement procedures—often interpret treaties when they are asked to oversee legal disputes.

What is the source of interpretive disagreements?[83] Just as domestic litigants may disagree about how to interpret ambiguous domestic legislation, so, too, states often disagree about the meaning of ambiguous treaties. For example, Australia sued Japan in 2010, arguing that a Japanese whale hunting program violated the International Convention for the Regulation of Whaling (ICRW). Japan argued that its program complied with the ICRW, which permits states to hunt whales "for purposes of scientific research."[84] Since the Japanese whales were used in scientific research and sold commercially as meat, the ICJ's ruling focused on a lengthy interpretation of the phrase "for purposes of scientific research." Interpreting these five words yielded a judgment that is over seventy pages long![85]

Additionally, international treaties are sometimes silent on legal obligations, either because states could not agree to a binding rule or because unexpected events create new circumstances for which the treaty lacks clear rules. Experts often refer to these silences as gaps or holes in international law. For example, a European migration crisis began in 2015 when conflicts in Libya, Syria, and other Middle Eastern countries prompted over a million individuals to flee their homes for Europe. Many of these individuals traveled on rafts from North Africa across the Mediterranean Sea. They frequently drowned during their journey, prompting debates about who (if anyone) was legally responsible for these deaths. Some scholars argue that international law has a "black hole" on this issue—no state has clear jurisdiction to prosecute deaths on the high seas on rafts, which are not registered by states.[86] This silence makes the regulation of migration very difficult.

Finally, states usually write treaties in multiple languages. All treaties that are negotiated under the United Nations are translated into six languages (Arabic, Chinese, English, French, Russian, and Spanish). Each of these translations is considered equally authentic, yet differences across translations sometimes cause disagreement. For example, the English translation of the ICJ Statute says that "The Court shall have the power to indicate ... any provisional measures which *ought to be taken*," suggesting that Court orders are optional.[87] In contrast, the French translation says that "La Cour a le pouvoir d'indiquer ... quelles mesures conservatoires du droit de chacun *doivent être prises*," suggesting that Court orders are mandatory and binding.[88] This small difference in translation—between "ought to be taken" and "*doivent être prises*" ("must be taken")—became important when Mexico sued the US in 1999.

What tools do treaty interpreters use to resolve such disagreements? The first, and most important, tool of legal interpretation is the treaty text itself. For example, the European Court of Human Rights mainly interprets the European Convention on Human Rights, which is the basis for its legal authority. Similarly, the dispute settlement system of the World Trade Organization focuses on WTO agreements, like the General Agreement on Tariffs and Trade.

A second tool for interpretation is a treaty's *travaux préparatoires*. As discussed above, these are the written documents from a treaty's negotiation. These documents include reports by the ILC or study groups, draft treaty texts, state responses, and negotiation memos. By consulting these documents, an actor can gain insight into the shared intentions of treaty negotiators. For example, when asked to resolve the conflict between English and French translations of the ICJ Statute, the Court consulted the *travaux préparatoires* to assess the intent of states that created the ICJ.[89]

Third, subsequent agreements can help define a treaty's meaning. For example, the Rome Statute gave the International Criminal Court authority to prosecute individuals for genocide, crimes against humanity, war crimes, and aggression.[90] However, the Rome Statute provided few details about these crimes. Instead, the

Rome Statute instructed its members to write a document called the Elements of Crimes to "assist the Court in the interpretation and application of" the Rome Statute.[91] This document is not a treaty, but it is an agreement that serves as "a key authoritative non-binding interpretive aid."[92] Such subsequent agreements to define treaty terms are relatively rare, yet they are an important tool when available.

A fourth, and related, tool of interpretation is other international agreements that are written either before or after the treaty in question. This tool is most useful when a state or court must consider relationships between multiple areas of law. For example, the European Court of Human Rights was asked to rule in 2010 on whether human trafficking is prohibited under the European Convention on Human Rights, which prohibits "slavery," "servitude," and "forced or compulsory labour."[93] Because human trafficking wasn't a common term when the European Convention was written, the Court consulted modern international agreements on human trafficking, even though not all members of the Court had joined these agreements.[94]

Fifth, actors sometimes use the subsequent practice of states to interpret a treaty. Such practice includes behavior between and within states, like domestic laws that implement the treaty. This tool is controversial because it can be difficult to separate practice that reflects a state's understanding of a treaty from practice that violates the treaty. Consider international rules that limit the use of force. Was the 2001 invasion of Afghanistan a reflection of the US understanding of those rules, or was it a violation of those rules? Experts who use subsequent practice to interpret treaties argue that state practice reflects political understandings of legal obligations, which may change over time. They believe that if we want to understand the UN Charter's prohibition of force, we should consider not only the 1945 text, but also how states have responded to that text since 1945. Such scholars believe in a "dialectical relationship between state policies and international rules," in which "practice towards a piece of international law can change the meaning of the obligations that it contains."[95] Scholars who oppose using subsequent practice argue that the 2001 invasion of Afghanistan does not change the meaning of the UN Charter. They believe that how states behave does not alter the obligations in the original text.

A final tool for interpretation is prior judicial rulings and academic scholarship. This tool reflects a delicate political compromise about the creation of international law. States with common law legal systems—like the UK and the US—use the principle of **precedent**, which is also called ***stare decisis*** ("let the decision stand"). This principle requires that judges defer to previous judicial rulings in similar cases. In contrast, states with civil law legal systems—like France and Germany—do not use precedent. Civil law judges must rule purely on the facts and law of a case, without relying on prior rulings. However, civil law judges often invoke academic scholarship in their rulings. As a compromise, the founders of the PCIJ and the ICJ included both judicial rulings and academic scholarship "as subsidiary means for the determination of rules of law."[96]

Methods

What methods do judges, states, and other actors use to interpret treaties? To illustrate the three major competing methods, consider the *Litwa* case, which was decided by the European Court of Human Rights in 2000. Witold Litwa was a Polish man who argued with post office clerks while collecting his mail. The clerks phoned the police and reported that Litwa "was drunk and behaving offensively."[97] Polish regulations allowed police to detain individuals believed to be drunk, so the police took Litwa to a government medical facility, where he waited for over six hours until a doctor verified that he was sober.

Litwa sued Poland, arguing that Poland had violated Article 5, paragraph 1, of the European Convention on Human Rights, which says:

Everyone has the right to liberty and security of person. No one shall be deprived of his liberty save in the following cases[:] ... the lawful detention of persons for the prevention of the spreading of infectious diseases, of persons of unsound mind, alcoholics or drug addicts ...

Litwa's case thus hinged on the legal meaning of "alcoholics." The Convention allowed a state to detain people who were "alcoholics," but did it allow a state to detain people who were believed to be drunk?

One method of treaty interpretation—known as the objective method—focuses on the ordinary meaning of a treaty. It focuses solely on the words in the text and asks: what would an ordinary person believe that the treaty says? Judges who use the objective method frequently refer to dictionary definitions, and the position and relationship of terms within the treaty.

In the *Litwa* case, Litwa's lawyers used the objective method: they argued that the ordinary meaning of the term "alcoholic" is a person who is addicted to alcohol. The Convention's mention of "drug addicts" reinforced this meaning. They then applied this meaning to the facts of the case. Litwa's lawyers argued that even if Litwa was drunk when he argued with the postal clerks, he was not addicted to alcohol. Additionally, Litwa did not have an "infectious disease," was not of "unsound mind," and was not a "drug addict." Therefore, they argued, the Polish government had violated his rights by detaining him.

Most experts believe that a treaty interpreter should begin with the objective method. Yet many experts also criticize judges who focus exclusively on ordinary meaning.[98] These experts point out that "almost any word has more than one meaning," and each disputant is "likely to consider the meaning it attaches to a particular word as the ordinary meaning."[99] Therefore, ordinary meaning alone is usually not enough to interpret a treaty because it probably has multiple competing ordinary meanings.[100] Additionally, treaty writers may have made mistakes in communicating their intent. For example, European Convention negotiators may have wanted police to have the authority to detain someone who was drunk, but used the word "alcoholic" because of a clerical or translation error.

A second method of treaty interpretation—known as the subjective method—encourages actors to look beyond the text to determine the subjective intent of states. Experts who support this method argue that states communicate their intentions in many different ways. They urge interpreters to consider the *travaux préparatoires*, the economic and political context of negotiations, and public statements by states.[101] Some of these experts believe that states continue to communicate their intent after a treaty is completed. They urge interpreters to examine subsequent agreements and practice "to give effect to the continuing consensus of the parties—that is, their contemporary shared expectations concerning problems of the type being disputed."[102] Experts who use the subjective method argue that states may have made clerical or translation errors, or may not have contemplated all possible scenarios when drafting the treaty.[103]

In the *Litwa* case, Poland argued that the ordinary meaning of the Convention "would lead to absurd or unreasonable results" because it would require that police make a medical diagnosis and it would allow police to detain alcoholics even if they are sober.[104] Poland argued that a more reasonable interpretation came from the *travaux préparatoires* for the Convention. Poland argued that negotiating states wanted to preserve "public morality and order" by preventing vagrancy and drunkenness.[105] Under this interpretation, which was ultimately supported by the Court, police had authority to detain drunk individuals until they are sober and no longer a threat to themselves and others.[106]

Critics of the subjective method often emphasize that states usually don't have a single, subjective intent when creating a treaty. *Travaux préparatoires* usually "reveal a good deal of divergence, disagreement, and lack of conclusive outcome as to meaning."[107] Allowing judges to probe detailed historical records gives them more discretion than focusing solely on a treaty's text. Additionally, a treaty reflects the outcome of debates among competing viewpoints. European states chose the word "alcoholic," not "drunk"—why should the European Court of Human Rights disregard that choice? Additionally, some critics note that reliance on the *travaux préparatoires* gives more deference "to the preferences of the most powerful actors."[108] For example, Poland did not participate in the European Convention negotiations in the late 1940s. When it joined the treaty in 1993, it did so based on the treaty text. Deference to the *travaux préparatoires* may therefore privilege the views of developed states that created the Convention, and discount the views of developing states that joined long afterwards.

Finally, a third method—known as the teleological method—emphasizes the object and purpose of the treaty. Its name comes from the Greek word *telos*, which translates as an end, goal, or purpose. Many ancient Greek philosophers viewed nature as a teleological process in which natural phenomena develop towards a final ideal outcome—a pinecone grows into a pine tree, a caterpillar develops into a butterfly, and so on.[109] They believed that humans also had a *telos*, which they associated with morality and virtue. Greek philosophers such as Aristotle asked: how should societies be designed to help humans achieve their *telos* of a virtuous life? Similarly, the teleological method of interpretation first asks: why did states write the treaty? It then asks: how can the text be interpreted to best achieve that objective? For example, the object and purpose of a trade agreement is usually to increase trade. Therefore, a judge who believes in the teleological method is likely to favor the interpretation that best promotes trade.

The object and purpose of the European Convention on Human Rights is to protect human rights.[110] The Preamble to the Convention invokes the 1948 Universal Declaration of Human Rights, and says that the Convention's members:

> [reaffirm] their profound belief in those fundamental freedoms which are the foundation of justice and peace in the world and are best maintained on the one hand by an effective political democracy and on the other by a common understanding and observance of ... Human Rights.

The Convention's reference to "effective political democracy" suggests that states must have the authority to maintain a functioning society. Yet the Convention's overall focus suggests that the individual right to be free from arbitrary detention arguably outweighs whatever social disruption is caused by Witold Litwa arguing with a postal clerk.

Critics of the teleological method note that international law does not define the meaning of "object and purpose." For example, scholars from different legal traditions disagree about whether "object" and "purpose" are two different concepts, or whether they jointly denote a single concept. Critics also note a paradox in the teleological method: an actor can only determine a treaty's object and purpose by examining the treaty's text, but the text is supposed to be interpreted using the object and purpose.[111]

International law experts disagree about which of these three methods—objective, subjective, or teleological—should be used for interpreting treaties. This disagreement partly stems from differences in how texts are interpreted in different domestic legal systems, and partly from differences in individual beliefs about the role of international law. When states drafted the Vienna Convention on the Law of Treaties, they wanted to include guidelines for treaty interpretation. However, they could not agree on which method of interpretation is best. Accordingly, the

VCLT reflects a compromise among all three methods. Article 31, paragraph 1, of the VCLT says "A treaty shall be interpreted in good faith in accordance with the ordinary meaning to be given to the terms of the treaty in their context and in the light of its object and purpose." The reference to "ordinary meaning" clearly favors the objective method, the reference to "context" alludes to the subjective method, and the reference to "object and purpose" is a nod to the teleological method. Scholars have intensely debated the VCLT text, but the ILC emphasized that the text does not contain a hierarchy among the three methods. The ILC argued that treaty interpretation is "a single combined operation" that incorporates elements of all three methods.[112]

Most international judges begin by examining the ordinary meaning of treaties. But if states could simply consult a dictionary to solve their problems, they would not go to court in the first place. Judges differ in whether they proceed next to subjective intent or to a treaty's object and purpose. In an ideal world, all three methods would yield the same outcome. Yet most international disputes do not work out so nicely. Different methods often lead to different outcomes, making the method of interpretation an important political choice.

Other Aspects

Aside from the method of treaty interpretation, experts disagree about two other aspects of treaty interpretation. First, should treaties be interpreted according to their original or evolutionary meaning? And second, how broadly should legal rules be interpreted?

Timing of Interpretation: Original versus Evolutionary Many factors of treaty interpretation can change over time, including: the meaning of words; state intentions; and the economic, political, and social context. Experts disagree about whether and how such changes affect treaty interpretation. Some experts believe in original interpretation—they believe that an "interpreter should seek the 'original meaning', trying to work out what the parties meant at the time of conclusion of the treaty."[113] Other experts believe in evolutionary interpretation—they believe that an interpreter should determine a treaty's "meaning at the time when an issue of interpretation … arises."[114]

To understand the difference between original and evolutionary interpretation, consider the *Dudgeon* case. In 1981, Jeffrey Dudgeon was a homosexual man in Northern Ireland, which prohibited male homosexual conduct. Dudgeon sued the UK at the European Court of Human Rights, arguing that Northern Ireland's laws violated Article 8 of the European Convention, which says:

1. Everyone has the right to respect for his private and family life …
2. There shall be no interference by a public authority with the exercise of this right except such as is … necessary in a democratic society … for the protection of … morals …

In its defense, the UK did not contest that private life includes sexual conduct. However, the UK argued that the law was justified under paragraph 2 of Article 8 because it was "necessary ... for the protection of ... morals" in Northern Ireland.

When the Convention was signed in 1950, European states routinely prohibited male homosexual conduct, suggesting that Dudgeon would have lost under an original interpretation of the Convention. However, the Court acknowledged in 1981 that social views toward homosexuality had evolved since 1950. The Court wrote:

> there is now a better understanding, and in consequence an increased tolerance, of homosexual behaviour ... In the great majority of the member states ... it is no longer considered to be necessary or appropriate to treat homosexual practices ... as in themselves a matter to which the sanctions of the criminal law should be applied.[115]

The Court noted changes in the domestic laws of other European societies (including England and Scotland) as evidence of changing social views towards homosexuality. The Court concluded that the Northern Ireland law violated Dudgeon's human rights.

An interpreter's personal ideology can shape her views about the timing of interpretation. Experts who believe in original interpretation tend to be more ideologically conservative. They tend to fear judicial activism, and believe in the primacy of state consent and sovereignty. In contrast, evolutionary interpretation tends to be more ideologically progressive because it gives the interpreter more freedom to move away from the meaning to which states originally consented. The importance of conservative versus progressive ideology can be seen also at the institutional level. For example, the European Court of Human Rights is well-known for evolutionary interpretation, while the International Court of Justice is more cautious.[116]

Either an original or evolutionary approach can be paired with all three methods of interpretation. However, some of these pairings make more sense than others. Original interpretation tends to be paired with more conservative methods, like the objective and subjective method.[117] Similarly, evolutionary interpretation tends to be used by interpreters who use the teleological method because both techniques are more progressive.[118]

Breadth of Interpretation: Narrow versus Broad The final major debate involves the breadth of interpretation. Some experts believe that international rules should be interpreted narrowly to minimize the constraints on states.[119] In contrast, other experts argue that legal rules should be interpreted broadly so that law is more effective in achieving the intent of states.

To understand the difference between narrow and broad interpretation, consider the *Golder* case. In 1969, Sidney Golder was an inmate in a UK prison. He was accused of assaulting a prison officer, but a later investigation found that Golder was not involved in the assault. Golder—who was upset by the false accusation—wanted to file a civil lawsuit for libel, but the UK government refused to allow him to communicate with a lawyer. Golder sued the UK government at the European Court of Human Rights, arguing that by denying him access to a lawyer, the UK had denied him access to a court.

Golder invoked Article 6, paragraph 1, of the European Convention on Human Rights, which reads:

> In the determination of his civil rights and obligations or of any criminal charge against him, everyone is entitled to a fair and public hearing within a reasonable time by an independent and impartial tribunal established by law ...

The UK argued that while the European Convention gave Golder "a right in any proceedings he may institute to a hearing that is fair," this did not imply that Golder had "a right of access to the courts."[120] The UK thus argued for a narrow interpretation of the text: that an individual has a right to a hearing that is fair, public, and timely, conditional on a judicial proceeding occurring. Alternatively, Golder's lawyers argued for a broad interpretation: that the Convention provides a right to the judicial proceeding itself.

If this distinction seems confusing, imagine that you are a university student and you discover a rule that says: "When reconsidering a student's final grade, a professor must provide the student with a written explanation of the grade in a timely manner." Does this rule mean that you have the right to a "written explanation of the grade in a timely manner" only if your professor agrees to reconsider your grade? Such a narrow interpretation would require little of a professor, who could simply announce, "I refuse to reconsider grades," and avoid a lot of extra work. Or does the rule imply that your professor has an obligation to reconsider your grade? Such a broad interpretation would require that your professor spend time reconsidering grades and writing explanations any time a student complains.

In the *Golder* case, the European Court carefully reviewed the *travaux préparatoires* and ultimately concluded that procedural guarantees—on fairness, publicity, and timeliness—could only be effective if a litigant could access a court to file a lawsuit. The Court explained:

> It would be inconceivable, in the opinion of the Court, that Article 6 para. 1 ... should describe in detail the procedural guarantees afforded to parties in a pending lawsuit and should not first protect that which alone makes it in fact possible to benefit from such guarantees, that is, access to a court. The fair, public and expeditious characteristics of judicial proceedings are of no value at all if there are no judicial proceedings.[121]

The Court thus adopted a broad reading of the Convention and found in favor of Golder.

The choice between narrow and broad interpretation is often affected by the ideology of individual judges. Some judges are more conservative in their view of the authority and limits of international law. They are more likely to show deference to state sovereignty by adopting narrow interpretations of treaties. Other judges are more progressive in their views towards international law. They believe that treaties should be effective in achieving their goals, and hence interpreted broadly. Similarly, institutions can vary in their ideology. Just as the European Court of Human Rights is more willing to adopt evolutionary interpretation than the International Court of Justice, so too it is more likely to adopt broader interpretations.

Additionally, the choice between narrow and broad interpretation has varied over time. Narrow interpretation is usually associated with older court rulings, while broad interpretation has become more common in more recent rulings. For example, deference to state sovereignty was more common in the Permanent Court of International Justice and in early cases heard by the International Court of Justice. This practice began to fall out of favor in the 1950s, and judges began to shift to a broader interpretation of treaties.[122]

**

In sum, judges, states, and other actors have many different tools and methods for interpreting international treaties. These options affect the outcome of disputes. Because treaty interpreters have so many options, some experts question whether any rules of treaty interpretation actually exist. They ask: do judges actually believe in principled treaty interpretation, or do they just use whichever method or approach leads to their most-preferred outcome? Yet most law experts do not believe that treaty interpretation is completely arbitrary. While individuals vary in their beliefs about how to interpret treaties, the interpretive process is not arbitrary. Just as individuals can have principled disagreements about political questions based on their individual ideology, so, too, can judges and other actors have principled disagreements about legal interpretation.

Treaty interpretation rules can also vary across different issue areas or legal questions. For example, states may want progressive interpretations of human rights treaties, but want conservative interpretations of trade agreements. Similarly, some experts believe that courts should be more progressive when interpreting treaties with more members because it is more difficult for states to renegotiate the terms of these agreements.[123] For example, despite broad support for LGBT rights in most European states, members of the European Convention on Human Rights are unlikely to ever renegotiate the Convention because it now has so many members. States may want the European Court to be more progressive, but want other courts to be more conservative.

Exit from Treaties

Just as states can join treaties to create legal obligations, they can often exit from treaties to end legal obligations.[124] For example, UK voters decided in a 2016 referendum to leave the European Union. The UK then invoked Article 50 of the Lisbon Treaty, which allows EU withdrawal and includes procedures for exit negotiations. International law gives states five methods for exiting from treaties, which are based on legal principles that govern private contracts.[125]

First, states can often exit a treaty by invoking a specific treaty provision, known as an **exit clause**, that specifies how a state may leave a treaty. Some treaties allow exit for any reason—like Article 50 of the Lisbon Treaty—while others limit withdrawal. For example, Article XV, paragraph 2, of the Antiballistic Missile (ABM) Treaty between the US and USSR stated that:

> Each Party shall ... have the right to withdraw from this Treaty if it decides that extraordinary events related to the subject matter of this Treaty have jeopardized its supreme interests. It shall give notice of its decision to the other Party ... Such notice shall include a statement of the extraordinary events the notifying Party regards as having jeopardized its supreme interests.

In December 2001, US President George W. Bush argued that the recent terrorist attacks showed that 2001 was "a vastly different world" from the one in which the ABM Treaty was signed.[126] Instead of fearing war with the USSR, the US feared "terrorist or rogue state missile attacks."[127] Bush argued that the ABM Treaty prevented the US from countering this threat by developing defensive military technology. Bush's rhetoric was crafted to describe the "extraordinary events [that] jeopardized its supreme interests," thereby justifying treaty withdrawal.

Second, states sometimes consent to treaty exit. The VCLT specifies that such exit can only occur "by consent of all the parties."[128] Ideally, such consent is explicit so that all states understand who is bound by a treaty and who is not. Yet states have occasionally argued that other states have tacitly consented to their exit either by creating new customary law or by acquiescing to their non-compliance.[129]

For example, in the 1970s, a German investor challenged Austrian limits on land purchases by foreigners. He argued that Austrian laws violated a 1930 Commercial Treaty between Austria and Germany. The Austrian Federal Constitutional Court argued in 1973 that Austria and Germany:

> have acted and conducted themselves in a manner which justifies the presumption that both states consider the provisions of the Commercial Treaty ... as no longer applicable.[130]

That is, the Court ruled that both states tacitly consented to the termination of the treaty by simply ignoring it.

Third, a state may exit from a treaty if another state has committed a **material breach**, which the VCLT defines as:

(a) a repudiation of the treaty not sanctioned by the present Convention; or
(b) the violation of a provision essential to the accomplishment of the object or purpose of the treaty.[131]

However, the VCLT clarifies that rules regarding material breach "do not apply to provisions relating to the protection of the human person contained in treaties of a humanitarian character."[132] For example, a state may not use a material breach as justification to exit from treaty obligations to respect human rights or to protect civilians during war.

Relatively few clear examples of material breach exist, perhaps because states don't join treaties that they believe they will later need to break. Yet states sometimes use the rhetoric of material breach during disputes. For example, Greece and Turkey reached an agreement over Cyprus in 1960. When Turkey later intervened militarily in Cyprus in 1974, many politicians argued that Turkey materially breached the 1960 agreement, thereby terminating it.[133]

Fourth, a state can exit from a treaty because of impossibility of performance—that is, if the state can no longer perform its obligations. The VCLT says:

> A party may invoke the impossibility of performing a treaty ... if the impossibility results from the permanent disappearance or destruction of an object indispensable for the execution of the treaty.[134]

However, a state may not use this excuse "if the impossibility is the result of a breach by that party" of the treaty.[135] Additionally, a state is still bound by a treaty if unexpected events make compliance more economically or politically costly, but not impossible.

For example, the ICJ ruled in 1997 that Hungary required to continue building a barrage system along its river border with Slovakia, even though Hungary discovered that the project would cause environmental damage.[136] Hungary could not terminate its treaty with Slovakia merely because compliance had become more costly. A few domestic courts have invoked impossibility of performance for economic treaties. For example, a German court ruled in 1930 that it did not need to apply a 1909 income tax treaty between Prussia and Luxembourg because Prussia no longer existed, and hence "could no longer collect the income tax."[137] Yet such circumstances are rare.

The final method of treaty exit comes from the doctrine of *rebus sic stantibus*, which translates from Latin as "things thus standing." This phrase has a long and troubled history in philosophy and politics because leaders used it as an excuse or justification to break their promises when economic or political circumstances changed. For example, Italian political philosopher Niccolò Machiavelli wrote in 1513: "a wise prince cannot and should not keep his pledge when it is against his interest to do so and when his reasons for making the pledge are no longer operative."[138] Machiavelli's advice reflected common practice during his time: political leaders often signed treaties of "perpetual peace" and abandoned them soon after.[139]

One of the most important examples of *rebus sic stantibus* involved Russian militarization in the Black Sea. After the Crimean War of 1853–1856, Russia was relatively weak and Central Europe was divided into multiple German states that shared a cultural heritage, but lacked unified military and political power. In its settlement to the Crimean War, Russia agreed not to develop its military in the Black Sea. Yet just fifteen years later, the distribution of power in Europe had changed. After the Franco-Prussian War of 1870–1871, Prussia absorbed numerous states to form a unified Germany. Russia claimed that this change entitled it to renegotiate its own legal rights. Russia demanded and was granted the right to remilitarize in the Black Sea. British philosopher John Stuart Mill commended Russia, writing that "Nations cannot rightfully bind themselves ... beyond the period to which human foresight can be presumed to extend."[140] He believed that leaders could not escape the risk that "the fulfilment of [an] obligation may, by change of circumstances, become either wrong or unwise."[141]

As international law developed in the early twentieth century, many states feared abuse of *rebus sic stantibus*.[142] Why did these states change their minds? Some scholars argue that Western imperialism caused the backlash against *rebus sic stantibus*. In the early twentieth century, China and Turkey renounced numerous economic treaties that had been imposed on them by European states. China and Turkey argued that their growing economic and military power entitled them to full membership as equal states in international society.[143] Western states—which had previously accepted European claims of *rebus sic stantibus*—feared Chinese and Turkish claims. For example, many scholars argued in the late 1920s that international organizations, like the League of Nations, should limit claims of *rebus sic stantibus*.[144] This limit was only proposed when non-Western states began to use the same tool as Western states. To some modern scholars, this behavior appears hypocritical.

Alternatively, perhaps states feared the abuse of *rebus sic stantibus* because of the overall progression of international law, which demanded more restrictions on state autonomy. If new international organizations—like the League of Nations—were going to be effective, states could not renounce their legal commitments at will. For example, the US government invoked *rebus sic stantibus* in August 1941 to suspend its obligations under the International Load Lines Convention, which restricted the cargo that could be loaded on a ship. The US declared that the suspension was necessary because of the war in Europe, even though the US had not yet joined World War II.[145] Contemporary observers described the US action as "reckless and unnecessary," and compared President Franklin D. Roosevelt to Adolf Hitler and Benito Mussolini for disregarding international law.[146] So while the standard for invoking *rebus sic stantibus* changed in the twentieth century, it changed for all states. Both developed and developing states were criticized for claiming *rebus sic stantibus*.

By the time of the VCLT negotiations, *rebus sic stantibus* had negative connotations for international lawyers. Yet many experts believed that states needed flexibility to exit from treaties that were too burdensome or no longer matched the need of states. The ILC speculated: "if international law provided no way to terminate an unduly burdensome treaty, it is likely that parties would take action outside of the law," rather than within it.[147] VCLT negotiators retained the overall concept of *rebus sic stantibus*, but changed its name and imposed limits.

The fifth method under the VCLT for states to exit treaties is to invoke a fundamental change in circumstances. The VCLT specifies four criteria for this mode of treaty exit:

1. *Change*: The current circumstances must differ from "those existing at the ... conclusion of a treaty."
2. *Unexpected*: The change must not have been "foreseen by the parties" to the treaty and must not be "the result of a breach by the party invoking it."
3. *Importance*: The circumstances must have been "an essential basis of the consent" of members.
4. *Magnitude*: The change must "radically ... transform the extent of obligations still to be performed."[148]

The VCLT thus preserves the essence of *rebus sic stantibus* while also limiting its use.

Because of these modern limits, states have rarely invoked fundamental changes of circumstances to alter their legal obligations. Yet at the end of the Cold War, East Germany voted to reunify with West Germany and notified the Soviet Union that it was withdrawing from the Warsaw Pact because of a fundamental change in circumstances.[149] Weeks later, East Germany no longer existed. Similarly, the European Court of Justice ruled in 1998 on a trade agreement between the European Economic Community and Yugoslavia. The Court ruled that "the break-up of Yugoslavia into several new states and the hostilities within Yugoslavia ... involved a fundamental change in the material circumstances underlying the consent of the contracting parties."[150] Therefore, the Court ruled that the trade agreement was suspended.

2.3 Customary International Law

Another way that states can make binding rules is using customary international law. Customary law was commonly used in domestic legal systems of medieval

Europe. At that time, most individuals lived in small, close-knit communities that fell under the jurisdiction of multiple overlapping authorities. With low literacy rates and high costs of copying documents, communities used unwritten laws based on local social practices, particularly for commercial transactions and property inheritance.[151] Medieval thinkers wrote extensively about how local practices could be transformed from social habits into binding laws.[152]

Customary law was subsequently adopted by international law scholars as a model of decentralized lawmaking. While early international law scholars believed that natural law was the most important source of law, later scholars placed more emphasis on voluntary law, which is the rules made by states. If international law was to be created by states themselves and all states were sovereign equals, then international rules could only be created through treaties or social practice. Customary law explained how such social practice could be transformed into binding rules.

Despite its long history, customary international law (CIL) is plagued by many contentious debates. One problematic aspect of CIL is the role of consent. During the classical and positivist era, many law scholars often emphasized consent because customary international law is made by state behavior, rather than derived from natural law principles. Yet most modern scholars acknowledge that customary international law is often non-consensual: states are often bound by rules to which they did not agree. While general state practice can lead to a legal rule, CIL does not require that every state consent to every rule. This issue of consent drives many of the modern debates about CIL, some of which are described below.

Additionally, CIL lacks clear standards regarding its formation and use. There is no international treaty that regulates CIL, and experts often disagree about how CIL is (and should be) made. Since 2012, the International Law Commission has focused on CIL, writing studies about its use and development. In 2016, the ILC issued a comprehensive report with conclusions that reflect delicate compromises between experts with diverging views.[153]

An additional complication is whether a subset of states can use customary international law to create obligations just among themselves. For example, can there be CIL that only applies to Latin American states? While the ICJ has acknowledged that regional CIL is theoretically possible, there are relatively few accepted examples.[154] Accordingly, we focus in this chapter on general CIL, which applies to all states.

One important case that illustrates how customary international law works is the *North Sea* case from the 1960s. In this case, the ICJ was asked to rule on a maritime border dispute between West Germany and its neighbors, Denmark and the Netherlands. All three states wanted to claim larger portions of the North Sea, but they disagreed about which rules applied to dividing up the territory. Denmark and the Netherlands argued that international law required use of the equidistance method.[155] This method was included in the 1958 Geneva Convention on the Continental

Shelf. While West Germany had signed this treaty, it had not ratified it. Accordingly, the ICJ could not rule based on treaty law. Denmark and the Netherlands therefore argued that the equidistance method was required under customary international law.

As explained by the ICJ in its *North Sea* ruling, a rule is part of customary international law if it satisfies two requirements. First, there must be state practice, in which states behave according to the rule. Second, there must be an acceptance by states that the behavior is required by law. This requirement is often referred to by the Latin phrase *opinio juris sive necessitatis*, which is usually shortened to *opinio juris*. As the ILC has argued, both elements—state practice and acceptance of law—are necessary for customary international law:

> the presence of only one constituent element does not suffice for the identification of
> a rule of customary international law. Practice without acceptance as law (*opinio juris*)
> ... can be no more than a non-binding usage, while a belief that something is ... the
> law unsupported by practice is mere aspiration; it is the two together that establish the
> existence of a rule of customary international law.[156]

In the following sections, we discuss each of these requirements—state practice and acceptance as law. We then discuss some of the conceptual challenges that lie at the core of customary international law.

State Practice
What Is State Practice?
The first requirement for a rule to be part of customary international law is **state practice**—states must behave in ways that match the proposed rule. For example, suppose you have arrived in a foreign state and do not know the traffic laws. You would probably begin by observing how drivers behave, such as how they approach red lights. In the US, you would see that drivers (usually) stop at red lights, so you would probably infer that the law requires this behavior. We must follow a similar process to determine the rules of customary international law—we must begin by observing how states behave.

Much of customary international law involves state interactions that have been repeated over long periods of time, like the treatment of foreign diplomats and commercial ships. In the modern era, customary international law also regulates how states treat their own citizens. Customary international law can also address rare events, like wars. For example, many rules from international humanitarian law, like the treatment of prisoners of war, are part of modern CIL. Historically, only the practice of states mattered in forming CIL, and not the practice of individuals, businesses, or non-governmental organizations. However, sometimes international organizations influence modern CIL.

Some experts argue that non-governmental organizations, like the International Committee of the Red Cross, should also shape CIL, but such arguments are controversial.[157]

What kinds of conduct contribute to state practice? Do only physical acts matter, or do verbal statements matter, too? These questions affect which states contribute to customary international law, and hence which states have power within the international system. For example, this chapter began by discussing North Korea's nuclear tests, which started in 2006. Prior to 1998, only China, France, the UK, the US, and the USSR/Russia conducted known nuclear tests, suggesting that few states had the capacity to conduct nuclear tests. If we don't take capacity into account, we might conclude that most states chose not to conduct nuclear tests. If we do take capacity into account, we might conclude that most states with the capacity to conduct nuclear tests did so. In 1998, India and Pakistan joined the nuclear club. Should the entry of developing states into the nuclear tests club affect our assessment of state practice? Do North Korea's tests strengthen state practice in favor of nuclear tests? What about verbal acts? States such as Australia and New Zealand challenged French nuclear tests in the South Pacific in the 1970s because they feared the health effects these would have on their nationals. Later tests by India, Pakistan, and North Korea were condemned for threatening regional stability. Do these verbal statements matter in shaping customary international law?

Some experts believe that only physical acts matter. They argue that law should be shaped by actual practice, and not by cheap talk, and that the rights of states should not be restricted by states that are unaffected by the relevant practice. Other experts believe that both physical acts and verbal statements should matter. They argue that if states must conduct nuclear tests to contribute to CIL on nuclear tests, then only rich and powerful states can influence CIL.

The ILC has adopted a compromise position by describing verbal statements as "verbal acts" that can influence state practice.[158] It defined state practice as including: "diplomatic acts and correspondence [and] conduct in connection with resolutions adopted by an international organization or at an intergovernmental conference."[159] It also declared: "There is no predetermined hierarchy among the various forms of practice."[160] However, given the long-standing preference for physical acts over verbal statements, many experts disagree with the ILC.

How Is State Practice Assessed?

How should state practice be assessed by judges, scholars, and states? To return to the traffic example, how would you, as a traveler to a foreign state, reach the conclusion that drivers should stop at red lights? You could use many different criteria:

- *Duration*: How long have you observed drivers stopping at red lights? Have you observed traffic for five minutes or for five weeks? The longer you have observed traffic, the more certain you would be about your conclusion.
- *Repetition*: How many times have you seen a car stop at a red light? Have you seen thousands of drivers stop at a red light, or only one? The more times the observed behavior is repeated, the more certain you would be.
- *Internal consistency*: Suppose that you followed an individual driver through multiple intersections. Did the driver stop their car every time they encountered a red light, or did they only stop sometimes? The more internally consistent the behavior of an individual driver is, the more certain you would be.
- *Generality*: Did all drivers stop when they encountered a red light, or only some drivers? The more general the behavior, the more certain you would be.
- *Representation*: Were the drivers who stopped at red lights representative of all drivers? Did both male and female drivers stop? Did the drivers of both sedans and trucks stop? The more representative the people following the behavior were, the more certain you would be.

As you satisfy more criteria, you would be more confident that you understand the traffic laws.

Because the rules of customary international law are not written down, there is no definitive checklist or formula that judges, scholars, and states use to assess state practice. But these five criteria—duration, repetition, internal consistency, generality, and representation—are often used in international disputes. For example, consider the *North Sea* case, in which Denmark, the Netherlands, and West Germany asked the ICJ to resolve a dispute over maritime delimitations. All three states wanted to claim more territory in the North Sea, but they disagreed about how to draw their boundaries. Denmark and the Netherlands favored the equidistance method, which gave them a large share of the territory. West Germany opposed the equidistance method, which gave it a small share of the territory. As part of the case, the ICJ asked whether customary international law required using the equidistance method.

In its majority opinion, the ICJ's discussion of state practice was relatively brief. The majority wrote:

> Although *the passage of only a short period of time* is not necessarily ... a bar to the formation of a new rule of customary international law ... an indispensable requirement would be that within the period in question ... State practice, including that of states whose interests are specially affected, should have been both *extensive and virtually uniform*.[161]

In its analysis, the ICJ focused on maritime delimitation—a physical act—as state practice. They asked: did states previously use the equidistance rule when drawing their boundaries?

Duration Note that the ICJ majority began by mentioning **duration**, which was one of the most important criteria for medieval customary law. While medieval scholars often referred to social behaviors that stretched back to "time immemorial," this usually meant only one or two generations. No one who was currently alive could remember society functioning differently.[162]

Duration is usually less important in modern customary international law. In the *North Sea* case, the ICJ acknowledged that while a longer duration of behavior would be stronger evidence of state practice, "the passage of only a short period of time" did not rule out CIL.[163] This element was particularly important in the *North Sea* case because new technologies enabled drilling for oil and minerals in the continental shelf, which lies below the ocean. States thus had financial incentives to claim larger shares of territory. In his dissenting opinion, Judge Lachs argued that the pressing need for new maritime delimitations should make duration less important than it had been in the past. He believed that law should change more quickly because of economic, political, and technological changes. He wrote:

> the great acceleration of social and economic change, combined with that of science and technology, have confronted law with a serious challenge: one it must meet, lest it lag even farther behind events.[164]

A state will still have a stronger legal claim under CIL if it can establish a longer duration of state practice.

Repetition A second criterion for assessing state practice is **repetition**, which is sometimes referred to as frequency. This criterion was also very important in medieval customary law because it demonstrated tacit consent to the prevailing behavior.[165] In some areas of customary international law, repetition remains important. For example, most states maintain diplomatic relationships with most other states. These repeated interactions provide clear standards for customary diplomatic relations law.

However, not all state interactions are repeated. For example, states rarely change their maritime borders. If these borders constantly changed, fishermen would not know where they could fish. As Judge Lachs wrote in his *North Sea* dissenting opinion: "Frequency may be invoked only in situations where there are many and successive opportunities to apply a rule."[166]

Internal Consistency A third criterion asks: how consistently does a state (or pair of states) follow a rule? Sometimes such **internal consistency** is referred to as continuity or uniformity.[167] In the *Right of Passage* dispute, the ICJ was asked whether Portugal had a right under CIL to pass through Indian territory in order to move goods and people between Portuguese territories. The Court examined Indian practice under British rule and after its independence. The ICJ ruled that "with regard to private persons, civil officials and goods in general there existed during the

British and post-British periods a *constant and uniform practice* allowing free passage between" the Portuguese territories.[168] However, the Court detailed numerous times when India restricted the movement of armed troops and police. Therefore, the Court concluded that Portugal had "no right of passage ... in respect of armed forces, armed police, and arms and ammunition."[169]

Generality A fourth criterion–**generality**–asks whether a practice is followed by many states. This criterion is sometimes referred to as consistency, although it differs from internal consistency because it focuses on behavior across states. In the *North Sea* case, the ICJ asked how many states used the equidistance principle in prior maritime delimitations. The majority found fifteen delimitations that used the equidistance rule, but suggested that these examples were not sufficiently general.[170]

International law lacks rules about how many states must follow a practice for it to be general, but as more states follow a practice, a claim of generality becomes stronger. However, not every state must follow a practice for it to be general. In his *North Sea* Dissenting Opinion, Judge Lachs wrote: "to become binding, a rule or principle of international law need not pass the test of universal acceptance ... Not all states have ... an opportunity or possibility of applying a given rule."[171] Modern experts often assert that CIL exists when only some states follow a rule.

Representation A final criterion for assessing state practice is **representation**–are the states that follow a practice representative of all states? Do both developed and developing states support the rule? Do states with different economic, legal, and political systems adhere to the rule? Are all regions of the world represented in the states that follow the rule?

This criterion rose to prominence in the 1960s during decolonization. Newly independent states were critical of many CIL rules that were formed before they could participate in lawmaking. In the *North Sea* case, Judge Lachs wrote:

> in the world today an essential factor in the formation of a new rule of general international law is ... that states with different political, economic and legal systems, states of all continents, participate in the process. No more can a general rule of international law be established by fiat of one or of a few, or ... by the consensus of European states only.[172]

New states and their supporters wanted to ensure that future CIL wasn't dominated by European states.

Representation continues to be important today. Since it is not necessary for all states, or even a majority of states, to agree to new CIL, representation may limit the abuse of lawmaking power. The ILC emphasized representation when it wrote: "It is important that ... states are representative of the various geographical regions and/or various interests at stake."[173]

Combining the Five Criteria These five criteria—duration, repetition, internal consistency, generality, and representation—guide assessments of customary international law. International law has no guidelines about how many criteria must be fulfilled (or how much they must be met) to conclude that state practice exists. But generally speaking, more is better: you would be more certain that state practice existed if more criteria were met.

If not all criteria are met, the context of a dispute can affect which criteria matter most. In the *North Sea* case, duration mattered less because of technology: states wanted to quickly claim new territory so that they could use new oil-drilling and mining technology to exploit more of the continental shelf. Similarly, repetition mattered less because states rarely draw new borders; maritime delimitation is rarely repeated. In contrast, representation mattered more because the *North Sea* case occurred during the height of decolonization. Judge Lachs, for example, did not want new CIL to be created solely by a few European states. A different context might have made different criteria more or less important.

What Practice Matters Most?

Specially Affected States If customary international law does not require all states to follow a particular rule, then which states matter most? In 1957, international law scholar Charles de Visscher used the metaphor of "the gradual formation of a road across vacant land" to describe the formation of customary international law.[174] He wrote:

> To begin with, the tracks are many and uncertain, scarcely visible on the ground. Then most users, for some reason of common utility, follow the same line; a single path becomes clear, which in turn gives place to a road henceforth recognized as the only regular way.[175]

De Visscher believed that this process was not democratic. He argued that "Among the users are always some who mark the soil more deeply with their footprints than others, either because of their weight ... or because their interests bring them more frequently this way."[176] De Visscher believed that "Every international custom is the work of power."[177]

Similarly, in the *North Sea* case, the ICJ suggested that some states matter more than others in shaping state practice. It wrote: "state practice, including that of *states whose interests are specially affected*, should have been both extensive and virtually uniform."[178] This sentence causes many experts to argue that international law has a **specially affected states doctrine**. Namely, these experts argue that customary international law gives (or should give) more deference to states that are more likely to be affected by a rule.

At first glance, this idea—that states that are more affected by a rule should have more power to shape that rule—might seem fair. Should all states have an equal voice in crafting rules that constrain only some states? For example, should landlocked states influence maritime delimitations? The ICJ did not write that powerful states matter more than weak states. However, for many experts—particularly those from developed states—specially affected states are inherently powerful states.

Not surprisingly, the idea of specially affected states has triggered intense debates. For example, the International Committee of the Red Cross issued a wide-ranging 2005 study of *Customary International Humanitarian Law*, which regulates armed conflict.[179] This study did not include a position on specially affected states. Yet parts of the study suggested that "*all* states are affected" by international humanitarian law, meaning that "states ... with greater capacity [in war] will not have any greater influence on the formation of custom than other states."[180] This study was heavily criticized by many powerful states. In an official response, the US wrote that the study:

> tends to regard as equivalent the practice of states that have relatively little history of participation in armed conflict and the practice of states that have had a greater extent and depth of experience or that have otherwise had significant opportunities to develop a carefully considered military doctrine. The latter category of states, however, has typically contributed a significantly greater quantity and quality of practice.[181]

The US argued that because it had more experience fighting than other states, it ought to have more influence on the relevant CIL.

The specially affected state doctrine may be unavoidable given the distribution of power within the international system. Realists often argue that international law will not succeed if powerful states will not uphold it. Can we have viable laws for armed conflict if the US—which has the strongest military in the world—refuses to follow them? On the other hand, it would be troubling for international law—which is based on the principle of equality—to explicitly grant some states greater authority. Harking back to de Visscher's metaphor, Bandeira Galindo and Yip wrote:

> if CIL is a path across a grass field, powerful states are the ones whose footprints lead the way. Third World countries hardly have the privilege of exploring alternative paths, being constrained to follow the trails developed by great powers ... From the perspective of the Third World, the fundamental norm of CIL can be read as follows: *Do not step on the grass.*[182]

Inaction and Counterexamples Thus far, we have focused on states that follow a particular rule. But how does customary international law consider states that do not follow the rule? What about states that do not act, neither confirming nor refuting a potential rule of CIL? And what about states that violate a proposed rule, creating counterexamples of state practice?

Most experts treat inaction as a form of state practice. For example, if a state repeatedly allows a foreign warship to pass through its territorial waters without taking action, this could be acceptance of the practice. However, inaction must be a choice to be state practice. A state's inaction would not count as consent if an undetected foreign submarine passed through the state's territorial waters. Inaction must be deliberate to count as state practice: a state must know about the behavior of others and have time to respond.[183]

Because inaction can represent support for a rule, silence can be costly in international law. A state's silence about the behavior of others can be interpreted as **acquiescence**, or tacit support for state practice. States thus have an incentive to engage in **active protest** when they disagree with an asserted rule. Active protest can be a physical act or a verbal statement, but states with more capacity are usually expected to take more costly actions to express their disagreement.

For example, China asserted rights in 2009 and 2011 over contested airspace, islands, and waterways in the South China Sea. China wants this territory for its oil and minerals, and to grow its air force and navy. The legal issues of the dispute are complex. Yet China mainly argues that it claimed the territory after World War II, and that from then until 2009, "China's territorial title and historic rights ... had never been protested by any state."[184] That is, China argues that its claims were tacitly supported by other states.

Many of China's neighbors—including Japan, the Philippines, and Vietnam—disagree with China's claims. They want to limit China's growing economic and military power, and they make alternative territorial claims. Yet they lack the capacity to challenge China militarily. Their more powerful allies—including Australia, France, the UK, and the US—have actively protested Chinese claims with freedom of navigation exercises, in which they fly military airplanes through contested airspace and navigate warships through contested waters. These protests have a legal purpose: they weaken China's claims of acquiescence.

More broadly, counterexamples often weaken claims of state practice. Yet experts sometimes disagree about how to interpret such counterexamples. In the *North Sea* case, the arguments of Denmark and the Netherlands (which wanted to use the equidistance principle) were weakened when West Germany showed that many maritime delimitations did not use the equidistance principle. Thus, counterexamples were treated by the *North Sea* majority as evidence against state practice. Yet in his dissenting opinion, Judge Lachs argued that counterexamples should be interpreted differently. He wrote:

> the fact that some states ... concluded agreements at variance with the equidistance rule ... represents a mere permitted derogation and cannot be held to have disturbed the formation of a general rule of law on delimitation.[185]

That is, Judge Lachs suggested that counterexamples may be violations of CIL.

Figure 2.3 A US military aircraft carrier sails through a portion of the South China Sea in February 2018. Many states routinely fly military airplanes and sail warships through the South China Sea to actively protest China's maritime claims. Such active protest ensures that China cannot claim that other states have acquiesced to its claims.

The *North Sea* case reflects a broader debate about counterexamples. Legal conservatives—who believe that it should be relatively difficult to create new CIL—usually treat counterexamples as evidence against state practice, as in the *North Sea* majority opinion. Legal progressives—who believe that it should be easier to create new CIL—often interpret counterexamples as violations of existing CIL, as in Judge Lachs's dissent. In 1969, the conservative view prevailed in the *North Sea* case. However, many courts have shifted over time towards the progressive view, particularly for human rights and the use of force.

This shift towards a more progressive view of counterexamples is apparent in the *Nicaragua* case, which challenged US military involvement in Nicaragua during the height of the Cold War. In 1979, a socialist government seized political power in Nicaragua, and the US feared that the USSR would gain power in Latin America. The US engaged in covert military activities and secretly supported rebels against the Nicaraguan government. Nicaragua sued the US at the ICJ, arguing (in part) that customary international law prohibits intervention and the use of force.

US supporters argued that while the UN Charter limits intervention and the use of force, both the US and the USSR frequently intervened and supported rebels in civil conflicts, including the Cuban Revolution; coups in Brazil, Chile, Guatemala, and Iran; and wars in Angola and Namibia. From the US perspective, all of these counterexamples were evidence against state practice. Yet the ICJ interpreted these counterexamples as violations of CIL. In its 1986 judgment, the ICJ wrote:

> It is not to be expected that in the practice of states the application of the rules in question should have been perfect, in the sense that states should have refrained, with complete consistency, from the use of force or from intervention in each other's internal affairs. The Court does not consider that, for a rule to be established as customary, the corresponding practice must be in absolutely rigorous conformity with the rule. In order to deduce the existence of customary rules, the Court deems it sufficient that the conduct of states should, in general, be consistent with such rules, and that instances of state conduct inconsistent with a given rule should generally have been treated as breaches of that rule, not as indications of the recognition of a new rule.[186]

That is, the ICJ viewed Cold War interventions (including US activities in Nicaragua) as violations of CIL, rather than as evidence against state practice. Yet over time, the *Nicaragua* approach has been confirmed by other courts, particularly for human rights. For example, experts usually argue that torture violates CIL, despite abundant evidence that governments often torture their political opponents. Human rights advocates argue that these counterexamples are violations of CIL, not evidence against state practice.

One way to reconcile the competing views on counterexamples is to note that publicity matters in assessing state practice. In maritime delimitations, states acted publicly: they did not hide their decisions about whether to use the equidistance method. In contrast, US military activities in Nicaragua were covert. Similarly, when governments torture their political opponents, they usually do so in secret, suggesting that they believe they are violating international law.

Acceptance as Law (*Opinio Juris*)

The second requirement for customary international law is that the rule be accepted as law. This requirement is often referred to by the Latin phrase *opinio juris sive necessitatis*, which is usually shortened to **opinio juris**. States want to distinguish legally binding rules from mere courtesy or habit. In the *North Sea* case, the ICJ wrote:

> The ... habitual character of the acts is not in itself enough. There are many international acts ... which are performed almost invariably, but which are motivated only by considerations of courtesy, convenience or tradition, and not by any sense of legal duty.[187]

Such acts include diplomatic protocols, like exchanging gifts or sending condolence notes when a foreign leader dies. States behave this way based on respect, not because of legal obligation. Similarly, the Court reasoned, states might have used the equidistance method out of courtesy or habit, rather than because they accepted it as law.

Opinio juris requires understanding why states behave in a particular way. As the ILC argued: "Evidence of acceptance as law ... may take a wide range of forms."[188] Such evidence includes:

> public statements ... ; official publications; government legal opinions; diplomatic correspondence; decisions of national courts; treaty provisions; and conduct in connection with resolutions adopted by an international organization or at an intergovernmental conference.[189]

This list emphasizes verbal statements because *opinio juris* relies on reasons for behavior. Yet states may not truthfully explain why they behave in a particular way. For example, governments often pledge to respect human rights while violating them in practice. Inaction can also be evidence of acceptance.[190] Just as a failure to physically or verbally act can be state practice, a failure to object to a rule can be a tacit acceptance of this rule.

Modern disputes over customary international law often involve complex debates over *opinio juris*. Namely: where does acceptance as law (or the belief that law exists) come from? These debates stem from the two major competing perspectives on modern international law: voluntary and communitarian law.[191] Under the voluntary law perspective, states must actually *consent* to rules for them to become laws. However, under the communitarian law perspective, the common *values* of the international community as a whole can become law, even absent explicit state consent.

This debate between consent and common values has important political implications. To understand these implications, one must first understand the historical context of the debate. International law's famous founding fathers—such as Grotius and Vattel—were all Europeans, and they were mainly focused on building stability within Europe, which was a relatively homogeneous society. European states varied in their attitudes towards Catholicism, but all were Christian and shared fundamental values.

Over time, European states began to interact more with non-European societies through commerce. These interactions forced European states to decide how (if at all) to incorporate non-Europeans into their regional system of law. Europeans usually viewed non-Europeans as primitive and unable to govern themselves.[192] Accordingly, European states usually did not view non-European societies as sovereign states with rights and responsibilities. The world outside of Europe was characterized as *terra nullius*—land belonging to no one—so Europeans felt justified in seizing resources and excluding native people from lawmaking.[193]

By the nineteenth century, major European states were building foreign empires, and international law was dominated by voluntary law. Most scholars thought that states must either tacitly or explicitly consent to a rule for it to become a legal obligation. Such law formation was possible because European states shared Christian values and common economic, legal, and political systems. In Latin America, European colonists displaced native populations. By the time of Latin American independence, the economic and political elite of these new states shared the Christian culture and history of European states. Australia, New Zealand, and the US were also settler colonies that easily integrated into the European system of international law.

Non-European and non-Christian states—like China, Japan, and Turkey—faced a more difficult path. As these states opened to Western technology and trade, they sought a growing voice. As the international system expanded, it became more difficult to create rules based on consent because of more diversity among its members. European states shifted from a consent-based view of law to one that emphasized common values. Since European states outnumbered non-European states, they determined what was a community value. Not surprisingly, these values included free trade, property rights for foreign investors, and European conceptions of due process. Institutions like the League of Nations were established to promote the spread of such values and the development of societies that were believed to be uncivilized.[194]

In the early twentieth century, developing states emphasized consent to resist being bound by European views.[195] They wanted international law to represent the views of all states, not just the views of strong states. In contrast, legal scholars who emphasized common values were usually promoting the views of developed and European states. Since these states were the majority, they could effectively control the agenda of the international community.

Decolonization in the 1950s to 1970s changed these dynamics. As the international system welcomed new developing states from Africa and Asia, powerful Western states lost their numerical majority. The UN General Assembly became a hotbed of legal activism as developing states promoted their preferred rules. For example, they claimed a right to permanent sovereignty over natural resources, implying that they could break drilling and mining contracts with foreign corporations.[196] The newly expanded international community challenged powerful states, which became alienated from the community that they had previously dominated. Perhaps not surprisingly, many powerful states shifted back to their earlier emphasis on consent.

In contemporary politics, powerful states routinely emphasize consent, while less powerful states usually emphasize common values. For example, small states have tried to limit the use and spread of nuclear weapons by larger and more powerful states. In 1996, the UN General Assembly persuaded the ICJ to issue an advisory opinion that challenged the *Legality of the Threat or Use of Nuclear Weapons*. And in 2014, the Marshall Islands filed numerous lawsuits arguing that nuclear states must give up their existing nuclear weapons and stop developing new ones. One of the Marshall Islands' arguments was that the Non-Proliferation Treaty of 1968 had become customary international law. The ICJ found that it lacked authority to rule on the case. However, in a dissenting opinion, Judge Cançado Trindade of Brazil argued for a view of *opinio juris* that privileged common values over consent. He wrote:

> *Opinio juris* became a key element in the formation itself of international law, *a law of conscience*. This diminished the unilateral influence of the most powerful states, fostering international law-making in fulfilment of the public interest and in pursuance of the common good of the international community.[197]

Judge Cançado Trindade, like many experts from developing states, thought that the international community should use law to challenge powerful states.

Given these dynamics, the ILC's effort to create guidelines on customary international law has been closely contested. ILC documents refer to "acceptance as law" and "a sense of legal right or obligation," without staking out a clear position on what creates such "acceptance" or "sense."[198] This ambiguity reflects political disagreements between states. In contemporary politics, the voluntary law perspective usually benefits powerful states, which can act unilaterally, while the communitarian law perspective usually benefits small and weak states, which outnumber powerful states. Whether acceptance as law comes from consent or common values is not merely a philosophical issue: it comes with political consequences about how international law is made.

Conceptual Challenges

We now consider some of the conceptual challenges at the heart of customary international law. We begin with the paradox of how CIL is created and changed. We then examine the influence of treaties and UN General Assembly resolutions on CIL. Finally, we ask whether states can opt out of CIL.

Paradox of Creation and Change

The first major conceptual challenge is: how can customary international law be created and changed if the acceptance of law comes from beliefs? How can a belief in law exist before the law itself exists? This paradox closely matches the adage: "Which came first, the chicken or the egg?" Just as chickens lay eggs, which hatch chickens, so, too, does belief create law, which creates belief.

Legal scholars often refer to this problem as the **chronological paradox**. Some experts argue that the only way to satisfy this paradox is if the states that initially believe in law are incorrect. If you accept the conventional framework for customary international law—and assume that acceptance of law must come before law itself exists—then you must explain how an egg can appear in a world without chickens.

Some critics therefore question the requirement of acceptance of law. In the *North Sea* case, Judge Lachs argued:

> to postulate that all states, even those which initiate a given practice, believe themselves to be acting under a legal obligation is to resort to a fiction—and in fact to deny the possibility of developing such rules. For the path may indeed start from voluntary, unilateral acts relying on the confident expectation that they will find acquiescence or be emulated ... It is only at a later stage that ... there develops ... international consensus.[199]

That is, Judge Lachs suggested that customary international law must be rooted in state practice alone.

Similar problems affect changes in customary international law. If a current rule requires behavior X, how can states change to a rule that requires behavior Y? How can states transition from the (correct) belief in X to the (incorrect) belief in Y?

Some experts argue that a state must break existing rules to generate new state practice. If those violations become common and are accepted by others, then customary international law has changed. Violations thus play a vital role in customary international law. Scholar Anthony D'Amato argued:

> an "illegal" act by a state contains the seeds of a new legality. When a state violates an existing rule of customary international law, it undoubtedly is "guilty" of an illegal act, but the illegal act itself becomes a disconfirmatory instance of the underlying rule. The next state will find it somewhat easier to disobey the rule, until eventually a new line of conduct will replace the original rule by a new rule.[200]

This logic is troubling to many lawyers because it suggests that law must be broken for it to adapt to changing economic and political environments. Yet it is difficult to explain how customary international law can change unless states violate existing rules. Verbal statements are rarely sufficient to change CIL.

Changes in customary international law are usually triggered by changes in economic and political power. When newly powerful states are dissatisfied with rules that were crafted by states that are declining in power, they often challenge these rules. For example, Portugal and Spain were the dominant maritime powers in the fifteenth century. They divided the world's oceans between themselves and declared a policy of *mare clausum* (or "closed sea")—no other states were permitted to travel through the world's oceans without Portuguese or Spanish permission. By the late sixteenth and early seventeenth centuries, Portugal and Spain had declined in power, and new states were rising. The Netherlands—which was fighting Spain for its independence—had a large commercial fleet that actively protested CIL by establishing new trading routes and engaging in privateering, which is state-sponsored piracy. Hugo Grotius—one of the founding fathers of international law—worked as a lawyer for the Dutch East India Company when one of its ships used force against a Portuguese merchant ship. This experience led him to write *Mare Liberum* (or "The Free Sea") in 1609, in which he argued that international law allowed all states to sail through the high seas.[201] Ultimately, the doctrine of *mare liberum* prevailed as Portuguese and Spanish power declined.

Similarly, new technology can prompt changes in customary international law. Most of the modern changes in the law of the sea were prompted by new technology for underwater drilling and mining. After World War II, US President Truman feared that the US lacked adequate oil for economic recovery. New technology promised to make offshore drilling into the continental shelf (the land mass below the ocean) economically viable. In September 1945, President Truman issued a public statement, in which he claimed control over the continental shelf adjacent to US territory. This policy violated CIL, but other states did not object. They were also economically devastated by World War II and seeking new resources for reconstruction. Rather than protesting the US action, many other states quickly copied it. By 1950, over thirty states had claimed expanded offshore territory, setting off new maritime delimitations like those in the *North Sea* dispute.[202]

These examples illustrate how political power affects the creation and change of CIL. While economic and technological changes create incentives for states to change CIL, the international system usually needs a powerful state, like the Netherlands in the seventeenth century or the US in the twentieth century, to assert leadership in creating and upholding new rules.

Influence of Treaties

A second conceptual challenge is: what role should treaties play in creating and identifying CIL? In the *North Sea* case, Denmark and the Netherlands argued that West Germany was bound by the 1958 Geneva Convention on the Continental Shelf, which included the equidistance rule. The ICJ dismissed this argument because West Germany had not ratified the Geneva Convention. Nonetheless, the ICJ then had to consider: what role (if any) did the Geneva Convention play in creating or identifying customary international law? First, perhaps the Geneva Convention codified rules that were already customary international law. Then the treaty would have reflected CIL without actually shaping it. Second, perhaps the Geneva Convention crystallized prior state practice into CIL. In this scenario, the treaty would have played a vital step in forming CIL. Finally, perhaps a customary rule formed after the Geneva Convention, meaning that the treaty might have influenced later CIL.

The first possibility—that a treaty codifies existing CIL—would require state practice and acceptance of law before the treaty was created. In its 2016 report, the ILC recommended examining a treaty's *travaux préparatoires* to see if states wrote rules that were generally accepted, or that were contested by many states.[203] Additionally, the ILC wrote that "participation in a treaty may be an important factor in determining whether it corresponds to customary international law; treaties that have obtained near-universal acceptance may be seen as particularly indicative."[204] However, even treaties that codify existing rules often contain new rules.

The second possibility—that a treaty crystallizes new CIL—comes with similar challenges. A treaty alone cannot create customary international law: state practice and *opinio juris* are also necessary. Judges may examine the *travaux préparatoires* and treaty membership. However, it is unlikely that states would spend effort writing down rules that are broadly accepted.

In the *North Sea* case, the ICJ quickly dispensed with these first two possibilities. The ICJ examined the Geneva Convention's *travaux préparatoires* and concluded that the equidistance method "was proposed ... with considerable hesitation, somewhat on an experimental basis."[205] The treaty allowed states to include reservations to the equidistance method, suggesting that negotiators did not regard it as part of customary international law. Accordingly, the Court concluded, the Geneva Convention neither reflected pre-existing CIL nor crystallized new CIL.

The final possibility was that perhaps CIL formed after the Geneva Convention. This third option forces experts to consider a difficult issue—how to assess the actions of states that join a treaty and comply with its terms? As a first step, judges can consider treaty membership as a form of state practice. In the *North Sea* case, the ICJ noted that the Geneva Convention had only existed for ten years by the time of the case. So the majority doubted that CIL could have formed over this short period. Additionally, the majority argued that too few states had ratified the treaty for it to serve as evidence of state practice and acceptance of law.[206]

As a second step, judges can consider how the treaty shapes other forms of state practice. Recall that Denmark and the Netherlands argued that many states used the equidistance method. However, the ICJ discounted these examples of state practice because many of these states were joining the Geneva Convention. It wrote:

> over half the states concerned ... were or shortly became parties to the Geneva Convention, and were therefore presumably ... acting actually or potentially in the application of the Convention. From their action no inference could legitimately be drawn as to the existence of a rule of customary international law.[207]

The majority argued that it was unclear whether these states were using the equidistance method because of the treaty, or because of CIL.

Some experts argue that after a treaty is completed, only non-members can affect CIL. This viewpoint essentially disregards all of the actions of treaty members.

Other experts argue that treaty members can influence subsequent CIL based on their behavior towards non-members. For example, the ILC argued that:

> when states act in conformity with a treaty by which they are not bound, or apply conventional obligations in their relations with non-parties to the treaty, this may evidence the existence of acceptance as law.[208]

Ironically, both perspectives imply that it is harder to create new CIL rules when more states agree to follow these rules by joining a treaty.

However, most contemporary international law experts believe that treaties play an important role in creating customary international law. They view treaty membership and compliance as inherently state practice and acceptance of law. Experts differ in how much they believe that treaties should affect custom. Overall, though, treaties have become a tool for forming both consensual obligations for treaty members and non-consensual obligations via customary international law.

Resolutions of the UN General Assembly

A third conceptual challenge is: how do UN General Assembly resolutions affect customary international law?[209] Each United Nations member has an equal vote in the General Assembly, meaning that it is very representative. The UN Charter allows the General Assembly to pass resolutions on a variety of issues using a two-thirds majority vote. But what legal force do these resolutions have?

The UN General Assembly is not an international legislature. When the UN was created in 1945, the General Assembly was viewed as a political body, while the ICJ was the UN's legal body. As states in Africa and Asia gained their independence in the 1950s and 1960s, they were optimistic that the ICJ would help them secure justice against colonialism. However, in two highly controversial lawsuits, the ICJ refused to rule on colonial disputes, making future colonial lawsuits unlikely.[210] Newly independent states shifted their focus to the UN General Assembly. While the General Assembly could not legislate, newly independent states believed that it could influence customary international law.

The 1960s and 1970s saw a flurry of activity in which newly independent states used their growing numerical power in the General Assembly. Much of their agenda focused on development, including trade, investment, finance, and foreign aid.[211] Over time, the ICJ began to invoke UN General Assembly resolutions as evidence of customary international law, particularly in cases that challenged powerful states. For example, General Assembly resolutions played a prominent role in the ICJ's ruling in the *Nicaragua* case, which found that the US had illegally intervened and used force in Nicaragua. Similarly, UN General Assembly resolutions were key to the ICJ's advisory opinion on the *Legality of the Threat or Use of Nuclear Weapons*. In both cases, the ICJ treated General Assembly resolutions as evidence of customary international law, thereby giving political influence to states that challenged US intervention and the power of nuclear states.

It is now commonly accepted that UN General Assembly resolutions influence CIL by serving as evidence of state practice and/or *opinio juris*. However, not all General Assembly resolutions are the same. In some areas, like the authorization of UN budgets, General Assembly resolutions are legally binding applications of the UN Charter.[212] In all other areas, they are not legally binding. So how do we know which resolutions influence customary international law, and which do not? The simple answer is: we don't. When lawyers use a General Assembly resolution as evidence of CIL, they must evaluate it carefully, taking into account the precise text, the political context in which it was passed, and other aspects of state behavior. They ask questions such as: Did states reach the text after extensive deliberation? How many states voted for and against the resolution? Did states pledge resources to uphold the resolution? Has the content been reinforced in other resolutions?

There is no official list of UN General Assembly resolutions that reflect customary international law. Yet Table 2.1 shows some prominent examples. Two resolutions from 1946 supported the Nuremberg Tribunal, which prosecuted Germans for World War II crimes, and condemned genocide. Both of these resolutions have influenced international criminal law. Similarly, the Universal Declaration of Human Rights was adopted as a UN General Assembly resolution in 1948. States often argue that many of its provisions reflect customary human rights law, although they disagree about which provisions are part of CIL and which are not. Similarly, developing states used General Assembly resolutions in 1962 and 1974 to challenge the rights of foreign investors. Finally, resolutions from 1970 and 1974 shaped law on the use of force.

Table 2.1 UN General Assembly Resolutions that Have Influenced CIL

Resolution	Year	Content
95	1946	Nuremberg Tribunal (international criminal law): "*The General Assembly* ... [a]ffirms the principles of international law recognized by the Charter of the [Nuremberg] Tribunal and the judgment of the Tribunal"
96	1946	Genocide: "genocide is a crime under international law which the civilized world condemns, and for the commission of which principals and accomplices ... are punishable"
217	1948	Universal Declaration of Human Rights: outlines many human rights*
1803	1962	Permanent Sovereignty over Natural Resources: economic agreements must be based on sovereign equality and self-determination of people living in a territory; states have a limited right to expropriate from foreign property owners**

Table 2.1 (cont.)

Resolution	Year	Content
2625	1970	Declaration on Principles of International Law Concerning Friendly Relations and Co-operation among States: prohibits use of force and intervention into domestic matters
3281	1974	Charter of Economic Rights and Duties of States: asserts various priorities of newly independent, developing states, including a limited right to expropriate from foreign property owners**
3314	1974	Definition of Aggression: defines various acts that qualify as aggression against a foreign state, including support of non-state actors

Notes:
* States disagree about which specific provisions are part of customary international law.
** Most often held to create evidence against CIL claims by developed states.

In contemporary debates, experts disagree over how much weight should be given to General Assembly resolutions. More progressive experts believe that General Assembly resolutions should have more influence over customary international law. These experts argue that the world has changed immensely since 1945, and our interpretation of the UN Charter should evolve to match new geopolitical realities. Now that developing states make up a majority of the international community, they should have more influence over international law. Since these states often lack the resources to influence CIL through physical acts, UN General Assembly resolutions should receive more deference.[213] These experts argue that the UN General Assembly is an ideal venue for shaping international law because its structure encourages deliberation and the equality of states, and its outcomes are representative.[214]

In contrast, more conservative experts believe that UN General Assembly resolutions should have less influence over CIL. They argue that these resolutions have always been non-binding. Since states do not believe they are making law when voting on UN General Assembly resolutions, we should not assume that their votes truthfully reveal their beliefs about law.[215]

The opinions of most experts lie in between these two extreme views. UN General Assembly resolutions are unlikely to prevail if they are the only evidence of a proposed rule. Yet they can supplement legal claims that are supported by other evidence of state practice and *opinio juris*. The ILC supported this moderate position, writing: "A resolution adopted by an international organization ... cannot, of itself, create a rule of customary international law," yet such a resolution "may provide evidence for establishing the existence and content of a rule of customary international law, or contribute to its development."[216]

Opting Out

A final conceptual challenge is whether states can opt out of CIL. As described above, states that don't object to new rules are believed to acquiesce to them. But if a state actively opposes a new rule, can it be bound by the rule?

Many experts believe that international law has a **persistent objector doctrine**—that a state that disagrees with a rule before it becomes CIL is not constrained by the rule after it becomes CIL. According to the ILC: "Where a state has objected to a rule of customary international law while that rule was in the process of formation, the rule is not opposable to the state concerned for so long as it maintains its objection."[217] A persistent objector does not keep the rule from becoming law, but it ensures that the law will not apply to itself. Some scholars argue that states are not bound by rules to which they have objected. Others argue that the international community merely tolerates violations by persistent objectors, making them "legally justified pariahs."[218]

Where does the persistent objector doctrine come from? Various scholars have traced the idea to classical international law, but most experts agree that it did not emerge as a fully developed doctrine until after World War II.[219] Two early ICJ cases suggested that a state can be exempt from CIL if it has consistently opposed the law. Yet the phrase "persistent objector" is believed to come from a 1966 textbook.

While the persistent objector doctrine has not been well-explored in legal cases, it has appeared in political disputes. For example, throughout most of the twentieth century, South Africa was governed by a white minority government that imposed apartheid. As decolonization spread, other states argued that apartheid violated human rights treaties and customary international law. South Africa claimed to be a persistent objector, and hence was allowed to continue apartheid. Similarly, in complaints to the Inter-American Commission on Human Rights, the US was accused of violating CIL by using the juvenile death penalty. In its defense, the US argued that it was a persistent objector.

Most of the development of the persistent objector doctrine—including procedural requirements and limits on its use—comes from law scholars. These scholars have argued that states can become persistent objectors by: making statements during treaty negotiations and international organization debates; issuing diplomatic communiqués and press releases on contemporary events; writing national laws; making arguments in domestic and international lawsuits; and adding reservations to treaties.[220] However, states must meet three criteria to be a persistent objector. First, they must be *persistent* by repeatedly objecting to a rule. Second, their actions must be *timely*—their objections must begin before a rule becomes CIL. Third, their opposition must be *consistent*—they must uniformly oppose the rule. For example, many activists argued in the 1990s that landmines violated customary international law. Turkey opposed this movement and used landmines on its borders with Iran, Iraq, and Syria. Yet activists argued that Turkey acted inconsistently when it agreed to remove landmines from its border with Bulgaria.[221] Similarly, human rights activists argued that the US position on the death penalty was inconsistent because only some parts of the US allowed the juvenile death penalty.

Scholars argue that sometimes states cannot be persistent objectors. First, new states–that are created after CIL–cannot become persistent objectors. Second, states cannot be persistent objectors to a peremptory norm. Just as states are not permitted to write treaties that violate a peremptory norm, so, too, are they prohibited from persistently objecting to a peremptory norm, like the prohibition of piracy or slavery.

The persistent objector doctrine has created major debates. First, many critics question whether the doctrine even exists, or whether it is the invention of law scholars. These critics argue that there is little state practice, and that the rule has never been successfully invoked as a defense in an international court. States that disagree with a possible legal rule usually deny that custom exists, rather than claiming status as a persistent objector. Additionally, most of the examples of persistent objectors have become moot because states eventually adopted the international norm. South Africa abandoned apartheid when it transitioned to black majority rule; Turkey prohibited landmines in 2003 when it signed the Mine Ban Treaty; and the US Supreme Court declared in 2005 that the juvenile death penalty violated the US Constitution. Thus, many examples of persistent objectors are no longer valid. Supporters of the persistent objector doctrine argue that international disputes rarely result in litigation, giving international courts few opportunities to address the issue. Also, given the uncertainty about whether/when a norm becomes CIL, it is not surprising that states would rather argue that a law does not exist than argue that they are "pariahs" that are exempt from the rule. The fact that South Africa, Turkey, and the US all changed their policies may simply reflect how difficult it is to remain a persistent objector.

Second, many critics argue that the persistent objector doctrine is a tool of power politics. They point out that the scholarship supporting the rule is biased in favor of the US, which often finds itself opposed to the international community on issues like the juvenile death penalty.[222] Additionally, the rule emerged when major Western states (like the UK and US) were challenged by new states in the UN General Assembly. Critics of the persistent objector doctrine also highlight that the timeliness criterion is biased against new states, which must accept rules that they did not shape.[223] Some judges and scholars from developing states argue that new states are not bound by existing rules of the international system. Rather, these scholars argue, new states should decide for themselves which rules of international law apply to them.

2.4   Other Important Factors

Finally, states can make international law using general principles, unilateral declarations, and peremptory norms. These methods are less common than treaties and customary international law, yet they are important nonetheless. We discuss each in turn.

General Principles

When states created the Permanent Court of International Justice (PCIJ) after World War I, they worried that it would not have enough treaties and customary international law to resolve international disputes. Some states argued that the PCIJ should be allowed to use "the general principles of justice and equity" or "rules which, in the considered opinion of the Court, should be the rules of international law."[224] Not surprisingly, this proposal was controversial to states that believed that only states can make international law. As a compromise, the final PCIJ Statute lists "general principles of law recognized by civilized nations" as a source of law, reflecting the European belief of the time that only "civilized" states should shape international law.[225] This text was later copied into the ICJ Statute.

Neither of these treaties defines "general principles" or describes how the Court should identify them. General principles only played a decisive role in one ICJ case. In the *Corfu Channel* case, the United Kingdom sued Albania after two UK warships were damaged by mines off the coast of Albania in 1946. Neither side could prove who had laid the mines, but the Court concluded that "the laying of the minefield which caused the explosions ... could not have been accomplished without the knowledge of the Albanian government."[226] The Court believed that Albania had a legal obligation to warn the UK government about the mines. The Court argued that Albania had violated:

> general and well-recognized principles, namely: elementary considerations of humanity
> ... ; the principle of the freedom of maritime communication; and every state's
> obligation not to allow knowingly its territory to be used for acts contrary to the rights
> of other states.[227]

Albania had not violated any treaties or customary international law, but it was nonetheless held responsible for the damage.

Experts disagree about how courts should use general principles. Two major approaches exist. First, most experts argue that the ICJ Statute's reference to "civilized nations" suggests that the Court may invoke domestic legal principles if they are used across different legal systems. These might include principles that regulate contracts between individuals.[228] For example, Iran and Iraq fought a prolonged war in the 1980s that disrupted trade in the Persian Gulf. Many ships were damaged by attacks and mines during the conflict, prompting the US to retaliate by bombing several Iranian oil facilities. Iran sued the US at the ICJ, arguing that the US violated international law. As in the *Corfu Channel* case, the Court did not know who laid the mines that damaged ships. In a separate opinion, Judge Bruno Simma analyzed multiple domestic legal systems and argued that Iran was responsible for the damage, even though the US could not prove that Iran laid the mines.[229] The majority of the Court did not agree with Judge Simma, but his opinion is notable because ICJ judges rarely invoke general principles of law.

The claim that general principles come from domestic legal systems has a few benefits. First, when states adopt a domestic legal principle, they implicitly consent to it. Second, such principles can help resolve disputes about new legal issues, such as environmental regulation. However, the major cost of this approach is that international judges are not experts on every legal system in the world. This limited knowledge can introduce bias into judicial decisions.[230]

Second, some experts argue that general principles allow judges to rule based on fairness and justice. Such arguments are controversial, suggesting a "contemporary revival of natural law."[231] Yet occasionally, judges invoke concepts like equity as a general principle of law. For example, in the *Frontier Dispute* case, the ICJ was asked to determine the border between Burkina Faso and Mali. The ICJ relied primarily on historical documents that were silent about the division of the pool of Soum, a small body of water that crossed the border. The ICJ wrote that "in the absence of any precise indication in the texts of the position of the frontier line, the line should divide the pool of Soum in two, in an equitable manner."[232]

Similarly, Argentina sued Uruguay in 2006 for constructing two mills along their common river border, arguing that the mills would cause environmental damage. The ICJ majority acknowledged that states have an obligation under customary international law to prevent transboundary harm to other states, but found that Uruguay had not breached any of its substantive treaty obligations by building the mills.[233] In a separate opinion, Judge Cançado Trindade argued that the majority overlooked numerous environmental principles that he believed were relevant. Judge Cançado Trindade could not argue that these principles were reflected in the relevant treaty or customary international law. Instead, he argued that they were binding as general principles. Echoing natural law theorists, he argued: "General principles of law emanate, in my perception, from human conscience, from the universal juridical conscience, which I regard as the ultimate material 'source' of all law."[234] Judge Cançado Trindade believed that environmental principles were a source of international law because they were necessary for law to "accomplish its fundamental function of providing justice."[235]

This approach to general principles also comes with benefits and costs. The key benefit is that judges can respond to issues not yet addressed by treaties and customary international law.[236] However, judges like Cançado Trindade risk the authority and legitimacy of international courts if they rule based on their own preferences, rather than the existing law.

Unilateral Declarations

In the early 1970s, Australia and New Zealand were upset with France for testing nuclear weapons in the atmosphere above the South Pacific. They were concerned about the health and environmental impact of the tests. Additionally, political organizations worldwide were pushing states to reduce their nuclear arsenals. Australia and New Zealand filed lawsuits at the ICJ in 1973, and the Court ordered France to temporarily cease atmospheric nuclear tests until litigation ended.[237] France quickly announced that it would not follow the ICJ order. Then France changed course and declared publicly that it would not conduct future atmospheric nuclear tests. This reversal was likely driven by domestic and international political pressure after it broke the ICJ's order, and technological developments that allowed France to switch to underground nuclear tests. Australia and New Zealand were not satisfied by this outcome, and continued with their cases.

France placed the ICJ in a very difficult position. The Court had been asked to rule against a powerful state on an important political issue. Rather than ruling on

Figure 2.4 France conducts an atmospheric nuclear test in French Polynesia in 1971. Australia and New Zealand sued France in 1973 over such tests, arguing that France had violated international law. France then made a unilateral declaration that it would not conduct future atmospheric nuclear tests. The ICJ ruled that this unilateral declaration created a binding obligation under international law.

the merits of the case, the ICJ argued that France had made a **unilateral declaration** that it would not conduct future atmospheric tests, thereby creating a legally binding obligation to end the tests. The ICJ wrote:

> It is well recognized that declarations made by way of unilateral acts ... may have the effect of creating legal obligations. Declarations of this kind may be, and often are, very specific. When it is the intention of the state making the declaration that it should become bound according to its terms, that intention confers on the declaration the character of a legal undertaking, the state being thenceforth legally required to follow a course of conduct consistent with the declaration. An undertaking of this kind, if given publicly, and with an intent to be bound ... is binding.[238]

Therefore, the Court reasoned, the dispute between these states no longer existed, and the Court did not need to rule on the legality of past tests.

Why did the Court believe that France's unilateral declaration created a binding legal obligation? Unilateral declarations are not listed as a source of law in the ICJ Statute, and they don't meet the definition of a treaty.[239] Prior to the *Nuclear Tests* case, there was almost no relevant state practice, suggesting that the Court's ruling was not supported by customary international law.[240] Under Anglo-American domestic law, unilateral declarations can create binding legal obligations if the listener acts in reliance on the statement, meaning that she commits "acts or abstentions based on the assumption that the unilateral promisor will keep his word."[241] However, this is not a rule under other domestic legal systems; and even if it were, Australia and New Zealand did not act in reliance on France's declarations. They continued their Court case even after France's declaration, indicating that they did not believe that France had created a legal obligation to stop atmospheric nuclear tests. Thus the ICJ's ruling in the *Nuclear Tests* case is not based on general principles of law.

The *Nuclear Tests* ruling is problematic for two additional reasons. First, if unilateral declarations can create legal obligations, then how can states know which declarations create law, and which do not? The ICJ argued that intention plays a key role in transforming a statement into a legal obligation:

> Of course, not all unilateral acts imply obligation; but a state may choose to take up a certain position in relation to a particular matter with the intention of being bound—the intention is to be ascertained by interpretation of the act.[242]

But how should such "interpretation" occur?

Second, if a unilateral declaration can create a legal obligation, can it also alter an obligation? That is, if France can unilaterally make international law one day, what stops it from unilaterally changing that law on the next day? The ICJ argued that the principle of **good faith**—which requires that parties to an agreement must act fairly and honestly towards one another—required that France must comply with its unilateral declaration:

> One of the basic principles governing the creation and performance of legal obligations, whatever their source, is the principle of good faith ... Just as the very rule of *pacta sunt servanda* in the law of treaties is based on good faith, so also is the binding character of an international obligation assumed by unilateral declaration. Thus interested states may take cognizance of unilateral declarations and place confidence in them, and are entitled to require that the obligation thus created be respected.[243]

Yet critics have found this argument unpersuasive. After all, if the principle of good faith cannot prevent states from sometimes exiting treaties, how can it bind a state that makes a unilateral declaration?

A few states tried to invoke unilateral declarations in later ICJ cases, but the Court did not support these arguments.[244] In response to the uncertainty generated by the *Nuclear Tests* ruling, the International Law Commission drafted principles for unilateral declarations.[245] The ILC identified past declarations that it believed had created legal obligations, including a 1957 proclamation by Egypt about the Suez Canal and a 1988 statement in which the King of Jordan waived territorial claims to the West Bank. However, the ILC's text is not itself a source of law. The legal status of unilateral declarations is thus ambiguous.

Peremptory Norms (*Jus Cogens*)

After World War II, a military tribunal at Nuremberg oversaw the criminal trials of Germans accused of war crimes.[246] Some of the defendants were accused of using French prisoners of war to manufacture armaments. As part of the defense, witnesses testified that Nazi Germany had negotiated an agreement with Vichy France that permitted the defendants to use the prisoners as labor. The Nuremberg judges doubted whether this agreement ever existed because there was no written copy. Nonetheless, the Tribunal ruled that even "if there was such agreement it was void under the law of nations."[247] The Tribunal argued that any such agreement "was manifestly **contra bono mores** [i.e. 'against good morals'] and hence void."[248] That is, the Tribunal concluded that international law prohibited France and Germany from writing a treaty that allowed prisoners of war to build armaments. In this ruling, the Nuremberg Tribunal reaffirmed the importance of natural law in international relations.

Early international law scholars believed that states were bound by higher rules that descended from natural law. Even Vattel, who emphasized state behavior, acknowledged "the necessary law of nations, which consists in the application of the law of nature to nations."[249] He argued:

> as this law is immutable, and the obligations that arise from it necessary and indispensable, nations can neither make any changes in it by their conventions,

dispense with it in their own conduct, nor reciprocally release each other from the observance of it.

> This is the principle by which we may distinguish lawful conventions or treaties from those that are not lawful, and innocent and rational customs from those that are unjust or censurable.[250]

These early international law scholars believed that certain man-made laws between states were not valid because they conflicted with higher-order natural law.

Natural law fell into disfavor during the positivist era when states and scholars emphasized voluntary law. However, the concept of natural law was revived by Alfred Verdross in the 1930s. As a native Austrian, Verdross was disturbed by many of the conditions placed on Austria and Germany by the Treaty of Versailles after World War I. He believed that it was immoral for victorious states to require losing states to disarm and pay war reparations that damaged their economies.[251]

Ironically, it was Germany's actions before and during World War II that created broad support for communitarian law, in which common values of the international community can trump the consent of states. Many experts were troubled by the Munich Agreement of 1938, in which France, Italy, and the UK agreed to give Germany land that belonged to Czechoslovakia without actually including Czechoslovakia in the negotiations. Additionally, observers were horrified by Nazi Germany's genocide against the Jews during World War II. After World War II, experts debated whether international law contained obligations and/or rights that were unconditional and could not be changed by states.[252] Verdross's arguments quickly gained support and were included in the Vienna Convention on the Law of Treaties.

Identification

The key concept that underlies peremptory norms is **derogation**, which is a decision by a pair or group of states to exempt themselves from a norm in their relations with one another. For example, imagine that you are a student in a class and your professor announces that one component of your grade is giving a presentation. If you have extreme anxiety about public speaking, you might ask your professor if you can complete an alternative assignment, like writing a paper. If she agrees, then you could derogate from the class syllabus.

Similarly, domestic legal systems sometimes contain default rules (or *jus dispositivum*) that individuals can change via contracts. Default rules provide useful standards that can be used in the absence of contracts, such as property inheritance rules. But individuals have autonomy to make alternative legal arrangements if they do not want to use default rules. In contrast, other rules in domestic legal systems are mandatory (or *jus cogens*). These mandatory rules limit the autonomy of individuals in exchange for promoting a social value. For example, if you hire an architect to design a new house, they must follow local building codes that protect homeowners from earthquakes, fires, and floods. While these building codes limit the plans that you and your architect can make, they keep you and your neighbors safe.

Similarly, many experts believe that states cannot derogate from certain international norms. The VCLT defines a peremptory norm as:

> a norm accepted and recognized by the international community of states as a whole as a norm from which no derogation is permitted and which can be modified only by a subsequent norm of general international law having the same character.[253]

The body of all peremptory norms is called *jus cogens*.

The VCLT defines peremptory norms based on their effect, not their content. Imagine that you are a student and you have this exchange with your professor:

PROFESSOR: A student who excels in my class will earn a grade of A+.
STUDENT: What must I do to excel in the class?
PROFESSOR: Earn an A+.

Would you know how to excel in the class? Being told to "Earn an A+" probably isn't very useful. Similarly, the VCLT definition of a peremptory norm isn't very useful.

Identifying peremptory norms is a highly contentious issue in international law. Any list of peremptory norms is likely to prompt disagreement from experts, who have diverse views. Yet to illustrate this diversity, Table 2.2 includes examples that are organized based on the level of support from the international community.

Overall, there is high support for some peremptory norms, including the prohibition of apartheid, genocide, piracy, slavery, torture, and the use of force.[254] Additionally, most experts argue that states have a non-derogable right to

Table 2.2 Examples of Proposed Peremptory Norms (*jus cogens*) and Level of Support from the International Community

Type of Norm	Low Support	Medium Support	High Support
Obligation	Prohibition of: • Use of economic force Protection of: • Environment	Prohibition of: • Human trafficking • Racial discrimination • Terrorism Protection of: • Civilians during war • Human rights* • Prisoners of war	Prohibition of: • Apartheid • Genocide • Piracy • Slavery • Torture • Use of force

Table 2.2 (cont.)

Type of Norm	Low Support	Medium Support	High Support
Right	Right to: • Permanent sovereignty over natural resources • Humanitarian intervention	Right to: • Defensive military • Provide diplomatic protection • Deep seabed resources as the "common heritage of mankind"	Right to: • Self-determination

Notes: This table summarizes possible peremptory norms (*jus cogens*) that have been proposed by courts, scholars, and/or states. The classification is based on the author's assessment of the academic literature and court rulings.

* States disagree about which specific human rights.

self-determination. Numerous other obligations and rights have been proposed as peremptory norms, but have received less support from the international community. For example, while many experts argue that some human rights protections have become peremptory norms, they disagree about which protections are peremptory.[255] Similarly, while the prohibition of apartheid is usually considered a peremptory norm, experts disagree about whether less extreme forms of racial discrimination violate a peremptory norm.[256]

One difficulty in identifying peremptory norms is limited state practice and court rulings. Statements about what is a peremptory norm are thus the opinions of politicians and scholars, which can lead to "false universalism," when individuals project their own values onto others.[257] Another difficulty in identifying peremptory norms is that beliefs about acceptable behavior can change over time. For example, in his 1937 German-language textbook, Verdross argued that the Versailles Peace Treaty, which ended World War I, was *contra bono mores* because it required Germany to surrender its citizens to face war crimes prosecutions by the victorious powers.[258] This argument implies that Verdross believed that a peremptory norm prohibited international tribunals for war crimes.[259] Yet eight years later, the Nuremberg Tribunal was prosecuting German war criminals.

Effects

International law scholars agree about one effect of peremptory norms: by definition, a treaty is invalid if it conflicts with a peremptory norm. While an international court has not yet invalidated a treaty based on a peremptory norm, experts have identified numerous examples of treaties that are possibly invalid. Table 2.3 shows some of these examples, including the 1956 Protocol of Sèvres, in which France, Israel, and the UK secretly agreed to attack Egypt after it nationalized the

Table 2.3 Examples of Possibly Invalid Treaties

Treaty	Purpose	Possible Conflict with a Peremptory Norm
Munich Agreement (1938)	France, Italy, and the UK agree to Germany's demands for territory that belongs to Czechoslovakia	Violates self-determination rights of Czech people living on the territory (but Czechoslovakia agrees to the demands soon after)
Molotov–Ribbentrop Pact (1939)	Germany and Soviet Union agree not to fight each other, and divide up land (that does not belong to them) in Eastern Europe and the Baltic	Violates self-determination rights of various people living on the territory
Protocol of Sèvres (1956)	France, Israel, and the UK write a secret pact to jointly attack Egypt after its nationalization of the Suez Canal	Violates UN prohibition on the use of force
Treaty of Guarantee (1960)	Cyprus, Greece, Turkey, and the UK agree to peaceful governance of contested territory on Cyprus; a treaty provision is later interpreted by Turkey as authorizing a military intervention	Violates UN prohibition on the use of force (but other parties disagree with Turkey's interpretation of the Treaty)
Exchange of Notes Concerning British Indian Ocean Territory (1966)	UK and US sign an agreement to create a US military base on a remote island; native population is removed by the UK	Violates self-determination rights of native people living on the island
Camp David Accords (1978)	Egypt and Israel resolve various territorial disputes	Violates self-determination rights of Palestinian people living on the territory
Timor Gap Treaty (1989)	Australia and Indonesia sign a maritime delimitation agreement that affects East Timor, a region that had asserted independence	Violates self-determination and natural resource rights of East Timorese people
EU–Morocco Fisheries Partnership Agreement (2013)	EU and Morocco sign fishing agreement with ambiguity about its application off the coast of Western Sahara, which is considered by the UN to be a non-self-governing territory	Violates self-determination and natural resources rights of Western Saharan people

Source: Examples from Daniel Costelloe (2017), *Legal Consequences of Peremptory Norms in International Law*, Cambridge University Press.

Suez Canal. When the treaty became public, experts condemned it for violating the international prohibition of the use of force.

Similarly, many experts believe that the Timor Gap Treaty of 1989 between Australia and Indonesia violated the self-determination rights of the East Timorese people, who sought independence from Indonesia.

In addition to invalidating treaties, some international law experts believe that peremptory norms can invalidate customary international law. In 1998, the International Criminal Tribunal for the former Yugoslavia (ICTY) argued that the prohibition of torture was a peremptory norm. The ICTY then argued that:

> Because of the importance of the values it protects, [the prohibition of torture] has evolved into a peremptory norm or *jus cogens*, that is, a norm that enjoys a higher rank in the international hierarchy than treaty law and even "ordinary" customary rules. The most conspicuous consequence of this higher rank is that the principle at issue cannot be derogated from by states through international treaties or ... even general customary rules.[260]

That is, the ICTY argued that the prohibition of torture invalidated treaties and customary international law.

For example, customary international law grants a state immunity from the jurisdiction of other states' domestic courts, provided that it is engaging in sovereign acts.[261] A person cannot, for example, go to an Italian domestic court to challenge German income taxes. But can someone go to an Italian court to sue Germany for violating a peremptory norm? That is, does violating a peremptory norm override Germany's right under customary international law to immunity from Italian courts? Both domestic and international courts have struggled with this question as individuals increasingly use domestic courts to challenge foreign states. Customary international law also protects some government officials from the jurisdiction of foreign courts. Yet human rights advocates have increasingly used domestic courts to sue foreign government officials for torture and war crimes. Some domestic courts have allowed peremptory norms to trump customary law rules on state immunity.

Some experts also argue that peremptory norms can invalidate treaty reservations. For example, the Democratic Republic of the Congo sued Rwanda at the ICJ in 2002 for genocide. When Rwanda joined the Genocide Convention, it included a reservation that limited the ICJ's jurisdiction to hear cases involving the Convention. The Democratic Republic of the Congo argued that the ICJ nonetheless had authority to hear the case because Rwanda was accused of violating a peremptory norm, thereby invalidating Rwanda's reservation to the Genocide Convention. While the ICJ acknowledged that genocide is a peremptory norm, it also ruled that this finding did not invalidate Rwanda's treaty reservation.[262]

Politicization

Due to their uncertain identification and effects, peremptory norms are highly politicized. Unlike treaties and customary international law, peremptory norms bind all states. A state cannot avoid a peremptory norm by refusing to sign a treaty or claiming to be a persistent objector. The stakes of peremptory norms are thus very high.

One common tactic is for states to try to use peremptory norms to bind states without their consent. For example, when states negotiated the 1982 UN Convention on the Law of the Sea (UNCLOS), they included rules for natural resources in the deep seabed, which lies outside of the territory of all states. During UNCLOS negotiations, developing states argued that deep seabed resources are the "common heritage of mankind"—meaning that they belong to all states collectively.[263] They believed that deep seabed drilling and mining should be conducted under international supervision with profit-sharing among states. In contrast, the US argued that if no state owns these natural resources, then any state can take them. To bind the US, Chile led an attempt to have UNCLOS declare that the common heritage of mankind was a peremptory norm.[264] Although the final UNCLOS text did not include any statements about peremptory norms, developing states continued to use the language of peremptory norms to try to constrain the US and other developed states.[265]

Additionally, states sometimes try to use peremptory norms to excuse or justify violations of other peremptory norms. For example, the international community widely believes that a peremptory norm prohibits the use of force unless a state is acting in self-defense or under UN Security Council authorization. Yet states also have a legal obligation to prevent international crimes like genocide. This obligation has led some experts to argue that states have a right to use force to prevent genocide and other international crimes.

For example, most states considered the 1999 NATO intervention in Kosovo to be a violation of international law.[266] Yet NATO members defended their actions as legal because of reports that Serbian troops were committing genocide against ethnic Albanians. These states believed that they could violate one *jus cogens* norm—the prohibition of the use of force—because another state previously violated another *jus cogens* norm—the prohibition of genocide.

A pessimist might conclude that peremptory norms are, at best, illusions, and, at worst, deceit. In contrast, an optimist might view peremptory norms as a law-creating process. For example, many scholars contemplate what should be peremptory norms, given their own conception of justice. Other scholars emphasize that courts and states use peremptory norms to "serve primarily rhetorical or aspirational ends."[267] Peremptory norms may thus be the rules that the international community needs, even if these are not the rules that it has.

2.5   Case Study Revisited: Are North Korea's Nuclear Tests Illegal?

This chapter began by describing the advocacy movement to ban nuclear weapons testing. By 1996, all of the states with known nuclear weapons—China, France, Russia, the UK, and the US—had agreed via unilateral declarations to halt nuclear tests. States had also negotiated the Comprehensive Nuclear-Test-Ban Treaty, which prohibits all nuclear tests. The CTBT was supported by the UN General Assembly and most states in the world.

In subsequent years, anti-nuclear advocacy groups faced three major setbacks. First, India and Pakistan conducted nuclear tests in 1998, but later vowed to stop nuclear tests under international pressure. Second, the US Senate refused to ratify the CTBT, meaning that the treaty could not enter into force. Finally, North Korea began a series of nuclear tests in 2006.

North Korea's behavior was widely condemned. Regional neighbors—including Australia, Japan, and South Korea—were particularly fearful that nuclear weapons would create instability in the Asia-Pacific region. Even the UN Secretary-General described the nuclear test as "a grave contravention of the international norm against nuclear testing."[268] But did North Korea actually break international law by conducting nuclear tests?

To answer this question, we had to learn how states make international law:

- *Treaties*: A treaty is a legally binding written agreement between states. International law contains complex and detailed rules for how treaties become binding international law. It also has rules for how states join treaties, interpret and apply their rules, and sometimes exit these treaties.
- *Customary international law*: Customary international law—which is formed through a combination of state practice and acceptance of law—is also a source of law. Experts assess state practice using criteria like duration, repetition, internal consistency, generality, and representation.
- *Other important factors*: General principles are also a source of international law, but experts disagree about the precise meaning of "general principles." The ICJ has ruled that unilateral declarations can also be a source of law, although it is difficult to know the difference between a unilateral legal obligation and a non-binding political promise. Finally, many experts believe that international law includes peremptory norms, which are norms that are "accepted and recognized by the international community of states as a whole as a norm from which no derogation is permitted."[269]

To know whether international law prohibited North Korea's nuclear tests, we must consider each of these possible sources of international law.

Table 2.4 Treaties that Regulate Nuclear Tests

Year	Name	Objective	Entered into Force?	Number of Members	Is North Korea a Member?
1963	Partial Test Ban Treaty	Prohibit nuclear tests in the atmosphere, outer space, or underwater	Yes	125	No
1968	Non-Proliferation Treaty (NPT)	Limit the arms control race and promote nuclear disarmament	Yes	190–191*	Maybe*
1974	Threshold Test Ban Treaty	Prohibit nuclear tests underground with force greater than 150 kilotons	Yes	2**	No
1996	Comprehensive Nuclear-Test-Ban Treaty (CTBT)	Prohibit all nuclear tests	No	170	No
2017	Treaty on the Prohibition of Nuclear Weapons	Eliminate and prohibit all nuclear weapons	Yes	55	No

Notes: Information accurate as of July 1, 2021.
* Sources disagree about whether North Korea is a treaty member.
** Bilateral treaty between the US and the USSR/Russia.

We can begin by examining the various treaties that govern nuclear tests. As shown in Table 2.4, five major multilateral treaties regulate nuclear tests. North Korea is not a member of most of these treaties, so it is not directly bound by these legal texts. However, it is unclear whether North Korea was a member of the Non-Proliferation Treaty (NPT) in 2006, when it began its nuclear tests.

Why don't we know whether North Korea is an NPT member? North Korea joined the NPT—by signing and ratifying the treaty—in 1985. Then North Korea threatened to withdraw in 1993 under the NPT's exit clause, which says:

> Each Party shall ... have the right to withdraw from the Treaty if it decides that extraordinary events, related to the subject matter of this Treaty, have jeopardized the supreme interests of its country. It shall give notice of such withdrawal ... three months in advance. Such notice shall include a statement of the extraordinary events it regards as having jeopardized its supreme interests.[270]

However, North Korea changed its mind and remained a member.

What North Korea likely did not anticipate was a provision of the NPT that reads: "Twenty-five years after the entry into force of the Treaty, a conference shall ... decide whether the Treaty shall continue in force indefinitely."[271] In 1995, treaty members declared after a majority vote that: "the Treaty shall continue in force indefinitely."[272] Most states interpreted this decision as eliminating the NPT's exit clause. In 2003, North Korea tried once again to withdraw from the NPT, but it was unclear whether it could do so given the 1995 vote. Could a majority vote by treaty members remove an exit clause? Even if the exit clause remained in force, many experts believed that North Korea did not face the "extraordinary events" to justify exit. While some experts believe that North Korea withdrew from the NPT in 2003, others believe that North Korea remains a member of the treaty.

Does the NPT prohibit nuclear tests? The NPT focuses on limiting the nuclear arms race and promoting nuclear disarmament. It does not directly address nuclear tests. However, Article VI requires that treaty members "pursue negotiations in good faith on effective measures relating to cessation of the nuclear arms race ... and to nuclear disarmament." Similarly, the Preamble expresses support for the Partial Test Ban Treaty of 1963. Some experts argue therefore that a nuclear test ban is necessary for the NPT to achieve its object and purpose.[273] North Korean nuclear tests may therefore have violated an international treaty.

A second possible source of legal obligation is customary international law. No international court has ruled (yet) on whether customary international law prohibits nuclear tests. However, we can examine state practice ourselves. As shown in Figure 2.5, nuclear tests were common in the 1950s to 1980s. Since the CTBT was completed in 1996, only three states—none of which have signed the CTBT—have conducted nuclear tests: India, Pakistan, and North Korea. How would you apply the various criteria for assessing state practice to this data? Do you think there is sufficient state practice for customary international law to exist?

Customary international law also requires acceptance as law (*opinio juris*). Should the treaty membership data shown in Table 2.4 count as evidence of acceptance as law? Nuclear tests have been condemned repeatedly in the UN General Assembly and the Security Council. Should these resolutions count as evidence? Even if customary international law prohibits nuclear tests, would North Korea qualify as a persistent objector? North Korea was (and possibly still is) an NPT member, and did not begin nuclear tests until 2006. Was this too late for North Korea to begin objecting?

Finally, we can examine whether any other important factors limit North Korean nuclear tests. While international law does not have well-developed general principles, domestic legal systems usually assign liability for damages caused by legal acts.[274] Perhaps general principles of law make North Korea responsible for the environmental and health effects of nuclear tests. It is not clear, however, whether such liability means that the test themselves would be illegal. Additionally, North Korea has not made any unilateral declarations to limit nuclear tests. The unilateral declarations made by other states—including China, France, Russia, the UK, and the US—do not directly bind North Korea. Finally, perhaps the prohibition of

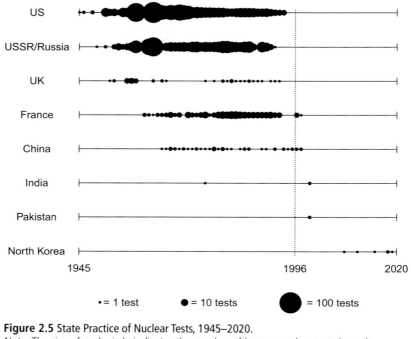

Figure 2.5 State Practice of Nuclear Tests, 1945–2020.
Note: The size of each circle indicates the number of known nuclear tests in each year. Almost all states ended nuclear tests by 1996. North Korea is the only state that continues to test nuclear weapons.
Data source: Arms Control Association.

nuclear tests is a peremptory norm. For example, more states illegally use force than conduct nuclear tests. So if the prohibition of the use of force is a peremptory norm, might the prohibition of nuclear tests also be a peremptory norm? All of these questions lack clear answers. But hopefully they illustrate the diverse ways that states can make international law.

3 Breaking International Law

3.1   Case Study: Estonia's Virtual War

In spring 2007, a sixty-year-old statue started a virtual war. At the end of World War II, Soviet soldiers expelled German forces from Tallinn, Estonia, a small city on the coast of the Baltic Sea. To celebrate this event, the Soviet Union created a memorial with a Bronze Soldier standing watch over the unclaimed bodies of Russian soldiers. For ethnic Russians, the monument symbolized their role in freeing Estonia from the Germans. For ethnic Estonians, the monument symbolized Estonia's subsequent oppression by the Soviet Union, which took control of Estonia.

After the Soviet Union collapsed in 1989, Estonia became independent and realigned with Western Europe, eventually joining the North Atlantic Treaty Organization (NATO). The Estonian government decided in 2007 to relocate the

Figure 3.1 An Estonian policeman stands guard near the Bronze Soldier of Tallinn in May 2007, after it was moved from central Tallinn to a military cemetery. This move provoked a massive cyberattack on the Estonian government and businesses.

Bronze Soldier and unclaimed bodies of Russian soldiers from central Tallinn to the edge of the city. Estonia's ethnic Russian community widely criticized this move. "Hacktivists"—political activists who use computer networks for subversive purposes—launched cyberattacks on the websites of Estonian government agencies, newspapers, and firms. These attacks lasted for weeks, shutting down many banks and government services. Legitimate websites were replaced with fake websites that called on ethnic Russians to riot against the Estonian government. An online battle even erupted for control over the "Bronze Soldier of Tallinn" Wikipedia page.

Many Estonians blamed Russia for the attack. Merit Kopli, the editor of a newspaper that was targeted in the attack, declared: "The cyber-attacks are from Russia. There is no question. It's political."[1] Anonymous NATO officials told reporters that the attacks were probably not the work of isolated individuals. They believed that the depth and sophistication of the attacks indicated that Russia was involved.[2] However, Russia denied responsibility for the attack. Russian officials argued that the cyberattacks were conducted by individuals who opposed the Estonian government, and were not an act of the Russian government.

In the aftermath of the attacks, NATO convened a group of international law experts to assess how international law applies to cyberattacks. They wrote: "The principle of state sovereignty applies in cyberspace ... In particular, states enjoy sovereignty over any cyber infrastructure located on their territory and activities associated with that cyber infrastructure."[3] They argued that international law on intervention and the use of force extended to cyberattacks. If Russia was indeed responsible for the cyberattacks, then it had broken international law.

But this assessment still leaves us with many open questions. First, was Russia actually responsible for the acts of individual hackers who opposed the Estonian government? If Russia was responsible for the cyberattacks, what could Estonia demand in response? And finally, how should states respond to incidents like the 2007 cyberattacks? For example, should they impose severe punishments, overlook legal violations, or pursue some other course of action?

Answering these questions requires that we first understand the following topics:

- *Determining responsibility*: How do experts determine whether a state has broken international law? Are states responsible for acts committed by non-state actors? And are there circumstances in which a legal violation is excused or justified?
- *Consequences of responsibility*: What are the consequences if a state is responsible for breaking international law? What can an injured state hope to gain by proving that another state has broken international law?
- *Why do states break international law?*: What factors explain when and why states violate legal commitments? Do states break law opportunistically, based on cost–benefit calculations? Or might they break law because of ambiguity about rules, limited capacity to comply, and other reasons?

The issues raised by the cyberattacks on Estonia are not unique to cybersecurity. This chapter asks: what happens when states break international law? States have attempted to answer this question by developing the international law of **state responsibility**. This body of law addresses the related issues of attribution, wrongfulness, and consequences; and it serves as a common basis for more specialized rules, like international trade, investment, and human rights law.

The law of state responsibility developed from international disputes about the treatment of individuals and firms in foreign states, particularly in the nineteenth and early twentieth centuries. When individuals and firms believed they had been mistreated in a foreign state, they sought diplomatic protection from their home states. These home states often pressured host states to use international **arbitration**, which is a legal process in which individuals consider the facts and laws relevant to an international dispute and then issue their findings. Usually these disputes involved investors from relatively rich countries, like France, the UK, and the US, who believed that their property rights had been violated by developing countries, usually in Latin America. These arbitration cases formed the historical basis of both the law of state responsibility and investment law.

After World War I, the League of Nations attempted to codify these rules about the treatment of foreign nationals. This effort was renewed after World War II by the United Nations, under the aegis of the International Law Commission (ILC). However, progress was stalled by disagreement between developed states, which favored strong legal protections for foreign nationals, and the growing number of newly independent developing states, which wanted to preserve their discretion and autonomy. In the mid-1960s, the ILC redefined its mandate: rather than writing rules for foreign investors, the ILC crafted a general framework for state responsibility under international law.

In 2001, the ILC completed the final version of its Articles on State Responsibility. Some states favored holding an international conference to transform the ILC Articles into a multilateral treaty. Other states opposed this plan, arguing that either such a treaty was not an important priority, or that such a conference was unlikely to yield a treaty because of a few controversial issues. As a compromise, the UN General Assembly passed a resolution in 2001 to show its support for the ILC Articles, but the Articles were never transformed into a treaty.[4]

The legal status of the ILC Articles is thus ambiguous: they are not treaty law, yet they reflect decades of negotiations and scholarship. Many critics believe that the Articles are (at most) a subsidiary source of international law because some provisions are progressive—that is, not well-established in state practice.[5] They argue that some provisions are what the ILC thinks *should be* international law, rather than what is actually customary international law. Nevertheless, the International Court of Justice (ICJ) treats the Articles as evidence of customary international law, giving (at least parts of) them great influence.

As shown in Figure 3.2, the ILC Articles (and the discussion in this chapter) begin with the assumption that an international legal obligation has already been broken. Such a breach could include a cyberattack on government agencies or the seizure of a foreign embassy. The law of state responsibility begins with attribution—or determining whether the breach is an act of a state. If the breach can be attributed to the state, the law of state responsibility then addresses wrongfulness. Namely, it asks whether the breach might be justified or excused. The combination of attribution and wrongfulness creates responsibility under international law. Finally, the law of state responsibility asks: what consequences should follow for

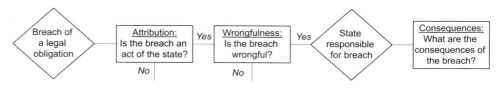

Figure 3.2 State responsibility concept map.
Note: The process of determining state responsibility begins with a legal breach. If the breach can be attributed to the state and it is wrongful, then the state is responsible. Responsibility then triggers consequences.

the breach? That is, what obligations does a responsible state have when it breaks international law?

A few important issues are missing from this conceptual framework. First, the ILC Articles do not consider the intentions of an actor who commits a legal breach. Some (but not all) domestic legal systems require that a plaintiff prove that a defendant intended to cause harm before holding the defendant responsible for a legal violation. International tribunals have historically been divided on this issue: some tribunals believed that intent was necessary to determine responsibility, while others did not.[6] The ILC Articles do not require a finding of intent, although the issue of intent is still a contested issue because of inconsistent state practice and because the ILC Articles are not treaty law.

Second, the ILC Articles do not explicitly address injury. Lawyers often distinguish between **material injury**, which negatively affects an individual's physical or economic well-being (such as medical expenses, lost income), and **moral injury**, which negatively affects an individual's conscience or mental well-being. Domestic legal systems vary in whether they allow plaintiffs to sue for moral damages, or only for material damages. These domestic differences often mirror international disagreement about when states can (and cannot) use litigation to uphold international law, particularly in disputes involving colonialism and human rights. The law of state responsibility does not require material injury: states can be responsible for breaking international law, even if no other state experiences physical or economic harm. However, as discussed below, injury often affects the consequences of responsibility.

Section 3.2 addresses the dual issues of attribution and wrongfulness, which jointly determine whether a state is responsible for a breach of international law. Section 3.3 then provides a brief overview of the consequences of responsibility, including the obligations to cease ongoing breaches, make reparation for past breaches, and prevent future breaches. Then, in section 3.4 we describe three competing perspectives about why states sometimes break international law: the enforcement, managerial, and flexibility perspectives. We describe the basic assumptions and arguments of each perspective, and then discuss how each perspective applies to state responsibility. Finally, we return in section 3.5 to the 2007 cyberattacks on Estonia.

3.2 Determining Responsibility

State responsibility for a legal breach is determined by two criteria. First, there must be attribution of the breach to the state. Second, the breach must be wrongful. We discuss each of these criteria in turn.

Attribution

Attribution rules determine when a legal breach is considered an act of a state. We begin by considering acts of government bodies and employees, which are evaluated using relatively clear and consistent criteria. We then discuss non-state actors, like rebel and terrorist groups, which have less clear and consistent attribution rules.

Government Bodies and Employees

Under international law, a state is responsible for the acts of all of its government bodies. The ILC Articles declare:

> The conduct of any state organ shall be considered an act of that state under international law, whether the organ exercises legislative, executive, judicial or any other functions, and whatever its character as an organ of the central government or of a territorial unit of the state.[7]

So states are responsible for many different types of acts, including laws, administrative regulations, and court rulings. International law does not distinguish between acts of a national government and acts of regional or local governments. A state is responsible for all of its units, meaning that states with federal governments, like Mexico and the US, often face special challenges when complying with international law. Even if the national government lacks authority to order a regional or local government to behave in a particular way, the state as a whole is responsible for regional and local governments. Similarly, even if a state's constitution prohibits the executive from ordering a court to rule in a particular way, the state is still responsible for all of its branches of government.

For example, Mexico was sued in 1993 by a US firm named Metalclad, which was building a hazardous waste landfill in Guadalcázar. Before purchasing the land, Metalclad was told by the federal and regional government that the seller had obtained all of the necessary permits to build the landfill. Shortly after its purchase, Metalclad began to have problems with the Guadalcázar local government, which insisted that Metalclad needed an additional construction permit, which the local government refused to issue. The national and regional governments argued that the local government lacked authority to block the project, and Metalclad sued Mexico for violating the North American Free Trade Agreement (NAFTA). During international arbitration, Mexico accepted responsibility for acts of the Guadalcázar local government, even though the national government had disagreed with the local government. Mexico wrote:

> [Mexico] did not plead that the acts of [Guadalcázar] were not covered by NAFTA. [Mexico] was, and remains, prepared to proceed on the assumption that the normal rule of state responsibility applies; that is, that the respondent can be internationally responsible for the acts of state organs at all three levels of government.[8]

After establishing that Mexico was responsible for Guadalcázar's actions, the US firm successfully argued that Mexico violated NAFTA protections against indirect expropriation.

Similarly, Germany sued the United States in 1999 for violating the Vienna Convention on Consular Relations. Two brothers—Karl and Walter LaGrand—were German nationals who were arrested in Arizona for attempted robbery, kidnapping, and murder. During the arrest, local police did not tell the LaGrand brothers that they could contact the German consulate and request assistance under the Vienna Convention. The brothers did not learn about the Vienna Convention until after they had been tried, sentenced to the death penalty, and exhausted all appeals within Arizona. When they tried to appeal their conviction at the national level, US federal courts refused to hear their arguments about international law. The federal courts argued that under US law, they could not hear legal arguments that were not first raised in Arizona courts. Germany sued the US at the International Court of Justice, alleging numerous legal breaches, including the failure of the Arizona police to contact the German consulate, and the failure of US federal courts to consider the LaGrand brothers' international law claims. In a complicated 2001 ruling, the ICJ found the US responsible for the acts of multiple government bodies.

It is usually more difficult to assess the acts of government employees, who have a sort of dual life: sometimes they represent the state, and sometimes they are private individuals, acting independently of their employer. For example, when a police officer issues a traffic ticket, she acts as an agent of the state; but when she rents an apartment, she acts as a private individual. More generally, which of these acts is attributable to the state, and which is not? International law manages these dual lives based on the authority and capacity of employees.

The terms "authority" and "capacity" are imprecise and sometimes confounded in practice. Authority refers to the types of actions that an individual is legally allowed to take. When asking whether a government employee is acting within their authority, we must ask: what powers has the state given to the employee? For example, most states give their police officers authority to arrest and detain suspected criminals. However, they usually do not give police officers the authority to torture. Such acts are considered ***ultra vires*** ("beyond the powers"): they exceed the authority given by a state to its employee.

In contrast, capacity refers to how a neutral observer would interpret the government employee's action in its context. For example, if an individual in a police uniform showed you their police identification, put you in a police car, and drove you to the police station, you would reasonably assume that you have been arrested by a police officer. The trappings of the government employee—their uniform, badge, car, and so on—would suggest that they are acting in their capacity as a police officer. If the same person approached you while wearing their personal, off-duty clothes and asked you to get into an unmarked car without showing you their government identification, you might think they were trying to kidnap you.

According to the ILC Articles:

> The conduct of a person or entity which is not an organ of the state ... but which is empowered by the law of that state to exercise elements of the governmental authority shall be considered an act of the state under international law, provided the person or entity is acting in that capacity in the particular instance.[9]

From the ILC's perspective, it does not matter whether a government employee is acting within their authority, provided that they are acting within their capacity as a government employee. Even if they exceed their legal authority (commit an *ultra vires* act), the state is responsible for their conduct if they act in their capacity as a government employee.

For example, in the *Velásquez Rodríguez* case, the Inter-American Court of Human Rights (IACHR) was asked to rule on a complaint against Honduras. The family of Manfredo Velásquez Rodríguez alleged that men in civilian clothes picked up Velásquez Rodríguez in an unmarked car and took him to an armed forces station where he was interrogated by law enforcement and military officials. While in captivity, he was tortured and then disappeared, meaning that he was presumed dead. This incident was part of a broader pattern in the early 1980s, when hundreds of people in Honduras were taken by police and security forces, and then never returned.

In its defense, Honduras argued that torture was illegal under its domestic laws. Honduras argued that it should not be responsible for the *ultra vires* acts of its officers. However, the IACHR disagreed. It argued:

> any exercise of public power that violates the rights recognized by the [Inter-American] Convention [on Human Rights] is illegal ... This conclusion is independent of whether the ... official has contravened provisions of internal law or overstepped the limits of his authority: under international law a state is responsible for the acts of its agents undertaken in their official capacity ..., even when those agents act outside the sphere of their authority or violate internal law.[10]

The Court emphasized that Velásquez Rodríguez was tortured while at an armed forces station, implying that the government employees were acting in their official capacity. Honduras was thus responsible for their actions.

Non-State Actors

What happens if non-state actors break international law? Recall that during the Estonian cyberattacks of 2007, the Russian government insisted that the attacks were committed by private individuals, not by government bodies or employees. Could Russia nevertheless be held responsible for the attacks? The ILC Articles say that:

> The conduct of a person or group of persons shall be considered an act of a state under international law if the person or group of persons is in fact acting on the instructions of, or under the direction or control of, that state in carrying out the conduct.[11]

Experts often disagree about how to interpret and implement this standard. Broadly speaking, international courts have articulated two competing approaches: the effective and the overall control standards.

The **effective control standard** was created by the ICJ in the *Nicaragua* case, which was decided before the ILC Articles were completed. The ICJ was asked to assess US military involvement in Nicaragua in the 1980s. During that time, the US government supported rebel groups that were challenging Nicaragua's Sandinista government, which the US perceived as a Communist threat. The Court was asked: which military activities were attributable to the US? In its ruling, the ICJ distinguished between three types of actors in the conflict. First, some acts were committed by employees of the US military and Central Intelligence Agency. Second, some acts were committed by "unilaterally controlled Latino assets" (UCLAs), who were "persons ... paid by, and acting on the direct instructions of, United States military or intelligence personnel."[12] Third, some acts were committed by rebel forces, known as the Contras. The US was clearly responsible for its employees, but was the US responsible for the other actors?

In its 1986 ruling, the ICJ argued that the US was responsible for the UCLAs. It reasoned:

> Although it is not proved that any United States military personnel took a direct part in the operations, agents of the United States participated in the planning, direction, support, and execution of the operations. The execution was the task rather of the "UCLAs," while United States nationals participated in the planning, direction and support. The imputability to the United States of these attacks appears therefore to the Court to be established.[13]

US involvement in planning and supporting UCLA activities was sufficient to create US responsibility.

In contrast, the ICJ found that the US had a more limited role in supporting the Contras, which Nicaragua accused of numerous crimes, including the kidnapping, killing, rape, and torture of civilians. The ICJ argued that the US provided funding, intelligence, supplies, and training for the Contras. However, the Court was not convinced that the Contra operations "reflected strategy and tactics wholly devised by the United States."[14] According to the ICJ, the US could only be responsible for the Contras if it had effective control over them:

> United States participation ... in the financing, organizing, training, supplying and equipping of the *contras*, the selection of its military or paramilitary targets, and the

planning of the whole of its operation, is still insufficient in itself ... for the purpose of attributing to the United States the acts committed by the *contras* ... All the forms of United States participation mentioned above ... would not in themselves mean ... that the United States directed or enforced the perpetration of the acts contrary to human rights and humanitarian law alleged by the applicant state. Such acts could well be committed by members of the *contras* without the control of the United States. For this conduct to give rise to legal responsibility of the United States, it would in principle have to be proved that that state had effective control of the military or paramilitary operations in the course of which the alleged violations were committed.[15]

While the US was responsible for its government employees and the UCLAs, the US was not found responsible for the crimes allegedly committed by the Contras.

The ICJ's *Nicaragua* ruling was challenged years later when the International Criminal Tribunal for the former Yugoslavia (ICTY) established an **overall control standard**. In the *Tadić* case, which was a criminal trial for war crimes, the ICTY argued that international courts can apply different attribution standards because: "The degree of control may ... vary according to the factual circumstances of each case."[16] The ICTY then argued that just as states were responsible for *ultra vires* acts of their employees, so, too, are they responsible for the non-state actors under their overall control, regardless of whether these actors are following explicit directions or instructions from a state. The ICTY argued:

In order to attribute the acts of a military or paramilitary group to a state, it must be proved that the state wields overall control over the group, not only by equipping and financing the group, but also by coordinating or helping in the general planning of its military activity. ... However, it is not necessary that ... the state should also issue, either to the head or to members of the group, instructions for the commission of specific acts contrary to international law.[17]

The overall control standard thus requires less than the effective control standard to establish that a state is responsible for non-state actors.

Which standard should international courts use when determining state responsibility for non-state actors: the effective control standard (from *Nicaragua*) or the overall control standard (from *Tadić*)? After the *Tadić* ruling, the ICJ revisited its *Nicaragua* ruling in a lawsuit over the *Bosnian Genocide* in Srebrenica. Rather than adopting the overall control standard, the ICJ reiterated its *Nicaragua* ruling, arguing that:

The "overall control" test has the major drawback of broadening the scope of state responsibility well beyond the fundamental principle governing the law of international responsibility: a state is responsible only for its own conduct ... the "overall control" test is unsuitable, for it stretches too far ... the connection which must exist between the conduct of a state's organs and its international responsibility.[18]

The ICJ believed that the ICTY standard was too strict in holding states accountable for non-state actors. Antonio Cassese—an expert on international criminal law and one of the *Tadić* judges—fiercely criticized the ICJ. He argued that the effective control standard is not supported by state practice and contradicts "a basic principle underpinning the whole body of rules and principles on state responsibility: states may not evade responsibility towards other states [by using] groups of individuals to undertake actions that are intended to damage ... other states."[19] Overall, there is little consensus on how to deal with this issue. The ICJ stuck with a conservative standard that limits state responsibility, while the ICTY used a more progressive standard that makes it easier to hold states responsible for legal breaches.

Even if a state has no control over non-state actors, sometimes it can become responsible for their behavior if the state "acknowledges and adopts the conduct in question as its own."[20] As the International Law Commission noted, such situations require that a state offer more than "mere support or endorsement" of acts.[21] In the *Iran Hostages* case, the International Court of Justice considered a 1979 attack by protestors on the US Embassy in Iran. The attack was launched by private individuals, so the ICJ ruled that Iran was not responsible for the attack itself.[22] However, the attack triggered an ongoing hostage crisis and numerous Iranian officials expressed their support. The ICJ argued that this public support "translated continuing occupation of the embassy and detention of the hostages into acts of" Iran.[23] Such examples of **acknowledgement** are rare, but they are nonetheless one way that states can become responsible for non-state actors.

Figure 3.3 In November 1979, protestors attacked the US Embassy in Tehran, Iran. While the attack was launched by private actors, numerous Iranian officials expressed their support for the taking and holding of hostages.

Wrongfulness

Even if a legal breach is attributable to a state, sometimes the breach will not be **wrongful**, meaning that a state will not be responsible for the breach. A factor that keeps a legal breach from creating responsibility is referred to as a **circumstance precluding wrongfulness** (CPW). Such circumstances are akin to excuses or justifications for legal breaches. While some domestic legal systems distinguish between an excuse and a justification, international law uses these terms interchangeably.[24]

The ILC Articles define six circumstances that preclude wrongfulness, which we can organize into two categories. First, sometimes a breach will not be wrongful because of actions taken by the injured state. The CPWs in this category include consent, self-defense, and countermeasures. Second, sometimes external forces will excuse or justify legal breaches. These CPWs include *force majeure*, distress, and necessity. Overall, these six circumstances allow states to sometimes break international law without incurring responsibility.

However, the ILC noted that none of these six circumstances precluding wrongfulness apply to breaches of peremptory norms. If a state breaks a peremptory norm of international law—for example, by permitting slavery or committing genocide—its action will always be considered wrongful. Additionally, once a temporary circumstance precluding wrongfulness has passed, a state is expected to return to compliance with its legal obligations. CPWs thus excuse or justify legal breaches, but do not invalidate or end legal obligations.

Actions of the Injured State

The first three CPWs all involve situations in which actions by the injured state prevent a breach from being wrongful. First, under the law of state responsibility, a legal breach is not wrongful if the injured state consents to the breach. Ideally, such consent should be given before a state breaks its obligations. However, this is not explicitly required by the ILC Articles, which say:

> Valid consent by a state to the commission of a given act by another state precludes the wrongfulness of that act in relation to the former state to the extent that the act remains within the limits of that consent.[25]

For example, in 1910 a UK ship was transporting Vinayak Savarkar—an Indian activist, lawyer, and politician—from England to India to face trial for assisting rebellion against UK rule in India. While en route, the ship stopped in Marseille, France. Savarkar jumped from a ship porthole into the ocean, swam to the French quay, and was captured by a French gendarme—a police officer—who returned him to the ship. France subsequently demanded that Savarkar be returned to French custody. However, the Permanent Court of Arbitration ultimately found that the UK had not violated French sovereignty.[26] The tribunal argued that "France had implicitly consented to the arrest through the conduct of its gendarme, who aided the [UK] authorities in the arrest."[27]

Second, the law of state responsibility includes self-defense as a circumstance that precludes wrongfulness of a legal breach. The ILC Articles say:

> The wrongfulness of an act of a state is precluded if the act constitutes a lawful measure of self-defence taken in conformity with the Charter of the United Nations.[28]

This provision ensures that the law of state responsibility is consistent with contemporary law on the use of force. For example, after Iraq invaded Kuwait in 1990, an international coalition fought back Iraqi forces during the Gulf War of 1990–1991 as an act of collective self-defense.

Even though self-defense is allowed under international law, some experts criticized its inclusion in the ILC Articles. These critics believe that by including self-defense as a CPW, the ILC risks encouraging states to invoke self-defense as an excuse for legal breaches. For example, one scholar argued that "self-defense is the legal recognition of the ineradicable human instinct of self-preservation. It is not a general residual right to protect interests, however major, by any appropriate means."[29]

Third, a legal breach is not wrongful under international law if it is a **countermeasure**, which is a legal violation taken in response to a prior wrongful act by another state. For example, France and the US signed a 1946 bilateral agreement on civil aviation. After a diplomatic dispute between the two states over commercial flights, France refused to allow passengers on flights by Pan American—a US airline—to disembark from their planes in Paris. The US believed that France broke the 1946 agreement, and responded by prohibiting many French airlines from flying to the US West Coast, thereby violating the 1946 agreement. In subsequent arbitration, a tribunal ruled that the US's breach was a legitimate response to France's prior breach.[30] The law of countermeasures—formerly called reprisals—has changed over time. This topic is addressed in Chapter 4 because countermeasures are one common tool for upholding international law.

External Forces

The final three CPWs involve external forces, which are beyond the control of the state that commits a breach. These forces are usually temporary disruptions to normal cooperation between states. Once the external force passes, states must return to cooperation. States tolerate breaches in such circumstances because "such an event, not being within the *de facto* control of the state, should not be allowed to disrupt cooperation if its effects are only temporary."[31]

The fourth circumstance precluding wrongfulness is **force majeure**, which the ILC Articles define as "an irresistible force or ... unforeseen event, beyond the control of the state, making it materially impossible ... to perform the obligation."[32] In the past, states often invoked *force majeure* opportunistically when compliance was merely costly or difficult. However, modern usage only includes circumstances in which compliance is not possible. States have successfully invoked *force majeure* in lawsuits involving the destruction of foreign investments during civil wars.[33] However, claims of *force majeure* are usually not successful because the standard for invoking it is so high.

Fifth, the law of state responsibility recognizes **distress** as a CPW. The ILC Articles define "distress" as a situation in which "the author of the act in question has no other reasonable way ... of saving the author's life or the lives of other persons entrusted to the author's care."[34] This CPW derives from the customary law of the sea, which allowed ships to enter foreign ports during dangerous storms. Emer de Vattel, a Swiss scholar of international law, wrote in 1758: "a vessel driven by stress of weather has a right to enter, even by force, into a foreign port."[35] This right to seek shelter from danger was a corollary to the freedom to navigate the high seas. Similarly, in modern times, an airplane in distress can make an emergency landing on foreign territory, even though states may restrict their airspace and landing rights under normal conditions.

The final circumstance that precludes wrongfulness is **necessity**, which comes from the natural law concept of self-preservation. One aphorism from ancient Rome was the Latin phrase *necessitas est lex temporis*, which translates as "necessity is the law of the moment." For example, Seneca the Elder discussed a soldier who lost his weapons during battle and took weapons from a corpse. Since theft was necessary for the soldier to survive, Seneca argued that it should not be punished. Similarly, medieval Christian theologians wrote commentaries on the Gospel of Mark, which tells the story of a starving man who stole holy bread that had been reserved for priests.[36] In the biblical account, Jesus treats the man's actions as excusable because they were necessary for him to survive.

Throughout the development of international law, states often invoked necessity to try to excuse or justify breaches of international law.[37] Yet when drafting the ILC Articles, many states believed that necessity had been abused by states, who tried to excuse non-compliance when it was merely inconvenient, and not when it was truly necessary to the state's survival. As a compromise, the ILC Articles allow states to invoke necessity subject to strict limits:

1. Necessity may not be invoked ... unless the act:
   (a) Is the only way for the state to safeguard an essential interest against a grave and imminent peril; and
   (b) Does not seriously impair an essential interest of the state or states towards which the obligation exists, or of the international community as a whole.

2. In any case, necessity may not be invoked ... if:
   (a) The international obligation in question excludes the possibility of invoking necessity; or
   (b) The state has contributed to the situation of necessity.[38]

One example provided by the ILC to support necessity is the *Torrey Canyon* incident of 1967. The *Torrey Canyon* was a Liberian ship transporting oil near (but outside of) British territorial waters. The ship was damaged after striking underwater rocks, causing a massive oil spill that threatened the British coast. After unsuccessful attempts to contain the spill, the British government bombed the ship to burn the oil before it could reach British soil. As the ILC noted, "The British Government did not advance any legal justification for its conduct, but on several occasions it stressed the existence of a situation of extreme danger and the fact that the decision to bomb the ship had been taken only after all the other means employed had failed."[39] The incident did not lead to litigation, but the ILC nonetheless concluded that if the British government had been sued, "the action taken by the British Government ... would have had to be recognized as internationally lawful, since the conditions for a 'state of necessity' were clearly fulfilled."[40]

After the ILC Articles were completed, Argentina invoked necessity as a defense in foreign investment lawsuits. These lawsuits challenged various policies that were implemented by Argentina after it faced a severe economic depression in 2001. In the *LG&E* case, US investors in the natural gas industry successfully argued that Argentina broke several international legal obligations to protect foreign investment. Yet the Tribunal found that Argentina's breaches were not wrongful because of necessity. The International Centre for Settlement of Investment Disputes wrote:

> The essential interests of [Argentina] were threatened in December 2001. It faced an extremely serious threat to its existence, its political and economic survival, to the possibility of maintaining its essential services in operation, and to the preservation of its internal peace. There is no serious evidence in the record that Argentina contributed to the crisis resulting in the state of necessity ... An economic recovery package was the only means to respond to the crisis.[41]

However, when a different tribunal ruled in another case with nearly identical facts, it reached the opposite conclusion. It argued that Argentina could not invoke necessity because

> the Tribunal is convinced that the Argentine crisis was severe but did not result in total economic and social collapse. When the Argentine crisis is compared to other contemporary crises affecting countries in different regions of the world it may be noted that such other crises have not led to the derogation of international contractual or treaty obligations.[42]

These rulings have created confusion about the meaning of necessity.

3.3   Consequences of Responsibility

Suppose that a state is responsible for breaking international law. What consequences follow? First, a state must cease ongoing breaches and prevent future breaches. Second, a state must repair the damage to injured states using reparations, such as restitution, compensation, and satisfaction. We discuss each of these issues in turn.

Cessation and Prevention

When a state is responsible for breaking international law, its first obligation is to cease any ongoing breaches. Unlike the rules of treaty invalidation and termination, the law of state responsibility does not alter legal obligations. As the ILC wrote: "The state responsible for [a] wrongful act is under an obligation … [t]o cease that act, if it is continuing."[43] Even if a circumstance precluded wrongfulness of a violation, legal obligations must be resumed once the circumstance passes.

Recall that in an arbitration case, an investment tribunal found that Argentina broke its legal obligations to US investors. These breaches were not found wrongful because of necessity and Argentina's severe economic depression. However, Argentina did not get a free pass on its promises to US investors. Once the crisis passed, Argentina's actions became wrongful and it had to resume its treaty commitments.

Many international disputes focus exclusively on cessation. As the ILC noted: "Cessation is often the main focus of the controversy produced by conduct in breach of an international obligation."[44] As such, "cessation is treated as an inherent obligation of the responsible state and not as a form of reparation."[45] In international trade, the World Trade Organization focuses purely on cessation of trade breaches. Members can sue each other for alleged trade breaches, but their objective is to stop the violation, not to receive compensation for past harm.

The law of state responsibility also seeks to prevent future breaches. The ILC Articles say that responsible states may be required: "To offer appropriate assurances and guarantees of non-repetition, if circumstances so require."[46] The ILC clarified that "assurances are normally given verbally, while guarantees of non-repetition involve something more—for example, preventive measures … designed to avoid repetition of the breach."[47] Such assurances and guarantees "are most commonly sought when the injured state has reason to believe that the mere restoration of the pre-existing situation does not protect it satisfactorily."[48]

States rarely seek assurances and guarantees of non-repetition in international disputes, and courts rarely demand them. An injured state that brings up repetition risks offending a state that committed previous breaches. Additionally, a court that orders assurances and guarantees could be viewed as pre-judging a dispute that has not yet occurred.

Assurances and guarantees of non-repetition were largely theoretical until the late 1990s, when Paraguay, Germany, and Mexico sued the US at the ICJ in the *Consular Relations* cases. They argued that the US violated the Vienna Convention on Consular Relations, which requires that law enforcement officials notify foreign consulates when one of their citizens has been arrested. After several foreign nationals from Paraguay, Germany, and Mexico were arrested, convicted, and sentenced to death by US state courts, they attempted to appeal their convictions and sentencing in US federal courts by arguing that they had not received consular assistance. However, these legal claims were barred in federal courts under the US doctrine of procedural default, because the foreign nationals had not raised these claims in state courts.

In its lawsuit, which is known as the *LaGrand* case, Germany demanded that "the United States should provide Germany a guarantee of the non-repetition of the illegal acts."[49] However, it was not clear how such an outcome could be guaranteed. The US, which feared that the ICJ would order it to revoke the procedural default doctrine, argued that the ICJ lacked jurisdiction to order assurances or guarantees of non-repetition. While the US acknowledged that the Court had authority to rule on past treaty breaches, the US believed that any Court order on non-repetition would create a new legal obligation, which the US believed the ICJ could not do. The US argued that a guarantee of non-repetition "goes beyond any remedy that the Court can or should grant, and should be rejected. The Court's power to decide cases ... does not extend to the power to order a state to provide any 'guarantee' intended to confer additional legal rights ... The United States does not believe that it can be the role of the Court ... to impose any obligations that are additional to or that differ in character from those to which the United States consented when it ratified the Vienna Convention."[50]

The ICJ ultimately adopted a moderate course. It first argued that it did have the authority to consider a guarantee of non-repetition, since this was a remedy for a past breach.[51] This ruling was a partial victory for Germany because it upheld the ICJ's authority to consider non-repetition. However, the ICJ also argued that the US had already taken adequate steps to prevent future breaches by running an education program for law enforcement officials about the Vienna Convention. The ICJ argued:

> If a state ... repeatedly refers to substantial activities which it is carrying out in order to achieve compliance with certain obligations under a treaty, then this expresses a commitment to follow through with the efforts ... The programme in question certainly cannot provide an assurance that there will never again be a failure by the United States to observe the obligation of notification under ... the Vienna Convention. But no state could give such a guarantee.[52]

The ICJ ruled that the US education program "must be regarded as meeting Germany's request for a general assurance of non-repetition."[53] This ruling was a partial victory for the US. When Mexico later raised non-repetition in its lawsuit, the ICJ refused to move any further. The Court reiterated its *LaGrand* ruling, and argued that the US education program "must be regarded as meeting the request by [Mexico] for guarantees and assurances of non-repetition."[54]

Reparation

A state that is responsible for breaking international law must repair the damage to injured states from its breaches. As the Permanent Court of International Justice ruled in 1928, "it is a principle of international law ... that any breach of an engagement involves an obligation to make reparation."[55] The ILC Articles elaborate on this principle by stating that:

1. The responsible state is under an obligation to make full reparation for the injury caused by the internationally wrongful act.
2. Injury includes any damage, whether material or moral, caused by the internationally wrongful act.[56]

The standard forms of reparation under international law include restitution, compensation, and satisfaction. All of these forms of reparation are based on remedial justice—they focus on repairing the damage caused by a legal breach, rather than deterring or punishing legal breaches.[57]

Restitution

The first form of reparation under international law is **restitution**, which is commonly referred to by the Latin phrase ***restitutio in integrum***. This form of reparation seeks to make the injured state whole by returning it to its *status quo ante*, which is the position that it was in before the breach. As the Permanent Court of International Justice wrote in 1928: "reparation must, as far as possible, wipe out all consequences of the illegal act and reestablish the situation which would, in all probability, have existed if that act had not been committed."[58] The ILC Articles reinforce the importance of restitution by stating:

> A state responsible for an internationally wrongful act is under an obligation to make restitution, that is, to re-establish the situation which existed before the wrongful act was committed, provided and to the extent that restitution:
> (a) Is not materially impossible;
> (b) Does not involve a burden out of all proportion to the benefit deriving from restitution instead of compensation.[59]

It is often difficult to apply this concept in international disputes. For example, in the *Consular Relations* cases, Paraguay, Germany, and Mexico all argued that the US violated the Vienna Convention on Consular Relations by failing to notify foreign consulates when their nationals were arrested. Since the consulates were not notified, they could not provide legal assistance to their nationals, who were convicted and sentenced to death. In the Paraguayan and German lawsuits, the relevant foreign nationals were executed before the ICJ ruled on the merits of either case. However, numerous Mexican nationals were still alive when the ICJ ruled on Mexico's lawsuit.

How could the US provide restitution in these cases? What actions would make the victims whole? Mexico argued:

> The primary form of reparation available to a state injured by an internationally wrongful act is *restitutio in integrum* ... The United States is therefore obliged to take the necessary action to restore the *status quo ante* in respect of Mexico's nationals detained, tried, convicted and sentenced in violation of their internationally recognized rights ... Restitution here must take the form of annulment of the conviction and sentences that resulted from the proceedings tainted by the [international legal] violations ... It follows from the very nature of *restitutio* that, when a violation of an international obligation is manifested in a judicial act, that act must be annulled and thereby deprived of any force or effect in the national legal system.[60]

Mexico thus believed that the US should annul the convictions and sentences, and set the prisoners free. Mexico believed that this would return the foreign nationals to the position that they were in before the breach.

In response, the US argued that its legal breach did not cause the foreign nationals to be arrested and convicted. Additionally, the Mexican nationals received fair trials with legal assistance, albeit not with assistance from their consulate. Therefore, the US argued, even if the police had notified Mexico of the arrests, the outcome of the trials would have been the same.

The ICJ took a moderate position. It argued that the US was not required to annul the convictions and sentences, as Mexico wanted, because "it is not the convictions and sentences of the Mexican nationals which are to be regarded as a violation of international law, but solely certain breaches of treaty obligations which preceded them."[61] However, the ICJ ordered the US to provide judicial review and reconsideration of the cases. This judicial process had to consider "the question of the legal consequences of the violation upon the criminal proceedings."[62]

Compensation

Even in simpler disputes, where it is clear what restitution would entail, international politics may keep restitution from being a feasible solution. For example, in the *Chorzów* case heard by the Permanent Court of International Justice in the 1920s, Germany sued Poland for the expropriation of a nitrogen factory. This factory was built during World War I on German land. However, after the war ended, the land was given to Poland. Both Germany and Poland agreed that restitution—the return of the factory to Germany—was not possible because the land on which the factory was built was now part of Poland.[63] The PCIJ therefore ordered Poland to compensate Germany by paying "a sum corresponding to the value which a restitution in kind would bear."[64]

Compensation is included in the ILC Articles, which say:

> The state responsible for an internationally wrongful act is under an obligation to compensate for the damage caused thereby, insofar as such damage is not made good by restitution.[65]

In some situations, a responsible state may be ordered to pay additional financial damages, like lost profits or interest. However, compensation may not be punitive, or designed purely to punish—the amount of compensation cannot be larger than the harm suffered by the injured state.

Compensation is usually considered a second-best solution under international law. Restitution is usually preferred to compensation because policy-makers don't want legal breaches to be commodified. They believe that the legitimacy of law is harmed if poor states are bound by law, while rich states can simply break the law and pay compensation.[66]

Nevertheless, compensation is routine in many areas of international law. For example, international investment law creates legal protections for firms that invest in foreign states. If a firm believes that it has been mistreated, it can sue the host government using international arbitration. In these disputes, firms seek compensation for the economic harm that they have suffered. Compensation is also common in property damage disputes. For example, UK warships patrolled the Mediterranean Sea after World War II. During one of these patrols, two UK ships struck mines in the Corfu Channel, off the coast of Albania. Dozens of sailors were killed and both ships suffered severe damage. Albania was held responsible for the explosions in an ICJ lawsuit and ordered to pay compensation to the UK.

Satisfaction

Many international disputes involve more symbolic issues than expropriation or property damage. One issue in the *Corfu Channel* case was the United Kingdom's response to the explosion. After its two ships were damaged, the UK conducted mine-sweeping operations in the Corfu Channel. Albania argued that these operations violated its sovereignty because it claimed the Corfu Channel as territorial waters. The UK operations did not cause any material damage, so Albania could not demand restitution or compensation. But Albania believed that it had suffered moral damage, so it asked the ICJ to declare that the UK had violated international law.[67] The ICJ agreed with Albania and wrote: "the action of the British Navy constituted a breach of Albanian sovereignty. This declaration ... is in itself appropriate satisfaction."[68]

In such situations, states often demand a verbal or written statement that acknowledges or apologizes for a legal breach. Such a statement is known as **satisfaction**. According to the ILC Articles:

1. The state responsible for an internationally wrongful act is under an obligation to give satisfaction for the injury caused by that act insofar as it cannot be made good by restitution or compensation.
2. Satisfaction may consist in an acknowledgement of the breach, an expression of regret, a formal apology or another appropriate modality.[69]

Such satisfaction "may not take a form humiliating to the responsible state," but an apology can heal the moral damage when a state breaks international law.[70]

3.4 Why Do States Break International Law?

International law experts usually focus on the content of legal rules, rather than state motivations for breaking them. But to have an effective system of international law—one in which law induces states to behave differently than they would in the absence of law—we must understand why states break international law. Three competing perspectives—the enforcement, managerial, and flexibility perspectives—offer different assumptions and arguments about state behavior. After introducing each perspective, we examine its implications for the law of state responsibility.

Enforcement Perspective
Assumptions and Arguments

The enforcement perspective questions whether international law can change state behavior. Scholars who adopt the enforcement perspective usually assume that states are rational actors. This assumption requires that leaders have preferences over the outcomes that can result from their choices. A change in leaders may result in a change in preferences. Yet whoever is leading a particular state is assumed to have preferences over his or her policy options. The rational actor assumption also requires that leaders act instrumentally to try to achieve their preferences, given their beliefs about how other states will act. Political leaders are not saints—while they may feel a moral desire to follow international law, they behave in a way that best protects the interests of their state (as they understand these interests), regardless of what international law requires. Any policy decision is therefore based on an assessment of the costs and benefits of possible alternatives.

The enforcement perspective assumes that breaking international law can sometimes give leaders a short-term benefit. For example, a leader with a strong domestic political opposition may benefit from violating human rights and suppressing his political opponents. Similarly, a leader with a weak economy may temporarily improve economic conditions by illegally raising trade barriers. A leader who is fighting a war may be tempted to use prohibited chemical weapons to gain a military advantage.

Political leaders must balance such benefits from breaking international law against their associated costs. The international system lacks a centralized body to enforce international law by imposing punishments on states that break it. Some scholars argue that this lack of centralized enforcement means that international law isn't actually law. For example, British legal scholar John Austin wrote in 1832 that law is a "rule laid down for the guidance of an intelligent being by an intelligent being having power over him."[71] He argued that the threat of punishment caused individuals to follow a sovereign's commands. Since international law lacks a sovereign who can compel actors to follow his command, Austin believed that international law wasn't actually law. He instead described it as a body of "rules set and enforced by *mere opinion*, that is, by the opinions or sentiments held or felt by an indeterminate body of men in regard to human conduct."[72] Austin believed that international law was morality thinly veiled by the analogy of law. To Austin and his followers, international lawyers are like the fabled emperor who wore no clothes: they may believe that their arguments are garbed in law, but their arguments are really moral and political, rather than legal.

More moderate scholars argue that Austin overemphasized the importance of command and coercion. Domestic legal systems often include customary law (which is not created by a political superior) and rely upon moral obligation to uphold legal commitments.[73] These scholars acknowledge that international law lacks powerful, centralized institutions to issue commands and compel states to follow them. Yet states often uphold international law in a decentralized way. For example, states that break human rights treaties are often "named and shamed" in international organizations to pressure them to maintain good reputations.[74] Similarly, when states unilaterally raise trade barriers, they usually face lawsuits and reciprocal breaches by other states as punishment. Finally, states that brazenly break the laws of war are sometimes attacked by international coalitions to retaliate for past breaches and deter future breaches. In all of these situations, states face negative consequences for breaking international law.

We use the term **punishment** to describe any response to a legal breach by states (either individually or collectively) that raises the cost of breaking international law. Possible punishments are shown in Table 3.1. Most of these punishments are political, rather than legal. When a leader evaluates the possible consequences of breaking international law, they must take into account both the likelihood and the magnitude of punishment.

Table 3.1 Punishment Mechanisms Under the Enforcement Perspective

Policy Tool	Description	Example
Domestic accountability	Leaders are accountable to domestic constituencies that favor compliance	Human rights advocates in El Salvador pressured their Supreme Court in 2016 to overturn a law that gave amnesty for crimes committed during the 1980–1992 civil war.
Legalized dispute settlement	Injured states use legal institutions to challenge violations and seek remedies	The Philippines sued China in 2013 in the Permanent Court of Arbitration over Chinese claims to territory in the South China Sea.
Linkage	Violating state loses benefits in other areas of international cooperation	In 2016, the EU cut aid to the Burundi government for systematic human rights abuses.
Reciprocity	Other states mimic violations	After the US imposed numerous trade barriers on Chinese goods in 2018, China imposed its own barriers on US goods.
Reputation	Violation reveals information to other states that makes future cooperation difficult	After its annexation of Crimea in 2014, Russia was excluded from G8 summits, in which the world's leading industrialized countries discuss international issues.
Retaliation	Other states adopt costly policies to punish, such as economic sanctions or military strikes	France, the UK, and the US launched military strikes against Syria in 2017 and 2018, in response to the Syrian government's use of chemical weapons on civilians and rebel forces.

The likelihood of punishment can be affected by many factors. First, a breach is unlikely to be punished if it is never detected. Other states may not notice minor breaches of environmental or human rights law, for instance; or domestic interests groups may not favor compliance with international rules, reducing the electoral pressure on leaders to comply. Second, other states may be unlikely to punish if a violator is powerful and punishment is costly. For example, many human rights activists fear that as more states become economically dependent on Chinese investment and trade, they will be less willing to pressure China into respecting civil and political rights.

Similarly, the expected magnitude of punishment affects compliance decisions. If a leader anticipates that the use of prohibited chemical weapons on civilians will only lead to negative publicity, then they will be less likely to comply than if they believe that their actions will trigger economic sanctions or military intervention. All else being equal, states that are more powerful can usually better tolerate punishment than states that are less so. For example, many developing states argue that international trade law is unfair because richer states can better tolerate economic punishments than poorer states.

The enforcement perspective argues that, all else being equal, the more likely a state is to be punished for breaking international law, the more likely it is to comply. Similarly, the greater the punishment, the more likely a state is to comply. Therefore, if states wish to bolster the effectiveness of international law, they should write rules and design institutions that increase the likelihood and magnitude of punishment. The enforcement perspective suggests that punishment is a key component for ensuring that international law works.

Implications for State Responsibility

Because most of the punishments that deter treaty breaches are political, enforcement scholars usually focus on how politics influences decisions about breaking international law.[75] Scholars who have analyzed state responsibility from the enforcement perspective have criticized international law as excessively weak because it creates several disconnects between a legal breach and punishment.[76] Such scholars argue that international law should have stricter attribution rules, fewer circumstances that preclude wrongfulness, and more severe consequences.

Attribution rules are important for enforcement because they determine whether states are responsible for non-state actors. These rules, in turn, affect the likelihood that states will be punished for legal breaches. The stronger the attribution rules, the more likely a state is to be held responsible and punished for a legal breach. The enforcement perspective therefore expects that states are less likely to break international law when they face stronger attribution rules.

For example, the effective control standard is a relatively weak attribution rule. Under this standard, a state is only responsible for non-state actors if they are "acting on the instructions of, or under the direction or control of, that state."[77] In contrast, the overall control standard is a relatively strong attribution rule. In the *Tadić* case, the ICTY argued that "it is not necessary that ... the state ... issue ... instructions for ... specific acts contrary to international law."[78] Instead, if a non-state actor "is under the overall control of a state, it must perforce engage the responsibility of that state for its activities, whether or not each of them was specifically imposed, requested or directed by the state."[79] By creating a tighter link between non-state actors and states, the overall control standard increases the likelihood that a state is punished for a legal breach.

Legal experts argue that weak attribution rules create incentives for states to outsource legal breaches to non-state actors. In the *Tadić* case, the ICTY justified the overall control standard by arguing:

> The rationale behind this rule is to prevent states from escaping international responsibility by having private individuals carry out tasks that may not or should not be performed by state officials ... States are not allowed on the one hand to act *de facto*

through individuals and on the other to disassociate themselves from such conduct when these individuals breach international law.[80]

Outsourcing legal breaches to non-state actors is often attractive when the anticipated breaches are relatively minor and difficult to monitor. Cyberattacks and other low-level military tactics can be used by a small number of actors, and it can be difficult for states to collect evidence about them.[81] However, if states are held more accountable for non-state actors, they will have less incentive to outsource legal breaches. Overall, the enforcement perspective suggests that stronger attribution rules increase compliance with international law.

The enforcement perspective also suggests that circumstances precluding wrongfulness affect state decision-making. States often invoke CPWs to test the boundaries of what is allowed. The enforcement perspective suggests that CPWs cause states to commit more breaches. If a state can excuse or justify breaking international law, then it can avoid punishments such as economic sanctions.

Similarly, many legal scholars argue that states abuse the doctrine of necessity.[82] As described above, Argentina repeatedly invoked necessity when it was sued by foreign investors and argued that its 2001 economic depression excused numerous legal breaches. Argentina had mixed success with this argument: while some tribunals found that Argentina's depression was not severe enough to excuse or justify its breaches, other tribunals agreed with Argentina's defense, thereby reducing Argentina's financial liability.[83] In sum, states often use CPWs to try to give legitimacy to actions that would otherwise be condemned and punished. The enforcement perspective suggests that CPWs thus decrease compliance with international law.

Finally, the enforcement perspective suggests that the consequences for legal breach are too weak. Recall that states that are responsible for legal breaches must make reparations to injured states. These reparations are based on remedial justice: international law seeks to make injured states whole by wiping away any damage, but it does not seek to punish the violator or deter future breaches, meaning that the magnitude of punishment is limited.[84] Additionally, it is often difficult for injured states to seek reparations. An injured state may not have access to an international tribunal that will hear the dispute, and litigation can be economically and politically costly, particularly for small or weak states. This reduces the likelihood that a violating state will be expected to make reparations.

Many experts argue that international law should allow punitive damages to deter legal breaches.[85] Because the likelihood that a breach will be punished is relatively small, these scholars believe that the optimal threat to deter a breach should be relatively large. Merely asking a state to make its victim whole is not sufficient: under the enforcement perspective, additional punitive damages are needed to offset the relatively small likelihood of punishment.

Managerial Perspective
Assumptions and Arguments

Scholars who adhere to the managerial perspective believe that the international system is characterized by order.[86] As one legal expert wrote:

> Violations of law attract attention and the occasional important violation is dramatic; the daily, sober loyalty of nations to the law and their obligations is hardly noted. It is probably the case that *almost all nations observe almost all principles of international law and almost all of their obligations almost all of the time.*[87]

Such scholars acknowledge that states sometimes challenge international rules, like NATO's 1999 intervention into Kosovo or Russia's 2014 intervention into Ukraine. However, managerial scholars believe that such challenges are outliers from most international behavior. The managerial perspective thus begins with the observation that states usually comply with international law.

This behavior leads managerial scholars to assume that states are predisposed to favor compliance with international law for many reasons. First, selection effects may make compliance relatively easy. If states only create legal obligations that match their interests, then a state is unlikely to agree to rules that are costly. States may thus comply with most international rules most of the time because they select into commitments that are easy to fulfill.[88] For example, critics of the Paris Climate Agreement argue that it is unlikely to be effective because each state set its own emissions levels, and states are unlikely to set standards that they know they will break. Any apparent compliance with the Paris Climate Agreement may therefore reflect the policies that states would have chosen, absent an agreement.

Second, states may want to comply with international law because it has normative force. If states perceive international law as legitimate or fair, then they may be likely to follow it even when compliance is costly.[89] For example, most individuals in the modern era consider war to be morally wrong. Domestic publics may still support wars in exceptional circumstances, such as to protect an ally or to stop a genocide. However, domestic publics no longer support wars launched purely for glory or to gain resources. The unconstrained use of force is no longer morally acceptable. Researchers have shown that individuals who have a stronger attachment to a global identity—as opposed to a national identity—are more supportive of international law.[90]

Finally, a state may find it more efficient to follow rules than to break them. For many states, international law is automatically incorporated into domestic law, meaning that a leader who breaks international rules can face domestic judicial consequences. In other states, international law is incorporated into domestic law via executive or legislative acts. International law is also often written into the standard operating procedures of government agencies and bureaucracies. For example, one of the most respected descriptions of the law of war is the UK's

Manual of the Law of Armed Conflict. This Manual was "intended to enable all concerned to apply the law of armed conflict when conducting operations and when training or planning for them."[91] By training its armed forces in the laws of war, the UK makes it easier for them to comply with the law.

If states are predisposed to compliance, why do they ever break international law? The managerial perspective provides three explanations. First, states may have principled disagreements about what the law requires because of ambiguity in legal rules. For example, in the *North Sea* dispute, Denmark and the Netherlands believed that Germany was required to use the equidistance method for maritime delimitations, while Germany believed that it was not required to do so. A managerial scholar would view this case as a principled disagreement about the meaning of law. Neither side opportunistically broke a clear rule. Rather, they disagreed about what rules should apply.

Second, states may break international law because they lack capacity to fully comply. Capacity is likely to be most important for states that are not economically developed or have weak governments. For example, Indian Prime Minister Narendra Modi said in 2017 that it would be a "morally criminal act" for states to ignore the growing threat of climate change.[92] However, the Indian government will find it difficult, both economically and politically, to comply with an agreement that halts or slows economic growth. Similarly, if a government lacks effective bureaucracies, it may not be able to force firms and consumers to adopt pollution-reducing technologies. A government's desire to comply may not be enough to ensure compliance, particularly when international law requires private actors to change their behavior.

Third, states may not comply fully with international law because they have not had enough time to change their policies. For example, the World Trade Organization (WTO) uses rules that were initially crafted in the late 1940s by a few relatively rich countries. As more states joined the trade regime over time, its members became more diverse, creating challenges for trade cooperation. When China joined the WTO in 2001, it promised to adopt reforms so that its economy would more closely resemble a market economy. Many of China's ongoing trade conflicts stem from the slow pace of Chinese reforms. For example, the EU and US often argue that China does not protect intellectual property, thereby harming foreign firms. Yet Chinese intellectual property laws have expanded dramatically since 2001, and are likely to continue growing stronger, particularly as Chinese companies develop new technology.[93] Some scholars defend China by arguing that it is moving in the right direction, and has not had sufficient time to change its domestic economic and legal system.[94]

Scholars who believe in the managerial perspective often argue that states should manage compliance by persuading one another to comply, rather than punishing each other for breaking international law. States, institutions, and non-state actors all participate in a transnational legal process in which interaction triggers the implementation of international rules and compliance by states.[95]

Implications for State Responsibility

Managerialist scholars believe that compliance with international law is driven by factors other than punishment. States want to comply, but sometimes cannot. Rather than punishing states for breaches, international law should help states to overcome their obstacles to compliance. Several aspects of state responsibility reflect the managerial perspective.

First, attribution rules only partially hold governments responsible. On the one hand, attribution rules are relatively strict for government bodies. For example, they presume that national governments can control regional and local governments. In the *Metalclad* case, Mexico was responsible for the Guadalcázar government, even though this local government defied the federal government. In contrast, attribution rules are more relaxed for government employees. States are responsible when their employees use their authority or capacity. In the *Velásquez Rodríguez* case, Honduras was responsible when police officers acted within their legal authority (by making arrests and detaining criminal suspects) and when they abused their status as government employees (by torturing a criminal suspect in a police station). By holding states responsible for such *ultra vires* acts, international law assumes that states can mostly control their employees. However, it does not assume that states can completely control their employees. When a government employee acts outside of her authority and capacity, the state is not responsible.

The law of state responsibility is most permissive for non-state actors. In the *Nicaragua* case, the US government was responsible for groups that acted under its effective control, but it was not responsible for the Contra rebels who merely received US assistance. The ICTY challenged the effective control standard by holding states responsible for non-state actors under their overall control. However, the ICJ argued that the overall control standard "stretches too far, almost to breaking point, the connection which must exist between the conduct of a state's organs and its international responsibility."[96] The ICJ's logic reflected the managerial perspective by questioning whether governments actually have capacity to control non-state actors, particularly during civil conflicts. Attribution rules therefore appear to match the managerial perspective. When states have less capacity to control actors, they are less responsible. Attribution rules ensure that states are not punished for outcomes that lie outside their control.

Second, many CPWs match managerial concerns about state capacity. The CPWs that involve external forces all contemplate that compliance may temporarily be cost-prohibitive or impossible. Under *force majeure*, a state's breach is not wrongful if the state cannot comply. Similarly, distress and necessity excuse/justify breaches when a state lacks capacity to both comply and protect a competing value, like human life or state survival. All of these circumstances reflect managerial concerns about capacity. Additionally, these CPWs reflect managerial concerns about the time needed to change behavior. They contemplate that a state may need to temporarily break international law. Once the external force passes, states must comply. These CPWs therefore give states extra time to meet their international obligations.

Finally, recall that the consequences for legal breaches are relatively limited. Reparations are intended to heal the injured state, but not to punish or deter future breaches. These rules match the managerial emphasis on persuasion, rather than coercion. Managerialist scholars usually question whether threats of punishment change state behavior. They note that punishment is often costly for states that uphold international law. Additionally, punishments can appear illegitimate because rich and powerful states can more easily threaten and withstand sanctions than poor and weak states.[97]

Overall, the managerial perspective believes that punishments are ineffective because they do not solve the problems of ambiguity, capacity, and insufficient time. States that want to promote compliance should clarify legal obligations, build state capacity, and give states more time to meet their obligations. The managerial perspective suggests that the legal disconnect between breaches and consequences is useful because states face a political disconnect between what they want and what they can achieve.

Flexibility Perspective
Assumptions and Arguments

A third approach towards why states break international law is the flexibility perspective. This perspective contains elements of both previous perspectives and was developed for international trade law.[98] Like the enforcement perspective, it emphasizes punishment. But like the managerial perspective, it also believes that states often have legitimate reasons for breaking international law.

The flexibility perspective begins with the assumption that economic and political pressure on governments to break international law can change unexpectedly over time.[99] Governments will usually benefit from complying with law. Yet sometimes unexpected events can tempt governments to break international law. For example, after the 2015 Paris terrorist attacks, France temporarily limited human rights by reducing judicial oversight of the police. The flexibility perspective assumes that sometimes unexpected events—like terrorist attacks—will make compliance with international law extremely costly.

The flexibility perspective also assumes that states can select into and out of their legal commitments. As emphasized by the managerial perspective, states join international treaties because they believe that the overall benefits of treaty membership outweigh the costs. Yet states often exit from treaties if these benefits and costs change.[100] Similarly, many states have exited the jurisdiction of international courts when they disagree with their rulings or cannot comply.[101] An optimal legal system is therefore one in which: states join treaties; states comply with treaties; and states do not exit treaties during economic or political crises.

The flexibility perspective argues that law should allow states to sometimes break their commitments without severe punishment. Imagine you are a student in a class in which you must attend lectures and complete assignments. The enforcement perspective would suggest that you will learn the most if you are threatened with extreme punishments. A professor who believes in the enforcement perspective might threaten that you will fail the class if you miss a lecture or an assignment deadline. However, perhaps you will get sick and miss a lecture, or perhaps a family emergency will cause you to complete an assignment late. If you fear an extreme punishment for an unexpected event, you may choose to not take the class rather than risk a bad grade. A professor who believes in the flexibility perspective would believe that it is better for a student to sometimes miss a lecture or turn in an assignment late than to never sign up for the class in the first place or to drop out of the class during tough times. Similarly, states know that they may sometimes face tough times, like terrorist attacks. If every breach triggers severe punishment, states may refuse to join treaties. Alternatively, they may join a treaty and then exit it if compliance becomes costly. Strong punishments can thus make treaties unstable over time.

The flexibility perspective argues that international law should include **escape clauses**, which allow states to sometimes temporarily break their commitments without severe punishment. For example, many human rights agreements allow states to suspend some civil liberties during temporary crises, like terrorist attacks.[102] Even though we want states to protect human rights, sometimes they need flexibility to temporarily break their commitments. Scholars who adhere to the flexibility perspective argue that escape clauses come with three benefits: they make states more likely to join treaties; they allow states to make deeper commitments; and they allow treaties to survive longer.[103]

How can we prevent states from abusing flexibility? How do we allow states to break international law during economic or political crises without encouraging them to do so any time law is inconvenient? Two techniques prevent abuse of escape clauses. The first technique is compensation. It is very difficult, if not impossible, to know how much pressure a government faces to break its legal obligations. While we may know macroeconomic indicators, we cannot truly know how much pressure a government faces to break international law. Accordingly, some experts argue that international law should put a price on breaches by requiring states to make injured states whole.[104] This technique is common in economic law, where states can calculate financial harm, but it is problematic for human rights.

An alternative technique to prevent abuse of escape clauses is appeals to exception. This technique requires that states define circumstances in which they can break the law without any punishment, and maintain a bureaucracy or court to adjudicate whether appeals to exception are legitimate. For example, the major multilateral human rights treaties each created a bureaucracy to oversee compliance.[105] Members must submit reports about their human rights records, and most of these treaties include legalized procedures that allow states and individuals to submit complaints about possible breaches. While a state may be allowed to temporarily restrict human rights after a terrorist attack, its appeal to exception is subject to oversight and challenge.

The flexibility perspective suggests that entry and exit dynamics should shape escape clauses. For example, escape clauses should be less important in customary international law—which binds (almost) all states—than in treaty law—which states can choose to enter or exit. Similarly, escape clauses should be less important when treaties are embedded into structures that make exit unattractive. For example, the European Union (EU) requires its members to join the European Court of Human Rights (ECHR). While EU members may be tempted to violate human rights, ECHR exit is not feasible because any state that leaves the ECHR would lose the benefits of EU membership. Overall, the flexibility perspective argues that escape clauses benefit international cooperation if they are designed and managed to prevent abuse.

Implications for State Responsibility

The flexibility perspective doesn't offer clear implications for attribution rules. Like the enforcement perspective, it views punishment as a tool for inducing compliance. So some flexibility scholars might view international law's attribution rules as weak and as creating incentives to outsource breaches to non-state actors. At the same time, the flexibility perspective echoes managerial concerns about capacity by arguing that sometimes states should overlook legal breaches. So other flexibility scholars might agree that states should be held less responsible when they have less capacity to control who commits a breach.

In contrast, circumstances precluding wrongfulness clearly align with the appeals to exception technique of the flexibility perspective. By defining when states may break international law without responsibility, CPWs allow states to avoid punishment. *Force majeure*, distress, and necessity all excuse or justify breaches caused by unexpected events that change the benefits and costs of compliance. Yet the ILC Articles limit the abuse of such appeals by creating criteria for invoking CPWs. For example, to invoke necessity, breach must be "the only way for the state to safeguard an essential interest against a grave and imminent peril."[106] Additionally, a state is not permitted to invoke necessity if it "has contributed to the situation of necessity," meaning that the pressure to break international law must lie outside of the state's control, thereby preventing abuse.[107]

In contrast, the consequences of state responsibility reflect concerns about compensation. Because international law does not require punitive damages, states can break their obligations temporarily and then return to compliance via restitution. If restitution is not possible, compensation must only make the injured state whole. Some scholars argue that putting a price on legal breaches makes reputation less important, thereby encouraging states to break international law.[108] While the enforcement and managerial perspectives consider this a negative aspect of compensation, the flexibility perspective views this as positive because it allows states to break international law when the costs of compliance outweigh the benefits. The flexibility perspective suggests that international law's focus on remedial justice (particularly its rejection of punitive damages) makes states more likely to join and remain in treaties.

3.5 Case Study Revisited: Is Russia Responsible for the Estonia Cyberattacks?

We began this chapter by examining the 2007 cyberattacks against Estonia, which caused widespread disruptions to daily life in Estonia. During and after the attacks, the Estonian government and numerous intelligence and technology experts blamed Russia for the attacks. NATO legal experts concluded that such attacks can be interventions that break international law. However, Russia argued that it was not responsible for the cyberattacks because they were conducted by "hacktivists," political activists who use computer networks for subversive purposes.

The 2007 cyberattacks on Estonia connect to each section of this chapter:

- *Determining responsibility*: The first criterion for establishing state responsibility is to prove that a legal violation can be attributed to the relevant state. The second criterion is to show that the violation is not excused or justified by a circumstance precluding wrongfulness. A state is only responsible for a legal violation if both of these criteria are met.
- *Consequences of responsibility*: If an injured state can prove that another state is responsible for a legal violation, then it is entitled to reparation from the responsible state. Such reparation can include restitution, compensation, and/or satisfaction. In some rare cases, states also seek assurances of non-repetition.
- *Why do states break international law?*: Three competing perspectives—with different assumptions and arguments—help to explain why states break international law. The enforcement perspective assumes that states are rational actors who make decisions based on their expected costs and benefits. The managerial perspective assumes that states are predisposed to comply with international law, but are sometimes limited by ambiguity, capacity, or insufficient times

to adapt to new rules. Finally, the flexibility perspective assumes that leaders sometimes face unexpectedly high economic or political pressure to break international obligations. This temporary pressure may make it optimal for states to sometimes overlook legal violations, rather than punishing them.

This information allows us to revisit our motivating questions. First, we asked: was Russia responsible for the acts of individual hackers who opposed the Estonian government? In the Estonian cyberattacks, Russia claimed that it was not responsible for "hacktivists" who attacked Estonian business and government websites. Russia portrayed the attacks as the work of isolated individuals, acting independently of Russia. The international law experts convened by NATO after the attacks agreed with Russia. They argued that the attacks could not be attributed to Russia under the effective control standard because "there is no definitive evidence that the hacktivists involved in the cyber operations against Estonia in 2007 operated pursuant to instructions from any state, nor did any state endorse and adopt the conduct."[109] Accordingly, they found that Russia was not responsible for the cyberattacks.

Even if the attacks had been attributed to Russia, the law of state responsibility allows states that break international law to avoid punishment if circumstances preclude wrongfulness of the breach. Such circumstances include some acts of the injured state and external forces. In the 2007 cyberattacks, Russia could not plausibly claim that Estonia had consented to the cyberattacks. Similarly, Estonia's decision to move the Bronze Soldier and Soviet graves could not justify Russian self-defense or countermeasures. Finally, no external forces—like *force majeure*, distress, or necessity—could be invoked to excuse or justify the cyberattacks. Therefore, if Estonia had been able to attribute the 2007 cyberattack to Russia, then Russia would have been responsible for the attack.

Second, we asked: if Russia was responsible for the cyberattacks, what could Estonia demand in response? While the cyberattacks were very disruptive for the people of Estonia, the legal consequences would have been minimal. A state is required to make reparations to injured states when it breaks international law, but it is usually only expected to provide restitution via a return to the *status quo ante*. Once a cyberattack has passed, the *status quo ante* has been restored. Estonia might have been entitled to some compensation for the harm that it suffered during

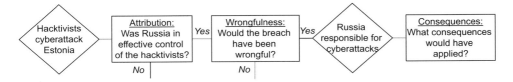

Figure 3.4 State responsibility for the 2007 Estonia cyberattacks.

the attack, such as disruptions to commercial activities, but punitive damages are not allowed under international law. A relatively powerful state like Russia could easily pay off a small country like Estonia for economic harm from a cyberattack. Finally, satisfaction is often required under international law. While a statement of Russian responsibility would have given the Estonian government and people some moral value, it would have provided little material value.

Finally, we asked: how should states respond to incidents like the 2007 cyberattacks? Your answer to this question would probably depend on your viewpoint about why states break international law. Enforcement scholars would view the 2007 cyberattacks in Estonia as an example of the weakness of international law. They would emphasize that despite a widespread belief that Russia was responsible, Russia faced no tangible punishment for the cyberattack. Additionally, enforcement scholars would likely argue that attribution rules gave Russia incentive to outsource legal breaches to individual hacktivists and "then hide behind a ... veil of plausible deniability."[110] They would also probably argue that the international community's failure to punish Russia likely encouraged Russia to commit further attacks. For example, Russia conducted cyberattacks during its 2008 conflict with Georgia and its 2014 conflict with Ukraine.[111] Overall, the enforcement perspective suggests that if states want effective laws, then they need to impose severe punishments for violations of those laws.

In contrast, the managerial perspective assumes that states want to comply with international law, but sometimes cannot because they are uncertain about the meaning of legal obligations, they lack capacity, or they have had insufficient time to comply. Managerial scholars would likely argue that there is ambiguity about the facts of the attack and the legal obligations involved. International law does not have any cybersecurity treaties. Rather, NATO had to gather legal experts to clarify the relevant legal obligations. If NATO leaders were uncertain in 2007 about what international law required, how could we expect Russia to know any better? Additionally, managerial scholars often argue that states lack capacity to control non-state actors. Attribution rules ensure that states aren't responsible for breaches that they cannot control. Finally, managerial scholars would probably argue that the fast pace of technological changes makes it very difficult for states to cooperate on cybersecurity. The 2007 cyberattack may be a temporary, but inevitable, disruption caused by insufficient regulation of new technologies. A supporter of the managerial perspective would likely argue that states should not punish one another for cyberattacks. Rather, they should overlook past violations and persuade each other to prevent future cyberattacks.

Finally, the flexibility perspective emphasizes that a state's temptation to break international law changes over time in response to unexpected economic and political pressure. While Estonia's decision to move the Bronze Soldier and Soviet graves did not legally excuse or justify a cyberattack, it does explain why individuals of Russian ethnicity were angry at Estonia. From Russia's perspective, Estonia created unexpected political pressure on Russia to respond. Flexibility scholars would also argue that states have weak rules on cybersecurity and state responsibility precisely because they do not want rules that fully prohibit cyberattacks. NATO members don't want Russia to attack Estonia, but they also want the flexibility to commit their own cyberattacks on China, North Korea, and Russia. Temptations to commit cyberattacks may simply be too large for cooperation.

For example, the US has criticized China, North Korea, and Russia for allegedly conducting cyberattacks on the US military and firms. Yet the US is also widely believed to have conducted the first ever cyberattack: in 1982, the CIA planted malicious code into Canadian software, causing a Soviet pipeline to explode.[112] Similarly, a 2010 computer glitch revealed the existence of Stuxnet, a sophisticated computer program that infiltrates computer operating systems and disrupts industrial control systems. Reporters later discovered that Stuxnet was jointly created by Israel and the US, and was used to hinder Iran's nuclear centrifuges.[113] US criticism of cyberattacks is therefore likely to be mere rhetoric, at best, and hypocrisy, at worst: states want to be able to use cyberweapons on others, even if they want others not to use these weapons. This perspective suggests that any apparent persuasion or threat after a cyberattack is merely political theater, rather than a genuine attempt to respond to a legal violation.

All three theoretical perspectives—the enforcement, managerial, and flexibility perspectives—therefore provide insight into why states sometimes break international law. Which perspective you find most compelling likely depends on your assumptions about how international politics works. Like any theory, these perspectives cannot be true or false; they can only be more or less useful. Which perspective is most useful may vary across different time periods, regions, or issue areas.

These theoretical perspectives matter for two reasons. First, they shape our understanding of why international law looks the way that it does. We can only understand the design of international law if we have a theory of state behavior. Second, they affect our beliefs about how international law can be made better. For example, when should states be held responsible for non-state actors? What is an acceptable excuse or justification for breaking international law? Should international law allow punitive damages? The answers to these questions depend on why states break international law.

4 Upholding International Law

4.1   Case Study: Argentina's $20 Million Standoff in Ghana

For a few months in fall 2012, Paul Singer—a Wall Street investment fund manager—was the proud owner of the *ARA Libertad*, a massive Argentine warship. This warship docked in Ghana—a small coastal state in West Africa—during military training exercises. Paul Singer asked a judge in Ghana to formally recognize a US court order that said Argentina owed Singer over $280 million in unpaid debts.[1] Singer estimated that the *ARA Libertad* was worth $20 million.[2] He accordingly asked for—and was awarded—the warship as a payment on Argentina's debt.

Argentina quickly challenged Ghana's actions, suing it at the International Tribunal for the Law of the Sea (ITLOS). ITLOS is an international legal body in the Netherlands. ITLOS does not hear debt disputes. Rather, it hears disputes about the international law of the sea, which includes rules about how states treat foreign

Figure 4.1 The *ARA Libertad*—an Argentine warship—arrives in Argentina in early 2013 after being detained in Ghana for many months by debt collectors.

warships. ITLOS ordered Ghana to release the warship immediately.[3] Ghana quickly complied and allowed Argentina to reclaim the *ARA Libertad*.

Like Argentina, most states routinely borrow money from global investors by issuing bonds, which are a kind of loan. Bond contracts are usually negotiated with large banks, who sell shares of the bond to investors. These shares can then be resold among investors. The price of these shares fluctuates based, in part, on the perceived likelihood that the original bond contract will be honored. Investors who own bond shares are entitled to interest payments and a final repayment when the contract ends.

In 2001, Argentina faced tough economic times. Overwhelmed by debt payments and domestic spending, Argentina decided to default on its debt, meaning that it stopped making payments to bond-holders. This default triggered complex negotiations between Argentina and major bond-holders. Many of these bond-holders agreed to a unilateral offer by Argentina in 2005: they would receive a small payment in exchange for their shares. However, some bond-holders became hold-out creditors, meaning that they did not accept the 2005 deal: they insisted that Argentina honor the original bond contract.

Many of the hold-out creditors were Wall Street investors like Paul Singer. These investors bought their shares after the 2001 default at a small fraction of their original price from prior investors who had given up hope of being paid. These investors then used legal and political tools to pressure Argentina into honoring its original bond contract. Critics describe such investors as "vultures" because they sweep into troubled situations and try to profit from them.

Why could Paul Singer seize an Argentine warship in Ghana, only to lose it a few months later? How did Argentina and Singer ultimately resolve their dispute? Finally, who won the Argentine debt dispute?

To answer these questions, we must first understand the following topics:

- *International legal enforcement*: What international legal bodies can hear disputes over international law? What factors affect their ability and willingness to rule on such disputes? Why didn't Paul Singer sue Argentina in an international legal body?
- *Domestic legal enforcement*: Can domestic courts uphold international law? When are states and their officials subject to foreign courts, and when are they immune? Why did domestic courts in the US and Ghana have authority over Argentina, and what were the limits of this authority?
- *Political enforcement*: How do individuals, states, and the international community use politics to uphold international law? What tools are available to these diverse actors? How did Paul Singer use politics to uphold Argentina's bond contract?

To answer these questions, we must first recognize that international law lacks a formal enforcement system. No international court has absolute authority to judge all possible violations of international law, and no international police force can compel individuals and states to follow a court ruling. Instead, individuals and states use many different legal and political tools to uphold international law. Sometimes they seek a **civil remedy**, which is a remedy primarily aimed at making a victim whole. For example, victims sometimes want financial compensation to help repair an injury, like an unpaid debt. At other times, they want a formal apology or acknowledgement of wrongdoing. Alternatively, individuals and states may seek a **criminal remedy**, which is a remedy primarily aimed at punishing a violator. For example, actors may seek the imprisonment of a politician or military leader who has violated international law. Finally, sometimes, actors uphold international law by preventing future legal violations.

This chapter examines how diverse actors—including individuals, states, and the international community—use both legal and political tools to uphold international law. Section 4.2 introduces international legal enforcement. We describe the International Court of Justice, international arbitration, and various specialized bodies that interpret and apply international law. Section 4.3 then discusses how and when domestic courts can uphold international law. In particular, it describes how the concepts of jurisdiction, admissibility, and immunity affect whether domestic courts can rule on international disputes. Next, section 4.4 describes common political tactics for upholding international law. Finally, section 4.5 returns to the standoff in Ghana between Argentina and Paul Singer.

4.2 International Legal Enforcement

The first tool for upholding international law is international legal enforcement. Many international bodies resolve disputes about the interpretation or application of international law. We begin by briefly describing major international legal bodies. We then discuss some common circumstances in which these bodies refuse to rule on legal questions. Finally, we discuss how non-state actors gain access to international legal institutions.

Major Bodies

International legal bodies are called many names, including courts, adjudicatory bodies, arbitration panels, and dispute settlement systems. These many names reflect the diverse powers and procedures of these bodies. Yet despite their differences, they all interpret and apply international law.

One key body for upholding international law is the **International Court of Justice** (ICJ), which is located in The Hague, Netherlands and is sometimes called the "World Court." The ICJ was created in 1946 as part of the United Nations system. It is the oldest international court that still exists, and its judgments are part of the bedrock of public international law.

Fifteen judges are chosen by UN elections to serve on the ICJ. These judges can hear every case during their terms. If the applicant or respondent state for a case does not have an elected judge currently serving in the ICJ, it may appoint an ad hoc judge, who hears only that particular case. These procedures ensure that most ICJ cases are decided by fifteen to seventeen judges. The five permanent members of the UN Security Council almost always have an ICJ judge. The other ten seats are allocated based on regional representation. In the ICJ's early decades, states often elected politicians as ICJ judges.[4] However, most contemporary ICJ judges have prior experience as academics, domestic judges, or government legal advisors.

The ICJ has no subject-matter restrictions, meaning that it rules on diverse issue areas using many sources of law. As shown in Table 4.1, most ICJ cases are land or maritime border disputes. These cases often involve oil or fishing rights. ICJ cases also often involve international conflicts, such as wars in the Democratic Republic of the Congo and the former Yugoslavia. Other ICJ cases involve property rights. For example, some ICJ disputes involve how governments treat foreign companies,

Table 4.1 Common Types of ICJ Disputes

Dispute Type	Number	Example
Border dispute	41	*Bakassi* (1994–2002): Cameroon sued Nigeria over the oil-rich Bakassi peninsula
International conflicts	25	*Armed Activities* (1992–2003): Democratic Republic of the Congo sued Uganda for invading and occupying its territory
Property rights	18	*Barcelona Traction* (1962–1970): Belgium sued Spain for mistreating foreign investors
Aviation	16	*ICAO Council* (2018–2020): Bahrain, Egypt, and UAE appealed a decision about an aviation blockade against Qatar
Diplomatic and consular relations	15	*Iran Hostages* (1979–1980): US sued Iran after protestors attacked the US Embassy and took hostages
Transnational justice	6	*Jurisdictional Immunities* (2008–2012): Germany sued Italy for allowing domestic lawsuits against Germany for war crimes
Environment	5	*Pulp Mills* (2006–2010): Argentina sued Uruguay for issuing construction permits without joint environmental review
Human rights	5	*South Ossetia and Abkhazia* (2008–2011): Georgia sued Russia for breaking human rights law in contested territories
Trusteeship and decolonization	4	*East Timor* (1991–1995): Portugal argued that an Australian treaty with Indonesia violated Portugal's colonial rights over East Timor

Note: This table categorizes all ICJ cases filed through 2020. It excludes attempts to revise or reinterpret a prior judgment. A single case can be classified in multiple categories, and some cases are classified as "other."

like the *Barcelona Traction* case discussed below. The ICJ also often adjudicates aviation disputes, such as the aviation blockade that many Gulf states imposed on Qatar in 2017, and diplomatic and consular disputes, like the *Iran Hostages* case of 1979–1980. These types of disputes have all been common throughout the ICJ's history.

Three new kinds of disputes have begun to appear at the ICJ in recent decades. First, some lawsuits involve transnational justice, which is the use of domestic courts in foreign states to uphold international law. For example, numerous victims of war crimes during World War II sued Germany in Italian domestic courts in the 2000s. As discussed below, Germany sued Italy at the ICJ in 2008, arguing that these lawsuits violated international law on state immunity. Second, some ICJ cases now involve environmental law. For example, Argentina sued Uruguay in 2006 for allowing the construction of factories that Argentina believed would pollute a shared river. Finally, a few ICJ cases involve human rights. For example, Georgia sued Russia in 2008 for human rights violations in South Ossetia and Abkhazia, which are contested territories. In contrast, ICJ disputes over trusteeship agreements and decolonization are no longer common. Nevertheless, several lawsuits in this category illustrate important legal principles that are discussed below.

Most ICJ cases are extremely complex, with intertwined legal questions. To manage this complexity, the ICJ usually divides each case into states, which can yield multiple judgments for each case. The Court often begins with state requests for provisional measures to preserve the political and economic situation until the Court rules on substantive matters.[5] Recall from Chapter 2 that the ICJ ordered France to stop all atmospheric nuclear tests until it had ruled on the arguments in the *Nuclear Tests* cases. Similarly, shortly after The Gambia sued Myanmar in late 2019 for allegedly committing genocide against the Rohingya people, the ICJ ordered Myanmar to "take all measures within its power to prevent the commission of all acts" covered by the Genocide Convention, and to "take effective measures to prevent the destruction and ensure the preservation of evidence related to allegations of acts" of genocide.[6] The ICJ then usually hears preliminary objections about whether the Court can and should rule on the case. During this stage, states often argue about issues like jurisdiction and admissibility, which are discussed in more depth below. Finally, the ICJ considers the merits of a case by interpreting and applying relevant law.[7]

Literally dozens of ICJ disputes are discussed throughout this book. Nevertheless, some exciting ongoing ICJ disputes (as of writing) include:

- *Relocation of the US Embassy* (2018–present): In late 2017, President Donald Trump moved the US Embassy in Israel from Tel Aviv to Jerusalem, meaning that the US formally recognized Jerusalem as the sovereign territory of Israel. Palestine—which is not recognized as a state by the US—sued the US, arguing that the move violated international law because Palestine claims Jerusalem as its own territory.
- *Myanmar Genocide* (2019–present): As mentioned above, The Gambia is suing Myanmar over its alleged genocide of the Rohingya people.
- *Certain Iranian Assets* (2019–present): The US has numerous domestic laws that allow victims of state-sponsored terrorism to sue foreign states in US domestic courts. Under these laws, victims of a terrorist bombing in 1983 have been trying to seize assets of the Iranian government located in the US. Iran argues that these US laws violate international law on state immunity (an issue discussed below).

Each of these disputes has the potential to develop and refine international law.

Another legal body that upholds international law is the Permanent Court of Arbitration (PCA), which was created in 1899 and is also located in The Hague. Despite its name, this organization is not actually a court because it does not have sitting judges. Instead, the PCA provides resources for **arbitration**, which is a process in which one or more individuals decide a dispute based on evidence and arguments. These resources include office space, procedural rules, and arbitrator recommendations. However, the litigants themselves decide who to hire as an arbitrator and how to conduct arbitration. Some important recent PCA disputes include:

- *South China Sea* (2013–2016): The Philippines challenged China over territorial claims in the South China Sea.
- *Arctic Sunrise* (2014–2017): The Netherlands challenged Russia over arrests and property seizures during a protest at sea near an offshore oil platform.

Note that both of these disputes involved the law of the sea, partly because the UN Convention on the Law of the Sea gives states relatively easy access to the PCA. The PCA also frequently hears disputes between investors and foreign states, which are possible under many investment treaties.

Many other international legal bodies help states to uphold specialized areas of international law. They include:

- the World Trade Organization's dispute settlement system, which oversees international trade disputes (discussed in Chapter 6);
- the International Centre for the Settlement of Investment Disputes, which hears arbitration cases about foreign investment law (discussed in Chapter 7);
- the European Court of Human Rights, which decides human rights cases (discussed in Chapter 8); and
- the International Criminal Court, which prosecutes individuals for international crimes, like genocide and war crimes (discussed in Chapter 11).

Finally, some international courts adjudicate regional disputes in multiple issue areas. For example, the European Court of Justice interprets and applies European Union law. A similar role is played by regional courts in Africa and Latin America. Each of these courts has its own unique rules that are set in their founding statutes.

Refusing to Rule

To interpret and apply international law, an international legal body must first establish that it has **jurisdiction** over the case, meaning that it has authority to rule on the dispute. International legal bodies have different jurisdictional rules. We focus here on how the ICJ works because of the inherent importance of the ICJ for international law, and because jurisdictional issues are usually very important and complex in the ICJ.

States can accept ICJ jurisdiction in multiple ways. First, a state can make a unilateral declaration that it accepts jurisdiction.[8] These declarations can define the scope of ICJ jurisdiction and be changed by states over time. For example, Australia accepted the ICJ's jurisdiction using a unilateral declaration in 1975. In 1999, East Timor voted to become an independent nation. Australia feared that it would be sued at the ICJ by East Timor over their shared maritime border, which affected underwater oil drilling.[9] Shortly before East Timor became independent in

2002, Australia changed its unilateral declaration. Australia wrote that it did not accept ICJ jurisdiction for "any dispute concerning or relating to the delimitation of maritime zones ... [or] the exploitation of any disputed area."[10] This new language protected Australia from being sued by East Timor.

Second, ICJ jurisdiction can be created by a **compromissory clause**, which is treaty text that gives authority to an international legal body to hear disputes about the treaty's interpretation or application. Sometimes a compromissory clause is included in the main treaty text, and sometimes it is included in an optional protocol. For example, the Vienna Convention on Consular Relations (VCCR) specifies state rights and responsibilities. A separate optional protocol gives the ICJ jurisdiction to hear disputes under the treaty. A state can join the VCCR without joining the optional protocol. This division allows a state to accept legal rights and responsibilities, but reject ICJ jurisdiction.

The US originally joined both the VCCR and its optional protocol. The US used this compromissory clause to file the *Iran Hostages* case in 1979. However, the US withdrew from the VCCR's optional protocol in 2002 after it was sued three times at the ICJ under the treaty. The US still has legal commitments under the VCCR, but the ICJ can no longer rule on alleged VCCR violations by the US. Similarly, the US can no longer sue other states at the ICJ for violating the VCCR.

Third, states can jointly agree to ICJ jurisdiction for a particular dispute. States can write a special agreement that defines the scope of the dispute. For example, states often write special agreements that create ICJ jurisdiction for land and maritime border disputes. Alternatively, one state can invite another state to accept jurisdiction for a particular dispute. The ICJ will only hear such a case if the respondent accepts the invitation.

Even if a legal body has jurisdiction to hear a case, it may refuse to rule by finding the case inadmissible. The concept of **admissibility** refers to criteria that affect a legal body's willingness to rule, usually based on the specific facts of the case. International law does not contain a definitive checklist of admissibility criteria. Instead, international legal bodies apply criteria from domestic legal systems.

For example, some international legal bodies will not rule on a case that affects the rights of an excluded third party. International lawyers sometimes call this criterion the "*Monetary Gold* principle" because of the *Monetary Gold* case in which many states claimed gold seized during World War II. Only some of these states wanted the ICJ to decide the dispute, so the Court refused to rule on the case.[11] In a more modern example, Portugal sued Australia in 1991 over a treaty that set the maritime border between Australia and Indonesia. This treaty assumed that Indonesia had sovereignty over East Timor, but Portugal believed that it had colonial authority over this territory. In 1995, the ICJ refused to rule on Portugal's lawsuit against Australia because any possible ruling would affect Indonesia, which was not included in the lawsuit.[12]

A second admissibility criterion is that the applicant have **standing**, meaning that the actor filing a case must have a legal interest in the dispute. International legal bodies define the concept of a legal interest in different ways.[13] The ICJ requires that an applicant state must identify how the responding state has violated a legal obligation to the applicant state. In one early ruling, the ICJ clarified: "only the party to whom an international obligation is due can bring a claim in respect of its breach."[14] Generally speaking, a state may not file a lawsuit on behalf of another state. For example, Belgium sued Spain in 1962 over Spain's treatment of the Barcelona Traction Company. This company was incorporated in Canada, but many of its shareholders were Belgian nationals. The ICJ argued that Spain had legal obligations to Canada, the home state of the company, but not to Belgium, the home state of the investors.[15] According to the Court, Belgium's case was inadmissible because Belgium did not have any legal rights that were affected by the dispute.

Third, many treaties require states to follow specific procedures before challenging violations at a court. If a state does not follow these procedures, an international legal body may rule the case inadmissible. For example, Georgia sued Russia in 2008 for violating human rights law in the contested territories of South Ossetia and Abkhazia. The International Convention on the Elimination of All Forms of Racial Discrimination required states to follow specific procedures before filing a lawsuit.[16] In 2011, the ICJ refused to rule on the alleged human rights violations because Georgia did not follow the treaty procedures for filing a lawsuit.[17]

Another admissibility criterion is timeliness. Many legal bodies will not rule if there has been an excessive delay between the time of a legal violation and the filing of a lawsuit. Second, an applicant must usually exhaust local remedies (like domestic administrative and legal procedures) before filing a case with an international legal body. Finally, the ICJ will only rule on a case if it can identify the existence of a legal dispute. Respondent states sometimes avoid substantive rulings by persuading the Court that a dispute does not actually exist.[18]

Even if jurisdiction exists and a case is admissible, a legal body may refuse to decide a particular legal question because of **judicial economy**, which is the principle that a legal body should decline to make a ruling that is not necessary to resolve a dispute. When judges are presented with complex cases, they often must consider multiple alternative arguments. Rather than deciding on each and every issue that is presented before them, a judge is encouraged to only make rulings that are actually needed.[19]

For example, in the *Barcelona Traction* case, Belgium tried to sue Spain on behalf of Belgian shareholders in a Canadian company. As one part of its argument, Belgium suggested that the Court could disregard the company's nationality if the company no longer existed, or if the company's home state lacked capacity to protect the company.[20] However, the Court concluded that neither of these circumstances was relevant—Barcelona Traction did still exist as a company, and Canada did have capacity to protect the company. The Court therefore exercised judicial economy and refused to rule on whether this particular part of Belgium's argument was valid.

Finally, a legal body may refuse to rule based on **judicial propriety**. This principle posits that a legal body should refuse to make a ruling that would not serve a judicial function. For example, Cameroon sued the UK in 1961 for violating a UN Trusteeship Agreement for the Northern Cameroons territory. Shortly after the lawsuit was filed, Northern Cameroons joined Nigeria and the relevant agreement was dissolved. The Court refused to hear the case because the relevant agreement was no longer in effect. The Court argued that any ruling "would be inconsistent with [the Court's] judicial function" because its judgment would serve no purpose.[21]

Access to Non-State Actors

Many international legal bodies—including the International Court of Justice—only allow states to file cases. Yet legal violations sometimes harm non-state actors. How do these actors access justice?

Individuals, Groups, and Non-Governmental Organizations

International law affects diverse actors within and across states, as discussed in Chapter 1. Some areas of international law create rights for individuals and groups, like racial and ethnic groups. International law also affects non-governmental organizations (NGOs), which operate independently of states to achieve political objectives. NGOs include advocacy groups, like Amnesty International, and multinational corporations, which practice international commerce.

Before the modern era, experts believed that international law created rights and obligations for states only. While international law might *affect* individuals, groups, and non-governmental organizations, experts believed that non-state actors did not have rights and obligations. These actors accordingly also lacked legal remedies.

Experts agreed that international law provided states with a **right to diplomatic protection**, which allows states to protect their nationals at the international level. For example, states often asserted this right to protect individuals traveling in foreign states and businesses producing or trading goods internationally. If these individuals or businesses believed that they were not treated fairly by a foreign state, they could ask their home state for diplomatic protection. Sometimes this protection yielded lawsuits in international legal bodies.

The right to diplomatic protection is a state right, not an individual right. As the Permanent Court of International Justice explained:

> It is an elementary principle of international law that a state is entitled to protect its subjects, when injured by acts contrary to international law committed by another state ... By taking up the case of one of its subjects and by resorting to diplomatic action or international judicial proceedings on his behalf, a state is in reality asserting its own rights—its right to ensure ... respect for the rules of international law.[22]

In the modern era, states continue to recognize and respect the right to diplomatic protection over nationals.

In rare circumstances, states can even protect non-nationals. Under international law, a ship falls under the jurisdiction of the state in which it is registered. A state can provide such a ship with diplomatic protection. For example, Greenpeace, an environmental advocacy group, used a Dutch ship called the *Arctic Sunrise* to conduct a protest at a Russian offshore oil platform in September 2013. Russia seized the *Arctic Sunrise*, arrested everyone on board, and charged them with crimes under Russian law. The Netherlands quickly filed a dispute against Russia at the Permanent Court of Arbitration, on behalf of the ship, its crew, and the protestors. Even though some of these individuals were not Dutch nationals, the Netherlands successfully invoked the right to diplomatic protection.[23]

However, states do not have an obligation to provide diplomatic protection under international law. For example, in the *Barcelona Traction* case, shareholders believed that a Canadian company was treated unfairly by Spain. Canada held diplomatic discussions with Spain about the company, but refused to sue Spain. While shareholders criticized Canada, the ICJ wrote:

> a state may exercise diplomatic protection by whatever means and to whatever extent it thinks fit, for it is its own right that the state is asserting. Should the natural or legal persons on whose behalf it is acting consider that their rights are not adequately protected, they have no remedy in international law.[24]

These was thus a separation between who was injured—a company and its shareholders—and who could access justice.

As international law became more inclusive of non-state actors, many experts believed that these actors should be able to access justice directly. As one expert wrote in 2011: "the recognition of [an individual's] rights, as a subject of international law, ought to correspond to the procedural capacity to vindicate them."[25] Many experts believed that empowering non-state actors could relieve tensions within the international system. For example, if multinational corporations could sue foreign states directly, then the home states of these corporations could credibly refuse to protect them. Diplomats could focus on maintaining peaceful relations between states, rather than representing commercial interests.

In some areas of international law, individuals now have direct access to international legal bodies. As discussed in Chapter 8, most states now allow **individual petition** for human rights violations, which allows individuals to complain directly to an international organization if they believe that their rights have been violated by a state. Many states also allow individuals to file lawsuits at regional human rights courts in Africa, the Americas, and Europe. Similarly, modern investment law often gives investors access to **investor–state dispute settlement**, which allows investors to directly sue foreign states using international arbitration.

However, individuals still lack access to justice for some other areas of international law. For example, the World Trade Organization only allows states to file trade disputes. Individual actors—like environmental groups, firms, industry organizations, and labor unions—must rely on diplomatic protection to uphold international trade law. Most states allow these actors to file complaints with domestic agencies that promote trade. However, these actors cannot file cases at the World Trade Organization. Similarly, non-state actors cannot file formal complaints with the International Criminal Court (ICC). The ICC Prosecutor often meets with advocacy organizations and crime victims. However, the Prosecutor is not legally obligated to give such access to the ICC.

The International Community

Traditionally, states conceived of international law as contracts that created legal obligations between pairs of states. Even multilateral treaties were believed to create bilateral obligations between their members. In modern international legal bodies, this bilateral structure is reflected in the concept of standing, which usually requires that the actor who files a case must have a legal interest in the dispute. Usually two criteria must be satisfied for a state to have a "legal interest" in a dispute. First, the applicant must have a legal right that was violated by the respondent. Second, the respondent must suffer an actual injury because of this violation. However, many violations of international law don't cause an actual injury to another state or its nationals.

For example, the Union of South Africa—a country governed by white minority rule—used to govern a territory called South West Africa.[26] After World War I, the Union signed a League of Nations agreement in which it pledged to promote the "well-being and the social progress of the inhabitants" of South West Africa.[27] In 1960, Ethiopia and Liberia sued the Union of South Africa at the ICJ for violating this agreement. Ethiopia and Liberia wanted to promote self-determination for the black natives of South West Africa and to eradicate apartheid. In a controversial 1966 ruling, the Court argued that Ethiopia and Liberia "did not, in their individual capacity as states, possess any separate self-contained right which they could assert, independently of, or additionally

Figure 4.2 A woman protests in 1948 outside the embassy of the Union of South Africa in London. For decades, states and non-governmental organizations challenged the Union's rule over South West Africa (modern-day Namibia). They argued that the Union—which was ruled by a white minority—was legally required to abolish apartheid and grant self-determination to the black native inhabitants of South West Africa. In 1960, Ethiopia and Liberia tried to sue the Union of South Africa at the ICJ, but the Court ruled in 1966 that Ethiopia and Liberia did not have standing to sue because their legal rights were not affected by the Union's behavior.

to, the right of the League."[28] That is, the ICJ ruled that Ethiopia and Liberia did not have standing to sue the Union.

Such disputes caused many legal experts to argue that international law can create legal obligations between a state and the international community.[29] While different experts conceptualize the international community in different ways, they usually define the **international community** as a group of global actors with legal interests and personality, independent of its members. These experts acknowledge that some international rules—like trade agreements—create only bilateral obliga- tions. But these experts also believe that international law can create an ***erga omnes obligation***, which is an obligation to the international community as a whole.[30]

A few years after the controversial *South West Africa* ruling, the ICJ endorsed the concept of an *erga omnes* obligation in an **obiter dictum**, which is a statement in a judgment that is not necessary to resolve the given legal dispute. In its 1970 *Barcelona Traction* judgment, the ICJ majority wrote:

> an essential distinction should be drawn between the obligations of a state towards the international community as a whole, and those arising *vis-à-vis* another state in the field of diplomatic protection. By their very nature the former are the concern of all states. In view of the importance of the rights involved, all states can be held to have a legal interest in their protection; they are obligations *erga omnes.*
>
> Such obligations derive, for example, in contemporary international law, from the outlawing of acts of aggression, and of genocide, as also from the principles and rules concerning the basic rights of the human person, including protection from slavery and racial discrimination. Some of the corresponding rights of protection have entered into the body of general international law ... Others are conferred by international instruments of a universal or quasi-universal character.[31]

This statement wasn't particularly relevant to the *Barcelona Traction* case. Belgium believed that its own rights had been violated, and it was suing over a foreign investment dispute, not over slavery or racial discrimination. Yet the ICJ's *obiter dictum* fueled intense debates about *erga omnes* obligations.

Politicians and legal experts now routinely refer to the international community as an actor with its own interests and rights. But no single person or organization represents the international community. So how do experts identify *erga omnes* obligations? Various ICJ rulings have provided five examples of *erga omnes* obligations: the prohibitions of aggression, genocide, racial discrimination, and slavery; and the right to self-determination.[32] But are there other *erga omnes* obligations?

Experts usually believe that all peremptory norms (*jus cogens*) are *erga omnes* obligations. Recall from Chapter 2 that a **peremptory norm** is "a norm accepted and recognized by the international community of states as a whole as a norm from which no derogation is permitted and which can be modified only by a subsequent norm of general international law having the same character."[33] As one expert wrote, "the character of a rule as *jus cogens* symbolizes the concern of the *omnes* in the sense of all states taken together."[34] Most experts therefore conclude that every peremptory norm is also an *erga omnes* obligation. However, this approach isn't very helpful in identifying *erga omnes* obligations because there is no widely accepted process for identifying peremptory norms.[35] Additionally, many experts believe that rules can be *erga omnes* obligations without being peremptory norms.

Some experts argue that other attributes of cooperation can help us to identify *erga omnes* obligations.[36] For example, some experts argue that a rule becomes an *erga omnes* obligation if it promotes an important community value. Other experts argue that *erga omnes* obligations must be non-reciprocal, meaning that a state cannot uphold the obligation by conditioning its own behavior on the behavior of another state. Still other experts argue that severe violations of law generate *erga omnes* obligations. In short, there is little consensus about how to identify *erga omnes* obligations.

Another important question is: how can *erga omnes* obligations be upheld? As some experts have noted, *omnes* has multiple meanings: "it can either refer to all others collectively, or to each of the others individually."[37] The specific meaning of *omnes* affects the appropriate mode of enforcement.

Some experts believe that every state has standing to unilaterally challenge the violation of an *erga omnes* obligation. These experts usually point to the ICJ's 1970 *Barcelona Traction* ruling, which says that "all states can be held to have a *legal interest*" in an *erga omnes* obligation.[38] Yet the ICJ has never allowed a state to establish standing using only the concept of an *erga omnes* obligation.

Other experts believe that only the international community—as a collective actor—can uphold *erga omnes* obligations. While the ICJ only hears cases between states, it can also issue an **advisory opinion**, which is a non-binding document that answers legal questions submitted by an international organization. These legal questions can be about any matter, not just *erga omnes* obligations. ICJ advisory opinions often address relatively narrow and technical issues, like the legal rights of UN employees. However, after the ICJ dismissed the claims of Ethiopia and Liberia in the *South West Africa* cases, the UN Security Council asked the ICJ for an advisory opinion on the matter.[39] The UN General Assembly has also requested advisory opinions on important legal topics, including:

- *Nuclear Weapons* ("Is the threat or use of nuclear weapons in any circumstance permitted under international law?");[40]
- *Israeli Wall* ("What are the legal consequences arising from the construction of the wall being built by Israel ... in the Occupied Palestinian Territory?");[41] and
- *Chagos Archipelago* ("What are the consequences under international law ... arising from the continued administration by the United Kingdom ... of the Chagos Archipelago?").[42]

While advisory opinions are non-binding, they help to clarify international law and reflect the concerns of international organizations.

4.3   Domestic Legal Enforcement

A second tool for upholding international law is domestic legal enforcement. Most states allow individuals, groups, and non-governmental organizations to challenge legal violations using law enforcement agencies and domestic courts. However, these government bodies are often limited by three important concepts: jurisdiction; state immunity; and diplomatic, consular, and official immunity. We discuss each of these concepts in turn.

Jurisdiction

Before hearing a dispute, a domestic court must first establish its jurisdiction. International law does not have clear rules about domestic court jurisdiction.[43] Each state sets its own rules about whether a domestic court can hear a particular case. There are five common ways in which contemporary domestic courts often assert jurisdiction.

The first basis for jurisdiction is territory. Since the rise of the modern state in seventeenth-century Europe, a core element of statehood has been sovereignty. This principle gives a state exclusive authority to rule on acts that occur within its borders. Domestic legal systems often have complicated rules for acts that occur across borders, like transnational business. Nonetheless, territorial jurisdiction is the most common and well-accepted basis for domestic jurisdiction.

The second basis for jurisdiction is active personality. This basis applies if the person who committed the relevant act is the state's national and the act occurred outside of the state's territory. Active personality jurisdiction therefore allows a state to regulate acts that occur in another state. Yet this form of jurisdiction is common and relatively uncontroversial in international politics.[44]

A third basis for jurisdiction is passive personality. This basis applies if a state's national was harmed by an act outside of the state's territory. Passive personality jurisdiction is usually more controversial than active personality jurisdiction. Yet states sometimes invoke passive personality jurisdiction to punish severe crimes, like genocide, terrorism, and torture.[45]

Fourth, domestic courts sometimes assert jurisdiction based on the **protective principle**. This principle claims that a state can regulate and punish acts with systematic and important effects on the state's national interests, like its security. Some legal experts view the protective principle as part of the right to self-defense.[46]

Finally, and most controversially, some states allow their domestic courts to assert **universal jurisdiction**, which is the claim that a state can sometimes use its domestic law and institutions to regulate behavior that occurs outside of its domestic territory, does not involve its nationals, and does not have systematic or important effects on itself.[47] Universal jurisdiction differs from the other four bases of jurisdiction because there is not a tangible link, or nexus, between the state asserting jurisdiction and the relevant act.

Domestic jurisdiction rules can depend on the remedy being sought. For example, US courts cannot assert universal jurisdiction for criminal remedies. However, they can sometimes assert universal jurisdiction for civil remedies using a US law called the Alien Tort Statute. This law allows US federal courts to have jurisdiction over "any civil action by an alien for a tort only, committed in violation of the law of nations or a treaty of the United States."[48] Non-US nationals have used the Alien Tort Statute to sue over matters such as: property taken by Germany during World War II; the killing and torture of political dissidents outside the US; and pollution caused by multinational corporations in foreign states.[49] Other US laws sometimes allow passive personality jurisdiction for civil remedies. For example, US nationals can use US domestic courts to seek compensation for terrorist attacks outside the US.[50]

Note that the same act can often qualify under multiple bases of jurisdiction. Thus international law violations can sometimes be challenged in the domestic courts of multiple states. For example, the Chilean government and military committed widespread human rights violations in the 1970s and 1980s under the autocratic rule of Augusto Pinochet. The perpetrators of these crimes were Chilean nationals, and the victims came from Chile and other states, including Spain. Under normal circumstances, Chilean courts would have territorial jurisdiction over these violations. However, Pinochet and other government actors were given amnesty for their alleged crimes when Chile transitioned to democratic rule in 1990. Many victims accordingly sought justice in other states. Some victims were Spanish nationals who lived in Chile. These victims and their families pressured a Spanish prosecutor to begin criminal proceedings against Pinochet using passive personality jurisdiction.[51] Other victims and family members who were Chilean nationals then persuaded the Spanish prosecutor to expand the proceedings to include Chilean victims. To justify this move, Spain invoked universal jurisdiction.

Overlapping jurisdiction can create political conflicts about who should hear a case. International law does not limit how many domestic courts can hear a case. In theory, Pinochet could have been prosecuted in multiple states. However, transnational lawsuits often require international cooperation. Under Spanish law, Pinochet could only be prosecuted if he was physically present in Spain. Spanish prosecutors therefore needed to arrest and extradite Pinochet to Spain. Chile refused to cooperate. When Pinochet traveled to the UK for medical treatment in 1998, Spain tried to convince the UK to arrest and extradite Pinochet. This situation created a complex legal battle within UK courts about whether the UK could (and should) extradite Pinochet to Spain.

State Immunity

Domestic courts are also limited by **state immunity**, which is the principle that a domestic court should not rule on a foreign state act without that state's consent. State immunity comes from the combination of sovereignty and the legal equality of all states within the international system. In 2012, the International Court of Justice wrote:

> state immunity occupies an important place in international law and international relations. It derives from the principle of sovereign equality of states, which ... is one of the fundamental principles of the international legal order. This principle has to be viewed together with the principle that each state possesses sovereignty over its own territory and that there flows from that sovereignty the jurisdiction of the state over events and persons within that territory.[52]

This logic suggests that when a domestic court rules on a foreign state's acts without that state's consent, there is "a departure from the principle of sovereign equality."[53] Immunity from jurisdiction protects a foreign state from being sued in a domestic court, while immunity from enforcement protects a foreign state's assets from being seized to enforce a court order.

Prior to World War II, most states accepted the **absolute theory of state immunity**, which protects all foreign state acts from domestic courts. For example, a US company sued *Transportes Maritimos Do Estado*, a Portuguese steamship owner, in US courts in the 1920s for not paying a repair bill. *Transportes* argued that it was a Portuguese government entity and hence entitled to immunity from US courts. In its petition to the US Supreme Court, Portugal wrote that it

> does not intend to avoid its just obligations to citizens of the United States, but it claims that, if there is any question between it and such citizens, they are matters for adjudication by the diplomatic departments of the two governments, and it does object to the violation of its sovereignty, contrary to all rules of international law and international comity.[54]

Portugal believed that disputes involving foreign governments should be resolved using diplomacy, not lawsuits.

After World War II, many governments became more involved in manufacturing, purchasing, and shipping goods across borders. This change affected how states perceived state immunity. Domestic courts and governments slowly whittled away the protections that they granted to foreign states, and private actors could more easily sue foreign states in domestic courts.

Many modern domestic courts divide state acts into two categories. Broadly speaking, domestic courts use the phrase ***acta jure imperii***—which is Latin for "sovereign act"—to describe an act that can only be undertaken by a state, not by a private company. Sovereign acts include:

- providing national security and law enforcement;
- issuing and regulating currency;
- providing universal education or health care; and
- taxing economic activities.[55]

In contrast, domestic courts use the phrase ***acta jure gestionis***—which is Latin for "commercial acts"—to describe an act that can be undertaken by a private company. Commercial acts by governments include:

- selling a good/service produced by a state-owned company (like an oil company or airline);
- buying a good/service that can also be purchased by a private company (like office supplies or clothing);
- issuing stock in a state-owned company; and
- leasing property for government offices.[56]

After classifying the foreign state act being challenged in a lawsuit, many modern domestic courts apply a **restricted theory of state immunity**, which only protects a foreign state's sovereign acts (and not its commercial acts) from domestic courts.[57] As shown in Table 4.2, domestic courts that adopt the restricted theory often allow lawsuits against foreign states. In some states, governments have written domestic laws that restrict state immunity. In other states, domestic courts use the restricted theory even without explicit domestic laws on the subject.

Table 4.2 Competing Theories of State Immunity

	Is a State Immune Under the ...	
Type of State Act	Absolute Theory?	Restricted Theory?
• *Acta jure imperii* (sovereign act)	Yes	Yes
• *Acta jure gestionis* (commercial act)	Yes	No

Figure 4.3 shows the gradual shift from absolute to restricted immunity across states and time. Only five states used the restricted theory of state immunity in 1945. However, seventy-six states had adopted restricted immunity by 2010.[58] This increase is partly explained by the growing number of states in the international system. Yet there is also a growing proportion of states that restrict state immunity.

Changing trends in state immunity have created two kinds of disagreement. First, experts often disagree about whether a particular state act is an *acta jure imperii* or an *acta jure gestionis*. State acts often involve a mixture of commercial and non-commercial activities and motives. Some examples include:

- hiring private companies to construct public buildings (e.g. schools and hospitals) or utility systems;
- loaning, leasing, or selling government-owned artwork or relics;
- buying and selling goods/services that cannot be purchased by private companies (e.g. missiles and nuclear reactors);

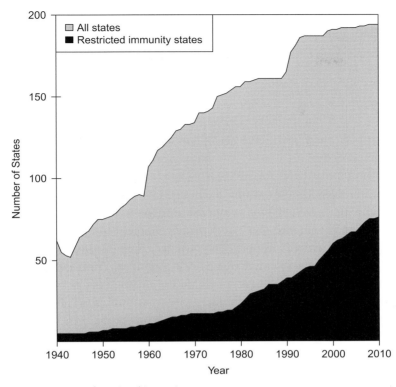

Figure 4.3 Rise of restricted immunity.
Source data: Correlates of War Project and Pierre-Hugues Verdier and Erik Voeten (2015),
"How Does Customary International Law Change? The Case of State Immunity," *International
Studies Quarterly* 59: 209–222, at 211.

- hiring private companies to help provide public education, health care, law
  enforcement, or national security; and
- issuing commercial bonds to finance sovereign acts.

Such acts often create disagreement about whether foreign states can be sued in
domestic courts that use restricted immunity.

For example, most foreign debt in the late twentieth century was issued in the
US.[59] For most of this period, US courts did not classify these debts as "commercial
acts."[60] To reassure investors, many foreign states began to waive their immunity
from US jurisdiction, thereby allowing investors to sue them in US courts. Some
states also waived their immunity from enforcement, allowing investors to seize
their assets in the US. By the 2000s, all foreign state bonds issued in New York
included a waiver of jurisdiction, and 78 percent also included a waiver from
execution.[61]

Second, experts often disagree about how international law governs state immunity rules. Two treaties—the European Convention on State Immunity (1972)

and the UN Convention on Jurisdictional Immunities (2004)—use the restricted theory of state immunity. However, few states have actually ratified these treaties.[62] Some legal experts believe that restricted immunity is now part of customary international law.[63] However, many states continue to use the absolute theory, as shown in Figure 4.3.

An international court has not yet resolved this disagreement. In 2008, Germany sued Italy at the ICJ over two sets of domestic lawsuits about German war crimes during World War II. One set of lawsuits involved Italian nationals who sued Germany in Italian courts. Germany argued that these lawsuits violated Germany's immunity from jurisdiction under international law. The second set of lawsuits involved Greek nationals. These individuals first convinced a Greek court to order Germany to pay compensation for war crimes. They then asked an Italian court to enforce the Greek order. Namely, they tried to seize Villa Vigoni, a German-owned property in Italy, as compensation. Germany argued that Italy had therefore violated Germany's immunity from enforcement under international law.

The Court had to rule using customary international law.[64] Importantly, both Germany and Italy agreed that war crimes were sovereign acts, rather than commercial acts. This agreement allowed the Court to avoid choosing between the absolute and restricted theories of state immunity because it was "not called upon to address the question of how international law treats the issue of state immunity in respect of *acta jure gestionis*."[65] States therefore continue to disagree about whether international law gives states absolute or restricted immunity. Different states use different rules.

Diplomatic, Consular, and Official Immunity

The oldest area of international law is diplomatic and consular relations law, which protects individuals who represent their governments in foreign states. These protections are provided by treaties and customary international law. Treaties protect two kinds of individuals: diplomats—who are political representatives of their home state; and consular officials—who are non-political representatives. Diplomats interact directly with top foreign government officials, and work out of embassies, which are located in the capital city of a foreign state. In contrast, consular officials promote cultural, economic, and educational exchanges, and help nationals from their state who are living or traveling in foreign states. They work in consulates, which are located in major commercial cities.

International law gives these individuals immunity from the domestic courts of foreign states. **Diplomatic immunity** protects diplomats from civil and criminal actions in domestic courts of a foreign state. A state can expel foreign diplomats for any reason, but it can not assert judicial or legal authority over them unless their home state waives diplomatic immunity. In contrast, **consular immunity** protects consular officials from criminal actions in domestic courts of a foreign state. Consular officials can be sued for civil violations, like broken contracts or traffic violations.

International law also gives other rights to facilitate diplomacy. Diplomats and consular officials may communicate with nationals of their home state and provide them with assistance. For example, states often help their nationals if they are arrested in a foreign state. Diplomats and consular officials can also privately correspond with their home government using couriers and other forms of communication. Finally, diplomats and consular officials can travel freely in most areas of foreign states.

Additional rules protect embassies and consulates. Treaties require that embassies and consulates be inviolable, meaning that government officials may not enter a foreign embassy or consulate without permission from the foreign state. Similar protections apply to the documents and property of a foreign embassy

Figure 4.4 Julian Assange—founder of Wikileaks—holds a 2012 press conference on the balcony of Ecuador's embassy in London. International law prohibited UK police from entering Ecuador's embassy to arrest Assange, who was wanted by Swedish police for an alleged sexual assault. Assange lived in the embassy for almost seven years until Ecuador finally gave the UK permission to enter the embassy and arrest Assange.

and consulate. Diplomats and consular officials do not have the right under international law to grant asylum to individuals in a foreign state. However, the rules that protect foreign embassies and consulates effectively allow individuals to stay within such buildings to evade arrest. For example, Julian Assange, founder of Wikileaks, lived in Ecuador's embassy in London from 2012 to 2019, to avoid arrest for sexual assault. Assange was ultimately arrested by the UK in 2019, only after Ecuador invited UK police to enter its embassy and remove Assange.

International law requires states to protect foreign embassies and consulates from attack. For example, rioters attempted multiple times in 1979 to seize control of the US Embassy and consulates in Iran. These rioters eventually seized control of the US Embassy and took over fifty US nationals as hostages, beginning a fourteen-month standoff. The US government pursued many tactics to free the hostages, including suing Iran at the ICJ. The US argued that Iran was responsible for numerous violations of diplomatic and consular relations law. The ICJ judgment carefully analyzed state responsibility for private actors, like rioters. The ICJ wrote that Iran had:

> the most categorical obligations ... to take appropriate steps to ensure the protection of the United States embassy and consulates, their staffs, their archives, their means of communication and the freedom of movement of the members of their staffs ...
>
> Despite repeated and urgent calls for help, [Iranian authorities] took no apparent steps either to prevent the militants from invading the embassy or to persuade or to compel them to withdraw. Furthermore, after the militants had forced an entry into the premises of the embassy, the Iranian authorities made no effort to compel or even to persuade them to withdraw from the embassy and to free the diplomatic and consular staff whom they had made prisoner.[66]

The ICJ therefore ruled that Iran broke international law by failing to adequately protect the US Embassy.

International law also protects other top government officials, such as presidents, prime ministers, and foreign ministers. These individuals are not diplomats or consular officials, meaning that they are usually not covered by treaties. However, states usually grant official immunity under customary international law. This immunity can hinder universal jurisdiction lawsuits over international crimes, like genocide, torture, and war crimes.

Recall that Spain claimed universal jurisdiction to prosecute Augusto Pinochet for crimes in Chile. When Pinochet traveled to the UK for medical treatment in 1998, Spain asked the UK to arrest and extradite him. For months, UK experts debated whether to extradite Pinochet. These debates revolved in part around whether Pinochet had official immunity. While some experts believed that Pinochet was immune for all acts, others argued that customary international law did not protect Pinochet from prosecution for international crimes or personal acts outside the scope of his official duties.[67]

Shortly after the *Pinochet* case in UK courts, the ICJ ruled on a similar dispute involving Abdulaye Yerodia, the Minister of Foreign Affairs for the Democratic Republic of the Congo (DRC). In 2000, Belgium issued an arrest warrant for Yerodia for inciting genocide in the DRC. The DRC sued Belgium, arguing that Yerodia had immunity from prosecution under customary international law. Belgian lawyers argued that:

> while Ministers for Foreign Affairs in office generally enjoy an immunity from jurisdiction before the courts of a foreign state, such immunity applies only to acts carried out in the course of their official functions, and cannot protect such persons in respect of private acts or when they are acting otherwise than in the performance of their official functions.[68]

However, the ICJ disagreed with Belgium and ruled in favor of the DRC:

> in international law it is firmly established that ... certain holders of high-ranking office in a state, such as the Head of State, Head of Government and Minister for Foreign Affairs, enjoy immunities from jurisdiction in other states, both civil and criminal ... In customary international law, the immunities accorded to Ministers for Foreign Affairs are not granted for their personal benefit, but to ensure the effective performance of their functions on behalf of their respective states.[69]

The ICJ argued that Yerodia had full immunity from Belgian courts while he was in office. The precise nature of his alleged crimes—as either personal or official acts—was irrelevant.[70] However, the ICJ did not rule on whether Yerodia had immunity after leaving office. The logic of the ICJ's ruling suggests that once a government official leaves office (and no longer represents a state), international law provides him with less protection from domestic courts in foreign states.

4.4 Political Enforcement

Diverse actors use political tools to uphold international law. These actors include individuals, groups, NGOs, states, and international organizations. These actors focus on preventing future legal violations, stopping ongoing violations, and sometimes punishing past violations. If actors are uncertain about whether a state has violated international law, they may use political enforcement after a ruling by a legal body. For example, states and other actors often use political tools to promote compliance with ICJ rulings.[71] We first discuss how actors sometimes use coercion to uphold international law, then discuss various forms of persuasion.

Coercion

When an actor uses coercion to uphold international law, it attempts to modify a government's cost–benefit calculation about following an international rule. Coercion implicitly assumes that leaders have preferences over the outcomes that can result from their choices, and make decisions that are consistent with their preferences and beliefs. Coercion includes both "sticks" that increase the cost of legal violations and "carrots" that increase the benefits of compliance. Actors can provide benefits—like foreign aid and trade concessions—to whomever they wish. International disputes therefore usually focus on costs—namely, when and how can actors threaten or punish governments to uphold international law?

Retorsion

The term **retorsion** describes a lawful act used to punish a state. Retorsion harms its target, which is the state that receives the punishment. However, retorsion is legal, and hence is not limited by international law.

For example, diplomatic and consular relations law allows states to cut off diplomatic relations and to expel foreign diplomats and consular officials for any reason. During the Iran hostage crisis of 1979–1981, Iran failed to adequately protect the US Embassy from attack, and endorsed the holding of US nationals as hostages.[72] In response, the US ended diplomatic relations with Iran and expelled Iran's representatives to the US. Iran could still send representatives to the United Nations in New York City. However, the US refused to communicate directly with Iranian officials.

Similarly, many states use foreign aid to uphold international law. For example, European Union members condition their foreign aid on human rights. In 2016, the European Union cut humanitarian and military aid to the Burundi government because of human rights abuses.[73] While such cuts come with ethical or moral concerns, they are usually lawful acts because international law does not include general obligations about foreign aid.

Non-state actors can also use retorsion to uphold international law. Recall the 1973 ICJ lawsuit filed by Australia and New Zealand against French atmospheric nuclear tests in the South Pacific. The ICJ ordered France to stop all future tests until the legal dispute had been resolved.[74] France quickly announced that it would ignore the ICJ order and continue its nuclear tests. In response, advocacy groups mobilized worldwide using protests, public criticism, and voluntary consumer boycotts. This pressure ultimately caused the French government to reverse its policy.

Countermeasures

States also sometimes punish prior legal violations by breaking their own obligations under international law. Historically, legal experts believed that an injured state could legitimately break international rules in reprisal for a prior legal violation. Modern international law continues to allow a modified form of this idea. International law defines a **countermeasure** as a legal violation taken in response to a prior wrongful act by another state. We describe a state that imposes a countermeasure as an "enforcing state," and the state that receives the countermeasures as the "target state." If certain criteria are satisfied, an enforcing state can impose a countermeasure without its behavior being wrongful, meaning that the enforcing state's violation is excused or justified.[75]

For example, France and the US joined a bilateral civil aviation agreement in 1946. After a disagreement between the two states, France refused to allow passengers on Pan American–a US airline–to disembark from their planes in Paris. The US believed that France broke the 1946 agreement. In response, the US also broke the 1946 agreement by prohibiting many French airlines from flying to the US West Coast. In subsequent arbitration, the US argued that its treaty violation was not wrongful because the US was responding to France's prior and ongoing treaty violation. The arbitration tribunal ultimately agreed with this argument.[76]

How do legal experts determine whether a legal violation is a countermeasure? No general international treaty regulates countermeasures, but a 2001 text by the International Law Commission (ILC) codified customary international law on countermeasures.[77] This ILC text provides four criteria for valid countermeasures by an injured state.

First, the objective of a countermeasure must be "to induce [the target state] to comply with its obligations."[78] Countermeasures cannot be used to punish a legal violation that has already stopped. Therefore, countermeasures must end when the target state complies with international law.

Second, international law limits the form of countermeasures. They cannot affect:

(a) the obligation to refrain from the threat or use of force ... ;
(b) obligations for the protection of fundamental human rights;
(c) obligations of a humanitarian character prohibiting reprisals; [and]
(d) other obligations under peremptory norms.[79]

Enforcing states must also comply with relevant dispute settlement procedures and "respect the inviolability of diplomatic or consular agents, premises, archives and documents."[80] Finally, countermeasures should be reversible, meaning that the enforcing state can return to compliance after the target state has complied.[81]

Third, international law limits the magnitude of countermeasures using proportionality. In the context of countermeasures, **proportionality** is the principle that coercion must be commensurate with a state's injury.[82] In a 1928 ruling, an arbitration tribunal wrote: "one should certainly consider as excessive and therefore unlawful reprisals out of all proportion to the act motivating them."[83] While countermeasures may escalate a dispute, they "must be commensurate with the injury suffered, taking into account the gravity of the internationally wrongful act and the rights in question."[84]

Finally, enforcing states must follow certain procedures for countermeasures. Before beginning countermeasures, an enforcing state must first "call upon the responsible State ... to fulfil its obligations."[85] It must then "notify the responsible State of any decision to take countermeasures and offer to negotiate with that State."[86] Finally, an enforcing state may need to suspend countermeasures during international legal proceedings.[87]

Despite the clarity of these criteria, countermeasures can be very murky in practice. For example, in June 2017, Saudi Arabia—in coalition with Bahrain, Egypt, and the United Arab Emirates—announced a blockade of Qatar, a small state in the Persian Gulf.[88] This blockade limited the flow of goods and people to Qatar, violating numerous treaties. To end the blockade, the Saudi coalition issued many demands. In part, they ordered Qatar to:

- curb diplomatic ties with Iran[;]
- sever all ties to "terrorist organisations", specifically the Muslim Brotherhood, Islamic State, al-Qaida and Lebanon's Hezbollah[;]
- immediately terminate the Turkish military presence in Qatar[; and]
- align itself with the other Gulf and Arab countries militarily, politically, socially and economically, as well as on economic matters, in line with an agreement reached with Saudi Arabia in 2014.[89]

The Saudi coalition did not fully justify the blockade using legal arguments. However, its reference to a 2014 secret treaty called the Riyadh Agreement suggested that the blockade was a countermeasure.

The Qatar blockade demonstrates one challenge with countermeasures: they require that states form their own assessments about whether another state has violated international law. The Saudi coalition did not ask an international legal body to rule on Qatar's behavior. They did not even provide a public text of the Riyadh Agreement. They simply declared that Qatar had violated international law, and proceeded to punish it. In response, Qatar filed numerous legal disputes (at the International Court of Justice, the Permanent Court of Arbitration, and the World Trade Organization), arguing that the Saudi coalition had violated international law, not Qatar. Yet the blockade continued until early 2021, when Kuwait and the US brokered a diplomatic settlement.

The Qatar blockade also demonstrates a second challenge with countermeasures: even if Qatar had broken the Riyadh Agreement, no state publicly identified how it had been injured by Qatar's action. This example illustrates a broader debate in international law about whether a state or group of states can use countermeasures if they have not been injured by the target state.

Recall that states traditionally conceived of international law as bilateral contracts that created legal obligations between pairs of states. Classical writers debated how this bilateral structure affected who could uphold international law. Hugo Grotius wrote in 1625 that kings "have a right to exact punishments, not only for injuries committed against themselves, or their subjects, but likewise, for those which do not peculiarly concern them, but which are ... grievous violations of the law of nature or nations."[90] In contrast, Emer de Vattel wrote in 1758 that a sovereign who grants "reprisals against a nation in favor of foreigners" acts "as judge between that nation and those foreigners; which no sovereign has the right to do."[91] Most classical experts agreed with Vattel—they believed that "it is up to each state to protect its own rights; it is up to none to champion the rights of others."[92]

However, modern experts now believe that international law includes *erga omnes* obligations to the international community as a whole. Can states that have not been injured by the violation of an *erga omnes* obligation use countermeasures to uphold international law? What is a legitimate response to aggression, genocide, racial discrimination, slavery, or the denial of self-determination? No general legal text clearly addresses countermeasures by non-injured states. In its 2001 text, the ILC wrote that "any state" can invoke responsibility for the violation of an *erga omnes* obligation.[93] The ILC also wrote that its text "does not prejudice the right of" such a state "to take lawful measures ... to ensure cessation of the breach and reparation in the interest of the injured State or of the beneficiaries of the obligation breached."[94] But the ILC text does not say whether a countermeasure is a "lawful measure."

In practice, non-injured states often use countermeasures to uphold important legal rules. States often describe such countermeasures as "sanctions," a term that has no specific meaning under international law. For example, from the 1950s to the 1990s, many states imposed sanctions on South Africa, arguing that apartheid and white-minority rule violated human rights and self-determination by the black majority in South Africa. Most of these sanctions included reprisals, like foreign aid cuts or voluntary consumer boycotts. But some states also violated their own obligations under aviation and trade agreements, meaning that some sanctions on South Africa were countermeasures by non-injured states.[95]

More recently, the ICJ ruled in 2019 that the UK's control over the Chagos Archipelago violated the right to self-determination of the Chagos people. The Court concluded:

> Since respect for the right to self-determination is an obligation *erga omnes*, all states have a legal interest in protecting that right ... The Court considers that, while it is for

the General Assembly to pronounce on the modalities required to ensure the completion of the decolonization of Mauritius, all member states must co-operate with the United Nations to put those modalities into effect.[96]

The Court did not clearly say why "all member states must co-operate" in this way. But some experts now believe that states have a legal obligation to uphold *erga omnes* obligations.[97] This interpretation of the ICJ ruling suggests that international law may sometimes require non-injured states to use coercion.

Persuasion

Persuasion aims to change a leader's preferences over choices. Persuasion can include social interactions that trigger discussions of government policy. It can also include educating leaders and their constituents. Finally, actors can try to shame leaders into changing their preferences. Actors usually use multiple forms of persuasion simultaneously. However, we discuss each of these approaches separately to better understand their underlying assumptions and causal processes.

Socialization

One approach to persuasion is **socialization**, which is an informal process in which diverse actors internalize social norms through their interactions. Leaders and diplomats routinely meet in conferences and international organizations to interact with their peers from other states. These interactions allow elite actors to share ideas on different topics. Some social interactions are inclusive, like the UN General Assembly, which allows all states to participate. Other social interactions are more exclusive, like the G7 ("Group of Seven"), which is a club of developed democracies that meet regularly to discuss common challenges.

The decision about who to include in social interactions can itself be a tool for persuasion. Throughout the nineteenth century, European states argued that international law only applied to "civilized states," and that societies that were not "civilized" were not full members of the international system.[98] European states never formally defined the concept of a "civilized state." In practice, European states wanted other societies to: mimic European standards of justice; protect private property, especially for foreign investors; and abolish cultural practices that Europeans found offensive, like polygamy.[99] European states pressured others—including China, Japan, and Siam—to change their domestic practices before participating in international conferences.

As a more recent example, consider the G7. Many observers hoped that Russia would transition to a capitalist democracy in the 1990s. After years of economic reforms, G7 members invited Russia to join their club in 1997, and the G7 became the G8 ("Group of Eight"). Like its predecessor, the G8 met regularly to share ideas and collaborate. However, the G8 was disbanded in 2014 after Russia annexed Crimea, which many experts viewed as a violation of international law. In effect, the original seven members kicked Russia out of the club, changing their name back to the G7.

Why might socialization matter? Regular interactions among elite actors may change their beliefs about what is appropriate behavior within domestic and international politics. Such interactions may change how leaders define their values or self-image. Additionally, such interactions may evoke feelings about prestige or status, thereby influencing government behavior.[100] Socialization might also affect other individuals. Many scholars argue that transnational advocacy groups share and spread ideas across borders.[101] These ideas may influence who domestic publics support as political leaders.

Some aspects of socialization may be negative, though. Most advocates for socialization want to spread Western values, like civil and political rights.[102] Yet socialization is rooted in a history of colonial oppression, in which states that challenged Western values were treated as inferior outsiders.[103] Are similar processes occurring today?

Additionally, socialization is often paired with coercion. Inclusion in social groups can come with material benefits, while exclusion comes with corresponding costs. For example, new European Union members receive aid, foreign investment, and trade concessions. States that rely on rich democracies for aid and investment may behave as though they are being socialized, when they are actually being bought.

Finally, socialization may sometimes lead to negative outcomes. For example, many critics of the UN General Assembly argue that its resolutions on the Middle East are motivated by anti-Semitism. Israel's conflict with the Palestinian Authority over Gaza and the West Bank is a complex and delicate issue. General Assembly resolutions that declare "zionism is a form of racism and racial discrimination" do not help to resolve this conflict.[104] Vigorous attempts at socialization may also trigger a backlash. In the 2010s, many states pushed back against globalization and international institutions. In the 2016 "Brexit" referendum, UK voters decided to withdraw from the European Union. Similarly, in 2016 the US elected President Donald Trump, who pledged to withdraw the US from numerous environmental and trade agreements. Excessive attempts to socialize states may therefore trigger nationalism.

Education

A second approach to persuasion assumes that states can be educated into changing their preferences. This approach sometimes uses reporting as an educational tool. Many international organizations—including human rights bodies and the World Trade Organization—require their members to self-report on their domestic policies. Similarly, many advocacy organizations—like Amnesty International, Freedom

House, and Human Rights Watch—compile annual reports to educate actors about international law violations. Finally, many domestic government agencies—like the US State Department—issue reports on legal violations by other states.

A second educational tool is **scorecard diplomacy**, which is the public grading of states to influence behavior. These grades represent state behavior using an ordered variable (e.g. 1/2/3).[105] For example, the UN Development Program and the World Bank issue grades for economic and social outcomes. Some states also have scorecard diplomacy programs. Scorecard diplomacy sometimes focuses on international law compliance, although grades also often reflect ideologies about good governance.[106]

For example, the US created a Trafficking in Persons (TIP) program in 2000. This program monitors how foreign states prevent and punish **human trafficking**, which is the use of force, fraud, or coercion to secure labor.[107] The US State Department classifies foreign states into three tiers based on their human trafficking policies. US officials then meet with elite actors to explain how they can improve their state's grade.

Why might reporting and grading matter? If elite actors do indeed want to be educated, reporting and grading can provide information about how to interpret and apply international law, and stimulate elite efforts to improve behavior.[108] Reporting and grading programs may also provide information to the domestic public in the state being graded. For example, the 2001 TIP report on Israel was heavily publicized by Israeli news media, creating public support for anti-trafficking reforms.[109] Finally, reporting and grading may affect individual behavior in other states. Economic performance grades affect how banks and investors perceive economic and political risks in foreign states.[110] These perceptions, in turn, might affect how banks and investors spend their capital.

Reporting and grading can also have drawbacks. First, reporting and grading programs can be affected by politics. Critics of the Trafficking in Persons program argue that its grades are subjective and influenced by political pressure. For example, Malaysia's TIP grade was raised in 2015 to ensure that it could participate in an important trade negotiation.[111] Education may not be effective if the "teacher" is using different grading standards for different "students."

Second, reporting and grading outcomes may reflect coercion, rather than persuasion. Some grading programs directly link costs and benefits—like foreign aid and trade agreements—to their scores. Grades can also have indirect costs and benefits. For example, the Financial Action Task Force is an international organization that focuses on money laundering and terrorist financing. It regularly announces grades to indicate which states have followed its recommendations. Some banks use these grades in their risk models and withdraw business from states with poor grades.[112]

Finally, while grades reflect underlying assumptions about how states should behave, they often do not reflect how states are legally obligated to behave. Sometimes these assumptions may be innocuous. Most individuals probably agree, for example, that human trafficking is normatively bad and should be limited. However, scorecard diplomacy can also focus on contested values, such as whether states adopt free market policies. Education is thus a tool of both law and politics.

Naming and Shaming

A third approach to persuasion is **naming and shaming**, in which actors publicly condemn non-compliant states. The naming and shaming approach assumes that leaders know how to follow international law, but must be shamed into changing their behavior. It thus differs in its baseline assumption from the education approach, although the two approaches are often intertwined in practice. Advocacy groups often use press releases to publicly name and shame states for legal violations. Human Rights Watch describes naming and shaming as "one of the most effective human rights tools."[113] States also often name and shame each other in international organizations.

For example, the UN Security Council (UNSC) has "primary responsibility for ... international peace and security."[114] The UNSC routinely monitors internal and international conflicts. It can authorize coercive sanctions, but it usually instead names and shames actors using public resolutions about legal violations such as aggression and civilian killings. The UNSC is not a legal body, and it only acts if it reaches a political consensus.

Similarly, the UN Human Rights Council is a political body that is elected by the UN General Assembly.[115] This institution conducts a regular Universal Periodic Review in which Council members publicly identify possible human rights violations. The Council is not a legal body. Its actions are not governed by treaty law, and its condemnations sometimes express political antagonism, rather than legal arguments. Yet it is an important forum for naming and shaming.

Naming and shaming might matter if leaders are genuinely motivated by shame and embarrassment. Naming and shaming might also affect how other actors treat a state. For example, human rights shaming by the UN appears to decrease foreign aid from the World Bank.[116] Additionally, public shaming may reduce trade flows and foreign direct investment if firms and individuals are less willing to buy goods from or invest capital in states that are publicly shamed.[117]

Yet naming and shaming also comes with limitations. First, politics fundamentally affects who is shamed and why. Geopolitical ideology, military alliances, arms sales, and foreign aid all affect shaming within the UN.[118] Additionally, advocacy groups can only name and shame if they can document legal violations, meaning that less transparent states (like China and North Korea) are less likely to be shamed than more transparent states (like Colombia and the US).[119] Politics can sometimes even yield outright mistakes. For example, a UN Security Council resolution mistakenly blamed the March 2004 bombings in Madrid, Spain on a Basque nationalist group rather than al-Qaeda, the true culprit.[120]

Second, we don't know whether leaders are actually motivated by shame and embarrassment. Aid, investment, and trade all affect a target state's economy. Naming and shaming may therefore be a form of coercion, rather than persuasion.

Finally, naming and shaming may come with perverse effects. For example, some evidence suggests that public condemnations of human rights violations increase political violence.[121] Naming and shaming may encourage states to offset improvements on some criteria against deterioration on others. Alternatively, naming and shaming may convince some states to abandon international norms because they have been branded as pariahs. Naming and shaming may also encourage governments to create and support pro-government militias as a way to benefit from repression while avoiding attribution and responsibility for illegal acts.[122]

4.5   Case Study Revisited: Who Won the Argentine Debt Dispute?

We began this chapter with Argentina's 2001 default on its debts to private investors. While many investors agreed to revised terms, some investors became hold-out creditors, meaning that they insisted that Argentina honor its initial bond contract. These hold-out creditors included Paul Singer, who purchased his bond shares after Argentina's 2001 default. Singer believed that he could force Argentina to comply with the original bond contract, even when other investors had given up such hope. Simply put, Singer believed that he could profit from upholding international law.

This example connects to each of the major topics in this chapter:

- *International legal enforcement*: Non-state actors have limited access to most international legal bodies, including the International Court of Justice, which only allows states to file disputes. Individuals can ask their home states to invoke their right to diplomatic protection, but states are not required under international law to provide such protection to their nationals.
- *Domestic legal enforcement*: Argentina's bonds were issued in New York, so US domestic courts had territorial jurisdiction over the dispute. Additionally, Argentina agreed to waive its state immunity in the original bond contract. In US legal proceedings, Argentina argued that its default should be excused and that its assets should be protected from creditors. However, US courts had clear

authority to hear these arguments, and domestic courts in other states had clear authority to enforce US court orders.

- *Political enforcement*: Hold-out creditors clearly used coercion against Argentina. Private investors have no legal obligation to make loans. As retorsion, private investors refused to issue new bonds for Argentina until the dispute was resolved. Similarly, the seizure of Argentina's assets was a countermeasure—an act that would normally be illegal under international law, but is not wrongful because of Argentina's prior legal violation. Persuasion is less apparent in this example. Paul Singer did not try to socialize or educate Argentina. However, Argentina's creditors tried to name and shame Argentina as a "deadbeat" debtor in the US financial press.[123] Argentina's president responded by labeling Singer and other hold-out creditors as "vultures" and "financial terrorists."[124]

We can now examine the big questions that motivated this chapter. First, we asked: why could Paul Singer seize an Argentine warship in Ghana, only to lose it a few months later? Paul Singer could not sue Argentina at the International Court of Justice, and the US government did not provide Singer with diplomatic protection, perhaps reasoning that Singer could protect himself.[125] Instead, Singer focused on domestic legal enforcement, suing Argentina in US courts. After a US court ordered Argentina to pay, Singer asked Ghana to enforce the US court order by awarding him the *ARA Libertad*, which was docked in Ghana.

While Paul Singer had legal justification to seize Argentine assets, the *ARA Libertad* was problematic because the international law of the sea includes rules about how states treat foreign warships. Argentina upheld these rules by suing Ghana at the International Tribunal for the Law of the Sea, an international legal body in the Netherlands. ITLOS ordered Ghana to return the warship to Argentina, and Ghana quickly complied. In contrast, investors can seize other assets—like airplanes, artwork, and bank accounts—more easily.

Second, we asked: how did Argentina and Singer ultimately resolve their dispute? The story of the *ARA Libertad*—while colorful—is not unique. Numerous hold-out creditors hunted for Argentine assets worldwide. They went after airplanes, artwork, and bank accounts located in numerous states. One hold-out creditor noted at the time that: "We will continue to seize assets, enforce judgments. Argentina can't isolate themselves from the US or in places where our claims are enforceable."[126] Yet this is precisely what Argentina tried to do. To protect its assets from seizure by foreign courts, Argentina kept its airplanes and artwork at home and tried to reroute its international payments away from US banks.

Argentina ultimately concluded that it was better to pay the hold-out creditors than to hide from them. In 2016, financial newspapers announced that Argentina had agreed to pay the hold-out creditors approximately $4.6 billion, about 75 percent of the amount claimed. The hold-out creditors accepted this payment, and the dispute ended.

This leaves one final question: who won the Argentine debt dispute? Paul Singer and many other hold-out creditors purchased their shares for a small fraction of the final $4.6 billion payout, causing most observers to conclude that the hold-out creditors had won. However, in a way, Argentina won, too. Most investors accepted either Argentina's 2005 settlement, or a similar deal in 2010. These deals allowed Argentina to escape most of its debt at a minimal cost. The remainder of the debt was paid off in 2016 at a 25 percent discount. With this task completed, Argentina went right back to private investors and borrowed another $16.5 billion.

The actors who won the Argentine debt dispute were those actors who understood the various legal and political tools for upholding international law. They leveraged global institutions and rules—like waivers of state immunity and the international law of the sea—to achieve their desired outcomes. They also had the patience and resources to maneuver within international law and politics. In contrast, the losers of the Argentine debt dispute were those investors who believed in Argentina's initial legal commitment without having the knowledge, patience, and resources to uphold international law. Ignorance comes with a cost.

PART II
Property Rights and Economic Exchange

5 Law of the Sea

5.1 Case Study: Chinese Militarization in the Spratly Islands

Throughout history, states have competed for dominance in the East and South China Seas. One ongoing dispute involves the Spratly Islands, a group of small land masses shown in Figure 5.1. Brunei, China, Malaysia, the Philippines, Taiwan, and Vietnam all claim ownership of parts of the Spratly Islands. Each of them also claims surrounding water and seabed areas. Figure 5.1 shows the complex overlapping maritime claims in this part of the South China Sea.[1]

Much of the Spratly Islands actually consists of underwater reefs. Those land masses that are above water cannot support a permanent human population. The native inhabitants of the Spratly Islands are mostly seabirds and turtles. The Spratly Islands may therefore seem unimportant. Yet they are located in one of the

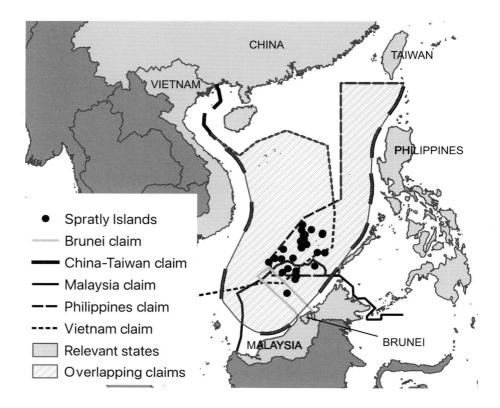

Figure 5.1 Conflicting maritime claims and the Spratly Islands.
Note: Many states in southwest Asia have made overlapping maritime claims in the South China Sea.
Source: Map drawn by author using QGIS. Data from Natural Earth and the Center for Strategic and International Studies.

world's most important trade corridors, and the surrounding water is an important fishing area. Additionally, the surrounding seabed is believed to contain valuable minerals, natural gas, and oil. The Spratly Islands also lie in a strategically important position between China and its neighbors.

As discussed in Chapter 2, many states with powerful militaries—including Australia, France, the UK, and the US—have tried to limit Chinese claims over the Spratly Islands and other parts of the East and South China Seas. Namely, they have actively protested Chinese claims with freedom of navigation exercises, in which they fly military airplanes through contested airspace and navigate warships through contested waters. These protests have a legal purpose: they weaken China's claims of acquiescence.

After Chinese President Xi Jinping came to power in 2012, he increased military spending and began building artificial islands throughout the East and South China Seas. China has built seven artificial islands in the Spratly Islands alone.

These artificial islands include military structures, like air strips, maintenance hangars, military barracks, and ports.[2]

China's artificial islands have been criticized by many actors. Many neighboring states fear that the islands will be used to fight or threaten wars. Business groups have warned that any disruption to transit in the South China Sea will have devastating consequences for global trade because the area is a major shipping route. And finally, many non-governmental organizations have denounced China for harming the environment by building artificial islands on top of natural reefs.

Why do states care about small, uninhabitable pieces of land, like the Spratly Islands? What are the implications of creating artificial islands? More generally, how should China and its neighbors resolve their competing maritime claims?

To answer these questions, we must first understand the following issues:

- *Governing the sea*: How has the international law of the sea evolved over time? What legal principles govern the sea?
- *Creating zones of authority*: How do states generate zones of authority in the sea? What rights do states have in various water and seabed areas?
- *Resolving maritime boundary disputes*: How do states resolve disputes over maritime areas? What principles and institutions govern conflicting legal claims over the sea?

The law of the sea is a large, multifaceted topic. In this chapter, we set aside more specialized issues such as archipelagos, landlocked states, and navigation within internal waters. Neither do we examine environmental law here, which is addressed in another chapter.

Section 5.2 provides a historical overview of the law of the sea and introduces key legal principles, including the freedom of the high seas, flag state jurisdiction, the prohibition of piracy and slavery, and the common heritage of mankind. Next, section 5.3 describes how states assert claims over maritime zones, and the rights and responsibilities that states have in these water and seabed zones. Section 5.4 then describes how states resolve maritime boundary disputes. Finally, section 5.5 revisits the example of China's artificial islands.

5.2 Governing the Sea

Evolution

Throughout human history, most of the sea was beyond human control. Merchants often traveled the sea, but no state had enough power to claim authority over the entire sea. However, when Portugal and Spain became naval powers in the 1400s, they began extracting resources from foreign lands and asserting control over sea trade routes. Portugal and Spain used international law to justify these activities. They proclaimed a policy of **mare clausum** ("closed seas"), meaning that they claimed exclusive jurisdiction over the sea. They enforced this policy by attacking foreign ships that challenged their authority.

Many Dutch merchants defied Portugal and Spain, causing violent skirmishes along trade routes. In 1603, Jacob van Heemskerck—a Dutch East India Company employee—attacked the *Santa Catalina*, a Portuguese ship full of valuable cargo near Singapore. Heemskerck took the *Santa Catalina* and sailed it to the Netherlands, where he tried to claim ownership of its cargo. Some observers accused Heemskerck of piracy, causing the Dutch East India Company to hire Hugo Grotius—a young Dutch lawyer and Heemskerck's cousin—to defend the attack.

This dispute inspired Grotius to publish a path-breaking book on the law of the sea in 1609. In this book, Grotius argued that natural law required free navigation on the sea. He argued that "those things which cannot be occupied or were never occupied can be proper to none," meaning that no one can claim ownership over them.[3] Even naval powers like Portugal and Spain could not occupy the entire sea. Grotius also argued that the sea was a common good because each state could take what it wanted "without the damage of one another."[4] Grotius did not contemplate overconsumption of sea resources, like fish and other wildlife. He thus concluded that international law included the principle of **mare liberum** (or "free sea"), meaning that no state can claim jurisdiction over the sea.

These arguments were controversial during Grotius's lifetime. For example, England claimed sovereignty over the waters surrounding its territory, prompting British scholar John Selten to challenge Grotius. Selten argued that a state could occupy portions of the sea, particularly water close to its shoreline.[5] Numerous other scholars entered this debate.

Over time, states reached a compromise between the various competing positions. Most of the sea was (and still is) considered the **high seas**, which is water in which no state has jurisdiction. However, many coastal states (like England) claimed jurisdiction over portions of the sea near their coastlines, which they called the territorial sea because the state had the same jurisdiction over this area as over its land territory. Swiss scholar Emer de Vattel explained this practice in the mid-1700s, when he wrote:

> When a nation takes possession of certain parts of the sea, ... [they] are within the jurisdiction of the nation, and a part of its territory: the sovereign commands there; he makes laws, and may punish those who violate them; in a word he has the same rights there as on land, and, in general, every right which the laws of the state allow him.[6]

The width of territorial seas varied across states and over time.[7] By the late 1800s, experts usually argued that a state could claim three nautical miles of the sea, as measured from its coastline.

States sometimes departed from this standard in their unilateral acts. States that were more economically dependent on fishing, like the Scandinavian states, would often claim a larger territorial sea.[8] Many states also wrote treaties to govern fishing and hunting in the high seas. These treaties began the development of international environmental law in the twentieth century.[9] Additionally, states agreed over time that piracy and slavery were prohibited on the high sea, and crafted customary international law for enforcing this prohibition.

These basic rules remained stable until 1945. After World War II, US President Truman feared that the US lacked adequate oil for economic recovery. New technology suggested that underwater oil drilling would soon be economically viable. In September 1945, President Truman issued two statements in which he unilaterally claimed control over fishing stocks and the seabed near the US coastline. He proclaimed:

> Having concern for the urgency of conserving and prudently utilizing its natural
> resources, the Government of the United States regards the natural resources of the
> subsoil and sea bed of the continental shelf beneath the high seas but contiguous
> to the coasts of the United States as appertaining to the United States, subject to its
> jurisdiction and control.[10]

Truman did not (and could not) provide any legal justification for this move. Yet other states quickly copied the US policy, rather than protesting against it. By 1950, over thirty states claimed expanded seabed rights.[11]

These new legal claims prompted states to write four treaties about the law of the sea, called the 1958 Geneva Conventions. These treaties codified many principles from customary international law. They also allowed states to claim portions of the seabed, and required states to protect fish and other natural resources. Finally, the Geneva Conventions contained guidelines for state disputes over water and the seabed. Numerous disputes involving the Geneva Conventions have been adjudicated by the International Court of Justice.

Yet states quickly developed new concerns that were not included in the Geneva Conventions. First, many governments became interested in the 1960s in mining to extract valuable minerals from the seabed, thousands of miles beyond territorial seas.[12] Developed states believed that any state could extract whatever it liked from the seabed under the high seas. In contrast, developing states believed that these minerals could not be taken for individual gain. Second, public concern about pollution grew dramatically, particularly after the 1967 *Torrey Canyon* incident. During this crisis, a Liberian ship called the *Torrey Canyon* hit underwater rocks in the high seas, spilling oil that threatened the UK coast.

In response to these important issues, states wrote the 1982 UN Convention on the Law of the Sea (UNCLOS). This treaty unified the topics in the four Geneva Conventions and created multiple water and seabed zones, which are described below. It also included rules for environmental protection and seabed mining. Some developed states, including the US, initially refused to join UNCLOS because they disagreed with its seabed mining rules, which favored developing states. After the collapse of the Soviet Union in 1989, developed states rolled back some of these rules in a 1994 Implementation Agreement.[13] Most developed states then joined UNCLOS, although the US refuses to do so. UNCLOS now has so many members that most of its rules have become customary international law.

States uphold the law of the sea using many different institutions. First, the International Court of Justice (ICJ) has heard many prominent disputes involving the law of the sea, especially maritime delimitation. Second, states sometimes use the Permanent Court of Arbitration (PCA) for sea disputes, particularly if they prefer more flexibility and privacy than the ICJ provides, or if they cannot establish ICJ jurisdiction. Finally, a specialized body called the International Tribunal for the Law of the Sea can hear disputes between UNCLOS members. These cases usually involve law enforcement operations against specific vessels. States usually go to this tribunal when they seek the quick resolution of an urgent problem, like the arrest of a crew or the seizure of a ship by law enforcement authorities. States usually go to the ICJ or PCA for cases involving complex findings of fact or legal interpretations.

Principles

Modern states have competing desires over the sea. On the one hand, states want to preserve the freedom of the *mare liberum*. On the other hand, states want order to protect their territory and limit heinous crimes on the sea. Four major principles balance these competing desires: the freedom of the high seas; flag state jurisdiction over ships; the prohibition of piracy and slavery; and the claim that high seas resources are the common heritage of mankind. We discuss each of these principles in turn.

Freedom of the High Seas

The spirit of *mare liberum* lives on in UNCLOS rules about the freedom of the high seas. UNCLOS proclaims that "the high seas are open to all states," and lists six key rights on the high seas:

(a) freedom of navigation;
(b) freedom of overflight;
(c) freedom to lay submarine cables and pipelines ... ;
(d) freedom to construct artificial islands and other installations permitted under international law ... ;
(e) freedom of fishing ... ; [and]
(f) freedom of scientific research.[14]

Of course, states must sometimes balance these rights against competing concerns. For example, the freedom of navigation does not entitle one ship to endanger the safety of another. Accordingly, UNCLOS requires that states exercise these freedoms "with due regard for the interests of other states in their exercise of the freedom of the high seas."[15]

For example, a large Italian commercial ship called the *Enrica Lexie* was sailing off the coast of India in February 2012, outside of India's territorial sea.[16] Two Italian naval officers who were guarding the ship shot at a small Indian fishing boat, killing two Indian fishermen. Italy claimed that the naval officers believed that the fishermen were pirates who were threatening the freedom of navigation for the *Enrica Lexie*. However, India claimed that the shooting violated its right to freedom of navigation. After years of diplomacy, India and Italy submitted the dispute to the Permanent Court of Arbitration. After a long legal process, arbitrators ruled that the evidence did not suggest that the fishermen were pirates. Therefore, they concluded that Italy had violated India's right to navigation (rather than vice versa).[17] The arbitrators ordered Italy to pay India compensation for "loss of life, physical harm, material damage to property ... and moral harm" to the fishermen.[18] The individual naval officers also faced a formal criminal investigation in Italy.

Freedom of navigation can include some activities that take place during navigation. Greenpeace, an environmental group, frequently used a Dutch ship called the *Arctic Sunrise* to conduct protests at sea. In September 2013, Greenpeace activists sailed the *Arctic Sunrise* to the Barents Sea to protest seabed drilling at a Russian offshore oil platform.[19] After a standoff, Russia seized the *Arctic Sunrise*, arrested everyone on board, and charged them under Russian law with the crime of hooliganism. Russia eventually released the protestors, but the incident triggered a dispute between the Netherlands and Russia at the Permanent Court of Arbitration. During diplomatic negotiations, Russia argued that the UNCLOS freedom of navigation did not include the right to protest at sea. However, the arbitrators disagreed with Russia's claim. They ruled that individuals have a right to protest under international human rights law, and that Russia did not give "due regard for the interests of" the Netherlands by arresting the protestors.[20] Therefore, they concluded, Russia violated their freedom of navigation.[21]

Flag State Jurisdiction

A second important principle is flag state jurisdiction. Under international law, a ship is subject to the jurisdiction of the state in which it is registered. This state is commonly called the **flag state** because ships usually fly national flags to indicate where they are registered. Flag states have two major rights under international law. First, flag states can set and enforce laws over their ships. These laws can include safety standards for the ship itself, labor rules for crew members, and taxes on ship activities. Because international law gives such broad authority to flag states, many ship-owners register their ships in states with relatively low taxes and lax regulations. For example, large commercial ships are often registered in states like Liberia, the Marshall Islands, and Panama. These states receive revenue from registration payments, even though many of these ships never even travel to their flag state.

Second, flag states can provide their ships with diplomatic protection if they become involved in an international dispute, meaning that the flag state can assert legal claims on behalf of the ship. This diplomatic protection also extends to individuals who are working on the ship, regardless of their nationality, because international law treats the ship and its crew as an individual unit.[22] In some circumstances, diplomatic protection can also extend to passengers on a ship, even if they are not crewmembers. For example, the Netherlands asserted diplomatic protection over all of the individuals arrested on board the *Arctic Sunrise*, even though some of the Greenpeace activists were not Dutch nationals. This diplomatic protection was later upheld during arbitration.[23] The arbitrators reasoned that:

> Even if some [individuals] did not engage directly in the functioning of the vessel as would a crewmember, they were all closely involved or interested in the ship's campaigning operations for Greenpeace through protest at sea. As such, they are properly considered part of the unit of the ship, and thus fall under the jurisdiction of the Netherlands as the flag State.[24]

Flag states also have responsibilities under international law. For example, the right to create safety and labor standards comes with the responsibility to ensure that these standards conform with international legal obligations. Similarly, flag states have a duty to prevent environmental harm by ships under their jurisdiction.[25] In some extreme circumstances, flag states can be legally responsible if their ships violate coastal state rules, like fishing regulations.[26]

Piracy and Slavery

While flag states have extensive rights over their ships, other states can override these rights to combat piracy and slavery. Historically, states relied on domestic courts to punish these crimes. To do so, these courts had to establish their jurisdiction over pirates and slave-traders. States usually assert one of four common bases of jurisdiction:

- territory—the action occurred on domestic territory;
- active nationality—the person who committed the action was a national of the state;
- passive personality—the person harmed by the action was a national of the state; or
- protective principle—the action had important and systematic effects on the state, like national security threats.

However, these concepts often don't cover piracy and slave-trading, which occur on the high seas. While the home state of a pirate could invoke active nationality jurisdiction, pirates often came from areas that were lawless or had weak governments.

Legal scholars developed the doctrine of **universal jurisdiction** to justify domestic trials and punishments for piracy. This doctrine posits that a state can sometimes use its domestic law and institutions to regulate behavior that occurs outside of its domestic territory, does not involve its nationals, and does not have systematic or important effects on itself. States supported universal jurisdiction over piracy for two reasons. First, piracy usually involved murder and theft, which all domestic legal systems prohibited. Cicero, the ancient Roman politician, described pirates as "a common foe" of the world.[27] Similarly, Alberico Gentili, a sixteenth-century Italian-British scholar, called pirates the "common enemies" of mankind.[28] These writings suggest that states found piracy morally abhorrent. Second, piracy usually occurred on the high seas. If no state had jurisdiction over the high seas, then pirates could easily escape punishment. This combination of common values and lack of enforcement led many scholars, including Swiss writer Emer de Vattel, to argue that all states could use domestic courts to punish pirates.[29] Over time, states extended this logic to slave-trading.

In UNCLOS, states implicitly recognized domestic courts by saying that "all states shall cooperate to the fullest possible extent in the repression of piracy on the high seas or in any other place outside the jurisdiction of any state."[30] UNCLOS defines "piracy" as:

> any illegal acts of violence or detention ... committed for private ends by the crew or the passengers of a private ship ..., and directed:
>
> (i) on the high seas, against another ship ..., or against persons or property on board such ship [or];
>
> (ii) against a ship, ... persons or property in a place outside the jurisdiction of any state.[31]

UNCLOS gives all states the right to board a ship if "there is reasonable ground for suspecting" piracy or slave-trading.[32] If there is evidence of piracy, a state can then "arrest the persons and seize the property on board."[33] These individuals can be prosecuted by the arresting state. UNCLOS also specifies that "any slave taking refuge on board any ship ... shall *ipso facto* be free."[34]

States face three major challenges when applying UNCLOS piracy rules. First, UNCLOS defines piracy as acts "committed for private ends." This clause protects government ships from being accused of piracy. However, it also means that non-state actors who use violence for political reasons can qualify as pirates. For example, the Sea Shepherd Conservation Society is a non-profit organization that repeatedly used violence against Japanese whaling ships. Members of this group—who call themselves "Sea Shepherds"—are motivated by policy goals, not financial rewards. Are Sea Shepherd attacks undertaken "for private ends?" Japan sued the Sea Shepherd Conservation Society in the US for financial damages in the early 2010s. Since the Sea Shepherds were private individuals (not a state), a US court ruled that they were pirates under UNCLOS. The court argued:

> "private ends" include those pursued on personal, moral or philosophical grounds, such as Sea Shepherd's professed environmental goals. That the perpetrators believe themselves to be serving the public good does not render their ends public.[35]

Similarly, a Belgian court ruled that Greenpeace activists were pirates after they blocked the passage of two ships, climbed onto their discharge pipes, and painted over their windows.[36] While most states agree that violence is not an acceptable form of political action, many experts question whether piracy law should apply to non-state actors who seek policy change. They believe that UNCLOS's reference to "private ends" is too broad.

Second, note that piracy must involve two ships. In 1985, four Palestinian terrorists disguised themselves as crew members on the *Achille Lauro*, a large Italian cruise ship. They then took control of the ship, holding its crew and passengers as hostages. During the resulting standoff, they murdered Leon Klinghoffer, a Jewish tourist. When the terrorists were later arrested, states had difficulty deciding who could prosecute them. The terrorists were not "pirates" under UNCLOS because the attack did not involve two ships. Many experts criticized UNCLOS for defining piracy too narrowly.

Finally, the UNCLOS definition covers acts in places "outside the jurisdiction of any state," but not acts within a territorial sea. Yet sometimes a coastal state is unwilling or unable to punish piracy in its territorial sea. For example, ships that travel between the Red Sea and the Indian Ocean must pass through a narrow sea corridor near Somalia. In the 1990s, Somali armed groups began attacking ships near this corridor and holding their crews hostage for ransom payments.[37] This often occurred in the territorial seas of Djibouti, Somalia, and Yemen, all of which lacked capacity to prevent and punish such attacks. The attacks grew more frequent and severe over time, but other states could not take action in these territorial seas. In 2008, the UN Security Council passed resolutions that gave other states—including France, the UK, and the US—authority to enter Somalia's territorial seas to capture pirates, who were then prosecuted in Kenya.[38] While this example of international cooperation is widely praised, it raises difficult questions about whether the UN Security Council can (and should) override treaty law.

Common Heritage of Mankind

States long believed that the freedom of the high seas included the right to fish, harvest and hunt without limit. However, this belief changed in the twentieth century because of two political factors. First, decolonization in the 1950s and 1960s allowed many new states in Africa and Asia to enter the international system.

These states usually lacked the capital and technology to take resources from the high seas, like gas, minerals, and oil. They feared that developed states would take these resources, widening inequality among states. Second, non-governmental organizations highlighted the negative impact of mankind on the natural environment. These organizations argued that excessive fishing, harvesting, and hunting could lead to animal and plant extinction. They also highlighted the effects of accidental and intentional sea pollution.

These two factors generated the principle of the **common heritage of mankind**, which posits that certain natural resources belong to mankind as a whole and should be protected from exploitation. By treating mankind as a collective entity—rather than with competing interests—states tried to bolster two kinds of fairness in international law. First, the common heritage of mankind aims to promote equity across states by giving all states legal rights to resources, even if they lack capacity to take these resources. Second, many states support **intergenerational equity**, which is the claim that current generations of humans should leave ample resources for future generations. UNCLOS explicitly uses the term "common heritage of mankind" to describe "the area of the seabed ... beyond the limits of national jurisdiction."[39] It contains extensive rules for exploiting this area, which must "be carried out for the benefit of mankind as a whole."[40] Some states even believe that these rules have become a peremptory norm under international law.[41]

5.3   Creating Zones of Authority

International law carefully balances the competing rights of states in international waters. It begins by establishing various zones in the water and seabed, and then specifies particular rules for these areas. We begin by describing how law creates these various zones. We then describe the allocation of rights for water-based activities, including navigation, regulation, and law enforcement. Finally, we summarize seabed-based activities, like drilling and mining for natural resources.

Maritime Zones

To create sea zones of authority, states begin by mapping the edges of their territory. This process yields a **baseline**, which is the boundary between a state's territory and international waters. Under UNCLOS, the first step for drawing baselines is to map the coastline when the sea is at low tide. This yields a low-water mark that separates land from water. The second step is then to draw closing lines across narrow natural indentations, like bays and river mouths. Finally, a state can draw straight lines between points on its coast if "the coastline is deeply indented and cut into, or if there is a fringe of islands along the coast in its immediate vicinity."[42] The combination of these lines forms a state's baseline.[43]

All water bodies within a state's baseline—such as lakes and rivers—are called **internal waters**. Each state has jurisdiction over its internal waters, meaning that it can create and enforce domestic laws.[44]

For example, Figure 5.2 shows a map of Ireland's baseline and internal waters claims. For most of Ireland's eastern coast, the baseline matches the low-water mark. However, along the northern, western, and southern coasts, Ireland's baseline departs from the low-water mark. The Irish baseline includes closing lines across natural bays and straight lines across many natural indentations and small islands.

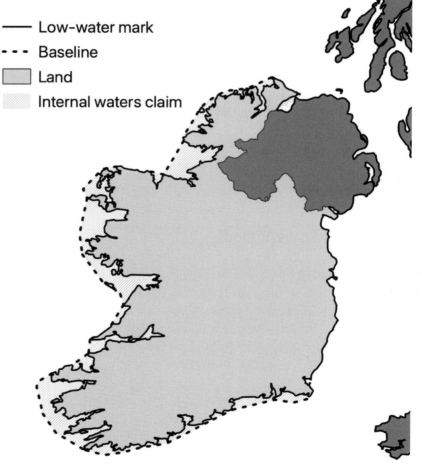

Figure 5.2 Ireland's baseline and internal waters claim.
Note: Ireland uses closing lines along its northern, western, and southern coasts. These lines make many natural bays and indentations into internal waters.
Source: Map drawn by author using QGIS. Data from Natural Earth and Maritime Boundaries, version 11.

While each state can draw its own baselines, other states often challenge these baselines using active protest and lawsuits. For example, Muammer Gaddafı, the former ruler of Libya, claimed a baseline in 1973 that became known as the "line of death." As shown in Figure 5.3, this baseline—which measured about 300 miles in length—enclosed the Gulf of Sidra, meaning that Gaddafı claimed a large portion of the Mediterranean Sea as Libyan internal waters. Gaddafı declared that "private and public foreign ships are not allowed to enter the Gulf without prior permission" from Libya.[45] Many states challenged this baseline, including Australia, France, Italy, Spain, the UK, and the US.[46] They believed that the baseline departed too much from Libya's low-water mark. To actively protest Libya's claim, the US military repeatedly sailed its Sixth Fleet through the Gulf of Sidra, provoking numerous military crises between Libya and the US in the 1980s.

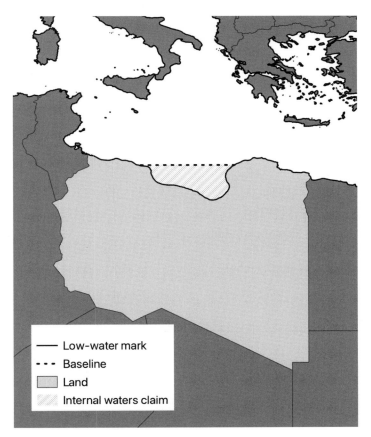

Figure 5.3 Libya's "line of death" and internal waters claim.
Source: Map drawn by author using QGIS. Data from Natural Earth and Maritime Boundaries, version 11.

After a state draws its baselines, it can then make legal claims over international waters. Figure 5.4(a) shows the four water zones under UNCLOS. The zone that is closest to a state's coastline is its **territorial sea**. This zone can extend up to 12 nautical miles (n.m.) from a state's baseline. In this zone, a coastal state has extensive rights, which are described below. The next possible region is the **contiguous zone**, which is water that lies outside of the territorial sea and can extend up to 12 additional nautical miles. In this zone, the coastal state has special law enforcement rights. The next region is the exclusive economic zone (EEZ), which begins at the edge of the territorial sea and extends for up to 200 n.m. from the baseline.[47] In this zone, coastal states can regulate natural resource conservation and exploitation. Finally, all water beyond a state's EEZ is the high seas, which is water over which no state has jurisdiction.

Figure 5.4(b) shows the two seabed zones defined by UNCLOS. First, a coastal state has exclusive rights over natural resources—like oil, minerals, and natural gas—in its **continental shelf**. The rules for measuring the continental shelf are very complicated and depend on seabed topography, but a coastal state can often claim

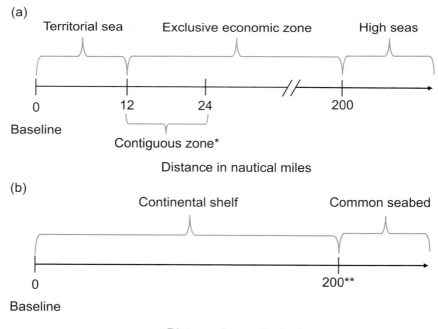

Figure 5.4 Zones of authority; (a) water; (b) seabed.
Notes: These graphs show the various zones of authority for water and the seabed under modern international law.
* Not all states claim a contiguous zone.
** Width varies based on seabed topography.

up to 200 n.m. or more from its baseline.[48] Second, no individual state has jurisdiction over the **common seabed**, which is the seabed beyond the continental shelf.[49] All states collectively own the natural resources in the common seabed, which are the common heritage of mankind.

One complicated issue is how islands and rocks that are not in the immediate vicinity of a state's main territory affect maritime claims. International law treats an "island" differently from a "rock." UNCLOS describes an island as "a naturally formed area of land, surrounded by water, which is above water at high tide."[50] States can claim a territorial sea, contiguous zone, EEZ, and continental shelf around each of their islands. However, UNCLOS says that "rocks which cannot sustain human habitation or economic life of their own shall have no exclusive economic zone or continental shelf."[51]

Because a tiny island can generate extensive water and seabed rights, states often disagree about who owns tiny pieces of land in the sea, and whether such land is an "island" or a "rock." For example, Japan claims ownership over Okinotorishima, which is about 100 square feet of land located over 1,000 miles south of Tokyo. Japan claims that Okinotorishima is an island, generating huge water and seabed claims in the Pacific Ocean. However, other states—including China and South Korea—believe that Okinotorishima is a rock, thereby invalidating Japan's water and seabed claims.[52] Such tiny pieces of land threaten peace in Southeast Asia by fueling maritime disputes in the East and South China Seas.

Water Rights

International law provides diverse rights that vary over water zones. We organize our discussion based on the nature of these rights. We first describe the navigation rights of foreign ships, then turn to the rights of coastal states to regulate water zones, and finally describe law enforcement by coastal states.

Navigation by Foreign Ships

Navigation rules balance the freedom of the high seas against the national security of coastal states, which often fear that foreign ships might be preparing for war, conducting espionage, or supporting terrorism.[53] Overall, coastal states have more authority to limit navigation in areas that are closer to their shores. However, states continue the tradition of *mare liberum* by giving foreign ships broad navigation rights.

UNCLOS proclaims that "the high seas are open to all states."[54] All ships can navigate freely on the high seas, regardless of their nationality. UNCLOS also allows foreign ships to sail freely in exclusive economic zones, provided that they:

> comply with the laws and regulations adopted by the coastal state in accordance with the provisions of this convention and other rules of international law.[55]

As discussed below, coastal states can regulate natural resources and create security zones around artificial structures in their EEZ. Foreign ships must follow these EEZ rules, but they can otherwise navigate freely in an EEZ.

However, the balance between competing rights is different in a territorial sea, where a coastal state has more authority. International law includes a **right to innocent passage**, which is the right of foreign ships to travel through a territorial sea, subject to specified constraints. UNCLOS defines innocent passage as navigation that "is not prejudicial to the peace, good order or security of the coastal state."[56]

It lists examples of prejudicial behavior, including:

* "any threat or use of force against ... the coastal state;"
* "any exercise or practice with weapons;"
* "any act aimed at collecting information to the prejudice of the defence or security of the coastal state;"
* "the launching, landing or taking on board of any aircraft;"
* "any act of wilful and serious pollution;" and
* "any other activity not having a direct bearing on passage."[57]

Coastal states can prohibit navigation in a territorial sea by foreign ships involved in such prejudicial activities.

Additionally, all foreign ships must follow valid territorial sea rules. Coastal states can limit navigation near delicate ecosystems, like natural reefs. They can also create safety rules to prevent maritime accidents and trade disruptions. The right to innocent passage allows a foreign ship to pass through a territorial sea, but it does not allow them to fish, enter ports, or conduct other activities. Finally, UNCLOS requires that innocent passage be "continuous and expeditious."[58]

One controversial issue is whether foreign warships have a right to innocent passage. Some states believe that foreign warships have a right to passage if they do not conduct military activities during transit. Other states believe that foreign warships are never "innocent." They argue that any foreign warship in a territorial sea poses a threat to the coastal state. Legal experts can make compelling arguments for both perspectives, and power politics clearly shapes these debates. States with powerful navies—including France, the UK, and the US—usually believe that warships have the right to innocent passage, while states without powerful navies—including most developing states—usually oppose this claim. For example, before the Soviet Union built a powerful navy, it argued that foreign warships were not entitled to innocent passage. However, the Soviet position changed after it built a strong navy: the Soviet Union (and now Russia) supported the right of warships to innocent passage. Courts have not resolved this controversial issue, in part because warships have **state immunity**, meaning that they are protected from the jurisdiction of domestic courts in foreign states.

Regulation by the Coastal State

Coastal states have limited rights to regulate maritime zones. Overall, coastal states have more authority to regulate areas that are closer to their shores. UNCLOS says that "the sovereignty of a coastal state extends [to] the territorial sea," suggesting that a coastal state can fully regulate its territorial sea.[59] It must still respect the right to innocent passage and flag state jurisdiction. But a coastal state can pass rules for issues like immigration, maritime safety, and taxation in its territorial sea.

However, coastal states have less authority to regulate their exclusive economic zones. UNCLOS says that in an EEZ, a coastal state has:

> sovereign rights for the purpose of exploring and exploiting, conserving and managing the natural resources, whether living or non-living, ... and with regard to other activities for the economic exploitation and exploration of the zone, such as the production of energy from the water, currents and winds.[60]

Simply put, a coastal state can only regulate natural resources in its EEZ.

First, UNCLOS allows (and requires) environmental regulations for EEZs. A coastal state must ensure that living resources, like fish and whales, in its EEZ are "not endangered by over-exploitation."[61] To achieve this objective, states can conduct scientific research and issue licenses for many economic activities. States can also ban fishing and hunting of endangered species. UNCLOS also requires coastal states to regulate pollution in their EEZ. Such pollution can come from ship accidents, routine discharges during navigation, and intentional waste dumping. Coastal states can create rules to prevent such pollution, like requiring ships to adopt technology that prevents accidents and routine discharges.[62] UNCLOS rules are reinforced by many water pollution treaties.[63]

Second, UNCLOS allows states to regulate natural resources for economic reasons. Coastal states can prohibit fishing by foreign ships, or sell fishing rights to generate government revenue. They also have exclusive rights to produce energy in their EEZs using wind and waves. States sometimes share or sell their EEZ natural resource rights to foreign states and/or companies. For example, fishing stocks in China's EEZ declined over recent decades, prompting China to use distant-water fleets. These fleets often operate in the EEZs of developing states—like Angola, Ghana, Mauritania, and Somalia—that give China fishing rights in exchange for Chinese investment in domestic infrastructure.[64]

Finally, UNCLOS also gives coastal states the exclusive right to create and use artificial structures—including artificial islands—in their EEZ.[65] States can create health and labor rules for these structures. They can also create small safety zones around these structures to protect navigation and the structure itself.[66] UNCLOS says that these structures "do not possess the status of islands," meaning that they do not change maritime zones.[67] Instead, artificial structures are intended to help states conserve and exploit their natural resources. For example, coastal states often construct offshore oil platforms in their EEZs to extract oil and natural gas from the seabed. In 2013, Greenpeace used the *Arctic Sunrise*, a Dutch ship, to protest an offshore oil platform called the *Prirazlomnaya* in Russia's EEZ. During the protest, Greenpeace activists entered the safety zone around the platform and two protestors tied themselves to the platform. A Russian coast guard ship chased the *Arctic Sunrise* away from the *Prirazlomnaya* and arrested everyone on board the *Arctic Sunrise* the next day. During legal proceedings about this incident, an arbitration tribunal noted that Russia had jurisdiction to create a safety zone around the *Prirazlomnaya* and that Greenpeace activists had therefore broken Russian law by entering the safety zone without permission.[68] The outcome of the case therefore hinged on how Russia enforced its law.

Law Enforcement by the Coastal State

How can coastal states enforce their rules for maritime zones? Coastal states are limited by flag state jurisdiction. Their ability to enforce law depends on where an alleged crime was committed, and where a foreign ship is located during enforcement. Generally speaking, a coastal state has more law enforcement authority over acts and ships that are closer to its shore.

If a crime occurs on state territory and the criminal flees on a foreign ship into the territorial sea, then the coastal state has relatively strong authority to arrest the individual.[69] However, if a crime occurs on a foreign ship in the territorial sea, then the coastal state can only enforce its law:

(a) if the consequences of the crime extend to the coastal State;
(b) if the crime is of a kind to disturb the peace of the country or the good order of the territorial sea;
(c) if the assistance of the local authorities has been requested by the master of the ship or by a diplomatic agent or consular officer of the flag State; or
(d) if such measures are necessary for the suppression of illicit traffic in narcotic drugs or psychotropic substances.[70]

If none of these criteria are met, then the coastal state cannot punish the crime and victims must rely on the flag state to provide justice.

Law enforcement is usually exclusive in the territorial sea, meaning that only the coastal or flag state can enforce law. This limit makes law enforcement difficult when the relevant states are unwilling or unable to uphold law. As mentioned earlier, piracy is common in the sea near Somalia. Some UN Security Council resolutions give other states authority to punish piracy in Somalia's territorial sea. However, it is unclear whether the UN Security Council has the power to issue such authority.

The contiguous zone is a portion of the EEZ that exists solely to bolster law enforcement over foreign ships. A coastal state does not have authority to regulate most activities in its contiguous zone. However, it can prevent and punish "infringement of its customs, fiscal, immigration or sanitary laws and regulations within its territory or territorial sea."[71] For example, a coastal state can prevent and punish human trafficking, smuggling, and tax violations in its contiguous zone.

In the rest of its exclusive economic zone, a coastal state can enforce its relevant rules on living resources, although it has limited power to detain foreign ships and punish their crews.[72] A coastal state must notify the flag state of any arrest or detention, which often provokes diplomatic disputes. Special enforcement rules apply to EEZ pollution, and a coastal state has more authority when pollution poses a greater threat.[73]

On the high seas, states have almost no enforcement authority whatsoever over foreign ships. If an accident causes pollution that threatens a state's "coastline or related interests," then the state can take action.[74] Otherwise, a state can only enforce law against a foreign ship on the high seas if "there is reasonable ground for suspecting" piracy, slavery, or specific acts.[75]

One law enforcement challenge is that ships can easily flee by traveling into zones where the state has less authority. To address this challenge, international law allows **hot pursuit**, which is a legal doctrine that allows a state to preserve its law enforcement authority if it follows certain procedures while pursuing crime suspects at sea. UNCLOS says that a coastal state retains enforcement authority if:

- the coastal state believes that a foreign ship has broken its law;
- pursuit begins in a zone where the coastal state has enforcement authority;
- the foreign ship is given an order to stop while it is in that zone;
- pursuit is not interrupted;
- pursuit is undertaken by "ships or aircraft clearly marked and identifiable as being on government service and authorized to that effect"; and
- the foreign ship does not enter the territorial sea of another state.[76]

All of these criteria must hold for a coastal state to retain its enforcement authority.

In the *Arctic Sunrise* case, arbitrators ruled that Greenpeace protestors had broken Russian law by entering the *Prirazlomnaya* safety zone and attaching themselves to the platform. A Russian coast guard ship gave the *Arctic Sunrise* an order to stop, chased it for three hours, and then watched it without taking any action for another thirty-three hours. Russian officials then seized the *Arctic Sunrise* in Russia's EEZ, towed it to Russian territory, and arrested everyone on board. A key question in arbitration was therefore: was this a valid hot pursuit? Two key questions were therefore: (1) was the stop order given while the *Arctic Sunrise* was in the safety zone?; and (2) was pursuit interrupted? Based on the available evidence, arbitrators could not determine where the *Arctic Sunrise* was located during the stop order. Additionally, they concluded that pursuit was interrupted because the coast guard ship watched the *Arctic Sunrise* without taking action for thirty-three hours. This interruption made Russia's law enforcement actions illegal. If Russia had acted more aggressively by immediately seizing the ship and arresting its crew and passengers, then Russia would have had a stronger legal claim.

One final challenge for law enforcement by coastal states is state immunity, which is the principle that a domestic court should not rule on a foreign state act without that state's consent. This protection extends to warships, government ships conducting non-commercial activities, and government officials. For example, recall the example of the *Enrica Lexie*, the Italian commercial ship that sailed through India's EEZ in February 2012. Two Italian naval officers guarding the ship shot at a fishing boat, killing two Indian fishermen. Arbitrators ruled that Italy violated India's freedom of navigation and must pay compensation for the killings. However, India could not prosecute and punish the Italian naval officers because they had immunity. Even though the Italian officers were protecting a commercial ship (rather than a naval vessel), arbitrators ruled that the officers were protected from Indian courts because they were "state officials who were acting in their official capacity during the incident."[77]

Seabed Rights

Historically, the law of the sea focused on water rights. However, the US and other states asserted seabed claims after World War II because new technology allowed gas and oil drilling in the seabed. Scientists also argued that seabed mining could provide states with valuable minerals. One important issue was therefore how to allocate rights over these natural resources. States agreed to divide the seabed into two zones: a continental shelf under coastal state jurisdiction; and a common seabed shared by all states.

Under UNCLOS, a coastal state has the exclusive right to explore and exploit its continental shelf.[78] Multinational corporations often purchase continental shelf rights from coastal states. For example, the De Beers Group purchased the right to extract diamonds from Namibia's continental shelf. In 2018 alone, the company extracted 1.4 million carats.[79] Similarly, private and state-owned oil companies often drill for gas and oil from the continental shelf.

In contrast, natural resources in the common seabed are described by UNCLOS as "the common heritage of mankind."[80] This means that "no state shall claim or exercise sovereignty or sovereign rights over any part of the [common seabed] or its resources."[81] UNCLOS created an international organization called the International Seabed Authority, with authority to make and enforce rules over the common seabed.[82] States planned for the Authority to write common seabed mining regulations and sell licenses to mining corporations. The revenue from these licenses would then be shared by all states. However, the Authority's work was delayed for decades because drilling and mining in the common seabed—which is much deeper than the continental shelf—was not economically and technologically feasible.

Thus far, the Authority has only written a few technical standards and issued about thirty licenses for common seabed exploration.[83] Many environmental activists fear that mining in the common seabed will damage animal and plant habitats.[84] They argue that common seabed mining violates international law if it does not provide an overall benefit for mankind.[85] Mining in the common seabed may therefore become an important legal and political issue in the future.

5.4   Resolving Maritime Boundary Disputes

When two states are located close together, international law can generate overlapping legal entitlements, which cause maritime boundary disputes. **Delimitation** is the allocation of legal rights when multiple states claim jurisdiction over the same area. Sometimes states resolve maritime boundary disputes through bilateral or regional negotiations. However, if negotiations fail, states often ask an international court or arbitration tribunal to resolve the dispute.

For example, Figure 5.5 shows a map based on the *Jan Mayen* case between Denmark and Norway at the International Court of Justice. This map shows Greenland, Iceland, and the small island of Jan Mayen in the northern Atlantic Ocean. Denmark represented Greenland at the ICJ, while Norway claimed Jan Mayen as its territory. Greenland and Jan Mayen are separated by about 250 nautical miles. As described above, Denmark and Norway each have a legal entitlement to a continental shelf and EEZ that are 200 n.m. wide. However, these entitlements overlap between Greenland and Jan Mayen. Denmark and Norway asked the Court to help them delimit this area. Denmark wanted 200 n.m. from the shore of Greenland, while Norway proposed using a median line to divide the shared resources. Because Iceland was not part of the lawsuit, Denmark and Norway asked the ICJ to consider only the area that did not overlap with Iceland's entitlement. The entitlement lines in Figure 5.5 thus stop approximately 200 n.m. from Iceland.

Maritime delimitation law is very complex. Recall that five multilateral treaties govern the seas: the four 1958 Geneva Conventions and the 1982 UN Convention on the Law of the Sea. These treaties create entitlements to a territorial sea, contiguous zone, exclusive economic zone, and continental shelf. However, these treaties lack consistent and uniform rules about how to resolve overlapping entitlements.[86] Additionally, many bilateral and regional agreements affect maritime delimitations. Customary international law can also affect maritime boundary disputes, as well as court judgments and arbitration awards from prior disputes.

We focus here on the two competing approaches to maritime delimitation, noting that the relevant law can vary across disputes. First, we discuss the equidistance method. We then discuss circumstances that can affect the equity of possible boundaries. Finally, we describe how procedures that use these two approaches have changed over time.

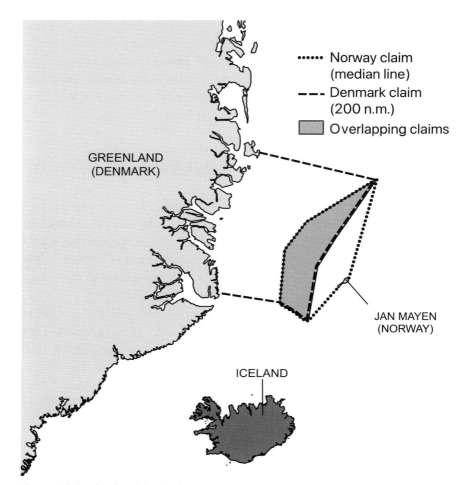

Figure 5.5 Overlapping claims in the *Jan Mayen* case.
Source: Map drawn by author using QGIS. Data from Natural Earth and ICJ documents.

Equidistance Method

One approach to maritime delimitation is the **equidistance method**, which is a geographic technique for drawing a line—called the equidistance or median line—that is equally distant from each state. States often use the equidistance method during negotiations because it generates a boundary that states often find equitable. For example, Costa Rica and Panama agreed in 1980 to use the equidistance lines shown in Figure 5.6. The lines mark the boundaries of their water and seabed areas.[87]

However, states sometimes argue that the equidistance method yields inequitable outcomes. For example, the dotted line in Figure 5.5 shows the median line between Greenland and Jan Mayen. Norway asked the ICJ to use this line as the maritime boundary between Greenland and Jan Mayen. However, Denmark argued that this outcome was inequitable because the equidistance method ignores the location of natural resources and differences between states, like the sizes of their

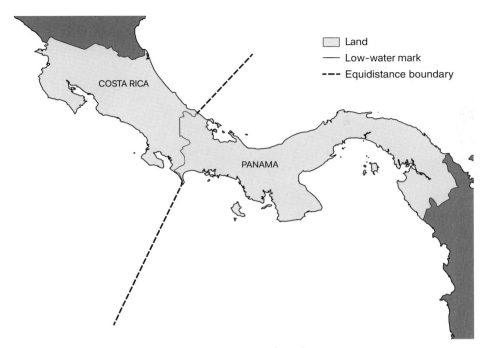

Figure 5.6 Equidistance method in the Costa Rica–Panama boundary.
Source: Map drawn by author using QGIS. Data from Natural Earth and treaty text.

economies, populations, and territory. Denmark sought a full 200 n.m. of maritime territory, as shown by the dashed line in Figure 5.5.

Similarly, the ICJ was asked to rule during delimitation negotiations between Denmark, the Netherlands, and West Germany, which have adjacent coastlines along the North Sea. Partial maritime boundaries had been set in prior negotiations, as shown by the solid lines in Figure 5.7. Denmark and the Netherlands wanted to use the equidistance method to project these boundaries outward into the North Sea, yielding the dashed lines in Figure 5.7. However, West Germany argued that the equidistance method was not equitable because it penalized West Germany for having a coastline that projected inward, thereby shrinking West Germany's portion of the water and seabed. Instead, West Germany wanted the dotted lines in Figure 5.7 to become its maritime boundary.

Circumstances that Affect Equity

The second approach to maritime delimitation focuses on equitable outcomes. For example, when US President Truman claimed expanded rights over sea resources in 1945, he wrote:

> In cases where the continental shelf extends to the shores of another state, or is shared with an adjacent state, the boundary shall be determined by the United States and the state concerned in accordance with *equitable* principles.[88]

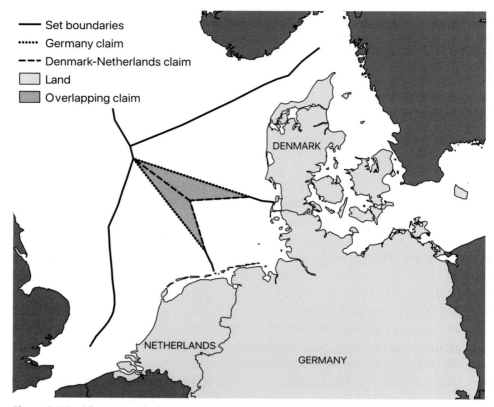

Figure 5.7 Equidistance method and the *North Sea* dispute.
Source: Map drawn by author using QGIS. Data from Natural Earth and ICJ documents.

In 1969, the ICJ ruled in the *North Sea* case that Truman's language—which was mimicked by other states when they too claimed larger portions of the sea—expressed an obligation under customary international law to reach equitable maritime delimitations.[89] International courts and arbitration tribunals have written extensively about "relevant circumstances" that affect the equity of possible boundaries. Similarly, two of the 1958 Geneva Conventions say that "special circumstances" can influence maritime delimitations, and UNCLOS requires "an equitable solution" to overlapping entitlements.[90]

International law does not define the terms "relevant circumstances" or "special circumstances" or specify how they differ. Additionally, it does not have a complete list of circumstances that affect equity. In the *North Sea* case, the ICJ ruled: "There is no legal limit to the considerations which states may take account of for the purpose of making sure that they apply equitable procedures."[91] However, the ICJ clarified in later rulings that circumstances must be "pertinent" to delimitation and should be consistent with state practice and prior cases.[92]

One circumstance that can affect equity is disparity between coastline lengths and maritime areas.[93] As shown in Figure 5.7, the coastlines of Denmark, the

Netherlands, and West Germany are similar in length. However, the equidistance method gave West Germany a much smaller share of maritime area than its neighbors because its coastline projected inward. The ICJ argued that this disparity was inequitable. The ICJ wrote:

> Equity does not necessarily imply equality. There can never be any question of completely refashioning nature, and equity does not require that a state without access to the sea should be allotted an area of continental shelf, any more than there could be a question of rendering the situation of a state with an extensive coastline similar to that of a state with a restricted coastline.[94]

However, the Court argued that when states have relatively equal coastline lengths, they should receive relatively equal maritime areas.

In contrast, Greenland has a very long coastline while Jan Mayen has a very short coastline. The ICJ calculated that the relevant coastline of Greenland was over nine times longer than the relevant coastline of Jan Mayen.[95] Yet the equidistance method gave them relatively equal maritime areas, as shown in Figure 5.5. The Court concluded that Greenland should receive a larger water and seabed area than the equidistance method would yield.[96]

A second circumstance that can affect equity is access to resources. In the *Jan Mayen* case, both Denmark and Norway wanted capelin, which are migratory fish that travel in the southeast region of the overlapping entitlements. The ICJ argued that the median line was "too far west for Denmark to be assured of an equitable access to capelin stock."[97] The location of continental shelf resources—like oil and natural gas—can also affect equity. However, the Court did not have enough information to consider these resources in the *Jan Mayen* case.[98]

Third, islands can affect equity. Recall that an island generates an entitlement to a territorial sea, contiguous zone, EEZ, and continental shelf. Yet states sometimes argue that islands should be ignored if they create overlapping entitlements with other states, particularly when they are small or uninhabited. For example, Jan Mayen is a small volcanic island with no permanent population. Denmark therefore argued that Jan Mayen should not limit Greenland's entitlement. The ICJ disagreed with Denmark and allowed Norway to have a share of the overlapping area. However, small islands are sometimes ignored during maritime delimitations.[99]

States often argue that other circumstances can affect equity. International courts and arbitration tribunals are often asked to consider the following criteria and questions:

- Population: Should states with more people receive more maritime area?
- Economy: Should states that are more economically dependent on the sea receive more maritime area?

- Environment: Should states that are more committed to environmental protection receive more maritime area?
- Security: Should states that are more vulnerable to attack receive more maritime area?

These factors usually do not change delimitation outcomes, but they are often discussed at length in court judgments and arbitration awards.

Delimitation Procedures

How do actors use these competing approaches? State practice and treaties require delimitation by agreement and equitable outcomes. States usually negotiate maritime boundaries using diplomats and legal advisors. When states cannot reach an outcome that both sides accept, they often ask an international court or arbitration tribunal for help. These courts and tribunals developed delimitation procedures over time, slowly generating rulings and awards that shaped later disputes.

For example, recall the *North Sea* case, which the ICJ decided in 1969. Denmark and the Netherlands argued that the 1958 Geneva Convention on the Continental Shelf required states to use the equidistance method for maritime boundary disputes. However, West Germany successfully argued that the equidistance method was not required because West Germany had not ratified the Convention, and because the equidistance method was not part of customary international law. Instead, the ICJ ruled that customary international law required equitable outcomes. The ICJ then described various circumstances that the states could consider during delimitation negotiations. The final maritime boundary was decided by the states themselves. This procedure—which emphasized case-specific circumstances that affect equity—dominated later disputes for many decades. States sometimes used the equidistance method, but they believed that this method was optional.

Delimitation procedure changed dramatically in 1993, when the ICJ ruled in the *Jan Mayen* dispute between Denmark and Norway. Unlike the *North Sea* case, both litigants in the *Jan Mayen* case had ratified the 1958 Geneva Convention on the Continental Shelf. The ICJ therefore departed from the delimitation procedure created by the *North Sea* case. Namely, the ICJ ruled that the Convention required that the Court use the median line as a provisional boundary between Greenland and Jan Mayen. The Court then asked whether this boundary should be adjusted to be more equitable. Figure 5.8 shows the final boundary set by the ICJ. Notice that the ICJ shifted the median line eastward because of the disparity between coastline lengths and maritime areas under the median line. Additionally, the ICJ shifted the median line further in the south because that was where the natural resources (capelin stocks) were more abundant. After 1993, international courts and arbitration tribunals began to follow the *Jan Mayen* procedure of using the equidistance method to set a provisional boundary, and then adjusting that boundary based on equity. This procedural change increased deference to the equidistance method and reduced the influence of case-specific circumstances.[100]

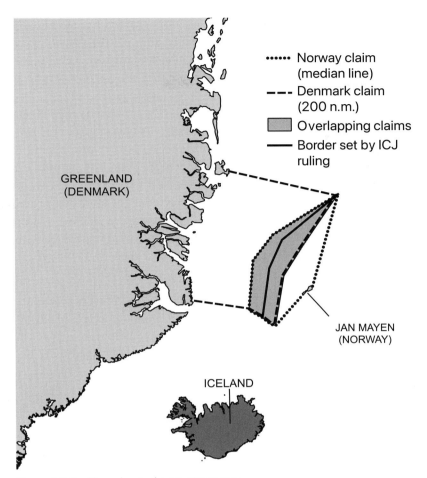

Figure 5.8 Final boundary in the *Jan Mayen* case.
Source: Map drawn by author using QGIS. Data from Natural Earth and ICJ documents.

5.5 Case Study Revisited: Why Did China Build Artificial Islands in the South China Sea?

In the introduction to this chapter, we briefly described the dispute between China and its neighbors over who controls the East and South China Seas. This dispute includes the Spratly Islands, a group of small land masses claimed (in part or in whole) by Brunei, China, Malaysia, the Philippines, Taiwan, and Vietnam. Since 2012, China has built seven artificial islands on top of underwater reefs in the Spratly Islands. These islands hold Chinese military structures and supplies. Many other Chinese artificial islands are now scattered throughout the East and South China Seas.

China's construction of artificial islands connects to each of the topics in this chapter:

- *Governing the sea*: The law of the sea includes many long-standing principles. However, this law changed dramatically after World War II, when new technology allowed states to extract minerals, natural gas, and oil from the seabed. At the same time, environmental activists pressured states to protect the sea and its resources.
- *Creating zones of authority*: Pieces of land, like the Spratly Islands, create legal entitlements to a territorial sea, contiguous zone, exclusive economic zone, and continental shelf. These zones come with rights to explore and exploit natural resources. International law also allows states to build and protect artificial structures—like islands—in their territorial sea and EEZ.
- *Resolving maritime boundary disputes*: The key goals of maritime delimitation are agreement and equity. States use two approaches to achieve these goals: the equidistance method and identifying case-specific circumstances that affect equity. Both approaches allocate water and seabed rights based on land-ownership.

The East and South China Seas disputes are one of the most complex in international politics. It is not possible to address every possible aspect of this dispute. Nevertheless, our discussion of the law of the sea should help us to answer the specific questions from the beginning of this chapter. First, we asked: why do states care about small, uninhabitable pieces of land, like the Spratly Islands? The key value of the Spratly Islands is not the land masses themselves, but rather the water and seabed around them. If a land mass is an island, then the state that owns the land can create a territorial sea, contiguous zone, exclusive economic zone, and continental shelf, thereby creating rights to explore and exploit natural resources. Many Southeast Asian states rely on fishing to support their populations, making the Spratly Islands very important. Rights to seabed mining, natural gas, and oil provide additional financial incentives to claim ownership of the Spratly Islands.

Second, we asked: what are the implications of creating artificial islands? A coastal state has the exclusive right to build and protect artificial structures in its territorial sea and EEZ. These structures are usually offshore platforms for gas and oil drilling, like the *Prirazlomnaya*. China cannot use its artificial islands to create new water or seabed zones. But China's artificial islands are nevertheless a legal tool for asserting its existing legal claims over nearby water and seabed areas. If other states ignore China's artificial islands, this acquiescence can be interpreted as state practice and *opinio juris* of Chinese claims over the Spratly Islands. China's artificial islands are also an important political tool that may intimidate China's neighbors into abandoning their own maritime claims. The artificial islands thus have both legal and political implications.

Finally, we asked: how should China and its neighbors resolve their competing maritime claims? Agreement is a key value of maritime delimitation, yet negotiations over the East and South China Seas have repeatedly failed. International agreement is usually more difficult to achieve when more states are involved. Additionally, standard delimitation approaches rely on ownership of land, which is sometimes contested for areas like the Spratly Islands. International courts and arbitration tribunals usually handle bilateral disputes. They are not designed or intended to resolve complex multilateral disputes.

For example, the Philippines filed an arbitration case against China in 2013 over maritime delimitations. The resulting 2016 arbitration award was widely described in the international news media as a major victory for the Philippines that refuted many Chinese legal claims. Yet the award is troubling because China had compelling objections to the tribunal's jurisdiction and refused to participate in the arbitration. Additionally, the award affected the legal rights of other actors—including Brunei, Malaysia, Taiwan, and Vietnam—that were not included in arbitration. Perhaps not surprisingly, the 2016 award did not change China's behavior. International law alone cannot solve the ongoing disputes in the East and South China Seas. Politics also matters.

6 Trade

6.1 Case Study: The European Union Saves (Some) Seals

In 2009, the European Union was caught between a rock and a hard place. On one side, animal rights advocacy groups were pushing the EU to ban the sale of all products made from seals. For decades, these groups tried to convince consumers worldwide to boycott goods made from seals, including: fur clothing; seal meat; and even some omega-3 dietary supplements. Animal rights activists argued that seals were gentle animals who suffered unnecessary and often cruel deaths. They also argued that laws to make hunting more humane were difficult to enforce and ineffective. The best solution, they believed, was a ban on the sale of all seal products.

On the other side of the debate were Nordic fishermen, who did not view the seals as gentle animals. They viewed the seals as noxious predators who competed

Figure 6.1 Activists in France participate in a 2006 worldwide protest against seal hunting in Canada. One protestor demonstrates the clubbing of a baby seal. Animal rights activists believe that some seal-hunting methods—like clubbing—are inhumane. However, Canada and Norway argued that their seal-hunting rules were more humane than the methods used by EU indigenous communities. They also argued that Canadian and Norwegian seal-hunting rules closely matched EU rules for commercial deer hunting.

with humans over dwindling fish stocks. Nordic fishermen pointed out that public campaigns to save the seals had created a glut of seals in many places. For example, the EU ran special programs in Finland and Sweden that paid hunters to kill seals to control their overpopulation. Nordic fishermen believed that it was wasteful for the EU to pay for seal hunts, while simultaneously banning the sale of seal products.[1]

Indigenous communities were also unhappy with the proposed EU seal ban. Many indigenous groups—including the Inuit people—viewed seal hunting as an important cultural practice that provided their communities with food and clothing.

These communities hunted and sold additional seals to earn money for supplies that they could not make themselves. They believed that an EU seal products ban would endanger their livelihoods.

As a compromise, the EU tried to please everyone. To please animal rights activists, it banned the sale of all seal products. However, it included two important exceptions to please the Nordic fishermen and indigenous communities. First, it included an indigenous communities (IC) exception, which allowed seal product sales by specified indigenous communities, including Inuit tribes. Second, it included a marine resources management (MRM) exception, which allowed sales from EU-sponsored seal hunting in Finland and Sweden.

While the EU managed to craft a delicate balance at home, its final policy created new international problems. Namely, both Canada and Norway were upset by the EU rules. Canada was home to many non-indigenous commercial seal hunters. These hunters were concentrated in areas with few alternative economic opportunities. Canada was also home to many animal rights advocacy groups that convinced Canadian voters to support strict regulation of seal hunts. Canadian politicians questioned why the IC exception allowed the sale of seals hunted by European indigenous communities, sometimes under inhumane conditions, while prohibiting seals hunted by non-indigenous Canadians who complied with "rigorous animal welfare principles."[2]

Similarly, Norway—which was not an EU member—was upset by the protections given to Finland and Sweden. All three of these Nordic states had a glut of seals that threatened their fish stocks. However, Norwegian seal hunters did not qualify for the MRM exception. The Norwegian government noted that its seal-hunting rules were designed to "inflict the least amount of suffering as possible on the animals."[3] Yet Norwegian seals were banned by the EU rules.

Soon after the EU passed its new rules, Canada and Norway filed complaints at the **World Trade Organization** (WTO), an international organization created in 1995 to promote international trade. They argued that the EU rules violated numerous international trade agreements that are overseen by the WTO. But why did Canada and Norway believe that the EU rules violated international trade law? How did the EU try to justify its policy? And, finally, what are the implications of the *Seals* dispute for international law more generally?

To answer these questions, we must first learn about the following topics:

- *Promoting international trade*: Why do states use international law to promote trade? How has this law evolved over time? What modern laws and institutions govern international trade?
- *Major obligations*: What are the major obligations that states have under international trade law? What kinds of commitments do states make about market access and the treatment of other states?

- *Major exceptions*: When are states allowed to break their commitments without violating international trade law? Can states restrict trade to address unfair trade, safeguard their economies from unexpected shocks, protect competing values, and preserve their national security?

The primary goal of international trade law is to advance **trade liberalization**, which is a set of policies designed to promote the trade of goods and services between states. Economists have long argued that international trade allows states to produce goods and services in which they have a comparative advantage, leading to greater aggregate wealth. Yet international trade comes with distributional consequences. If a state can more efficiently import a good than produce it, then domestic producers will face competition from foreign producers. Businesses and workers that can compete in the global market will benefit from trade liberalization, while those that cannot compete will be harmed. This distributional effect creates pressure on governments to protect many businesses and workers from foreign competition.

After World War II, the US and other developed states believed that the world would become more peaceful and prosperous if states became more economically interdependent. They created a new multilateral treaty in 1947 to promote trade liberalization, known as the **General Agreement on Tariffs and Trade** (GATT). Over time, GATT grew both deeper and larger, with more members pledging more trade cooperation. In 1995, the GATT was transformed into the modern-day World Trade Organization. Almost all states in the world are now members of the GATT and the WTO. Additionally, most states are members of preferential trade agreements, which aim to promote trade amongst a limited group of states.

Modern international trade law is an extremely complex body of rules. For example, the GATT/WTO has special rules that apply to developing states, which have more flexibility to restrict trade to promote economic growth. Additionally, trade agreements often contain specialized rules to protect foreign investment and intellectual property. Politically sensitive areas—like agriculture and textiles—are also often governed by their own special rules. Below we focus on GATT/WTO rules that apply to most goods and services. Readers who want more details on specific issue-areas or other trade agreements are encouraged to consult more specialized texts.

Section 6.2 discusses why states use international law to promote international trade. It describes concepts that inform and shape international rules, and how these rules have evolved over time. Section 6.3 then outlines the major obligations under international trade law. These include ensuring market access and complying with various treatment standards. We then describe major exceptions in international trade law in section 6.4. These exceptions allow states to respond to unfair trade conditions, safeguard their economies from economic shocks, balance trade liberalization against competing values, and protect their national security. Finally, we conclude in section 6.5 by returning to the EU ban on seal products.

6.2   Promoting International Trade

We begin by describing some of the key concepts that motivate international trade law. Most experts agree that international law can help states to promote trade liberalization. However, they disagree about how law should be designed to achieve this objective. We then provide a brief overview of the evolution of international trade law.

Concepts

Economists have long argued that international trade poses a **collaboration problem** for states.[4] While states would benefit from jointly choosing free trade, each state has a temptation to defect from such cooperation by unilaterally protecting its market using trade barriers. One common barrier is a **tariff**, which is a tax on a foreign good that is imported into a state. If states focus solely on their short-term individual incentives, then the likely outcome is for both states to protect their markets. However, if states can focus on the long-term and how their interests align, then they have an incentive to create rules and institutions that promote trade liberalization.

How does international law help to solve this collaboration problem? First, international trade law creates expectations about how much a state must open up its market by reducing trade barriers. Most trade agreements allow states to restrict trade somewhat. For these agreements to work, states must have clear expectations about which restrictions are allowed, and which are not. Second, institutions created by international trade law can provide information about the meaning of legal rules and whether a given state has broken these rules. This information helps states to uphold international law using economic and political tools.

Of course, a state's temptation to defect by restricting trade can change over time in response to economic, political, and social pressure. Unexpected economic downturns, closely fought elections, and changing social values (like environmental or animal rights activism) can increase the pressure on governments to restrict trade. If states face unexpected pressure to protect their markets, then punishing states for temporary legal violations may be counterproductive. For example, suppose a government is facing a severe recession and must restrict trade to temporarily protect its own businesses and workers. How should its trading partners respond?

Many scholars argue that rather than focusing purely on punishment, states have injected flexibility into the international trade rules, by allowing states to respond to exigent circumstances (like unexpected economic, political, and social changes) without destroying overall trade cooperation.[5] They argue that international trade law explicitly allows limited and/or temporary unilateral protection without cooperation collapsing as a whole. States can sometimes unilaterally break various trade rules without violating their trade law obligations as a whole. This flexibility is usually enshrined in a treaty provision that political scientists refer to as an **escape clause**, which is a treaty provision that allows a state to break a trade rule without violating the treaty as a whole.[6] Lawyers refer to these same rules as "exceptions." As described below, there are four major types of escape clauses—or exceptions—in international trade law. States are usually allowed to break their major obligations to respond to unfair trade; to safeguard their economies from unexpected economic shocks; to protect competing values; and to protect national security.

How do states ensure that flexibility provisions are not abused? After all, a government will always be tempted to defect in a collaboration problem. What keeps a government from claiming that it is under extreme pressure to escape, even if it is not? Scholars of trade cooperation have put forth various solutions that fall into two broad categories: compensation and appeals to exception.

Scholars who adhere to the compensation perspective usually believe that it is extremely difficult, if not impossible, to know how much pressure a government faces to protect its market. While outside observers may know a state's GDP, unemployment rate, and other macroeconomic indicators, they cannot truly know how much political pressure is put on a government to protect its market. Additionally, if a government is given leeway to restrict trade, then the government has incentive to overstate its pressure to gain cooperation from others while protecting its own businesses and workers. Rather than trying to elicit a true understanding of how much pressure a government faces, the international trade system can simply put a price on protectionism by requiring some form of compensation for trading partners that are harmed by it.[7]

For example, GATT/WTO rules require states to compensate their trading partners when they apply a **safeguard**, which is a trade restriction that protects a domestic industry from an unexpected import surge. This practice was common in the early decades of the GATT. Usually states offered to lower their taxes on other goods that flowed between the two states as a form of compensation.[8] This practice has become less common over time. Under the WTO, safeguards can now be used for a limited period of time without compensation. Yet the criteria for when safeguards can be used are also now much more stringent, making the abuse of safeguards more difficult. For example, if a state is experiencing a drought that has dramatically increased the price of cattle feed, trading partners can be confident that a government is not abusing flexibility when it restricts beef imports. Compensation is less necessary when it is harder to abuse flexibility in the system.

Outside of safeguards, GATT/WTO does not explicitly require compensation to offset trade protectionism. Yet the politics of international trade is such that states sometimes use compensation to manage trade disputes. For example, consider the *Cotton* dispute, which was initiated by Brazil against the US over cotton subsidies.

Instead of removing its subsidies, the US paid $147.3 million a year to the Brazilian Cotton Institute, a fund for technical assistance to foreign farmers. Brazil had full discretion over how to allocate this money. In exchange, Brazil suspended its case. There was little disagreement about what this deal amounted to. As US Congressman Jeff Flake of Arizona stated, "Because our subsidies violate WTO rules, we're now paying millions to subsidize Brazilian agriculture."[9]

Trade disputes also often involve blatant threats of retaliation as a form of compensation. For example, US President George W. Bush dramatically raised tariffs on imported steel in March 2002 during the run-up to a congressional election. These tariffs drew wide condemnation from many states, including the EU. As part of its diplomatic efforts, the EU released a list of specific products on which it would be raising tariffs if it won its case at the WTO and the US did not back down.[10] The retaliatory tariffs targeted textiles from South Carolina, where the Republican Party was facing a close Senate election, and orange juice from Florida, which was led by Governor Jeb Bush, the US president's brother. At a summit with EU leaders, President Bush reportedly asked a top EU leader, "Why are you attacking my family?"[11] The tactic worked: just days before the retaliation was set to begin, President Bush revoked his steel tariffs.

The common theme behind both of these examples is that they require a government to compensate its trade partners if it pursues policies that violate WTO rules. Situations like these cause some economists to argue that international trade law implicitly allows efficient breach: when a government is under high pressure to protect, it can violate its commitments and compensate its trading partners, making all states better off than they would have been under free trade.[12]

Scholars who are critical of the compensation perspective point out that this is not how the system is supposed to operate. States are supposed to comply with their GATT/WTO obligations—they are not supposed to buy each other off with checks for $147.3 million. While this behavior might be common, that does not make it acceptable. These scholars point out that flexibility is apparent in other aspects of the international trade system, like GATT/WTO rules for protecting competing values. In this realm of trade law, governments can make "appeals to exception," arguing that trade liberalization must be balanced against competing values that are included in GATT/WTO texts.

The interpretation of these texts about competing values has changed dramatically over time. Prior to 2000, the GATT/WTO was widely accused of having a pro-trade bias: complainants—who seek more open trade—almost always won their cases, and competing values almost never prevailed in trade disputes. For example, in the early 1990s, multiple states complained at the GATT about US rules for tuna. These disputes involved US rules to reduce the number of dolphins killed in tuna fishing nets. These cases involved complex interpretations of many areas of GATT law. The US argued that its policies were allowed because they protected competing values. The US lost the tuna disputes, prompting broad worldwide criticism from environmental organizations and threatening the stability of the new World Trade Organization.

Just a few years later, the WTO was presented with a nearly identical dispute in which numerous states challenged US rules that protected turtles from being killed in shrimping nets. Once again, the US invoked competing values to defend its policy. As described below, the WTO ultimately issued a ruling that expanded the prior interpretation of rules on competing values. The WTO has since gained a reputation for being more willing to give governments latitude to balance trade against competing social values.

One benefit of the appeals to exception perspective is that it is more insulated from power politics than the compensation perspective. If states can appeal to exceptions and the WTO is a neutral arbiter, then their success in gaining flexibility will hinge on the merits of their legal arguments. In contrast, under the compensation perspective, states must have the power to demand compensation or threaten retaliation in order to keep governments from abusing flexibility. For example, few states have the market power or legal resources to challenge the US when it acts opportunistically in international trade. In the *Cotton* dispute, small cotton producers (like Ghana) relied on Brazil to challenge US policies. Accordingly, the compensation perspective may bias the international trade system against developing states.

However, one cost of the appeals to exception perspective is that it requires a bureaucracy with the capacity to oversee compliance. If a state can only protect its market when it can make a principled argument about legal exceptions, then the trading system must have an international legal body to oversee legal challenges. This judicial system must be able to discern when leaders are truly seeking to balance competing values and when they are protecting their economies for purely opportunistic reasons. Additionally, developing states must have the resources to use the system to protect their interests. So the appeals to exception perspective does not erase the influence of power politics within the international system.

Evolution

Before World War II, international law played a small role in regulating trade between states. Trade relationships were generally determined by power politics, rather than binding legal commitments. Sometimes international trade was included in more general treaties between states. For example, after declaring its independence from Great Britain in 1776, the US sought international support from France. In 1778, France and the US signed a treaty that recognized the US's claim to political independence. This treaty covered diverse topics, including the treatment of ships during wartime, fishing rights, and a pledge "not to grant any particular favor to other nations in respect of commerce ..., which shall not immediately become common to the other party."[13]

As international trade grew over the nineteenth century, many powerful states used the threat of military force to coerce weaker states into opening their markets to trade. For example, the US sent a squadron of ships under Commodore Perry to negotiate with Japan in the early 1850s. During diplomatic exchanges, Perry offered "gifts" to Japanese officials that included a white flag of surrender, American weapons, and books about Perry's recent victory in the Mexican-American War.[14] Perry's message was unmistakable: Japan must either fight or trade with the US. Japan promptly signed a treaty that opened Japanese ports to US trade. The US was not alone in this practice. After its victory in the Opium Wars of 1839–1842, the UK demanded that China sign a treaty that opened Chinese ports to UK merchants.

International agreements also reinforced—or at least reflected—colonial relationships prior to World War II. Most colonizing states wanted access to raw materials and export markets in their colonies. Accordingly, colonizing states often required that their colonies join a **customs union**, which is a trade agreement that requires free trade within members states and common trade policy with outside states. These trading relationships were often reinforced by imperial control over local currency.

GATT/WTO System

International trade law changed dramatically after World War II, when a group of industrialized states wrote the General Agreement on Tariffs and Trade. The GATT includes broad legal principles to govern international trade and contains detailed lists of the maximum taxes that each state can impose on imported goods. In 1947, twenty-three states agreed to join the GATT immediately, pending the completion of a separate treaty to create a new international organization to oversee the GATT. However, this separate treaty was ultimately abandoned, leaving states with binding trade rules, but no institution to oversee and manage these rules.

GATT members slowly developed new agreements over time. They initially focused on reducing tariffs on goods. In a series of negotiations, members progressively lowered their tariffs, leading to deeper trade cooperation. Then in the mid-1960s, they began writing new rules for other trade policies. GATT members could pick and choose which of these rules they followed, creating a complex web of legal commitments in which different rules applied to different pairs of members.[15]

GATT members also gradually developed an informal organization with committees and procedures for settling trade disputes. Over time, this informal organization grew stronger and more developed. As shown in Figure 6.2, more states joined the GATT and the organization began overseeing more trade disputes between its members. By the 1980s, the GATT system had become sufficiently complicated, large, and unwieldy that its members agreed to redesign the international trade system.

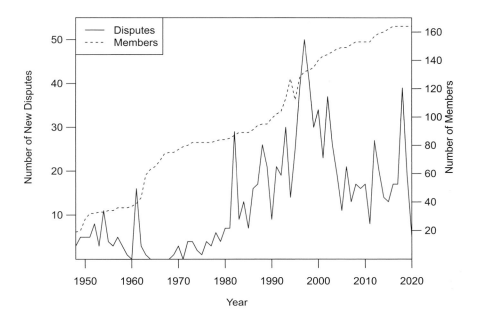

Figure 6.2 Trade disputes in the GATT/WTO.
Source: Figure drawn by author using WTO data.

International trade law began a new era in 1995 with the creation of the World Trade Organization. The WTO retained the basic rules from the 1947 GATT. However, additional WTO texts addressed new issues, like foreign investment, intellectual property, and services. WTO texts also refined pre-existing GATT rules on issues like unfair trade. These new rules applied to all WTO members—states could no longer pick and choose which rules to follow.

One of the most important elements of the modern WTO is its dispute settlement system (DSS). This international judicial body is not called a "court," yet it functions like a court. As shown in Figure 6.3, the DSS is divided into two stages. The first stage—the "legal stage"—begins with formal negotiations (called "consultations") between states in a trade dispute. If disputants cannot reach a settlement, then the complaining state can request a "panel." This panel functions like a court, with each side presenting factual and legal arguments that are assessed by three experts in trade law in a document called a "panel report." If neither party requests appellate review, then the panel report becomes legally binding. However, if either party disagrees with part of the panel report, it can request review by the "Appellate Body" (AB), which functions like an appellate court. The AB is a group of trade law experts who review the legal arguments and then issue their own document, the "Appellate Body report." This AB report then becomes legally binding.

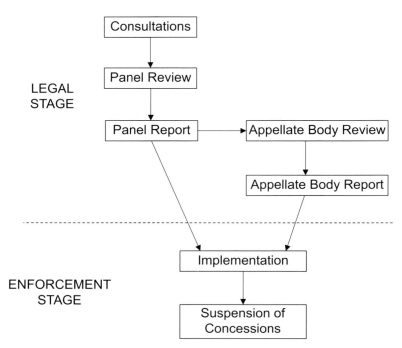

Figure 6.3 WTO dispute settlement system.

The second stage of the DSS—the "enforcement stage"—focuses on compliance with the final WTO report for the dispute. If the respondent has violated WTO law, it must either change its policies or financially compensate the complainant. Panels and the Appellate Body rule on whether a legal violation occurred, but they do not specify how the respondent must behave in the future. There are thus often disputes over "implementation," or how the respondent should change its policies to comply with WTO rules. The WTO has elaborate implementation procedures. If these procedures do not yield a satisfactory outcome, the complainant can request authorization to "suspend concessions," meaning it can ask for permission to punish the respondent using various policy tools. As shown in Figure 6.2, litigation is common in the WTO. On average, states filed 23 new disputes each year between 1995 and 2020.

Preferential Trade Agreements

In addition to joining the GATT/WTO system, a state can also join a **preferential trade agreement** (PTA), which is an international trade agreement with limited membership, like bilateral and regional agreements. For example, the European Union is a customs union that operates based on a PTA. These agreements are explicitly allowed under GATT/WTO rules.

PTAs have grown in popularity since the early 1990s, as shown in Figure 6.4. The two declines in the number of PTAs shown in Figure 6.4 (in 2005 and 2008) were caused by EU expansion. When states join the EU, they leave their pre-existing

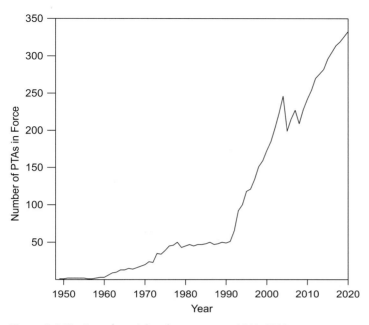

Figure 6.4 Rise in preferential trade agreements, 1948–2020.
Source: Figure drawn by author using WTO data.

PTAs and join the PTAs already in force between the EU and its trading partners. This results in a decline in the number of PTAs.

Why did PTAs become so popular beginning in the 1990s? First, the collapse of the Soviet Union in 1989 prompted many states in Central Asia and Eastern Europe–that were previously under Soviet political control–to sign new trade agreements. Second, further trade liberalization within the WTO was stymied by disagreements over issues like agricultural subsidies and intellectual property. Finally, PTA growth was affected by economic competition. For example, one objective of the *Mercado Común del Sur*–a PTA that includes multiple South American states and is often called "MERCOSUR"–was to improve the bargaining power of its members vis-à-vis the EU and other regional groups.[16] Its members believed that they would have more leverage if they negotiated as a group.

6.3 Major Obligations

International trade law is built upon a set of core legal principles that were first articulated in the GATT, and then subsequently expanded under the WTO and various PTAs. This body of law creates two major kinds of obligations. First, states have crafted rules about market access, which limit the ability of states to use tariffs and other trade restrictions. Second, international law contains treatment standards, which set standards for how governments treat imported goods and services.

Market Access

States often try to restrict access to their domestic markets using many different kinds of policies. Recall that a tariff, which is sometimes called a customs duty, is a tax on a foreign good that is imported into a state. A **non-tariff barrier** is a policy that is not a tariff, but that restricts trade. These can include quantitative restrictions, technical barriers to trade, and restrictions on government procurement.

Tariffs

Most trade agreements allow their members to restrict trade using tariffs. Governments usually choose different tariff rates for different products, based on economic and political factors. When they negotiate trade agreements, states hold set limits on the tariffs that they will charge for different products. For example, one state may agree to lower its tariff on oranges if another state lowers its tariff on cotton. Negotiated maximum tariff rates are usually included in a document called the Schedule of Concessions.

Quantitative Restrictions

Throughout the twentieth century, governments often limited trade by imposing quantitative restrictions. A **quantitative restriction** is either a ban of a particular good or a **quota** which limits the amount of a particular good that can be imported into a state. For example, when Turkey negotiated a customs union with the EU in the mid-1990s, it limited the amount of textiles that could be imported from other states, including India. States sometimes implement quotas by limiting the number of import licenses that they grant to businesses.

Quantitative restrictions are illegal under the GATT for most goods. GATT Article XI(1) reads:

> No prohibitions or restrictions other than duties, taxes or other charges, whether made effective through quotas, import or export licences or other measures, shall be instituted or maintained ... on the importation of any product of the territory of any other contracting party or on the exportation ... of any product destined for the territory of any other contracting party.

Yet this rule was often ignored during the early decades of the GATT, with states blatantly violating Article XI. States also attempted to evade Article XI using a tool known as a **voluntary export restraint** (VER). Under a VER, an exporter voluntarily limits the amount of a good that it sells in a foreign market.[17] Since the exporter (not the importer) limits the sale of goods under a VER, importers do not directly violate Article XI. For example, US automobile manufacturers suffered a massive downturn in the late 1970s and early 1980s. Poor economic conditions and an oil crisis reduced car sales. Consumers who could afford new cars favored Japanese models, which were smaller and more fuel-efficient than US models. In May 1981, the Reagan Administration signed a VER in which Japan limited the number of automobiles that it exported to the US. This limitation on supply increased car prices in the US and temporarily protected the US automobile industry as it shifted to producing smaller cars and adopted new technology. Meanwhile, Japanese car manufacturers increased their profits because of the higher car prices. During the 1980s and early 1990s, many GATT members tried to crack down on the use of VERs and violations of Article XI. States ultimately agreed to limit quantitative restrictions on agricultural products (which were originally exempted from Article XI), and the WTO explicitly prohibited VERs.

When states limit market access, they usually want to restrict imports. Yet states also sometimes want to restrict the export of goods. For example, the components in many modern electronics, like laptop computers and cell phones, are made using rare earth minerals. Ironically, these minerals are not particularly rare, but environmental and health regulations make them expensive to mine in most parts of the world. As demand for consumer electronics grew, China aggressively promoted the mining of these minerals, driving down the cost of the minerals and forcing mines to close in most other states. By 2010, China alone accounted for 97 percent of the world production of rare earth minerals.[18] Once it had secured monopoly power over global production, China restricted the export of these minerals. These export restrictions were intended to raise the world price of the minerals and to encourage technology companies to manufacture their products in China, where they could easily obtain the minerals. Multiple states successfully sued China at the WTO, arguing that China violated GATT Article XI.

Technical Barriers to Trade

Governments also sometimes restrict market access using technical barriers to trade, which are government regulations and standards that obstruct trade. These regulations and standards often pertain to product characteristics, production methods, and labeling requirements. While these policies may ostensibly be crafted to protect public health and the environment, they can often be a disguised restriction on trade. For example, in the 1980s, France required government inspections of all facilities that manufactured pharmaceutical products, yet France refused to allow its government inspectors to travel abroad. This regulatory policy effectively banned pharmaceutical imports into France.[19] More recently, the US has faced legal problems because of its agricultural labeling rules, which required that retailers inform consumers about the country of origin of any beef and pork that they sell. US country-of-origin labeling rules were extremely complicated, with multiple categories based on where animals were born, raised, and slaughtered. Since cows and pigs were often raised in Canada or Mexico and then slaughtered in the US, additional rules regulated "commingling," which is the slaughtering and processing of meat from animals of multiple nationalities. To sell a single package of ground beef, a US grocery store thus had to know where the cow had been born, where it was raised, where and when it was slaughtered and processed, and what other nationalities of cows were slaughtered and processed in the same facility on the same day. Canada and Mexico successfully sued the US at the WTO, arguing that the US labeling rules were so burdensome that many private companies would only process and sell domestic livestock, thereby restricting trade.

Government Procurement

Finally, government procurement rules can be non-tariff barriers if they limit purchases of imported goods and services by businesses and government agencies. For example, following the 2008 Financial Crisis, the US government passed an economic stimulus bill that poured approximately $800 billion into the US economy. The bill included a "Buy American" provision, which stated that "None of the funds appropriated ... by this Act may be used for a project for the construction, alteration, maintenance, or repair of a public building or public work unless all of the iron, steel, and manufactured goods used in the project are produced in the United States."[20] The US isn't alone in crafting such rules: states often require that government spending go towards domestic goods and services. The WTO's Agreement on Government Procurement is a first step towards limiting such NTBs. But many critics argue that trade agreements have been relatively ineffective in liberalizing government procurement practices.[21]

Treatment Standards

Modern trade law has two major treatment standards. Both are relative standards: they regulate the treatment of a good/service, relative to another comparable good/service. The first standard—known as **most-favored-nation (MFN) treatment**—regulates how imported goods from one state are treated relative to imported goods from another state. GATT Article I provides:

> With respect to customs duties ... any advantage ... granted by any contracting party to any product originating in or destined for any other country shall be accorded ... to the like product originating in or destined for the territories of all other contracting parties.

This treaty provision means that any time a GATT member makes a trade concession on a product to a particular state, all other GATT members must receive the same concession. For example, if the US lowers its tariff on Spanish oranges, it must lower its tariff on oranges from all other GATT members.[22] In the *Bananas* dispute, numerous states challenged rules on imported bananas that were passed by the European Economic Community (EEC), the precursor of the modern EU. These rules were ultimately found to violate GATT rules because they gave more favorable treatment to bananas that came from former European colonies.

The second standard—known as **national treatment**—regulates how imported goods are treated relative to domestic goods. As stated in GATT Article III(4):

The products of the territory of any contracting party imported into the territory of any other contracting party shall be accorded treatment no less favourable than that accorded to like products of national origin.

An imported good can still be subject to a tariff, which is not charged on domestic goods. Additionally, imported goods may face different regulations than domestic goods. For example, a state may require inspections to ensure that imported products meet safety requirements that are applied to domestic goods. However, a state may not use such regulations "to afford protection to domestic production."[23] For example, the EEC rules that were challenged in the *Bananas* dispute allocated import licenses based on a firm's past banana imports. Other states argued that the EEC rules "gave operators an incentive to purchase EEC ... bananas because, by doing so, they could obtain ... a larger share of the quota rents."[24] Put simply, the EEC licensing rules allowed banana importers to make more money if they sold EEC bananas than if they sold imported bananas from Costa Rica and Nicaragua. The GATT panel agreed with the complainants, finding that the EEC rules violated the national treatment standard.

One of the most controversial issues in international trade law is the meaning of two key words: "like product." Because both the MFN and national treatment standards are relative treatment standards, they require the use of structured comparisons. Sometimes this is a simple endeavor, as with primary agricultural products. In the *Bananas* case, the complainants could very easily argue that a banana grown in Costa Rica is "like" a banana grown in the EEC or a former European colony. However, for more complex goods, especially those that involve manufacturing, it is harder to argue that two products are "like." For example, is sparkling wine from the Napa Valley of California "like" sparkling wine from the Champagne Valley of France? In the *Alcohol* dispute, the EEC challenged Japanese regulations for alcoholic beverages. These regulations charged internal taxes on imported vodka that were four to seven times higher than the taxes on shochu, a Japanese-produced liquor. The panel ruled that "Japanese shochu ... and vodka could be considered as 'like' products ... because they were both white/clean spirits, made of similar raw materials, and their end-uses were virtually identical (either as straight 'schnaps' type of drinks or in various mixtures)."[25]

6.4 Major Exceptions

International trade law also includes four kinds of exceptions, which are situations in which a state can break a trade rule without violating international trade law. First, international law allows states to sometimes increase tariffs on imported goods in response to practices called "unfair trade." Second, states can break their trade obligations to safeguard their economies from unexpected shocks. Third, states can sometimes restrict trade to accommodate competing values, like protecting human health and the environment. And fourth, states can restrict trade to preserve their national security. We discuss each of these topics in turn.

Preventing Unfair Trade

The GATT/WTO and most PTAs allow states to restrict trade in response to two common practices that are commonly described as unfair trade.

Subsidies and Countervailing Duties

First, governments often provide subsidies to their industries. The GATT defines a **subsidy** as "any form of income or price support" provided by a government.[26] Subsidies usually lower—directly or indirectly—the market price of a good, which can create distortions in economic markets. For example, if an imported good is subsidized, then it can become more difficult for domestic producers to compete. The GATT/WTO has elaborate rules regarding subsidies that have evolved considerably over time.[27]

Regardless of whether a given subsidy is considered legal under international law, the GATT/WTO and most PTAs allow states to impose a **countervailing duty** (CVD) if a domestic industry is harmed by a subsidized imported good. These additional duties are intended to offset any "subsidy bestowed directly, or indirectly, upon the manufacture, production or export of any merchandise."[28] To impose a CVD, a state must first establish that an injury has occurred because of a foreign subsidy, and then determine the size of the subsidy so that it imposes a CVD of the appropriate magnitude.

Subsidies and CVDs have been routinely challenged in the GATT/WTO's dispute settlement system. For example, the US and Canada have been in a dispute over softwood lumber for over thirty-five years! Both states allow lumber companies to purchase logging rights on government-owned lands. However, Canada charges below-market prices, so lumber production costs are significantly lower in Canada. The US argues that Canada has granted a subsidy that harms the US lumber industry. So the US imposes a countervailing duty that raises the price of Canadian lumber. Canada has filed multiple disputes at the WTO to challenge the legality of the CVD.

Dumping and Antidumping Duties

Second, producers sometimes engage in **dumping** their goods in foreign markets by selling them "at less than [their] normal value."[29] Consumers in the importing state benefit from the low price of these goods. However, domestic producers that compete with imported goods are harmed by dumping if they are unable to match these prices. Dumping is legal under GATT/WTO rules, but is nonetheless considered unfair.

Most trade agreements allow their members to impose an **antidumping duty**, which raises the price of the dumped good, if dumping harms domestic producers. Rules on antidumping duties have also evolved greatly over time.[30] Antidumping duties can offset the injury caused by dumping, but they cannot be used for punitive purposes. Antidumping disputes thus usually involve complex economic arguments about how to calculate a good's export price and its normal value, which determine the size of an antidumping duty. These calculations are particularly difficult when goods are imported from a non-market economy.

Exporters often challenge antidumping duties by arguing that their goods were not dumped, or that the importer's domestic producers have not experienced sufficient harm to justify trade restrictions. After China joined the WTO in 2001, it filed many disputes to challenge the methods that other states used to determine the normal value of Chinese goods. For example, the EU imposed an antidumping duty on Chinese leather shoes in 2006. China then filed a complaint at the WTO to challenge the EU's calculations.

In practice, states can both subsidize and dump goods simultaneously, meaning that states often impose both countervailing and antidumping duties on the same product. For example, while the US–Canadian softwood lumber dispute began over subsidies, the US government also argued that Canadian firms dumped lumber in the US. As such, the US imposed both countervailing and antidumping duties on Canadian lumber. The tariffs were broadly supported by the US lumber industry, which argued that the tariffs were necessary to combat unfair trade practices. However, the tariffs were opposed by the construction industry, which argued that they significantly raised the price of commercial and residential construction.

Safeguarding Economies from Unexpected Shocks

The second kind of exception allows states to safeguard their economies from unexpected shocks by raising their tariffs during economic emergencies. GATT Article XIX(1)(a) reads:

> If, as a result of unforeseen developments ..., any product is being imported ... in such increased quantities and under such conditions as to cause or threaten serious injury to domestic producers in that territory of like or directly competitive products, the contracting party shall be free ... to suspend the obligation in whole or in part or to withdraw or modify the concession ...

When a state responds to such import surges by restricting trade, its resulting policy is usually referred to as a safeguard since the intention of the restriction is to protect domestic producers from unexpected events. States usually implement safeguards through tariff increases or import quotas. Under GATT rules, any state that imposed a safeguard was required to compensate its trading partners, usually by granting trade concessions on other goods that flowed between the two states.

Such compensation was common in the early GATT.[31] However, this practice faded over time, and WTO members now often use safeguards without providing any compensation at all.

If a GATT/WTO member believes that a safeguard is not allowed, it can challenge the safeguard through the GATT/WTO dispute settlement system. These disputes often involve arguments about whether an "unforeseen development" caused an import surge, and whether domestic producers have experienced or been threatened with "serious injury." For example, a fashion trend in the late 1940s increased the popularity of women's felt hats with fur trimmings. US milliners could not compete effectively with foreign producers because these hats were labor-intensive and the US had relatively high labor costs. The US increased its tariff on these hats so that milliners would be protected from foreign competition. The United States viewed its tariff as legitimate under GATT safeguard rules, but Czechoslovakia—a major exporter of these hats to the US—disagreed and filed a complaint. Part of the dispute involved the legal interpretation of the term "serious injury," which was not defined in the 1947 GATT text. But more importantly, the US and Czechoslovakia disagreed about whether changes in women's fashion were "unforeseen developments," as required by Article XIX. When the US prevailed in the dispute, the door opened to widespread use of safeguards.

Over time, GATT/WTO members cracked down on such practices, creating more precise definitions of legal terms and stricter standards on when states can use safeguards to restrict trade. They also developed procedures to govern the use of safeguards. States still routinely use safeguards to restrict trade, although states can usually successfully challenge these trade restrictions at the WTO. As described earlier, President George W. Bush raised tariffs on imported steel prior to the 2002 US Congressional elections. Bush described the tariffs as safeguards. However, his tariffs were widely viewed as an attempt to boost political support for Republican candidates in Ohio and Pennsylvania. Numerous states sued the US at the WTO. They successfully argued that the US violated WTO procedures, including failing to show that "unforeseen developments" had caused an import surge.

Protecting Competing Values

Third, trade law allows states to sometimes restrict trade to protect competing values. For example, GATT/WTO members are allowed to choose policies that otherwise violate their legal obligations if these policies address specific competing values. GATT Article XX reads:

> Subject to the requirement that such measures are not applied in a manner which would constitute a means of arbitrary or unjustifiable discrimination between countries where the same conditions prevail, or a disguised restriction on international trade, nothing

in this Agreement shall be construed to prevent the adoption or enforcement by any contracting party of measures:

(a) necessary to protect public morals;

(b) necessary to protect human, animal or plant life or health ...

(g) relating to the conservation of exhaustible natural resources if such measures are made effective in conjunction with restrictions on domestic production or consumption ...

Disputes that involve Article XX involve a two-step legal test. If the respondent violated any of its GATT obligations, such as imposing illegal quantitive restrictions or violating treatment standards, the dispute settlement system will first ask: does the trade restriction satisfy any of the specific provisions of Article XX? For example, is it "necessary to protect public morals?" The dispute settlement system will then ask: does the trade restriction violate the **chapeau**—or introductory text—of Article XX? Namely, is the trade restriction "a means of arbitrary or unjustifiable discrimination between countries where the same conditions prevail, or a disguised restriction on international trade?"

Article XX(a)—the "public morals" exception—was historically interpreted as justifying bans on alcohol and pornography.[32] Yet this provision was rarely discussed and was not even invoked in a trade dispute until the early 2000s. In 2003, Antigua and Barbuda filed a WTO dispute, challenging US restrictions on online gambling.[33] The US defended its policies by arguing that gambling restrictions were a valid means of protecting "public morals." The US ultimately lost the case: the Appellate Body ruled that the restrictions on online gambling violated the *chapeau* because the US allowed similar gambling services to be provided by US firms. Yet the panel report opened the door to future invocations of the public morals exception, stating:

the content of [public morals] can vary in time and space, depending upon a range of factors, including prevailing social, cultural, ethical and religious values ... Members should be given some scope to define and apply for themselves the [concept] of "public morals" ... in their respective territories, according to their own systems and scales of values.[34]

This statement became important when Canada and Norway sued the EU over rules that restricted the sale of products made from seals, as discussed in the case study that frames this chapter.

Article XX(b)—which covers measures "necessary to protect human, animal or plant life or health"—has been very thoroughly explored in GATT/WTO disputes. These types of disputes usually involve disagreements over the safety of particular goods or services. For example, the EU and US have a long-standing dispute over the use of growth hormones in beef. The dispute stems in part from disagreement about how governments should assess the risk of particular products. Loosely speaking, the US—which commonly uses hormones to promote growth in cattle—believes that governments should allow the sale of goods unless there is scientific evidence that they are not safe. The EU—which opposes the use of hormones in beef—believes that governments should not allow the sale of products unless there is scientific evidence that they are safe.[35] The WTO sided with the US in 1998, but the EU refused to comply and continued to restrict US beef imports. The standoff between the two states has lasted for over twenty years, with periodic flareups and negotiations.

Even if the GATT/WTO agrees that a policy aims "to protect human, animal or plant life or health," the policy must also be "necessary" to achieve this objective. For example, in the *Cigarettes* dispute, the US challenged Thai laws that imposed quantitative restrictions on imported cigarettes. The panel report noted "that smoking constituted a serious risk to human health and that consequently measures designed to reduce the consumption of cigarettes fell within the scope of Article XX(b)."[36] However, the panel noted:

> the import restrictions imposed by Thailand could be considered to be "necessary" in terms of Article XX(b) only if there were no alternative measure consistent with the General Agreement, or less inconsistent with it, which Thailand could reasonably be expected to employ to achieve its health policy objectives.[37]

For example, rather than limiting the import of foreign cigarettes, the Thai government could have imposed labeling requirements, or banned advertisements for all cigarettes.

Article XX(g)—which pertains to "exhaustible natural resources"—was originally believed to apply to mineral and non-living resources. For example, in the *Gasoline* dispute, Venezuela challenged US regulations on imported gasoline. The panel ruled "that clean air was an exhaustible natural resource within the meaning of Article XX(g)," although the US regulation was ultimately found to violate the Article XX *chapeau*.[38] However, the interpretation of "exhaustible natural resources" has evolved over time to also include living resources, like animals and plants.

For example, in the *Shrimp* case, multiple states challenged US laws that restricted the import of shrimp. At the time, the US wanted these states to adopt technology that would reduce the number of turtles killed in shrimping nets. Existing rulings on the meaning of "necessary" in Article XX(b) set a high legal standard. To hedge its case, the US argued that the shrimp restrictions were permissible under Article XX(g) by arguing the turtles were an "exhaustible natural resource." The WTO Appellate Body agreed:

> We do not believe that "exhaustible" natural resources and "renewable" natural resources are mutually exclusive. One lesson that modern biological sciences teach us is that living species, though in principle, capable of reproduction and, in that sense,

Figure 6.5 In November 1999, many protestors in Seattle wore turtle costumes to argue that the newly formed WTO prioritized free trade over competing values, like the protection of wildlife. A year earlier, the WTO ruled that turtles were "exhaustible natural resources," but that US laws to protect turtles were nonetheless "arbitrary or unjustifiable discrimination." Since the Seattle protests, the WTO has slowly given states more flexibility to restrict trade to protect competing values.

"renewable", are in certain circumstances indeed susceptible of depletion, exhaustion and extinction, frequently because of human activities. Living resources are just as "finite" as petroleum, iron ore and other non-living resources.[39]

By successfully invoking Article XX(g), the US no longer needed to prove that its rules were "necessary" to protect turtles. Instead, it needed to prove that the rules were "relating to the conservation of" turtles, a much lower legal standard. Additionally, Article XX(g) requires that "such measures are made effective in conjunction with restrictions on domestic production or consumption," which is sometimes referred to as "even-handedness."[40] This test was easily satisfied by the US law, which also required that the domestic shrimping industry use the special nets that protect turtles.

As in the *Gambling* dispute, the US ran into some problems, though, with the Article XX *chapeau*. Namely, the WTO identified several details of US shrimp regulations that created "arbitrary or unjustifiable discrimination."[41] For example, the US provided financial assistance to some (but not all) states to help them purchase the new shrimping nets. The US declared the case a major victory for turtles, and revised problematic details of its regulations. However, many animal rights activists criticized the WTO for not completely supporting the US regulations.

Preserving National Security

Finally, the GATT/WTO allows its members to violate their major legal obligations to preserve national security. GATT Article XXI reads:

Nothing in this Agreement shall be construed ...

(b) to prevent any contracting party from taking any action which it considers necessary for the protection of its essential security interests
  (i) relating to fissionable materials ... ;
  (ii) relating to the traffic in arms, ammunition and implements of war and to such traffic in other goods and materials as is carried on directly or indirectly for the purpose of supplying a military establishment;
  (iii) taken in time of war or other emergency in international relations; or
(c) to prevent any contracting party from taking any action in pursuance of its obligations under the United Nations Charter for the maintenance of international peace and security.

Note that Article XXI allows both specific and general restrictions on trade. Under Article XXI(b), GATT/WTO members may restrict trade on specific goods—such as guns and military equipment—at any time. States can generally restrict trade of any goods "in time of war or other emergency." Article XXI(c) expands the exception even further, allowing any UN member to restrict trade in order to maintain "international peace and security."

Many states believe that Article XXI is a self-judging provision. Article XXI(b) allows any state to take actions "which it considers necessary." While this phrase is not included in Article XXI(c), the text does not actually require any official action or determination by the UN. For example, a state that participates in UN Security Council sanctions is surely protected by Article XXI(c). However, sanctions need not be authorized by the UN Security Council for a state to invoke Article XXI(c).

Yet despite its broad reach, Article XXI was one of the least-used provisions of the GATT. It was only invoked six times from 1948 to 2015, and it was never formally adjudicated by the GATT/WTO's dispute system.[42] For example, the US imposed a trade embargo on Nicaragua in 1985 as part of its attempt to destabilize the Nicaraguan government. Nicaragua argued that the US embargo violated numerous GATT provisions, but the US argued that its actions were legitimate under Article XXI(b)(iii). Under GATT rules at the time, states had tremendous discretion in shaping the dispute settlement process. While the US allowed a panel to hear the dispute, the panel was not allowed to assess "the validity of or the motivation for the invocation of Article XXI."[43] Because of this restriction, the panel ultimately concluded in late 1986 that it was unable to determine whether the US had violated the GATT.[44] Because it was so rarely invoked in disputes and never formally adjudicated, Article XXI received relatively little attention from trade lawyers, policy-makers, and scholars.

However, a series of recent WTO disputes brought Article XXI to the forefront of international trade law. Qatar filed numerous WTO disputes after a group of Middle East states—led by Bahrain, Egypt, Saudi Arabia, and the United Arab Emirates—imposed a blockade against the small Gulf state in 2017 over various policy disagreements. Saudi Arabia publicly justified its blockade using Article XXI.[45] However, the WTO did not rule on Qatar's complaints because the relevant states reached a diplomatic solution in 2021 and the blockade was removed.

Similarly, Russia and Ukraine descended into a trade conflict in 2014 after multiple states accused Russia of military operations in eastern Ukraine (which Russia denied) and Russia annexed Crimea, a piece of land on the Black Sea. In 2016, Ukraine filed a complaint against Russian trade policies, which Russia sought to justify under Article XXI. Seventeen WTO members joined the legal proceedings for the dispute, suggesting the systemic importance of the case.[46]

As part of the legal proceedings, the US laid out a traditional interpretation of Article XXI, stating:

> Issues of national security are political matters not susceptible for review or capable of resolution by WTO dispute settlement. Every member of the WTO retains the authority to determine for itself those matters that it considers necessary to the protection of its essential security interests, as is reflected in the text of Article XXI.[47]

In contrast, the EU took a more moderate position. It argued that when a state invokes Article XXI, its decision should be subject to review:

> Panels must review ... whether [the] invoking member can plausibly consider that the measure is necessary. This limited review is necessary in order to ensure that the exception is applied in good faith by the invoking member and prevent abuses.[48]

The WTO ultimately agreed with the EU, arguing that the dispute settlement system had authority to review Russia's interpretation of whether Article XXI applied.[49] This ruling implicitly limits how and when states can invoke national security to justify trade restrictions.

6.5 Case Study Revisited: Can the EU Ban Seal Products?

We began this chapter by describing how animal rights advocacy groups pressured the EU in 2009 to ban the sale of seal products, including fur, meat, and various by-products. Animal rights activists believed that the ban was necessary to prevent animal cruelty because seals are sometimes killed in inhumane ways. However, other EU interest groups pointed out many indigenous groups rely on the sale of seals, and that seals are not endangered animals. In fact, the EU was funding regular seal hunts in Finland and Sweden to protect fishing stocks!

To accommodate these diverse interest groups, the EU included two important exceptions to its import ban. First, the indigenous communities exception allowed the sale of products from seals hunted by indigenous communities. Second, the marine resources management exception allowed the sale of seals hunted by specific programs that managed wildlife populations in places like Finland and Sweden.

Both Canada and Norway criticized the EU rules. Both states had extensive domestic laws that banned inhumane hunting practices. These laws closely matched EU rules for commercial deer hunting. Yet most Canadian and Norwegian seal hunters could not sell their products under the IC or MRM exceptions. Canada and Norway therefore argued that the EU rules violated international trade law.

This example connects to each of the following topics:

- *Promoting international trade*: The European Union is a customs union that was created by a preferential trade agreement. The EU requires that its member states remove barriers to trade within the EU and set a common trade policy for outside states, like Canada and Norway. Canada and Norway believed that the EU law violated GATT rules, and they challenged the EU by filing a complaint at the WTO's dispute settlement system.
- *Major obligations*: The GATT sets out basic rules for market access and treatment standards. In particular, the GATT and related WTO agreements limit tariffs, quantitative restrictions, technical barriers to trade, and government procurement. The GATT also requires that its members provide most-favored-nation and national treatment to one another. These legal obligations gave Canada and Norway multiple ways to challenge the EU's laws.
- *Major exceptions*: The GATT provides four major exceptions, which allow states to escape from their trade obligations without violating international trade law. These exceptions allow states to address unfair trade, safeguard their economies from unexpected shocks, protect competing values, and preserve their national security. The EU tried to justify its trade policies using these exceptions.

We can now return to the motivating questions from the introduction. We began by asking: why did Canada and Norway believe that the EU rules violated international trade law? During legal proceedings, Canada and Norway made many different arguments using WTO agreements. Two of these arguments focused on GATT treatment standards. First, they argued that the EU rules violated GATT rules on most-favored-nation treatment. To make this argument, Canada and Norway analyzed the impact of the EU rules on Greenland, which is not an EU member. Greenland is populated by a large Inuit community that hunts seals and exports seal products to the EU. These products were allowed into the EU under the IC exception. Therefore, they argued, EU rules treated Greenland more favorably than Canada and Norway.

The WTO agreed with Canada and Norway on most-favored-nation treatment. A WTO panel first reasoned that a seal product from Canada and Norway was "like" a seal product from Greenland. The panel then argued that the EU rules gave an "advantage" of market access to Greenland because of its large Inuit population. The WTO panel wrote:

> the vast majority of seal products from Canada and Norway do not meet the [indigenous communities] requirement ... In contrast, virtually all of Greenlandic seal products are likely to qualify under the IC exception.[50]

Therefore, the WTO panel concluded that Greenland's "advantage" of market access was not "accorded immediately and unconditionally to the like product" from Canada and Norway, as required by GATT Article I. This logic was later upheld by the WTO Appellate Body.

Second, Canada and Norway argued that EU rules violated GATT rules on national treatment. To make this argument, Canada and Norway argued that the EU rules favored seal products from Finland and Sweden relative to imported seal products from Canada and Norway. Because Finland and Sweden were EU members, their seal products were "domestic products."

Once again, the WTO agreed with Canada and Norway. It wrote that a seal product from Canada and Norway was "like" a seal product from Finland or Sweden, and EU rules ensured that:

> the vast majority of seal products from Canada and Norway are excluded from the EU market by the terms of the MRM exception. In contrast, evidence shows that virtually all domestic seal products are likely to qualify for placing on the market.[51]

Therefore, the WTO panel concluded that seal products from Canada and Norway were given treatment "less favourable than that accorded to like products of national origin," thereby violating GATT Article III. After reading the panel report, the EU declined to even appeal this part of the ruling.

We then asked: how did the EU try to justify its policy? The EU could not invoke GATT/WTO exceptions about unfair trade, economic shocks, or national security to justify its rules. Instead, the EU argued that the seal ban was created to protect competing values. Namely, it argued that protecting seals was "necessary to protect public morals" under Article XX(a). Recall that in the *Gambling* dispute, the WTO ruled that:

> the content of [public morals] can vary in time and space, depending upon a range of factors, including prevailing social, cultural, ethical and religious values ... Members should be given some scope to define and apply for themselves the [concept] of "public morals" ... in their respective territories, according to their own systems and scales of values.[52]

Figure 6.6 Cuddly friend or ruthless predator? A seal pup rests on Canadian ice in 2008. The EU banned the sale of seal products in 2009, arguing that the protection of seals was "necessary to protect public morals." But Canada and Norway disagreed—they argued that seal hunting was necessary to protect fishing stocks and provide revenue to Arctic communities.

The EU reasoned that if the US public could find gambling to be immoral, then the EU public could find seal hunting to be immoral. This argument worked! The EU convinced both the panel and the Appellate Body that its objective was to "address the moral concerns of the EU public with regard to the welfare of seals," and that this objective was legitimate under Article XX(a) of the GATT.[53] However, like the earlier US lawsuits on *Gambling* and *Turtles*, the EU ran into some difficulties with the Article XX *chapeau*. The WTO ruled that both the IC and MRM exceptions created "arbitrary or unjustifiable discrimination" and hence violated Article XX.

This outcome allowed both sides to claim a partial victory. The EU could claim a partial victory because the WTO had agreed that banning seal products could be "necessary to protect public morals." Meanwhile, Canada and Norway could claim a partial victory because the WTO had found that the IC and MRM rules were "arbitrary or unjustifiable discrimination." The final Appellate Body report prompted the EU to revise its policy by eliminating the MRM exception and revising the IC exception.

Finally, we asked: what are the implications of this example for international trade law more generally? Many trade law experts were surprised that the WTO gave the EU such broad discretion in defining "public morality." They fear that the *Seals* case opens the door to abuse by states, who have been given broad discretion in defining what is a public moral.[54] For example, WTO members have long debated whether trade policy can be used to promote social objectives, like climate change mitigation or high labor standards. Thus far, the WTO has not allowed its members to "discriminate between products on the basis of the underlying processes and production methods if these leave no physical trace in the final product."[55] So a state cannot give more favorable treatment to an imported t-shirt made from sustainably farmed cotton by unionized workers. But what if a state claims that fighting climate change and protecting labor rights is a public moral? International trade experts aren't sure whether the WTO would accept such a policy. How do you think the WTO should rule?

7 Investment

7.1   Case Study: Uruguay Limits Cigarette Sales

In 2005, Uruguayan voters elected Tabaré Vázquez, a former oncologist, as their president. After decades of watching his patients battle cancer, one of Vázquez's priorities was to create new rules to limit cigarette sales. Vázquez was supported in his efforts by advocacy groups and international organizations. For example, the World Health Organization (WHO) had recently helped states to write the Framework Convention on Tobacco Control, a multilateral treaty in which states pledged to implement new domestic rules to reduce tobacco consumption. The WHO also wrote detailed guidelines about policies that had been proven to benefit public health.

Figure 7.1 A young woman hands out anti-smoking information during a 2010 meeting of the World Health Organization in Montevideo, Uruguay. The WHO supported Uruguay during its arbitration with Philip Morris over anti-smoking regulations.

Vázquez's government adopted two new anti-smoking rules. First, numerous scientific studies had shown that consumers were often misled by the design of cigarette packages. For example, they believed that cigarettes in lighter-colored boxes or labeled as "low tar" were healthier than cigarettes in darker-colored boxes. Uruguay used this evidence as justification to create a rule called the single presentation requirement (SPR). This rule prohibited cigarette companies from selling multiple varieties of a single brand. Each brand could only be associated with one product. Second, Uruguay passed a rule called the 80/80 Regulation. This rule increased the size of warning labels on cigarette packages.

One company that was affected by this rule was Philip Morris, a US firm that sold cigarettes worldwide. Prior to the new anti-smoking rules, Philip Morris sold many varieties of cigarettes in Uruguay through its local subsidiary. For example, it sold four different varieties under the brand name of "Marlboro." These included "Marlboro Red," "Marlboro Gold," "Marlboro Blue," and "Marlboro Green (Fresh Mint)."[1] Under the new SPR rule, Philip Morris had to eliminate three of these varieties because it could only sell one kind of "Marlboro" cigarette. Additionally, the new 80/80 Regulation ensured that almost the entire cigarette package was covered by a warning label, giving Philip Morris little space to display its logo and product information.

Other states were were also debating whether to pass new anti-smoking rules being promoted by the WHO, including Canada, Ireland, and New Zealand. So Philip Morris decided to make an example of Uruguay. In early 2010, it filed an arbitration case against Uruguay. In this case, Philip Morris argued that Uruguay had broken international investment law.

But why exactly did Philip Morris believe that Uruguay had broken international law? And why did Uruguay believe that Philip Morris had been treated fairly and appropriately? More generally, is international investment law good for society? Should you support international investment law or oppose it?

To answer these questions, we must first understand the following topics:

- *Protecting foreign investment*: Why do states sign treaties that protect foreign investors? How has international investment law evolved in response to international economics and politics?
- *Foreign investor rights*: What major protections does international law give to foreign investors? How do foreign investors uphold these rights?
- *Preserving state authority*: How does international investment law balance investor rights against a state's authority to regulate its economy? What aspects of international investment law are controversial in domestic politics?

This chapter focuses on **foreign direct investment** (FDI), which involves the investment of capital from a firm in one state into business activities that take place in another state.[2] For an investment to qualify as FDI, the firm must have a long time-horizon and be directly involved in the management of business activities abroad.[3] For example, when a US firm drills an oil well in Venezuela or builds a factory in Mexico, it expects to conduct business abroad for many years. A firm that engages in FDI is often called a multinational corporation.

FDI usually involves the purchase of **immobile assets**, which are assets that cannot be easily moved or redeployed for other activities. For example, drilling a new oil well requires that a firm sink millions of dollars into the ground. Similarly, building a new manufacturing plant can involve developing infrastructure, installing utilities, purchasing heavy machinery, and training workers. These activities all involve high upfront costs that cannot be easily reclaimed. An investor must have a relatively long time-horizon to be profitable with these high upfront costs.

Foreign investors like Philip Morris face inherent political risk because they conduct their activities in multiple states. As shown in Figure 7.2, most FDI flows into developed states, which tend to have strong legal protections for property rights. Yet a growing amount of FDI goes into developing states. These developing states can offer foreign investors profitable economic opportunities, yet they also often have weak domestic legal systems. Historically, many foreign firms that invested in developing states have had difficulty protecting their property,

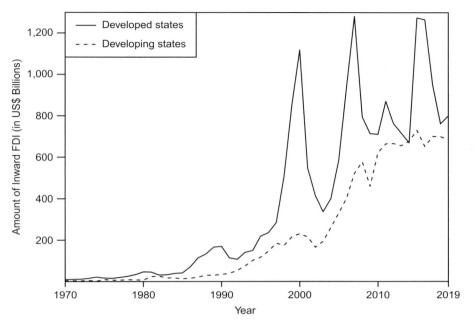

Figure 7.2 Inward foreign direct investment.
Source: Figure drawn by author using data from UNCTAD.

particularly when they had immobile assets. Foreign investors that could not easily leave a state and reclaim their upfront costs were targets for mistreatment by their host governments.

Section 7.2 begins by describing key concepts that underlie foreign direct investment and discusses two competing perspectives on why states sign investment treaties. It then describes the historical evolution of international investment law with an emphasis on economic and political factors. Section 7.3 outlines major foreign investor rights under international law. Next, section 7.4 discusses legal and political attempts to balance foreign investor rights against the state authority to regulate. Finally, section 7.5 returns to the example of Uruguay's cigarette rules.

7.2   Protecting Foreign Investment

Investment law is one of the most controversial areas of international law. This controversy stems from two major sources. First, experts often disagree about why states use investment law. Second, investment law has a complex and highly politicized past.

Concepts

Both supporters and opponents of investment law usually agree that foreign direct investment comes with benefits for developing states. After all, foreign investors pay taxes, create jobs, train workers, and develop local infrastructure. All of these activities create positive externalities, or benefits that spill over to other areas of the economy. However, opponents of investment law also emphasize the costs that can come with FDI, like pressure from foreign investors on the government to have weak environmental and labor regulations.

Most economic and political disagreements over international investment law can be analyzed using two competing explanations for why states sign investment treaties. Supporters of investment law generally believe that developing states use investment law to solve a commitment problem, while opponents of investment law generally believe that investment law reflects competition between developing states for limited capital. These two competing perspectives—commitment versus competition—are based on different assumptions about the challenges faced by states that seek foreign capital. Accordingly, they each generate different conclusions about the economic and political effects of international law.

Commitment Perspective

Supporters of international investment law tend to argue that developing states face a **commitment problem**, which is a situation in which sequential decision-making ensures that the plan of action that is initially optimal becomes suboptimal as time passes.[4] From this perspective, strategic interactions between a foreign firm and host government unfold sequentially over time. As shown in Figure 7.3, the firm must first decide whether to invest in the host state. If the firm decides to invest, then the host government must decide whether to take the firm's investment.

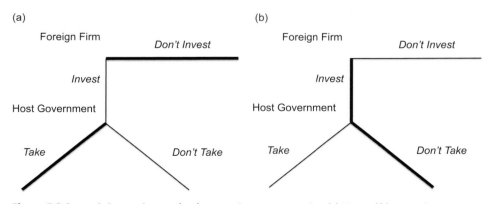

Figure 7.3 Strategic interactions under the commitment perspective. (a) No credible commitment to protect foreign investment; (b) Credible commitment to protect foreign investment.
Notes: Panel (a) shows expected decisions by rational actors if the host government cannot credibly commit to protecting foreign investment. Panel (b) shows expected decisions by rational actors if the host government can credibly commit. Thick lines show the expected behavior of rational actors.

The commitment perspective is built upon three key assumptions about foreign direct investment. First, it implicitly assumes that FDI involves predominantly immobile assets. That is, the foreign firm cannot invest its capital in the host state and then easily recover its capital if it suspects that the host government is going to take. Investment is essentially a one-time choice. Second, it assumes that taking is an all-or-nothing choice. That is, the host government cannot take a small portion of the investment by increasing taxes or regulation. Finally, the commitment perspective focuses on the interactions between a foreign firm and one potential host state. For example, the foreign firm cannot ask two different states to compete with each other.

From the firm's perspective, the investment is only profitable if its property rights are respected. The worst outcome is accordingly to invest and have its assets taken; the better outcome is to not invest in the first place (and presumably pursue other investment opportunities); and the best outcome is to invest and not experience expropriation. From the host government's perspective, the worst outcome is to not receive the investment. However, if the firm does invest, then the host government will be tempted to take the investment.

A firm that is a rational actor should be able to infer the consequences of its investment decision, given these incentives. The thick lines in Figure 7.3(a) show the expected decisions of each actor if the host government cannot credibly commit to protecting the foreign investment. If the firm invests, then the host government has incentive to take, yielding the firm's worst possible outcome. The firm is accordingly better-off if it refuses to invest in the first stage. However, note that this is a suboptimal outcome for both the firm and the host government. After all, the host government prefers receiving the investment to not receiving it.

Why do the foreign firm and host government end up in a suboptimal outcome? Since the host government stands to benefit from this investment, it has an incentive to make promises to the firm about how the firm will be treated. However, if these promises aren't credible, it will be tempted to renege after the investment is made.

Now suppose that the host government can write a contract in which it pledges not to expropriate from the foreign firm. If this contract can be enforced, then there will be a cost associated with breaking the contract. If the cost of taking the foreign investment is sufficiently large, then the host government will find it better to not take the foreign investment. The thick lines in Figure 7.3(b) show the expected decisions of each actor in this revised scenario: the firm will invest and its property will not be taken by the host government. Comparing outcomes from the two scenarios shows that both players are better-off when the host government can credibly commit to protecting foreign investment.

How can such credible commitments be made? How do we move from the decisions in Figure 7.3(a) to the decisions in Figure 7.3(b)? Put differently, what makes it costly for host governments to take property from foreign firms? In states with independent domestic courts, the host government can simply write a contract and know that if it breaks the contract, it will face costly court cases that it is likely to lose. Yet many developing states lack independent domestic courts. In such states, the government can break contracts knowing that domestic courts will uphold its actions.

Some scholars argue that the global market for capital inherently constrains host states. Suppose that foreign firms are unwilling to invest in a state where a government has previously broken its contract with another foreign firm. If past government behavior affects future investment decisions, then a capital-seeking government may honor its commitments to foreign firms even if it is not constrained by a domestic court. When a government must repeatedly seek foreign capital, it has an incentive to cultivate a reputation for honoring its contracts with foreign firms.

While this argument about the constraining effect of global capital is both compelling and plausible, reputation is only effective—that is, induces a government to honor a commitment that it would otherwise break—if future firms change their investment decisions based on a government's past behavior. Even if firms are simple profit-maximizing actors, the host government's past behavior may not change firm decision-making. For example, the potential return on capital may be so large that firms will take the risk that the government will break its promises in the future. Or firms may believe that the government broke its previous promises because of extraordinary circumstances that are unlikely to recur. Alternatively, firms may not be able to observe the host government's treatment of previous firms, or may be uncertain about whether the government has broken a contract. Finally, even if a firm knows for certain that a host government has broken its past promises to others, it may believe that this past behavior is irrelevant to how it will be treated in the future. Differences in nationality, industry, government composition, and other factors might lead a firm to disregard past behavior. For example, a US software firm that invests in a state ruled by a right-wing government may not care whether a previous left-wing government broke its contract with a European energy firm.[5]

Supporters of international investment law argue that signing investment treaties and accepting the jurisdiction of international legal bodies make it more costly for states to take property from foreign firms. Under this perspective, international law solves the commitment problem faced by states that lack independent domestic courts. Put differently, international law may allow a state to solve its commitment problem, which in turn stimulates FDI and benefits the developing state.

Competition Perspective
Critics of international investment law tend to argue that developing states face a **collaboration problem**, which is a situation in which states jointly benefit from

choosing the same action, but each state is tempted to unilaterally deviate to a different action.[6] Under this theoretical perspective, multiple developing states must compete to secure foreign investment by choosing their taxes and regulations. Lower taxes and less stringent regulations are assumed to yield higher profits for foreign investors. This perspective tends to emphasize simultaneous decision-making by competitive states.

The competition perspective is built upon three key assumptions about FDI. First, it implicitly assumes that foreign direct investment involves predominantly **mobile assets**—which can be easily moved or redeployed for other activities—because it assumes that if a host state changes its policies, then foreign investors can quickly change their investment strategies. For example, if one state lowers its tax rate, it will benefit and other potential host states will be harmed because investors will redeploy their assets. Investment is therefore an ongoing choice and capital can move easily across different host states. Second, the competition perspective usually assumes that host governments can choose to incrementally take value from foreign firms using taxes and regulations. Taking is not an all-or-nothing choice because states compete over how much they take from foreign investors. Finally, the commitment perspective focuses on the interactions between multiple potential host states.

Under the competition perspective, two or more states that want foreign capital must simultaneously decide whether to make binding promises to protect foreign investment. All else equal, the firm will prefer to send its FDI wherever it will receive the highest profit. So as one state lowers its taxes or weakens its regulations, more capital will flow into the state from foreign investors.

The competition perspective suggests that the expected outcome is a "race-to-the-bottom," in which the states set low taxes and weak regulations to lure in FDI. A state that chooses higher taxes or stronger regulations will be "punished" by losing access to foreign capital. The outcome of the competition perspective is thus one that benefits foreign investors (who can expect high profits), but harms states, which end up with little tax revenue and lax regulations.

Why can't the host states cooperate by jointly raising taxes and increasing socially beneficial regulations? Under the competition perspective, cooperation is difficult because each state will be tempted to undercut the other to secure more foreign investment. The main conclusion of the competition perspective is that investment law privileges foreign firms at the expense of developing states. States that seek FDI are not helped by investment law; they are harmed by it.

Evolution

The evolution of international investment law has been closely connected to economic and political changes worldwide. Here we provide a chronological account of this evolution.

Early Investment Law

Early investment law was grounded in the economic development of Latin America. After the Napoleonic Wars ended in 1815, European firms began to seek new investment opportunities abroad. As new states in Latin America achieved their independence, they attracted investment from firms in France, Germany, and the UK. These investments came in the form of both foreign direct investment—often for railroads, canals, and other large infrastructure projects—and loans to the newly independent governments.

Despite the large potential for growth in these Latin American states, these investments came with high levels of political risk. Newly independent states in Latin America faced frequent international and civil conflicts, as well as chronic economic instability. Many European and US firms that faced difficulties in Latin America sought help from their home governments. This help often came in the form of gunboat diplomacy, in which European and US governments used the threat of military force to protect the economic interests of their firms abroad. Developed and developing states were divided on an important legal question: what international legal obligations do states have regarding the treatment of foreign firms?

On one side, developed states—predominantly European states and the US—believed that international law provided basic protections to foreign firms, or a minimum standard of treatment. These developed states believed that even if a developing state lacked a well-functioning domestic court or was involved in a civil conflict, foreign firms were entitled to the basic rule of law and security. Additionally, developed states believed that customary international law provided them with the **right to diplomatic protection**, which is the doctrine that states have the right to protect their nationals at the international level. They believed that they could intervene diplomatically (and even militarily) to ensure that their firms were treated fairly by other states.

The viewpoint of developed states was most clearly articulated in 1940 by Cordell Hull, the US Secretary of State. In a series of letters to the Mexican Foreign Minister, Hull advocated for US firms that had their property taken by the Mexican government. After decades of negotiations and legal proceedings, not a single claim was paid to US investors.[7] In response, Hull wrote:

> The Government of the United States readily recognizes the right of a sovereign state to expropriate property for public purposes ... [Yet] the right to expropriate property is coupled with and conditioned on the obligation to make adequate, effective and prompt compensation.[8]

Hull's claim that states must provide prompt, adequate, and effective compensation if they expropriate property from foreign firms quickly became known as the **Hull Doctrine**. From the US perspective, foreign firms were entitled to compensation, regardless of how Mexico treated its own firms. The implication of this

Figure 7.4 The cover of the French publication, *Le Petit Parisien*, from 9 February 1903, shows German warships bombing Venezuela. Venezuela had previously defaulted on its foreign debt and refused to compensate foreign investors for the damages that they suffered during a civil war. In response, Germany, Italy, and the UK blockaded Venezuelan ports in 1902–1903. Scholars use the term "gunboat diplomacy" to describe such use of force to protect the economic interests of foreign investors.

perspective was that international law protected foreign firms, but did not protect comparable domestic firms.

On the other side, the developing states of Latin America argued that when developed states (like the US) asserted diplomatic protection, they were asserting political power, not inherent legal rights. They argued that when developed states used diplomacy and force to protect their firms in developing states, they violated the principles of the sovereign equality of states and the right to non-intervention. This viewpoint was articulated by Carlos Calvo, a noted Argentine diplomat and legal historian in the late 1800s. Both his publications and his private letters led to the development of the **Calvo Doctrine**. In its narrow form, the Calvo Doctrine asserts that foreigners are not entitled to more favorable treatment than domestic nationals. In its broad form, the Calvo Doctrine asserts that the principle of sovereign equality allows all states to set their own economic policies without interference by other states.

Many Latin American states promoted the Calvo Doctrine using their domestic constitutions.[9] While a domestic constitution is not a source of international law, it does constrain how a state's domestic courts treat foreign firms. Additionally, widespread practice at the domestic level can indicate customary international law or a general principle of law. Therefore, Latin American states tried to promote the Calvo Doctrine at the international level by adopting it at the domestic level. For example, the 2009 Bolivian Constitution prohibits foreign firms from seeking diplomatic protection from their home governments and mandates that foreign firms are not entitled to more favorable treatment than domestic firms.[10]

Additionally, Latin American states promoted the Calvo Doctrine by requiring that foreign firms renounce their right to diplomatic protection in contracts that they signed with Latin American states. States disagreed over whether these contract terms, commonly known as Calvo Clauses, were legally valid under international law. For example, in the *Dredging* case, an international arbitral tribunal was asked to rule in 1926 on the validity of a Calvo Clause signed by a US firm operating in Mexico. The tribunal issued a mixed ruling, finding that while the US firm had renounced its own right to diplomatic protection in the contract dispute, it did not have authority to renounce the right of the US government to provide diplomatic protection. While the ruling was criticized by legal scholars, who found it "inconsistent and illogical," it was supported by states as a political compromise.[11]

Neither developed nor developing states were able to embed their preferred legal standards into international treaties. This led to much disagreement about what constraints (if any) international law created on states and foreign investment. Latin American states could point to their own domestic constitutions and written contracts with foreign firms. In contrast, developed states could point to the *Dredging* ruling (and other related arbitration cases), which upheld the fundamental right of states to provide diplomatic protection to their nationals.

Changing Patterns After World War II

The politics of foreign investment disputes changed after World War II. The spread of communism in Eastern Europe and the decolonization of Africa and Asia led to a surge in expropriation of foreign investments. States that adhered to communist ideology believed in collective, rather than private, ownership of property. Furthermore, states that were newly independent often viewed the existing property rights of foreigners as the spoils of colonialism. They often equated decolonization with expropriation, and believed that by taking foreign-owned property, they were merely reclaiming what had been taken from them by their colonizers.

After World War II, most developing states actively promoted economic policies referred to as **import substitution industrialization** (ISI). States that adopted ISI believed that the key to economic growth was economic self-sufficiency. Rather than exporting raw goods (usually to their former colonial ruler) and importing manufactured goods, these developing states wanted to break their economic dependence on developed states by manufacturing their own goods. To implement ISI policies, governments actively managed their domestic economies, and often engaged directly in business activities by creating state-owned entities, like government-owned oil firms. Developing states financed these activities largely by issuing long-term government bonds. They believed that government debt was preferable to FDI and its potential for external political influence.

At the same time, these developing states formed a political coalition within the UN known as the **Group of 77**. This coalition of 77 developing states tried to promote common interests by using their voting power in the UN General Assembly (UNGA), which gives each state in the international system an equal vote. While the General Assembly does not have the legal authority to create international law, international courts often refer to UNGA resolutions when assessing customary international law. Since developed states often insisted that the Hull Doctrine was binding under customary international law, the Group of 77 sought to refute this claim by passing a series of UNGA resolutions in which they put forth their own preferred legal standards for foreign investment.

In the early 1960s, UNGA resolutions emphasized that "economic and financial agreements between the developed and the developing states must be based on the principles of equality and of the right of peoples and nations to self-determination."[12] Developing states asserted the right to expropriate under limited circumstances, provided that the state "paid appropriate compensation, in accordance with the rules in force in the state taking such measures in the exercise of its sovereignty and in accordance with international law."[13] However, by the early 1970s the rhetoric grew more heated, as the Group of 77 asserted an "inalienable right ... to the full exercise of national sovereignty over ... natural resources."[14] Rather than being constrained by international law, the Group of 77 argued that states could decide for themselves "the amount of possible compensation and the mode of payment."[15]

In 1974, the Group of 77 declared the formation of a **New International Economic Order**, which was a set of trade, investment, development, and assistance policies to promote the interests of developing states. These policies were articulated in a document called the Charter of Economic Rights and Duties of States, which was adopted as a UNGA resolution. The Charter asserted that "every state has and shall freely exercise full permanent sovereignty, including possession, use and disposal, over all its wealth, natural resources and economic activities."[16] It explicitly rejected the minimum standard of treatment for foreign firms, stating that "no state shall be compelled to grant preferential treatment to foreign investment."[17] Additionally, it asserted that states had the right "to nationalize, expropriate or transfer ownership of foreign property, in which case appropriate compensation should be paid by the State adopting such measures, taking into account its relevant laws and regulations and all circumstances that the State considers pertinent."[18] So while the Charter said that a state "should" compensate a foreign firm for an expropriation, the Charter did not require compensation. Additionally, the amount of compensation was self-judging: a state that took foreign property could determine for itself how much to pay based on any criteria it chose. The Charter was a clear renunciation of the Hull Doctrine.

Rise of Modern Investment Law

In the 1980s, the politics of international investment law once again changed in response to changes in the global economy. The fifteen- and twenty-year government bonds that developing states had issued in the 1960s and 1970s to finance import substitution industrialization began to mature, meaning that the developing states had to pay back the money they had borrowed. Yet developing states had not grown quickly enough to pay back their debts. State-owned enterprises were generally inefficient compared to their privately owned competitors, in part because they lacked the technology and expertise of the privately owned firms in developed states. Additionally, while the oil crises of the 1970s were a boon for states that produced oil, they were a major financial hardship for states that relied on foreign oil. These factors led to a major debt crisis in the 1980s in which developing states were unable to repay their debts.

This debt crisis caused most developing states to become reliant on massive financial assistance from the International Monetary Fund and other international organizations. However, this money came with conditions—later coined the **Washington Consensus**—that were intended to prevent future economic crises. One major Washington Consensus policy was to encourage FDI in order to stimulate growth without raising government debt. Other Washington Consensus policies included lowering trade barriers and privatizing state-owned enterprises. These policies were highly contentious. Critics of the Washington Consensus argued that developed states and the International Monetary Fund used their economic power to coerce poor states into adopting policies that privileged rich states. Supporters of the Washington Consensus argued that the experiences of developing states showed that ISI doesn't work, and that development requires that a state be integrated into the world economy, not isolated.

The Washington Consensus received a further boost when the Soviet Union collapsed in 1989. States that were formerly under the political control of the Soviet Union had to decide how to move forward. After decades of socialist rule and economic stagnation, states in Eastern Europe and Central Asia began to adopt Washington Consensus policies. In particular, they wanted to attract FDI to fuel economic development.

These economic and political forces led to a surge in investment treaties. Most of these agreements are bilateral investment treaties, in which pairs of states create legal rights and remedies for one another's firms. However, other kinds of treaties sometimes include special protections for foreign investment. For example, the Energy Charter Treaty, which is a multilateral agreement that aims to promote cooperation in the energy industry, contains protections for some foreign investors. Also, many international trade agreements contain investment provisions. For example, the North American Free Trade Agreement (NAFTA) has rules to protect foreign investment between Canada, Mexico, and the US. Figure 7.5 shows the rise in the number of investment treaties over time. As of 2020, almost 2,700 investment treaties were in force, creating a complex web of treaty protections for foreign firms. Nearly every state in the world now belongs to at least one investment agreement, and large economies like China and the US belong to well over a hundred investment treaties each.

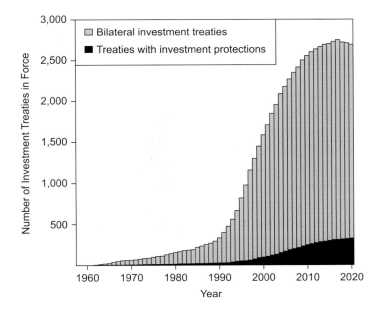

Figure 7.5 Rise in investment treaties.
Notes: The number of investment treaties in force grew dramatically from the 1990s. Beginning around 2016, there is a slight decline in investment treaties that reflects some of the political backlash against international investment law.
Source: Figure drawn by author using data from UNCTAD.

7.3   Foreign Investor Rights

Because of the proliferation of bilateral and regional investment treaties, modern international investment law lacks the standardization and coherence of other areas of international law. Disputes often hinge on the details of specific treaties and firm-specific contracts. Yet most modern investment treaties contain four kinds of foreign investor rights: expropriation rules; treatment standards; limits on performance requirements; and legal remedies.

Expropriation

Modern international law recognizes two types of expropriation. **Direct expropriation** occurs when a government's actions deprive a firm of the full value of its investment. This is also sometimes called "outright expropriation." For example, foreign investment flowed into Russia in the late 1980s and early 1990s as the Soviet Union transitioned into modern-day Russia. Franz Sedelmayer, a German citizen with a law enforcement background, invested in the Russian security industry. In 1990, he formed a joint-venture with the local police department in Leningrad. They created a firm that sold law enforcement equipment and training to government bodies, and provided security services to private individuals and businesses. Over time, the firm became caught up in ongoing disputes between the local and the national government over the ownership of government property. Then in 1994, Boris Yeltsin, President of Russia, seized ownership of the building in which Sedelmayer's firm operated. After unsuccessfully challenging the government seizure in Russian courts, Sedelmayer filed a request for international arbitration. During the international proceedings, Sedelmayer successfully argued that the Russian directive violated a 1989 investment treaty between West Germany and the Soviet Union, and that Sedelmayer was entitled to compensation for the expropriation of his property.[19]

In contrast, **indirect expropriation** occurs when a government's actions violate pre-existing contracts or laws, and substantially reduce the value of a foreign firm's property, often via taxation or regulation. Because indirect expropriation involves reduced value, rather than outright taking, it is sometimes called "creeping expropriation." For example, a US firm named Metalclad purchased a site in 1993 being used to construct a hazardous waste landfill in Mexico. Before making the purchase, Metalclad received assurances from both the federal and state governments that the previous Mexican owners had obtained all necessary permits and authorizations for the landfill. Shortly after its purchase, Metalclad began to experience difficulties with the local government, which insisted that Metalclad needed an additional construction permit to build the landfill. The local government refused to issue this permit on environmental grounds, effectively halting all construction. After years of negotiations, Metalclad filed a request for international arbitration, arguing that Mexico had violated the investment protections included in the NAFTA. The Mexican government's actions were not direct expropriation because Metalclad continued to own the land. Yet Metalclad argued that the local government's actions were indirect expropriation because the denial of a construction permit reduced the value of the land, which could no longer be made into a hazardous waste landfill. An arbitration tribunal agreed with Metalclad:

> expropriation under NAFTA includes not only open, deliberate and acknowledged takings of property, such as outright seizure …, but also covert or incidental interference with the use of property which has the effect of depriving the owner, in whole or in significant part, of the use or reasonably-to-be-expected economic benefit of property even if not necessarily to the obvious benefit of the host state.[20]

Even though indirect expropriation does not require outright taking by the government, investment tribunals are usually unwilling to make a finding of expropriation if a host government's actions are temporary or only slightly reduce the value of an investment. In another dispute, a NAFTA tribunal ruled that "expropriation requires a 'substantial deprivation'" of the value of an investment.[21] Minor changes in regulation that reduce the profitability of an investment are unlikely to meet the legal definition of "expropriation," especially if a firm remains in full control of its investment.

It is difficult to make broad assertions about the politics and practice of expropriation, particularly based on arbitration cases. We can only observe disputes in which foreign firms have legal remedies and the financial resources to pursue those remedies. Additionally, not all legal claims that are brought by firms are successful. Nonetheless, claims of indirect expropriation are much more common than claims of direct expropriation, suggesting that much of the contemporary politics over foreign direct investment involves regulation and taxation, rather than outright taking.

Treatment Standards

Modern international law has four major treatment standards, which are rules that set standards for how a government treats foreign investors. The first two standards—national and most-favored-nation treatment—are relative standards: they constrain how a host government treats a particular firm, relative to how it treats other comparable firms. The second two standards—full protection and security, and fair and equitable treatment—are absolute standards: they are not influenced by how the government treats other firms.

National Treatment

The **national treatment** standard requires that a foreign investor receive treatment that is at least as favorable as the treatment received by a similar domestic investor, who is usually defined as an investor in "like circumstances." This relative standard closely matches the concept of national treatment under international trade law.

For example, in *Cargill* v. *Poland*, a US company challenged Polish rules that limited the production of isoglucose, a food and beverage sweetener. Since Cargill was the only producer of isoglucose in Poland, the Polish government argued that its rules did not discriminate against the company based on its nationality. However, Cargill successfully argued to an arbitration tribunal that it was "in like circumstances" with domestic sugar producers, which received more favorable treatment. The tribunal ruled that the Polish rules violated the national treatment standard, since they treated isoglucose less favorably than they treated sugar.[22]

Most–Favored–Nation Treatment
The **most-favored-nation treatment** standard requires that a foreign firm must receive treatment that is at least as favorable as the treatment received by a foreign national from another state. This relative standard mimics the most-favored-nation principle under international trade law.

For example, in *ATA Construction* v. *Jordan*, a Turkish firm attempted to sue Jordan, arguing that it was not treated fairly by a domestic court. Jordan's international investment agreement with Turkey didn't directly give the firm very strong legal claims, but it granted most-favored-nation treatment to Turkish firms in Jordan. ATA Construction was accordingly able to invoke more favorable legal protections in treaties that Jordan signed with other states. Namely, ATA argued that Jordan had violated provisions of its investment treaties with Croatia, Spain, and the United Kingdom.[23]

Cases that successfully invoke most-favored-nation treatment are relatively rare. Most investment treaties contain common core legal standards, which perhaps make it unnecessary to invoke treaties signed with other states.[24] Alternatively, the detail-oriented nature of investment disputes may make it difficult for firms to argue that they are being treated worse than a foreign firm from a different state that is in otherwise like circumstances.[25]

Full Protection and Security
The third treatment standard requires that host governments provide **full protection and security** to foreign firms. This absolute treatment standard requires that host governments refrain from military attacks against foreign firms and their property.

For example, in *Asian Agricultural Products* v. *Sri Lanka*, a UK firm that operated a shrimp farm in Sri Lanka sought compensation after a military operation in which Sri Lankan forces seized control of its shrimp farm and killed several staff members. The Sri Lankan government argued that the shrimp farm was under the control of rebel forces, who were responsible for the damage. The UK firm could not prove that the military caused the property damage. Yet the investment tribunal found that the host government was responsible for the damage because it did not take sufficient action to protect human life and property.[26]

Fair and Equitable Treatment

Finally, and most controversially, modern investment law usually requires that host governments provide **fair and equitable treatment** to foreign firms. This absolute treatment standard is also sometimes referred to as the modern-day "minimum standard of treatment." The precise meaning of "fair and equitable treatment" has evolved over time, but legal claims under this standard often include:

- violations of due process in judicial and administrative proceedings;
- non-transparency about government policies and procedures;
- arbitrary, unreasonable, or discriminatory treatment;
- policy changes that violate the legitimate expectations about the regulatory environment; and
- acting in bad faith towards foreign firms.

Recall that in the *Metalclad* case discussed above, a US firm sued Mexico after the local government refused to issue the firm a construction permit. One major question in the dispute was whether the local government even had the legal authority to require and issue such a construction permit. The tribunal wrote that the lack of transparency about government regulations violated Metalclad's right to fair and equitable treatment:

> all relevant legal requirements for the purpose of initiating, completing and successfully operating investments made, or intended to be made, under [NAFTA] should be capable of being readily known to all affected investors ... There should be no room for doubt or uncertainty on such matters. Once the authorities of the central government ... become aware of any scope for misunderstanding or confusion in this connection, it is their duty to ensure that the correct position is promptly determined and clearly stated so that investors can proceed with all appropriate expedition in the confident belief that they are acting in accordance with all relevant laws.[27]

Similarly, in *Micula* v. *Romania*, Swedish investors sued the Romanian government for revoking financial incentives that were designed to promote investment in underdeveloped portions of the state.[28] Romania argued that its actions were reasonable because they were required in order to join the European Union, which was one of Romania's major policy objectives at the time. The arbitral tribunal found that even though Romania acted reasonably when it revoked the financial incentives to pursue EU membership, this nonetheless "undermined the Claimants' legitimate expectations" about access to the financial incentives.[29] As such, Romania failed to provide fair and equitable treatment to the investors.

Limits on Performance Requirements

Host governments often attempt to protect their local economies and promote development by imposing **performance requirements**, which are specific policies pertaining to production and sales. For example, if a foreign firm wants to build a factory to manufacture shoes, the host government may require that the foreign firm export its goods so that domestically owned shoe producers are protected from economic competition. Alternatively, the host government may require that the foreign firm purchase local materials (called domestic content), or hire a minimum number of local workers. The host government may also mandate that the firm share its manufacturing technology with local shoe producers.

Many developed states have tried to limit such performance requirements. For example, NAFTA Article 1106 says:

(1) No Party may impose or enforce any of the following requirements ...
   (a) to export a given level or percentage of goods or services;
   (b) to achieve a given level or percentage of domestic content;
   (c) to purchase, use or accord a preference to goods produced or services provided in its territory, or to purchase goods or services from persons in its territory; ...
   (f) to transfer technology, a production process or other proprietary knowledge to a person in its territory ...

Limits on performance requirements are not as common as the expropriation rules and treatments standards discussed above. Yet they are sometimes included in investment treaties and invoked in arbitration disputes between foreign firms and their host governments. For example, in *Mobil Investments* v. *Canada*, a US oil firm challenged Canadian rules that required the firm to invest a minimum amount of expenditure on "research and development" and "education and training" in Newfoundland, the site of offshore drilling. In a 2012 decision, an arbitration tribunal ruled that both "research and development" and "education and training" constituted "services" under NAFTA Article 1106(1)(c).[30] Accordingly, the tribunal found that Canada had violated investment law.

Legal Remedies

Finally, and perhaps most importantly, modern investment law provides foreign firms with legal remedies via **investor–state dispute settlement** (ISDS). Prior to the 1980s, foreign firms had to rely primarily on diplomatic protection when they experienced problems with their host states. This diplomatic protection sometimes resulted in arbitration, as in oil nationalization disputes involving Libya and Kuwait in the 1970s. Additionally, states tried to use the International Court of Justice a few times to protect their foreign investors.

However, ISDS eschews these traditional forms of diplomatic protection. While foreign firms may sometimes seek assistance from their home state, particularly in the early stages of a dispute, ISDS gives firms legal standing to represent their own interests in investment disputes. As illustrated by the numerous arbitration cases described above, most modern investment treaties allow foreign firms to file arbitration cases if a host government violates its legal obligations.

Just as legal obligations are highly fragmented under modern investment law, so, too, are legal remedies. Most ISDS cases are currently overseen by the **International Center for the Settlement of Investment Disputes** in Washington, DC. This international organization was created under the auspices of the World Bank in 1966 to promote foreign investment. Yet investment treaties usually give firms multiple options about where and how to pursue arbitration cases. Other institutions that regularly oversee ISDS cases include: the International Chamber of Commerce in Paris, the London Court of International Arbitration, the Permanent Court of Arbitration in The Hague, and the Stockholm Chamber of Commerce. None of these institutions has a sitting panel of judges to hear cases. Rather, cases are heard by three-person panels of arbitrators that are selected ad hoc, on a case-by-case basis. Each side is allowed to appoint a single arbitrator, with the third person chosen jointly by the two appointees.

Investment arbitration is often a private process. Even if litigants publicly disclose that arbitration has occurred, they still often refuse to disclose the actual outcome of arbitration.[31] Yet the stunning rise in the number of known ISDS cases (shown in Figure 7.6) suggests the growing importance of arbitration in enforcing international investment law. Arbitration is not easy. Recent studies found that foreign firms demand, on average, US$884 million in damages, and average reported litigation costs are approximately 10 percent of the value of the award, suggesting that foreign firms often pay tens of millions of dollars for enforcement.[32] This pattern presents a major political problem, as it suggests that international investment law primarily benefits powerful and rich firms, who arguably have the most political influence even without legal protection.

When a firm successfully sues its host state using ISDS, does it actually get compensated? The privacy that surrounds investment arbitration makes it difficult to know how often host states voluntarily pay compensation. However, the ISDS system was set up to facilitate the enforcement of arbitration awards. Any state that is a member of the ICSID is required to recognize and enforce its awards at the domestic level. Additionally, most states are members of the 1958 New York Convention, which is an international treaty that requires its signatories to recognize and enforce arbitration awards. These rules allow investors to use domestic courts to seize the assets of a foreign state—such as foreign bank accounts and real estate—if the government refuses to pay the investor compensation after losing an investment arbitration case. In theory, the threat of domestic enforcement should make host governments more willing to pay firms in the first place. Yet in practice, it is often difficult for investors to successfully seize assets because states can invoke domestic and international rules regarding state immunity to try to protect their assets.[33]

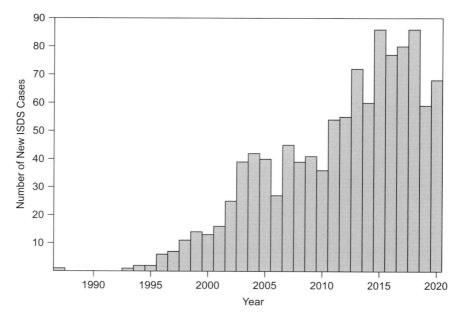

Figure 7.6 Rise of investor–state dispute settlement.
Notes: ISDS cases have grown in popularity since the late 1990s. Some of these cases—including the *Philip Morris* case—have prompted a political backlash against international investment law.
Source: Figure drawn by author using data from UNCTAD.

7.4   Preserving State Authority

The rise in investment treaties with foreign investor rights was driven by the rhetoric of the Washington Consensus, and the belief that states faced a commitment problem when seeking FDI. However, some states and advocacy groups have pushed back against this trend. In international judicial bodies, they argue that customary international law allows states to sometimes break their treaty commitments. Outside of these judicial bodies, they stoke a political backlash to international investment law. We discuss each of these trends in turn.

Police Powers Doctrine

Many states have tried to defend themselves in investment arbitration by arguing that international law includes the **police powers doctrine**, which is the principle that a state has an inherent right to protect the public interest. They argue that this customary right trumps any conflicting investor rights under treaty law. Some modern investment treaties explicitly include the police powers doctrine. However, states that assert this doctrine in international arbitration usually must invoke customary international law, meaning that they must prove state practice and acceptance of law. Some historical examples suggest that a state can violate foreign investor rights without paying compensation if the state is acting to protect public health, morals, or order.

In the clearest examples, states used their police forces to preserve public order. For example, when a foreign investor is suspected of a crime, police forces often search and seize evidence (like business documents) from her home and office. If a foreign investor is convicted of a crime, domestic law may allow the state to seize the investor's property as punishment. All of these actions would be considered legitimate under the police powers doctrine if the state provided due process to the investor.[34]

Another example of the police powers doctrine would be the many economic shutdowns worldwide that began in 2020 during the global pandemic. In early 2020, many states had outbreaks of COVID-19, a newly discovered deadly virus with no proven medical treatment. In response, many states imposed temporary economic closures in areas with high infection rates. These shutdowns generated enormous financial losses for both domestic and foreign investors. While no international judicial body has assessed these shutdowns under international investment law, states viewed the temporary economic closures as a legitimate and necessary use of their authority to protect public health.

What limits do states face when they invoke the police powers doctrine? Legal experts argue that states must satisfy three requirements to invoke the police powers doctrine. First, states must act in **good faith** when they assert the police powers doctrine, meaning that states must act fairly and honestly towards foreign investors.[35] Second, laws and regulations must be non-discriminatory, meaning that they treat all comparable investors in the same manner. Finally, laws and regulations must be proportionate, meaning that they clearly relate to their intended objective, and are neither overly broad nor under-inclusive.

For example, imagine that you live in a state that is experiencing an outbreak of a highly contagious disease in its capital. Suppose that the state orders a temporary economic closure of businesses in the capital. Additionally, suppose that the state allows certain businesses—like grocery stores and pharmacies—to continue operating so that people in the capital city can get the necessary supplies to survive. This policy would likely be justified under the police powers doctrine. However, other policies would be more problematic. Suppose that the state claimed permanent control of foreign-owned petroleum refineries during the closure. Such an action would be discriminatory (because it targets only foreign-owned refineries) and disproportionate (because taking permanent control of refineries does not clearly relate to a temporary public health emergency). Similarly, a nationwide economic closure would probably be overly broad if the outbreak of the contagious disease were geographically contained.

One important challenge in investment arbitration is reconciling the police powers doctrine with foreign investors' rights in investment treaties. After all, the "public interest" can be defined very broadly—any taking of foreign investor property helps the public interest if the investor's property is used to finance government services. Historically, most arbitration tribunals were very hesitant to uphold the police powers doctrine, reasoning that states deliberately limited their regulatory authority by signing investment treaties. However, some recent arbitration cases suggest growing support for the police powers doctrine. This shift in legal reasoning has occurred at the same time as a growing backlash against international investment law.

Backlash to Investment Law

The historical evolution of international investment law was primarily driven by clashes between developed states—which wanted more protection for their firms that invested abroad—and developing states—which wanted foreign capital. These dynamics are sometimes still apparent in modern politics. Yet much of the modern politics of investment law involves a backlash within developed states from diverse ideological groups.

On the left, activists often view ISDS as an assault on legitimate government regulation on issues like the environment and labor rights. For example, the *Metalclad* case—in which a US firm successfully sued the Mexican government for refusing to grant it a construction permit on environmental grounds—has been widely criticized for privileging big business over environmental protection. Similar concerns have fueled opposition in the EU to new investment treaties. In 2015, the EU trade commissioner declared that "ISDS is now the most toxic acronym in Europe."[36]

On the right, some fiscal conservatives argue that ISDS distorts economic decision-making by giving firms more incentive to make risky decisions. For example, in an October 2017 interview, US Trade Representative Robert Lighthizer characterized ISDS as an unfair subsidy of foreign investment. When discussing US corporations that were lobbying to promote ISDS, he said:

> instead of buying political risk insurance, or instead of calculating political risk into their decision about a dollar and cents decision, what they're doing is saying "no, we want a thumb on the scale" ... It's always odd to me when the business people come around and say "oh, we just want our investments protected." I thought, "well so do I." I mean don't we all? I would love to have my investments guaranteed. But unfortunately it doesn't work that way in the market. It does work that way when you're talking about special interests.[37]

Additionally, by making it easier for companies to produce goods and services abroad, ISDS encourages large corporations to outsource their activities, potentially reducing employment at home.

These ideological critiques have been exacerbated by two major concerns about the behavior of foreign investors. First, some investors have engaged in "treaty

Figure 7.7 Politicians participate in a February 2019 session of the European Parliament in Strasbourg, France. The "Stop ISDS" signs indicate opposition to investor–state dispute settlement.

shopping." Recall that specific investment protections vary across agreements, which are usually signed at the bilateral level. Large multinational corporations usually operate in many different states, giving them access to multiple sets of treaty rules. In some controversial cases, foreign investors have manipulated their corporate nationality to try to obtain more favorable international legal protection.

For example, the Australian government announced in 2010 that it would be following the example of Uruguay by adopting stricter anti-smoking laws. Philip Morris is a US corporation that produces and sells cigarettes in over 180 states, including Australia. It conducts these business activities using a vast network of subsidiaries and partners, giving it flexibility in defining its corporate nationality. At the time that Australia announced its new policy in 2010, Philip Morris's Australian subsidiaries were owned by a Swiss holding company. Switzerland did not have an investment agreement with Australia, meaning that Philip Morris could not sue Australia using its Swiss holding company. Similarly, the US's agreement with Australia did not allow ISDS, so Philip Morris could not sue Australia based on its US nationality. However, Philip Morris discovered that an Australia–Hong Kong investment agreement allowed Hong Kong companies to file international arbitration cases against Australia. So Philip Morris tried a clever tactic: it transferred the ownership of its Australian operations from the Swiss holding company to a subsidiary in Hong Kong and filed an arbitration case under the Australia–Hong Kong agreement. Philip Morris's tactic was ultimately unsuccessful: the arbitral tribunal refused to hear its case against Australia because the company changed its corporate nationality after the announcement of the new anti-smoking rules. Yet many other foreign investors have successfully changed their nationality in order to "shop" for more favorable international legal provisions.[38]

A second concern about the behavior of foreign investors is that they may be using international law to file "nuisance" cases with little legal merit. Even if a large foreign firm is unlikely to prevail in investment arbitration, the firm may benefit from threatening arbitration as a bargaining tool. For example, some scholars believe that the rise in fair and equitable treatment claims over time suggests that foreign investors are using ISDS to file "weaker" cases and possibly abusing international investment law.[39]

Investment arbitration can have a chilling effect on new government regulations. When Philip Morris sued Uruguay to challenge its anti-smoking laws, numerous states announced that they would postpone implementing new tobacco regulations until the case was resolved. These chilling effects may be most severe for developing states, which have fewer resources to defend controversial policies. During the *Philip Morris* dispute, Uruguay had to rely upon a charitable fund set up by Bill Gates and Michael Bloomberg to pay its legal bills.[40] Philip Morris ultimately lost both of its investment arbitration cases and was forced to compensate Australia and Uruguay for most of their legal costs. However, researchers have provided strong evidence that the *Philip Morris* arbitration against Uruguay delayed and even stopped new anti-smoking rules in many states.[41]

Some observers believe that these three factors—ideological critiques in developed states, treaty shopping, and nuisance lawsuits—will weaken investment law in the future. After all, the backlash against ISDS has prompted some states to withdraw from international obligations. For example, Bolivia, Ecuador, and Venezuela all unilaterally withdrew from ICSID jurisdiction because they believed that ISDS unfairly constrained their domestic economic policies.

Yet despite its critics, international investment law is broadly supported by foreign investors, who benefit from its legal protections. Additionally, investment provisions are supported by many moderate politicians in developed states, who want to protect their firms in the global economy. Some states, including Canada and the EU, want to protect investment law by promoting greater institutionalization. These states argue that by creating a new international organization (like an investment court system), they can ensure that there is more accountability and transparency than currently exists under investment arbitration. Rather than weakening investment law, Canada and the EU want to make the investment system even stronger. It is too early to tell which approach will prevail, yet the history of international economic law suggests that any rollbacks of investment law are probably only temporary setbacks in the move toward ever-greater legalization.

7.5   Case Study Revisited: Should We Feel Sorry for Cigarette Companies?

It's hard to feel sorry for the merchants of death. But we can also probably understand why cigarette company executives were upset in 2005, when Uruguayan voters chose Tabaré Vázquez, a former oncologist, to serve as their president. Vázquez promised to fight the tobacco industry by creating strict new anti-smoking rules. First, Vázquez imposed a single presentation requirement, which prohibited cigarette brands from selling multiple varieties of their products. Second, Vázquez implemented the 80/80 Regulation, which increased the size of warning labels on cigarette packages.

These new policies in Uruguay coincided with a broader effort by the World Health Organization to get states to pass new anti-smoking laws. Diverse states—including Canada, Ireland, and New Zealand—were all considering new legislation to implement WHO guidelines. Philip Morris anticipated a wave of restrictive new laws and decided to fight back by suing Uruguay in international arbitration. This case caused many states to pause their proposed new anti-smoking rules until the case was resolved.[42]

The Philip Morris example connects to each of the topics in this chapter:

- *Protecting foreign investment*: Experts disagree about why states sign investment treaties. Some experts believe that investment law helps states to solve commitment problems that deter FDI. Other experts believe that investment law reflects competition between states and a "race to the bottom," in which states destroy their regulatory authority. The historical evolution of international investment law was marked by clashes between developed states—which wanted more protection for foreign investors—and developing states—which wanted more FDI.
- *Foreign investor rights*: Specific legal protections vary across treaties, but most investment agreements protect foreign investors from expropriation and provide various treatment standards. They also often limit when states can impose performance requirements, and give foreign investors the right to file international arbitration cases against states.
- *Preserving state authority*: Many states have pushed back against investor rights using a legal argument called the police powers doctrine, which asserts that states have an inherent right to protect the public interest. Many developed states are also experiencing a backlash against international investment law from diverse ideological perspectives. This backlash is motivated, in part, by attempts by foreign investors to manipulate their corporate nationality to obtain favorable legal protections, and by the fear that foreign investors are using investment arbitration to deter legitimate regulation by states.

We can now return to the big questions from the introduction. First: why exactly did Philip Morris believe that Uruguay had broken international law? Philip Morris made two legal arguments. First, it argued that the Uruguay rules were indirect expropriation because they reduced the value of Philip Morris's property. This argument was grounded in the claim that Philip Morris would have sold more cigarettes without the rules, and in the belief that the Uruguay rules diminished the value of Philip Morris's intellectual property.

Second, Philip Morris argued that Uruguay had not provided fair and equitable treatment to the company. Namely, Philip Morris highlighted several aspects of the Uruguayan rules that it believed were "arbitrary." First, Philip Morris argued that the SPR was not recommended by WHO guidelines and was not supported by any scientific evidence that it reduced smoking. Indeed, no other state had previously implemented a rule like the SPR. Second, it noted that the new anti-smoking rules were passed "without due consideration by public officials."[43] Finally, Philip Morris argued that the SPR was not proportionate because it "did not further its stated objective" of protecting public health.[44]

In particular, Philip Morris argued that the SPR allowed companies to evade its restriction by simply changing the brand name of its product varieties. For example, the Mailhos tobacco company had previously sold three varieties of Coronado cigarettes in distinctive gold, silver, and blue boxes. Each of these boxes had the same crown logo. To comply with the SPR, Mailhos continued selling its cigarettes in its distinctive gold, silver, and blue boxes with a crown logo. It simply changed the brand names for the silver and blue boxes to "Madison" and "Ocean." Consumers who saw the boxes in Uruguayan stores could easily recognize their preferred cigarettes based on the box color and crown logo.

Philip Morris also argued that the SPR was not proportionate because it prohibited behavior that could not be interpreted as deceptive to consumers. For example, cigarette companies could not include seasonal decorations or promotions on their packages. Philip Morris believed that these restrictions did not protect public health, they merely constrained advertising and sales tools.

Second, we asked: Why did Uruguay believe that Philip Morris was treated fairly and appropriately? Uruguay believed that both the SPR and the 80/80 Regulation complied with international investment law. First, it countered Philip Morris's claim of indirect expropriation with evidence that Philip Morris profits increased after the new rules were implemented. While Philip Morris believed that it would have made more profit without the rules, the arbitration panel agreed with Uruguay. It ruled that Philip Morris could not claim indirect expropriation if its profits had increased.

Second, Uruguay argued that the police powers doctrine was part of customary international law. Accordingly, Uruguay argued that any possible violations of its investment treaty were excused or justified by the fact that Uruguay was attempting to promote the public interest by reducing smoking. This argument was ultimately accepted by the arbitration panel, in part because the WHO submitted a legal brief arguing that it believed that the Uruguay rules would be effective. This component of the ruling has broad significance for international investment law because the arbitration panel clearly and strongly supported the police powers doctrine.

Finally, we asked: Is international investment law good for society? Should you support international investment law or oppose it? Whether you support or oppose international investment law will probably depend on which of the competing perspectives for why states use investment law you find most compelling. Both the commitment and competition perspectives are "true" in that they present an internally consistent narrative about how economic and political factors influence state decisions about whether to use international investment law. Yet they are built on very different assumptions about the nature of economic exchange and they yield dramatically different implications.

Recall that the commitment perspective is based on sequential moves: the firm must first decide whether to invest, and the host government can then decide whether to take. The commitment perspective thus views FDI as an investment in immobile assets, which cannot be easily moved or sold after threat of mistreatment. In contrast, the competition perspective is based on simultaneous moves by multiple developing states. Foreign investors can easily move and divide up their investment across multiple states, meaning that FDI is assumed to be mobile.

Most prominent historical examples of expropriation involve highly immobile industries, like mining and oil wells. However, modern foreign investors also often invest in more mobile industries, like legal services and software development. So the commitment and competition perspectives may both be apt, but only in relation to specific industries. That is, investment law may help developing states with respect to foreign investment in immobile industries, while harming them with respect to foreign investment in mobile industries.

Second, the commitment and competition perspectives have different conceptions of foreign investor rights. The commitment perspective is based on direct expropriation, in which the host government seizes complete control over the foreign investment. In contrast, the competition perspective is based on government regulation and taxation, which are incremental decisions that lower an investment's value. The commitment perspective may accordingly be more useful for understanding the historical development of investment law after World War II when direct expropriation was relatively common. In contrast, the competition perspective may be more useful for understanding contemporary debates over indirect expropriation.

Where does this leave us? Overall, international investment law is probably neither inherently good nor inherently bad for society. Rather, different economic and political contexts will shape its likely effect on governments, firms, and consumers. What is good for Australia is probably not the same as what is good for Azerbaijan.

PART III
Peace and War

8 Human Rights

8.1 Case Study: Child Workers in Bolivia

In 2013, the streets of La Paz erupted in riots between Bolivian police and protestors, who were challenging child labor laws. As a member of the 1989 Convention on the Rights of the Child, Bolivia had prohibited all hazardous labor by children below the age of eighteen and severely limited labor by children below the age of fourteen. Yet the protestors and their objectives might surprise you: they were children seeking a lower legal working age.

Children are an important part of Bolivia's economy. In urban areas, children sell candy, gum, and newspapers on the street. They also work in family-run bakeries, markets, and restaurants, preparing produce and washing dishes. Many of these children also attend school full-time. Yet some children in Bolivia are less fortunate. Some children, particularly in rural areas, work in dangerous conditions in agriculture, mining, and the oil industry. Girls can be particularly vulnerable—many are sexually abused and impregnated by adult workers.

Most advocacy organizations and the international community emphasize the human cost of child labor, arguing that all children should be protected from work, regardless of where they live. However, the Bolivian public—including the children themselves—mostly support child labor. As Jade Sanjinez, a fourteen-year-old newspaper seller, said: "I feel good about myself because I am helping my family."[1] Many Bolivians view child labor as a cultural tradition and economic necessity because of Bolivia's high poverty rate. Dr. Jorge Domic, Director of the Fundación La Paz, a Bolivian advocacy group that supports child rights, explained:

> In the Western world, the meaning of being a child is centered around the ideas of family security, education and play. For us, that is a romantic vision. Children living in

Figure 8.1 A boy helps his siblings wash cars in La Paz, Bolivia in 2014. Many children in Bolivia work jobs to help support their families. Such labor violates international human rights law. However, Bolivian children believe that such international laws limit their autonomy and independence.

the Andean world—in Bolivia particularly—have duties and obligations. But besides that, they have an active role in society ... In Bolivia, to eradicate child labor you would have to eradicate Andean culture.[2]

Domic and other Bolivians clearly believe that child workers play an important economic and social role.

Should children like Jade Sanjinez be protected from work, or should they have a right to work? Should we be surprised that Bolivia—a well-functioning democracy—blatantly violates international law on child labor? Should every society follow the same universal standards for child labor, or should human rights vary based on their social context?

Answering these questions requires that we understand and address the following issues:

- *Creating human rights*: What are the major components of international human rights law? How does this law apply to children?
- *Physical integrity rights*: What obligations do governments have to protect the physical integrity of individuals, and of children specifically?
- *Civil and political rights*: What civil and political rights are protected under international human rights law? Do these rights extend to children?
- *Economic, social, and cultural rights*: Does international law provide children with economic, social, or cultural rights to work?

Before answering these questions, we should recognize that there is no single definition for the term "human right." Some experts believe that these rights come from natural law and basic conceptions about what it means to be human. Other experts emphasize voluntary law, arguing that individual rights are granted by governments. Finally, many experts view human rights as a manifestation of communitarian law, in which common values and evolving standards govern how states should treat individuals.

What do human rights entail? Most experts agree that international law includes physical integrity rights, which focus on life and physical well-being. However, experts often disagree about other kinds of human rights, as shown in Table 8.1. Most developed democracies emphasize civil and political rights, which closely resemble individual rights under their constitutional laws. However, developing states often emphasize cultural, economic, and social rights. Real-life applications of human rights often involve multiple categories. For example, if an indigenous group wants to teach its native language in public schools, it is making a claim with civil, cultural, political, and social dimensions. Numerous institutions also uphold human rights law. These overlaps present both a challenge and an opportunity: they make human rights law more complex, but also give individuals multiple ways to assert and uphold their legal rights.

Table 8.1 Human Rights Typology

Type	Meaning
Civil	Preserve individual autonomy
Cultural	Permit expression of collective identity
Economic	Allow individuals to earn livelihoods and gain economic self-sufficiency
Physical integrity	Protect life and physical well-being
Political	Allow participation in governance
Social	Guarantee basic survival and development

Regardless of their source, international law distinguishes between derogable and non-derogable rights. **Non-derogable rights** are rights that a state must uphold in all circumstances, like the prohibition of genocide and torture. These rights are so fundamental that states may not excuse or justify violations of them. In contrast, states may suspend **derogable rights** during public emergencies.[3] States must declare such emergencies in advance, describe how they will derogate, and end the derogation within a reasonable period of time. For example, after the Paris terrorist attacks in fall 2015, France declared a temporary emergency, derogated from international human rights agreements, and expanded police powers.[4]

Finally, states must often balance human rights against competing values. For example, states that oppose racial discrimination often prohibit hate speech, thereby restricting freedom of expression. International institutions usually defer somewhat to states when they balance competing values, although this deference varies across institutions. The European Court of Human Rights often asserts the **margin of appreciation** doctrine, which posits that because states have more knowledge about their own social context, a court ought to defer to states when applying legal standards. In contrast, the Inter-American Court of Human Rights does not use this doctrine.

This chapter is organized as follows. Section 8.2 provides a historical overview of human rights, including major multilateral and regional treaties. Section 8.3 then discusses physical integrity rights, including: genocide and ethnic cleansing; torture; and human trafficking. Section 8.4 focuses on civil and political rights, such as: expression, assembly and association; religion; and criminal justice. Then section 8.5 describes cultural, economic, and social rights involving: labor; economic and social assistance; and cultural rights and marginalized groups. Throughout each of these sections, we introduce various institutions that monitor and uphold human rights. Finally, section 8.6 returns to the case of child workers in Bolivia.

8.2 Creating Human Rights

To provide context for contemporary international law, we describe the processes that created modern human rights law. We begin with the origins of human rights in philosophical debates and the history of colonialism. We then describe multilateral human rights treaties after World War II. Finally, we examine regional human rights agreements in Europe, the Americas, and Africa.

Origins of Human Rights

Societies have long believed that individuals possess certain inherent rights. Early scholars often argued that such rights came from God and were revealed to mankind through religious texts. For example, Francisco de Vitoria lectured in the mid-1500s about Spanish exploration in the Americas. The Bible describes Jesus as instructing his followers, "Go ye into all the world, and preach the gospel to every creature," prompting Vitoria to believe in the divine right of Christians to proselytize in foreign lands.[5] He argued that if native Americans "obstruct the Spaniards in their free propagation of the Gospel, the Spaniards ... may preach and work for the conversion of that people even against their will."[6] Yet Vitoria did not believe that all individuals had rights to religious freedom and speech; he believed that only Christians had such rights.

Some early scholars challenged this viewpoint, arguing that non-Christians might have competing norms and rights that were just as valid. For example, French intellectual Michel de Montaigne wrote numerous essays reflecting on life and politics in sixteenth-century France. Montaigne lived in a society torn apart by religious conflict between Catholics and Protestants, each of which claimed to understand God's divine truth. In a famous essay entitled, "On Cannibals," Montaigne reflected on contemporary reports of cannibalism in other societies.[7] Montaigne believed that despite their departures from European mores, these societies demonstrated a nobility and respect for life that he suggested was missing from sixteenth-century France: "each man calls barbarism whatever is not his own practice; for indeed it seems that we have no other test of truth and reason than the example and pattern of the opinions and the customs of the country we live in."[8] Montaigne was fundamentally a sceptic; he questioned claims by men to understand God's will.

In contrast, Enlightenment philosophers of the 1700s—such as David Hume, Immanuel Kant, and Jean-Jacques Rousseau—provide the foundation for modern claims of **universalism**. These philosophers argued that natural law provides a basis for individual rights. For example, in *The Social Contract*, Rousseau famously wrote: "Man is born free, and everywhere he is in chains."[9] He believed that men were inherently free by nature, and that governments could only validly limit such freedom if their constraints reflected the will of the people. Such arguments are reflected in historic texts like the US Declaration of Independence (1776), the French Declaration of the Rights of Man (1789), and the US Bill of Rights (1791). While these texts are part of domestic law, their intellectual basis is not constrained by national borders. If human rights are truly inherent and bestowed by God or nature, then they are not conferred on only Americans or Frenchmen. To universalists, all humans have fundamental rights, regardless of where they live. If child labor violates human rights in France, a universalist would argue, then it also violates human rights in Bolivia.

Yet many modern scholars and politicians have questioned the intellectual and political basis for universalism. Many modern ethical, moral, and political theories instead advocate for **relativism**. Scholars who adopt a relativist view on human rights argue that rights must be understood within their social context. For example, the American Anthropological Association issued an official statement in 1947 in which it questioned "philosophical systems that have stressed absolutes in the realm of values and ends."[10] It argued that debates about human rights should have "respect for cultural differences" because "standards and values are relative to the culture from which they derive."[11] As described above, many Bolivians believe that child labor is an economic necessity and a cultural practice that should be allowed, rather than prohibited. Relativists believe that many different factors—including culture, economics, and politics—can shape conceptions of human rights.

One challenge of the intellectual debate between universalism and relativism is knowing when individuals are making principled ideological arguments, and when they are using rhetoric to advance their own interests. During the colonial era, European states frequently made relativist arguments to deny basic human rights to native populations in Latin America, Africa, and Asia. Many Europeans believed that native populations were less civilized, and hence less capable or deserving of rights than Europeans.[12] Other Europeans invoked relativist claims about native culture to justify slavery and forced labor.[13] In contrast, African and Asian leaders who sought independence frequently invoked universalism.[14] However, after these societies gained independence, many of them transitioned into autocratic rule, replacing foreign domination with despotic local rule. These autocratic rulers then frequently invoked relativism to stymie democracy and challenges to their power.[15]

Just as the intellectual foundations of human rights are based partly in imperialism and political power, so, too, are many of its other components. One key component of the modern human rights system is non-governmental organizations that promote human rights within their own societies and abroad. Many of these organizations have their roots in the anti-slavery movement, which began in the late eighteenth century. This movement was driven by the universalist claim that Africans had the same inherent rights as Anglo-Europeans. Most anti-slavery advocacy focused on prohibiting slavery under domestic law. A few states created international treaties and tribunals to restrict the slave trade.[16] Yet the anti-slavery movement's main international significance comes from the creation of advocacy organizations that sought to enhance and protect the rights of individuals in other societies. As colonialism grew in the nineteenth century, organizations like the Anti-Slavery Society (in the UK) and the *Bureau International pour la Défence des Indigènes* (in France) pressured colonial states to respect the basic rights of the colonized. While they did not always succeed, they informed domestic publics about conditions in overseas territories and the human cost of colonial authority.[17]

A second key component of the modern human rights system is the weakening of claims to state sovereignty. This trend is apparent in evolving norms about domestic jurisdiction, minority rights, and consular jurisdiction. During the colonial era, powerful states did not directly project their domestic laws onto foreign

Figure 8.2 The most recognized image of the British anti-slavery campaign is this 1787 engraving, which was widely used in public education campaigns. Anti-slavery campaigns (in Great Britain and elsewhere) were grounded in the universalist claim that Africans had the same inherent rights as Anglo-Europeans.

territories. For example, long after slavery was abolished in the UK, it persisted in many parts of the British Empire. The practice of exerting political control over foreign territories, which had their own domestic laws, required states to develop complex legal doctrines for overlapping jurisdictions. These doctrines weakened the sovereignty of foreign territories.[18]

States also often used their economic and military power to write treaties that protected ethnic and religious minorities in foreign states, thereby eroding sovereignty. For example, Russia and numerous Western European states included minority protection clauses in their economic treaties with the Ottoman Empire. Under Ottoman law, non-Muslims faced different legal rights from Muslims. For example, Ottoman law often barred non-Muslims from entering certain professions and required them to pay higher taxes.[19] Russia and Western European states, which were predominantly Christian, believed they had a moral obligation to protect Christian minorities in Muslim lands. Similar treaties protected religious minorities in places like Poland and Transylvania, particularly when land was transferred between Catholic and Protestant states.[20]

Additionally, many economic treaties created **consular jurisdiction** in foreign states, which were separate legal systems for foreigners that were overseen by consular officials from the foreigners' home state. These systems challenged the sovereignty of foreign states. In the nineteenth century, many powerful trading states (including France, the UK, and the US) convinced weaker states (like China, Japan, and Thailand/Siam) that foreigners should not be subject to local laws and legal institutions, which they considered "uncivilized." These powerful states pressured their weaker trading partners into setting up consular jurisdiction.[21] These systems remained until states revised their domestic laws to reflect Western legal concepts, procedures, and punishments, such as Western norms about due process, cruel and unusual punishment, and freedom of religion. Consular jurisdiction was thus a tool for coercing many states into adopting Western conceptions of human rights, and an early precedent for international monitoring and adjudication of human rights.

A third key component of the modern human rights system is the creation of international institutions to monitor and challenge state compliance with human rights. This process began after World War I, when the League of Nations monitored minority rights in Europe and native populations in many colonial territories. Throughout the 1920s and 1930s, the League slowly developed a bureaucracy that required states to submit reports about their domestic governance and laws. Additionally, the League system created the process of **individual petition**, which allows individuals to directly complain to an international organization if they believe that their rights have been violated by a state. Both processes—monitoring and individual petition—challenged state sovereignty and encouraged non-governmental organizations, like the Anti-Slavery Society and the *Bureau International pour la*

Défence des Indigènes, to monitor and publicize human rights in societies without strong judicial institutions. One historian described this process as "internationalization" because "certain political issues and functions [were] displaced from the national or imperial, and into the international, realm."[22]

Multilateral Human Rights

World War II was a transformational event for human rights. After the war ended, many Europeans feared the revival of fascism and the spread of communism.[23] Contemporary observers widely believed "a new world order should be established," based on the primacy of individual rights.[24] Yet states disagreed about the content of these individual rights. Western states believed that civil and political rights for individuals were key to freedom. In contrast, the USSR and its allies emphasized economic and social rights for groups, such as labor rights for workers. Finally, newly independent states and territories seeking independence cared most about racial equality and self-determination.[25]

In the late 1940s, states could not reach a consensus on the definition of human rights, so they wrote a compromise document that reflected all of these views: the 1948 Universal Declaration of Human Rights. Today, the Universal Declaration is considered a foundational document in human rights law, but it was not regarded as such in 1948. Because of disagreement about its content, the Universal Declaration was adopted as a UN General Assembly resolution, rather than a treaty.[26] Additionally, it reflected many of the biases of colonial states. For example, it did not explicitly include the right to self-determination.[27] After decades of subsequent human rights treaties and practice, most experts now believe that the Universal Declaration binds all states under customary international law. But in 1948, the document expressed diverse aspirations, rather than legal rights.

States were more successful in uniting to condemn the Holocaust via the 1948 Genocide Convention, shown in Table 8.2. In one sense, the Genocide Convention is the most broadly supported human rights treaty. Only three years after its creation, the International Court of Justice suggested that it already reflected customary international law, binding members and non-members alike.[28] Yet in another sense, the Genocide Convention is also the weakest modern human rights treaty, because it lacks an institution to monitor state behavior and it does not give individuals a way to challenge violations. Many states have accepted the Court's jurisdiction to adjudicate disputes under the Genocide Convention, and the ICJ has ruled on many genocide cases, including Bosnia's lawsuits against Serbia. But no institution monitors treaty compliance and assesses individual petitions about possible violations.

The creation of multilateral human rights institutions had to wait until the mid-1960s. States initially tried to negotiate a single human rights treaty within the UN, but ultimately concluded that disagreements about human rights

Table 8.2 Key Multilateral Human Rights Treaties

Signature Year	Treaty Name
1948	Genocide Convention
1965	International Convention on the Elimination of All Forms of Racial Discrimination (ICERD)
1966	International Covenant on Civil and Political Rights (ICCPR)
1966	International Covenant on Economic, Social and Cultural Rights (ICESCR)
1979	Convention on the Elimination of All Forms of Discrimination against Women (CEDAW)
1984	Convention against Torture (CAT)
1989	Convention on the Rights of the Child (CRC)
1990	International Convention on the Protection of the Rights of All Migrant Workers and Members of Their Families
2007	International Convention for the Protection of All Persons from Enforced Disappearance
2007	Convention on the Rights of Persons with Disabilities (CRPD)

were too large. Accordingly, they drafted three separate treaties that form the core of modern human rights law. Each of these treaties appealed to a different constituency of states, based on their own particular conceptions of human rights. While they sometimes have overlapping provisions, they have dramatically different emphases.

First, the International Convention on the Elimination of All Forms of Racial Discrimination condemns "any distinction, exclusion, restriction or preference based on race, colour, descent, or national or ethnic origin."[29] This treaty was strongly supported by newly independent states in Africa and Asia, who believed that it condemned apartheid and colonialism. However, many of these states did not believe that the treaty constrained their treatment of minorities who were also African or Asian. Many such populations, like the Kurds in Iraq and the Tutsis in Rwanda, faced systematic persecution after their states gained independence.[30] This treaty also gained support from the USSR and its allies, who viewed it as a condemnation of race relations in the US.

In contrast, Western states preferred the International Covenant on Civil and Political Rights, which focuses on topics like free expression, assembly and association, the right to religion, and criminal justice. Most ICCPR provisions closely mimic constitutional protections in Western states like France and the US. Not surprisingly, autocracies usually either refused to join this treaty or simply ignored it.

Finally, the USSR and its allies supported the International Covenant on Economic, Social and Cultural Rights. This treaty emphasizes labor rights and social assistance programs, like health care and housing. In practice, most states joined the ICCPR and the ICESCR at the same time. Yet the political rhetoric behind these treaties often revealed sharply different ideologies about human rights.

Many prominent advocates for the ICESCR argued that there was a fundamental tension between the ICCPR's emphasis on political democracy, which protects individual rights, and the ICESCR's emphasis on economic justice, which privileges the needs of all people. For example, Mohammed Reza Pahlavi, an autocrat who ruled Iran from 1941 until 1979, wrote in 1967 that "political rights which are divorced from social rights, and legal justice that does not include social justice, ... are devoid of real meaning."[31] Such leaders often believed that political rights should take a backseat to economic development, particularly in developing states. They also often supported the redistribution of wealth from rich to poor states as a human right.

Later multilateral human rights treaties focused on the rights of protected groups, including women, children, migrant workers, and people with disabilities. These treaties clarified that earlier rights conferred in the ICCPR and the ICESCR applied to groups that were frequently excluded from economic and political power. They also sometimes extended additional rights based on the presumption that these groups require additional protection. For example, the Convention on the Rights of the Child (1989) limits child labor based on the belief that children lack physical and mental capacity. Additionally, the Convention against Torture (1984) and the International Convention for the Protection of All Persons from Enforced Disappearance (2007) both prohibit government officials—including police officers and the military—from violating the physical integrity of individuals, including political opponents.

Each of these multilateral human rights treaties (except the Genocide Convention) created its own **special treaty body**, which is an international institution that monitors compliance with the treaty and assesses individual petitions about possible violations. All treaty members agree to submit regular reports to these bodies about their relevant domestic laws and practices, although the frequency and quality of these reports varies.[32] International law experts usually argue that this monitoring generates elite socialization, in which policy-makers are persuaded or shamed into protecting human rights. This process is often reinforced by UN political bodies.[33]

Special treaty bodies usually only have jurisdiction to hear individual petitions if a state joins both the treaty and an additional optional protocol. For example, the Human Rights Committee is the special treaty body that oversees compliance with the ICCPR. When the Committee receives a complaint against an ICCPR member, it conducts a quasi-judicial process in which it assesses the facts, considers legal arguments, and then shares its views in a non-binding public document. These views are usually considered authoritative interpretations of the ICCPR.

They shape how states understand their legal commitments and create precedents for future disputes.[34]

Regional Human Rights

After World War II, various states also pursued regional human rights agreements to complement the multilateral system. Table 8.3 lists the major regional human rights treaties and their associated courts. The common thread connecting each of these regional systems was the desire by newly democratic states in Europe, the Americas, and Africa to reinforce rights that were recently granted under domestic law.

The European human rights system was created to promote democratic stability within Western Europe and prevent future wars. Western European observers feared a resurgence of fascism and the spread of communism in Eastern Europe. Accordingly, the European human rights system was a conservative enterprise because "Western Europe was anxious to preserve the freedom it currently enjoyed," rather than pushing new, progressive agendas.[35] Initial support for the European system was strongest in states transitioning from autocratic to democratic rule in the late 1940s, like Austria, France, and Italy.[36] In contrast, most well-established democracies (like the UK) supported a treaty with weak institutions, while most autocratic states (like Portugal and Spain) did not support any European human rights treaty.[37]

The 1950 European Convention on Human Rights outlines major civil and political rights that were common within democracies at the time. States also created the European Court of Human Rights to oversee legal disputes about the Convention. In the Convention's early decades, states could choose whether or not to accept jurisdiction of the Court and to allow individual petitions, which were called applications. After an initial screening process, these applications could become cases at the European Court of Human Rights. Over time, the European system grew stronger as more states accepted the Court's jurisdiction and allowed individual petitions, and the Court established its reputation in interpreting human rights

Table 8.3 Regional Human Rights Treaties

Signature Year	Name	Associated Court
1950	European Convention on Human Rights	European Court of Human Rights
1969	American Convention on Human Rights	Inter-American Court of Human Rights
1981	African Charter on Human and Peoples' Rights	African Court on Human and Peoples' Rights

law. Beginning in 1998, all members of the European Convention were required to both accept jurisdiction of the European Court of Human Rights and allow individual petitions.

Membership in the European system continued to grow, particularly after the collapse of the Soviet Union in 1989 and democratization in Eastern Europe. The European human rights system is technically independent of the European Union. For example, Russia is a member of the European system, but not of the European Union. Yet all members of the European Union are required to be members of the European Convention on Human Rights. Therefore, many states that want to join the European Union (like Albania, Serbia, and Turkey) have joined the European human rights system.

Similar regional integration has occurred in the Americas. After World War II, many states in North and South America created the Organization of American States. Its founding documents include the American Declaration of the Rights and Duties of Man, which pre-dates the Universal Declaration of Human Rights. Like the Universal Declaration, the American Declaration reflected human rights aspirations, but was not legally binding.[38] The Organization included an Inter-American Commission to monitor human rights conditions in its members, but it lacked authority to issue legally binding rulings.

In 1969, many Organization members joined the American Convention on Human Rights, a binding human rights treaty that mimics the European Convention. Compliance with the American Convention is overseen by the Inter-American Court of Human Rights, which can issue binding rulings on human rights disputes.[39] As in the European system, most of the Court's early support came from states transitioning from repressive autocracies to democratic rule.[40] Stable democracies, like Canada and the US, refused to join the American Convention and accept the jurisdiction of the Inter-American Court.

Finally, the 1981 African Charter on Human and Peoples' Rights was created by African Union member states. Once again, this system was stimulated by growing support within African states for democracy.[41] Like its predecessors, the African system initially included a Commission to monitor compliance with human rights obligations. In the mid-2000s, member states created the African Court on Human and Peoples' Rights, which can issue legally binding rulings on disputes.

Most human rights scholars focus on the European system, which now routinely issues over a thousand judgments per year. In contrast, the Inter-American and African courts issue a handful of judgments each year. The long history and large caseload of the European Court has led experts to call it "the pre-eminent system of international human rights protection."[42]

But we should consider a few caveats. First, the European system has existed far longer than the Inter-American and African systems, leading to advocacy groups and lawyers that specialize in the European system. It has also generated a large body of case law that can easily be extended and applied to new disputes, and it has a relatively large budget and experienced staff who can process cases. In its early decades, the European Court issued fewer than a dozen judgments each year, making it more closely resemble the other regional courts. With time, the Inter-American and African courts are likely to become more prolific.

Second, while it is difficult to compare substantive content across courts, the European Court may be hearing different kinds of cases than the Inter-American and African courts. For example, Chapter 2 discussed the case of *Litwa* v. *Poland*, in which a Polish man was arrested by police because postal clerks believed that he was intoxicated. This case reflects broader trends—most of the European Court's cases involved legal violations that are relatively minor and/or unintentional in highly democratic states.[43] In contrast, cases heard by the Inter-American Court routinely involved "authoritarian regimes, mass atrocities, and violent human rights violations, such as massacres in indigenous communities and prisons, as well as widespread forced disappearances of political dissidents."[44]

Differences are also apparent in compliance with court rulings. When a state loses a human rights judgment, the court will usually provide a remedy by telling the state how to make a human rights victim whole. States are much more likely to comply with rulings by the European Court than by the Inter-American Court.[45] However, this pattern overlooks the fact that the Inter-American Court issues more severe remedies than the European Court. For example, in *Litwa* v. *Poland*, the European Court ordered Poland to cover Litwa's court costs and pay him modest compensation.[46] Poland was not ordered to change its domestic laws or reform its police forces. In contrast, the Inter-American Court routinely orders more dramatic remedies. In addition to paying compensation, states are often ordered to change domestic laws, reform government bureaucracies, and even sometimes to change constitutional provisions to prevent future violations.[47] Because the Inter-American Court orders more aggressive remedies, each case that it hears can have a larger impact than a European case.

8.3 Physical Integrity Rights

Physical integrity rights protect life and physical well-being, placing them at the core of international human rights law. These rights are outlined in many different treaties, including: the Genocide Convention (1948); the International Covenant on Civil and Political Rights (1966); the International Covenant on Economic, Social and Cultural Rights (1966); the Convention against Torture (1984); and regional human rights treaties. Therefore, disputes over physical integrity rights often involve many different treaty texts. Here, we discuss some contemporary physical integrity concerns: genocide and ethnic cleansing; torture; and human trafficking.

Genocide and Ethnic Cleansing

Growing up in Poland in the early twentieth century, Raphael Lemkin witnessed routine violence against Jews.[48] Yet the transformative political event of his youth was learning about the Ottoman massacre of Armenians. Lemkin was horrified to read newspaper accounts of the mass deportation and killing of over one million people, "for no other reason than they were Christians."[49] As a young adult, Lemkin feared Germany's anti-Jewish laws. He fled Europe, and wrote an influential book documenting the German persecution of Jews.[50] He described this persecution as "genocide," a term he invented from the Greek word for nation/race/tribe (*genos*) and the Latin word for kill (*caedere*). After World War II, Lemkin formed an advocacy called the World Movement to Outlaw Genocide, to pressure governments to create a treaty that criminalized genocide.

Lemkin used the term genocide to refer broadly to actions and policies that persecuted a group. Yet the Genocide Convention (1948) sets relatively narrow parameters on the legal meaning of the term. Under international law, **genocide** is defined as:

> any of the following acts committed with intent to destroy, in whole or in part, a national, ethnical, racial or religious group, as such:
> (a) Killing members of the group;
> (b) Causing serious bodily or mental harm to members of the group;
> (c) Deliberately inflicting on the group conditions of life calculated to bring about its physical destruction in whole or in part;
> (d) Imposing measures intended to prevent births within the group;
> (e) Forcibly transferring children of the group to another group.[51]

While the main motivating force behind the Genocide Convention was the Holocaust, the Genocide Convention clarifies that genocide is a crime that is prohibited "in time of peace or in time of war."[52] The prohibition of genocide is therefore a human right, rather than a law of armed conflict. It is included in customary international law, and considered a non-derogable right.

Genocide has three elements—group identification, physical acts, and a destructive intent. First, genocide is acts against "a national, ethnical, racial or religious group." The Genocide Convention does not protect other possible groups from persecution, like economic, ideological, linguistic, or political groups. For example, we could not call the mass persecution of homosexuals a "genocide," because sexuality is not protected by the Genocide Convention. Yet nationality, ethnicity, race, and religion are often malleable concepts that are defined and activated for political reasons. Many tribunals and experts therefore argue that perceptions and stigmatization affect whether a group is protected under the Genocide Convention.[53]

For example, the majority Hutu group in Rwanda massacred the minority Tutsi group in 1994. Many scholars documented that the differences between the Hutu and Tutsi groups are artificial.[54] They share the same culture, language, and religion; they mainly differ based on economic class. Historically, "Tutsi" individuals owned more cattle and had more economic and political power, while "Hutu" individuals were agricultural workers with less economic and political power. Prior to colonization, "if a Hutu could acquire sufficient wealth, he would be considered a Tutsi."[55] Belgian colonial officials often could not tell who belonged to which group because of generations of intermarriage. Belgian officials therefore issued identity cards, which labeled Rwandans as Hutu or Tutsi, based on how many cattle their family owned.[56] Yet the International Criminal Tribunal for Rwanda (ICTR) found that the Tutsis were protected as an ethnic group under the Genocide Convention because they were "a group identified as such by others."[57]

Given the malleability in defining groups, some legal experts believe that the prohibition of genocide should protect other groups. For example, in the 1970s, Ugandan dictator Idi Amin slaughtered his political opponents, and the Cambodian Khmer Rouge massacred economic groups—including business owners,

Figure 8.3 A collection of human remains fill a church in Kigali, Rwanda. Many experts question whether the Hutu and Tutsi people of Rwanda are in fact distinct ethnic groups. However, the mass killing of approximately 800,000 Rwandans in 1994 has been widely recognized as a genocide because the Tutsi were identified as an ethnic group by others (namely, by the Hutu extremists who slaughtered them).

intellectuals, and urban elites—while trying to create a Maoist agricultural state. Yet these massacres are not "genocides" under international law because the victims were not a protected group. Many critics accordingly view the Genocide Convention's group identification criteria as a weakness of international law.[58]

Second, the Convention identifies five physical acts of genocide, listed above as items (a)–(e). Some of the included acts are straightforward, such as killing and the forcible transfer of children. Others are more ambiguous and require careful interpretation. For example, the Guatemalan army believed in the 1980s that indigenous Mayans were supporting armed opposition groups, so it launched a counterinsurgency campaign in Mayan communities. According to the Guatemalan Commission for Historical Clarification, "whole villages were burnt, properties were destroyed and the collectively worked fields and harvests were also burnt, leaving the communities without food."[59] The Genocide Convention does not prohibit property destruction, but the Guatemalan army starved the Mayans by destroying their crops. The Commission concluded that the army inflicted "conditions of life calculated to bring about [the] physical destruction" of the Mayans.

Some critics argue that the Genocide Convention should prohibit more forms of persecution. For example, activists often describe the destruction of cultural or religious monuments as "cultural genocide" that destroys social communities.[60] Similarly, sexual violence is not explicitly a genocidal act, but women's rights advocates argue that "mass rape is a tool, a tactic, a policy, a plan, a strategy, as well as a practice" of genocide.[61] Some tribunals have found that mass rapes, such as those in Rwanda in 1994, cause "serious bodily or mental harm" that qualifies as genocide.[62]

Third, the Convention says that physical acts must be "committed with intent to destroy" the protected group. This means that genocide is a systematic action—spontaneous acts of violence do not satisfy the intent requirement. Experts have two competing approaches for proving intent. Some experts focus on purpose, or individual motives for a particular act. Others focus on knowledge, or whether a plan directed behavior. Most experts agree that the "intent to destroy" must involve physical or biological destruction. The destruction of social or cultural identities does not (currently) qualify as genocide.[63]

A more challenging provision is the Convention's reference to destruction "in whole or in part." For example, Nazi Germany never attempted to destroy all Jews worldwide. Even Hitler had his limits. But consider the Srebrenica massacre of 1995, in which Serbian armed groups attacked a Bosnian territory that was a UN safe haven for refugees. Serbian armed groups separated the inhabitants based on their gender and age. Women, small children, and the elderly were forcibly evacuated to Muslim-controlled territory. The remaining men and teenage boys—over 8,000 people—were slaughtered over four days. Was this massacre a genocide? No evidence suggests that Serbians wanted to kill all Muslims (or even all male Muslims) in Bosnia, or even in Srebrenica. Yet international tribunals have consistently described Srebrenica as a genocide because of the mass killings.

The Genocide Convention does not have a special treaty body to challenge treaty violations. However, there are several other tools for upholding international law against genocide. First, one tool upholding these rules is the criminal prosecution (at either the domestic or international level) of individuals who participate in a genocide. Such participation includes direct acts (like killing) and indirect acts (like conspiracy, complicity, and incitement). To facilitate such trials, the Genocide Convention requires states to extradite individuals who face prosecution for genocide.[64]

Another tool for upholding international law is the International Court of Justice.[65] However, attribution is a major challenge in such cases.[66] For example, Bosnia sued Serbia at the ICJ for the Srebrenica genocide. While the ICJ agreed that a genocide occurred, it argued that the killings by armed groups could not be attributed to Serbia as a state. Serbia provided financial and military assistance to the armed groups, but the ICJ did not believe that Serbia had effective control over the genocide.[67]

The Genocide Convention declares that "genocide ... is a crime under international law," but it places few direct obligations on states.[68] It says that people who commit genocide "shall be punished," and that member states must write domestic legislation "to provide effective penalties for persons guilty of genocide."[69] If a member state suspects that a genocide is occurring, then it "may call upon the competent organs of the United Nations to take such action ... as they consider appropriate for the prevention and suppression of acts of genocide."[70]

Modern experts interpret these provisions as creating a legal obligation to prevent genocide. In the *Bosnian Genocide* case, the ICJ ruled:

> a state's obligation to prevent, and the corresponding duty to act, arise at the
> instant that the state learns of ... the existence of a serious risk that genocide will be
> committed. From that moment onwards, if the state has available to it means likely to
> have a deterrent effect on those suspected of preparing genocide ... it is under a duty to
> make such use of these means as the circumstances permit.[71]

It thus ruled that Serbia violated the Genocide Convention because it had "undeniable influence" over armed groups, but did not make "the best efforts within [its] power to try and prevent the tragic events."[72] But how far does the duty to prevent extend? Powerful states like France, the UK, and the US also had influence over Serbian armed groups. Did they violate international law by failing to prevent genocide?

Some experts even argue that the legal obligation to prevent genocide may require states to use force in order to stop or prevent a genocide. For example, many Western lawyers and diplomats argue that international law includes the **responsibility to protect**.[73] This principle posts that (1) every state has a responsibility to protect its population from severe violations of human rights and humanitarian law; and (2) failure to meet this responsibility can trigger force by the international community. Canada created an International Commission on Intervention and State Sovereignty to analyze major recent humanitarian crises, like the 1994 Rwandan genocide and the 1995 Srebrenica massacre. The Commission issued a major 2001 report that identified genocide as one possible justification for the use of force by other states.[74]

These factors cause many states to avoid the "g-word." For example, many governments initially refused to call the 1994 Rwandan massacres a "genocide" because they did not want to be under a legal obligation to respond.[75] Alternatively, many advocates use the word "genocide" strategically to highlight historical and ongoing injustice, or as a justification for the use of force.[76] The label "genocide" thus has legal and political implications—it may enable states to behave in ways that would otherwise be inappropriate or illegal.[77]

A related concept is **ethnic cleansing**, which is the compelled removal of an ethnic group using intimidation or violence. While this tactic was common throughout history, it became an important legal issue in the 1990s.[78] During the breakup of Yugoslavia, there was extensive ethnic cleansing as three different ethnic groups—Croatians (Catholics), Muslims, and Serbians (Orthodox Christians)—fought for territory. One important region was Prijedor, a Muslim majority district located between Serbian majority districts.[79] Serb forces pressured Muslim residents to leave Prijedor and move to other Muslim-controlled areas. Serb forces bombed Muslim businesses, homes, and mosques, while leaving Serb properties untouched. After gaining control over Prijedor's villages, Serb groups forcibly deported and/or imprisoned civilians in camps, where they were beaten, sexually abused, and tortured. Table 8.4 shows official census figures from the time. Roughly 49,454 Muslims lived in Prijedor before the violence began. Two years later, only 6,124 Muslims remained. Roughly 88 percent of Muslims disappeared in only two years. Similarly, almost half of Prijedor's Roman Catholic population and over 70 percent of the other non-Serbs (such as Roma populations) disappeared in just two years.

Table 8.4 Ethnic Cleansing in Prijedor, Bosnia

Ethnic Identity	1991 Population	1993 Population	Percentage Change
Serbs (Eastern Orthodox)	47,745	53,637	12.3%
Muslims	49,454	6,124	−87.6%
Croats (Roman Catholics)	6,300	3,169	−49.7%
Others	8,971	2,621	−70.8%

Source: Data from UN Document S/1994/674, p. 37.

When the International Criminal Tribunal for the former Yugoslavia (ICTY) prosecuted Serbs for the Prijedor attacks, it refused to describe these actions as "genocide." While many of the Serbs' acts—such as forcible deportations, sexual violence, and torture—are crimes under international law, the ICTY did not believe that Serb forces tried to "destroy" the Muslims. Similarly, the ICJ ruled in the *Bosnian Genocide* case: "Neither the intent ... to render an area 'ethnically homogeneous', nor the operations that may be carried out to implement such policy, can *as such* be designated as genocide."[80] Yet despite the distinction within international law between genocide and ethnic cleansing, states often use these terms interchangeably and describe ethnic cleansing as "a form of genocide."[81]

Torture

Most international law experts believe that torture is prohibited under customary international law. This prohibition is a non-derogable right that is included in numerous treaties, including the ICCPR (1966) and the UN Convention against Torture (1984). Additionally, the African, Inter-American, and European human rights systems also prohibit torture.[82] Yet despite this widespread prohibition, states often disagree about the definition of torture.

The ICCPR and regional human rights treaties do not define torture or terms like "cruel, inhuman or degrading treatment or punishment."[83] Institutions that uphold these treaties, including the Human Rights Committee and regional human rights courts, have interpreted these terms in numerous disputes. These institutions use evolutionary interpretation, meaning that what constitutes torture and severe ill-treatment changes over time. These institutions consider torture to be the most severe act, while other ill-treatment—that is "cruel, inhuman or degrading"—includes less severe acts.

In contrast, the UN Convention against Torture (CAT) provides a detailed definition:

> "torture" means any act by which severe pain or suffering, whether physical or mental, is intentionally inflicted on a person for such purposes as obtaining from him or a third person information or a confession, punishing him for an act he or a third person has committed or is suspected of having committed, or intimidating or coercing him or a third person, or for any reason based on discrimination of any kind, when such pain or suffering is inflicted by or at the instigation of or with the consent or acquiescence of a public official or other person acting in an official capacity.[84]

To qualify as torture under the CAT, an act must therefore fulfill many different criteria:

- Nature—does the act impose "severe pain or suffering, whether physical or mental?"
- Intent—is the act "intentionally inflicted on a person?"

- Purpose—is the act performed to obtain "information or a confession," to punish the victim, to intimidate or coerce the victim, or as an act of discrimination?
- Official capacity—is the "pain or suffering ... inflicted by or at the instigation of or with the consent or acquiescence of a public official or other person acting in an official capacity?"

These criteria often give states wiggle-room to argue that torture has not occurred.

For example, Peru suffered widespread violence in the 1980s and 1990s between the government and a revolutionary group called Sendero Luminoso (Shining Path). In 1991, a Peruvian woman—known by her initials, GRB, to protect her identity—was captured by Sendero Luminoso, held prisoner, and raped. After she escaped, she fled Peru and her family's home was bombed by Sendero Luminoso in retaliation. GRB applied for asylum in Sweden, arguing that if she returned to Peru, she would be tortured. Sweden denied her claim, arguing that "there were no indications that she was persecuted by the Peruvian authorities, and that the acts by Sendero Luminoso could not be considered as persecution by authorities, but criminal activities."[85] Because GRB's persecution did not involve a government official, it did not qualify as "torture" under the CAT. GRB filed a complaint against Sweden with the Committee Against Torture, which agreed with Sweden's reasoning.[86]

International disputes about torture often involve prisoners, who are especially vulnerable to mistreatment by government officials. Two important topics often come up in these disputes. First, many torture disputes involve prison conditions, including restrictions on prison visitors, sensory deprivation, and solitary confinement. Rulings on these topics have varied over time and across institutions.[87] However, the overall trend is a broader interpretation of torture and ill-treatment. Practices that were acceptable in the past are often found to violate human rights.

Second, experts disagree about the legality of the death penalty. Many experts believe that the death penalty is torture. They argue that death is the most severe form of physical suffering, and that the death penalty satisfies the CAT criteria of intent, purpose, and official capacity. However, when states negotiated the ICCPR, they explicitly allowed the death penalty under limited circumstances.[88] States that use the death penalty accordingly argue that the death penalty is not torture or severe ill-treatment because the ICCPR allows it. Legal disputes over the death penalty therefore usually involve the procedural and mechanical details of execution. Numerous disputes have addressed physical suffering from the method of execution (e.g. hanging, lethal injection), and mental suffering from delay caused by legal appeals. Ironically, some of the major legal victories for anti-death penalty campaigners involve delays that protect prisoners from wrongful execution—if states simply executed convicts more quickly, they would be in compliance with international law.[89]

Human rights treaties that address torture usually include provisions about prevention and punishment. First, states usually have a duty to prevent torture by both public officials and private actors. States must accordingly enact legislation to deter torture, train public officials (like police and prison guards), and create procedural safeguards. The obligation to prevent torture has also created a prohibition on **re-foulement**, which is the forced return of migrants to states where they are likely to suffer severe human rights violations, like torture.[90] When GRB complained to the Committee Against Torture about Sweden, she was making a legal claim about refoulement—she argued that Sweden should grant her asylum because she would be tortured if she returned to Peru. States and human rights bodies vary in their interpretation of which human rights violations are covered by refoulement, and how likely these violations must be for a migrant to receive protection. In GRB's dispute, the Committee Against Torture argued that returning to Peru did not put GRB at risk because Sendero Luminoso was not active throughout Peru, and therefore "the threat from Sendero Luminoso ... [was] of local character."[91] Even if GRB were at risk in some parts of Peru, she wouldn't be at risk everywhere in Peru.

Second, states have a duty to punish torture and ill-treatment. Numerous disputes have established that states must thoroughly investigate possible violations and fully enforce their domestic laws. States must also make adequate reparation for torture and ill-treatment, which can include compensation, medical care, and policy changes to prevent future violations.

One issue with the obligation to punish torture involves political transitions. States that transition from autocracy to democracy often create **amnesty** laws in which they agree not to prosecute individuals for certain offenses, and to pardon individuals already convicted of those offenses. Numerous Latin American states—including Argentina, Chile, and Uruguay—passed amnesty laws when they transitioned to democracy in the 1980s and 1990s. South Africa and Spain followed a similar pattern during their political transitions. Many experts believe that amnesties help to promote peaceful political transitions.[92] As one scholar explains: "transitions to democracies are usually brokered processes, with the outgoing leaders exerting considerable power and the incoming regime being necessarily sensitive to their demands."[93] Yet numerous human rights bodies—including the Committee Against Torture, the Human Rights Committee, and the Inter-American Court of Human Rights—have argued that amnesties violate the legal obligation to punish torture and ill-treatment.[94]

An additional issue is whether states should punish torture that occurs outside their territory. In most domestic legal systems, a state can use its domestic courts to punish a crime if at least one jurisdictional criterion applies:

- Territory—did the crime occur on state territory?
- Nationality—was the accused or the victim a state national?
- National security—did the crime threaten the state's national security?

If none of these criteria apply, then domestic courts usually lack jurisdiction over a crime. However, states sometimes assert **universal jurisdiction** so that their domestic courts can prosecute severe crimes that: (1) occurred on foreign territory; (2) involved only foreign nationals; and (3) did not threaten the state's national security. Such prosecutions are rare, but sometimes address torture.

For example, when Chilean leader Augusto Pinochet stepped down from power, he was promised immunity from criminal prosecution. Years later, torture victims persuaded Spanish officials to prosecute Pinochet in Spanish courts, leading Spain to try to extradite Pinochet while he was visiting the UK. Ironically, Spanish amnesty laws protected members of the Franco regime, so many Spanish torture victims asked Argentina to prosecute their torturers. The overall result has been that many military and political leaders who are accused of crimes like torture face impunity at home, but prosecution abroad.[95] These cases raise complicated questions about the limits of state power, but they remain an important way to uphold international law.[96]

How can we understand the widespread use of torture, despite its broad condemnation? We can begin by thinking about those states that have not joined any of the relevant treaties, like Malaysia, Oman, and Singapore. A small minority of law scholars question whether torture is actually prohibited under customary international law.[97] Recall that customary international law is formed by a combination of state practice and acceptance as law (*opinio juris*). As discussed in Chapter 2, judges and scholars often disagree about whether treaties are evidence of custom. As one expert argues: "arguments for the illegality of torture [under customary international law] depend entirely on … rhetorical evidence of law rather than on a demonstration of the actual behavior of states with regard to torture."[98] That is, if state practice comes from how states actually behave—rather than the pledges they make—then perhaps torture is allowed under customary international law. States that have not ratified torture treaties therefore may not be breaking international law when they commit torture.

Second, many states disagree about what constitutes torture. For example, after the 2001 terrorist attacks against the US, the Bush Administration asked US government lawyers for clarification about the rights of suspected terrorists held in a military prison at Guantanamo Bay, Cuba.[99] The US reservation to the CAT limits the interpretation of mental suffering.[100] Some tactics in US military prisons—like threatening prisoners with dogs, forcing male prisoners to stand naked before female guards, or isolating them from other prisoners—did not cause physical suffering, so US officials argued that they were permitted under the US treaty reservation. Other tactics—like forced standing and sleep deprivation—were not considered severe enough to be torture.[101] The Bush Administration believed that the US did not violate international law, although most human rights advocates disagree with this conclusion.

Finally, even though the prohibition of torture is non-derogable, some experts nonetheless argue that necessity or self-defense can preclude the wrongfulness of torture.[102] For example, a prominent 2002 US government memo argued that if US officials were accused of torture, they could escape US criminal liability because torture was necessary and used in self-defense to prevent terrorist attacks.[103] Other states that used torture during international crises, including France during the Algerian War of Independence, have made similar arguments.[104] Many US voters—including military veterans—believe that torture can sometimes be excused or justified.[105] However, public support for torture diminishes when individuals are more informed about international law.[106]

Human Trafficking

International law scholars consider the prohibition of slavery to be a peremptory norm. Yet throughout the world, individuals are held in slave-like conditions—forced to work dangerous jobs with little to no compensation or freedom. We use the term **human trafficking** to describe the use of force, fraud, or coercion to secure labor. This definition includes the recruitment, movement, harboring, or sale of individuals, both domestically and across international borders. Most anti-trafficking efforts focus on protecting women in the commercial sex industry. But under contemporary international law, anti-trafficking rhetoric is often used to describe child labor and forced marriages. We categorize human trafficking as a physical integrity issue because trafficking victims are often forced into organ and tissue donation, prostitution, and surrogacy.

Human trafficking is usually hidden from public view, but it often begins with voluntary transactions in which individuals from developing states agree to move to developed states for work opportunities.[107] Some trafficking victims pay employment agencies or smugglers to arrange their transportation and jobs, while others agree to give up a portion of their future salaries. Occasionally, trafficking victims are kidnapped or sold by family members into forced labor. Some trafficking victims know that they will be entering dangerous professions, like prostitution, while others are deceived. After arriving at their destinations, trafficking victims are usually unable to leave their jobs and are treated inhumanely. Employers or smugglers often seize the passports of trafficking victims, and refuse to pay them sufficient wages to earn their release, leading to indentured servitude. Human trafficking thus "blurs the lines of where slavery ends and economics begins."[108]

Given the horrors of human trafficking, why hasn't the international community combatted it more aggressively? One obstacle is ideology—human trafficking connects to broader political debates about the commercial sex industry and immigration. In some conservative societies, sex workers are viewed as unworthy of legal protection, even if they are subjected to force, fraud, or coercion. Even in very liberal societies, women's rights activists often disagree about commercial sex. Some activists believe that prostitution is "an inherently oppressive practice that stems from women's inequality" and should be illegal.[109] Others believe that prostitution is a legitimate form of labor that should be protected, and that only coerced or forced sex should be illegal. Immigration debates also hinder international cooperation. While some politicians believe that human trafficking victims should be allowed to remain and work legally in their destinations, others believe that victims should be deported back home.

Instrumental factors also prevent international cooperation to combat human trafficking. Regulating black markets is costly and difficult, distracting law enforcement from other priorities. Additionally, human trafficking victims are often illegal migrants with little influence over politicians, while the beneficiaries of human trafficking often have political power. Sometimes the beneficiaries are even governments themselves! For example, Belarus, Japan, and Uzbekistan all have government-run labor programs that violate human trafficking standards.[110]

Human trafficking rose to global attention in the 1990s, after the fall of the Soviet Union stimulated economic migration. Argentina pushed for human trafficking to be included in a UN agreement on transnational organized crime because of concerns about child pornography and prostitution.[111] By 2001, labor and women's rights activists had built an international coalition with religious groups, including evangelical Christians. This coalition pressured states to join the Palermo Protocol on Human Trafficking. This treaty requires states to criminalize human trafficking and to assist and protect victims.[112] It thus treats human trafficking as primarily a criminal issue, rather than a human rights issue.[113]

Yet the most successful anti-trafficking effort has probably been a domestic US law. Under the Trafficking Victims Protection Act of 2000, the US government began monitoring and reporting on anti-trafficking efforts in other states. This program is based on the concept of **scorecard diplomacy**, in which states are publicly assessed and graded to influence their behavior. When the US program began in 2001, it assigned its lowest grade to Israel, which had extensive human trafficking for prostitution and low-skilled manual labor. US State Department officials privately pressured government leaders to pass and enforce stronger criminal laws that prohibited human trafficking.[114] Additionally, Israeli newspapers publicized Israel's low grade, noting that the US would likely cut foreign aid unless Israel passed and enforced new laws.[115] The pressure worked and Israel adopted reforms until it earned a top grade in 2012. This pattern was not unique to Israel: scorecard diplomacy can be an effective way to pressure states to change their behavior.[116]

Most states have now either partially or fully criminalized human trafficking. Yet many anti-trafficking experts believe that states should address the conditions that make individuals willing to migrate for dangerous work. One expert argues: "The problem of trafficking begins not with the traffickers themselves, but with the conditions that caused their victims to migrate."[117] Such conditions include home state corruption, poverty, sexual violence, and the lack of political and social rights.[118] These conditions also include weak labor protections in destination states, which allow employers to exploit trafficking victims.[119] To combat human trafficking, states may need to promote civil and political rights, as well as economic and social rights.

8.4   Civil and Political Rights

Civil and political rights are a separate area of human rights from physical integrity rights. The key treaty that defines these rights is the 1966 International Covenant on Civil and Political Rights (ICCPR). This treaty is overseen by a special treaty body called the Human Rights Committee (HRC). States sometimes temporarily derogate from ICCPR provisions. For example, after the Paris terrorist attacks in fall 2015, France declared a temporary state of emergency that expanded police powers and limited ICCPR protections for freedom of assembly and criminal justice. Nonetheless, states are required "to respect and to ensure" ICCPR protections.[120] States may not claim that they lack capacity to fully protect these rights.

International civil and political rights closely correspond to the domestic rights provided within most advanced democracies. However, international rules are compromises between competing domestic conceptions about how to balance rights. For example, while some states (like the US) believe in nearly absolute protections for free speech, other states (like Germany) are willing to restrict free speech to promote competing objectives, like racial and religious equality. International rules thus grant states flexibility to balance competing values. In the text below, we first discuss the related rights of expression, assembly, and association. Second, we discuss religion, including the right to manifest beliefs through "worship, observance, practice and teaching."[121] We then consider criminal justice, including rules for arrests, trials, and humane prison conditions.

Expression, Assembly, and Association

The ICCPR establishes that individuals have a human right to hold opinions and express them in a variety of ways. This freedom of expression includes the right "to seek, receive and impart information and ideas of all kinds … either orally, in writing or in print, in the form of art, or through any other media."[122] The ICCPR also establishes the related rights of assembly and association.[123] Under international law, assembly is the public gathering of individuals "intentionally and temporarily for a specific purpose."[124] Assembly is related to expression because it involves the transmission of ideas within a group or to audiences.

For example, the HRC has argued that freedom of assembly protects public protests against government officials.[125] The freedom of association allows individuals "formally to join together in groups to pursue common interests."[126] Legally protected associations include advocacy groups, political parties, and trade unions.

However, the ICCPR does not allow unconstrained rights to expression, assembly, and association. The ICCPR allows states to limit expression if such limits "are provided by law and are necessary ... for the protection of national security or of public order ..., or of public health or morals."[127] Similar provisions limit assembly and association.[128] Because limits must be "provided by law", states must follow their national laws when restricting individual rights. For example, states may not arbitrarily suppress protests, but they can have laws that require protest permits so that police can protect public safety. Such limits must be "necessary" to achieve a legitimate competing objective. To meet this requirement, a state must establish "a direct and immediate connection between the expression and the threat," and the limit must be proportionate, meaning that it "must not be overbroad."[129] Additionally, the ICCPR requires states to prohibit hate speech, which it defines as the "advocacy of national, racial or religious hatred that constitutes incitement to discrimination, hostility or violence."[130]

The competing objectives of national security and public order can be used to prohibit "speech which may incite crime, violence, or mass panic."[131] For example, radio broadcasters helped direct the 1994 Rwandan genocide by urging their Hutu listeners to murder Tutsis.[132] They directed militias to organize roadblocks and to kill both specific enemies and individuals who would not produce their government identity cards.[133] These broadcasts were not protected under human rights law. Rather, radio broadcasters were later prosecuted by an international criminal tribunal for inciting genocide.[134]

Similarly, many states limit expression, assembly, and association that promotes anti-Semitic, fascist, and neo-Nazi viewpoints. The HRC has repeatedly supported such limits:

- the HRC refused to hear a legal challenge to Canadian telecommunications rules that prevent anti-Semitic speech;[135]
- the HRC upheld the firing of a Canadian public school teacher who published anti-Semitic books and pamphlets;[136] and
- the HRC upheld an Italian ban on a fascist political party.[137]

These cases involved a combination of justifications about national security, public order, and hate speech.

The European Convention on Human Rights also allows states to restrict rights for the sake of "national security" and "public safety."[138] Recall that its creation was driven by the fear that newly democratic states might revert to fascism in the aftermath of World War II.[139] This fear has also shaped the European Court's case law. For example, the European Court upheld a Turkish law that banned a political party that advocated for theocratic law. In its ruling, the European Court wrote:

> it is not at all improbable that totalitarian movements, organised in the form of political parties, might do away with democracy, after prospering under the democratic regime, there being examples of this in modern European history.[140]

However, the European Court later overturned a Romanian law that banned a communist political party, reasoning that:

> there can be no justification for hindering a political group that complies with fundamental democratic principles ... solely because it has criticised the country's constitutional and legal order and sought a public debate in the political arena.[141]

These rulings suggest that under European human rights law, national security and public safety relate to the preservation of democracy.[142]

Another competing objective in the ICCPR is public health. The HRC has not (yet) heard a dispute involving public health. Yet the 2020 worldwide outbreak of COVID-19, a contagious virus, shows how states can use public health concerns to restrict expression and assembly. Some states—including India—passed laws permitting press censorship about COVID-19. Ostensibly, these laws prevent the broadcast of false health information, but they also prevent the press from criticizing government health policies.[143] Other states—including China, Italy, and the US—prohibited assemblies, arguing that these limits would constrain the spread of the virus. However, these laws also prohibited individuals from protesting government policies and attending religious services.

States routinely use the ICCPR's morals clause to limit pornography and other materials that are considered obscene. For example, Finland's government restricted radio and television broadcasts about homosexuality in the late 1970s, reasoning that homosexuality violated "prevailing moral conceptions in Finland."[144] Complainants at the HRC argued that Finland violated their right to free expression. However, the HRC supported Finland, noting that "public morals differ widely" across societies and that homosexual behavior was criminal in Finland.[145] In similar lawsuits, the European Court of Human Rights has invoked the margin of appreciation doctrine, reasoning that European states have different conceptions of morality, and hence that courts should give deference to states when deciding which restrictions are necessary.[146]

The final, and most controversial, competing value in the ICCPR is the prohibition of hate speech. Many states—including Belgium, Denmark, Finland, Iceland, and the US—believe in strong protections for the freedom of expression and used treaty reservations to opt out of ICCPR rules on hate speech.[147] For example, US domestic courts have repeatedly invalidated laws that restrict hate speech.[148] Other states—like Canada, South Africa, Sweden, and the UK—are more willing to limit expression that promotes hatred.[149]

All of these competing values—of national security and public order, public health, morality, and hate speech—require that states balance the rights of different individuals. This balancing can be particularly challenging for three contemporary political issues. First, the rise of groups like al-Qaeda and ISIL has prompted many states to try to limit speech that supports terrorism. For example, the UN declared in 2015 that "eliminating extremist speech" was an important political goal.[150] Similarly, the UK announced in 2015 that it was drafting legislation to limit "vocal or active opposition to fundamental British values including democracy, the rule of law, individual liberty, mutual respect and tolerance of different faiths and beliefs, as well as calling for the deaths of members of the armed forces."[151] However, such legislation never appeared, reportedly because "government lawyers had found it impossible to find a 'legally robust' definition of extremism that would have any chance of surviving a free speech challenge in the courts."[152] While speech that directly incites terrorist attacks can threaten public order, should states prohibit speech that supports groups like al-Qaeda and ISIL? Does supporting Sharia law and an Islamic caliphate fundamentally threaten national security or qualify as hate speech? International law has struggled to answer these questions.

Second, many states have tried to ban speech that denies the Holocaust and other genocides. These states argue that denying the Holocaust and other genocides makes future violence more likely. For example, a controversial 1990 French law called the *Loi Gayssot* makes it illegal to question the findings of the 1945 Nuremberg Tribunal, which prosecuted Nazi officials for the Holocaust. When this French law was challenged for violating the ICCPR, France argued that "racism did not constitute an opinion but an aggression, and that every time racism was allowed to express itself publicly, the public order was immediately and severely threatened."[153] The HRC ultimately accepted France's argument and did not find that the *Loi Gayssot* violated international law.[154] However, when Switzerland later prohibited denial of the Armenian genocide, the European Court of Human Rights ruled that Switzerland had violated freedom of expression.[155] Differences in treaty law, case facts, and national legislation can lead to diverging outcomes, but the European Court ruling suggested to some observers that "from a legal viewpoint, Holocaust denial remains unique, such that it may justify restrictions on free speech that the denial of other grave crimes may not."[156]

In a more recent case, the African Court on Human and Peoples' Rights was asked to evaluate a Rwandan law that criminalized the "minimisation of genocide."[157] The African Court ultimately ruled that the law did not violate the African

Charter or the ICCPR because it "served the legitimate interests of protecting national security and public order."[158] In particular, the Court noted that:

> Rwanda suffered from the most atrocious genocide in the recent history of mankind and this is recognised as such internationally. This grim fact of its past evidently warrants that the government should adopt all measures to promote social cohesion and concordance among the people and prevent similar incidents from happening in the future.[159]

However, the African Court ruled that Rwanda violated individual rights when it used the law to imprison an opposition politician.[160] These rulings suggest that genocide denial laws will continue to raise important human rights issues, particularly in societies that experienced mass violence.

One final contemporary political issue is the relationship between freedom of expression and religion. For example, numerous Middle Eastern states imposed blasphemy laws after the Arab Spring protests in the early 2010s.[161] Other states with blasphemy laws include Ireland, Pakistan, and Russia. These laws often prohibit the questioning of religious beliefs, "the destruction of holy books [and] depictions deemed disrespectful of God or holy figures."[162] States with blasphemy laws often argue that they protect public order and morality, or that blasphemy is hate speech. Some states even argue that restrictions on blasphemy are necessary to protect freedom of religion. Yet critics of blasphemy laws argue that these laws are frequently used to persecute religious minorities, and to suppress criticism of religious leaders. How can states balance the rights of believers and non-believers? Is the protection of "morality" the same as the protection of religion? Once again, international law does not provide easy answers.

Religion

Religion is also protected by human rights law. This right is based on the individual freedom to choose and express an identity, rather than the protection of religious groups or traditions.[163] The ICCPR says:

> Everyone shall have the right to freedom of thought, conscience and religion. This right shall include freedom to have or to adopt a religion or belief of his choice, and freedom, either individually or in community with others and in public or private, to manifest his religion or belief in worship, observance, practice and teaching.[164]

Similar provisions are included in the European, Inter-American, and African regional agreements.[165] These treaties generate three important political questions.

First, what kinds of beliefs qualify as a religion? The ICCPR does not define the term "religion." However, the HRC wrote that the ICCPR:

> protects theistic, non-theistic and atheistic beliefs, as well as the right not to profess any religion or belief ... [The ICCPR] is not limited in its application to traditional

religions or to religions and beliefs with institutional characteristics or practices analogous to those of traditional religions. The Committee therefore views with concern any tendency to discriminate against any religion or belief for any reason, including the fact that they are newly established, or represent religious minorities.[166]

Nonetheless, states often define what is (and what is not) protected as a religion under their domestic laws. For example, Indonesia recognizes six religions: Buddhism, Catholicism, Confucianism, Hinduism, Islam, and Protestantism. Individuals who follow the official doctrines of these religions are legally protected, but individuals who deviate from these doctrines can be punished under Indonesian law.[167] While some experts view Indonesia's laws as religious protection, others believe that these laws violate religious freedom.

A second related political question is: how broad is the right to manifest beliefs? The ICCPR does not define the term "manifest," mentioning only "worship, observance, practice and teaching." However, the HRC has adopted a very broad interpretation of the right to manifest beliefs:

> The freedom to manifest religion or belief in worship, observance, practice and teaching encompasses a broad range of acts. The concept of worship extends to ritual and ceremonial acts giving direct expression to belief, as well as various practices integral to such acts, including the building of places of worship, the use of ritual formulae and objects, the display of symbols, and the observance of holidays and days of rest. The observance and practice of religion or belief may include not only ceremonial acts but also such customs as the observance of dietary regulations, the wearing of distinctive clothing or head coverings, participation in rituals associated with certain stages of life, and the use of a particular language customarily spoken by a group. In addition, the practice and teaching of religion or belief includes acts integral to the conduct by religious groups of their basic affairs, such as the freedom to choose their religious leaders, priests and teachers, the freedom to establish seminaries or religious schools and the freedom to prepare and distribute religious texts or publications.[168]

Nonetheless, this broad interpretation is sometimes difficult to apply.

Some disputes over religious manifestation are rooted in differences between religious doctrine and cultural traditions. For example, many Jewish communities celebrate Sukkot, a nine-day harvest festival, by constructing temporary hut-like outdoor structures. Many Jewish families throw elaborate parties during Sukkot, decorating their structures with lights and ornaments. Neighbors have friendly competitions over who has the most beautiful Sukkot structure, just like Christian families often compete over their Christmas decorations. But are these decorations protected religious symbols or merely cultural traditions?

No religious text requires Jews to build Sukkot structures or instructs Christians to decorate their homes at Christmas. However, when a Canadian court was asked to assess a Sukkot structure built illegally on an apartment balcony, it argued that the lack of a religious mandate did not matter. Instead, the court ruled that the Sukkot structure was a protected religious symbol because the individuals who built it had a sincere belief that it was related to their religion. This approach suggests that individuals, not governments, should determine how to manifest their beliefs. While some states—such as South Africa and the US—have used a similar approach, other states—like Greece and India—give their governments more power to determine what is a protected manifestation.[169]

A third political question is: how should states balance religion against competing values? The ICCPR recognizes such competing values by saying:

> Freedom to manifest one's religion or beliefs may be subject only to such limitations as are prescribed by law and are necessary to protect public safety, order, health, or morals or the fundamental rights and freedoms of others.[170]

But how do states strike a balance between religion and these competing values? Can this balance vary across different societies?

Concerns about public safety and order can justify many different kinds of limits on religious manifestation. Many states limit hate speech about religion, particularly states with religious violence.[171] Similarly, states sometimes limit religious dress because of safety concerns. For example, the HRC upheld Canadian regulations that required railway electricians to wear hard hats, even though this required a Sikh to remove his religious turban.[172]

But does religious dress in general—like Islamic headscarves and Sikh turbans—threaten public order? Many European states have struggled to answer this question, yielding conflicting jurisprudence. The German Constitutional Court ruled in 2003 that Muslim schoolteachers could wear headscarves at work.[173] However, just two years later, the European Court of Human Rights upheld a Turkish law that prohibited university students from wearing Islamic headscarves. The European Court noted that "the supporters of secularism [in Turkey] see the Islamic headscarf as a symbol of a political Islam."[174] These two rulings suggest that different societies can (and perhaps should) balance competing values in different ways because an Islamic headscarf has a different meaning in Germany than in Turkey.

Complicating matters, sometimes different legal bodies interpret the same facts in different ways. For example, French law requires individuals to remove head coverings for all government-issued photo identification cards, including driver's licenses and passports. Police officers and customs officials can then ask individuals to remove their head coverings to verify their identity. Mann Singh—an observant Sikh—believed that these French regulations violated his freedom of religion since they required him to remove his religious turban. In a series of cases, Mann Singh challenged the French law at the European Court of Human Rights and the HRC. The European Court upheld the French law under the European Convention on Human Rights, while the HRC ruled against France under the ICCPR.[175] Yet the European Convention and ICCPR texts on religious freedom are nearly identical. The main difference between the two cases was that the European Court usually grants more deference to states (through its margin of appreciation doctrine) than the HRC.

States also sometimes restrict religious manifestation because of health concerns. For example, some religious groups manifest their faith by using hallucinogenic drugs. Members of the Rastafari faith smoke cannabis during religious ceremonies, and some Native American tribes use peyote for religious purposes. Many governments worry that individuals may claim membership in these groups solely to use drugs that would otherwise be illegal. States with large populations of these groups—like South Africa and the US—have carefully crafted laws that balance the religious use of drugs against public health concerns.[176]

Finally, while the ICCPR lists religious "teaching" as a protected activity, many states restrict proselytism, which is trying to convert a person to a faith.[177] These states often argue that proselytism limits the "rights and freedoms of others," including the right to freely choose a faith. When considering a Greek law that criminalized proselytism, the European Court of Human Rights wrote that proselytism can "take the form of ... exerting improper pressure on people in distress or need; it may even entail the use of violence or brainwashing."[178]

Criminal Justice

Many ICCPR provisions address criminal justice. First, the ICCPR prohibits the "arbitrary arrest or detention" of all individuals, and requires that arrest or detention must be "on such grounds and in accordance with such procedure as are established by law."[179] Individuals who are arrested or detained must be "promptly informed of any charges against" them.[180] If these include criminal charges, the individual must be "brought promptly before a judge or other officer authorized by law to exercise judicial power and shall be entitled to trial within a reasonable time or to release."[181] Additionally, the ICCPR says that "anyone who is deprived of his liberty by arrest or detention shall be entitled to take proceedings before a court, in order that that court may decide without delay on the lawfulness of his detention and order his release if the detention is not lawful."[182] The HRC has clarified that this right includes access to lawyers who can assist with court proceedings.[183]

Yet states often allow arrests or detentions that international law experts believe are "arbitrary." For example, Australia is a common destination for asylum seekers from Asian states—like Afghanistan, Cambodia, Sri Lanka, and Vietnam—who flee war and poverty. Many of these individuals arrive in Australia without prior authorization. Australia requires that these individuals remain in government detention centers while they apply for refugee status. The HRC has repeatedly condemned Australia for this policy and for the long delays faced by migrants when they apply for legal residency.[184]

Human rights advocates also criticize the US for its detention camps along the US–Mexico border, which house migrants who are fleeing violence and poverty in Latin America. US laws require the mandatory detention of many migrants, including those caught illegally crossing the border.[185] In a harsh report, UN human rights experts criticized US policies:

> the mandatory detention of immigrants, especially asylum seekers, is contrary to international human rights ... Individuals held in immigration detention shall be brought promptly before a judicial authority empowered to order their release or to vary the conditions of release. If detention is ordered, it should be subject to regular, periodic reviews to ensure that it is reasonable, necessary, proportional and lawful, and that alternatives to detention are considered.[186]

These migrants cannot challenge their detention at the HRC because the US does not accept its jurisdiction to hear complaints against the US.

Second, the ICCPR contains extensive rules to ensure that individuals who face criminal charges receive a fair trial.[187] It says:

> All persons shall be equal before the courts and tribunals ... Everyone shall be entitled to a fair and public hearing by a competent, independent and impartial tribunal established by law.[188]

In numerous disputes, the HRC has clarified aspects of this right, focusing on the presumption of innocence, adequate legal defenses, expeditious proceedings, witness examination, and the right to appeal a conviction.[189]

Many states—particularly in poor or war-torn societies—struggle to provide criminal justice.[190] As one legal expert writes:

> A mere failure to bolt the doors to the courtroom will not guarantee access without discrimination to the courts. The provision of information about legal services, the holding of courts in accessible locations and perhaps also ... the provision of legal aid, may all be needed.[191]

These resources are important both to criminal defendants and to victims. For example, the Democratic Republic of the Congo experienced multiple wars in the 1990s and 2000s, leading to extreme sexual violence. Numerous Western aid organizations helped to build special criminal courts for sexual violence. These efforts included training police officers to conduct investigations, providing prosecutors, hiring and training judges, and even constructing courtrooms in remote areas.[192]

But what is the meaning of "a competent, independent and impartial tribunal established by law?" In many states, governments interfere in domestic courts.

For example, one study of Pakistani courts has shown that judges are more likely to rule in favor of the government when they are chosen by the executive branch than when they are chosen by their peers.[193] This evidence reinforces broader concerns about the decline of judicial independence, particularly in states like Hungary and Poland.[194]

Even when judges are independent from the executive and legislature, other factors may affect their impartiality. Many judges in the US are elected by voters, rather than selected using neutral assessments of their competence. Political scientists have shown that US judges give harsher criminal punishments when they are subject to electoral pressure.[195] Additionally, the HRC has repeatedly questioned the impartiality of military trials. In a 1999 review of Chile, the HRC wrote that "the wide jurisdiction of the military courts ... contribute[s] to the impunity which [military] personnel enjoy ... for serious human rights violations."[196]

Third, ICCPR rules govern the humane treatment of prisoners. As discussed in section 8.3, the ICCPR is one of many treaties that prohibit "torture" and "cruel, inhuman or degrading treatment or punishment."[197] The ICCPR additionally requires that "All persons deprived of their liberty shall be treated with humanity and with respect for the inherent dignity of the human person."[198] The HRC has clarified that these rules apply to all forms of detention, including "prisons, hospitals—particularly psychiatric hospitals—detention camps or correctional institutions."[199]

ICCPR members are required to follow UN guidelines on detention conditions, which were drafted in 1957 and updated in 2015.[200] These rules prohibit discrimination in the treatment of prisoners. They additionally require sleeping accommodations with adequate heating, lighting, and ventilation. Finally, these rules require states to provide bedding, clothing, food and medical care. The ICCPR additionally says that "the essential aim" of criminal detention should be "reformation and social rehabilitation," rather than punishment.[201]

Given that the ICCPR seeks "reformation and social rehabilitation," how does it address the death penalty? The ICCPR allows the death penalty within limits. It says that the "sentence of death may be imposed only for the most serious crimes," and that "anyone sentenced to death shall have the right to seek pardon or commutation of the sentence."[202] It additionally requires that the death penalty cannot "be imposed for crimes committed by persons below eighteen years of age" and cannot "be carried out on pregnant women."[203]

However, as described above, many states believe that the death penalty is inherently torture or "cruel, inhuman or degrading treatment or punishment."[204] The HRC has ruled that prolonged detention while awaiting the death penalty causes mental distress that violates the ICCPR.[205] It has also criticized states for using the death penalty for crimes that the HRC does not consider sufficiently serious.[206] States that use the death penalty therefore face extreme political pressure to discontinue it. Some states—including Guyana, Jamaica, and Trinidad and Tobago—have even withdrawn from the HRC's jurisdiction to hear individual complaints after being repeatedly chastised about the death penalty.[207]

8.5   Economic, Social, and Cultural Rights

The 1966 International Covenant on Economic, Social and Cultural Rights (ICESCR) was completed in the same year as the ICCPR, and international labor laws pre-date World War II. Yet economic, social, and cultural rights receive less attention from the international community than physical integrity, civil, and political rights.[208] While the ICCPR requires its members "to respect and to ensure" its provisions, the ICESCR says only that each member must "take steps ... to the maximum of its available resources, with a view to achieving progressively the full realization of the rights" in the ICESCR.[209] The ICESCR thus acknowledges that states can have limited capacity to uphold economic, social, and cultural rights.

Compliance with the ICESCR is overseen by the Committee on Economic, Social and Cultural Rights (CESCR). This institution declared that the ICESCR creates "a minimum core obligation to ensure the satisfaction of ... minimum essential levels of each of the rights," and it has drafted guidelines about these minimum core obligations for many rights.[210] Additionally, the CESCR routinely reminds states that all rights in the ICESCR "will be exercised without discrimination of any kind as to race, colour, sex, language, religion, political or other opinion, national or social origin, property, birth or other status."[211] So states cannot withhold ICESCR rights on the basis of criteria like race, sex, and religion.

In the text below, we begin with labor, one of the oldest areas of human rights law. We then discuss economic and social assistance, including rights to social security, food, housing, health, and education. Finally, we consider cultural rights and marginalized groups.

Labor

After World War I, states created the International Labour Organization (ILO) to help draft international labor standards. In part, the ILO stemmed from the anti-slavery movement and criticism of forced labor in colonial territories. However, states also believed that labor protections would help achieve social justice and prevent future wars.[212] Throughout its history, the ILO has created literally hundreds of treaties that outline labor rights for diverse groups—like child workers—and related topics—like labor unions. The ILO additionally drafts standards that serve as non-binding guidelines for states. These treaties and standards are often invoked as evidence of customary international law, which binds all states. To reinforce the ILO, states included labor rights in the ICESCR. We focus here on ICESCR provisions because they establish the broad principles that guide other treaties and standards on more specialized topics.

First, the ICESCR guarantees a right to work. Its members pledge to "recognize the right to work, which includes the right of everyone to the opportunity to gain his living by work which he freely chooses or accepts."[213] The CESCR clarified that this obligation creates a right to "decent work," which it defines as "work that respects the fundamental rights of the human person as well as the rights of workers in terms of conditions of work safety and remuneration."[214] The ICESCR does not guarantee individuals the right to a job for which they lack necessary training or credentials. You do not have the right to work as a doctor without medical training and certification. But the ICESCR asks states to reduce unnecessary restrictions on employment, and to increase employment opportunities.

According to the CESCR, states have three minimum core obligations regarding the right to work:

(a) To ensure the right of access to employment, especially for disadvantaged and marginalized individuals and groups ...

(b) To avoid any measure that results in discrimination and unequal treatment in the private and public sectors of disadvantaged and marginalized individuals and groups ... [and]

(c) To adopt and implement a national employment strategy.[215]

Broader aspirational goals include full employment (of individuals who want to work) and judicial remedies for labor law violations. The CESCR encourages states to support vocational training programs and track employment indicators for policy decision-making.

Very few international disputes have involved these legal protections. However, many states debated the labor rights of former government officials after the fall of communism in the Soviet Union and Eastern Europe. For example, after gaining its independence from the Soviet Union, Lithuania prohibited individuals who had served in Soviet security and intelligence institutions from working for the government, including working as police officers. Numerous lawsuits in international bodies challenged these restrictions as political discrimination on employment. These international bodies ruled that while Lithuania could deny employment based on an individual's former affiliation with the Soviet regime, it had to evaluate each situation on its own merits; it could not issue a blanket prohibition on employment.[216]

Similarly, many states restrict female labor by arguing that women are too vulnerable and weak to work at night or in dangerous industries, like mining.

Modern international law experts usually believe that such laws violate the ICESCR. Employers may refuse to hire workers who lack specific job requirements (like the ability to carry heavy equipment), but outright bans on female employment are now considered illegal discrimination.

Second, the ICESCR requires favorable work conditions. It requires that its members "recognize the right of everyone to the enjoyment of just and favourable conditions of work," including:

(a) Remuneration which provides all workers, as a minimum, with:
    (i) Fair wages and equal remuneration for work of equal value ... ;
    (ii) A decent living for themselves and their families ... ;
(b) Safe and healthy working conditions;
(c) Equal opportunity for everyone to be promoted in his employment ... ;
(d) Rest, leisure and reasonable limitation of working hours and periodic holidays with pay, as well as remuneration for public holidays.[217]

The ICESCR does not set specific wages, conditions, or hourly limitations, but the CESCR and the ILO issue guidelines on these issues. Minimum core obligations on work conditions include protection from pay discrimination (particularly for women and other protected groups), and the adoption of domestic legislation that sets minimum wages, caps daily/weekly working hours, protects worker health and safety, and prohibits sexual harassment.[218] As an aspirational goal, states are expected to progressively improve safety standards and work conditions.

Finally, the ICESCR creates a right to unionize. It says that its members "undertake to ensure":

(a) The right of everyone to form trade unions and join the trade union of his choice, subject only to the rules of the organization concerned, for the promotion and protection of his economic and social interests. No restrictions may be placed on the exercise of this right other than those prescribed by law and which are necessary in a democratic society in the interests of national security or public order or for the protection of the rights and freedoms of others ...

(c) The right of trade unions to function freely subject to no limitations other than those prescribed by law and which are necessary in a democratic society in the interests of national security or public order or for the protection of the rights and freedoms of others;

(d) The right to strike, provided that it is exercised in conformity with the laws of the particular country.[219]

The CESCR has not written guidelines for union rights, although it is usually critical of domestic laws that restrict or limit trade unions.[220] Numerous regional human rights bodies have ruled that individuals may not be compelled to join a union to practice their profession, although these cases were decided under regional human rights treaties.[221]

Some critics argue that labor rights are incompatible with democracy and free market capitalism. After transitioning to democracy in the early 1990s, many Eastern European states incorporated many international rules into their new domestic constitutions. Cass Sunstein, a prominent legal scholar, criticized these constitutions, arguing that "Governments should not be compelled to interfere with free markets."[222] Access to work, favorable work conditions, and labor unionization are laudable goals, yet their realization depends on government policies. Sunstein believed that labor rights decreased the power of elected legislatures, and increased the power of judges as upholders of rights. He believed that judges were ill-suited for regulating work conditions, and that such tasks "should be subject to democratic debate."[223]

Economic and Social Assistance

International law also recognizes rights to economic and social assistance. Throughout history, families, guilds, and religious groups protected individuals from accidents, illness, and unemployment. As states grew in capacity, they began to provide economic and social assistance, like education, health care, and unemployment insurance. In the mid-1960s, the ICESCR said that such assistance had become a human right.

First, the ICESCR establishes "the right of everyone to social security."[224] The ICESCR does not define the term, but states usually interpret **social security** as financial assistance to protect individuals from unexpected outcomes that harm their livelihoods, including accidents, disability, illness, involuntary unemployment, and the death of a spouse.[225] In some states, social security also includes benefits for the elderly and pregnant women. The ICESCR's right to social security is supplemented by numerous ILO conventions and recommendations, regional treaties, and specialized treaties on women, children, and other protected groups.

The CESCR requires every state to provide a minimum core level of social security, regardless of its resources.[226] As a state has more resources, it must provide more social security benefits. For example, the CESCR routinely urges poor states (like Kyrgyzstan and the Democratic Republic of the Congo) to increase social security spending, and criticizes rich states (like Canada and Sweden) when they reduce spending.[227] It also sometimes criticizes taxation and spending decisions that determine the resources available for social security.

States often require employers and workers to help finance social security benefits through employment taxes. States can also impose "reasonable, proportional and transparent" conditions on social security.[228] For example, a state may require an able-bodied individual to attend vocational training or provide evidence that she is seeking employment in exchange for social security payments. It may also require that children attend school for their families to receive assistance.[229]

Second, the ICESCR recognizes the right to food as part of "an adequate stand-ard of living."[230] This right is arguably the most important economic and social right because, in the words of one diplomat who helped draft the ICESCR, "no hu-man right was worth anything to a starving man."[231] The ICESCR does not create a right to be fed—states are not required to provide free food to all people. Rather, states must ensure that people have access to food.[232]

Access to food is driven by governments, which control the movement of food across borders, and build transportation networks within states. They can also subsidize or tax food production, and shape agricultural prices through controls or large-scale purchases of crops. Such agricultural policies are driven by domestic politics.[233] Economist Amartya Sen wrote in 1982: "Starvation is the characteristic of some people not *having* enough food to eat. It is not the characteristic of there not *being* enough food to eat."[234] In his work, Sen described how many govern-ments had caused mass starvation through poor policy choices.

Numerous domestic and international courts have agreed with Sen, finding governments responsible for violating the right to food. In 2001, the Indian Su-preme Court ruled that the government violated individual rights by not distribut-ing the government's ample grain stockpiles to communities harmed by massive droughts.[235] Similarly, the Inter-American Court of Human Rights ruled in 2005 that Paraguay violated the rights of an indigenous group by removing it from native lands where it practiced subsistence agriculture, fishing and hunting.[236] Numerous lawsuits against Nigeria have alleged that oil production destroyed the soil and water of native Ogoni communities, causing starvation.[237] All of these cases illustrate violations of the right to food in the ICESCR and regional human rights treaties.

Third, the ICESCR says that housing is part of "an adequate standard of liv-ing."[238] Once again, the ICESCR does not require states to provide free housing to everyone. Rather, it requires states to enable the private sector to develop access-ible, adequate, and affordable housing. Housing rights disputes can involve zon-ing restrictions, price controls, mortgage rules, and utility services (like electricity, sanitation, and water).[239]

One area of international housing law that has been well-developed involves forced evictions, which the CESCR defines as "the permanent or temporary re-moval against their will of individuals ... from the homes and/or land which they occupy, without the provision of, and access to, appropriate forms of legal or other protection."[240] Forced evictions are common during wars, when armed forces often destroy civilian homes, and when states promote large public infrastructure projects and private development. The CESCR condemned China when it forcibly evicted individuals to build facilities for the 2008 Olympic Games.[241] Similarly, Nigeria forcibly evicted the Ogoni people from the Nigerian Delta to promote pri-vate oil drilling.[242]

The right to housing also requires states to assist the homeless. In the *Grootboom* case from 2000, the South African Constitutional Court used both domestic and international law to address South Africa's housing crisis. In this case, homeless individuals illegally constructed shelters on private land.[243] The government evicted them and destroyed their shelters without giving them alternative housing. In its ruling, the South African Constitutional Court detailed the "intolerable conditions" faced by individuals waiting to receive subsidized government housing.[244] While the Court acknowledged "that the state is not obliged to go beyond available resources or to realize [housing] rights immediately,"[245] it argued that South Africa violated individual rights because "it failed to provide for any form of relief to those desperately in need of access to housing."[246]

Fourth, the ICESCR asserts "the right of everyone to the enjoyment of the highest attainable standard of physical and mental health."[247] The ICESCR requires access to medical care, including emergency and preventive treatment. The right to health can justify mandatory vaccines and restrictions on the freedom of assembly to prevent the spread of diseases.[248] For example, many states mandated quarantines during the COVID-19 pandemic of 2020 to protect public health. The

Figure 8.4 A 2006 photograph shows conditions in a squatter camp in Soweto, South Africa. The small plastic structure in the center foreground of the photo is a toilet shared by the people living in the surrounding shacks. While South Africa has above-average levels of wealth, a large portion of South Africa's population lives in conditions that the South African Constitutional Court described in 2000 as "intolerable" and contrary to international human rights law.

right to health has also been used to support access to water, sanitation, and a clean environment.[249]

The CESCR noted that marginalized populations—including women, children, and persons with disabilities—are often denied health rights. Many states provide inadequate reproductive and maternal care, leading to the unnecessary deaths of children and mothers.[250] Additionally, the CESCR has condemned states like The Gambia for imprisoning individuals with mental illness, rather than providing them with medical treatment.[251] Another major health challenge has been HIV/AIDS. Many Western drug companies have provided anti-retroviral drugs to developing states at little-to-no cost, yet states like South Africa have struggled to distribute these drugs because of inadequate medical infrastructure.[252] Also, many states have refused to prevent HIV/AIDS by creating sexual education programs that promote condoms.[253] The right to health thus includes access to medical care and diverse policies, including criminal laws and education policy.

Finally, the ICESCR recognizes "the right of everyone to education."[254] Yet it requires more access to lower levels of education. While primary education "shall be compulsory and available free to all," secondary education only needs to be "generally available," and higher education must be "equally accessible."[255] The ICESCR recognizes that many states do not have the capacity to provide comprehensive education.

States that violate education rights usually fail to invest in public education or deny education to marginalized groups. These marginalized groups are often removed from mainstream education and provided with alternative services that are inadequate. For example, the Supreme Court of Colombia found the government guilty of violating education rights by suspending girls for becoming pregnant, thereby stigmatizing them and removing them from school.[256] Similarly, many minority groups (like the Roma in Eastern Europe) cannot attend mainstream schools if they don't speak a state's official language.[257] International disputes have also examined the education of children with autism and other special needs.[258] Finally, many international bodies have also focused on low female literacy and education rates as a violation of education rights.[259]

Cultural Rights and Marginalized Groups

International law aims to protect human rights for all individuals. Yet marginalized groups often face special challenges in realizing their rights. International law deals with this challenge in two ways. First, international law creates cultural rights, which are associated with minority groups. Second, numerous treaties address marginalized groups like women, children, persons with disabilities, and migrants. We discuss each of these topics in turn.

Cultural rights permit the expression of collective identity, particularly by minority groups. The ICESCR recognizes "the right of everyone ... to take part in cultural life."[260] Similarly, the ICCPR addresses minority groups:

> In those states in which ethnic, religious or linguistic minorities exist, persons belonging to such minorities shall not be denied the right, in community with the other members of their group, to enjoy their own culture, to profess and practise their own religion, or to use their own language.[261]

While the ICCPR refers to religion and language, neither treaty defines the term "culture." The CESCR interprets the term "culture" broadly, writing that "culture is a broad, inclusive concept encompassing all manifestations of human existence."[262] This includes:

> ways of life, language, oral and written literature, music and song, non-verbal communication, religion or belief systems, rites and ceremonies, sport and games, methods of production or technology, natural and man-made environments, food, clothing and shelter and the arts, customs and traditions through which individuals, groups of individuals and communities express their humanity and the meaning they give to their existence, and build their world view representing their encounter with the external forces affecting their lives.[263]

Cultural rights therefore build on numerous individual rights (like expression, assembly, and religion) to protect group identities.

Disputes over cultural rights often involve minority languages. When public education is not offered in minority languages, individuals are excluded from education.[264] The CESCR argues that states must allow individuals to use their preferred language when communicating with public authorities so that they can access public services, like education.[265] Cultural disputes also often involve indigenous group access to land and resources. For example, the Endorois people lived near Lake Bogoria (in modern-day Kenya) for centuries.[266] In the 1970s, Kenya evicted the Endorois people to build a national game reserve. Kenya later leased mining rights and resold part of this land to third parties.[267] After decades of trying to secure compensation, the Endorois people filed a complaint at the African Commission on Human and Peoples' Rights. They alleged numerous treaty violations, including their right to "cultural development."[268] The African Commission supported the Endorois's claim that Kenya's land seizure violated their cultural rights.[269] Similar lawsuits against Canada, Finland, and New Zealand have examined access to native land as a cultural right.[270]

Because cultural rights are rooted in collective identity, they can sometimes yield conflicts between individual and group rights. For example, Canadian law in the late 1970s specified that Canadian Indian women who married outside of their tribe lost their legal status as members of the tribe. This law matched traditional tribal practices, which emphasized patrilineal ancestry. Sandra Lovelace was born into the Maliseet Indian tribe, but lost her legal status as a Maliseet Indian when she married outside her tribe and left her native reservation. Years later, she divorced her husband and tried to move back to tribal lands. However, she was prohibited from doing so by the Tribal Council, which did not consider her a Maliseet Indian. Lovelace successfully filed a complaint against Canada, arguing that Canadian law violated her cultural rights under the ICCPR.[271] In its decision, the HRC ignored the tension between individual and group rights. Lovelace believed that she was a Maliseet Indian, but the Tribal Council believed that she was not. Who should prevail in such conflicts—individuals or groups?

Numerous treaties also address marginalized groups, including women, children, migrants, and persons with disabilities. These treaties echo rights in the ICCPR and ICESCR, meaning that they largely reinforce existing rights rather than create new rights. Yet human rights advocates argue that these treaties are important because they create "special measures of protection and assistance to enable" marginalized groups "to enjoy rights on an equal footing with everyone else."[272]

For women's rights, international law often faces a tension between infantilizing and empowering women. Early international labor law tried to protect women by prohibiting them from working at night or in dangerous industries. A rhetoric of vulnerability has slowly yielded to a rhetoric of equality, with contemporary treaty law prohibiting "discrimination against women in all its forms."[273] The Convention on the Elimination of All Forms of Discrimination against Women mainly reiterates the ICESCR's economic and social rights, including access to education, employment, and health care. Yet treaty disputes often emphasize gender differences. Numerous cases have treated inadequate reproductive and maternity care as violations of women's rights, rather than as a violation of the general right to health. Similarly, many recent disputes address domestic and sexual violence against women.[274] The classification of these issues as women's rights, rather than physical integrity rights, suggests that women are inherently weak and require different rights than men.

Similarly, tensions appear in the Convention on the Rights of the Child, which proclaims that "childhood is entitled to special care and assistance."[275] This treaty extends physical integrity rights to children, and grants them civil and political rights that mimic those of adults under the ICCPR. It also extends numerous social and cultural rights under the ICESCR. Yet children are provided with few labor rights. This treaty requires that states:

> recognize the right of the child to be protected from economic exploitation and from performing any work that is likely to be hazardous or to interfere with the child's education, or to be harmful to the child's health or physical, mental, spiritual, moral or social development.[276]

But the ICESCR already protects all individuals from exploitation and hazardous work. In contrast, the Convention on the Rights of the Child does not provide a right to work, fair wages, and unionization because most states believe all labor harms a child's education and development. Accordingly, international law provides children with few economic rights, despite their important economic role in many states.

Migrant rights under treaty law are addressed in the International Convention on Migrant Workers. This treaty creates rights for any "person who is to be engaged, is engaged or has been engaged in a remunerated activity in a state of which he or she is not a national," regardless of whether he has complied with domestic laws, including migration laws.[277] The treaty extends physical integrity, civil, and political rights to migrants. It also requires "treatment not less favourable than that which applies to nationals ... in respect of remuneration" and other work conditions. Finally, it requires access to economic and social assistance, like education, health care, and social security.[278]

To understand the politics of migrant rights, we must recognize that all states are either labor-exporting (meaning that they have a net outflow of workers to other states) or labor-importing (meaning that they have a net inflow of workers from other states). For example, many Latin American nationals migrate to the US to work. Similarly, many North African nationals migrate to Europe for work. Most of the fifty-five member states of the International Convention on Migrant Workers are labor-exporting states. By signing the treaty, they create few obligations for themselves (because they do not receive many migrants) while promoting the interests of their nationals abroad.[279] In contrast, most labor-importing states—like France, the US, and the UK—do not support this treaty because they do not want to extend rights to migrants who are illegally living and working in their state.

A more recent treaty with broad political support is the Convention on the Rights of Persons with Disabilities. This treaty aims to protect individuals with "long-term physical, mental, intellectual or sensory impairments" that "hinder their full and effective participation in society on an equal basis with others."[280] This treaty prohibits discrimination and requires states "to enable persons with disabilities to live independently and participate fully in all aspects of life."[281] It additionally clarifies that basic individual human rights apply to individuals with disabilities.

8.6 Case Study Revisited: Do Children Have a Right to (Be Protected from) Work?

We began this chapter with a description of the 2013 La Paz protests over Bolivia's child labor laws. Political pressure from child workers, families, and employers was ultimately successful. In 2014, Bolivia amended its laws to allow children to work independently at the age of ten, and to sign employment contracts at the age of twelve. While these laws were condemned by many international groups, they were supported by Bolivia's voters and the child workers themselves.

The case of child labor in Bolivia connects to each of the major topics of this chapter:

- *Creating human rights*: Throughout the early history of human rights law, children fell outside of the rhetoric of rights. The International Labour Organization's child labor standards from the 1970s and the Convention on the Rights of the Child in 1989 marked a dramatic change in the status of children under international law.[282] Yet these laws reflect a key tension: should children be protected, or should they be empowered?
- *Physical integrity rights*: Most opponents of child labor argue that labor threatens the physical integrity of children. They argue that all labor threatens the life and physical well-being of children. Additionally, they believe that child labor places girls at particular risk of sexual exploitation and human trafficking.
- *Civil and political rights*: One stunning aspect of this case is the role of children as civil and political actors in Bolivia. The 2013 La Paz protests were not isolated or unique. Many child workers in Bolivia organize themselves politically to lobby policy-makers on labor issues.[283] Children also participated in negotiations over the 2009 constitution, which includes child rights. Bolivian children thus exercise their international rights of expression, assembly, and association, although they do not have the right to vote.
- *Economic, social, and cultural rights*: Child labor is most clearly related to economic, social, and cultural rights. Many Bolivian child workers belong to labor unions. These child workers believe that they have the right to work so that they can provide for themselves and their families. Their labor helps them and their families to realize their additional rights to social security, food, housing, health, and education. Many Bolivians also view child labor as a cultural right.[284]

We can now return to the big questions from the beginning of the chapter. First, we asked: should children like Jade Sanjinez be protected from work, or should they have a right to work? Opponents of child labor argue that labor threatens the physical integrity of children, who lack the mental and physical capacity of adults. Most supporters of child labor acknowledge that it can sometimes threaten the life and well-being of children, particularly in dangerous industries.[285] Additionally, the human trafficking of girls in the sex industry is an important challenge worldwide. However, supporters of child labor argue that the physical integrity of children is better protected by legal regulations than by forcing children—who must often work to survive—into illegal work arrangements. Additionally, they argue that most child labor—like selling newspapers or washing dishes—does not threaten physical integrity. Your answer to the question of whether children need to be protected from work will likely depend on your perspectives about childhood itself. Should children be protected from the harsh realities of the world, or empowered to strive for personal autonomy and economic freedom? There is no correct answer to this question.

We next asked: should we be surprised that Bolivia—a well-functioning democracy—blatantly violates international law on child labor? If you live in a democratic state, you probably believe that democracy inherently leads to respect for human rights.[286] Yet the brutal truth is that democracy sometimes hinders human rights. Democratic publics often support torture and amnesty laws, which protect individuals who violate physical integrity rights.[287] Democratic publics sometimes want children to work, regardless of international standards. They often oppose the redistribution of wealth via taxes, which is necessary to provide poor individuals with social security, food, housing, health, and education. Bolivia is not unique—many democracies break international human rights law.

Finally, we asked: should every society follow the same universal standards for child labor, or should human rights vary based on their social context? Put differently: does a child in France have the same rights as a child in Bolivia? Or do Bolivia's economic, social, and cultural differences from France justify differing conceptions of rights? Even within developed states—with comparable economic and social traditions—conceptions of rights can vary dramatically. For example, in some fishing communities in Norway, children as young as six years old routinely work as *tungeskjærerne* ("tongue-cutters"), using sharp knives and hooks to remove the tongues from locally caught fish.[288] These communities—particularly the child workers themselves—are proud of this tradition. As one former *tungeskjærerne* explained: "It's a great tradition mainly because you learn the value of money. We were never given pocket money when we were younger—if we wanted something, we had to earn the money to buy it."[289] Should the cultural traditions of these Norwegian communities outweigh the universal standard that young children should not work, particularly with dangerous equipment like sharp knives and hooks? International law does not provide a simple solution to the tension between universalism and relativism. Yet these questions matter because they require us to consider our own conceptions of rights and the purpose of law.

9 Use of Force

9.1 Case Study: Saudi Arabia Bombs Yemen

After the 2011 Arab Spring protests, Yemen began a political transition overseen by the Gulf Cooperation Council (GCC) and the UN Security Council, including drafting a new constitution and holding elections.[1] In 2012, Abdrabbuh Mansur Hadi—the leader of the transition—won 99.8 percent of the vote in a one-candidate election. Despite the lack of political competition, other states considered President Hadi to be the legitimate leader of Yemen.[2]

The Houthis, a Shiite tribe, were excluded from the Sunni-led transition and government. They rebelled against President Hadi and slowly seized territory.

Meanwhile, numerous terrorist groups grew in power, including al-Qaeda and Islamic State of Iraq and the Levant (ISIL).[3] When the Houthis gained control of Sana'a, Yemen's capital, they placed President Hadi under house arrest and forced him to resign from power. Hadi eventually escaped, fled to Aden, and claimed that he was still Yemen's president. As the Houthis attacked Hadi in Aden, terrorist bombings caused mass civilian deaths at Sana'a mosques. Yemen's neighbors feared the growing power of the Houthis, al-Qaeda, and ISIL. In particular, Saudi Arabia feared that the Houthis were linked to Iran, Saudi Arabia's main regional rival, and that its border with Yemen was threatened by the Houthis. By March 2015, Yemen was in total chaos.

Throughout the conflict, the UN Security Council supported President Hadi. It passed numerous resolutions that condemned violence by the Houthis, al-Qaeda, and ISIL, and imposed economic sanctions on these groups.[4] But in March 2015, the GCC asked the Security Council to do more. Qatar asked the Security Council to invoke Chapter VII of the UN Charter, which allows it to authorize force in response to "any threat to the peace, breach of the peace, or act of aggression." Yet the Security Council refused to authorize force. Instead, it urged "all sides to refrain from any further use of military force, any offensive military actions and other uses of violence."[5]

Hadi then wrote to the GCC, asking for help. He described the Houthi "campaign of aggression," and argued that they violated the Security Council's calls to end their violence.[6] He asked the GCC "to provide immediate support in every form and take the necessary measures, including military intervention, to protect Yemen and its people" from the Houthis, al-Qaeda, and ISIL.[7]

Then the bombing began. A Saudi-led coalition—including GCC members, Egypt, Jordan, Morocco, and Sudan—attacked Yemeni targets. Additional support came from Australia, the UK, and the US. Criticism of the bombing was "noticeably absent."[8] When the Security Council discussed the bombing, it restated "its support for the [GCC] in assisting the political transition in Yemen."[9] However, did the decision by GCC members to bomb Yemen violate international law?

To answer this question, we must understand the following topics

- *Restricting force*: What major legal principles govern decisions about whether to use force? How have these rules evolved over time?
- *UN Security Council authorization*: What role does the UN Security Council play in legalizing the use of force? Did the UN Security Council's support for the GCC count as a valid authorization?
- *Self-defense*: When can states use force in self-defense under international law? Was the bombing of Yemen a legitimate act of self-defense against the Houthis, al-Qaeda, and/or ISIL?
- *Other possible justifications*: Does international law allow the use of force under any other circumstances? For example, did President Hadi's request for military support make the GCC's bombing of Yemen a legal use of force?

Figure 9.1 A Saudi army unit fires shells towards Yemen in April 2015. Saudi Arabia and other members of the Gulf Cooperation Council began using force in Yemen after President Hadi requested assistance in fighting various non-state actors, including Houthi rebels, al-Qaeda, and ISIL.

These questions are not unique to Yemen. In this chapter, we examine ***jus ad bellum***, which regulates the initiation of armed conflict. Chapter 10 describes *jus in bello*, which regulates behavior during armed conflicts. As shown in Figure 9.2, interstate wars have become rare since 1945, while civil wars have grown more common. International law does not govern the initiation of civil wars. However, international law affects when and how other states decide to intervene in civil wars and fight non-state actors, like al-Qaeda and ISIL.

The figure shows the number of armed conflicts per year from 1946 to 2020. Colonial wars ceased in the mid-1970s, and interstate wars are now relatively rare. In contrast, civil wars—with and without foreign intervention—have become more common since 1945.

Section 9.2 describes major principles and historical attempts to prohibit force. Then we discuss exceptions to this prohibition. Section 9.3 discusses UN Security Council authorization, while section 9.4 describes self-defense, including preventing armed attacks and defending against non-state actors. Section 9.5 then examines other possible exceptions to the prohibition on force, including: protecting nationals abroad; humanitarian intervention and the responsibility to protect; and consent to intervention. Finally, section 9.6 applies lessons from this chapter to the bombing of Yemen.

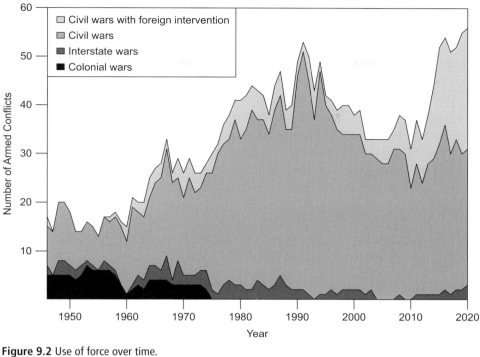

Figure 9.2 Use of force over time.
Data source: Uppsala Conflict Data Program.

9.2 Prohibiting Force

Attempts to limit force stretch back to ancient times. Historical and religious texts all reveal limits on the authority of leaders to wage war in places like ancient Babylon, China, India, and Greece.[10] During the Middle Ages in Europe, religious scholars such as Augustine of Hippo and Thomas Aquinas wrote about just war, discussing when war was consistent with Christian theology. While classical scholars continued to debate the morality of war, states considered war a fundamental right during the positivist era.[11] Modern law in the use of force rests on three pillars: the long-standing principles of military necessity and proportionality; treaties that progressively prohibited force in the early twentieth century; and the more recent prohibition of intervention under customary international law. We discuss each of these topics in turn.

Principles

Modern states must follow two major principles of customary international law. First, force must be necessary for a state to achieve its goals. Second, force must be proportionate to these goals. These principles bind all states, regardless of whether their actions are otherwise legal.

Military Necessity

The principle of **military necessity**[12]—which posits that force is only lawful if it is necessary to achieve a legitimate military objective—is usually illustrated by a dispute between the UK and the US in the mid-1800s. At that time, Canada was ruled by the UK, and the US was sympathetic to Canadian independence. In 1837, Canadian rebels began collecting arms and recruiting volunteer fighters in Buffalo, New York. A group of US volunteers crossed into Canada and seized Navy Island near Niagara Falls. They transported men and supplies from Buffalo to Navy Island along the Niagara River, on a steamboat called the *Caroline*. One night, UK forces decided to destroy the *Caroline*, which was docked on US territory. UK forces crossed into US territory, boarded the ship, set it on fire, towed it into the river, and then let it float down to Niagara Falls, destroying the ship and killing two US volunteers.

The US viewed the raid on the *Caroline* as an illegal attack on its territory. Afterwards, the US Secretary of State and the UK Foreign Minister exchanged letters, trying to resolve the dispute. The UK repeatedly claimed that the raid was justified because UK forces were acting in self-defense. In an 1842 letter, the US Secretary of State established what has become known as the ***Caroline test***. Namely, he wrote that the UK needed to prove a "necessity of self-defence, instant, overwhelming, leaving no choice of means, and no moment of deliberation."[13] After more letters, the US Secretary of State accepted an apology from the UK government.

The *Caroline* became legendary in international law because the dispute transformed claims of self-defense "from a political excuse to a legal doctrine."[14] The *Caroline* test limited when states could argue that force is necessary for self-defense or other reasons. It thus ensured that "necessity was a limiting factor at a time when there were no other limits, and took the place of restraints on the resort to force."[15]

The *Caroline* test's requirement that action be "instant" implies that a state must face an immediate need to act. Significant delay between when a state is threatened and when it responds weakens a state's claim to self-defense. The term "overwhelming" implies that a state must be upholding an important right when it uses force, such as survival of the state itself.[16] Finally, the reference to "no choice of means, and no moment of deliberation" suggests that arbitration, diplomacy, and other non-military options won't work in achieving a state's objective. A state must demonstrate "that reasonable non-forcible measures are unavailable to a state before resorting to the use of force."[17]

For example, Nicaragua sued the US at the International Court of Justice (ICJ) in the 1980s, arguing that the US had illegally used force by supporting anti-government rebels. In its defense, the US claimed that it was responding to Nicaraguan support for rebels in El Salvador. However, the ICJ questioned whether the US response was necessary because it began after El Salvador quelled its own rebels. The ICJ wrote that the US actions:

> were only taken … several months after the major offensive of the armed opposition against the Government of El Salvador had been completely repulsed … Thus it was possible to eliminate the main danger to the Salvadorian Government without the United States embarking on activities in and against Nicaragua. Accordingly, it cannot be held that these activities were undertaken in the light of necessity.[18]

The ICJ questioned whether US actions were militarily necessary because they were not "instant"–there was a delay between the threat to El Salvador and the US response.

Customary international law also uses the term "military necessity" to evaluate the choice of specific military targets. For example, in the *Oil Platforms* case, Iran sued the US for attacking two oil complexes in the late 1980s. The US argued that the attacks were "necessary to protect [its] essential security interests" because of a previous missile attack on a US-flagged oil tanker and the mining of a US warship.[19] The ICJ disagreed with the US decision to target the oil complexes, which were not conventional military targets. The ICJ argued that the attacks were not necessary for the US's self-defense because they were not military targets.[20]

Proportionality

A second principle from customary international law is **proportionality**–which posits that force must be commensurate with a state's objectives. Religious scholars long urged states to consider "whether the overall evil of resorting to war was balanced by the overall good that would arise."[21] However, proportionality received little attention from states until the modern era. For example, the League of Nations issued a 1927 report stating: "Legitimate defence implies the adoption of measures proportionate to the seriousness of the attack and justified by the seriousness of the danger."[22] Concerns about proportionality grew after the development of nuclear weapons.

In the *Oil Platforms* dispute, the ICJ considered two sequences of attacks and counterattacks. The US responded to a 1987 attack on a US-flagged oil tanker by bombing an oil complex. While the ICJ questioned the necessity of this response, it acknowledged that the 1987 counterattack "might … have been considered proportionate."[23] However, the US responded more dramatically to the 1988 mining of a warship by counterattacking multiple targets. The ICJ wrote that the 1988 counterattack on an oil complex was:

> executed as part of a more extensive operation entitled "Operation Praying Mantis" … The Court cannot … close its eyes to the scale of the whole operation, which involved … the destruction of two Iranian frigates and a number of other naval vessels and aircraft.

As a response to the mining ... of a single United States warship, which was severely damaged but not sunk, and without loss of life, neither "Operation Praying Mantis" as a whole, nor even that part of it that destroyed the [oil complex], can be regarded ... as a proportionate use of force.[24]

Both military necessity and proportionality therefore constrain whether and how states use force.

Evolution

The idea that war could be illegal slowly developed during a bloody, dangerous time in Europe. In the nineteenth century, European states fought several devastating conflicts, including the Crimean War of 1853–1856 and the Franco-Prussian War of 1870–1871. Additionally, European states fought extensively in Africa and Asia as they built empires. States held the Hague Conventions of 1899 and 1907 to write agreements that regulated war. Most of these agreements regulated the conduct of war, yet states attempted to prevent and regulate the initiation of war in two ways:

- *Peaceful settlement*: Both Hague Conventions required states "to use their best efforts to ensure the pacific settlement of international differences" by seeking mediation or arbitration.[25] The Hague Convention of 1899 also created the Permanent Court of Arbitration to hear international disputes.
- *Declaring war*: The Hague Convention of 1907 required members to publicly declare war before starting hostilities.[26]

Despite these attempts to prevent conflict, World War I demonstrated the need for more comprehensive rules to limit force. When states subsequently joined the League of Nations, they pledged "to achieve international peace and security by the acceptance of obligations not to resort to war."[27] While the League did not outlaw war, it included procedures to prevent wars between its members. For example, it required states to attempt to resolve their disputes using legalized procedures, and imposed a mandatory waiting period before the use of force.[28] Despite its minimal requirements, the League reflected a shift in international values: war had become a community concern rather than an individual right of states.

Transnational activists pressured states to create a treaty that prohibited war.[29] After years of activism, numerous states pledged their support in 1928 for the Pact of Paris (also known as the Kellogg–Briand Pact). In a remarkably short text, signatories first agreed to "condemn recourse to war for the solution of international controversies, and renounce it, as an instrument of national policy in their relations with one another."[30] Then they pledged that "the settlement or solution of all disputes or conflicts of whatever nature or of whatever origin they may be, which may arise among them, shall never be sought except by pacific means."[31]

The Pact's brief text was full of holes. First, the text did not mention self-defense, but states submitted reservations clarifying that the Pact of Paris did not apply to defensive wars.[32] One critic wrote that no "conceivable wars have been excluded from the list of permitted wars" because states could simply claim to be acting in self-defense.[33] Other critics argued that the prohibition of wars "of national policy" implied that states could still fight wars for international policy, such as to punish a state or enforce a court order.[34] Finally, the Pact did not prohibit force generally; it only applied to wars. Despite its weaknesses, states accepted similar declarations and treaties at the regional level. For example, Argentina helped draft the Saavedra Lamas Pact, a 1933 anti-war treaty that was widely supported in the Americas and Europe.[35]

State practice at this time rarely matched the ideals of international law. Numerous conflicts challenged peace activists, including the 1931 Japanese invasion of Manchuria and the 1935 Italian invasion of Ethiopia. Yet legal rhetoric shaped responses to these incidents. Japan was widely condemned for violating the Pact of Paris during its invasion of Manchuria, and China called upon treaty members for their support as it descended into war with Japan.[36] Some experts believed that by 1939 customary international law prohibited the use of force.[37] Such experts interpreted World War II as "a war of collective defense ... against ... aggression and lawlessness" by the Axis Powers.[38] This view was reflected in the post-war criminal trials of Axis officials in Nuremberg and Tokyo.

At the end of World War II, the Allied Powers drafted a treaty that built on the ideals of the Pact of Paris and the structure of the League of Nations. The result was the United Nations Charter of 1945. Article 2(4) of the Charter says:

> All Members shall refrain in their international relations from the threat or use of force against the territorial integrity or political independence of any state, or in any other manner inconsistent with the Purposes of the United Nations.

Importantly, Article 2(4) prohibits not merely war, but "the threat or use of force," to avoid the criticisms of the Pact of Paris.

But what exactly is the "use of force?" During the UN Charter negotiations, Brazil tried to include economic coercion as a use of force.[39] However, experts agree that Article 2(4) only applies to armed force used by states via conventional military forces or non-state actors, like mercenaries, rebels, and terrorists. Providing financial support to armed groups usually is not considered a use of force, although providing weaponry and/or military training usually is considered a use of force.[40] Accordingly, many states that supported the Free Syrian Army, a rebel group in the Syrian civil war, provided "non-lethal aid"—like body armor, food, and medicine—rather than military equipment, to avoid direct involvement in the war.[41]

However, experts disagree about many issues relating to the use of force. One view, which I call the restrictive view, interprets Article 2(4) as dramatically constraining states. It places heavy emphasis on institutions as interpretive actors, and on plain text interpretation. An alternative view, which I call the permissive view, believes that Article 2(4) imposes minimal constraints. It believes that states are the main interpretive actors, and that subsequent (post-1945) state practice affects interpretation of Article 2(4).[42] Perhaps not surprisingly, relatively powerful states (like France, the US, and UK) tend to believe in the permissive view, while states that are less powerful tend to believe in the restrictive view. Table 9.1 compares these views on multiple issues.

First, restrictive scholars argue that Article 2(4) prohibits all armed force, regardless of its severity.[43] They believe that even relatively minor uses of force are legal violations. In contrast, permissive scholars believe that Article 2(4) only applies to severe armed force.[44] They argue that abductions, assassinations, and rescue missions are not a "use of force" under Article 2(4). In practice, states usually argue that such incidents violate their sovereignty, rather than that they are illegal uses of force. However, this rhetoric may indicate that states do not want to escalate a minor incident into an outright war.

An additional debate has come from the second half of Article 2(4). In the early years of the UN, experts sometimes argued that Article 2(4) allowed states to use force if they did not threaten another state's "territorial integrity or political independence" or act inconsistently with the UN's purpose. Some experts

Table 9.1 Comparing Views on Article 2(4)

Question	Restrictive View	Permissive View
Who should interpret the treaty?	Institutions	States
Which tools should be used for interpretation?	Plain text	State practice
What is a "use of force?"	All armed force is prohibited.	Only serious armed force is prohibited. Minor acts (like abductions, assassinations, and rescue attempts) are not a "use of force."
Are uses of force allowed that do not threaten "territorial integrity or political independence?"	All force is prohibited, regardless of its objectives/effects.	Force is allowed if it is consistent with the UN's purposes.
Does the UN context affect the prohibition?	States are bound by the prohibition, regardless of whether the Security Council acts.	Failure of collective security excuses or justifies force to achieve the UN's purposes.

argued that states could use force to uphold judicial rulings.[45] Others believed that states could use force to recover territory. For example, in 1961, India sent troops into Goa, which was a Portuguese colony. India's representative to the UN argued, "There is no legal frontier—there can be no legal frontier—between India and Goa."[46] Therefore, India argued, its troops did not challenge Portugal's "territorial integrity," because Goa did not rightfully belong to Portugal. Still other experts argued that states could use force to promote democracy. For example, after the US invaded Grenada in 1983, it argued in the UN Security Council that "the prohibitions against the use of force in the Charter are contextual, not absolute. They provide justification for the use of force in pursuit of other values also inscribed in the Charter, such values as freedom, democracy, and peace."[47] In contemporary politics, restrictive scholars reject these arguments, while permissive scholars often invoke values like human rights to justify humanitarian intervention.

A final debate involved Article 2(4)'s institutional context. Article 2(4) is "part and parcel of a complex collective security system" that was intended to help states resolve disputes peacefully.[48] Yet the UN system has never operated as planned. The restrictive view believes that any weaknesses of the UN do not erase the legal obligation in Article 2(4). States prohibited force via treaty, and this legal act cannot be undone simply because some states disagree with UN outcomes. Permissive scholars argued in the past that Article 2(4) was "dead" because it was "founded on an invalid premise: that the Security Council would be able to discharge its responsibility ... for world peacekeeping."[49] Such experts believe that force should be allowed—or at least excused/justified—when it serves a good end, such as self-determination, human rights, or democracy.

After 1945, many states tried to reinforce Article 2(4). Throughout the Cold War, both the US and the USSR used low-level force, such as funding rebels, in proxy wars. Developing states, which were often caught between these two great powers, pushed the UN General Assembly to condemn intervention.[50] This activism led to the 1970 Declaration on Friendly Relations, which said:

> No State ... has the right to intervene, directly or indirectly, ... in the internal or external affairs of any other State. Consequently, armed intervention and all other forms of interference ... are in violation of international law.[51]

Additionally, the UN General Assembly wrote:

> no State shall organize, assist, foment, finance, incite or tolerate subversive, terrorist or armed activities directed towards the violent overthrow of the regime of another State, or interfere in civil strife.[52]

While this resolution is not directly binding on states, it is now widely accepted that customary international law prohibits intervention.

For example, recall the 2007 cyberattack on Estonia discussed in Chapter 3. This incident involved distributed denial of service attacks, which make computer networks unavailable to their intended users. Legal experts consider such attacks to be interventions because they interfere with technology located in the target state. However, such attacks are not a use of force because they do not cause physical destruction of property. In contrast, the Stuxnet worm, which was planted by Israel and the US in Iran's computer network, ultimately resulted in the destruction of 1,000 nuclear centrifuges. Legal experts accordingly believe that Stuxnet was a use of force.[53]

Figure 9.3 shows the relationship between the use of force and intervention. While all uses of force qualify as intervention, only the most serious interventions qualify as uses of force. International law does not clearly delineate which acts fall into each category. However, my careful reading of UN General Assembly resolutions, ICJ cases, and academic scholarship suggests the classification in Figure 9.3. While both intervention and the use of force are illegal, states generally consider intervention to be less serious than use of force. This explains why states that oppose the Syrian government, for example, provided the Free Syrian Army with "non-lethal" aid, but not weapons or troops. While these policy options all break international law, intervention comes with less severe political consequences than an outright use of force.

The UN Charter explicitly includes two exceptions to Article 2(4)'s prohibition of force. First, the Charter allows the Security Council to use force. Second, the Charter allows for self-defense. Many experts believe that other possible exceptions exist under international law, including the right to protect nationals abroad, humanitarian intervention and the responsibility to protect, and intervention via consent. The remaining sections of this chapter discuss each of these topics in turn.

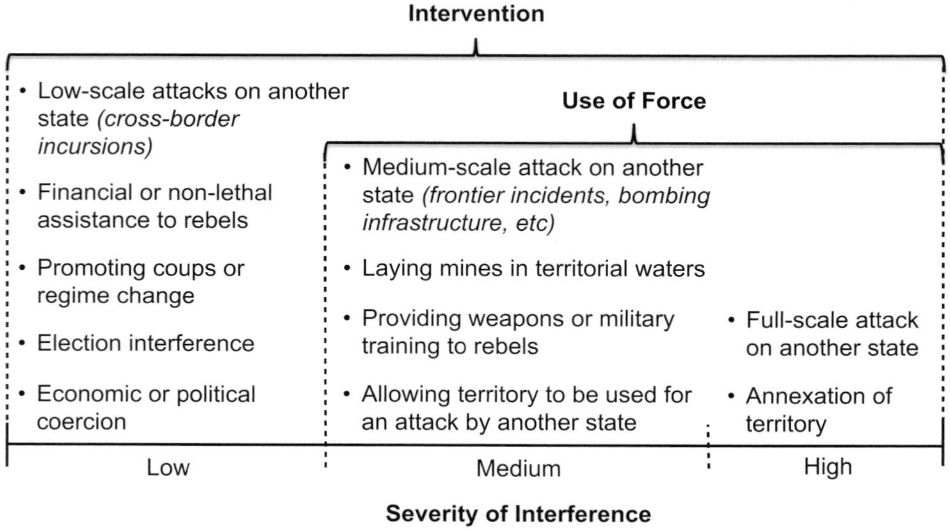

Intervention

Low	Medium	High
• Low-scale attacks on another state *(cross-border incursions)*	**Use of Force**	
• Financial or non-lethal assistance to rebels	• Medium-scale attack on another state *(frontier incidents, bombing infrastructure, etc)*	
• Promoting coups or regime change	• Laying mines in territorial waters	
• Election interference	• Providing weapons or military training to rebels	• Full-scale attack on another state
• Economic or political coercion	• Allowing territory to be used for an attack by another state	• Annexation of territory

Severity of Interference

Figure 9.3 Relationship between intervention and the use of force.

9.3   Using Force with UN Security Council Authorization

When the UN was created, states envisioned an institution with authority and resources to use force. The UN Charter gives the Security Council broad powers to counter "any threat to the peace, breach of the peace, or act of aggression."[54] It urges states to provide the Security Council with troops, and creates an administrative structure for managing these troops. However, no state ever provided such troops. Thus the collective security system envisioned in 1945 was never realized.

Throughout the Cold War, the Security Council routinely ordered non-forcible measures like economic sanctions. However, rivalry between the US and USSR—both of which had Security Council veto power—ensured that it only authorized force twice. First, when North Korea attacked South Korea in 1950, the Security Council urged states to "furnish such assistance … as may be necessary to repel the armed attack."[55] Second, when Southern Rhodesia declared independence from the UK in 1965, the Security Council imposed economic sanctions and ordered the UK to enforce them "by the use of force if necessary."[56] The Security Council also oversaw peacekeeping operations throughout the Cold War, but these forces had extremely limited authority to use force. Experts accordingly view these early peacekeeping operations as "non-coercive measures."[57]

After the Cold War ended, Security Council practice changed dramatically. It began to authorize force regularly by:

- ad hoc coalitions of states—such as the coalition that liberated Kuwait from Iraq in the 1991 Gulf War;
- regional international organizations—such as the European Union's 2007 humanitarian mission in Chad and the Central African Republic; and
- UN peacekeeping operations—such as numerous UN operations in Haiti.

Some scholars criticized this change, arguing that authorization allows states "to act with the Security Council's blessing but without its control."[58] Yet states overwhelmingly support the current system. We focus here on post-Cold War authorization. We do not explore the legal issues unique to UN peacekeeping operations, which require the consent of the state in which they operate.[59]

Explicit Authorization

The UN Charter does not give the Security Council clear authority to authorize force by member states. Two relevant provisions are Article 39 and Article 42. The first reads:

> The Security Council shall determine the existence of any threat to the peace, breach of the peace, or act of aggression and shall make recommendations, or decide what measures shall be taken … , to maintain or restore international peace and security.

Article 42 reads:

> Should the Security Council consider that [non-forcible] measures ... would be inadequate
> or have proved to be inadequate, it may take such action by air, sea, or land forces as
> may be necessary to maintain or restore international peace and security. Such action
> may include demonstrations, blockade, and other operations by air, sea, or land forces ...

While Article 42 refers to force, Security Council practice suggests that authorizations are "recommendations" per Article 39, rather than mandatory orders that
bind all states. Most experts therefore believe that Security Council authorization is
implied by Chapter VII as a whole, rather than any specific provision.[60] They describe
the UN Charter as a "living instrument"—when collective security didn't work as
planned, states reinterpreted the Charter to create new Security Council powers.[61]

Authorization begins with a determination of "the existence of [a] threat to the
peace, breach of the peace, or act of aggression" under Article 39. For example, after Iraq invaded Kuwait in 1990, the Security Council issued Resolution 660, which
declared that "there exists a breach of international peace and security as regards
the Iraqi invasion of Kuwait" and demanded that Iraq withdraw from Kuwait. The
Security Council then usually encourages diplomacy and non-forcible measures.
Only when such tactics fail does it authorize force. For example, after the Iraqi

Figure 9.4 The UN Security Council (UNSC) votes in November 1990 on Resolution 678. This historic
document was the first explicit authorization of armed conflict by the Security Council. The UN Charter
does not explicitly allow the UNSC to authorize force, yet broad support for the 1990 vote changed
understandings about the scope of UNSC authority.

invasion of Kuwait, the Security Council imposed economic sanctions to pressure Iraq into withdrawing. Only after months of delay and failed negotiations did the Security Council issue an ultimatum backed by force. Resolution 678 said:

The Security Council ...

Determined to secure full compliance with its decisions ...

1. *Demands* that Iraq comply fully with resolution 660 ... and decides ... to allow Iraq one final opportunity, as a pause of goodwill, to do so;

2. *Authorizes* Member States co-operating with the Government of Kuwait, unless Iraq on or before 15 January 1991 fully implements ... the above-mentioned resolutions, to use all necessary means to uphold and implement resolution 660 ... and all subsequent relevant resolutions and to restore international peace and security ...

The US-led coalition had to wait six more weeks before they could use force. As in Resolution 678, the Security Council usually adopts the phrase "all necessary means" or "all necessary measures" to denote that states may use force. Other examples in which the Security Council authorized force by states include conflicts in Rwanda (1994), Albania (1997), East Timor (1999), the Democratic Republic of the Congo (2003 and 2006), and Mali (2013).

Note that Resolution 678 is relatively open-ended. The Security Council did not limit how long states could use force. Instead, it granted broad authority "to uphold and implement resolution 660 ... and all subsequent relevant resolutions." When Iraq withdrew from Kuwaiti territory a few months later, it agreed to cease-fire terms included in a Security Council resolution.[62] These terms included regular weapons inspections. Iraq later hindered inspections, prompting the US to claim that Resolution 678 continued to authorize "all necessary means to uphold and implement ... all subsequent relevant resolutions," including the 1991 ceasefire.[63]

In response, the Security Council has become more cautious in how it authorizes force.[64] Resolutions now routinely limit the type and duration of force. Additionally, they usually require reports to the Security Council. For example, Resolution 1973 of 2011 expressed "grave concern at ... the heavy civilian casualties" in Libya's ongoing civil war. It authorized "all necessary measures ... to protect civilians and civilian populated areas," while prohibiting "a foreign occupation force of any form." A coalition of states—including France, the UK, and the US—began military operations. But instead of guarding civilians, they bombed Libyan troops and facilities, assisting Libyan rebels with regime change.[65]

Fear of such overreach can hinder Security Council cooperation. When the 2011 Syrian civil war began, disorder allowed ISIL to seize territory. While all Security Council members opposed ISIL, they couldn't craft a resolution that explicitly authorized force during ISIL's rise to power. States that supported the Syrian government—like Russia—feared that states that opposed the government—like France, the UK, and the US—would use an authorization to justify attacks on the Syrian government.[66]

The Security Council is fundamentally a political body. Its five permanent members—China, France, Russia, the UK, and the US—do not represent the world as a whole. Each of these countries can unilaterally veto resolutions. The political nature of the Security Council affects its activities in many important ways.

First, the Security Council asserts expansive authority. Rather than limiting itself to international peace and security, it has interpreted Article 39's reference to "threat to the peace" quite broadly.[67] It regularly intervenes in civil conflicts and authorizes force to uphold democratic elections, human rights, and humanitarian conditions. While these may be valid political reasons for intervention, they differ from the Security Council's legal purpose: "the maintenance of international peace and security."[68]

Second, the Security Council does not make legally principled decisions about whether and how to intervene in disputes. It frequently refuses to become involved in disputes, such as the Syrian civil war, and is often criticized for failing to protect individuals from war.[69] It is also often criticized for its bias in who it protects—many experts criticize the Security Council for neglecting the interests of women and developing states.[70] Unlike a legal institution, which should be impartial in administering justice, the Security Council is a political body in which states pursue their own interests.

Third, because of the difficulty of securing Security Council approval, authorization is arguably most likely when it is least needed. Almost all authorizations involve UN peacekeeping operations, which the Security Council will only authorize with the consent of states that receive peacekeepers. Other authorized uses of force usually involve self-defense that does not require authorization, like the 1991 Gulf War. Political scientists have therefore argued that Security Council approval is fundamentally a political signal.[71] Authorization can convey that a state has good intentions and wise policies.[72] It can also constrain powerful states, like the US.[73] Security Council authorization may thus be less about legal authority, and more about information transmission to domestic and international audiences.

Finally, Security Council politics often yields intentionally ambiguous resolutions. When states cannot agree to precise terms, they often write vague rules that allow all sides to claim victory.[74] For example, many Security Council resolutions condone force without explicitly authorizing it.[75] After a wave of terrorist attacks in fall 2015 (including the November attack in Paris), the Security Council passed Resolution 2249, which asked states:

> to take all necessary measures, in compliance with international law, in particular with the United Nations Charter, ... on the territory under the control of ISIL ... in Syria and Iraq.

Did this resolution authorize force against ISIL? Some states believed it did so because of its reference to "all necessary measures," while others believed that it did not because it required that measures be "in compliance with international law, in particular with the United Nations Charter."[76] Such ambiguity sometimes allows states to argue that the Security Council has given implied authorization of force.

Implied Authorization?

When states use force without first gaining explicit Security Council authorization, they sometimes argue that their actions are legal because the Security Council has given implied authorization. Sometimes states argue that resolutions passed before (*ex ante*) a use of force indicate implicit authorization. For example, Resolution 2085 of 2012 included procedures to create an African peacekeeping force to combat terrorism in Mali, and called on all states "to provide ... any necessary assistance ... to reduce the threat posed by terrorist organizations." However, before the African peacekeeping force was deployed, terrorists gained control over important territory. In response, France sent troops to fight in Mali until the African peacekeeping force was ready. Given that African preparations for authorized force were under way, France had a compelling case that it had implied authority to assist Mali.[77]

Yet such arguments can be abused. When the North Atlantic Treaty Organization (NATO) bombed Kosovo in 1999, some states argued that the bombings were justified by earlier Security Council resolutions that condemned the violence in Kosovo and imposed an arms embargo.[78] However, none of these resolutions authorized force by NATO. Kosovo and other prominent examples (such as the 2003 US war against Iraq) make most law scholars dubious of *ex ante* implied authorization.[79]

Alternatively, sometimes states argue that resolutions passed after (*ex post*) a use of force can serve as implied authorization. For example, the Economic Community of West African States (ECOWAS) intervened in civil conflicts in Liberia and Sierra Leone in the 1990s. In both situations, ECOWAS acted without explicit Security Council authorization. Yet the success of the interventions prompted the Security Council to express support for ECOWAS after the interventions began. During the Liberian intervention, Resolution 788 said that the Security Council "*Commends* ECOWAS for its efforts to restore peace, security and stability in Liberia." Similarly, during the Sierra Leone intervention, Resolution 1132 said that the Security Council "*Expresses* its strong support for the efforts of [ECOWAS] to resolve the crisis in Sierra Leone." In both conflicts, the Security Council ultimately created peacekeeping operations to assist ECOWAS.

Do such examples indicate that *ex post* implicit authorization is possible? Most experts believe that states must secure explicit authorization before force occurs. Yet many experts acknowledge that regional organizations like ECOWAS "might be carving out a role [of] legal and political independence ... in matters pertaining to regional peace and security."[80] *Ex post* resolutions may therefore indicate that certain interventions are tolerated violations of international law.[81]

9.4   Using Force in Self-Defense

The second exception to Article 2(4)'s prohibition of force is self-defense. Article 51 of the UN Charter says:

> Nothing in the present Charter shall impair the inherent right of individual or collective self-defence if an armed attack occurs ... Measures taken by Members ... shall be immediately reported to the Security Council.

Three important questions affect self-defense. First, how can states respond to prior armed attacks? Second, can states prevent armed attacks using force? And third, how can states respond to attacks by non-state actors, like rebels or terrorists? We discuss each of these questions in turn. In this section, we focus on attacks on a state's territory. Some experts argue that states can also act in self-defense of their nationals when they are on foreign territory. We discuss this issue below.

Responding to Armed Attacks

For the UN's early decades, states disagreed about the meaning of "armed attack." Some states believed that the terms "use of force" and "armed attack" were interchangeable, while others believed that a higher standard applied to armed attacks. The ICJ decided this issue in the *Nicaragua* case. Nicaragua sued the US for using covert force to destabilize the Nicaraguan government. Some US actions were direct, such as mining Nicaraguan harbors, while others were indirect, such as funding Nicaraguan rebels called the Contras.[82] The US argued that its actions were justified as collective self-defense because Nicaragua committed armed attacks against Costa Rica, El Salvador, and Honduras. More specifically, the US argued that: (1) Nicaragua had provided arms to rebels in El Salvador; and (2) Nicaraguan troops had illegally crossed into Costa Rica and Honduras. The Court asked whether Nicaragua's actions were an "armed attack" that justified self-defense.

In its ruling, the Court argued that force varies in its gravity, and that only the "most grave forms of the use of force ... constitut[e] an armed attack."[83] It noted that in UN General Assembly resolutions: "Alongside certain descriptions which may refer to aggression, ... others ... refer only to less grave forms of the use of force."[84] None of these resolutions actually defined an "armed attack." However, these resolutions repeatedly refer to "aggression," or "*agression*" in French. Because the French text of Article 51 uses the term "*agression armée*," experts who use French texts naturally conclude that an "armed attack" is a severe form of "aggression."[85] The ICJ argued that force had to meet a **gravity threshold** to qualify as an armed attack—only the most serious force qualified as armed attacks, as shown in Figure 9.5.

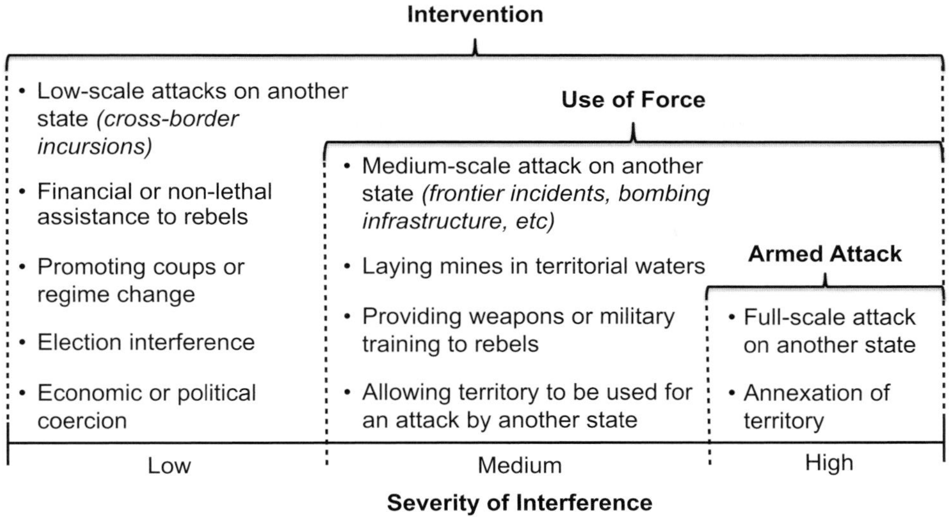

Figure 9.5 Relationship between intervention, use of force, and armed attacks.

The ICJ elaborated on force that did and did not satisfy this gravity threshold. It argued that an armed attack could include conventional forces or non-state actors under effective control of a state:

An armed attack [includes] action by regular armed forces across an international border, [and] "the sending by or on behalf of a state of armed bands, groups, irregulars or mercenaries, which carry out acts of armed force against another State of such gravity as to amount to" ... an actual armed attack conducted by regular forces ... But the Court does not believe that the concept of "armed attack" includes ... assistance to rebels in the form of the provision of weapons or logistical or other support. Such assistance may be regarded as a threat or use of force, or amount to intervention in the internal or external affairs of other states.[86]

It also suggested that "a mere frontier incident" would not meet the gravity threshold.[87]

The *Nicaragua* ruling suggests a few criteria for evaluating whether a use of force meets the gravity threshold.

- *Scale and effects*: How large in magnitude was the force? How many troops and what kinds of weapons were used? How destructive was the force? The larger the scale and effects of force, the more likely it is to be an armed attack.
- *Circumstances and motivations*: Was the force well-planned and intentional, or was it accidental? For example, if troops crossed a border, did they intend to do so? The more intentional the force, the more likely it is to be an armed attack.

In the *Nicaragua* case, the Court concluded that Nicaragua did not commit an armed attack on El Salvador because Nicaragua only provided arms to rebels.[88] The

ICJ had more difficulty assessing whether Nicaragua's "transborder incursions" into Costa Rica and Honduras were an armed attack.[89] To assess this argument, the Court turned to procedural requirements.

Recall that Article 51 of the UN Charter requires that "self-defence shall be immediately reported to the Security Council." Prior to the *Nicaragua* case, such reports were rare.[90] Nonetheless, the ICJ argued: "The absence of a report may be one of the factors indicating whether the State in question was itself convinced that it was acting in self-defence."[91] It noted that the US had not "addressed to the Security Council ... the report which is required by Article 51."[92] It argued that "this conduct ... hardly conforms with the [US's] avowed conviction that it was acting in ... collective self-defence."[93]

Additionally, the Court argued that collective self-defense came with additional requirements not included in Article 51. First, it argued that a state that is attacked must declare itself a victim. It wrote: "Where collective self-defence is invoked, it is to be expected that the State for whose benefit this right is used will have declared itself to be the victim of an armed attack."[94] Second, it argued that the victim must request assistance: "there is no rule permitting the exercise of collective self-defence in the absence of a request by the State which regards itself as the victim of an armed attack."[95] The Court did not specify how such declarations and requests should be made. But it focused on public communications, ruling out private declarations and requests.[96] It also emphasized timeliness, which is often used to assess the necessity of self-defense. El Salvador declared itself a victim and requested assistance in 1984, but the Court argued that it acted too late.[97]

After examining the public record, the Court argued that Costa Rica, El Salvador, and Honduras had not satisfied either of these requirements in a timely manner.[98] Based on these three procedural elements—declaring victimhood, requesting assistance, and reporting self-defense—the Court concluded that Nicaragua had not committed an armed attack, and accordingly that US force was not allowed.

Many experts question elements of the *Nicaragua* ruling. First, some experts question the ICJ's gravity threshold.[99] They believe that self-defense is constrained by proportionality. For example, they believe that relatively minor uses of force, like a cross-border incursion by a small number of troops, can trigger self-defense provided that the response is proportionate. They argue: "The gravity of an attack may affect the proper scope of the defensive use of force ..., but it is not relevant to determining whether there is a right of self-defense."[100] Additionally, they argue that by setting a high standard for armed attacks, the ICJ created incentives for states to commit low- and medium-scale attacks, knowing that they can avoid defensive responses.[101]

Second, many experts criticize the ICJ for creating procedural requirements for collective self-defense. Article 51 requires reporting for self-defense, but it does not require that victims declare they were attacked and request assistance. While states often requested assistance for collective self-defense prior to the *Nicaragua* ruling, they almost never declared themselves victims.[102]

Despite these criticisms, the *Nicaragua* case reflects the consensus view on how states can respond to armed attacks. It led to a dramatic change in state behavior. While states rarely reported self-defense before *Nicaragua*, they now routinely report self-defense, "even when this seems entirely implausible and to involve the stretching of Article 51 beyond all measure."[103]

Preventing Armed Attacks

Can states use force to prevent armed attacks?[104] Figure 9.6 shows contrasting views about self-defense before, during, and after an attack. The restrictive view is that Article 51 only allows self-defense during an attack, but not before or after. For example, imagine a neighboring state has invaded your territory. Once you regain your territory, you have returned to the *status quo ante* and the attack is over. A restrictive view would suggest that crossing into your neighbor's territory after the attack is over would not be valid self-defense. However, a permissive view would allow states to continue fighting after the attack ends to prevent future attacks. Some experts argue that states that have repelled a prior attack need not sit at the border, waiting to be attacked again.[105] Crossing into your neighbor's territory and destroying its army may be justified, given the prior attack, if you can prevent future attacks. As shown in Figure 9.6, the permissive view allows for the possibility that force may be justified immediately after an attack ends, if only to prevent another future attack. As more time passes after the attack, fighting is less likely to be justified.

If self-defense can continue after an attack has ended, then can self-defense begin before an attack? Suppose that an attack has not occurred, but you see an army on your border preparing to attack. Must you wait for the army to attack before you defend yourself? Experts usually believe that this type of self-defense to such imminent attacks is allowed. In 1967, Egypt expelled UN peacekeeping forces from its border with Israel and began amassing troops there. It also blockaded a

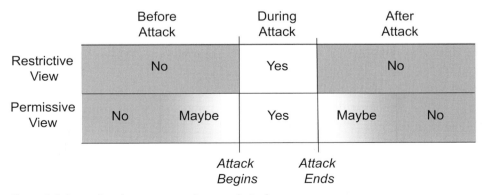

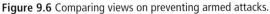

Figure 9.6 Comparing views on preventing armed attacks.

waterway leading to southern Israel. Fearing an imminent invasion, Israel attacked Egypt, Jordan, and Syria, causing the Six Day War. Israel initially claimed that Egypt attacked first, but later admitted: "we were the ones to fire the first shot."[106] States condemned Israel, yet some experts argued that Israel's response was legal.[107]

After the 2001 terrorist attacks, the US revived these arguments. It argued:

> For centuries, international law recognized that nations need not suffer an attack before they can lawfully take action to defend themselves against ... an imminent danger of attack ... The greater the threat, the greater is the risk of inaction—and the more compelling the case for taking anticipatory action to defend ourselves ... The United States will not use force in all cases to preempt emerging threats, nor should nations use preemption as a pretext for aggression. Yet ... the United States cannot remain idle while dangers gather.[108]

Experts disagree about whether this argument has affected international law. Some cling to the restrictive view, believing that international law continues to prohibit the use of force to prevent armed attacks.[109] Other experts believe that states have shifted to the permissive view since 2001.[110]

Consider two nearly identical Israeli airstrikes. The first airstrike occurred in 1981, when Israel bombed the Osirak nuclear reactor, which was under construction outside Baghdad. Iraq claimed that the reactor was for scientific research, but Israel argued that Iraq was building nuclear weapons that would pose an existential threat to Israel. Additionally, it argued that it needed to bomb before the nuclear reactor was completed and to avoid spreading radioactive fallout over Baghdad. Israel's UN representative argued:

> a state's right to self-defense ... took on new and far wider application with the advent of the nuclear era ... That is particularly true for small states whose vulnerability is vast and whose capacity to survive a nuclear strike is very limited.[111]

Israel's 1981 airstrike was widely condemned. Some states condemned any force without a prior armed attack. Others states supported self-defense to imminent attacks, but believed an Iraqi attack was not imminent.[112]

The second airstrike occurred in 2007, when Israel bombed Syria. Both states initially refused to discuss the incident, but information slowly emerged that the airstrike targeted the al-Kibar nuclear facility, which was under construction.[113] Israel never provided a legal justification for the attack; but it was never asked to do so.[114] The 2007 airstrike was largely ignored, suggesting that other states tacitly agreed with the strike.[115]

Why did states condemn the 1981 airstrike, but ignore the 2007 airstrike? One explanation is that international law may have changed. States may have changed their beliefs about the legality of preventive attack, particularly against nuclear facilities, which threaten all states. An alternative explanation is that perhaps international law has not changed, but states grew more willing to tolerate violations of the law. As one expert wrote of the 2007 airstrike:

> While states do not wish to see pre-emptive self-defence take its place ... within the law of self-defence, there may be times when they wish to say nothing ... By comparison to the [Osirak] incident, [the response to the 2007 attack on Syria] may indicate that states are more tolerant of pre-emptive action.[116]

As suggested by the flexibility perspective on compliance, states may have preferred to tolerate the 2007 airstrike rather than accept another state into the nuclear club.

Defending Against Non-State Actors

How can states defend themselves from armed attacks by non-state actors, like rebels or terrorists? Traditionally, non-state actors were not subjects of international law, meaning that they had neither international rights nor responsibilities regarding force.[117] Attacks by non-state actors can be attributed to a state with effective control over the non-state actor.[118] Such attribution would transform the attack into an interstate dispute governed by the international law of self-defense. However, what happens if a state does not have effective control over the non-state actor? If ISIL operates independently in Syria and commits an attack in Paris, can France lawfully use force in self-defense in Syria?

Before 2001, most experts believed that only states could launch "armed attacks" that justified self-defense.[119] Attacks by non-state actors were governed by domestic criminal law, rather than international law. The use of force after attacks by non-state actors was usually condemned as illegal. Yet states routinely used force against non-state actors, as shown in Table 9.2.

Table 9.2 Defending Against Non-State Actors

Year	Intervening State	Non-State Actor	Territorial State	Description
1985	Israel	Palestinian Liberation Organization (PLO)	Tunisia	After PLO attacks, Israel bombed PLO headquarters in Tunisia.
1998	US	al-Qaeda	Afghanistan and Sudan	After al-Qaeda bombed US embassies in Kenya and Tanzania, the US bombed al-Qaeda-linked targets in Afghanistan and Sudan.
1998*	Uganda	Allied Democratic Forces (ADF)	Democratic Republic of the Congo (DRC)	ADF rebels in the DRC committed cross-border attacks against Uganda, prompting Uganda to attack rebel and government targets in the DRC.

Table 9.2 (Cont.)

Year	Intervening State	Non-State Actor	Territorial State	Description
2001	US	al-Qaeda	Afghanistan	After the 2001 terrorist attacks, the US invaded Afghanistan.
2006	Israel	Hezbollah	Lebanon	After a cross-border Hezbollah attack, Israel launched a month-long war.
2008	Colombia	Fuerzas Armadas Revolucionarias de Colombia	Ecuador	After decades of civil conflict, Colombia attacked rebels in Ecuador.
2011	US	al-Qaeda	Pakistan	US forces entered Pakistan without permission to kill Osama Bin Laden, the leader of al-Qaeda.
2014	US-led coalition	ISIL	Syria	US-led coalition attacked ISIL targets in Syria.

* Prior to 1998, Uganda used force with the DRC's consent.
Source: Tom Ruys and Olivier Corten, eds. (2018), *The Use of Force in International Law*, Oxford University Press.

For example, after Palestinian Liberation Organization (PLO) attacks, Israel bombed the PLO headquarters in Tunisia in 1985. Israel argued that Tunisia "knowingly harbored the PLO and allowed it complete freedom of action in planning, training, organizing, and launching murderous attacks from its soil."[120] Thus, Israel concluded, Tunisia bore "considerable responsibility" for the PLO's attacks.[121] Similarly, when al-Qaeda bombed US embassies in Kenya and Tanzania in 1998, the US responded by bombing al-Qaeda-linked targets in Afghanistan and Sudan. US President Clinton explained that, "Our target was terror," not the states of Afghanistan or Sudan, but he also argued that "countries that persistently host terrorists have no right to be safe havens."[122] Other pre-2001 examples include:

- Portugal used force in Guinea, Senegal, and Zambia in the 1960s and 1970s, arguing that non-state actors were attacking Portuguese colonies;
- Senegal crossed into Guinea–Bissau territory in 1992 and 1995 to fight opposition forces;
- Tajikistan fought rebels in Afghanistan in 1993; and
- Thailand fought guerrillas in Burma in 1995.[123]

In sum, state practice often departed from international law before 2001.

The 2001 terrorist attacks by al-Qaeda in the US dramatically changed the politics of self-defense against non-state actors. The US Ambassador to the UN announced: "We will make no distinction between the terrorists who committed these

Figure 9.7 On September 11, 2001, al-Qaeda—a terrorist group—hijacked US civilian airplanes and used them to conduct suicide attacks on the Twin Towers office buildings in New York City. A similar attack also partially destroyed the Pentagon in Washington, DC. Approximately 3,000 people died in the coordinated attacks. The US ultimately argued that these attacks justified the use of force against Afghanistan, which had sheltered al-Qaeda prior to the attacks.

acts and those who harbour them. We will bring those responsible to account."[124] The Security Council then adopted Resolution 1368, which condemned the attacks and explicitly invoked "the inherent right of individual or collective self-defence," implying that non-state actors could indeed commit an "armed attack." Soon after, Resolution 1373 reiterated the right to self-defense against terrorism and called on states to cooperate in suppressing terrorism.

The US's response was to attack Afghanistan. The US did not claim that Afghanistan had effective (or overall) control over al-Qaeda—it argued that the Taliban government, which governed Afghanistan, had harbored al-Qaeda, but was unable or unwilling to prevent their attacks. The US argued that the attacks:

have been made possible by the decision of the Taliban regime to allow the parts of Afghanistan that it controls to be used by this organization as a base of operation. Despite every effort by the United States and the international community, the Taliban regime has refused to change its policy. From the territory of Afghanistan, the Al-Qaeda organization continues to train and support agents of terror who attack innocent people throughout the world.[125]

Unlike its 1998 attacks on al-Qaeda targets in Afghanistan, the US attacked both al-Qaeda and the Afghan government. Support for the US response was widespread.[126] About one-quarter of UN General Assembly speeches explicitly supported US claims to self-defense, while the remaining speeches acquiesced by making no mention of self-defense.[127]

But did the US response to the 2001 attacks change customary international law? Can the victim of an armed attack use force against a state that is unable or unwilling to control non-state actors in its territory? Or was the Afghanistan war an idiosyncratic example in which states tolerated a violation of international law by a powerful state?

Subsequent state practice suggests that international law may have changed in 2001. The Afghanistan war opened the door to many similar claims, some of which are shown in Table 9.2. For example, by 2014, ISIL had seized control of territory in Iraq and Syria. Iraq notified the Security Council that ISIL "has repeatedly launched attacks against Iraqi territory from eastern Syria," and requested military assistance.[128] A US-led coalition began attacking ISIL targets in Iraq. Then the US announced that it was expanding its attacks into Syria:

> The Syrian regime has shown that it cannot and will not confront [ISIL] effectively itself. Accordingly, the United States has initiated necessary and proportionate military actions in Syria in order to eliminate the ongoing ISIL threat to Iraq.[129]

Other states issued similar statements, including Australia, Canada, and Turkey. Not all states in the coalition were willing to attack ISIL in Syria. For example, France initially hesitated to expand its operations into Syria. After the November 2015 attacks in Paris, France invoked its right to individual (rather than collective) self-defense and expanded its airstrikes.[130] The coalition was careful to attack only ISIL targets and to avoid confronting the Syrian government. This suggests that the evolving international law of self-defense may only permit attacks *within* states that harbor terrorist groups, and not attacks *against* such states.[131]

Despite this state practice, many experts cling to the pre-2001 view. They argue that no international treaty or court has upheld the new norms. For example, shortly after the Afghanistan war, the ICJ ruled on the *Armed Activities* case between the Democratic Republic of the Congo (DRC) and Uganda. Ugandan rebels had been launching cross-border attacks from within the DRC, and Uganda responded by attacking both rebel and government targets in the DRC. The DRC sued Uganda for use of force, arguing that the DRC had not committed an "armed attack" on Uganda that would justify self-defense. The ICJ majority ruled that because Uganda had attacked government targets and the DRC government did not control the rebels, Uganda had illegally used force. Therefore, the ICJ reasoned, it did not need to decide whether Uganda was allowed to attack rebel targets in the DRC.[132] Some experts interpret this refusal to rule as support for the traditional doctrine.[133] Yet some ICJ judges criticized the majority. These judges agreed that Uganda had acted illegally by attacking government targets. But they also suggested that states can use force in self-defense against non-state actors.[134]

In addition to debating whether the law of self-defense against non-state actors *has* changed, experts also debate whether law *should* change. If non-state actors can commit "armed attacks" within the meaning of Article 51, then are they subjects of international law? Does a non-state actor have a right to self-defense when it is the victim of an "armed attack?" Some experts believe that this logic leads to a "manifestly absurd and unreasonable result"—namely, that it "promotes [terrorists] from the status of common criminals to being subjects of international law with a degree of legal capacity."[135] Similarly, one expert warned in 2001 that recognizing self-defense against non-state actors would open "a Pandora's box" that legitimized methods like the "extra-judicial assassination of terrorists."[136] His warning would prove apt—after the 2001 attacks, many states began targeted killings, including the 2011 killing of Osama Bin Laden in Pakistan.[137]

Despite these consequences, most states now support self-defense against non-state actors, reversing pre-2001 state practice. Why have the views of states changed so quickly? Probably because the politics of fighting terrorism have changed so dramatically. While a few states—including Israel and the US—long supported force against non-state actors, terrorism lacked global salience. The 2001 terrorist attacks triggered broad support for global cooperation against terrorism, which threatens statehood itself. As one expert argued: "terrorism is something that many states face in one form or another, particularly with the advent of global terrorist groups, meaning that greater flexibility in the response may be permitted."[138] As long as states view terrorism as a global threat, they will likely continue to allow self-defense against non-state actors.

9.5 Other Justifications for Using Force?

Experts agree that UN Security Council authorization and self-defense are exceptions to Article 2(4)'s prohibition of force—that is, they make force legally permissible. But does international law have other exceptions? We examine here three possibilities. First, can states use force to protect their nationals abroad? Second, do states have a right to humanitarian intervention or a responsibility to protect foreign nationals? Finally, can states consent to foreign intervention?

Protecting Nationals Abroad?

Throughout history, states used force to protect their nationals when they were on foreign territory. Statehood was usually linked to both territory and a population, so states were often believed to have jurisdiction over their population, even when they traveled abroad. Emer de Vattel wrote in 1758:

> Whoever uses a citizen ill, indirectly offends the state, which is bound to protect this citizen; and the sovereign of the latter should avenge his wrongs, punish the aggressor, and, if possible, oblige him to make full reparation; since otherwise the citizen would not obtain the great end of the civil association, which is safety.[139]

Vattel and others believed that a state could punish anyone who harmed its nationals. As international commerce grew in the nineteenth century, states frequently used force to protect both the physical security and economic well-being of their nationals. States that expropriated foreign-owned property or defaulted on foreign debt were often threatened with military force.[140] States widely believed that they had international legal obligations to protect foreigners in their territory.[141] Sometimes these obligations were established under customary international law, and sometimes they were included in treaties, particularly between European and non-European states.[142] Failure to uphold these obligations was considered a just cause of war.

After states prohibited war in the Pact of Paris, protecting nationals abroad was considered self-defense. In 1933, international lawyer Quincy Wright argued:

> Invasion of territory, destruction of nationals abroad, or the destruction of government prestige, authority, or agencies, are types of irreparable injury threats to which have most frequently called forth defensive action. A state cannot exist without territory, without nationals, or without government.[143]

Wright and others believed that by protecting its nationals, a state was protecting its own existence.

Even after states expanded on the Pact of Paris to prohibit the use of force in the UN Charter, experts often argued that states only had the right to non-intervention if they upheld their obligation to protect foreigners within their territory. In 1957, UK lawyer Gerald Fitzmaurice argued:

> the protection which international law affords to the territorial sovereignty ... of a state within its own territory, has as its necessary corollary the corresponding duty of the state thus protected, not itself to endanger the lives or persons of foreign nationals in its territory ... If international law, generally speaking, prohibits foreign intervention of a forcible or coercive character, this is because it imposes a corresponding duty on states not themselves to create, or to tolerate in their territory, the conditions which might call for and justify such intervention. If there is a failure to carry out this duty, the prohibition can no longer be maintained, and intervention becomes legitimate.[144]

All of these scholars—Vattel, Wright, and Fitzmaurice—argued that the right to protect nationals was a part of customary international law.

These arguments were reflected in state practice: many states used force to protect their nationals long after 1945. For example, four terrorists hijacked an Air France flight in 1976. They diverted the plane to Uganda and landed at Entebbe airport. Ugandan dictator Idi Amin oversaw negotiations with the terrorists, who wanted multiple states to release terrorists from prison. Ugandan troops provided the hostages with food and supplies, but they did not attempt a rescue operation. Instead, they assisted with guarding the hostages and preventing their escape. The terrorists initially released some non-Israeli passengers because they believed that these passengers were not Jewish. However, the terrorists continued to hold ninety-four passengers (who they believed were Jewish) and twelve crew members as hostages.

A week after the crisis began, Israel launched a rescue mission called Operation Thunderbolt.[145] Israel flew soldiers to Entebbe and launched a surprise attack. After rescuing the hostages, they destroyed military airplanes to prevent a retaliatory attack by Uganda. While Idi Amin claimed to be neutral, details suggest that he supported and colluded with the terrorists. After the attack, Ugandan soldiers murdered

Figure 9.8 This 1976 photograph shows the safe return of Israeli hostages after Operation Thunderbolt, in which the Israeli military attacked an airport in Entebbe, Uganda to free over a hundred individuals held as hostages. While some states condemned that Israeli attack as "state terrorism," the US argued that Israel had a "well established right" to protect its nationals.

Dora Bloch, an Israeli hostage who was at a hospital during the Israeli raid. Amin also ordered the murder of hundreds of Kenyans living in Uganda in retaliation for Kenya allowing the Israeli planes to land and refuel on their way home.

Israel's rescue mission prompted intense debate at the UN Security Council, where Uganda argued that Israel had committed an "act of naked aggression."[146] Israel defended itself by arguing that "The right of a state to take military action to protect its nationals in mortal danger is recognized ... in international law."[147] Israel's raid was condemned by numerous African and Arab states. While some states, like Kenya, were moderate in their criticisms, others, like Libya, accused Israel of "state terrorism" and invoked anti-Semitic rhetoric.[148] Some states—like France, Japan, Sweden, the UK, and West Germany—were ambivalent in their responses, neither condemning nor supporting Israel. Only the US wholeheartedly supported Israel, arguing that Israel had a "well established right" to protect its nationals.[149] The Security Council debate lasted four days, but ultimately achieved little. The UK and the US failed to gain support for a resolution that condemned hijacking, while Benin, Libya, and Tanzania failed to pass a resolution that condemned Israel's raid as a "flagrant violation of Uganda's sovereignty and territorial integrity."[150]

While few states supported Israel in 1976, many states have behaved similarly. Table 9.3 contains numerous examples in which states used force to protect their

Table 9.3 Rescuing Nationals Abroad

Intervening State(s)	Target State	Year	Description
France and UK	Egypt (Suez Canal)	1956	After Egypt nationalized the Suez Canal, Israel attacked Egypt. France and the UK then intervened. The UK justified its action domestically as protecting UK nationals.
Belgium	Congo	1960	Days after gaining independence, conflict began in the Congo. Belgium sent troops to protect Belgian nationals until a UN peacekeeping force arrived.
Israel	Uganda (Entebbe airport)	1976	Israel intervened in Uganda to rescue Jewish hostages from an airplane hijacked by terrorists.
US	Iran	1980	During the Iran hostage crisis, the US launched a failed mission to save its hostages.
US	Liberia	1990	During civil conflict, rebels ordered the arrest of all foreigners in Monrovia. The US evacuated over 1,600 nationals of Canada, France, Iraq, India, Italy, Korea, Lebanon, the UK, the US, and other states.

Sources: Natalino Ronzitti (1985), *Rescuing Nationals Through Military Coercion and Intervention on Grounds of Humanity*, Martinus Nijhoff; Richard Lillich (1992), "Forcible Protection of Nationals Abroad: the Liberian 'Incident' of 1990," *German Yearbook of International Law* 35: 205–223.

nationals abroad. How do states reconcile such examples with the UN Charter? First, these examples are consistent with a permissive view of Article 2(4). Recall that some experts believe that Article 2(4) only prohibits severe force. They regard the Entebbe raid and similar actions as extraterritorial police actions, rather than uses of force.[151] Other experts argue that rescue operations do not threaten a state's "territorial integrity or political independence" and are consistent with the UN Charter's emphasis on human rights.[152]

Second, these examples have been historically consistent with a broad interpretation of Article 51. If an attack on a state's nationals is an attack on the state itself, perhaps rescuing nationals is legitimate self-defense. While this view had a long history, it has been abandoned by modern scholars. Attacks on nationals abroad are not included in UN General Assembly resolutions that have developed the international law on force. Additionally, the ICJ's *Nicaragua* ruling suggests that hostage-taking does not qualify as an "armed attack" under Article 51. While states frequently use the political rhetoric of self-defense to justify protecting nationals, one expert concluded in 1985 that "it is a mere pretext to consider an attack against nationals abroad as an attack on the State itself."[153]

Many modern experts believe that the examples in Table 9.3 are violations of international law, and that Article 51 only permits self-defense from armed attacks on a state's territory. Even in the Entebbe hostage crisis, such experts could argue that the Entebbe rescue mission was illegal because Uganda did not attack Israel. Rather, non-state actors hijacked a French airplane and forced an emergency landing in Uganda. They could additionally argue that even if Idi Amin was responsible for the hijacking, Israel did not have a right to defend a French airplane.

Of course, some experts within this camp recognize that politics may require that states tolerate force to protect nationals abroad. Since the violation of sovereignty is temporary, the benefits of rescuing nationals may outweigh the costs of temporarily breaking international law.[154] It may therefore be politically beneficial to ignore the disconnect between what the law requires and how states actually behave.[155] Such views match the flexibility perspective on compliance from Chapter 3.

However, other experts fear that ignoring legal violations will tempt states to abuse flexibility.[156] For example, Russia began granting citizenship and passports in 2006 to ethnic Russians in South Ossetia, a region of Georgia. Two years later, Russian troops invaded South Ossetia and expelled ethnic Georgians. Russian President Dmitry Medvedev claimed that Russian troops were protecting Russian nationals living abroad. He stated: "I am obligated to defend the life and honor of Russian citizens, wherever they may be. We will not let those responsible for the deaths of our people go unpunished."[157] While Russia can grant citizenship as it likes, legal scholars have routinely condemned Russia's actions as an abuse of international law.[158] Russia also claimed it was protecting ethnic Russians when it intervened in Ukraine in 2014.[159]

Regardless of one's perspective about the UN Charter, force must conform with the principles of military necessity and proportionality. Military necessity requires that force only be used when nationals can be rescued—force cannot be used to punish a state for prior harm that has ceased.[160] Proportionality requires that "intervention ... be limited in time and space ... it must have the sole aim of safeguarding foreign citizens by evacuating them rapidly."[161] For example, force should be "directed specifically at the site where the hostages are being held," and "casualties, especially civilian casualties, should be minimized to the absolute extent possible."[162]

Humanitarian Intervention and the Responsibility to Protect?

In the nineteenth century, states agreed that international law allowed **humanitarian intervention**—namely, they believed that states could use force to protect foreign nationals from mistreatment by their own government. Historical examples usually involved powerful Christian states—like France, Russia, and the UK—using force to protect Christian minorities in places like the Ottoman Empire. Sometimes intervening states could invoke treaties in which the Ottoman Empire pledged to protect Christian minorities from mistreatment. However, these interventions all occurred before the Pact of Paris and the UN Charter.[163] By the early 1960s, most international experts could confidently argue that humanitarian intervention "has disappeared from modern state practice."[164]

Yet three conflicts in the 1970s persuaded some experts to revive the doctrine of humanitarian intervention.[165] The first example was India's intervention in East Pakistan in 1971. After its independence, Pakistan was split into two separate territories. West Pakistan—where political power was concentrated—was primarily occupied by Muslims, while East Pakistan was primarily occupied by Bengalis, who had multiple religions and their own language and ethnic identity. When West Pakistan refused to grant East Pakistan more political autonomy, a secessionist movement broke out, triggering mass killings of Bengalis and a migration crisis into India. Many scholars consider West Pakistan's actions in East Pakistan to be a genocide.[166] In response to the conflict, India invaded East Pakistan, ultimately leading to the formation of Bangladesh.

Since East Pakistan was part of Pakistan, India could not claim that it was assisting with collective self-defense—no foreign state had attacked East Pakistan. India instead emphasized the humanitarian nature of the crisis, arguing that it was promoting self-determination and protecting the Bengalis. India also argued that it acted in individual self-defense in relation to the migration crisis, although it did not claim that Bengali refugees or Pakistan attacked India. Many experts highlight India's geopolitical motivations: India was (and continues to be) a rival of Pakistan. Nonetheless, the humanitarian crisis appears to be a key factor behind India's intervention.

The second example from the 1970s involved Kampuchea (now Cambodia). In 1975, the Khmer Rouge seized power and attempted to create a communal

Figure 9.9 Individuals from East Pakistan flee violence in 1971. The massacre of Bengali civilians in East Pakistan triggered a massive refugee crisis in India. In response, India invaded East Pakistan, stopped the massacre of the Bengalis, and supported the creation of Bangladesh as an independent state.

agricultural nation based on Maoist principles. It tortured and murdered intellectuals, business owners, urban elite, religious leaders, ethnic minorities, and former government officials. In late 1978, Vietnam invaded and helped remove the Khmer Rouge from power.

Vietnam justified its actions in two ways. First, it claimed self-defense against cross-border attacks. However, such attacks occurred before 1975 as Vietnam fought its own civil war. Second, Vietnam emphasized the Khmer Rouge atrocities. While it did not claim humanitarian intervention, it clearly believed that the humanitarian crisis was a compelling political justification.

The final example is Tanzania's 1979 invasion of Uganda. During his eight-year reign, Uganda dictator Idi Amin tortured and killed about 300,000 Ugandans.[167] In late 1978, Amin declared war on and invaded Tanzania. While he never provided a coherent justification for the invasion, he had long feuded with Tanzania because it provided sanctuary to Amin's political opponents.[168] Tanzania defended its territory and counter-invaded in early 1979. It then assisted rebels with deposing Amin.

Tanzania justified its counter-invasion primarily as self-defense against Uganda's prior attack. However, experts question whether self-defense can fully justify Tanzania's counter-invasion and its involvement in deposing Amin. To bolster its justification, Tanzania emphasized Amin's widespread human rights violations.

All three of these examples—East Pakistan in 1971, Kampuchea in 1978, and Uganda in 1979—are linked by their emphasis on humanitarian concerns as a justification for force. Scholars who do not believe in a right to humanitarian intervention can easily pick these examples apart. For example, no state explicitly argued that it could intervene based on humanitarian motives. They cloaked their actions in rhetoric about self-defense. Additionally, all of these actions were criticized by observers. Yet scholars who believe in an emerging right to humanitarian intervention see these examples as "lawful" interventions that reflect changing views about the use of force.[169]

These examples complemented the growing emphasis on human rights in international law. Experts argued that law about force and intervention should be balanced against "the equally strong and complementary norms of international human rights law," and that governments that violated human rights had "forfeited their legitimacy."[170] Advocates of humanitarian intervention argued that individual states should respond to "clear violations of rights when multilateral possibilities do not obtain."[171] Some even argued that states have a "right to provide humanitarian assistance," which can sometimes include intervention.[172]

When Liberia descended into civil war in 1989, it drew little attention from the Security Council, which was focused on the Soviet Union's collapse, Germany's reunification, and Iraq's invasion of Kuwait in 1990. In response to the UN's inertia, ECOWAS stepped up. It created an intervention force that entered Liberia in 1990 without prior authorization from the Security Council. ECOWAS argued that it was "going to Liberia first and foremost to stop the senseless killing of innocent civilian nationals and foreigners, and to help the Liberian people to restore their democratic institutions."[173] Broad support for ECOWAS led many scholars to argue that customary international law now permitted humanitarian intervention.[174]

Similarly, after the US-led coalition liberated Kuwait from Iraq in 1991, Kurdish populations in northern Iraq rebelled, prompting mass repression and refugee flows into Turkey. France, the UK, and the US created and enforced a no-fly zone to allow humanitarian aid deliveries and the return of Kurdish refugees. A similar no-fly zone was created in southern Iraq to protect Shiite populations. While the US and its allies claimed to be supporting a Security Council resolution, this resolution did not actually authorize force.[175]

Advocates of humanitarian intervention faced their biggest challenge yet in Kosovo in 1999. Throughout the 1990s, multiple conflicts tore apart Yugoslavia, a multiethnic state in southeastern Europe. Kosovo was a small territory that was part of Serbia, one of the Yugoslavian territories, but Kosovo's population was mostly ethnic Albanian. The Yugoslavian conflict sparked a separatist movement within Kosovo, which escalated into full-blown conflict with Serb forces by 1998. The Security Council passed multiple resolutions in 1998, condemning violence in Kosovo, but it did not authorize force.[176]

The Security Council conducted multiple peacekeeping operations in Yugoslavia in the early years of the war. However, by the late 1990s, the Security Council was widely viewed as dysfunctional and ineffective in Yugoslavia. Security Council members routinely disagreed about the nature and scope of UN activities. The result was peacekeeping forces with extremely limited authority to intervene in the conflict. For example, in July 1995, Serbian forces massacred approximately 8,000 Bosnian men and boys in just eleven days near the town of Srebrenica, which had been previously designated a UN Safe Area under the protection of a peacekeeping operation. UN peacekeepers watched the violence, but did little to halt the massacre. Additionally, international politics often interfered with the peacekeeping operations. For example, the mandate for a UN peacekeeping force located in Macedonia expired in February 1999. Despite support for the operation within Macedonia, China refused to reauthorize the operation because it was upset at Macedonia for its diplomatic relationship with Taiwan.[177]

As the Kosovo conflict deepened, military intelligence suggested that Serbian forces were planning an imminent ethnic cleansing of Kosovo. With the Security Council in disarray, NATO members decided to act on their own by conducting extensive bombing in Kosovo in March to June 1999. The bombing campaign pressured Serbian leaders to accept a diplomatic settlement that was endorsed by the Security Council.[178]

Some NATO members emphasized that the bombings were intended to enforce earlier Security Council resolutions. Yet most NATO members emphasized the overwhelming need for humanitarian intervention. In a Security Council debate in March 1999, the UK argued:

> The action being taken is legal. It is justified as an exceptional measure to prevent an overwhelming humanitarian catastrophe. Under present circumstances in Kosovo, there is convincing evidence that such a catastrophe is imminent. Renewed acts of repression by the authorities of [Serbia] would cause further loss of civilian life and would lead to displacement of the civilian population on a large scale and in hostile conditions.
>
> Every means short of force has been tried to avert this situation. In these circumstances, and as an exceptional measure on grounds of overwhelming humanitarian necessity, military intervention is legally justifiable. The force now proposed is directed exclusively to averting a humanitarian catastrophe, and is the minimum judged necessary for that purpose.[179]

Similarly, Canada argued:

> Humanitarian considerations underpin our action. We cannot simply stand by while innocents are murdered, an entire population is displaced, villages are burned and looted and a population is denied its basic rights merely because the people concerned do not belong to the "right" ethnic group.[180]

Similar reasoning was given by Belgium, the Netherlands, and the US.

After the Kosovo intervention, many Western lawyers and diplomats campaigned to rebrand humanitarian intervention under the principle of the **responsibility to protect**. This principle posits that (1) every state has a responsibility to protect its population from severe violations of human rights and humanitarian law; and (2) failure to meet this responsibility can trigger force by the international community. Canada created an International Commission on Intervention and State Sovereignty to analyze major recent humanitarian crises, like the 1994 Rwandan genocide and the 1995 Srebrenica massacre. The Commission issued a major 2001 report that sought to change "the emphasis from a politically and legally undesirable right to intervene for humanitarian purposes to the less confrontational idea of a responsibility to protect."[181] This report emphasized the rights of individuals who need protection, and argued that sovereignty is linked to the responsibility of states to protect their nationals.[182] As experts emphasized, the ideas in the report "are nothing new but the way they are presented and interconnected is."[183] Components of the report were subsequently adopted in UN documents, including a 2005 UN General Assembly resolution.[184]

What is the current status of the doctrine of humanitarian intervention? Some states continue to support the primacy of sovereignty and non-intervention, and fear that claims of humanitarian intervention will be abused by states that act opportunistically. Yet there is relatively broad international support for humanitarian intervention under the authority of the Security Council.[185] Most experts seem to agree "that no individual state can be trusted with authority to judge and determine wisely" whether humanitarian intervention should occur.[186] But can NATO be trusted to make a wise decision? Some experts supported the Kosovo intervention because NATO was itself a multilateral organization.[187] Given the failure of the UN to prevent or even respond to the 1994 Rwandan genocide and the 1995 Srebrenica massacre, perhaps other international organizations should have leeway to respond.

Yet many experts are troubled by the symbolism of rich, Western states claiming the right to intervene in poor, Eastern or Southern states. In her discussion of the Kosovo intervention, Christine Chinkin suggested the hypocrisy of NATO's claim to legality: "the West continues to script international law, even while it ignores the constitutional safeguards of the international legal order." Similarly, feminist legal theorist Anne Orford argued that humanitarian interventions are based on problematic "heroic narratives" in which white, male characters save "the black, native, or colonized subject."[188] Some scholars suggested that the Kosovo intervention increased support from developing states for humanitarian intervention because it showed predominantly Christian states intervening against Orthodox Christian Serbs on behalf of Muslim Albanians.[189] Yet Orford's analysis suggests that we should ask: why do Christians need to save Muslims? A more compelling example may be ECOWAS's intervention in Liberia. When African soldiers save African victims, we avoid the implication that Africans are "starving, powerless, suffering, abused, or helpless victims ... in need of rescue and salvation."[190]

Those experts and states that support humanitarian intervention, absent Security Council authorization, generally argue: what's the alternative? If the Security Council won't act, should states ignore genocide, ethnic cleansing, and other atrocities? They generally argue: "If it is morally right to use force to prevent a humanitarian emergency, then it should be legally permissible as well."[191] As the Netherlands argued in UN Security Council debates in June 1999:

> We sincerely hope that the few delegations which have maintained that the [NATO] air strikes ... were a violation of the United Nations Charter will one day begin to realize that the Charter is not the only source of international law.[192]

As the Netherlands suggested, states are bound not only by the UN Charter, but also by human rights law and their own moral values.

Consent to Intervention?

Can a state consent to another state's intervention on its territory? If so, what limits (if any) does international law impose? Consider the Syrian civil war.[193] In 2011, the Arab Spring, a wave of anti-government protests, spread across the Middle East. Syrians were inspired to challenge President Bashar al-Assad. Assad brutally suppressed the protests, spurring widespread violence by rebels with competing agendas. By late summer 2011, ISIL expanded from its base in Iraq and began to capture Syrian territory. Assad requested military assistance from Iran and Russia, and both states sent troops and weapons. States that oppose Assad—including France, the UK, and the US—began supporting rebels, including the Free Syrian Army. These states also feared the growth of ISIL.

Most international law experts agree that governments can consent to interventions, but they do not agree about why this is allowed. Under collective self-defense, a state that has been attacked can ask other states to help it to defend itself. However, Syria wasn't attacked by another state: its conflict stemmed from internal opposition. Recall that consent is a circumstance precluding wrongfulness of a legal breach.[194] So if Syria consents to the force by Iran and Russia, then perhaps the breach of Article 2(4) is not wrongful. However, recall that most experts argue that the prohibition of force is a peremptory norm. States may not derogate from peremptory norms, so the law of state responsibility treats breaches of peremptory norms as inherently wrongful. Other experts argue that intervention by consent is not a "use of force" and hence does not violate Article 2(4) or a peremptory norm.[195] Still others adopt a permissive view of Article 2(4), and argue that if Syria consents to force, then Iran and Russia are not acting "against the territorial integrity or political independence of" Syria.

As part of their consent, governments set limits on where and how force is used. For example, states routinely allow other states to station troops on their territory. Under its 1997 treaty with Ukraine, Russia was allowed to station up to 25,000 troops in Crimea.[196] However, Ukraine did not consent to the use of these troops to destabilize its own rule, as occurred in 2014 when Russia annexed Crimea. In the *Armed Activities* case, the ICJ ruled that states may withdraw their consent to intervention "at any time ... without further formalities being necessary."[197]

If Assad can invite Iran and Russia to intervene, can the Free Syrian Army invite France, the UK, and the US to intervene as well? Most scholars would say: no. Under international law, a government has authority to consent, but rebels do not. For example, the ICJ was asked to rule in the *Nicaragua* case on US support for the Contras. The ICJ ruled:

> the principle of non-intervention derives from customary international law. It would certainly lose its effectiveness ... if intervention were to be justified by a mere request for assistance made by an opposition group ... it is difficult to see what would remain of the principle of non-intervention in international law if intervention, which is already allowable at the request of the government of a state, were also to be allowed at the request of the opposition.[198]

The Court both acknowledged that governments can consent to intervention, and argued that rebels cannot.

This logic shaped international support for the Syrian rebels. When EU members provided aid to the Free Syrian Army, they gave "non-lethal" goods—such as armored vehicles, night-vision goggles, and protective gear—to avoid breaking international law.[199] When speaking to Syrians in 2016, US Secretary of State John Kerry expressed frustration with the different standards for Russian and US activities in Syria. When discussing intervention, Kerry said:

> we don't have a basis, our lawyers tell us, unless we have a UN Security Council resolution ... or unless we are under attack from the folks there, or unless we are invited in. Russia is invited in by the legitimate regime.[200]

States that support a government face different rules than states that support rebels.

Given the imbalance between what governments and rebels can do, some experts argue that special rules apply to conflicts involving self-determination. The 1970 Declaration on Friendly Relations says:

> Every state has the duty to refrain from any forcible action which deprives peoples ... of their right to self-determination and freedom and independence. In their actions ... in pursuit of the exercise of their right to self-determination, such peoples are entitled to seek and to receive support in accordance with the purposes and principles of the Charter.[201]

Similarly, the 1974 Definition of Aggression reaffirms "the duty of states not to use armed force to deprive peoples of their right to self-determination, freedom and independence."[202] Of course, these statements must be understood in their historical context: they supported decolonization, not necessarily all rebellion.[203]

Nevertheless, the principle of self-determination has led some scholars to argue that international law has a **negative equality doctrine**. Namely, they argue that outside states must remain neutral during civil wars, and can only provide assistance to offset outside assistance from other states. This doctrine has complex historical roots in the nineteenth century.[204] It was reinforced in 1975 when the Institut de Droit International—a professional association of international lawyers—issued guidelines declaring:

> the violation of the principle of non-intervention for the benefit of a party to a civil war often leads in practice to interference for the benefit of the opposite party ... States shall refrain from giving assistance to parties to a civil war which is being fought in the territory of another state.[205]

While the negative equality doctrine is sometimes invoked, there is relatively little modern support in treaties or customary international law for this doctrine.

Because of uncertainty over the legality of consent to intervention, states are cautious when they explain their decisions to intervene. Table 9.4 shows that states frequently use force based on consent. However, it is unclear whether these examples are legal, or whether they are tolerated violations of international law. For both legal and political reasons, states often refer to domestic opponents as

Table 9.4 Consenting to Intervention

Intervening States	Target State	Start Year	Note
Ethiopia	Somalia	2011	Ethiopia sent troops after Somalia asked for help fighting al-Shabaab, a jihadist organization.
Saudi Arabia and GCC members	Bahrain	2011	Bahrain asked GCC members for help in suppressing Arab Spring protests.
France	Mali	2013	Mali invited France to fight al-Qaeda.
Australia, Belgium, Canada, Denmark, France, Iran, Jordan, Netherlands, Russia, UK, and US	Iraq	2014	Iraq asked for help in fighting ISIL within Iraq.
Russia	Ukraine	2014	Deposed President Yanukovych gave Russia consent to intervene in Ukraine.
Iran and Russia	Syria	2015	President Assad invited Iran and Russia to assist in fighting rebels.

Table 9.4 (Cont.)

Intervening States	Target State	Start Year	Note
Saudi Arabia and GCC members	Yemen	2015	Deposed President Hadi gave GCC members permission to fight Houthi rebels.
Egypt and US	Libya	2015	Libya invited Egypt and the US to fight ISIL within Libya.

Sources: Karine Bannelier-Christakis (2016), "Military Interventions against ISIL in Iraq, Syria and Libya, and the Legal Basis of Consent," *Leiden Journal of International Law* 29: 743–775; Christine Gray (2018), *International Law and the Use of Force*, Oxford University Press; Christian Henderson (2018), *The Use of Force and International Law*, Cambridge University Press.

terrorists, suggesting that foreign states are assisting them with law enforcement, rather than helping to suppress political dissent. Sometimes these labels are plausible, like when Mali asked for French assistance in 2013 in fighting al-Qaeda. Yet sometimes they are questionable, like when Bahrain described Arab Spring protestors as terrorists. States also often claim that rebels are supported by outside states to justify their own use of foreign troops to suppress dissent.

States face two additional questions about consent to intervention. The first question is: who has authority to consent? It can be difficult to identify legitimate governments during civil conflicts. Historically, international law relied on an effective control test—if a group had control over territory, it had authority to represent that territory.[206] This test "serve[d] as a rough proxy for ... congruity between the government and the larger political community of the state."[207] However, many experts now question the **effective control test**, particularly when "local impositions ... defy popular will or the rule of law."[208]

Instead, states have begun to emphasize democratic legitimacy. Even if a democratically elected government lacks territorial control, it may have authority to consent to intervention. For example, The Gambia unexpectedly voted in late 2016 to remove incumbent President Jammeh from power. On the 2017 transition date, Jammeh refused to step down and his opponent, Adama Barrow, took the oath of office while in exile in Senegal. Then Barrow requested that ECOWAS intervene with troops from Senegal and Nigeria.[209] Shortly after ECOWAS troops entered The Gambia, Jammeh agreed to surrender power. As observers noted, "President Barrow ... never exercised any control or government authority in The Gambia," but he had international support from the African Union and the UN Security Council because he was democratically elected.[210]

Even if states can agree on who makes up the legitimate government, states often disagree about which specific officials have authority to consent to intervention. Can an executive, like a president or a prime minister, consent? Does a legislature need to approve? Experts often disagree about whether valid consent was given in specific cases because of this ambiguity.[211]

The second question is: can states give *ex ante* consent before the need for intervention arises? Before 1945, states often signed treaties in which they allowed other states to intervene on their territory.[212] After 1945, such agreements were believed to violate the UN Charter and a peremptory norm prohibiting force.[213] Yet in the late 1990s, African states revived *ex ante* consent to intervention. This revival was driven by the UN's failure to effectively intervene in the Rwandan genocide and a growing sense of marginalization within the UN.[214]

After ECOWAS's successful interventions in Liberia in 1990 and Sierra Leone in 1996, its members agreed to the Lomé Protocol in 1999. This document gives ECOWAS power to "authorise all forms of intervention and decide particularly on the deployment of political and military missions."[215] Similarly, the African Union's founding treaty says:

The Union shall function in accordance with …

(h) the right of the Union to intervene in a member state pursuant to a decision of the Assembly in respect of grave circumstances, namely: war crimes, genocide and crimes against humanity …

(j) the right of member states to request intervention from the Union in order to restore peace and security.[216]

Many experts believe that these agreements conflict with the UN Charter. After all, Article 103 of the UN Charter says: "In the event of a conflict between the obligations of the members of the United Nations under the present Charter and their obligations under any other international agreement, their obligations under the present Charter shall prevail." What will happen if ECOWAS or African Union members approve force without the support of the UN Security Council? Would such an intervention be legitimate because the target state gave *ex ante* consent to intervention? Scholars disagree about these questions, suggesting that states will experience future disputes over consent to intervention.[217]

9.6　Case Study Revisited: Was the Saudi-Led Bombing of Yemen Legal?

We began this chapter with the 2015 bombing of Yemen. Recall that the Houthis, a Shiite tribe, were excluded from the Sunni-led political transition after the 2011 Arab Spring. In 2012, Abdrabbuh Mansur Hadi—a Sunni leader—won 99.8 percent of the vote in a one-candidate presidential election. Houthi rebels rose up against President Hadi and began slowly to seize territory. At the same time, both al-Qaeda and ISIL grew in parts of Yemen. Saudi Arabia—Yemen's neighbor—believed that the Houthi rebels were supported by Iran, its regional rival. It feared that growing Houthi strength would threaten Saudi Arabia.

In spring 2015, Qatar asked the UN Security Council to authorize force in response to the growing strength of the Houthis, al-Qaeda, and ISIL. However, the UN Security Council instead urged "all sides to refrain from any further use of military force, any offensive military actions and other uses of violence."[218] President Hadi then wrote a letter asking the Gulf Cooperation Council for help. He claimed that Houthi forces had violated the UN Security Council resolution and asked the GCC "to provide immediate support in every form and take the necessary measures, including military intervention, to protect Yemen and its people" from the Houthis, al-Qaeda, and ISIL.[219] A Saudi-led coalition—including GCC members, Egypt, Jordan, Morocco, and Sudan—then began a massive bombing campaign within Yemen.

This case study relates to each of the major topics in this chapter:

- *Restricting force*: International law requires that any use of force satisfy the principles of military necessity and proportionality. Additionally, Article 2(4) of the UN Charter prohibits "the threat or use of force against the territorial integrity or political independence of any state." Modern customary international law also prohibits intervention in a foreign state.

- *UN Security Council authorization*: Since the end of the Cold War, most experts agree that the UN Security Council can authorize the use of force. Explicit authorization makes otherwise illegal uses of force into legal acts.

- *Self-defense*: States are permitted under international law to use force in either individual or collective self-defense. However, self-defense can only occur if a state is first subject to an armed attack by another state. Legal experts debate whether states can legally use force to prevent an armed attack. They also debate how rules about international wars apply to conflicts with non-state actors, like the Houthis, al-Qaeda, and ISIL.

- *Other possible exceptions*: Finally, some legal experts argue that international law allows the use of force under other special circumstances. These circumstances include: protecting nationals abroad; humanitarian intervention; and consent to intervention.

This information allows us to answer our motivating question for this chapter: did the decision by GCC members to bomb Yemen violate international law?

We can begin by asking: was the bombing a "use of force" under international law? While Article 2(4) does not define the "use of force," the Saudi-led coalition conducted a massive bombing campaign over a prolonged period of time. When the bombing was unsuccessful, conflict escalated: the Saudi-led coalition implemented a naval blockade and sent ground troops into Yemen. The magnitude and duration of force suggest that the Saudi-led coalition clearly used force, per Article 2(4).

Secondly, we must ask: did the UN Security Council authorize the bombing? The UN Security Council often monitors and exerts authority over internal conflicts. Multiple Security Council resolutions imposed non-forcible measures on Yemen, such as economic sanctions. Two days before the bombing began, the Security Council urged "*all sides* to refrain from ... military force."[220] The UN Security Council did not give explicit authorization for the bombing. However, the UN Security Council also did not condemn the bombing after it began. Instead, it stated "its support for the [GCC] in assisting the political transition in Yemen."[221] Reasonable people may disagree on whether the Saudi-led bombing was approved by the UN Security Council. Most experts would probably conclude that the bombing was not authorized. However, some experts might argue that there was implied authorization for the GCC to use force.

Next, we should consider: was the bombing allowed as self-defense against the Houthis, al-Qaeda, and/or ISIL? When Hadi requested GCC assistance, he invoked "the right of self-defence set forth in Article 51," and asked for protection from "the ongoing Houthi aggression."[222] However, the Houthis were not a foreign state that attacked Yemen. Additionally, Hadi presented no evidence that Houthi attacks could be attributed to Iran.[223] Hadi therefore lacked a clear basis for invoking Article 51.

When the Saudi-led coalition notified the UN Security Council of its bombing, it invoked Saudi Arabia's right to self-defense, arguing:

> the acts of aggression have also affected Saudi Arabia, and the presence of heavy weapons and short and long-range missiles ... poses a grave and ongoing threat ... The Houthi militias have already carried out a bare-faced and unjustified attack on the territory of Saudi Arabia, in November 2009, and their current actions make it clear that they intend to do so again.[224]

Saudi Arabia's self-defense claim thus rested on an isolated incident from five years earlier, and fear of a possible future attack. Neither factor suggests that bombing was necessary for Saudi Arabia's self-defense. There is thus a very weak case for the claim that the Saudi-led bombings were an act of self-defense.

Finally, we can ask: was the bombing allowed under any other exception to the prohibition of force? The Saudi-led coalition never claimed to be protecting nationals abroad or intervening for humanitarian reasons, but perhaps Hadi legally consented to the bombings. Recall that consent must be given by a valid domestic authority. When Hadi requested assistance, he had declared himself president after previously surrendering power. Additionally, he lacked effective control over most of Yemeni territory, weakening his authority to consent to intervention. Also recall that many experts believe that outside states are legally obligated to remain neutral during civil conflicts. Under the negative equality doctrine, outside states can only provide assistance to offset outside assistance from other states. Neither Yemen nor the Saudi-led coalition presented evidence of Iranian involvement in 2015.

Overall, this reasoning suggests that the 2015 bombing of Yemen violated international law. Yet most states "expressed sympathy towards the Saudi-led coalition's actions from a legal perspective."[225] How do we account for the dramatic difference between international law and politics in this case? In 1977, political theorist Michael Walzer described debates over the use of force as "utopian quibbling," writing that "lawyers have constructed a paper world, which fails at crucial points to correspond to the world the rest of us still live in."[226] Such criticism may still ring true.

However, Saudi Arabia did not simply bomb Yemen on a whim. It spent years working with the GCC and the UN to help Yemen with its political transition. It supported economic sanctions to hinder the Houthis, al-Qaeda, and ISIL. It sought Security Council authorization in spring 2015. And when these efforts failed, it built a broad coalition to use force in consultation with an elected leader. International law is clearly more than a "paper world."

10 Armed Conflict

10.1   Case Study: Barrel Bombs and Chemical Weapons in Syria

In 2011, Syria spiraled into a civil war between autocratic President Bashar al-Assad and various rebel groups that wanted to remove Assad from power. Images and interviews from Syria were broadcast worldwide, showing the immense brutality and suffering unleashed by the civil war. One dominant theme of news coverage was the impact of the war on civilians. While some cities, like Damascus,

Figure 10.1 A man and boy assess the damage from a barrel bomb attack by government forces in Aleppo, Syria in March 2014. While barrel bombs can cause immense damage and suffering, they are not explicitly prohibited by an international treaty.

were shielded from fighting, Assad's forces attacked major cities, like Aleppo and Homs, causing massive civilian casualties and displacement. These attacks often involved indiscriminate bombings that destroyed civilian targets, like apartment building and hospitals.

A second dominant theme of the war was Assad's refusal to recognize the rebel fighters as legitimate combatants. Terrorist groups, like ISIL, were fighting in some regions of Syria.[1] However, many rebel groups in the conflict were seeking political change, rather than mass terror. For example, many outside states, including the UK and US, treated the Free Syrian Army as a legitimate combatant, rather than a terrorist organization.

One final theme was Assad's choice of two important weapons. First, the Syrian government used barrel bombs, which are containers filled with non-explosive materials like sharp pieces of metal. When dropped by a plane or helicopter, the barrel breaks, scattering its contents at a high velocity. Second, the government used chlorine gas, a chemical weapon that is immensely destructive and easily produced.[2]

The international response to Syria's conduct was mixed. President Assad received significant military support from Iran and Russia in fighting against the rebels. Many states—including France, Turkey, the UK, and the US—condemned the war's cruelty and gave financial assistance to the Free Syrian Army. But none of these states would directly use force against Assad.

Public criticism of Assad by outside states predominantly focused on one aspect of the fighting: the use of chemical weapons. For example, US President Obama condemned Syrian chemical weapons in 2012:

> We have been very clear to the Assad regime ... that a red line for us is we start seeing a whole bunch of chemical weapons moving around or being utilized. That would change my calculus. That would change my equation.[3]

Obama's reference to a "red line" was widely interpreted as a threat: if Assad used chemical weapons, then the US would intervene. However, Obama did not follow through. After reports of extensive chemical weapons attacks in Syria, US Senator John McCain wryly noted: "the red line ... was apparently written in disappearing ink."[4]

No external military action was taken against Syria until April 2017, when newly elected US President Donald Trump launched a missile strike against a Syrian airbase days after a well-publicized chemical weapons attack by Assad. In a letter to the US Congress, Trump wrote:

> I directed this action in order to degrade the Syrian military's ability to conduct further chemical weapons attacks and to dissuade the Syrian regime from using or proliferating chemical weapons, thereby promoting the stability of the region and averting a worsening of the region's current humanitarian catastrophe.

Trump's letter did not mention other troubling aspects of the conflict, including indiscriminate attacks against civilians, the labeling of political opponents as "terrorists," or the brutality of barrel bombs.

Why didn't states like France, Turkey, the UK, and the US challenge the Syrian attacks on civilians more vocally? Why did they overlook the description of political opponents as "terrorists?" And why did they focus so much attention on chemical weapons, while ignoring other destructive weapons, like barrel bombs?

To answer these questions, we must consider the following issues:

- *Regulating armed conflict*: What legal principles and treaties apply during armed conflicts?
- *Protected people*: What obligations does Assad have towards civilians and other protected people?
- *Military conduct*: What rules constrain Assad's choice of targets, methods, and weapons?
- *Non-international armed conflict*: Does it matter that Assad was fighting a civil war? Is international law for internal war different from the law for international war?

The chapter examines ***jus in bello***, which regulates behavior during armed conflicts. Before the twentieth century, this body of law was called the law of war because it only regulated violence between states. However, in the twentieth century, states and scholars began to call it the law of armed conflict, as it expanded to regulate international and non-international conflicts. The term **humanitarian law** describes those laws that address suffering during war.

The law of armed conflict applies very broadly. International law does not define armed conflict, but experts agree that international law applies whenever two states use armed force against each other. States need not formally declare war for the law of armed conflict to apply.[5] International law also sometimes regulates **non-international armed conflict**, which is the legal term for a civil war or other significant internal violence, like the Syrian civil war. As the International Criminal Tribunal for Yugoslavia ruled in the *Tadić* case:

> an armed conflict exists whenever there is ... protracted armed violence between governmental authorities and organized armed groups or between such groups within a state.[6]

Rules during conflict do not depend on whether a state complied with *jus ad bellum*, described in Chapter 8. A state's initial decision to use force does not affect legal restrictions during conflict.

This chapter is organized as follows. Section 10.2 describes the major customary principles of armed conflict law and the historical development of relevant treaty law. Section 10.3 then discusses special protections for civilians and combatants. Section 10.4 provides an overview of rules for military conduct, including targets, methods, weapons, and belligerent occupation. Section 10.5 then describes how international law governs non-international armed conflicts. Finally, section 10.6 revisits the Syrian case. We apply international law to help us understand how other states responded to Assad's conduct.

10.2   Regulating Armed Conflict

The law of armed conflict stretches back for millennia. Many ancient societies had rules for wartime conduct. In the Middle Ages, European nobles followed rules of chivalry, a moral code for war. Classical international law scholars like Grotius and Vattel wrote their own accounts of the laws of war, although we don't know how much these accounts matched actual state behavior. Then, in the positivist and modern eras, states began writing treaties that govern war. This history yielded four major principles and dozens of treaties. We discuss each of these topics in turn.

Principles

The law of armed conflict is built upon four major principles of customary international law—distinction, humanity, military necessity, and proportionality. These principles are closely intertwined without a clear hierarchy between them, and bind all states simultaneously. The principle of **distinction** separates civilians and combatants into different groups, and limits force against civilians. It is also sometimes called the principle of discrimination or identification. States must distinguish between these groups to apply many international rules that aim to protect civilians from the effects of war.

Distinction is included in many different treaties. For example, the Geneva Conventions of 1949 designate civilians as protected persons with legal rights that differ from those of combatants. Similarly, Additional Protocol I of 1977 requires that:

> Parties to the conflict shall at all times distinguish between the civilian population and combatants and between civilian objects and military objectives and accordingly shall direct their operations only against military objectives.[7]

This treaty describes distinction as a "basic rule" of armed conflict.[8]

If a state does not adequately separate civilians and combatants during armed conflict, it violates the principle of distinction. For example, the Democratic Republic of the Congo (DRC) sued Uganda in the *Armed Activities* case at the ICJ. The DRC argued that Uganda violated the law of armed conflict during the Great African War of 1996–2003. The ICJ ultimately found that Uganda "committed acts of killing, torture and other forms of inhumane treatment of the civilian population, destroyed villages and civilian buildings, [and] failed to distinguish between civilian and military targets."[9]

The principle of **humanity** requires states to avoid unnecessary suffering during war. Such suffering includes needless death, injury, and property damage. Scholars sometimes use the term "public conscience" when discussing humanity because of the belief that needless suffering—for both civilians and combatants—is immoral.

Some of the earliest treaties on armed conflict included this principle. For example, the St. Petersburg Declaration of 1868 says:

> the progress of civilization should ... alleviat[e] as much as possible the calamities of war ... This object would be exceeded by the employment of arms which uselessly aggravate the sufferings of disabled men, or render their death inevitable ... The employment of such arms would, therefore, be contrary to the laws of humanity.[10]

Humanity is often invoked in treaties that ban weapons.

For example, the UN General Assembly asked the ICJ in 1994: "Is the threat or use of nuclear weapons in any circumstance permitted under international law?"[11] In the *Nuclear Weapons* Advisory Opinion, the ICJ argued that the threat or use of nuclear weapons was not directly prohibited. However, it also argued that human-ity prohibited "unnecessary suffering to combatants."[12] The Court concluded that "the unique characteristics of nuclear weapons" suggested that "the use of such weapons ... seems scarcely reconcilable with respect for" distinction and human-ity.[13] Accordingly, the Court concluded that "the threat or use of nuclear weapons would generally be contrary to the rules of international law applicable in armed conflict."[14]

A third major principle is **military necessity**, which posits that force is only lawful if it is necessary to achieve a legitimate military objective.[15] This principle applies to both the initial decision to use force (*jus ad bellum*) and subsequent decisions during armed conflict (*jus in bello*). States may only use violence "to achieve the legitimate purpose of the conflict, namely the complete or partial sub-mission of the enemy at the earliest possible moment with the minimum expend-iture of life and resources."[16] Military necessity constrains armed conflict; it does not excuse or justify violence.

Military necessity can affect a state's choice of weapons. For example, the St. Petersburg Declaration of 1868 says:

> The only legitimate object which States should endeavor to accomplish during war is to weaken the military forces of the enemy ... For this purpose it is sufficient to disable the greatest possible number of men.

States can kill and wound soldiers to achieve their military objectives. Yet they may not use weapons that increase suffering without increasing military value.

Military necessity also affects the choice of targets. During the 1991 Gulf War, a US-led coalition fought Iraq after it invaded Kuwait. The coalition's objective was "to restore international peace and security in the area."[17] As the coalition advanced into Kuwait, Iraqi troops withdrew along Highway 80, which connect-ed Kuwait City to Basra, Iraq. During this withdrawal, the coalition bombed Iraqi troops, killing hundreds of soldiers and forcing others to flee on foot. Highway 80 soon became known as the "Highway of Death." While soldiers are legitimate military targets, many critics questioned whether it was militarily necessary to kill the retreating troops.[18] If the coalition wanted to remove Iraqi troops from Kuwait, why did it kill them as they retreated?

The final major principle is **proportionality**, which requires that force must be commensurate with a state's objectives. More specifically, states must balance an operation's expected military advantage against its expected civilian harm, in-cluding death, injury, or property damage. Proportionality became a well-estab-lished principle of customary international law after World War II.[19]

While early treaties hint at proportionality, its most explicit statement comes in Additional Protocol I of 1977. This treaty does not use the word "proportionality," but it prohibits attacks that:

may be expected to cause incidental loss of civilian life, injury to civilians, damage to civilian objects, or a combination thereof, which would be excessive in relation to the concrete and direct military advantage anticipated.[20]

However, most states believe that proportionality "does not itself require the attacker to accept increased risk" for its own troops.[21]

In practice, proportionality affects decisions about targets, weapons, and timing. Attacks on targets with both military and civilian uses, such as factories and power grids, often occur at night or on weekends to minimize civilian deaths.[22] Unfortunately, proportionality can create perverse incentives for combatants to deter attacks by increasing risk to their own civilians. During the 1991 Gulf War, Iraq stored military equipment in hospitals, mosques, residential areas, and schools to deter attacks by the US-led coalition.[23]

Evolution

In the 1860s, states and non-governmental organizations (NGOs) began writing treaties limiting armed conflict. The first modern codification was the **Lieber Code**, which was issued by US President Abraham Lincoln in 1863 to the northern army during the US Civil War. It was written to help professionalize the northern army, which rapidly expanded during the war from thirteen thousand to a million soldiers.[24] Since these new soldiers lacked extensive training, the Lieber Code educated them about the rules of warfare.

At the same time, humanitarian activists—including Clara Barton, Henry Dunant, and Florence Nightingale—raised public awareness of the suffering caused by war.[25] For example, Henry Dunant, a Swiss businessman, helped to create the International Committee of the Red Cross after witnessing the 1859 Battle of Solferino, in which over twenty thousand dead and wounded soldiers were abandoned on the battlefield. This organization subsequently drafted agreements to protect civilians and combatants. These parallel efforts—by states and NGOs—led to numerous treaties on armed conflict, many of which are shown in Table 10.1.

The first systematic international rules are collectively called **Hague law**. These numerous agreements from 1899 and 1907 regulate military operations and limit weapons. Most of these agreements are short conventions and declarations that establish broad principles. They mainly focus on state (or belligerent) rights, yet they include some civilian protections and clarify that customary international law—particularly humanity—also governs armed conflict. In a famous provision called the **Martens clause**, states declared:

Until a more complete code of the laws of war has been issued, ... the inhabitants and the belligerents remain under the protection and the rule of the principles of the law of nations, as they result from the usages established among civilized peoples, from the laws of humanity, and the dictates of the public conscience.[26]

Table 10.1 Key Armed Conflict Treaties

Year(s)	Name	People	Methods	Weapons
1899/1907	Hague Conventions, Declarations, and Regulations*		X	X
1949	Geneva Conventions**	X		
1972	Biological Weapons Convention (BWC)			X
1977	Additional Protocols I and II (AP/I & AP/II)	X	X	X
1980	Conventional Weapons Convention			X
1993	Chemical Weapons Convention (CWC)			X
1997	Mine Ban Treaty			X
2008	Convention on Cluster Munitions			X
2017	Treaty on the Prohibition of Nuclear Weapons			X

* Includes four declarations and sixteen conventions. The Hague Regulations are a set of detailed rules included in an annex to Hague Convention IV ("Laws and Customs of War on Land") of 1907.
** These four conventions address: "Wounded and Sick in Armed Forces in the Field" (I); "Wounded, Sick and Shipwrecked Members of Armed Forces at Sea" (II); "Treatment of Prisoners of War" (III); and "Protection of Civilian Persons in Time of War" (IV).

International courts later invoked the Martens clause—especially its reference to humanity and public conscience—as justification for evolutionary interpretations of the law of armed conflict. Some experts argue that these terms have become "rhetorical and ethical code words" that judges use to incorporate morality and public opinion into their rulings.[27] Hague law also includes a document known as the Hague Regulations (1907), which is a set of detailed rules that apply during wars on land.[28]

States initially enforced the law of armed conflict using reciprocity.[29] For example, some of the states that Germany fought in World War II—including France, Poland, and the UK—belonged to a treaty protecting prisoners of war, while others—including the Soviet Union—did not.[30] This variation affected how Germany treated prisoners of war.[31] French, Polish, and UK prisoners all received relatively humane treatment in German camps, while Russian prisoners received far worse treatment. This treatment was reflected in mortality rates: a UK solider in a German camp had a 96 percent chance of surviving the war, but a Russian soldier had only a 43 percent chance of survival.[32]

After World War II, states enforced the law of armed conflict using legal proceedings. Many states held civil and criminal trials in their domestic courts. For example, Dutch courts prosecuted Hanns Albin Rauter in 1949 for violating Hague law as a Nazi official in the German-occupied Netherlands.[33] Additionally, the victorious Allied Powers created the Nuremberg and Tokyo Tribunals to prosecute military and political leaders from Germany and Japan for war crimes and crimes against humanity. These proceedings changed the future applicability of Hague law. In 1946, the Nuremberg Tribunal declared that Hague law was customary international law. Therefore, Hague obligations shifted from reciprocal promises to unconditional, universal pledges.[34] This shift led to a "widespread and growing ambivalence ... about the practical utility and moral defensibility of reciprocity," and states began to emphasize individual rights.[35]

This shift—from state rights to individual rights—is apparent in the **Geneva Conventions**, which are four 1949 treaties that focus on protected people, including civilians and combatants who are captured, sick, or wounded. Most states interpret the Geneva Conventions as unconditional obligations, which bind states regardless of how others behave.[36] Most Geneva provisions are now considered customary international law.[37]

The final major development was a 1977 treaty called **Additional Protocol I** (AP/I). This treaty expands prior rules about military conduct and protected people. While AP/I unifies Hague law and the Geneva Conventions, it also contains some controversial provisions. Some powerful states—like Australia, France, and the UK—joined AP/I with detailed reservations, while others—including Israel, Turkey, and the US—refuse to join. Accordingly, states often debate which parts of AP/I reflect customary international law.

These three major bodies of law—Hague law, the Geneva Conventions, and AP/I—all focus on international armed conflict. Yet states also wrote some rules for non-international armed conflict (NIAC), which is the international law term for a civil, internal, or intrastate war. As discussed below, Common Article 3 of the Geneva Conventions establishes basic protections during NIACs. States developed and expanded these rules in **Additional Protocol II** (AP/II) of 1977 and have written many additional treaties for special topics in armed conflict. These include treaties that prohibit certain weapons, such as biological and chemical weapons. Examples are listed in Table 10.1 and discussed below.

10.3   Protected People

International law regulates the treatment of people and property during international armed conflicts. We begin this section by examining legal definitions of civilians and combatants, and how states classify people who participate in armed conflicts but are not clearly combatants. We then discuss civilian protections under international law and political factors that affect compliance with these rules. Finally, we next proceed to combatant protections, including immunity from prosecution and prisoner-of-war treatment.

Who Is the Enemy?

International law treats civilians differently than combatants, so a key task is defining these categories. This task might seem simple. You might argue that combatants belong to a state's armed forces, while civilians do not. This basic definition was initially sufficient, with the addition of some other armed groups as combatants.

For example, the 1907 Hague Regulations applied:

> not only to armies, but also to militia and volunteer corps fulfilling the following conditions:
> (1) To be commanded by a person responsible for his subordinates;
> (2) To have a fixed distinctive emblem recognizable at a distance;
> (3) To carry arms openly; and
> (4) To conduct their operations in accordance with the laws and customs of war.[38]

This definition was reiterated with minor changes in the Geneva Conventions. Criteria (1)–(4) create obligations for fighters that want combatant protections. These obligations include distinguishing themselves from civilians—criteria (2) and (3)—because states believed that when fighters "conceal their identity ... to gain the advantage of surprise, [they] violate the principle of humanity underlying the laws of war and are undeserving of legal recognition and protection."[39]

But how should we classify fighters who do not meet these criteria? During World War II, French Resistance fighters covertly challenged the Nazi occupation of France while hiding as civilians. The UK and US argued that these fighters were combatants who should have prisoner-of-war status if captured. Yet Germany argued that they were terrorists because they violated criteria (2) and (3).[40] After World War II, such **guerrilla warfare**, in which armed groups do not distinguish themselves from civilians, increased. In conflicts like the Vietnam War, armed groups often violated criteria (2)–(4). Should such armed groups qualify as combatants?

In response to guerrilla warfare, AP/I has a broader definition of combatants. It includes "all organized armed forces, groups and units which are under a command responsible ... for the conduct of its subordinates."[41] Additionally, it requires that combatants "shall be subject to an internal disciplinary system which ... shall enforce compliance with the rules of international law applicable in armed conflict,"[42] and requires combatants "to distinguish themselves from the civilian population while they are engaged in an attack or in a military operation preparatory to an attack."[43] These provisions mimic criteria (1)–(4).

However, AP/I provides wiggle-room to armed groups:

> Recognizing ... that there are situations in armed conflicts where ... an armed combatant cannot so distinguish himself, he shall retain his status as a combatant, provided that ... he carries his arms openly:
> (a) during each military engagement, and
> (b) during such time as he is visible to the adversary while he is engaged in a military deployment preceding the launching of an attack in which he is to participate.[44]

This language allows fighters to hide as civilians when they aren't fighting, weakening criteria (2) and (3).[45] AP/I also says that "violations of [international law] shall not deprive a combatant of his right to be a combatant."[46] This weakens criterion (4), allowing fighters to violate international law while still receiving combatant protections. Many states that oppose AP/I—like India, Israel, Pakistan, and the US—dislike these provisions.[47] Some critics even describe AP/I as "a pro-terrorist treaty masquerading as humanitarian law."[48]

Even when states agree about how to identify combatants, they sometimes disagree about how to treat fighters who aren't combatants. For example, the US accepts Hague and Geneva law, but opposes AP/I. During the 2001 Afghanistan War, the US fought al-Qaeda members who: did not wear fixed, distinctive emblems; did not carry arms openly; and did not comply with Hague and Geneva law. Were these fighters combatants? By participating in war, including killing US troops, most experts agree that they were not civilians. Yet the US did not want to treat them as combatants.[49]

Some experts argue that international law has three categories: civilians, "legal combatants," and "illegal combatants."[50] These experts argue that when individuals fight in an international armed conflict without meeting criteria (1)–(4), they are neither (lawful) combatants nor civilians. Such individuals exist in a "legal black hole," with ambiguous rights, because treaties do not mention illegal combatants.[51]

An alternative position—that is more widely supported—is that international law has two categories (civilians and combatants), but civilians can lose some protections in some circumstances. AP/I says: "Civilians shall enjoy ... protection ..., unless and for such time as they take a direct part in hostilities." For example, a civilian who delivers weapons to combatants might be targeted for killing or criminally prosecuted. However, no treaty defines "direct part in hostilities" or specifies how such individuals should be treated. Some domestic and international courts have issued relevant rulings,[52] and the International Committee of the Red Cross adopted guidelines in 2009 on this topic.[53] These rules might evolve into customary international law over time. In the meantime, states debate how to classify individuals who participate in armed conflicts without meeting criteria (1)–(4).

The broader question—who is the enemy?—will probably grow even more important. Many states use private contractors during armed conflicts for tasks such as: building infrastructure; operating mess halls and prisons; and providing services and supplies. Additionally, new technologies—like drones and cyberattack programs—are often created, maintained, and operated by civilians.[54] Are these individuals directly participating in armed conflict? Are they legitimate targets during war? Should they receive combatant protections? International law does not (yet) provide clear answers.

Civilian Protections

Early armed conflict treaties largely ignored civilians. The Hague Regulations prohibit "the attack or bombardment ... of towns, villages, dwellings, or buildings which are undefended."[55] This rule placed the burden for protecting civilians on defending states.[56] If each state separated its combatants from its civilians, then attacking states would focus on combatants—who were defended—and not on civilians—who were undefended. In contrast, the Geneva Conventions explicitly address civilians. All four Geneva treaties include rules to protect "persons taking no active part in the hostilities."[57] Additionally, Geneva Convention IV focuses on civilian protections during hostilities and belligerent occupations.

Geneva rules encourage states to create "hospital and safety zones ... to protect from the effects of war, wounded, sick and aged persons, children under fifteen, expectant mothers and mothers of children under seven."[58] These rules required defending states to display "emblems indicating civilian hospitals ... to obviate the possibility of any hostile action."[59] They also encourage states to jointly create "neutralized zones ... to shelter" civilians from war.[60] These provisions give defending and attacking states joint responsibility for protecting civilians.

Geneva rules also protect civilian relief supplies. They require all states to "allow the free passage of all consignments of medical and hospital stores ... intended only for civilians," and "all consignments of essential foodstuffs, clothing and tonics intended for children under fifteen, expectant mothers and maternity cases."[61] Yet an attacking state can restrict relief supplies if it fears that they "may be diverted from their destination" or that "a definite advantage may accrue to the military efforts or economy of the enemy."[62]

Finally, many Geneva rules require special treatment for women and children. Detailed rules govern children who are "orphaned or are separated from their families," and correspondence between family members.[63] Geneva rules also protect women from "any attack on their honour, in particular against rape, enforced prostitution, or any form of indecent assault."[64]

Geneva rules carefully balance civilian protection against military necessity. For example, they say that civilians "may not be used to render certain points or areas immune from military operations."[65] They also allow states to imprison civilians during armed conflict because of security concerns.[66] States must provide humane treatment, but they do not need to provide judicial review to such prisoners. These rules affect contemporary debates about the imprisonment of suspected terrorists in Guantanamo Bay, Cuba.

AP/I expands civilian protections and shifts the burden of compliance to attacking states.[67] It says that civilians "shall not be the object of attack."[68] It also prohibits **indiscriminate attacks**, which are:

(a) those which are not directed at a specific military objective;

(b) those which employ a method or means of combat which cannot be directed at a specific military objective; or

(c) those which employ a method or means of combat the effects of which cannot be limited ... and consequently ... are of a nature to strike military objectives and civilians or civilian objects without distinction.[69]

Civilians may still be killed during combat, but AP/I requires that states use proportionality to balance military advantage against civilian harm. AP/I also prohibits attacks on "objects indispensable to the survival of" civilians, including agriculture, livestock, and irrigation.[70] Finally, AP/I requires that states take precautions to avoid and minimize harm to civilians, which can include advance warning of attacks.[71]

These rules can create "perverse incentives for nations with less-developed armed forces to use civilians to shield their military operations."[72] In 2014, ISIL used Raqqa, a Syrian city, as its operational base. When a coalition of states fought ISIL they had to decide: how would they attack Raqqa? If Raqqa were a military base, the coalition could have bombed it with little risk for coalition forces. But because Raqqa was full of civilians, coalition ground troops fought a slow, bloody battle for Raqqa in 2016–2017. Of course, allowing states to attack civilians is not an acceptable solution to such dilemmas. But many experts argue that AP/I provides little incentive for armed groups like ISIL to distinguish themselves from civilians.[73] Such experts argue that AP/I constrains attacking forces too much, and constrains defending forces too little.

When are civilians more or less vulnerable? We don't know exactly how many civilians have died during war. Yet credible analyses suggest that about 60 percent of the deaths in twentieth-century interstate wars were civilians.[74] One possible factor can be quickly rejected: regime type. Democracies are not more humane than non-democracies. In prolonged conflicts, the opposite is true: democracies kill more civilians than non-democracies. Some scholars therefore argue that voter accountability causes governments to target civilians when they need a quick victory.[75]

Another possible factor is cultural, ethnic, or religious differences between states. In the nineteenth century, Western states often argued that international law did not apply in conflicts with "barbaric" or "uncivilized" people.[76] Many military commanders were more humane towards civilians of their own ethnicity than civilians of a different ethnicity. For example, the Lieber Code—which constrained fighting during the US Civil War in 1861–1865—was ignored during later government attacks against Native American populations.[77] Similarly, European states were more likely to provide humane treatment to European civilians than to non-European civilians.[78] In contemporary wars, civilians are more likely to be killed in territorial conflicts between different ethnic groups, such as the Kosovo conflict between Serbians and ethnic Albanians in the late 1990s.[79]

The most important factor in contemporary politics is the strategic attributes of warfare. Numerous scholars show that guerrilla warfare increases civilian deaths.[80] Such deaths are also more likely in prolonged wars of attrition, perhaps because military targets have already been destroyed or publics become desensitized to civilian deaths.[81] This evidence does not explain why states use guerrilla tactics or fight wars of attrition, yet these strategic attributes can alert NGOs and states to risk factors for civilian suffering.

How are civilian protections likely to evolve in the future? One important development is likely to be new military technology that affects how states target combatants and how publics perceive civilian deaths. Military operations have already changed dramatically because of computer databases with targeting information, technology-based surveillance, and drones that allow more precise killing.[82] These technologies suggest that states will better protect civilians. Yet technology will also affect how civilian deaths are perceived by mass publics. Television dramatically increased awareness of civilian deaths in the Vietnam War, and the Internet and cell phones are doing the same for contemporary conflicts. When anti-government Syrian rebels sought outside intervention from France, Turkey, the UK, and the US, they posted cell phone videos of chemical weapons attacks against civilians on Internet platforms like Facebook and Twitter.[83] These videos created domestic pressure on foreign governments to support the rebels.

A second important development will probably be changing gender norms. International law often associates civilians with "women, children and other vulnerable groups," ignoring the fact that women and children are frequently combatants.[84] This gender-based discourse can be problematic if it reinforces biases about who is and is not likely to be a combatant. For example, Serbian groups fought in 1995 to reclaim Srebrenica, a contested territory under UN protection. After gaining control, Serbian armed groups forcibly evacuated women and young children. They then massacred thousands of men and adolescent boys. This massacre reflects a broader pattern in armed conflict. Numerous studies show that adult civilian males between sixteen and sixty years old are more likely to be killed during war than other civilians.[85] Experts argue that armed groups perceive adult males as more dangerous than women and children. Also, NGOs and IOs often provide more protection to women and children, who are perceived as more vulnerable than adult males.[86] Finally, while international law protects women and children from sexual violence, it has largely overlooked sexual violence against men.[87] As gender norms change across societies, international law must adapt.

Combatant Protections

International law also protects combatants. One important principle is **combatant immunity**—combatants may not be criminally prosecuted for their legal acts during armed conflict. A combatant can be prosecuted for illegal acts—like theft, sexual violence, or war crimes—but a combatant cannot be prosecuted for murder, assault, or property damage.[88] As one expert explains: "immunity for warlike acts that fit within the law of armed conflict turns a murderer into a soldier."[89]

Such immunity is important to contemporary debates about whether al-Qaeda and ISIL members are (lawful) combatants. If they are combatants, then they cannot be criminally prosecuted for murder; but if they are not, then they "are not entitled to participate in the hostilities and consequently may be prosecuted and punished for doing so."[90] The US refused to recognize al-Qaeda fighters in Afghanistan as combatants because it wanted them to be criminally prosecuted as terrorists.[91]

Second, the Geneva Conventions protect combatants who are wounded, sick, or shipwrecked. They require that such combatants "shall be respected and protected in all circumstances" and "treated humanely and cared for."[92] They may not be killed and are entitled to medical assistance. When allocating such medical treatment, decisions must be based on need—a state cannot treat its own combatants first if enemy combatants have more urgent medical needs.[93] AP/I adds that medical assistance must be "to the fullest extent practicable and with the least possible delay."[94]

The Geneva Conventions also address **prisoners of war** (POWs). Winston Churchill once quipped: "A prisoner of war is a man who tries to kill you and fails, and then asks you not to kill him."[95] Under international law, POWs are combatants "who have fallen into the power of the enemy," usually by surrendering or being captured.[96] Various individuals who accompany combatants—such as chaplains, medical personnel, and reporters—also qualify as POWs. POWs are entitled to food, medical assistance, and supplies like clothing and soap. They may be compelled to work, but only in certain industries not associated with war.[97] After armed conflict ends, they must be released and returned to their home state.

The Geneva Conventions require that POWs "must at all times be humanely treated."[98] Yet it does not define humane treatment, instead saying:

> Any unlawful act or omission ... causing death or seriously endangering the health
> of a prisoner of war ... is prohibited ... Likewise, prisoners of war must at all times be
> protected, particularly against acts of violence or intimidation and against insults and
> public curiosity.[99]

This suggests that humane treatment requires protecting a POW from severe danger, but not necessarily shielding them from discomfort or pain. In contrast, AP/I provides much more extensive rules, including the prohibition "at any time and in any place whatsoever" of "violence to the ... physical or mental well-being of persons."[100] AP/I also prohibits "outrages upon personal dignity, in particular humiliating and degrading treatment."[101]

POW treatment came to public attention in the 2001 war against Afghanistan. The US was a member of the Geneva Conventions, but not AP/I. This shaped its interpretation of acceptable POW treatment. News media revealed many abuses of Afghan and al-Qaeda fighters in US military prisons that were deeply shocking and clearly violated Geneva standards.[102] Yet some US activities fell into gray areas of international law, about which reasonable people can disagree. For example, the US military subjected Afghan and al-Qaeda fighters to forcible sleep deprivation during interrogations. This would probably not violate Geneva standards, yet it does violate AP/I because it is a form of "violence to the ... physical or mental well-being of persons." Similarly, the US released photographs in 2002 of Guantanamo Bay prisoners wearing eye masks and earmuffs while kneeling on the ground. It hoped that the photographs would deter Afghans from supporting al-Qaeda.[103] The US did not believe that sensory deprivation or kneeling violated Geneva standards, and it did not believe that the photographs were "insults and public curiosity" because the prisoners were not publicly identifiable. Yet in many European states that belonged to AP/I, both sensory deprivation and the release of photos were interpreted as illegal.[104]

Figure 10.2 Suspected members of the Taliban and al-Qaeda are held during processing at Camp X-Ray—a US military facility in Guantanamo Bay, Cuba—in January 2002.

When are states more or less likely to protect combatants? One possible factor is regime type. On average, democracies treat combatant prisoners more humanely than non-democracies.[105] Some scholars argue that because democracies face voter pressure to secure victory quickly, they benefit most from persuading enemy forces to surrender.[106] Voter accountability may therefore explain why democracies are more likely both to follow international law on POWs and to break international law on killing civilians during prolonged wars.

A second possible factor is cultural, ethnic, or religious differences between states. One study of World War II POWs concluded that humane treatment was most likely when "a sufficient degree of respect for the foe as part of a common humanity existed—that is, where ideological considerations tended toward benevolence—or, even more important, where concern existed for the well-being of friendly prisoners in enemy hands."[107] Many historians argue that POW treatment was most brutal on the eastern European front (between Germany and the USSR) and in the Pacific (between US and Japan) because of cultural differences, while more humane treatment was given on the western European front because of cultural similarities.[108]

Once again, though, the most important factor is likely the strategic attributes of warfare. Prisoner abuse is most likely in prolonged wars of attrition.[109] Additionally, it is affected by reciprocity—states are more likely to treat their enemy combatants humanely when their enemy holds POWs who can be punished in retaliation.[110] For example, Allied treatment of German POWs grew worse at the end of World War II as fears of German retaliation declined.[111]

10.4 Military Conduct

International laws vary for fighting on land, in water, or in the air. Rather than exploring these differences, we focus on broad rules about military conduct. We organize this discussion into four parts. First, we discuss rules for choosing targets. Then we discuss methods for attacking such targets. Third, we discuss rules about weapons. Finally, we discuss state obligations during the occupation of foreign territory.

Targets

Early treaties limit targets based on their defenses. As mentioned previously, the Hague Regulations prohibit "the attack or bombardment ... of towns, villages, dwellings, or buildings which are undefended" because states did not defend illegitimate targets.[112] However, as states accepted more responsibility for protecting civilians under the Geneva Conventions, they began defending illegitimate targets. This change prompted new targeting rules.

AP/I limits attack to **military objectives**, which are:

> those objects which by their nature, location, purpose or use make an effective contribution to military action and whose total or partial destruction, capture or neutralization, in the circumstances ruling at the time, offers a definite military advantage.[113]

This rule creates a two-tiered definition. First, a target must "make an effective contribution to military action" based on its "nature, location, purpose or use." Second, an attack must create "a definite military advantage," based on "the circumstances ruling at the time." A target can only be attacked if both of these criteria are met.

How do states interpret and apply this definition? The first tier of the definition uses criteria that are interpreted in the following ways:

- *Nature*: What is the intrinsic character of the target? For example, a tank or military base inherently contributes to military action, while a church or school does not.
- *Location*: Does the target's geographic position give it military value? Destroying a bridge may limit troop movements, while destroying a portion of open land would not.
- *Purpose*: What future use is intended for the target? For example, the construction site for a weapons factory may provide military value even if the factory is not yet operational.
- *Use*: What is the current use of the target? If a state requisitions a church, school, or hospital for the military, this target is transformed from protected civilian property into a legitimate target.

The term "effective contribution" sets a threshold for each criterion. For example, a bridge may theoretically be used to move troops. However, if fighting is far away and the bridge isn't actually being used this way, then it isn't making an "effective contribution to military action."

The second tier of the definition requires that "total or partial destruction, capture or neutralization, in the circumstances ruling at the time, offers a definite military advantage." This advantage cannot be speculative or hypothetical—a state can only attack if the military advantage is "definite." While targets may sometimes have political or symbolic value, they cannot be attacked unless they also provide military value. Destroying public morale or political support for a war is usually not believed to provide a military advantage.[114] Additionally, destroying cultural property—such as art, architecture, and manuscripts—that is unrelated to war is specifically prohibited.[115]

What about dual-use objects, which serve both military and civilian uses? Consider a power grid that serves both a military base and nearby civilians. For such objects, states usually first ask whether it qualifies as a military objective, and then assess proportionality by asking whether civilian harm would outweigh the military benefit from an attack.

To understand how international law defines military objectives, consider a few examples. Before the 1991 Gulf War, the US military created a list of possible targets.[116] This list included statues of Iraqi leader Saddam Hussein that military planners considered political symbols.[117] However, the statues did not "make an effective contribution to military action" and their destruction would not have provided "a definite military advantage." The US military ultimately removed the statues as possible targets. While the US did not explain this decision, experts agree that the statues were not military objectives.

Second, during its 1999 intervention in Kosovo, NATO bombed the headquarters of Radio Television of Serbia (RTS), a state-owned broadcasting corporation.[118] NATO argued that RTS was part of Serbia's command, control, and communications network, meaning that it coordinated fighting. RTS also sent pro-government messages to the Serbian public. NATO argued: "Strikes against TV transmitters and broadcast facilities are part of our campaign to dismantle the [Serbian] propaganda machinery."[119] Within hours of the attack, RTS resumed broadcasting. Some experts criticize NATO statements about propaganda as irrelevant and argue that even if RTS coordinated fighting, its bombing did not provide "a definite military advantage" because RTS resumed broadcasting so quickly.[120] Other experts believe that the benefit of disrupting propaganda did not negate RTS's "effective contribution to military action." These experts note that the RTS bombing was part of broader attacks on Serbian military communications, suggesting that RTS was a military objective.[121]

Finally, UK forces fought in 2003 in Basra, Iraq's second-largest city.[122] After weeks on the city outskirts, UK troops moved into the city. Defending forces retreated to the College of Literature, with guns and rocket-propelled grenades. The Irish Guards and Scots Dragoon Guards led an attack on the College, successfully gaining control of Basra. Experts widely agree that this attack was legal. While the College would normally be a civilian building, it was transformed by defending troops into military use. Securing control over the defensive stronghold gave "a definite military advantage" to the UK.

Recall that not all states have joined AP/I—some object to its definition of military objectives. For example, the US believes that it can attack targets that directly or indirectly sustain war.[123] During military strikes against ISIL, the US chose economic targets that indirectly helped ISIL maintain power. During a 2016 speech, US President Obama argued:

Thanks to our wave of strikes against its oil infrastructure, tanker trucks, wells and refineries, ISIL's oil production and revenues are significantly reduced. We're destroying the storage sites where ISIL holds its cash—its money is literally going up in smoke. As a result, ISIL has been forced to slash the salaries of its fighters, which, increasingly, diminishes their morale.[124]

Such strikes violate AP/I because economic targets only indirectly help ISIL in armed conflict.[125] However, numerous recent examples, including NATO's decision to target Afghan narcotics production in 2008–2014, cause some experts to argue that the US position has broad political support.[126]

Methods

International law constrains acceptable methods of conflict, which change dramatically over time. For example, before the rise of modern naval fleets, states often relied on **privateering**—they gave private actors authority to attack foreign vessels and seize them as prizes during war. Hugo Grotius's first case as a lawyer was defending the Dutch East India Company after it seized a Portuguese merchant vessel. Grotius argued that the Company's actions were legal because Portugal had restricted the freedom of the seas by limiting Dutch trade.[127] While this argument worked in the 1600s, most states strongly opposed privateering by the mid-1800s. After building their own naval forces, states no longer wanted private actors to wage war. Accordingly, one of the first armed conflict treaties is an 1856 agreement that says, "Privateering is, and remains abolished."[128]

As states developed the international law of armed conflict, they prohibited new methods. For example, the Geneva Conventions prohibit "all measures of intimidation or of terrorism" and "the taking of hostages," while AP/I prohibits attacking "a person parachuting from an aircraft in distress."[129] Because international law changes in response to technology and beliefs about appropriate behavior, we focus here on three methods of contemporary warfare: child soldiers, pillage of natural resources, and sexual violence.

Child Soldiers

International law defines a **child soldier** as a person below fifteen in an armed group. Yet human rights and humanitarian law give individuals below eighteen special protection as children. This inconsistency in standards reflects the practice in some states of allowing individuals between fifteen and seventeen to serve in militaries.

Why do armed groups use child soldiers? Many NGOs and scholars describe how child soldiers are kidnapped from their families, incapacitated by alcohol and drugs, and then forced to commit atrocities.[130] These experts often emphasize African child soldiers in places like Sierra Leone, Sudan, and Uganda.[131] Some experts argue that children are less skilled at fighting than adults, so their recruitment and use implies that "children are easier to mislead and indoctrinate, cheaper to retain, and more responsive to coercive methods" than adults.[132] This narrative is based on passivity, poverty, and victimhood.

While this narrative is undoubtedly true for some child soldiers, other experts argue that the full picture is more complex. Many child soldiers are born into armed groups or voluntarily join them as an economic opportunity. Most child soldiers do not actually fight—they work as cooks, messengers, or other support roles.[133] Girls are commonly overlooked as child soldiers.[134] Yet they often face the worst conditions, serving as sexual partners for adult male fighters. Finally, child soldiers are not unique to Africa. They are common in Asia (Myanmar, Nepal, and Sri Lanka), Latin America (Colombia, Mexico, and Peru), and the Middle East (Iran, Iraq, and Yemen).[135]

International law prohibits states from using child soldiers. The Convention on the Rights of the Child (1989)—one of the most broadly supported human rights treaties—says:

> States Parties shall take all feasible measures to ensure that persons who have not attained the age of fifteen years do not take a direct part in hostilities ... States Parties shall refrain from recruiting any person who has not attained the age of fifteen years into their armed forces.[136]

Figure 10.3 A Yemeni boy poses as part of a Houthi rebel group in July 2017. Despite broad opposition by the international community, child soldiers are routinely used in armed conflicts worldwide. This practice raises complicated legal questions about the rights and responsibilities of children under international law.

Similar requirements are included in AP/I.[137] Additionally, the International Criminal Court includes "conscripting or enlisting children under the age of fifteen years into the national armed forces or using them to participate actively in hostilities" as a war crime.[138]

Many NGOs want to further prohibit military service by anyone below eighteen. This advocacy movement—called "Straight-18"—argues that international law should use consistent standards to protect children. This movement pushed many states to join the Optional Protocol to the Convention on the Rights of the Child, which limits military service for individuals below eighteen, although many members continue to allow individuals who are sixteen and seventeen to serve in their military.[139] These NGOs have also pressured international criminal tribunals to grant de facto immunity to individuals who were below eighteen when they committed war crimes.[140]

However, some critics question this advocacy movement. They note that child soldiers advocacy is driven by a broader "politics of age" in which "there is a tension between the protection of children and the participatory rights of children."[141] While some individuals below eighteen surely are compelled into military service, many voluntarily choose to fight and commit war crimes. Critics question whether states should excuse such crimes based on a "legal fiction of faultless passive victimhood."[142]

Child soldier culpability has taken on renewed importance because many children have been recruited online from the UK and US to join armed groups like al-Shabaab and ISIL.[143] If these children are passive victims, do they have a right to return home after war? Should they face criminal prosecution? What makes children more or less culpable for their actions? Policy-makers remain divided on these important questions.

Pillage and Natural Resources

International law also prohibits **pillage**, which is the unlawful taking of property during conflict for private ends.[144] This includes the seizure of public or private property by civilians or combatants. However, pillage does not include the legal taking of property, such as tax collection or requisitioning property for war, both of which are regulated separately by international law. Pillage was common until the modern era. Hugo Grotius wrote in 1625: "by the Law of Nations ... every Man in a solemn War acquires the Property of what he takes from the Enemy."[145] Property was a spoil of war, and victorious states took what they liked. Some states prohibited pillage in their military codes. However, pillage was not prohibited under international law until modern times.

The Hague Regulations say: "the pillage of a town or place ... is prohibited."[146] Similar protections are included in the Geneva Conventions and AP/I.[147] Finally, the International Criminal Court includes "extensive ... appropriation of property, not justified by military necessity and carried out unlawfully and wantonly," and "pillaging a town or place, even when taken by assault," as war crimes.[148]

The conventional interpretation of these rules is that they prohibit taking moveable property, like art, artifacts, and money. But can states take natural resources, like diamonds, timber, and oil? Does it matter whether new timber will grow over time? If armed groups must invest to extract resources like diamonds and oil, are they pillaging? Legal scholars debate these questions because of policy concerns about the causes of armed conflict.[149]

Many experts believe that natural resources fuel conflict in states like Angola, Liberia, and Sierra Leone.[150] These examples illustrate a broader phenomenon called the **resource curse**, which is the claim that states with more natural resource wealth tend to experience worse economic, political, and social outcomes, including more armed conflict. Many studies show that states with greater wealth from natural resources—including diamonds, oil, and minerals—are more likely to experience armed conflict.[151] Additionally, natural resources affect conflict severity. For example, regions with more diamond mines experienced more attacks during Sierra Leone's civil war, and changes in the global price of goods affect violence.[152]

Yet relatively few legal disputes have addressed natural resources. The most important case thus far is the *Armed Activities* case. In this case, the Democratic Republic of the Congo (DRC) sued Uganda at the ICJ for pillage of its natural resources during the Great African War of 1996–2003. After reviewing the evidence, the Court concluded that "officers and soldiers of the [Ugandan Army] were involved in the looting, plundering and exploitation of the DRC's natural resources."[153] The Court invoked rules prohibiting pillage and concluded that Uganda had violated international law.[154]

As a preventive measure, some international rules aim to disrupt trade of conflict diamonds, which are extracted by armed groups to finance conflicts. After years of advocacy, including consumer awareness campaigns, NGOs persuaded businesses and states to create the Kimberley Process in 2003. This international certification system assures consumers that they are not supporting armed conflict when they purchase a certified diamond. Such certification would probably not be feasible for goods like timber and oil, which are traded in higher volumes by more businesses.[155]

As an alternative, many experts believe that states should more aggressively deter corporations from purchasing pillaged commodities. These experts argue that:

> corporate purchasers of illicit resources are the essential links in the entire supply chain: without the knowledge that they would make valuable use of the illicit resources, there would be no market for the resources, the conflict would lose its most important source of financing, and the conflict would therefore be smaller, shorter, and less lethal.[156]

Such experts believe that corporations should face severe penalties for making armed conflict profitable.

Sexual Violence

Finally, sexual violence[157] has long been prohibited by many military codes, including the Lieber Code.[158] However, states varied in their definitions of terms like "rape" and "sexual assault," leading to conflicting domestic rules that were under-enforced during armed conflict.[159] Sexual violence rose to international attention in the 1990s for multiple reasons. First, the end of the Cold War prompted cooperation in the UN Security Council on issues like the rights of women and children. Second, the 1990s conflict in Yugoslavia, which was widely reported in Western media, included "deliberate, massive and egregious" sexual violence.[160] Finally, public awareness grew that men and boys are also sexual violence victims.[161] Policy-makers began to understand that sexual violence was not an isolated criminal act, but rather a tool of "power and control" used systematically by armed forces.[162]

Prior to the 1990s, international law included few references to sexual violence. The Hague Regulations say "family honour and rights ... must be respected."[163] Additionally, the Tokyo Tribunal prosecuted rapes committed during World War II. The Geneva Conventions mention sexual violence against women, saying: "women shall be especially protected against any attack on their honour, in particular against rape ... or any form of indecent assault."[164] A similar provision was included in AP/I.[165]

However, these legal provisions were problematic. First, they did not define or prohibit "rape" or "indecent assault." They simply required that women be protected from them. Second, by focusing on women, these rules ignored that children and men can also experience sexual violence. Finally, these rules were usually simply ignored.[166]

Dissatisfaction led NGOs to pressure states to develop and enforce rules that define and prohibit sexual violence.[167] The International Criminal Court wrote legal standards on sexual violence that its members must include in their domestic laws. Additionally, many NGOs help war-torn states, like the Democratic Republic of the Congo, to prosecute sexual violence. They help states to write domestic laws on sexual violence; they train judges on domestic and international standards; and they fund trials.[168] Another NGO priority is providing justice for historical crimes that went unaddressed. For example, NGOs organized a Women's International War Crimes Tribunal in 2000 to hold mock trials for rape and sexual slavery that occurred in the 1930s to 1940s, when Japan engaged in war throughout the Asia Pacific region.[169] This tribunal could not issue binding legal orders, but it publicized sexual violence that had previously been ignored. Finally, increased attention has revealed sexual violence by peacekeeping troops sent to war-torn states by the UN and regional organizations. The complex legal status of peacekeeping missions has complicated attempts to address this problem. An important NGO priority is developing new law to prevent and prosecute sexual violence by peacekeeping troops.[170]

Weapons

A state's choice of weapons during armed conflict is always governed by customary international law principles, like distinction and humanity. Yet many treaties also regulate specific weapons. Experts usually differentiate **conventional weapons**, which have relatively limited and precise effects in combat, from weapons that have more massive effects, like biological, chemical, and nuclear weapons. Because the characteristics of weapons affect how they are regulated, we separate our discussion into four parts. First, we examine conventional weapons. Second, we discuss biological and chemical weapons. Third, we examine nuclear weapons. Finally, we discuss possible explanations for why some weapons are regulated by treaties, while other weapons are not. We do not address arms control agreements, which limit the number and kinds of weapons that states accumulate.

Conventional Weapons

One of the oldest rules of weaponry is the prohibition of poison during war.[171] The Lieber Code says: "The use of poison in any manner, be it to poison wells, or food, or arms, is wholly excluded from modern warfare. He that uses it puts himself out of the pale of the law and usages of war."[172] Additionally, Hague law reinforced customary rules that prohibited applying poison to weapons, like arrowheads or bullets.[173] States believed that such behavior caused unnecessary suffering and death.

Second, Russian Tsar Alexander II convinced states in 1868 to ban the use of bullets that exploded or set on fire when they hit their targets. Once again, states believed that such weapons—which were only theoretically possible at the time—would cause unnecessary suffering. They wrote that such bullets would "uselessly aggravate the sufferings of disabled men, or render their death inevitable."[174]

Third, Hague law prohibits the use during war of "bullets which expand or flatten easily in the human body, such as bullets with a hard envelope which does not entirely cover the core or pierced with incisions."[175] In many states, these are called dum-dum bullets and are allowed under domestic law. Because these bullets expand or flatten after hitting their target, they are less likely to exit a body and hit bystanders. Accordingly, they are often used by police forces during riots or hostage situations. However, they are prohibited in war because states believe that they cause unnecessary internal damage in individuals.

After Hague law, relatively little law was made on conventional weapons for several decades. Then, in 1980, states finalized the Conventional Weapons Convention, which is an umbrella treaty made up of multiple protocols, each of which prohibits a specific type of weapon. Protocol I says simply: "It is prohibited to use any weapon the primary effect of which is to injure by fragments which in the human body escape detection by X-rays." The goal of this provision is to ensure that battlefield doctors can easily diagnose and treat injuries.

Fifth, Protocol II of the Conventional Weapons Convention includes detailed rules on the placement and maintenance of mines. States that use such mines are also required to deactivate or remove them when war ends. States expanded these rules after an NGO advocacy campaign in the 1980s and 1990s that highlighted the danger of anti-personnel mines.[176] Civilians are frequently injured, maimed, or killed by anti-personnel mines, even long after conflicts end. In 1997, states completed the Mine Ban Treaty, which requires states to destroy their stockpiles of anti-personnel mines and "destroy ... all anti-personnel mines in mined areas under its jurisdiction or control."[177] Over 80 percent of states have signed and ratified this treaty, leading many activists to argue that anti-personnel landmines are now banned under customary international law. However, other kinds of mines, like anti-vehicular mines, are still allowed under international law.

Sixth, international law limits the use of incendiary weapons. These rules were motivated by the Vietnam War, in which US aircraft dropped napalm—a highly flammable gasoline-based bomb—on Vietnamese villages. Protocol III of the Conventional Weapons Convention defines an incendiary weapon as "any weapon or munition which is primarily designed to set fire to objects or to cause burn injury to persons."[178] Protocol III does not ban these weapons, but it limits how they can be used. States disagree about whether Protocol III applies to white phosphorus, which is used to create smoke screens that protect military personnel and equipment.[179] Even those states that believe that white phosphorus is allowed, like the UK, use it with extreme caution.[180]

Seventh, states created rules for blinding laser weapons in 1995 in Protocol IV of the Conventional Weapons Convention. Since many weapons systems use lasers to mark targets, Protocol IV only prohibits "laser weapons specifically designed, as their sole combat function or as one of their combat functions, to cause permanent blindness."[181] For example, Australia complained in 2019 that China targeted military helicopters with lasers in the South China Sea.[182] No injuries were reported, but Australia's complaint echoed a 2018 US complaint that China was pointing lasers at military jets in Djibouti, causing serious injuries to pilots. The Chinese Defense Ministry denied both events, saying that China "strictly abides by international law."[183]

States added one more set of rules in 2003 to the Conventional Weapons Convention. Protocol V requires states to remove or deactivate any "explosive remnants of war"—such as unexploded bombs and grenades—after hostilities end.[184] For example, Cambodia, Laos, and Vietnam have all struggled to clear explosive remnants from the Vietnam War in the 1960s and 1970s. These remnants have injured, maimed, and killed tens of thousands of civilians since the war ended. Additionally, remnants harm economic growth by preventing farming and other development.

Finally, international law prohibits cluster munitions, which are explosive weapons that contain smaller explosive weapons within them. When the outer shell of a cluster munition breaks, smaller explosive devices are scattered across a broad area. These weapons are highly efficient at spreading the destructive impact of a single weapon, but they inherently cannot distinguish between civilians and combatants. In 2008, states began joining the Convention on Cluster Munitions, which has attracted broad international support. Some states—including the US—refuse to join because they believe that some uses of cluster munitions are legitimate.[185] For example, if a battlefield is isolated from civilians, then distinction may not be relevant. However, NGOs have convinced many states that cluster munitions are inherently harmful to civilians.

Biological and Chemical Weapons

International law also restricts biological and chemical weapons. These restrictions began with the Hague law prohibition of "the use of projectiles the sole object of which is the diffusion of asphyxiating or deleterious gases."[186] After widespread use of gas weapons during World War I, states recommitted to banning gas warfare in 1925 and agreed "to extend this prohibition to the use of bacteriological methods."[187] While states did not define bacteriological methods, experts interpret this term as weaponized viruses and other living organisms. These 1925 rules were considered massively successful when states refrained from using gas during World War II.

In modern law, a **biological weapon** is a weapon that uses a living organism—such as a fungus or virus—to wound or kill animals, humans, or plants. Examples include anthrax and weaponized measles. In 1972, states completed the Biological Weapons Convention (BWC), committing "never in any circumstances to develop, produce, stockpile or otherwise acquire or retain" biological weapons.[188] While this prohibition is now part of customary international law, some experts view the BWC as ineffective because it does not require inspections and monitoring.[189] Additionally, many states possess anthrax and measles for medical research, causing fear about covert biological weapons development.[190]

A **chemical weapon** is a weapon that uses a toxic chemical—in gas, liquid, or solid form—to wound or kill animals or humans. Examples include chlorine, mustard, and tear gases. Many states believe that chemicals should also be banned from destroying plants during armed conflict. They argue that while pesticides may be useful in battle, they can cause long-term environmental and medical damage. Nonetheless, when states negotiated the Chemical Weapons Convention (CWC) of 1993, they excluded pesticides at the US's insistence. The CWC is arguably the strongest weapons treaty. Its members unambiguously pledge "never under any circumstances":

(a) To develop, produce, otherwise acquire, stockpile or retain chemical weapons, or transfer, directly or indirectly, chemical weapons to anyone;

(b) To use chemical weapons;

(c) To engage in any military preparations to use chemical weapons;

(d) To assist, encourage or induce, in any way, anyone to engage in any activity prohibited to a State Party under this Convention.[191]

The CWC created an institution called the Organization for the Prohibition of Chemical Weapons to conduct weapons inspections and verify that members were destroying their stockpiles. In recognition of its important and thorough work, this organization was awarded the Nobel Peace Prize in 2013. Nearly every state in the world is now a member of the CWC, and the chemical weapons ban is part of customary international law.

Nuclear Weapons

Since the US developed the first nuclear weapon in 1944, states have progressively limited the spread and testing of nuclear technology. The key treaty that limits nuclear technology is the 1968 Non-Proliferation Treaty (NPT). Additional treaties include: the 1963 Partial Test Ban Treaty, which prohibits nuclear tests in the atmosphere, outer space, or underwater; the 1974 Threshold Test Ban Treaty, which prohibits large underground tests; and the 1996 Comprehensive Nuclear Test Ban Treaty, which will prohibit all nuclear tests if it enters into force. Despite these treaties, states disagree about whether they can actually use a nuclear weapon under international law. The UN General Assembly asked the ICJ in 1994 "to render its advisory opinion on the following question: 'Is the ... use of nuclear weapons in any circumstance permitted under international law?'"[192]

In its 1996 Advisory Opinion, the ICJ began by examining treaty law. It discussed two regional treaties in which states pledged not to use nuclear weapons in Latin America and the South Pacific, but noted that "the nuclear-weapon States have reserved the right to use nuclear weapons in certain circumstances; and ... these reservations met with no objection from the [treaty] parties."[193] It then noted that many states with nuclear weapons provided security assurances to NPT members without nuclear weapons. However, these assurances had conditions, so the Court did not "view these elements as amounting to a comprehensive and universal conventional prohibition."[194]

The ICJ then examined customary international law. No state has used nuclear weapons since 1945. Some states believed that this state practice meant that the use of nuclear weapons is prohibited. However, other states argued that "if nuclear weapons have not been used since 1945, it is not on account of an existing or nascent custom but merely because circumstances that might justify their use have fortunately not arisen."[195] The Court also examined General Assembly resolutions as possible evidence of *opinio juris*. While numerous resolutions condemn nuclear weapons, many states opposed these resolutions, suggesting that *opinio juris* did not exist.

The Court then examined principles of armed conflict law. It argued that nuclear weapons had "certain unique characteristics" that render them extremely destructive.[196] It noted that nuclear weapons are "vastly more powerful than ... other weapons" and that nuclear radiation has widespread and long-lasting effects on humans and the environment.[197] These characteristics suggested to the ICJ that nuclear weapons cannot be used without violating the principles of distinction and humanity. In particular, the ICJ invoked the Martens Clause to argue that the absence of a treaty prohibition does not imply that use is legal under customary international law.

In its conclusions, the Court acknowledged that there might be extreme scenarios in which states could legally use nuclear weapons.[198] However, outside of such extreme scenarios, it argued that "use of nuclear weapons would generally be contrary to the rules of international law applicable in armed conflict."[199]

The Court declined to address tactical nuclear weapons, which use nuclear technology with more contained effects than normal nuclear weapons. Many states—including the UK and the US—believe that such weapons can be developed and used in some circumstances without violating distinction and humanity. However, this debate remains theoretical because such weapons have never been used.

Anti-nuclear activists continue to pressure states to abandon their nuclear weapons. In 2014, the Marshall Islands sued NPT members with nuclear weapons, arguing that these states violated their NPT obligations to stop the nuclear arms race and disarm. However, these cases were dismissed in 2016 because the ICJ lacked jurisdiction over them. Then in 2017, many states signed the Treaty on the Prohibition of Nuclear Weapons, which requires states to eliminate and prohibit all nuclear weapons, including pre-existing stockpiles. This Treaty currently has seventy signatories, but none of these states actually has nuclear weapons.

Explaining Weapons Treaties

What explains which weapons are regulated by treaties, and which are not? One possible explanation is that customary principles—distinction, humanity, military necessity, and proportionality—underlie these treaties. Yet many scholars question this explanation. For example, some World War II strategists argued that gas weapons were more humane than bombing because they could wound without killing or destroying infrastructure.[200] Similarly, some experts argue that "poison is cruel and barbarous but so are other weapons that are not so indelibly stamped with moral opprobrium."[201] If customary principles guide treaty-making, then why is poison prohibited, but not bombs and bullets? Similarly, why are chemical weapons prohibited by treaty while nuclear weapons are not?

An alternative explanation is that public opinion and NGO advocacy affect treaty-making and compliance. For example, some experts argue that the UK complied with the Geneva Gas Protocol during World War II because of domestic political opinion. One expert writes that "among the English no weapon was more reviled than poison gas," and UK military policy was "a prisoner of the popular revulsion against such weapons."[202] Similarly, treaties like the Mine Ban Treaty and the Convention on Cluster Munitions were heavily influenced by public opinion and NGO advocacy. Because NGOs have idiosyncratic agendas and political power, this can generate idiosyncratic outcomes in weapons treaties.[203] For example, NGOs pressured states to limit cluster munitions, which the US uses, but ignored comparable weapons, like barrel bombs, that developing states use.

A third explanation emphasizes military culture and doctrine. For example, Germany's decision not to use gas weapons during World War II was likely driven by military strategy. At that time, German military strategists emphasized speed—they tried to invade and consolidate control as quickly as possible. Gas weapons slowed down this process because they required long supply lines and their victims died relatively slowly.[204] The logistical difficulties of using certain weapons may therefore help explain which weapons are limited by treaties, and whether states comply.

One final explanation emphasizes power. Sometimes weapons treaties appear driven by powerful states. Early weapons treaties often mention "civilization."[205] While European states constrained their conduct with each other, they did not constrain themselves against non-European states.[206] Similarly, some scholars argue that the prohibition of poison limited who could wage war.[207] If warfare required costly weapons, then only kings and rich nobles could fight. If poison—which was easily accessible throughout history—were permissible, then anybody could fight, including women and the poor. Yet sometimes weapons treaties reflect the opposite pattern: weak states use law to constrain powerful states. For example, states that join weapons treaties often lack the regulated weapons. Of the 193 states that belong to the Chemical Weapons Convention, only eight had declared chemical weapons as of 2019.[208]

While states have limited or banned many weapons, some politically contentious weapons are not regulated by treaties. While customary international law may fill these gaps, the absence of treaty law may create the appearance of permissibility.[209] For example, **drones**—which are unmanned aerial vehicles—have generated intense legal debates.[210] Because drones allow states to kill with relatively little risk, many experts question whether states use them for killings that are not militarily necessary and proportionate.[211] Similarly, because drones have been used extensively against terrorist targets, many experts question whether states are adequately distinguishing between civilians and combatants.[212] Evidence suggests that drones have killed many civilians.[213]

Additionally, many NGOs and states are concerned about autonomous weapons. Even the most sophisticated weapons currently use human operators to choose targets and decide when to detonate. Technology experts believe that computers may soon be able to decide for themselves who and when to kill using artificial intelligence. Such weapons are often called "killer robots." Most states don't object to the mechanization of killing, but rather to the mechanization of decision-making. They ask: can a machine ever distinguish between civilians and combatants, and understand human suffering? Should human consciousness be removed from armed combat?[214] As technology develops, states will need new laws for regulating autonomous weapons.

Belligerent Occupation

International law also regulates **belligerent occupation**, which occurs when one state has authority over another state's territory without its consent.[215] These rules specify the rights and obligations of the **occupying power**, which is the state whose military has authority over its enemy. According to the Hague Regulations:

> Territory is considered occupied when it is actually placed under the authority of the hostile army. The occupation extends only to the territory where such authority has been established and can be exercised.[216]

These rules don't define "authority," causing debates about when the law of belligerent occupation applies.[217] Because international law creates extensive obligations for occupying powers, states often claim that they are not an occupying power.

For example, in the *Armed Activities* case, the Democratic Republic of the Congo (DRC) sued Uganda at the ICJ for activities during the Great African War of 1996–2003. The DRC argued that Uganda was the occupying power for Ituri, which is DRC territory located near Uganda, because a Ugandan general appointed a governor for Ituri.[218] Uganda acknowledged that its troops were present in Ituri, but argued that they lacked authority over it.[219] Uganda also claimed that its general acted beyond his authority by appointing a governor. The Court ultimately sided with the DRC, arguing that Uganda was legally responsible for its general's actions, even if he acted beyond his authority. Additionally, the Court argued that appointing a governor indicated that Uganda exercised authority over Ituri.

What are the rights and obligations of an occupying power? Legal provisions fall into two categories: ensuring stability and protecting civilians. First, many international rules promote stability by limiting occupying powers.[220] For example, Hague Regulations require respect for the internal laws of occupied territory. They require an occupying power to:

> take all the measures in [its] power to restore, and ensure ... public order and safety, while respecting, unless absolutely prevented, the laws in force.[221]

For example, after the US invaded Iraq in 2003, it created the Coalition Provisional Authority (CPA), which had administrative authority over Iraq. To promote "public order and safety," the CPA dissolved the Iraqi military, which it then replaced with its own forces.[222] It also wrote new criminal laws that were consistent with international human rights standards.[223] Some experts believe that such sweeping changes violated international law, and that the CPA needed UN Security Council authorization.[224]

International law also promotes stability by forbidding an occupying power from confiscating private property and pillaging occupied territory.[225] An occupying power may collect taxes in accordance with existing laws "to defray the expenses of the administration of the occupied territory."[226] However, it may not use these taxes to enrich itself, to fund war outside of occupied territories, or to punish occupied territories.[227]

In the *Armed Activities* case, the DRC argued that Uganda was legally responsible for pillaging by both Ugandan armed forces and private individuals in Ituri. The Court agreed, writing:

> The fact that Uganda was the occupying Power in Ituri … extends Uganda's obligation to take appropriate measures to prevent the looting, plundering and exploitation of natural resources … Rather than preventing the illegal traffic in natural resources, including diamonds, high-ranking members of the [Ugandan military] facilitated such activities by commercial entities.[228]

The Court accordingly ordered Uganda to make reparation for the pillaging. In subsequent negotiations, the DRC sought $10 billion in compensation.

Second, many international rules require an occupying power to protect civilians in occupied territory. Most of these provisions are contained in the Geneva Conventions and AP/I.[229] An occupying power must respect basic human rights, although it can restrict the freedom of press, speech, and movement to protect the security of the territory.[230] Additionally, the law of armed conflict provides extensive safeguards for individuals who are arrested and prosecuted for crimes in occupied territory.[231] Occupying powers may also have additional international obligations under human rights law. Finally, an occupying power must provide for civilian needs in occupied territory, including education, food, supplies, medical care, and shelter.[232] This can include cooperating with international relief organizations on the distribution of food and supplies.[233]

10.5   Non-International Armed Conflict

Most contemporary conflicts are civil wars. International law describes such full-scale internal conflicts as non-international armed conflicts (NIACs). NIACs do not include "internal disturbances and tensions, such as riots, isolated and sporadic acts of violence and other acts of a similar nature."[234] For example, the 2010 and 2011 Arab Spring protests in Bahrain, Egypt, and Tunisia were not NIACs because they were not sustained violence.[235]

Most NIACs occur between governments and **armed opposition groups**, which are non-state actors that fight to achieve political goals. Such political goals include: removal of the government; independence from foreign control; greater regional autonomy; and secession. Non-state actors that use violence for solely non-political reasons, such as the illicit drug trade or human trafficking, are not armed opposition groups.

NIACs also sometimes involve foreign states that intervene to support the government. For example, both Iran and Russia have fought in the Syrian civil war to support the Assad government. This intervention is a use of force under international law, but it is not an international armed conflict because Iran and Russia are attacking non-state actors.

What rules apply to NIACs? We begin by discussing the legal obligations that apply to NIACs under treaties and customary international law. We then discuss the legal and political issues faced by armed opposition groups.

Legal Obligations

In early armed conflict treaties, states focused on international conflicts. Many states believed that international rules for NIACs would threaten their sovereignty.[236] For example, many states that wrote Hague law had overseas empires in Africa and Asia. They feared that international rights and obligations for armed opposition groups would encourage rebellion. Most early armed conflict treaties therefore ignored NIACs.

The first treaty obligation for NIACs was **Common Article 3**, a provision included in all of the Geneva Conventions. It requires that:

(1) Persons taking no active part in the hostilities ... shall in all circumstances be treated humanely ... To this end the following acts are and shall remain prohibited at any time and in any place whatsoever with respect to the above-mentioned persons:

    (a) violence to life and person, in particular murder of all kinds, mutilation, cruel treatment and torture;

    (b) taking of hostages;

    (c) outrages upon personal dignity, in particular humiliating and degrading treatment;

    (d) the passing of sentences and the carrying out of executions without previous judgment pronounced by a regularly constituted court ...

(2) The wounded and sick shall be collected and cared for ...

Common Article 3 has "glaring omissions and ... abstract generalities."[237] Individuals who fight for armed opposition groups have no right to combatant immunity or prisoner-of-war status. Additionally, Common Article 3 does not restrict NIAC attacks on hospitals or other targets that are protected in international conflicts.

When states decided to negotiate further NIAC rules, they crafted AP/II of 1977. Developing states—many of which fought NIACs—insisted on relatively weak rules.[238] AP/II mimics the structure of AP/I, but it includes few constraints. It does not prohibit indiscriminate attacks, require proportionality, or grant combatant immunity or prisoner-of-war status.[239] AP/II also only applies to disputes in which armed opposition groups are very well-organized. It says:

> This Protocol ... shall apply to all armed conflicts which are not covered by [AP/I] and which take place in the territory of a High Contracting Party between its armed forces and dissident armed forces or other organized armed groups which, under responsible command, exercise such control over a part of its territory as to enable them to carry out sustained and concerted military operations and to implement this Protocol.[240]

Therefore, AP/II applies when part of a state's existing armed forces split from the state (becoming "dissident armed forces"). For example, during Yugoslavia's wars in the 1990s, many regional military units were associated with regional governments that claimed independence. Alternatively, AP/II applies if an armed opposition is "organized"—meaning that it is "under responsible command," has sufficient control over territory for "sustained and concerted military operations," and has capacity "to implement this Protocol." If an armed opposition group is not "dissident armed forces" or "organized," then AP/II does not apply. For example, Russia—which ratified AP/II—faced persistent violence in Chechnya in the 1990s. Russia refused to acknowledge this violence as an NIAC; it insisted that the violence was domestic terrorism.[241]

Some other armed conflict treaties include NIAC rules. For example, many weapons treaties—including the Biological Weapons Convention (1972), the Chemical Weapons Convention (1993), the Mine Ban Treaty (1997), and the Convention on Cluster Munitions (2008)—apply to NIACs. A supplemental agreement to the Conventional Weapons Convention extends those rules to NIACs.

What rules constrain NIACs under customary international law? Experts agree that Common Article 3 has become customary international law. However, they disagree about which AP/II rules have become customary international law. Many experts—like the International Committee of the Red Cross—argue that most customary rules for international armed conflicts also apply to NIACs.[242] They point out that most states have ratified AP/I and AP/II, and incorporated these rules into their domestic laws.[243] Additionally, they note that numerous international human rights and criminal tribunals—including the International Criminal Court—hold governments and individuals accountable for their actions during NIACs. These tribunals have yielded many rulings that apply AP/I rules to NIACs. One criminal tribunal explained: "What is inhumane and consequently proscribed, in inter-national wars, cannot but be inhumane and inadmissible in civil strife."[244]

However, other experts disagree about whether customary international law regulates NIACs. They argue that treaty ratifications and domestic laws should not count as state practice and *opinio juris* because most states that ratified AP/II haven't actually fought NIACs.[245] For example, 168 states have ratified AP/II, as shown in Table 10.2, suggesting strong support for its rules. Approximately 33 percent of these states experienced civil conflict on their territory after their ratification. In some of these conflicts, such as Russia's conflict in Chechnya, rat-ifying states refused to acknowledge that they were fighting NIACs. Other states that have begun fighting new NIACs, such as Croatia and Bosnia, ratified AP/II to gain international support for their conflicts. In contrast, thirty states have not ratified AP/II, but 60 percent of these states have experienced civil conflict on their territory since 1977. Many of these states—including Indonesia, Iraq, and Somalia—have faced repeated civil conflicts since 1977. This data suggests that states that join AP/II are fundamentally different than the states that do not join AP/II. If we focus on simply counting treaty ratifications, we may overemphasize the practice of states that rarely fight NIACs, and underemphasize the practice of states that often fight NIACs. We also implicitly treat the practice of small, peace-ful states—like Barbados and Fiji—as equivalent to the practice of larger states with more civil conflict—like Indonesia and Turkey.

Some experts argue that we should examine instead how states and armed op-position groups actually behave during NIACs. Recent NIACs in Syria and Yemen suggest that states and armed opposition groups rarely follow AP/II rules when they actually fight. Additionally, these experts point out that international human rights and criminal tribunals rule based on their own treaties, which don't fully coincide with the law of armed conflict. This can yield "a patchwork of norms" that are "incoherent, unworkable, and ineffective."[246] Experts thus disagree about which rules govern NIACs under customary international law.

Table 10.2 State Practice and Ratification of AP/II			
	Yes	No	Total
Civil conflict*	55	18	73
No civil conflict	113	12	125
Total	168	30	

* For ratifying states, includes count of states that fought a civil war on their own territory after their ratification year. For non-ratifying states, includes count of states that fought a civil war on their own territory after 1977.
Sources: Civil conflict data from the Uppsala Conflict Data Program; ratification data from the ICRC.

Armed Opposition Groups

Historically, international law constrained governments, the legitimate representatives of states. But does international law also constrain armed opposition groups? This question reflects broader debates about whether non-state actors are subjects of international law.[247] When NIAC rules were originally developed, many armed opposition groups argued that treaties did not bind them. They objected to being bound by rules that they did not participate in creating. For example, the National Liberation Front—a Vietnamese armed opposition group—informed the International Committee of the Red Cross in 1965 that it "did not participate in the Geneva Conventions … and is not bound by" them.[248]

This understanding—that international law constrains states, but not armed opposition groups—was also reflected in legal scholarship. For example, one expert argued in 1981 that AP/II "does not confer rights or impose obligations on rebels, in that it does not permit them formally to become a party to it … States are the only international entities to which the Protocol applies."[249] However, this understanding changed over time, in part because of the behavior of armed opposition groups in accepting and complying with international rules.

First, many armed opposition groups accept armed conflict rules using special agreements and declarations. As shown in Table 10.3, these examples span all regions of the world. In many states—like Algeria and Angola—armed opposition

Table 10.3 Armed Opposition Groups that Accepted Armed Conflict Rules

Years	State	Armed Opposition Groups	Description
1954–1962	Algeria	Front de Libération Nationale	Accepted the Geneva Conventions
1961–1975	Angola	União Nacional para a Independência Total de Angola	Accepted the Geneva Conventions
1964–present	Colombia	Ejército de Liberación Nacional and Fuerzas Armadas Revolucionarias de Colombia	Agreed to numerous humanitarian rules
1980–1991	El Salvador	Frente Farabundo Martí para la Liberación Nacional	Accepted Common Article 3 and AP/II
1984–present	Turkey	Partiya Karkerên Kurdistanê	Accepted the Geneva Conventions and AP/I
1992–1995	Bosnia	Various groups	Wrote rules for prisoner exchanges and humanitarian assistance
1996–2006	Nepal	Communist Party of Nepal–Marxist	Agreed to numerous humanitarian rules
2000s	Myanmar	Karenni Army and Karen National Liberation Army	Renounced child soldiers and anti-personnel mines

Table 10.3 (Cont.)			
Years	State	Armed Opposition Groups	Description
2003–present	Sudan	Justice and Equality Movement	Agreed to numerous humanitarian rules
2004–present	Yemen	Houthi	Agreed to numerous humanitarian rules

Source: Sandesh Sivakumaran (2012), *The Law of Non-International Armed Conflict*, Oxford University Press, pp. 144–151.

groups used international law as a political tool when they sought independence from colonial rule.[250] In others—like Myanmar and Turkey—geographically concentrated ethnic groups wanted to secede and form new states. These agreements and declarations are not treaties, but some experts believe that they should affect customary international law.[251]

Second, many armed opposition groups comply with international rules. Research shows that when armed opposition groups seek legitimacy from the international community, they are more likely to comply with international law. This compliance pattern includes rules about targeting civilians, using child soldiers, and granting access to detention centers to monitor humane conditions.[252] Similarly, armed opposition groups are less likely to target civilians when they are financially dependent on outside states that value human rights.[253]

Most contemporary experts now believe that international law constrains armed opposition groups, even if these groups have not consented to these rules.[254] However, they disagree about which rules bind these states. Some experts argue that armed opposition groups can legally detain individuals who fight against them.[255] Others argue that armed opposition groups should receive combatant immunity if they follow international humanitarian law.[256] An important future task for international law is specifying the rights and obligations of armed opposition groups.

10.6 Case Study Revisited: Did Assad Violate International Law During the Syrian Civil War?

This chapter began describing the outbreak of the Syrian civil war in 2011. We described three key themes in the war. These were: indiscriminate attacks by the Syrian military on major cities, like Aleppo and Homs; Assad's refusal to recognize rebel groups as legitimate combatants; and the use of highly destructive weapons, like barrel bombs and chlorine gas. President Assad received support from Iran and Russia, but the Free Syrian Army—the main rebel group—struggled to gain support from states. Many states—including France, Turkey, the UK, and the US—condemned the government's cruelty and gave financial assistance to the Free Syrian Army. But the first outside attack against Assad didn't occur until 2017, when US President Trump bombed a Syrian airbase in retaliation for an earlier chemical weapons attack.

This case study relates to each of the major topics in this chapter.

- *Regulating armed conflict*: Conduct during armed conflict is governed by numerous principles and treaties. Table 10.4 summarizes Syria's obligations under armed conflict treaties. This includes treaties that are directly binding because Syria ratified them, and treaties that are indirectly binding because their rules have become part of customary international law. While Hague and Geneva law are part of customary international law, they have limited application to NIACs like the Syrian civil war. Additionally, Syria has ratified AP/I, but not AP/II.
- *Protected people*: Treaties and customary international law create obligations for a government to protect civilians and other protected people. These obligations include both a prohibition on civilian attacks and an obligation for military forces to distinguish themselves from civilians. Additionally, states are required to provide combatant immunity and prisoner-of-war status to foreign troops during international armed conflicts.

Table 10.4 Syria's Obligations Under the Law of Armed Conflict

Year(s)	Treaty Name	Directly Bound via Ratification?	Indirectly Bound via Custom?
1899/1907	Hague Conventions, Declarations, and Regulations	No	Yes
1949	Geneva Conventions	Yes	Yes
1972	Biological Weapons Convention (BWC)	No	Yes
1977	Additional Protocol I (AP/I)	Yes	Maybe*
1977	Additional Protocol II (AP/II)	No	Maybe*
1980	Conventional Weapons Convention	No	No
1993	Chemical Weapons Convention (CWC)	Yes (since 2013)	Yes
1997	Mine Ban Treaty	No	Maybe*
2008	Convention on Cluster Munitions	No	No
2017	Treaty on the Prohibition of Nuclear Weapons	No	No

* Experts have principled disagreements about whether these rules are part of customary international law.
Source: Ratification data from UN records.

- *Military conduct*: Barrel bombs are not regulated by existing treaties. While they have horrific effects, states cannot identify a treaty that prohibits them. However, chlorine gas is prohibited in all circumstances by the Chemical Weapons Convention. This treaty is part of customary international law and Syria even ratified the treaty in 2013.

- *Non-international armed conflict*: International rules differ for international armed conflicts and non-international armed conflicts. Some experts believe that most rules for international conflicts can be applied to internal conflicts as customary international law.[257] Other experts disagree. While many tactics during the Syrian civil war are horrific and deeply troubling on moral grounds, they are not necessarily illegal.

This information allows us to return to the questions that we posed at the introduction of this chapter. We began by asking: Why didn't states like France, Turkey, the UK, and the US challenge the Syrian attacks on civilians more vocally? While Assad's attacks on major cities were horrific, he might argue that Syrian rebels placed civilians at risk by not distinguishing themselves. Like most guerrilla movements, the Free Syrian Army does not have military bases and does not wear uniforms when fighting. Civilian deaths are somewhat inevitable when troops cannot distinguish between who is a civilian and who is not.

Additionally, if Assad were fighting an international armed conflict, the attacks on Aleppo and Homs would clearly be prohibited as indiscriminate attacks under AP/I, which Syria has joined. However, Assad is fighting a non-international armed conflict. Syria is not a member of AP/II, and even if it were a member, AP/II does not prohibit indiscriminate attacks for NIACs.

Secondly, we asked: Why did outside states overlook the description of political opponents as "terrorists," rather than legitimate combatants? By refusing to recognize rebel groups as legitimate combatants, Assad denied rebel fighters combatant immunity and prisoner-of-war status.[258] Syria still has a legal obligation to treat rebel fighters humanely under human rights and armed conflict law. However, it is allowed to treat rebel fighters as criminals, rather than protected combatants.[259]

Perhaps not coincidentally, Assad's legal position towards the Syrian rebel groups matches Turkey's own legal position towards Kurdish rebels, and the US's position towards al-Qaeda and ISIL. While Turkey, the US, and many other states do not consider the Free Syrian Army to be terrorists, it is difficult for these states to make principled arguments that Syrian rebels should be given combatant immunity and prisoner-of-war status. Doing so would undermine Turkey's policy on Kurdish rebels and the US's policy on al-Qaeda and ISIL.

Finally, we asked: why did the US and and other outside states focus so much attention on chemical weapons, while ignoring other destructive weapons, like barrel bombs? Most individuals who have learned about the brutality of the Syrian civil war would probably think, "How could such horrific violence be allowed? Assad must be violating international law." Yet a diligent lawyer knows that law and morality do not always coincide. All military attacks are destructive; that does not make them illegal. We can have informed and principled debates about whether Assad has violated rules that protect civilians and combatants. However, there is only one action during the Syrian civil war that clearly and irrefutably violated international law: Assad's use of chemical weapons. Accordingly, the only action of the Assad government that has triggered a military response by another state is his use of chemical weapons. Barrel bombs and the destruction of major cities triggered no concrete response. The details of international law matter.

Figure 10.4 Nikki Haley—the US Ambassador to the UN—presents evidence of a Syrian chemical weapons attack during a meeting of the UN Security Council in April 2017. The US refused to participate directly in the Syrian civil war and did not respond militarily to the widespread use of barrel bombs and general attacks on civilians. However, the US launched limited retaliatory attacks after the chemical weapons attacks in 2017.

PART IV
New Challenges

11 Criminal Responsibility

11.1 Case Study: An African Dictators's Day in Court

In May 2016, Hissène Habré awaited his verdict.[1] For months, Habré had watched victims testify about mass killings, rape, and torture. Throughout the trial, he did not speak. He simply watched from a black leather armchair, wrapped head-to-toe in white with his eyes shielded by dark sunglasses. When the guilty verdict finally came, the courtroom erupted in cheers of "*Vive la victoire!*" But Habré remained silent. His only reaction to the outcome was to raise his fist in protest as he left the courtroom.

Hissène Habré seized control of Chad, a state in central Africa, in 1982. He was supported throughout his rule by France and the US, both of which wanted Habré to limit Libya's growing regional power. While Habré proved a trusty ally to France and the US, his rule was marked by extreme internal violence. Habré oversaw a security agency that engaged in widespread killings, rape, and torture of

Figure 11.1 Hissène Habré—former dictator of Chad—gestures to onlookers as he leaves a courtroom in Dakar, Senegal in June 2015. Habré was prosecuted by the Extraordinary African Chambers for multiple international crimes.

armed groups that opposed Habré and of civilians from rival ethnic groups.[2] Habré even converted his swimming pool into an underground prison where his rivals were tortured. In 1990, Idriss Déby—Habré's former army commander—overthrew Habré in a coup. Habré quickly raided Chad's treasury and fled to Senegal, a state in West Africa that granted him asylum.

For Habré's victims, justice was a long time coming. Many of them spent decades working with non-governmental organizations to compile evidence of Habré's atrocities.[3] They filed complaints in numerous states, including Belgium and Senegal, asking that Habré be prosecuted for international crimes. Eventually, Chad's government (still led by Déby) declared that Habré had no immunity from prosecution, and Habré faced trial at a criminal tribunal created by the African Union.

What gave the African Union, Belgium, and Senegal authority to get involved in a domestic dispute in Chad? Why was Habré prosecuted for crimes, while Déby, an army commander, was not tried? Why weren't France and the US also responsible for assisting (or at least ignoring) Habré's crimes? More generally, is the Habré trial an example of justice or political retribution?

To answer these questions, we must understand and address the following issues:

- *Creating international crimes*: What major principles govern international criminal law? Where did this body of law come from?

- *Establishing guilt*: Which acts are crimes under international law—are all legal violations crimes, or only some? How do we know when individuals (rather than states) should be punished for legal violations? What possible defenses could Habré assert?
- *Enforcing international criminal law*: What institutions prosecute individuals like Habré? Why was he prosecuted by an African Union court, rather than a domestic court or the International Criminal Court?

In this chapter we focus on international law that creates duties for individuals, like military and political leaders.[4] These individual duties often overlap with state duties under international law, yet they are analytically distinct. While international criminal law builds on concepts from international law on human rights, use of force, and armed conflict, it has its own distinct rules. We focus here on the four core crimes that can be prosecuted by the modern International Criminal Court—aggression, crimes against humanity, genocide, and war crimes.

Section 11.2 describes how states developed international criminal law over time. It discusses relevant legal principles and the historical use of international tribunals to prosecute individuals. Section 11.3 then discusses how states and tribunals establish guilt. This section addresses core crimes, modes of individual responsibility, and possible defenses to prosecution. Next, section 11.4 describes the two important ways that states enforce international criminal law: the International Criminal Court and universal jurisdiction. Finally, section 11.5 revisits the case of Hissène Habré and asks whether the outcome was justice or political retribution.

11.2 Creating International Crimes

In this section, we discuss how states developed international criminal law over time. We begin with an overview of the major principles of international criminal law, some of which came from domestic law. We then provide a brief history of international criminal law, focusing on international tribunals that have prosecuted individuals.

Principles

One major principle of international criminal law is that crimes consist of two elements. First, the **material element** is the physical act prohibited by law. Such physical acts are usually both objective and observable. Second, the **mental element** typically requires individual knowledge of relevant facts and intent to commit a crime. This element is inherently more subjective and less observable than the material element because it is based on the defendant's beliefs. In terms of knowledge, a defendant usually cannot claim that he is innocent of a crime because he did not know international law. However, a defendant may be acquitted if he can prove that he misunderstood the law or relevant facts. The second component of the mental element—intent—is usually the most difficult to understand and prove because it requires that we understand *why* an individual takes a particular action.

For example, suppose that a military commander is accused of the war crime of using child soldiers. To establish the material element of this crime, a prosecutor must prove that an individual below the age of fifteen participated in the armed group. Even if this is proven, the commander could argue that he is not guilty because the mental element is not satisfied. The commander might argue that he made a mistake of law because he believed that fourteen-year-olds could legally fight in wars.[5] Alternatively, the commander might argue that he made a mistake of fact because he genuinely believed that the soldiers were at least fifteen years old. Finally, and relatedly, he might argue that he did not intend to commit a crime. For example, he might argue that the participation of a few isolated children was accidental, rather than intentional.

Another major principle of international criminal law is **non-retroactivity**. This principle has two parts. First, it requires that individuals may not be convicted for acts that were not illegal at the time that they were committed. Second, it requires that individuals may not be punished for acts unless law provided for such punishment at the time that the act was committed. These components are often referred to by two Latin phrases:

- ***Nullum crimen sine lege*** ("no crime without law"): the principle that law cannot be applied retroactively;
- ***Nulla poena sine lege*** ("no punishment without law"): the principle that punishments cannot be applied retroactively.

Non-retroactivity posed challenges for early international criminal tribunals.

For example, the Allied Powers gave the Nuremberg Tribunal authority after World War II to prosecute Nazi German officials for "crimes against peace," which they defined as the "planning, preparation, initiation or waging of a war of aggression, or a war in violation of international treaties, agreements or assurances."[6] The Nuremberg Tribunal dated the beginning of World War II to the German invasion of Poland in 1939. German defense lawyers argued that non-retroactivity required that the Tribunal assess the defendants based on legal standards from 1939. They argued that the defendants could not be convicted of crimes against peace because aggression was not illegal in 1939. The only relevant treaty at that time was the Pact of Paris (1928), in which states "condemn[ed] recourse to war for the solution of internatonial controversies and renounce[d] it as an instrument of national policy in their relations with one another." But states did not write in 1928 that "planning, preparation, initiation or waging" war was illegal or a crime.

When addressing this argument, the Nuremberg Tribunal reviewed various attempts by states to prohibit war before the Pact of Paris. It obliquely concluded:

> All these expressions of opinion ... reinforce the construction which the Tribunal placed
> upon the Pact of Paris that resort to a war of aggression is not merely illegal, but is
> criminal. The prohibition of aggressive war demanded by the conscience of the world finds
> its expression in the series of pacts and treaties to which the Tribunal has just referred.[7]

The Nuremberg Tribunal thus suggested that its interpretation (or "construction") of the Pact of Paris was based on what "the conscience of the world" demanded in 1928, rather than the actual text of the treaty. Many legal experts find this logic unconvincing and criticize the Nuremberg Tribunal for applying law retroactively. To avoid such situations, modern international criminal tribunals include non-retroactivity rules in their statutes.

A final major principle is **individual criminal responsibility**, which is the principle that individuals have duties under international criminal law. Throughout history, legal experts have debated who exactly has duties and rights under international law. In the nineteenth century, most experts believed that international law created legal obligations for states, but not for individual leaders. How, then, could individuals be held criminally accountable for breaking international law? Early international criminal tribunals had to address this important hurdle.

At the Nuremberg Tribunal, German defense lawyers argued that:

> international law is concerned with the actions of sovereign states and provides no
> punishment for individuals; and further, that where the act in question is an act of
> state, those who carry it out are not personally responsible, but are protected by the
> doctrine of the sovereignty of the state.[8]

Nuremberg judges dismissed this argument. They argued that states had long punished military soldiers and commanders for violating the laws of war, and therefore international tribunals could do the same. They adopted a broad interpretation of relevant law, reasoning that:

> Crimes against international law are committed by men, not by abstract entities,
> and only by punishing individuals who commit such crimes can the provisions of
> international law be enforced.[9]

Once again, the Nuremberg Tribunal's logic was widely criticized. And once again, modern international criminal tribunals have sought to avoid this criticism by including individual criminal responsibility in their statutes.

Evolution

The evolution of international criminal law began in the early twentieth century. After World War I, states tried—but failed—to hold individuals accountable for war using international trials. In the Treaty of Versailles, Germany agreed to surrender Kaiser Wilhelm II—the German emperor—to face trial for violating international law. However, he escaped prosecution when the Netherlands granted him asylum. Germany also pledged to surrender its citizens for prosecution by Allied Power military tribunals. But Germany then persuaded the Allied Powers to allow it to hold domestic trials in Leipzig for alleged war crimes. An Allied commission recommended that Germany prosecute nearly 900 individuals for violating existing laws of armed conflict. This list was slowly whittled down to just forty-five names, which yielded only twelve trials and six convictions.[10] Similarly, the UK demanded that Turkey—the successor of the Ottoman Empire—surrender Ottoman officials to face prosecution for the wartime massacre of Armenians. But Turkey ultimately persuaded the UK to drop its demands. No individual faced international prosecution for violating armed conflict treaties during World War I.

World War II Military Tribunals

After World War II, the Allied Powers tried again to use international criminal tribunals. As shown in Table 11.1, they created two international military tribunals to prosecute German and Japanese leaders in Nuremberg and Tokyo, respectively. These tribunals were created without the explicit consent of Germany or Japan, although some scholars argue that such consent was not necessary because both states were occupied. Many observers accordingly criticized the Nuremberg and Tokyo Tribunals as victor's justice, rather than a legitimate exercise of international authority.

These tribunals faced three key legal challenges. First, the principle of international criminal responsibility was not well-established in the 1940s. Many experts questioned whether international law constrained individuals.[11] They believed that international law only constrained states. For example, while states routinely punished individuals for war crimes, they did so under domestic law, like military

Table 11.1 International Criminal Tribunals Examples

Type	Years	Name
Military	1945–1946	Nuremberg Tribunal
Military	1946–1948	Tokyo Tribunal
Ad hoc	1993–2017	International Criminal Tribunal for the former Yugoslavia (ICTY)
Ad hoc	1995–2015	International Criminal Tribunal for Rwanda (ICTR)
Permanent	2002–present	International Criminal Court (ICC)
Mixed	2002–2013	Special Court for Sierra Leone
Mixed	2006–present	Extraordinary Chambers in the Courts of Cambodia
Mixed	2009–present	Special Tribunal for Lebanon
Mixed	2013–2017	Extraordinary African Chambers

codes of conduct. Therefore, many experts believed that international law did not create legal duties for individuals. Many German and Japanese defendants argued that they had complied with domestic law, and that international law did not apply directly to them.

Second, as discussed above, many experts argued that the Nuremberg and Tokyo Tribunals applied law retroactively.[12] The Hague Regulations—which codified the laws of war—did not explicitly create individual criminal responsibility. Similarly, the Pact of Paris—which condemned war—did not criminalize war or create any punishments for violations. While most experts believed that Germany and Japan had violated international law as states, it was less clear whether German and Japanese officials could be held criminally responsible for these violations and punished by an international court. Possible justifications for these prosecutions, like the legal documents that created the tribunals, were written after the war was completed.

Finally, many experts questioned whether the Nuremberg and Tokyo Tribunals had jurisdiction over their defendants. The Nuremberg Tribunal was created by a treaty between France, the UK, the US, and the USSR.[13] Similarly, the Tokyo Tribunal was created by an Allied military order. Neither Germany nor Japan accepted the jurisdiction of these two tribunals. Some experts argued that these tribunals were allowed under the international law of belligerent occupation. Alternatively, other experts argued that the tribunals were legitimate based on the surrender by Germany and Japan. This uncertainty about the tribunals' jurisdiction caused the Allied Powers to seek formal support from the United Nations. In late 1946, after the Nuremberg Tribunal issued its judgment, the UN General Assembly affirmed "the principles of international law recognized by the" Nuremberg Tribunal.[14]

Despite these challenges, the Nuremberg and Tokyo Tribunals were probably the best options at the time. The international community did not trust German and Japanese courts to conduct genuine prosecution of military and political leaders. The United Nations was barely functioning and no alternative venue existed for international criminal trials. Whatever their faults, the tribunals provided more justice than granting impunity or executing leaders without trial. The tribunals demonstrated the possibilities of international criminal law and created important case law on concepts such as individual criminal responsibility. Their work was used by later military tribunals run by Australia, Canada, China, France, the Netherlands, Norway, Poland, the UK, and the US. For example, the Allied Powers oversaw fifty-one war crimes tribunals in former Japanese territories, like Hong Kong, Kuala Lumpur, Manila, and Singapore. These tribunals prosecuted over 5,700 individuals for war crimes in the Asia-Pacific region.[15]

Throughout the late 1940s to 1990s, states made periodic attempts to further develop international criminal law and institutions. The International Law

Commission drafted numerous reports to establish international criminal responsibility, define international crimes, and create a permanent international criminal tribunal. However, states made little progress until the early 1990s, when the Cold War ended and armed conflicts began in Yugoslavia and Rwanda.

Modern Criminal Tribunals

Before the 1990s, Yugoslavia was a federation of six territories in southeastern Europe. Many of these territories began declaring their independence, creating interwoven conflicts. Most of the violence occurred in Bosnia, Croatia, and Serbia.[16] Most individuals in these territories belonged to three ethnic groups—most Bosnians were Muslim; most Croatians were Roman Catholic (Christian); and most Serbians were Eastern Orthodox (Christian). However, the territories of Bosnia, Croatia, and Serbia did not perfectly align with the ethnic and religious identities of their inhabitants. For example, many people living in Bosnia belonged to the Eastern Orthodox faith and called themselves "Bosnian Serbs." Similarly, Roman Catholics who lived in Bosnia called themselves "Bosnian Croats."

All sides in the conflict committed international crimes. However, most of these crimes were committed against Muslims in Bosnia. The Yugoslavian conflict popularized the term **ethnic cleansing** because armed groups sought to establish military control by forcibly removing rival ethnic groups. The Yugoslavian conflict was also characterized by mass civilian deaths, sexual violence, torture, and the destruction of important cultural and historical centers.

Meanwhile, civil violence was simmering in Rwanda, a small state in central Africa. Most native Rwandans belonged to the Hutu and Tutsi ethnic groups. These two groups share the same culture, language, and religion. They historically differed based on socio-economic class: the Tutsi, a minority group, were usually richer than the Hutu, the majority of the population.[17] Decolonization led to a long-term power struggle between the two groups, which erupted into a civil war in 1990. The two sides initially reached a peaceful agreement, but the assassination of Rwanda's leader in 1994 triggered intense violence for approximately one hundred days. During this period, extremist Hutus killed an estimated 500,000–1,000,000 people. Most of the victims were Tutsi, but many moderate Hutus who refused to slaughter Tutsis were also killed. Extremist Hutus also committed mass sexual violence. These one hundred days in 1994 are commonly labeled a genocide.

International attention became focused on both Yugoslavia and Rwanda in the 1990s. Western news broadcasts publicized both conflicts, sharing images and accounts that shocked Western audiences and revived memories of the Holocaust. Horrified domestic publics in France, the UK, and the US pressured their leaders to respond. These leaders acted through the UN Security Council (UNSC) because

Russia, the successor of the USSR, was focused on internal economic issues and willing to cooperate with Western states. Meanwhile, China wanted a good relationship with the US to maintain favorable trade conditions. The UNSC authorized peacekeeping missions in Yugoslavia and Rwanda, and created two **ad hoc criminal tribunals**. These tribunals—the International Criminal Tribunal for the former Yugoslavia (ICTY) and the International Criminal Tribunal for Rwanda (ICTR)—were empowered to punish individuals for international crimes committed during the two conflicts. These tribunals were temporary institutions that ultimately ended their operations. Yet their case law became foundational to international criminal law, and prompted states to subsequently clarify legal issues as they developed new criminal rules and institutions.

The Yugoslavian and Rwandan conflicts also prompted the international community to complete the Rome Statute of 1998. This treaty created the **International Criminal Court** (ICC), which is a permanent court that prosecutes aggression, crimes against humanity, genocide, and war crimes. Unlike the ICTR and ICTY—which were temporary tribunals created by the UNSC after major crimes occurred—the ICC is a permanent institution meant to deter and prosecute future international crimes. We discuss the details of how the ICC works later in this chapter.

Finally, many modern conflicts have prompted states to create **mixed criminal tribunals**, which are institutions that prosecute individuals using a blend of domestic and international law, personnel, and/or procedures. Most of these tribunals have prosecuted crimes that occurred before the ICC was created. Examples include:

- *Special Court for Sierra Leone* (2002–2013): created by a treaty between Sierra Leone and the UN; it prosecuted international and domestic crimes committed during the civil war between 1996 and 2002.
- *Extraordinary Chambers in the Courts of Cambodia* (2006–present): a domestic Cambodian court that uses international assistance and standards; it prosecutes crimes committed by the Khmer Rouge regime between 1975 and 1979.
- *Special Tribunal for Lebanon* (2009–present): created by the UN Security Council; it investigates and prosecutes a 2005 assassination and related bombings in Lebanon.
- *Extraordinary African Chambers* (2013–2017): created by a treaty between Senegal and the African Union; it prosecuted Hissène Habré, the former President of Chad, for international crimes.

Other mixed criminal tribunals prosecuted crimes in Bosnia, Kosovo, and East Timor. All of these states were sufficiently stable that they could conduct judicial proceedings. Yet they all also desired or needed international assistance and/or expertise to prosecute serious crimes.

11.3   Establishing Guilt

Now that we understand the major principles and history of international criminal law, we can focus on how modern international criminal tribunals establish guilt. We begin by describing the core crimes of international law. We then discuss how tribunals establish whether individuals are responsible for these crimes. Finally, we discuss possible defenses to alleged crimes.

Core Crimes

Many acts are crimes under international law, including slavery and terrorism. But only some have been prosecuted by international criminal tribunals. These acts are the core crimes of international law: aggression; crimes against humanity; genocide; and war crimes. The definitions of these crimes vary across time and sources. Here, we give a brief overview of each crime, focusing on the definitions in the Rome Statute.

Aggression

After World War I, transnational activists pressured states to prohibit war.[18] This activism pushed numerous states to join the 1928 Pact of Paris, in which they pledged that "the settlement or solution of all disputes or conflicts ... shall never be sought except by pacific means." While the Pact did not contain any enforcement mechanisms, Allied Powers sought to hold German and Japanese leaders accountable after World War II for going to war. The Allied Powers argued that violating the Pact of Paris was a crime against peace. The Nuremberg and Tokyo Tribunals executed many German and Japanese leaders for participating in the decision to begin World War II. This element of the Nuremberg and Tokyo judgments has been highly criticized for violating the principle of non-retroactivity because the Pact of Paris did not say that violations were punishable crimes.

After World War II, states restricted war in the 1945 UN Charter. They also developed extensive customary international law on the use of force. This law included UN General Assembly Resolution 3314 (1974), which defines aggression. This text basically defines **aggression** as a severe violation of international law on the use of force. Therefore, aggression is the use of a significant level of force that is not legally justified as self-defense or by a prior UN Security Council authorization.

When states negotiated the Rome Statute, they agreed that the ICC would prosecute aggression as a crime. However, they could not agree on a definition of aggression. After years of negotiations, ICC members included a definition in a legal document called the Kampala Amendments to the Rome Statute. Under the Kampala Amendments, an individual who is "in a position effectively to exercise control over or to direct the political or military action of a state" can be criminally responsible for "the planning, preparation, initiation or execution" of a use of force that, "by its character, gravity and scale, constitutes a manifest violation" of the UN Charter.[19] The Kampala Amendments list annexation, blockades, bombardments, and invasion as examples of aggression.[20]

The ICC has not yet prosecuted anyone for the crime of aggression. Because of the delay in defining the crime, the ICC can only prosecute aggression that occurred after July 2018. Additionally, many experts debate the ICC's authority over this crime because the Kampala Amendments were written after many states ratified the Rome Statute. Are these states bound by the later Kampala Amendments? While some ICC members have taken special action to ratify the Kampala Amendments, other states have not. It is unclear whether the latter are bound by the original Rome Statute (which did not define aggression) or by the amended text.

Crimes Against Humanity

The term "crimes against humanity" comes from the 1915 massacre of ethnic Armenians in the Ottoman Empire (modern-day Turkey). France, Russia, and the UK condemned the killings, but did not describe them as "war crimes" because Ottoman officials killed their own nationals, rather than foreign civilians or soldiers. France, Russia, and the UK accordingly invented the term "crimes ... against humanity and civilization," and threatened to prosecute Ottoman officials for these crimes.[21]

After World War II, the Allied Powers instructed the Nuremberg Tribunal to prosecute crimes against humanity as the mistreatment of civilians. However, Nuremberg prosecutors believed that they could not punish mistreatment of civilians that occurred before the war.[22] Accordingly, they did not prosecute German mistreatment of Jews and other civilians before 1939. This omission generated intense pressure to expand the interpretation of the term "crime against humanity" to include severe mistreatment of civilians during peace. In later decades, numerous states adopted domestic laws to prohibit crimes against humanity, but no treaty defined this term.[23] Domestic courts and international criminal tribunals therefore used slightly different definitions.

Under the Rome Statute, a **crime against humanity** is an act "committed as part of a widespread or systematic attack directed against any civilian population" during peace or armed conflict.[24] These physical acts include:

- ethnic cleansing, which is the compelled removal of an ethnic group using intimidation or violence;
- killing and **extermination**, which is "the intentional infliction of conditions of life ... calculated to bring about the destruction of part of a population";[25] and
- **persecution**, which is "the intentional and severe deprivation of fundamental rights contrary to international law" of "any identifiable group or collectivity on political, racial, national, ethnic, cultural, religious, gender ..., or other grounds that are universally recognized as impermissible under international law."[26]

Other physical acts that can be crimes against humanity include: apartheid; enforced disappearances; enslavement; sexual violence; and torture.[27]

Experts debate whether crimes against humanity include a **state policy requirement**—that is, whether a state must have a common and preconceived policy for committing an attack.[28] The ICTY and ICTR did not require a state policy for crimes against humanity.[29] This omission allowed them to prosecute non-state actors, like members of paramilitary groups that were not under the control of a state.[30] However, many experts believe that crimes against humanity, particularly at the ICC, must satisfy the state policy requirement.[31] They note that the Rome Statute says that an attack against civilians must be "pursuant to or in furtherance of a state or organizational policy to commit such attack."[32]

For example, the ICC prosecutor charged Laurent Gbagbo, the former president of Côte d'Ivoire, with crimes against humanity. The prosecutor presented extensive evidence of murders, persecution, and sexual violence by pro-Gbagbo groups after a 2010 presidential election. However, ICC judges argued that the prosecutor had "failed to demonstrate the existence of the alleged policy to attack a civilian population."[33] They ordered that Gbagbo be acquitted and released. This outcome suggests that a state policy to attack civilians is a necessary component of crimes against humanity. Such policies can be made by a state or by one of its sub-bodies, such as an intelligence service, military, or police.

But what about non-state actors, like criminal organizations, multinational corporations, political parties, and terrorist groups? Al-Qaeda, a terrorist group, repeatedly announced its plans to attack civilians. Can its members be prosecuted for crimes against humanity? Similarly, some multinational corporations that drill for oil in the Nigerian Delta have been accused of mistreating civilians. Can corporate officers be prosecuted for crimes against humanity? Experts debate the answers to these unresolved questions, which challenge the boundary between international and domestic criminal law. They will likely play an important role in the future development of international law.

Genocide

The 1948 Genocide Convention provided the ICC's definition of **genocide**:

> any of the following acts committed with intent to destroy, in whole or in part, a national, ethnical, racial or religious group, as such:
> (a) Killing members of the group;
> (b) Causing serious bodily or mental harm to members of the group;
> (c) Deliberately inflicting on the group conditions of life calculated to bring about its physical destruction in whole or in part;
> (d) Imposing measures intended to prevent births within the group;
> (e) Forcibly transferring children of the group to another group.[34]

Genocide has three elements. The first element is group identification—genocide must be directed against "a national, ethnical, racial or religious group." The second element is physical acts—genocide must involve at least one of the five acts listed above in (a)–(e). Finally, genocide requires destructive intent—physical acts must be "committed with intent to destroy, in whole or in part" a protected group.[35] If an incident does not satisfy all three criteria, then it is not a genocide.

In some ways, this definition is very broad. Genocide can occur during peace or war. It can be committed by state agents or by private individuals. It may be planned or spontaneous, although prosecutors often use state or group policies to prove intent.

However, genocide is very hard to prove because of its intent requirement. For example, Goran Jelisić was a Bosnian Serb who abused and killed Muslim civilians in a detention camp during the Yugoslavian War. ICTY prosecutors indicted Jelisić for both crimes against humanity and genocide. Jelisić pled guilty to crimes against humanity, but claimed that he was innocent of genocide. ICTY judges ultimately acquitted Jelisić of genocide. They argued that prosecutors had proven that Jelisić intended to abuse and kill Muslim civilians, but they had not proven that Jelisić "intended to destroy" Muslims as a group.[36] In particular, the judges noted that Jelisić allowed two Muslim witnesses to live.[37]

War Crimes

Finally, **war crimes** are serious violations of the law of armed conflict that create individual criminal responsibility. Many treaties specify the law of armed conflict, but not all states have ratified all of these treaties. Therefore, state sometimes disagree about which physical acts qualify as war crimes. Most states define and punish war crimes under domestic law, including military codes of conduct.

The Rome Statute contains a long and dense definition of war crimes. Physical acts that are criminal during international armed conflict include: attacks against civilians, those providing humanitarian assistance, or peacekeeping forces; and killing protected persons (including civilians, wounded combatants, and prisoners of war). It also includes warfare tactics such as: sexual violence; torture; and the use of child soldiers and prohibited weapons. The Rome Statute also contains rules for non-international armed conflicts that largely mimic the rules for international armed conflicts.

To qualify as war crimes, these physical acts must satisfy two requirements. First, they must occur during an armed conflict. Acts that occur during "internal disturbances and tensions, such as riots, isolated and sporadic acts of violence or other acts of a similar nature" are not war crimes.[38] Second, they must have a nexus—that is, a link—to the armed conflict. Namely, the ICC requires that "the conduct took place in the context of and was associated with" an armed conflict.[39]

This nexus requirement means that not all crimes that occur during conflict are war crimes. Murder or sexual violence during an armed conflict is not a war crime if the act is unrelated to the conflict.

Recall that the international law of armed conflict has different rules for international and non-international armed conflicts.[40] Prior to the creation of the Rome Statute, war crimes prosecutions sometimes involved arguments about the nature of a conflict. During the Yugoslavian War in the 1990s, numerous regions—including Bosnia and Croatia—claimed independence from the Yugoslavian government. These regions are now considered independent states. Yet experts disagreed about their status during the conflict. This disagreement affected war crimes prosecutions because it affected which acts were illegal.[41] The Rome Statute distinguishes between international and non-international armed conflicts. Yet its definitions of war crimes for the two types of armed conflict are similar, thereby avoiding some debates about the nature of armed conflicts. For example, it is a war crime under the Rome Statute to use child soldiers, regardless of the type of conflict.

Responsibility and Liability

International crimes are usually committed by groups of individuals who act jointly to achieve a common purpose. For example, attacks on civilian villages often involve political leaders, commanders, soldiers, and individuals who recruit, train, and equip these soldiers. International criminal tribunals prosecute individuals, not groups. So how do we establish individual responsibility for a group act? Domestic legal systems use different forms of responsibility. Because international law is a synthesis of these different systems, different international criminal tribunals have used different approaches.[42] Here we introduce the forms of responsibility at the ICC.

Perpetrators

Under international criminal law, **perpetrator responsibility** exists when an individual has control over whether a crime will occur.[43] The simplest way to establish perpetrator responsibility is if someone commits a crime "as an individual."[44] This form of responsibility requires that one person is in direct and sole control of all elements of a crime.

For example, Dražen Erdemović was a soldier in the Yugoslavian War. He helped attack Srebrenica—a village in Bosnia—and then participated in the mass killing of over 8,000 Muslim men and boys. These killings were labeled a genocide by multiple international tribunals. After the war, Erdemović confessed to television reporters about his actions in Srebrenica. He was then arrested and indicted by the ICTY for the individual acts that he committed. Erdemović pled guilty to crimes against humanity for murdering approximately seventy civilians.[45] Erdemović was not the only individual who killed Muslim civilians in Srebrenica, but he was responsible as an individual for the specific killings that he committed.

International law also creates responsibility when an individual directly commits a crime "jointly with another ... person."[46] This form of responsibility is often called co-perpetration because the elements of the crime involve acts by multiple people. When a prosecutor accuses a defendant of co-perpetration, she must usually prove two elements. First, she must prove that multiple individuals have a common plan that results in the commission of the crime. Second, she must prove that the defendant made an essential contribution to this common plan, which might include deciding whether and how the crime is committed. The defendant is only guilty of co-perpetration if both of these elements are proven.

The ICC's first completed trial—the *Lubanga* trial—involved co-perpetration. Thomas Lubanga was a rebel leader in the Democratic Republic of the Congo (DRC) during the Great African War of 1996–2003. In 2002, Lubanga became president of the *Union des Patriotes Congolais* (UPC), a rebel group that used child soldiers. The ICC prosecutor did not have evidence that Lubanga recruited and trained child soldiers himself, so the prosecutor could not accuse Lubanga of committing a crime as an individual. Instead, the ICC prosecutor argued that Lubanga committed a crime jointly with other UPC members. First, the ICC prosecutor argued that Lubanga "endorsed a common plan to build an effective army" that included child soldiers.[47] Second, the ICC prosecutor argued that Lubanga served as commander-in-chief of the UPC's military. After considering evidence about UPC operations, the ICC judges concluded that "the accused's function within the hierarchy ..., along with his involvement in planning military operations and his key role in providing logistical support ... resulted in his role being essential" to the UPC military.[48] This combination of a common plan and an essential contribution caused ICC judges to find Lubanga guilty via co-perpetration of the war crime of using child soldiers.

Even if an individual is not directly involved in a crime, he may be a perpetrator if he is in control of the crime. Namely, the Rome Statute says that an individual can commit a crime "through another person."[49] This form of responsibility is sometimes called indirect co-perpetration. In theory, indirect co-perpetration requires more than merely ordering another person to commit a crime. An indirect co-perpetrator must cause a crime to occur via his control over another person. As the ICC argued, an "indirect perpetrator has the power to decide whether and how the crime will be committed."[50]

The ICC's second completed trial—the *Katanga* trial—began as an indirect co-perpetration case. This trial focused on a 2003 brutal attack on Bogoro, a DRC village, during the Great African War. During this attack, rebel forces killed and raped civilians, destroyed property, and pillaged. Germain Katanga helped multiple rebel commanders to coordinate the attack on Bogoro, and stored and distributed weapons before the attack. At Katanga's trial, the ICC prosecutor argued that Katanga had control over all of the combatants during the attack. Therefore, the prosecutor argued, Katanga had committed crimes against humanity and war crimes through another person. Defense lawyers argued that Katanga lacked control over the combatants. After extensive witness testimony, the ICC judges ruled that Katanga "was a seasoned and well-known soldier" with some "military authority" within his group.[51] However, they could not "find beyond reasonable doubt that Germain Katanga wielded powers of command and control in all areas of military life and over all the commanders and combatants" within his group.[52] The ICC judges therefore ruled that Katanga was not responsible for the Bogoro attack based on indirect co-perpetration.

Accessories

Accessory liability exists when an individual provides material or moral assistance that has a substantial effect on the crime, even though he does not have control over the crime. An individual is only an accessory if "the power to decide on the execution of the crime remains the preserve of another person."[53] For example, the Rome Statute says that an individual is responsible if he "orders, solicits or induces the commission of … a crime."[54] Such actions could include offering a reward or encouragement to someone who commits a crime, or threatening to punish someone who does not commit a crime. The Rome Statute also creates responsibility for "facilitating the commission of … a crime," which is also often called aiding, abetting, and/or assisting in a crime.[55] Finally, the Rome Statute creates responsibility for an individual who "in any other way contributes to the commission [of] a crime by a group of persons acting with a common purpose."[56] The ICC has not yet developed enough jurisprudence to firmly distinguish between these kinds of accessory liability. For example, the difference between facilitating and contributing to a crime is unclear.

In the *Katanga* trial at the ICC, Germain Katanga was found guilty of crimes during the Bogoro attack based on accessory liability. Recall that Katanga coordinated the attack and stored and distributed weapons. The ICC judges argued that these weapons were specifically intended for the attack and played "a truly significant part in bringing about the crimes."[57] They therefore concluded that Katanga was guilty because he made an "intentional contribution to the crimes" committed during the attack.[58]

Other international criminal tribunals have also ruled on accessory liability. These include the following examples:

- The ICTR convicted Jean-Paul Akayesu—a Rwandan mayor—of being an accessory to crimes against humanity and genocide because he ordered killings and sexual violence.[59]
- The ICTY convicted Radislav Krstić—a commander in a Bosnian Serb armed group—of being an accessory to the Srebrenica genocide because he allowed his soldiers to participate in the killings.[60]

- The Extraordinary Chambers in the Courts of Cambodia convicted Kaing Guek Eav—a Khmer Rouge prison head—of being an accessory to crimes against humanity because he trained and supervised prison staff who committed crimes.[61]
- The Special Court for Sierra Leone convicted Charles Taylor—the President of Liberia—of being an accessory to crimes against humanity and war crimes because he sold weapons to rebel groups.[62]

In each of these scenarios, prosecutors could not prove that the defendant perpetrated a crime. Instead, they proved that the defendant had accessory liability because his assistance had a substantial effect on crimes committed by others.

Commanders and Superiors

International law often holds military commanders responsible for their subordinates. If a commander orders a subordinate to kill a civilian, the commander can be responsible as either a perpetrator or accessory, depending on the ability of the subordinate to refuse the order. But what happens if a subordinate commits a serious international crime without receiving an order to do so? Is the commander responsible for the crime? The principle of **command responsibility** says that military commanders are criminally responsible if they fail to prevent or punish crimes committed by the troops under their effective control. Because command responsibility is based on a commander's obligations to prevent and punish crimes committed by others, it falls outside of perpetrator responsibility and accessory liability, creating its own form of criminal responsibility.[63]

Different tribunals have used different standards when applying command responsibility. Some tribunals only hold a commander responsible if she *knows* that her subordinates have committed a crime or were likely to commit a crime. Other tribunals hold a commander responsible if she *should have known* such information. Similarly, most tribunals only hold a commander responsible for her subordinates if she has effective control over them. Yet in some extreme scenarios, tribunals have held a commander responsible even when she lacked effective control.

For example, Japanese troops committed widespread crimes—including civilian killings and rapes—in the Philippines in 1944. After the war, a US military tribunal in the Philippines prosecuted Tomoyuki Yamashita for these crimes. Yamashita was a Japanese general who was assigned command over these troops only ten days prior to the outbreak of violence. During the trial, US prosecutors documented the crimes, but could not prove that Yamashita ordered or assisted in the crimes. Defense lawyers argued that the US military had previously destroyed Japanese communications in the Philippines, meaning that Yamashita could not receive messages from the battlefield or send instructions to his troops. Yamashita therefore did not know that the crimes were occurring, and had no way to exert control over his troops.[64] Yet Yamashita was nonetheless held responsible under the principle of command responsibility and sentenced to death.

While many experts criticize such extreme cases, the principle of command responsibility is an important part of modern international criminal law. The Rome Statute says:

> A military commander or person effectively acting as a military commander shall be criminally responsible for crimes ... committed by forces under his or her effective command and control ... as a result of his or her failure to exercise control properly over such forces, where:
>
> (i) That military commander or person either knew or, owing to the circumstances at the time, should have known that the forces were committing or about to commit such crimes; and
>
> (ii) That military commander or person failed to take all necessary and reasonable measures within his or her power to prevent or repress their commission or to submit the matter to the competent authorities for investigation and prosecution.[65]

Historically, command responsibility only applied to military commanders, meaning that it only created responsibility for crimes committed by a state's armed forces. However, the Rome Statute extends this principle to any "person effectively acting as a military commander," which includes leaders of rebel groups and other non-state actors.

These rules were applied by the ICC in the *Bemba* case. In this case, the ICC prosecuted Jean-Pierre Bemba Gombo (known as "Bemba"), leader of the *Mouvement de libération du Congo* (MLC). The MLC was a rebel group based in the DRC during the Great African War of 1996–2003. During this war, MLC soldiers were sent to the Central African Republic to help suppress a coup attempt. While there, some MLC soldiers committed crimes against humanity and war crimes, including murder, pillaging, and rape.

In Bemba's trial ruling, ICC judges found that: crimes were committed by MLC troops; Bemba knew about these crimes; and Bemba had effective command and control over these troops. Bemba's defense lawyers argued that after learning about the crimes, Bemba created an inquiry, met with UN officials, and asked the Central African Republic to investigate the crimes. However, the ICC's trial judges believed that Bemba had not taken "all necessary and reasonable measures within his or her power to prevent or repress" the crimes.[66] Accordingly, they concluded that Bemba was criminally responsible based on command responsibility.[67]

Bemba's lawyers appealed the ruling. They argued that Bemba—who operated in the DRC—had limited ability and authority to conduct investigations in the Central African Republic, a separate sovereign state. The ICC appellate judges agreed, writing:

> The scope of the duty to take "all necessary and reasonable measures" is intrinsically connected to the extent of a commander's material ability to prevent or repress

the commission of crimes or to submit the matter to the competent authorities for investigation and prosecution. Indeed, a commander cannot be blamed for not having done something he or she had no power to do.[68]

These judges additionally noted that "it is not the case that a commander must take each and every possible measure at his or her disposal"—a commander need only do what is "reasonable" in the circumstances.[69] Based on the trial evidence, the ICC appellate judges concluded that Bemba was not guilty under the principle of command responsibility.

Some international tribunals have extended the concept of command responsibility to cover hierarchical relationships outside of militaries. The principle of **superior responsibility** says that civilian superiors are criminally responsible if they fail to prevent or punish crimes committed by the subordinates under their effective control. For example, in the *Čelebići* case, the ICTY prosecuted numerous individuals who worked at a Bosnian prison camp that held Serbian civilians. One of the defendants was Zdravko Mucić, the head of the prison camp. Many Serbian civilians in the Čelebići camp were killed, raped, and tortured by prison guards. The ICTY prosecutor could not prove that Mucić was a perpetrator or accessory to any of these crimes. Additionally, the ICTY prosecutor could not prove that Mucić was a military commander. The ICTY judges nonetheless argued that Mucić was responsible for failing to prevent and punish crimes that occurred in the Čelebići camp because civilians can have hierarchical relationships that are akin to a military chain of command.[70]

Similarly, the ICTR prosecuted Ferdinand Nahimana, co-founder of a Rwandan radio station. The ICTR prosecutor argued that this radio station broadcast messages that encouraged the killings of Tutsis, thereby inciting genocide. Defense lawyers argued that Nahimana did not participate in the day-to-day operations of the radio station during this period, and that he therefore was neither a perpetrator nor an accomplice. They additionally argued that only civilian leaders with public authority could be convicted based on superior responsibility, not business officials.[71] However, the ICTR judges ruled that Nahimana had superior responsibility because he had "authority to intervene with [the radio station's] employees and journalists."[72]

The Rome Statute gives the ICC authority to invoke superior responsibility. For situations that do not involve military hierarchies, it says:

A superior shall be criminally responsible for crimes ... committed by subordinates under his or her effective authority and control, as a result of his or her failure to exercise control properly over such subordinates, where:
(i) The superior either knew, or consciously disregarded information which clearly indicated, that the subordinates were committing or about to commit such crimes;

(ii) The crimes concerned activities that were within the effective responsibility and control of the superior; and

(iii) The superior failed to take all necessary and reasonable measures within his or her power to prevent or repress their commission or to submit the matter to the competent authorities for investigation and prosecution.[73]

The combination of prior ICTY/ICTR jurisprudence and the Rome Statute suggests that superior responsibility is now part of customary international law.

***

Note that there can be overlap between these three categories—an individual who plans and leads an attack on a civilian village may be simultaneously responsible for international crimes as a perpetrator, accessory, and commander. Since a set of facts can generate multiple forms of responsibility, prosecutors often charge an individual for crimes in multiple ways. Judges must then decide which specific charges should apply.

Possible Defenses

How can defendants avoid punishment by international criminal tribunals? Domestic legal systems vary in their conceptions of authority. Because international law balances these competing conceptions, international law often uses terms like defense, excuse, and justification interchangeably. We use the term **defense** to describe any legal argument made by a defendant to avoid or minimize punishment.[74]

Defendants often argue that prosecutors lack sufficient evidence for a conviction. This defense often works because international prosecutors frequently lack forensic evidence and reliable witnesses. Many alleged criminals have avoided punishment by arguing that international prosecutors lacked sufficient evidence to hold a trial.[75] Defendants also try to avoid or minimize punishment using legal arguments. International law allows defenses that are common under domestic criminal law.[76] For example, defendants can argue that they acted in self-defense or had diminished capacity because of mental illness.[77] However, more interesting defenses involve limits on tribunal authority or defendant autonomy. We discuss each of these factors in turn.

Tribunal Authority

One defense that challenges a tribunal's authority is to claim that a defendant is immune from prosecution. Domestic laws often limit domestic prosecutions of government officials. These laws usually grant government officials immunity from prosecution because acts of government officials are considered acts of state. Similarly, government officials sometimes argue that they are immune from prosecution for international crimes because they acted on behalf of their state.

Immunity defenses are usually unsuccessful in international criminal tribunals. For example, recall that the Special Court for Sierra Leone prosecuted Charles Taylor—the President of Liberia—for being an accessory to international crimes because he sold weapons to rebel groups in Sierra Leone. Taylor argued that his status as a Liberian official gave him immunity from international prosecution. In its ruling, the Special Court argued that it could prosecute Taylor because immunity is inconsistent with individual criminal responsibility.[78] To support this argument, it invoked the practice of numerous earlier tribunals—including the Nuremberg Tribunal and the ICTY—in prosecuting government leaders.

However, immunity defenses are sometimes successful in domestic courts that try to prosecute international crimes. An important principle of customary international law is **official immunity**: individuals who are government officials are not subject to another state's jurisdiction. Some experts believe that official immunity does not apply to international crimes.[79] However, the ICJ upheld official immunity from domestic courts in cases involving international crimes.[80]

Another possible defense is that a tribunal has limited authority because of an **amnesty**, which is an agreement not to prosecute individuals for certain offenses and to pardon individuals already convicted of those offenses. Amnesties are often included in peace agreements, and many experts believe that amnesties end conflicts by convincing combatants to stop fighting.[81] Yet legal experts question whether amnesties are consistent with international law. For example, the Inter-American Court of Human Rights ruled that amnesties violate the international legal obligation to punish human rights violators.[82] Similar arguments apply to international criminal law.

After a long civil war, the Sierra Leone government signed a 1999 peace agreement with rebels called the Lomé Agreement. In this agreement, the government pledged to grant amnesty to rebel fighters. One year later, Sierra Leone's president requested that the UN Security Council create the Special Court for Sierra Leone to prosecute crimes committed during the civil war. The Court's statute said: "An amnesty granted to any person falling within the jurisdiction of the Special Court ... shall not be a bar to prosecution."[83] During his trial before the Special Court, Morris Kallon—a former rebel fighter—argued that he could not be prosecuted because of the Lomé Agreement. The judges disagreed, writing:

> The Lomé Agreement is not a treaty or an agreement in the nature of a treaty. The rights and obligations it created are to be regulated by the domestic laws of Sierra Leone. In the result, whether it is binding on the Government of Sierra Leone or not does not affect the liability of the accused to be prosecuted in an international tribunal for international crimes.[84]

The judges believed that while the Lomé Agreement may have prohibited domestic prosecutions, it did not limit international prosecutions.

Would the outcome have been different if the amnesty had been included in an international treaty? We don't know. The Rome Statute does not explicitly address amnesties, and ICC cases have not (yet) involved amnesties. The ICC would likely uphold the logic of the *Kallon* case if a defendant claimed amnesty under domestic law. But it is unclear how the ICC would behave if an international treaty included an amnesty.

One final defense that challenges tribunal authority is to invoke the principle of **complementarity**, which is the principle that an international criminal tribunal should complement, rather than replace, domestic criminal tribunals. The principle comes from the notion that it is better that the domestic courts of the state where international crimes were committed should prosecute those crimes. Complementarity implies that individuals who undergo genuine domestic prosecutions should not be prosecuted again for the same crime at the international level.

According to the Rome Statute, the ICC cannot hear a case if:

(a) The case is being investigated or prosecuted by a State which has jurisdiction over it, unless the State is unwilling or unable genuinely to carry out the investigation or prosecution;

(b) The case has been investigated by a State which has jurisdiction over it and the State has decided not to prosecute the person concerned, unless the decision resulted from the unwillingness or inability of the State genuinely to prosecute;

(c) The person concerned has already been tried for conduct which is the subject of the complaint ...[85]

ICC judges have power to determine whether a state is "genuinely" investigating and/or prosecuting an individual. This careful language is intended to prevent states from holding show trials, in which defendants are always acquitted, to protect alleged criminals from international prosecution.

The ICC has applied complementarity a few times. For example, the ICC issued an arrest warrant for Abdullah Al-Senussi—the former intelligence chief for the Gaddafi government in Libya—for the murder and persecution of civilians during the 2011 uprising against Gaddafi. Al-Senussi fled Libya, but was arrested in 2012 in Mauritania and returned to Libya to face trial under the new government. After learning about the Libyan proceedings, ICC judges ruled that:

the same case against Mr Al-Senussi ... is currently subject to domestic proceedings being conducted by the competent authorities of Libya ... Libya is not unwilling or unable genuinely to carry out its proceedings in relation to the case against Mr Al-Senussi. The case against Mr. Al-Senussi is therefore inadmissible before the Court.[86]

Somewhat ironically, this ruling was unsuccessfully appealed by Al-Senussi, who preferred an ICC trial to a Libyan prosecution.

Defendant Autonomy

An alternative defense is to argue that a defendant lacked full autonomy in her decision-making. International law provides two major ways to make such an argument. First, a defendant may claim that she acted under **duress**, which is pressure to perform an illegal act to avoid serious harm. The Rome Statute says that a person is not criminally responsible if her conduct:

> has been caused by duress resulting from a threat of imminent death or of continuing or imminent serious bodily harm against that person or another person, and the person acts necessarily and reasonably to avoid this threat, provided that the person does not intend to cause a greater harm than the one sought to be avoided.[87]

Such threats can come from "other persons" or "circumstances beyond that person's control."[88]

Second, a defendant may claim that she was obeying orders from a superior. Historically, states often allowed military subordinates to avoid punishment for war crimes if they were following superior orders. These states believed that military orders transferred responsibility from subordinates to superiors.[89] However, such arguments were dismissed by the Nuremberg Tribunal, which argued that defendants were fully responsible for their acts, regardless of superior orders.[90]

The ICC strikes a compromise, allowing the defense of obedience to superior orders in certain narrow circumstances. The Rome Statute says:

> The fact that a crime within the jurisdiction of the Court has been committed by a person pursuant to an order of a government or of a superior, whether military or civilian, shall not relieve that person of criminal responsibility unless:
> a. The person was under a legal obligation to obey orders of the government or the superior in question;
> b. The person did not know that the order was unlawful; and
> c. The order was not manifestly unlawful.[91]

It additionally clarifies that "orders to commit genocide or crimes against humanity are manifestly unlawful" and hence cannot be excused by superior orders.[92]

Recall Dražen Erdemović, the soldier who participated in the Srebrenica genocide. Erdemović pled guilty to crimes against humanity at the ICTY, but his lawyers attempted to reduce his punishment using several defenses. When confessing his guilt, Erdemović told the Court:

> I had to do this. If I had refused, I would have been killed together with the victims. When I refused, they told me: "If you're sorry for them, stand up, line up with them and we will kill you too. ..." I could not refuse because then they would have killed me.[93]

After extensive legal proceedings, the ICTY judges ruled that neither duress nor obedience to superior orders could fully excuse Erdemović's actions—he was still guilty of a crime. However, these factors could mitigate his punishment.

In the *Erdemović* sentencing judgment, ICTY judges detailed many factors that affected their sentence, including the number of people that Erdemović had killed, his remorse for his actions, and his cooperation in testifying against others. They paid little attention to superior orders, noting that Erdemović disobeyed his commander on other occasions.[94] However, they believed Erdemović's claims of duress, writing:

> The evidence reveals the extremity of the situation faced by the accused. The Trial Chamber finds that there was a real risk that the accused would have been killed had he disobeyed the order. He voiced his feelings, but realised that he had no choice in the matter: he had to kill or be killed.[95]

We do not know how much duress affected the sentencing outcome. But ICTY judges ultimately sentenced Erdemović to five years in prison for committing approximately seventy murders, which amounted to less than one month per victim. This relatively lenient punishment suggests that Erdemović's claims of duress were compelling.

11.4   Enforcing International Criminal Law

Thus far we have described the legal principles that criminal tribunals use to establish whether an individual is guilty of an international crime. We now turn to the enforcement of international criminal law. We focus on the two major modes of contemporary enforcement. First, we provide an overview of the International Criminal Court. Second, we describe how domestic courts can assert universal jurisdiction to prosecute international crimes.

International Criminal Court
We first discuss the ICC's jurisdiction and procedures for investigating and prosecuting cases, providing illustrations from existing investigations and cases. We then describe the obligations of states that join the Court.

How the ICC Works
The Rome Statute gives the International Criminal Court authority to prosecute the four core international crimes (aggression, crimes against humanity, genocide, and war crimes), if the Court has at least one basis of jurisdiction. First, the ICC can pursue a case if it has territorial jurisdiction, meaning that a crime was committed

on a member state's territory, regardless of who committed the crime. Second, the ICC has active nationality jurisdiction, meaning that it can prosecute a crime committed by member state nationals, regardless of where the crime occurred. Most ICC prosecutions have involved both territorial and national jurisdiction, like the prosecutions of Congolese rebels who committed crimes in their home state. Finally, the ICC has jurisdiction over crimes referred to the Court by the UN Security Council (UNSC), regardless of whether affected states have accepted ICC jurisdiction. For example, the UNSC asked the ICC to investigate crimes that occurred in Darfur (a region of Sudan) and Libya. These UNSC referrals usually impose limits on the ICC. For example, the UNSC limited prosecutions against African Union peacekeeping forces that served in Darfur and NATO troops that fought in Libya.[96]

The ICC has time limits on its jurisdiction. It cannot prosecute crimes that occurred before 2002, when the Rome Statute came into effect. The Court cannot, therefore, prosecute historical crimes, such as massacres in the 1970s in East Pakistan (now Bangladesh), Kampuchea (now Cambodia), and Uganda. Additionally, if the Court asserts territorial or active nationality jurisdiction, it cannot prosecute crimes that occurred before the relevant state accepted the Court's jurisdiction. Finally, the ICC is bound by the principle of complementarity, which is discussed above. The ICC cannot take action if a domestic legal system is willing and able to conduct criminal proceedings against the same individual.

Some of the Court's current investigations face jurisdictional challenges. The first investigation concerns Myanmar's persecution of the Rohingya ethnic group. Following an upsurge in violence, which many experts consider a genocide, the Rohingya fled Myanmar, creating a refugee crisis in neighboring Bangladesh. While Bangladesh has accepted ICC jurisdiction, Myanmar has not. Bangladesh asked the ICC to investigate the mistreatment of the Rohingya. However, the Rome Statute only allows the ICC to prosecute crimes committed either by Bangladeshi nationals or on Bangladeshi territory. The ICC investigation thus hinges on the claim that deportation of the Rohingya partially took place on Bangladeshi territory.

Second, the ICC is investigating the Afghanistan War, including war crimes allegedly committed by US nationals. However, the US has not accepted ICC jurisdiction. Many experts believe that US nationals may face criminal charges for torturing terrorism suspects in Afghanistan, Lithuania, Poland, and Romania, all of which are ICC member states.[97] While the US argues that the ICC should not prosecute US nationals, the ICC argues that its territorial jurisdiction is sufficient for it to bring criminal charges.[98]

The ICC's procedures are laid out in the Rome Statute and other core legal texts. The key actors in this process are the ICC Prosecutor, who oversees a staff of

Figure 11.2 A group of Rohingya migrants cross the river border between Myanmar and Bangladesh in October 2017. The Myanmar government has been widely accused of committing extensive atrocities against the Rohingya people, causing a massive refugee crisis. While Bangladesh has accepted ICC jurisdiction, Myanmar has not. In late 2019, the ICC's Pre-Trial Chambers argued that the ICC Prosecutor had authority to investigate allegations of forced deportation because this crime partially took place on Bangladeshi territory.

investigators and lawyers, and the ICC judges, who are grouped into three different chambers: the Pre-Trial Chambers, the Trial Chambers, and the Appeals Chambers. Figure 11.3 shows the major steps in an ICC investigation.

First, the Court must learn about an alleged crime. Member states and the UNSC can make formal referrals to the Court, and the ICC Prosecutor can make a motion to examine a crime. However, individuals and NGOs have no formal ways to alert the Court about alleged crimes. In practice, individuals and NGOs often meet with the ICC Prosecutor in the hope that they will take action.

Second, the ICC Prosecutor can open a preliminary inquiry. During this inquiry, ICC staff interview witnesses, collect evidence, and assess whether the Court has jurisdiction over possible crimes. The Prosecutor then assesses whether they believe that the alleged crimes are sufficiently important to justify using the ICC's limited resources.

Third, the Prosecutor can then open an investigation. To prevent a possible abuse of power, the ICC Prosecutor must seek authorization from the Pre-Trial Chambers to open an investigation if the case began under their own motion.

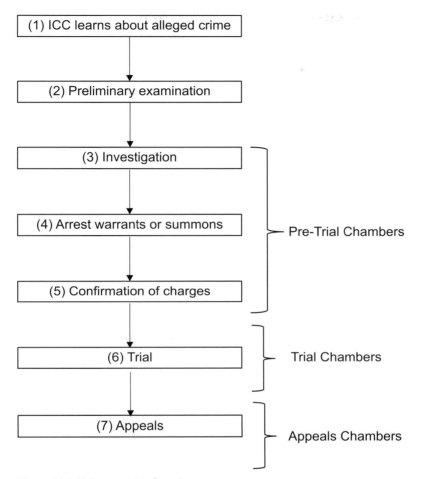

Figure 11.3 ICC prosecution flow chart.

As shown in Table 11.2, most of the ICC's early investigations involved internal conflicts that states referred to the ICC. For example, the Central African Republic, Democratic Republic of the Congo, Mali, and Uganda asked the ICC to investigate crimes that were committed on their own territory by rebel groups. Governments were therefore asking the ICC to investigate their political opponents, not themselves. In contrast, most recent investigations have been initiated by the ICC Prosecutor, including investigations in Afghanistan, Bangladesh, and Burundi.

Fourth, the Prosecutor can ask the Pre-Trial Chambers to begin a case against an individual defendant by issuing a warrant or summons. The Pre-Trial Chambers issues an arrest warrant when it believes that an individual will not voluntarily appear before the Court. The ICC relies upon states to enforce these warrants by capturing and surrendering defendants. The ICC does not have police officers who

Table 11.2 ICC Investigations			
Place	Start Date	Referral Mode	Situation
Democratic Republic of the Congo	2004	State	Internal and international conflict
Uganda	2004	State	Internal conflict
Sudan	2005	UN Security Council	Internal conflict
Central African Republic I	2007	State	Internal conflict
Kenya	2010*	Prosecutor	Post-election violence
Libya	2011	UN Security Council	Internal conflict
Côte d'Ivoire	2011*	Prosecutor	Post-election violence
Mali	2013	State	Internal conflict
Central African Republic II	2014	State	Internal conflict
Georgia	2016*	Prosecutor	International conflict
Burundi	2017*	Prosecutor	Violence after an electoral announcement
Bangladesh/Myanmar	2019*	Prosecutor	Persecution of the Rohingya people of Myanmar, which triggered refugee flows into Bangladesh
Afghanistan	2020*	Prosecutor	International conflict
Palestine	2021	State	International conflict

Pre-Trial Chambers approval date.

Note: This table displays all known ICC investigations and their mode of referral as of July 1, 2021.

can make arrests. If a defendant is likely to voluntarily appear at the Court, then the Pre-Trial Chambers will issue a summons, which is considered less adversarial than an arrest warrant.

Once an individual enters the Court's custody (by arrest or voluntary appearance), the defendant can try to get the case dismissed by the Pre-Trial Chambers. For example, the defendant might argue that the Prosecutor has insufficient evidence or that the ICC lacks jurisdiction to hold a trial. If these arguments are successful, the Pre-Trial Chambers will dismiss the warrant or summons. However, if these arguments are not successful, then the Pre-Trial Chambers will confirm the charges.

The sixth step is a trial by the Trial Chambers. All ICC cases are decided by judges, not juries. Trials usually last for many years. The Prosecutor and defense lawyers present evidence, question witnesses, and present expert testimony. After both the prosecution and defense have offered their arguments, the Trial Chambers writes a judgment that provides its findings of facts and law. If a defendant is found guilty, then he/she is sentenced by the Trial Chambers.

If either the defense or prosecution disagrees with the trial judgment or sentencing, they can appeal the case to the Appeals Chambers. During appeals, judges usually focus on legal questions, such as how to interpret a treaty text. They usually do not review factual findings, meaning that lawyers usually cannot offer new evidence or witnesses. After reconsidering any open legal questions, the Appeals Chamber then issues its judgment, which is final and binding.

Member State Obligations

States that ratify the Rome Statute create legal obligations to the ICC. First, they accept the ICC's jurisdiction. Member states thus make their nationals, including government officials, vulnerable to criminal prosecutions. However, most of the ICC's early prosecutions focused on rebel leaders, rather than government officials. Every state referral to the ICC (including referrals by the Central African Republic, Democratic Republic of the Congo, Mali, and Uganda) has yielded rebel prosecutions. Government officials have only been targeted in situations referred by the UN Security Council (in Darfur and Libya) or the ICC Prosecutor (in Côte d'Ivoire and Kenya). Therefore, when governments join the ICC, they may expect to constrain their political opponents, rather than themselves.

Second, member states of the Rome Statute must "cooperate fully with the Court in its investigation and prosecution of crimes."[99] For example, the ICC can ask its members to locate victims and witnesses. Once those individuals are found, member states must make them available for questioning and testimony, and provide them with protection from intimidation. ICC member states must also provide documents and forensic evidence of crimes.

Sometimes states refuse to fully cooperate with the ICC, particularly when the Court targets government elites. For example, the ICC tried to prosecute Kenyan politicians for 2007 post-election violence. The Kenyan government allowed ICC officials to make site visits and provided documents to the ICC. Yet it also delayed prosecutions through legal challenges, intimidated witnesses, and tampered with evidence.[100] The ICC ultimately dropped criminal charges because of insufficient evidence. Some scholars believe that the Kenya example reflects a broader trend—namely, that prosecution decisions are affected by the level of state cooperation.[101]

Finally, and perhaps most importantly, ICC member states must enforce ICC warrants by arresting and surrendering defendants. This area of cooperation has been difficult for the ICC. International law does not contain global extradition rules. Rather, states have built a network of bilateral treaties on criminal cooperation. These treaties can sometimes conflict with the Rome Statute. For example, the ICC issued an arrest warrant for Omar Al Bashir, the sitting president of Sudan, in 2009. Al Bashir visited many ICC member states (including Kenya, Malawi, and South Africa) after the warrant was issued, yet none of these states arrested and surrendered him to the ICC. Some experts argue that sitting heads of state are immune from arrest in foreign states under both customary international law and treaty law.[102] Other experts argue that the Rome Statute should override other international legal commitments.[103]

International law lacks clear answers about how a state should behave if it faces such conflicting rules. On the one hand, the Rome Statute clearly says that members "shall, in accordance with … the procedure under their national law, comply with requests for arrest and surrender."[104] On the other hand, Article 98 of the Rome Statute says:

> The Court may not proceed with a request for surrender which would require the requested state to act inconsistently with its obligations under international agreements pursuant to which the consent of a sending state is required to surrender a person of that state to the Court, unless the Court can first obtain the cooperation of the sending state for the giving of consent for the surrender.

Simply put, the ICC cannot demand the arrest and surrender of a defendant under the Rome Statute if another treaty prohibits this outcome and if the defendant's home state refuses to grant an exception.

The US—which is not an ICC member—has used this treaty provision to protect its nationals from ICC prosecution. Since 2002, the US has aggressively pushed other states to sign **Article 98 agreements** with the US, which are bilateral agreements in which states pledge not to surrender each other's nationals to the ICC.[105] For example, Afghanistan, Colombia, and Sierra Leone are ICC members that signed an Article 98 agreement with the US. Legal experts debate the legality and implications of these agreements. Thus far, the ICC has not issued an arrest warrant for a US national. However, this situation may change as the ICC investigates the Afghanistan War.

Universal Jurisdiction

We begin with an overview of how universal jurisdiction works, including its intellectual foundations and practice over time. We then discuss how treaties affect universal jurisdiction cases.

How Universal Jurisdiction Works

When states create and enforce domestic laws, they must establish their jurisdiction over actions that they want to regulate.[106] States usually assert one of four common bases of jurisdiction:

- Territory—the action occurred on domestic territory;
- Active nationality—the person who committed the action was a national of the state;

- Passive personality—the person harmed by the action was a national of the state; and
- Protective principle—the action had important and systematic effects on the state, like national security threats.

In contrast, if a state asserts **universal jurisdiction**, it uses its domestic law and institutions to regulate actions that occur outside of its domestic territory, do not involve its nationals, and do not have important and systematic effects on itself. Universal jurisdiction differs from the four common bases of jurisdiction because there is not a tangible link between the regulated action and the state when the action occurs. Many experts agree that customary international law allows states to assert universal jurisdiction to prosecute crimes against humanity, genocide, torture, and war crimes.[107]

The intellectual foundations of universal jurisdiction trace back to the historic practice of piracy, which had two key attributes. First, piracy usually involved murder and theft, which all domestic legal systems prohibited. Cicero, the ancient Roman politician, described pirates as "a common foe" of the world.[108] Similarly, Alberico Gentili, a sixteenth-century Italian-British scholar, called pirates the "common enemies" of mankind.[109] These writings suggest that states believed that piracy was morally abhorrent.

Second, piracy usually occurred on the high seas, outside of the territorial jurisdiction of any state. If no state asserted domestic jurisdiction over the high seas, then pirates could easily escape punishment. This combination of common values and lack of enforcement led many scholars, including Swiss writer Emer de Vattel, to argue that states could use domestic courts to punish pirates, even if they lacked jurisdiction based on territory or nationality.[110]

As international law developed in the twentieth century, states returned to universal jurisdiction as a tool for upholding international criminal law. Some states argued that they could use domestic courts to punish serious international crimes if no other state or international body was willing or able to uphold international law. For example, Raphael Lemkin, the Polish activist who pressured states to create the Genocide Convention, supported universal jurisdiction:

> If the destruction of human groups is a problem of international concern, then such acts should be treated as crimes under the law of nations, like piracy, and every state should be able to take jurisdiction over such acts irrespective of the nationality of the offender and of the place where the crime was committed.[111]

Universal jurisdiction is thus based on a fundamental tension: anyone can prosecute serious international crimes if no one else is willing or able to do so.

States differ in how they invoke universal jurisdiction. Some states can use customary international law and treaties to justify domestic prosecutions. Other states must incorporate international law into their domestic laws for prosecutions to occur. Table 11.3 shows four examples of domestic laws that allow universal jurisdiction. The details of these laws vary. For example, UK law allows the prosecution of crimes that occurred during World War II in Germany or German-occupied territory. In contrast, Canadian law allows the prosecution of genocide, crimes against humanity, and war crimes that occur anywhere.

The first and most notorious example of universal jurisdiction over core international crimes was the trial of Adolph Eichmann in Israel. Eichmann was a Nazi official who helped orchestrate the Holocaust. After World War II, he fled Germany and moved to Argentina. When Israel learned Eichmann's location, it sent intelligence officers to Argentina to kidnap Eichmann and bring him to Israel for trial. Most observers believed that Eichmann deserved trial and punishment, yet many questioned Israel's actions. Eichmann's crimes occurred before Israel became a state. Israel therefore could not assert jurisdiction based on territory,

Figure 11.4 In 1961, Adolph Eichmann—a former Nazi official—faced trial in Jerusalem for his role in planning the Holocaust.

Table 11.3 Examples of Domestic Laws that Allow Universal Jurisdiction

State	Name	Text
Canada	Crimes Against Humanity and War Crimes Act (2000)	"Every person who ... commits outside Canada (a) genocide, (b) a crime against humanity, or (c) a war crime, is guilty of an indictable offence and may be prosecuted for that offence" *(para. 6(1))*
France	Code of Criminal Procedure (2006)	• "In accordance with the international conventions quoted in the following articles, a person guilty of committing any of the offences listed by these provisions outside the territory of the Republic and who happens to be in France may be prosecuted and tried by French courts" *(Art. 689-1)* • Includes UN Convention against Torture and other international treaties *(Art. 689-2–10)*
New Zealand	International Crimes and International Criminal Court Act (2000)	• Defines genocide, crimes against humanity, and war crimes • "Proceedings may be brought for an offence ... regardless of— (i) the nationality or citizenship of the person accused; or (ii) whether or not any act forming part of the offence occurred in New Zealand; or (iii) whether or not the person accused was in New Zealand at the time that the act ... occurred or ... a decision was made to charge the person with an offence" *(Section 8(1)(c))*
UK	War Crimes Act (1991)	• "Proceedings for murder, manslaughter or culpable homicide may be brought against a person in the United Kingdom irrespective of his nationality at the time of the alleged offence if that offence— (a) was committed during the period beginning with 1 September 1939 and ending with 5th June 1945 in a place which at the time was part of Germany or under German occupation; and (b) constituted a violation of the laws and customs of war" *(Art. 1(1))* • "No proceedings shall ... be brought against any person unless he was on 8th March 1990, or has subsequently become, a British citizen or resident in the United Kingdom" *(Art. 2)*

nationality, or national security effects. Instead, Israeli prosecutors asserted universal jurisdiction. They argued that the international community had condemned genocide, and that Israel could prosecute Eichmann because no other state or international body had done so.

How common are universal jurisdiction prosecutions? The *Eichmann* trial is not a unique or isolated example. Experts have identified sixty-one universal jurisdiction trials from 1957 to 2017.[112] This number only includes examples in which states collected sufficient evidence for a trial, such as the *Eichmann* trial. This number does not include examples in which a state used universal jurisdiction to investigate crimes, but no trial was held. The number of universal jurisdiction complaints—which are attempts by victims, NGOs, or state officials to begin criminal investigations—is much higher: 1,990.[113] These complaints matter because they generate evidence, such as witness testimony, that documents international crimes. Also, highly publicized complaints can influence public opinion and pressure governments to provide other forms of justice.

For example, in the mid-1990s, a Spanish judge asserted universal jurisdiction to prosecute Augusto Pinochet, the former dictator of Chile, for torture and other crimes. The Spanish government spent many years documenting Pinochet's past actions. Court hearings, which included witness testimony, publicized Pinochet's actions to domestic and international audiences. Pinochet was not actually tried by Spain because other states refused to arrest and extradite him to Spain.[114] However, Spain's actions ultimately led to criminal proceedings against Pinochet in Chile.[115]

Which states assert universal jurisdiction? Many critics of universal jurisdiction argue that powerful states use universal jurisdiction to control poor and weak states, especially former colonies.[116] Most states that assert universal jurisdiction are advanced industrial states, like Germany and Spain. However, middle-income and even lower-income states—like Argentina, Senegal, South Africa, and Turkey—have received universal jurisdiction complaints. Universal jurisdiction is not therefore a purely European phenomenon. While many states that assert universal jurisdiction are former colonial powers (such as Belgium, France, Germany, and Spain), others are themselves former colonies (such as Argentina, Canada, and Senegal).

Where do universal jurisdiction defendants come from? Many cases involve wars with large-scale human rights abuses, like the Great African War, the Syrian civil war, and the Yugoslavian War. Other cases involve authoritarian repression. For example, many universal jurisdiction defendants participated in authoritarian violence in places like Argentina and El Salvador. Finally, some defendants are nationals of world powers that engage in foreign military intervention, like France, the UK, and the US. Universal jurisdiction is therefore a global practice.

Treaty Obligations

No international treaty creates global rules for domestic criminal jurisdiction, but many treaties affect universal jurisdiction. One early example is the Genocide Convention (1948), which says:

Persons charged with genocide ... shall be tried by a competent tribunal of the state in the territory of which the act was committed, or by such international penal tribunal as may have jurisdiction with respect to those [treaty members] which shall have accepted its jurisdiction.[117]

This text clearly allows territorial jurisdiction over genocide. But does it allow universal jurisdiction?

In the mid-1990s, Germany arrested and prosecuted Nicola Jorgić, a Bosnian Serb, for genocide during the Yugoslavian War. After his trial, Jorgić challenged Germany at the European Court of Human Rights, arguing that Germany had violated his human rights because it lacked jurisdiction over his case. Germany acknowledged that the Genocide Convention did not explicitly authorize German jurisdiction because Jorgić's actions did not occur on German territory. However, Germany argued that the Genocide Convention did not prohibit universal jurisdiction, either.[118] Germany therefore concluded that universal jurisdiction did not violate international law. The Court supported Germany, ruling that Germany's interpretation of the Genocide Convention was "reasonable" given the object and purpose of the treaty.[119]

Many other treaties create an obligation to prosecute or extradite individuals who are accused of serious international crimes. For example, the UN Convention against Torture (1984) says:

Each state party shall ... [grant its courts] jurisdiction over [acts of torture] in cases where the alleged offender is present in any territory under its jurisdiction and it does not extradite him.[120]

The state party in the territory under whose jurisdiction a person alleged to have committed [torture] is found shall ... if it does not extradite him, submit the case to its competent authorities for the purpose of prosecution.[121]

The UN Convention against Torture thus requires states to create and exercise jurisdiction if they do not extradite an alleged torturer to another state for prosecution.

For example, recall the example from the introduction of Hissène Habré, the former dictator of Chad. During his time in power, state authorities tortured both armed groups that opposed Habré and civilians from rival ethnic groups. After leaving power, Habré fled to Senegal, which was a member of the UN Convention against Torture. Habré's victims invoked universal jurisdiction and filed criminal complaints in numerous states, including Belgium and Senegal. Belgian authorities tried to pursue such charges, but Senegal refused to extradite Habré to Belgium and refused to prosecute him in Senegalese courts. After numerous diplomatic exchanges, Belgium successfully sued Senegal at the ICJ for violating the UN Convention against Torture.[122] This ICJ ruling created political pressure on Senegal to take action against Habré. Senegal ultimately agreed to a compromise and surrendered Habré to the Extraordinary African Chambers for trial.

11.5   Case Study Revisited: Did Chad Get Justice or Political Retribution?

We began this chapter with the trial of Hissène Habré, who ruled Chad from 1982 to 1990. During his rule, the Chad government committed mass killings, rape, and torture of armed groups and civilians. Habré was ultimately removed from power by Idriss Déby, his former army commander, and fled to Senegal. Habré's victims and non-governmental organizations pressured states for decades to hold Habré accountable. This pressure finally resulted in the creation of the Extraordinary African Chambers, a mixed criminal tribunal based in Senegal and overseen by the African Union. In 2016, Hissène Habré was convicted of international crimes and sentenced to life in prison.

The Hissène Habré trial connects to each of the topics in this chapter:

- *Creating international crimes*: Habré's conviction was based on individual criminal responsibility. This major principle of international criminal law ensured that Habré could not claim that legal violations were acts of the Chadian state. Rather, they were crimes committed by individuals with duties under international law. Habré's trial by the Extraordinary African Chambers reflects the historical trend of tribunals prosecuting international crimes.

- *Establishing guilt*: Habré was convicted of two core international crimes: crimes against humanity and war crimes.[123] One witness testified that Habré was a direct perpetrator of a rape.[124] The rest of the prosecution's case relied on indirect responsibility. Namely, prosecutors argued that Habré planned, oversaw, and ordered crimes committed by his security agency.[125] Additionally, prosecutors argued that the principle of command responsibility ensured that Habré could be punished for acts of his armed forces. Habré's court-appointed defense lawyers challenged various documents and witnesses. However, Habré's main defense strategy was to challenge the authority of the tribunal by refusing to cooperate. As his conviction shows, non-cooperation was not an effective defense.

- *Enforcing international criminal law*: Recall that the International Criminal Court has temporal limits: it cannot prosecute conduct before 2002, when the Court was created. Belgium tried to assert universal jurisdiction over Habré, but could not get Senegal to extradite Habré to Belgium. Instead, Senegal agreed to create a new mixed tribunal to prosecute Habré.

We can now answer the big questions from the introduction. First, what gave the African Union, Belgium, and Senegal the authority to intervene in a domestic dispute in Chad? Belgium's attempt to prosecute Habré was based on a claim to universal jurisdiction. Because Habré was credibly accused of serious international crimes and had not faced prosecution elsewhere, Belgium asserted its own authority to prosecute Habré. Senegal's involvement was based on the fact that Habré was living in Senegal. While Senegal was not willing to prosecute Habré using its normal domestic criminal courts, it was willing to participate in the Extraordinary African Chambers, a mixed criminal tribunal created by the African Union.

Second, why was Habré prosecuted for crimes, while Déby, an army commander, was not tried? The international community was selective about who was prosecuted by the Extraordinary African Chambers. As one Chad national told journalists: "[Habré] didn't kill on his own, he didn't torture on his own, he didn't cut people's throats on his own."[126] Habré's rule was supported by thousands of officials serving in the armed forces and the security agency, as well as elite co-ethnics who benefitted both economically and politically from Habré's rule. Yet almost none of these individuals were punished for the mass killings, rape, and torture. In particular, Idriss Déby faced no accountability for his role as Habré's army commander. Additionally, Déby mimicked Habré's tactics for oppressing rival groups after he came to power. However, Habré was available for trial—he had been removed from power and was living in Senegal. Déby was not available because he remained in power in Chad. Additionally, the international community needed Déby's support to ensure that prosecutors could gain access to the evidence and witnesses that they needed to prosecute Habré.

A third question was: why weren't France and the US also responsible for assisting (or at least ignoring) Habré's crimes? Recall that France and the US helped Habré to gain and maintain his power in Chad. Namely, they provided Habré with financial assistance, military training, and weapons, even though his crimes were well-documented and circulated in Western news media.[127] Many experts therefore view France and the US as partially responsible for Habré's crimes. Yet France and the US have faced no tangible consequences for their role in Habré's crimes because of their power within the international system. Some critics even argue that individual prosecutions (like the Habré trial) allow powerful states (like France and the US) to shield themselves from justice.[128]

Finally—and most importantly—is the Habré trial an example of justice or political retribution? Reasonable people can disagree on the answer to this question, but many of us would probably respond that both answers are correct. Hissène Habré was involved in truly horrendous acts that deserved punishment. At one point, Senegal offered to extradite Habré to Chad, but human rights NGOs strongly opposed the move, arguing that Habré would not get a fair trial.[129] Others argued that Chad would simply execute Habré without any trial because Habré had previously been convicted and sentenced to death by a Chadian court for supporting an attempted coup against Idriss Déby. When he appeared before the Extraordinary African Chambers, Habré received far more legal protections during his trial and sentencing than his victims did. These factors suggest that Habré's trial and conviction are an example of justice.

At the same time, Habré's trial definitely contained elements of political retribution. Idriss Déby donated money to the Extraordinary African Chambers and offered to testify for prosecutors against his political rival.[130] Yet Déby committed similar crimes and escaped punishment. Additionally, no French or US leaders were punished for their role in assisting and/or ignoring Déby's crimes. This selectivity in prosecution suggests that politics matters because it determines *who* is punished. Idriss Déby may someday have his own day in court. But this is unlikely to happen until Déby loses political power. Justice and politics go hand-in-hand.

12 Environmental Protection

12.1   Case Study: Japan Legalizes Commercial Whale Hunts

In July 2019, Japan held its first commercial whale hunt in thirty years. Japan's fishing minister celebrated that Japanese "culture and way of life will be passed on to the next generation."[1] Meanwhile, international environmental groups criticized Japan for breaking international norms against whale hunting, with one activist describing the hunt as "pirate whaling."[2] The day of the hunt coincided with Japan's withdrawal from an important treaty for whale protection.

States wrote the 1946 International Convention for the Regulation of Whaling (ICRW) "to protect all species of whales from further over-fishing."[3] In the 1940s,

Figure 12.1 A worker poses next to a whale captured after Japan resumed commercial whale hunting in July 2019. Many environmental activists condemn these hunts, but Japan views the hunts as an important part of its cultural heritage.

states viewed marine animals as economic resources that should be managed to ensure their long-term survival. The ICRW required states to manage whale stocks, saying that "increases in the size of whale stocks will permit increases in the number of whales which may be captured without endangering these natural resources."[4] It created the International Whaling Commission as an international organization to oversee whale stock management. Major whaling states—like Iceland, Japan, and Norway—supported the ICRW and the Commission.

However, environmental attitudes changed in the 1960s and 1970s. Most states began to believe that living resources should be protected regardless of their economic value. Environmental activists pressured the International Whaling Commission to ban commercial whaling.[5] They convinced landlocked states (like Mongolia and Switzerland) to join the ICRW to shift voting power away from states with commercial whaling (like Iceland, Japan, and Norway). After decades of pressure, the International Whaling Commission banned commercial whaling in 1986. ICRW members could only allow whale hunts by indigenous groups or scientific programs monitored by the Commission.

Some ICRW members (like Iceland and Norway) simply continued commercial whale hunts. For decades, Japan tried to comply with the ban by creating a scientific whaling program. Then in 2010, Australia sued Japan at the ICJ. Australia asked the Court to interpret ICRW text that allows a member to "kill ... whales for purposes of scientific research."[6] The Court found that aspects of Japan's program "cast doubt on its characterization as a program for purposes of scientific research."[7] The Court then ruled that Japan had violated the ICRW, prompting Japan to exit the ICRW in 2019.

Do Japan's actions suggest that it disdains whale protection, or that it defines protection differently than ICRW members? Does Japan's exit from the ICRW mean that it can kill an unlimited number of whales, or does international law still constrain Japan? What tools can other states use to discourage commercial whale hunts?

To answer these questions, we must examine the following issues:

- *Environment as a common resource*: Why does international law address some aspects of the environment, but not others? What legal principles bind states? Where did international environmental law come from?
- *Protecting the environment*: What international rules govern protection of the atmosphere, water, and living resources?
- *Interaction with other areas of law*: What other areas of international law have implications for environmental protection? Would international law about trade, investment, human rights, or armed conflict affect how we assess Japan's actions?

International environmental law is grounded in scientific knowledge. Since the Enlightenment, humans have believed that nature is governed by fixed processes. **Science** is the intellectual claim that natural processes can be understood by human reason based on observation and experimentation. For example, science allows experts to track whale stocks over time, make inferences about the causes and effects of changing stocks, and recommend policies to preserve these stocks.

While science aspires to political neutrality, the interpretation and use of science are fundamentally political. In choosing policies, we must decide: Who should choose the optimal size of whale stocks? How should we evaluate the claims of individuals who want to eat whale meat? Do whales have intrinsic value, regardless of economics? Do whales have inherent rights, irrespective of the desires and needs of humans?

Most environmental challenges are rooted in **industrialization**, which is the shift from agrarian production to manufacturing. Industrialization allows humans to support larger populations that consume more goods and services over longer time-spans. However, the transformation of raw materials into manufactured goods creates **pollution**, which is the release of substances that harm the atmosphere, water, and/or living resources.

Industrialization also comes with political challenges. States in the Americas and Europe industrialized much earlier, on average, than states in Asia and Africa.

In part, this variation in industrialization was driven by the location of natural resources needed for industrialization, such as coal.[8] States in the Americas and Europe therefore bear more responsibility, on average, for past and current pollution than states in Asia and Africa. How should this historical inequality affect future industrialization? Should all states limit industrialization? Should developed states bear more costs because of their past conduct? These are fundamentally political questions that require international cooperation.

All of these questions are apparent in contemporary debates about climate change, a political issue that currently receives extensive public attention, particularly from young activists. Some readers might therefore expect that this chapter would focus primarily on climate change and the Paris Climate Agreement, a relatively recent international treaty. However, this topic represents only one small sliver of international environmental law, which focuses on diverse complex issues. In this chapter, section 12.2 analyzes why states create international environmental law. It describes the rise in treaties and explains common principles of environmental law. Section 12.3 then discusses the specific treaty rules that govern the atmosphere, water, and living resources. Next, section 12.4 examines how other areas of law—including trade, investment, human rights, and armed conflict law—affect the environment. Finally, section 12.5 applies all of this information to Japan's commercial whale hunts.

12.2   Environment as a Common Resource

We now consider why and how states make international environmental law. We start by explaining why environmental protection is often framed as a collaboration problem. We then examine the evolution of environmental law, including the growth in environmental agreements after World War II, changing beliefs about the purpose of environmentalism, and the creation of UN General Assembly documents that articulate environmental principles. We then describe many of these principles in detail, highlighting which of these principles have become part of customary international law.

Concepts

Most environmental challenges stem from collaboration problems. Recall from Chapter 1 that in a collaboration problem, states jointly benefit from choosing the same action, but each state is tempted to unilaterally deviate to a different action. These incentives ensure that all states are worse off than if they jointly cooperated. Two types of collaboration problems are common in environmental politics.

The first type is called the **tragedy of the commons**. In this situation, a group of actors collectively benefit from protecting a common resource, but each individual actor is tempted to overconsume the resource. For example, the high seas contain fish, whales, and other animals that individuals want to consume. However, if individuals consume too much, then animals can become extinct. Absent a binding agreement to protect a common resource, states will be tempted to satisfy their own desires, thereby endangering the survival of the common resource.

Even if states have well-defined property rights, they can face a tragedy of the commons over **fugitive resources**, which are resources that move across borders, such as migratory birds, fish, and whales. For example, a state that allows hunters to kill a migratory bird may not fully account for the impact of that decision on other states where the bird travels. The tragedy of the commons also affects the **global commons**, which are resources that belong to no specific state, like the earth's atmosphere, the high seas, and even outer space.

The second type of collaboration problem in environmental politics is public goods provision. A **public good** is a good that is non-excludable—meaning that all actors benefit from its existence—and non-rivalrous, meaning that consumption of the good by one actor does not limit consumption of the good by another actor. For example, consider the earth's atmosphere. All humans need clean air to survive, and when one individual breathes, ample clean air remains for others. However, individuals also want manufactured goods, like cell phones, laptop computers, and televisions. Making and using these goods releases pollution into the atmosphere. In a public goods problem, actors collectively benefit from a public good, like clean air. However, each individual actor is tempted to take actions that diminish the public good, like producing and consuming manufactured goods. These incentives lead to **free-riding**, which is a situation in which actors provide less cooperation than would be optimal for society as a whole. Free-riding therefore prioritizes individual outcomes over collective social outcomes.

When are states more likely to overcome such collaboration problems? One important factor is the number of actors involved in a collaboration problem.[9] Generally speaking, scholars have shown that cooperation is easier when fewer actors are involved. For example, some kinds of air pollution travel a few hundred miles or less, affecting only a pair of states. Other kinds of air pollution travel thousands of miles to the outer layers of the atmosphere, affecting all states. All else being equal, it should be easier for two states to negotiate and comply with an agreement to stop pollution than it would be for all states to cooperate. This strategic logic suggests that some kinds of air pollution can be more easily limited than others.

Another important factor is how actors assess the benefits and costs of collaboration. This assessment can be driven by the relative wealth and capacity of states. For example, excessive hunting has endangered many elephant species in sub-Saharan Africa. International rules aim to protect these species, but elephant hunting remains common in some African states. People living in poorer states usually have fewer economic opportunities than individuals living in richer states. Also, poorer states usually have fewer resources for upholding law than richer states. Accordingly, evidence suggests that elephant poaching is more likely to occur in areas with poorer populations and more government corruption.[10] To overcome such challenges, states often use **linkage**, which is the use of conditional economic benefits and punishments to encourage compliance with international agreements. For example, poorer states that join treaties to protect endangered species (like elephants) often receive financial assistance from richer states to help them comply with treaty rules. Changes in domestic political power can also affect how actors assess the benefits and costs of collaboration. For example, non-governmental organizations (NGOs) often pressure states to cooperate on environmental issues. Governments that are more responsive to the demands of these NGOs should be more willing to join environmental treaties and implement them using domestic policies.[11]

One final important factor is the ability of actors to monitor whether cooperation occurs. For example, states can monitor water pollution in shared rivers by testing water at their shore. These same tests are not effective, however, in measuring pollution in the high seas, thousands of miles from the shore. Because states can more easily monitor pollution for smaller bodies of water, they can more accurately assess whether various actors are complying with environmental agreements. States routinely require regular monitoring and reporting in environmental agreements. To facilitate this process, they usually create an international body that is responsible for collecting and assessing data about environmental conditions. These monitoring bodies, in turn, enable environmental NGOs to hold governments accountable when they violate environmental agreements.[12]

Evolution

For centuries, states have written bilateral agreements to regulate their interactions in shared spaces, like rivers and lakes along shared borders. These agreements usually focused on navigation and commerce, including fishing and other economic activities. For example, after purchasing Alaska in 1867, the US claimed jurisdiction over large portions of the Bering Sea, including exclusive rights over seal hunting. Yet Canadian fishermen routinely killed seals in the Bering Sea, leading to a depletion in seal stocks. The US complained to the UK, which had authority over Canada's foreign relations. The dispute ultimately went to arbitration, which the US decisively lost in 1893. The arbitration tribunal ruled that Canadian seal hunting was occurring in the high seas, outside of US jurisdiction.[13] Seal stocks then continued to decline as Japanese hunters began capturing the prized seals. Eventually, Japan, Russia, the UK, and the US agreed to sign the North Pacific Fur Seal Convention of 1911, which limited seal hunting in the Bering Sea. While this treaty is often described as an early example of environmental law, the main concern of states was the economic well-being of commercial hunters. States protected the environment because it provided raw materials for economic exchange.

After World War II, international environmental politics was affected by three trends. First, international organizations became more important and independent in all areas of politics. The new United Nations system contained numerous forums for environmental politics, including the General Assembly. Other institutions, like the General Agreement on Tariffs and Trade, also became involved in environmental politics over time.

Second, the ideology of environmentalism changed. Activists and NGOs began to argue that the environment has inherent value to human well-being, irrespective of its economic value. There are diverse modern views about how to trade off human consumption and environmental protection. For example, some environmental advocates believe that states must limit population growth to help protect the environment. However, the overwhelming majority of modern environmentalists are anthropocentric, placing human well-being at the center of ethical and moral debates.

Finally, the number of environmental agreements grew dramatically after World War II. Figure 12.2 shows this growth over time. The solid line shows new multilateral agreements, while the dotted line shows new bilateral agreements, beginning

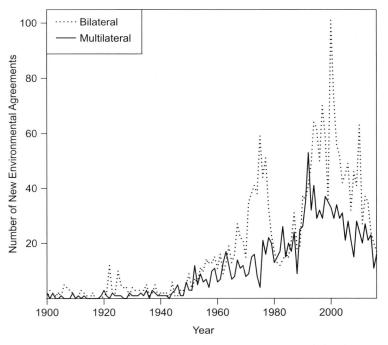

Figure 12.2 Growth in international environmental agreements, 1900–2016.
Source: Data is from the International Environmental Agreements Database Project (https://iea.uoregon.edu).

in 1900. Because each line represents new agreements, the cumulative number of environmental agreements is huge. States have signed over 1,200 multilateral agreements and over 2,200 bilateral agreements that address environmental issues![14] Most bilateral agreements regulate the use of a specific shared resource. For example, the 1975 Statute of the Uruguay River was negotiated by Argentina and Uruguay to govern use of the river along their shared border. In contrast, most multilateral agreements address larger environmental issues, like protection of the atmosphere, water, or living resources. These agreements sometimes overlap with each other and yield disagreements.[15]

Activists in developed states drive most environmental politics. To build broad support for international environmental law, developed states had to accommodate developing states, which had their own distinct objectives. Many developing states gained their independence from colonial rule in the 1950s to 1970s. These states used international organizations to advance the **New International Economic Order**, which was a set of trade, investment, development, and assistance policies to promote the interests of developing states in the 1970s. For example, developing states proclaimed that every state had permanent sovereignty over its natural resources and a **right to development**, meaning that every state had the right to create its own policies for exploiting its natural resources. These legal claims were intended to reduce the economic and political influence of foreign-owned oil and mineral companies in developing states. Additionally, developing states argued that all states had shared rights to valuable minerals (including gold and silver) in ocean floors. While these claims were rooted in economics, rather than ecology, they offered an opportunity for political compromise with the environmental concerns of developed states.

Developed and developing states discussed their concerns in numerous international organizations and conferences. One major challenge in this discussion was fear about possible conflicts between domestic regulations and international standards.[16] Also, states recognized that the capacity and interests of developing states differed significantly from those of developed states.[17] Because states wanted universal support for new environmental rules, they initially wrote non-binding principles that were overseen by bureaucratic institutions, rather than legally binding rules that were enforced by an international court.

These discussions ultimately yielded the **Stockholm Declaration**, which is a non-binding document from 1972 that includes general principles about development and the environment. The Stockholm Declaration was adopted by consensus. It is not a legally binding treaty that was ratified by individual states. Much like the Universal Declaration of Human Rights, not every state agrees with every principle included in the document. Nonetheless, many principles in the Stockholm Declaration are now part of customary international law. States also negotiated an action plan to help implement these principles and created new international organizations to assist states on environmental issues.

Environmental advocates continued to push states to write stronger and more detailed environmental principles. In the 1980s, the UN created a group called the Brundtland Commission to further study the environment. Under the leadership of Gro Harlem Brundtland, the former Prime Minister of Norway, the Commission popularized the concept of "sustainable development" as a way to reconcile the competing demands of environmental protection and economic growth. The work of the Brundtland Commission led to a new set of expanded and refined environmental principles contained in the **Rio Declaration**, which is a non-binding document from 1992.

While the Stockholm and Rio Declarations have similar content and goals, they differ in three important ways. First, the Stockholm Declaration often uses aspirational and imprecise language, such as "States *should* adopt an integrated and co-ordinated approach to their *development planning* so as to ensure that development is compatible with the need to protect and improve environment."[18] In contrast, the Rio Declaration uses more precise and obligatory language, such as "States *shall* enact effective *environmental legislation*."[19] Second, the Rio Declaration has procedures for including public participation in rule-making, evaluating scientific risk, and compensating environmental damage.[20] Finally, the Rio Declaration places more emphasis on the demands of developing states, which wanted financial and technical assistance from developed states.[21] We now turn to an overview of the most important principles contained in the Stockholm and Rio Declarations.

Principles

Legal principles for environmental protection fall into two groups. The first group involves **transboundary harm**, which occurs when an act in one state causes or threatens harm to the persons, property, or environment of another state. The second group involves sustainable development, which involves balancing development and the environment. We discuss each of these groups in turn.

Transboundary Harm

An important transboundary harm dispute is the *Trail Smelter* dispute. In the 1890s, a Canadian firm built a smelter, which is a factory that uses heat to extract metal from ore, in Canada near the US border. For decades, this smelter emitted sulfur dioxide that damaged crops, livestock, and timber in the US. No international law prohibited smelters, but the US argued that Canada was financially responsible for the harm caused by the smelter to the US. After decades of diplomacy, Canada accepted responsibility for the damage in 1935 by agreeing to arbitration over damages.[22]

Over time, other states accepted the principle of responsibility for transboundary harm, even if the acts that cause this harm are not illegal. For example, the Stockholm Declaration proclaims: "States have ... the responsibility to ensure that activities within their jurisdiction or control do not cause damage to ... areas beyond the limits of national jurisdiction."[23] Similar language is also included in the Rio Declaration.[24] In 2001, the International Law Commission completed draft articles on this topic.[25] State responsibility for transboundary harm is now part of customary international law, although states often disagree about exactly how to define transboundary harm.

This legal principle has led to numerous other related legal principles. First, states have an obligation to prevent transboundary harm. In 2010, the International Court of Justice wrote:

> the principle of prevention, as a customary rule, has its origins in the due diligence that
> is required of a state in its territory ... A state is thus obliged to use all the means at
> its disposal in order to avoid activities which take place in its territory, or in any area
> under its jurisdiction, causing significant damage to the environment of another state.[26]

As the ICJ indicated, the obligation to prevent transboundary harm is also now part of customary international law.

Second, if a policy or project risks significant transboundary harm, then states should conduct an **environmental impact assessment**, which is a process for evaluating the impact of a policy or project on environmental outcomes. International law does not have detailed rules for how and when states should make such assessments. States usually conduct assessments using their own domestic laws and procedures. Additionally, international law does not require states to conduct environmental impact assessments for every project that might cause harm.[27] However, projects that are larger or risk more significant harm should be assessed more rigorously and systematically.[28] The ICJ has not (yet) decided whether assessments are required under customary international law, but bilateral and multilateral environmental agreements usually require these assessments.

Third, states should assess environmental risk using a precautionary approach. International law does not have a clear and consistent definition of precaution.[29] Some states strongly support a precautionary approach, while others question its implications. For example, the European Union routinely bans the production and sale of agricultural products (like genetically modified crops) unless these products are proven to be safe.[30] In contrast, the US believes that such bans unduly limit commerce and technological innovation. The US argues that farmers should be able to produce and sell products (including genetically modified crops) unless they are proven to be dangerous.

Fourth, if a state's environmental impact assessment reveals a risk of significant transboundary harm, then the state should notify and consult with other states that are likely to be affected. Many bilateral and multilateral environmental agreements contain specific procedures for such notification and consultation. However, even in the absence of treaty rules, the ICJ has ruled that notification and consultation are part of the "obligation to exercise due diligence in preventing significant transboundary harm."[31] This language suggests that notification and consultation are now required under customary international law.

Finally, if transboundary harm actually occurs, the responsible state must provide compensation. This principle is well-established under customary international law and is sometimes called the "polluter pays" principle.[32] This obligation to compensate holds even if the act that caused the harm was not illegal and was committed by a private actor, like a smelting operator.[33]

The ICJ applied many of these principles in the *Pulp Mills* case. In 1975, Argentina and Uruguay signed a bilateral environmental agreement called the Statute of the Uruguay River. The Statute requires each state to inform the other about new projects that might affect the river, which forms part of the border between Argentina and Uruguay. The Statute also includes consultation rules to promote cooperation over possible adverse effects. Finally, it requires states to prevent river pollution, which it defines as "the direct or indirect introduction by man into the aquatic environment of substances or energy which have harmful effects."[34]

In the early 2000s, two firms applied in Uruguay for permits to build two factories along the river. Uruguay issued preliminary permits without first notifying

Figure 12.3 This 2007 photograph shows the Botnia pulp mill on the Uruguay River, which is the boundary between Argentina and Uruguay. In the center foreground, a small Argentine boat sails along the river. Argentina sued Uruguay at the ICJ for allowing the construction of the mill. Argentina feared that the mill would generate pollution that would harm commercial and recreational activities on the river.

Argentina and seeking its input. Argentina then successfully sued Uruguay at the ICJ for breaking the 1975 Statute by not informing Argentina about the projects. Argentina also argued that Uruguay violated its obligation to prevent pollution. Argentina argued that the precautionary approach required Uruguay to prove that the factories were not causing pollution.[35] However, the ICJ disagreed and required that Argentina prove that the factories were causing pollution.[36] After reviewing the scientific evidence, the ICJ concluded that Argentina could not prove that the factories "had deleterious effects or caused harm to ... the river."[37] Accordingly, Uruguay was not found guilty of failing to prevent pollution.

Sustainable Development

States often use the phrase "sustainable development" to describe the process of balancing development and the environment. Experts interpret this concept in many different ways.[38]

Some experts emphasize the principle of fairness over time. This approach states that sustainable development requires **intergenerational equity**, which is the claim that current generations of humans should leave ample resources for future generations. For example, climate activist Greta Thunberg and fifteen other children filed a complaint in 2019 at the UN Commission for the Rights of the Child.[39] They argued that states violated human rights under the UN Convention on the Rights of the Child by failing to combat climate change. They also suggested that future humans—who had not yet been born—possessed human rights to natural resources. In their complaint, they invoked the 1992 UN Framework Convention on Climate Change, which says that states "should protect the climate system for the benefit of present and future generations of humankind."[40]

Second, some experts emphasize the principle of fairness across states. These experts argue that states have **common but differentiated responsibility** for the environment, meaning that while the environment is a common concern, states have different levels of responsibility for protecting the environment. Usually these experts emphasize historical responsibility, arguing that developed states should contribute more resources to environmental protection than developing states because developed states have both consumed more natural resources and generated more pollution in the past than developing states. Sometimes these experts also emphasize state capacity, arguing that developed states can enforce rules more cost-effectively than developing states. For example, many environmental agreements—including the 2015 Paris Climate Agreement—contain common principles, but create different pollution targets for different states. Developing states (like India) usually do not face the same standards as developed states (like Germany).

A third set of experts emphasizes the principle that natural process should offset human consumption. These experts view sustainable development as an obligation to maintain current environmental conditions, meaning that humans should consume only what can be replaced through natural processes. These experts often encourage consumers to limit their consumption of goods that come with high environmental costs.

One final group of experts support the principle that economic policy-makers should consider environmental effects. This approach treats sustainable development as a process, rather than an outcome. For example, many environmental advocates push for more accountability and transparency in policy-making. They also argue that governments should consult with populations that may be harmed by new development. This view of sustainable development is reflected in the 1998 Aarhus Convention, which requires states to provide public information about the environmental impact of policies, to incorporate the public into decision-making, and to allow the public to challenge policies in domestic courts.

12.3   Protecting the Environment

The earth's systems are all interconnected. For example, land-based activities, like burning coal to produce electricity, can create air and water pollution that harms living resources, like animals and plants. We nonetheless organize our discussion of environmental rules into three topics. First, we introduce international law about the atmosphere, including rules on transboundary air pollution, ozone depletion, and climate change. Second, we discuss rules for the earth's shared water, including watercourses and seas. Finally, we provide an overview of international law for living resources.

Atmosphere

Pollution changes the composition of the earth's atmosphere, generating complex effects. International law addresses three atmospheric problems: transboundary air pollution; ozone depletion; and climate change. Table 12.1 shows major atmosphere agreements.[41]

Transboundary Air Pollution

Scientific research in the 1960s and 1970s showed that cars, manufacturing, and power plants were releasing atmospheric pollution—including nitrogen oxide and sulfur—that increased rain acidity throughout Europe and North America. This pollution harms animals and plants thousands of miles from its source. Acid rain was therefore an environmental problem that required international cooperation. Since many states contributed to this problem, they decided to craft a multilateral agreement on emissions levels.

Table 12.1 Key Atmosphere Agreements

Year	Name	Primary Motivation	Framework	Protocol
1979	Long-Range Transboundary Air Pollution Convention (LRTAP)	Transboundary air pollution (acid rain)	X	
1985	Ozone Convention	Ozone depletion	X	
1987	Montreal Protocol	Ozone depletion		X
1992	UN Framework Convention on Climate Change (UNFCCC)	Climate change	X	
1997	Kyoto Protocol	Climate change		X
2015	Paris Climate Agreement	Climate change		X

States created a **framework agreement**, which contains objectives and principles, and creates an institution to promote these objectives and principles. A framework agreement does not, however, include specific limits on state behavior, like pollution emissions. Framework agreements are often used when states face considerable uncertainty about the science underlying an environmental challenge, and when states seek to build broad support for cooperation.[42]

Namely, states created the 1979 Long-Range Transboundary Air Pollution (LRTAP) Convention as a framework for reducing transboundary air pollution. The objective of LRTAP is to "gradually reduce and prevent air pollution including long-range transboundary air pollution."[43] It includes the principles that states should:

- promote research about transboundary air pollution;
- exchange information about emissions; and
- adopt pollution-reducing policies that require "the best available technology which is economically feasible."[44]

To support its objective and principles, LRTAP created an institution to periodically review domestic regulations and emission levels. LRTAP has fifty-one members in Europe and North America, all of which are relatively developed states.

States then used the LRTAP framework agreement to negotiate eight different **protocols**, which are agreements that contain detailed rules for a specific issue. The first LRTAP protocol created procedures for monitoring and evaluating pollution in Europe. The subsequent protocols limited specific pollutants, including nitrogen oxide and sulfur. LRTAP members chose which protocols to join based on their circumstances.

Why could states solve the collective action problem of transboundary air pollution? One key factor is the regional nature of transboundary air pollution. For example, Canadian pollution causes acid rain in the US, but not in South Africa. States could therefore cooperate in small groups of geographic neighbors. For example, Canada and the US negotiated a bilateral agreement on sulfur that differs from the relevant LRTAP protocol, which applies to Europe. In Europe, cooperation nominally entailed more states, but the European Economic Community—a precursor of the modern European Union—coordinated the responses of most Western European states. Cooperation thus involved a relatively small number of actors.

Ozone Depletion

Second, scientific research in the 1970s and 1980s examined the **ozone layer**, which is the outer layer of the atmosphere that filters dangerous radiation from sunlight. It creates a protective skin around the earth's atmosphere. Scientists discovered that some pollutants—called ozone-depleting substances—can reduce the thickness of the ozone layer, allowing more sunlight to pass into the earth's atmosphere and causing harmful effects on the earth's surface.

Scientists initially identified chlorofluorocarbons as an ozone-depleting substance. These chemicals were used in consumer goods from the 1980s, like aerosol hair spray, air conditioners, and refrigerators. Environmental activists pushed states to ban these chemicals, but states initially disagreed about how to respond to ozone depletion because scientists did not fully understand how ozone-depleting substances worked. As a compromise, states began writing a framework agreement.

The 1985 Ozone Convention is a framework agreement whose objective is "to protect human health and the environment against adverse effects resulting or likely to result from human activities which modify or are likely to modify the ozone layer."[45] Like LRTAP, the Ozone Convention includes the principles that states should promote research, exchange information, and adopt domestic policies to limit ozone depletion. The Ozone Convention also created a new institution to encourage future cooperation. Finally, the Ozone Convention identifies scientific research priorities and likely ozone-depleting substances.[46] Unlike LRTAP, the Ozone Convention is a truly global agreement, with 198 members.

The Ozone Convention only has one protocol: the 1987 Montreal Protocol. This agreement reflects the principle of common but differentiated responsibility by setting different rules for developed and developing states. Namely, developed states agreed to reduce their ozone-depleting emissions, while developing states only agreed to freeze their emissions. In later years, states strengthened the Montreal Protocol by including new ozone-depleting substances and requiring a complete phaseout of banned substances. Throughout this process, developing states were given special accommodations. They received more time to phase out banned substances, and developed states gave them financial assistance and technology transfers to ease this transition.

In some ways ozone depletion was a more challenging problem than transboundary air pollution. The ozone is truly part of the global commons, rather than the more localized regional atmosphere affected by transboundary air pollution. Successful cooperation therefore required coordinated involvement by more actors. So why could states cooperate successfully on ozone depletion? States used linkage to connect the issues of environmentalism and international trade. Many of the consumer goods that used ozone-depleting substances—including aerosol hair spray, air conditioners, and refrigerators—were sold internationally. The Montreal Protocol allows states to ban such imported goods. Many firms that produced these consumer goods were able to shift to alternatives that were less harmful to the environment. The ban on ozone-depleting substances reduced the economic benefit of free-riding, thereby easing the collective action problem.

Climate Change

Finally, scientists discovered in the 1980s that pollution affects how sunlight travels within the earth's atmosphere (after it crosses the ozone layer). They identified **greenhouse gases**, which are atmospheric substances—including carbon dioxide and methane—that modify the impact of sunlight on the earth's surface. These gases have complex effects on diverse phenomena, including ocean currents and sea levels. Scientists use the term **climate change** to describe changes in the earth's climate patterns, including increases in the global average temperature.

Greenhouse gas emissions from human activities can be partially offset through natural processes. A **sink** is any system that absorbs more greenhouse gases than it releases. For example, a healthy tree consumes carbon dioxide from the atmosphere and releases oxygen. Environmental activists therefore push states both to limit greenhouse gas emissions and to protect sinks that offset human emissions, like the Amazon rainforest. While existing sinks cannot fully offset the impact of human activities, the further destruction of sinks would exacerbate climate change even more.

Once again, early scientific uncertainty about climate change prompted states to write a framework agreement: the 1992 UN Framework Convention on Climate Change (UNFCCC). The objective of this agreement is the "stabilization of greenhouse gas concentrations in the atmosphere at a level that would prevent dangerous ... interference with the climate system."[47] The UNFCCC refers to many principles, including intergenerational equity, common but differentiated responsibility, precaution, and the right to sustainable development.[48] As in prior atmospheric agreements, states also pledge to promote research, exchange information, and adopt domestic policies about greenhouse gas emissions. Finally, the UNFCCC created an institution to oversee climate change cooperation.

In accordance with differentiated responsibility, the UNFCCC classifies its members into two groups. One group—known as the "Annex I States"—contains mostly developed states, including Australia, Canada, EU members, Japan, New Zealand, Russia, and the US. These states pledged to return "individually or jointly to their 1990 levels" of greenhouse gas emissions.[49] However, this pledge is not legally binding. All other states—including most UNFCCC members—agreed to the importance of climate change, but did not make specific pledges to cut greenhouse gas emissions.

The UNFCCC has two protocols. First, the 1997 Kyoto Protocol limits six greenhouse gases, including carbon dioxide and methane, for the Annex I States. These states can either reduce emissions or increase sinks to meet their limits. Some Annex I States, like Japan and the EU members, pledged to reduce their emissions. Other states, like New Zealand and Russia, pledged not to increase their emissions. Finally, a few Annex I States, including Australia, Iceland, and Norway, could increase their emissions by a fixed amount. Most Kyoto members faced no limits on their greenhouse gas emissions.

Annex I States can meet their emissions goals by cooperating with other states. For example, an Annex I State can receive credits by financing projects that reduce emissions in other states. They can also purchase credits through emissions trading. All Kyoto members have equal voting rights in the monitoring organization, even though they do not have equal legal responsibilities.

Second, the 2015 Paris Climate Agreement set a global target "to limit the [global average] temperature increase to 1.5 °C above pre-industrial levels."[50] However, the Paris Climate Agreement does not include any emissions limits. Instead, it asks each state to make a voluntary "nationally determined contribution" to cutting emissions, acknowledging that states face "different national circumstances."[51] An international institution can review whether states meet their contributions, but these contributions are not binding under international law. Supporters describe this agreement as an innovation because states set standards, rather than the international community. However, many critics question whether this agreement will actually change behavior, or merely reflect how a state would have behaved absent a treaty.[52]

Why haven't states overcome the collective action problem of climate change? One key factor is that climate change involves the global commons—it affects all states. It is particularly hard to persuade and coordinate so many states to change their policies. In contrast, only a few states needed to cooperate to reduce transboundary air pollution. A second key factor is that states have not (yet) linked the environment and international trade, as they did for ozone depletion. Ozone-depleting substances were used in relatively few consumer goods that were banned based on their product characteristics. In contrast, all products generate greenhouse gas emissions. Some states, including EU members, want to use carbon tariffs to encourage environmentally friendly production technology. While international trade law allows states to tax imported products based on their characteristics, it does not allow taxes based on how products are produced. Unless states change World Trade Organization rules, they cannot use the same linkage politics as they used to combat ozone depletion.

Water

International environmental law protects two water sources. First, it protects seas, which are made of salt water. Second, it protects **international watercourses**, which are freshwater resources—including lakes and rivers—that are shared by multiple states. We discuss each of these areas in turn. Table 12.2 shows major water agreements.

Seas

States have long used international law to protect seas.[53] Early agreements focused on economic activities in seas, like fishing and whale-hunting. New challenges arose after World War II, in response to new technology, like the development of container ships, oil tankers, and nuclear power.

First, new technology required the disposal of new forms of waste, including container ships, oil tankers, and by-products from nuclear power plants. For example, Japan, the UK, and the US all routinely dumped radioactive waste into the high seas after World War II.[54] To prevent such activities, developed states negotiated the 1972 Dumping Convention. Its members pledged:

> to take all practicable steps to prevent the pollution of the sea by the dumping of waste and other matter that is liable to create hazards to human health, to harm living resources and marine life, to damage amenities or to interfere with other legitimate uses of the sea.[55]

Over time, states expanded and strengthened the Dumping Convention. Current rules prohibit dumping of nearly all waste into the sea. States can issue special permits only if the waste is harmless and no alternative disposal methods exist.[56] All developed states are now members of the Dumping Convention. States that are not members of the Convention are bound by other global and regional dumping rules.[57]

Table 12.2 Key Water Agreements		
Year	Name	Primary Motivation
1972*	Dumping Convention	Waste dumping
1978**	MARPOL Convention	Ship-based pollution
1982	UN Convention on the Law of the Sea	General
1997	International Watercourses Convention	Watercourse management

* Revised in 1993 and 1996.
** Based on a 1973 draft. Revised in 1997.

Second, new technology created pollution from ship operations and accidents. Larger and larger ships began crossing the seas more and more frequently, carrying traded goods, including oil. These ships release oil and other pollution into the sea during their routine operations. Additionally, they can damage the environment during accidents. For example, the *Torrey Canyon* was a Liberian ship transporting oil near the UK. In 1967, the ship hit underwater rocks, causing a massive oil spill that threatened the UK coast. After unsuccessful attempts to contain the spill, the UK government bombed the ship to burn the oil before it reached the coast.

Under the law of the sea, every ship must be registered in a flag state, which has jurisdiction over the ship. Most developed states have domestic laws for the design and operation of their ships, yet firms often avoid these laws (and high corporate taxes) by registering their ships in flag-of-convenience states, which have lax domestic laws. International rules are therefore essential to reducing pollution from ship operations and accidents.

States began writing rules about such pollution in the 1950s. These rules ultimately led to the 1978 MARPOL Convention.[58] This treaty contains detailed rules for ship construction, equipment, and inspections. Over time, states revised these rules because of new technology and aging ships. MARPOL allows ships to discharge some pollution, but it limits where this discharge can occur. For example, it prohibits almost all discharges into enclosed or semi-enclosed seas like the Black Sea and the Mediterranean. Most commercial ships are now governed by MARPOL, and experts consider MARPOL rules to be customary international law.

Despite the broad acceptance of MARPOL, state-based enforcement is sometimes difficult. Ships registered in flag-of-convenience states (including most oil tankers) rarely visit their flag state, thereby reducing state inspections.[59] The shipping industry therefore uses private organizations to inspect ships and verify that they meet international standards. Firms participate in such certification so that they can obtain private insurance and enter foreign ports.[60] Non-state actors therefore play an important role in enforcing environmental rules for ships.

In response to environmental activism in the 1960s and 1970s, states also included many environmental principles in the 1982 UN Convention on the Law of the Sea (UNCLOS). UNCLOS clearly includes transboundary harm principles that were well-established in the 1970s. Namely, UNCLOS includes obligations to prevent pollution of the seas, conduct environmental impact assessments, and provide legal remedies for transboundary harm.[61] UNCLOS is more ambiguous, though, about principles that developed after the 1970s. It does not clearly include a precautionary approach or require states to notify and consult about possible environmental risks. It only requires states to notify other affected states and international organizations if "the marine environment is in imminent danger of being damaged or has been damaged by pollution."[62]

UNCLOS also includes principles for balancing development and the environment. It says: "states have the sovereign right to exploit their natural resources pursuant to their environmental policies and in accordance with their duty to protect and preserve the marine environment."[63] UNCLOS emphasizes the concept of fairness across states by recognizing the concept of common but differentiated responsibility. Namely, it requires states "to prevent, reduce and control pollution," using "the best practicable means at their disposal and in accordance with their capabilities."[64] It also treats environmental protection as a process by including rules about planning, notification, and monitoring of environmental conditions. However, UNCLOS does not reflect fairness across time (i.e. intergenerational equity) or the view that human consumption must be offset via natural processes.

Another source of environmental rules are regional sea agreements, which have developed since the 1970s. These agreements currently cover eighteen different regional seas, including portions of the Atlantic and Pacific Oceans, as well as smaller bodies of water, like the Black Sea. Some regional seas have binding international treaties, while others have non-binding principles for cooperation. Each regional sea has an associated institution to promote environmental protection. For example, the Regional Organization for the Protection of Marine Environment (ROPME) has eight member states: Bahrain, Iran, Iraq, Kuwait, Oman, Qatar, Saudi Arabia, and the United Arab Emirates, shown in Figure 12.4. These states have worked from the 1970s to protect the ROPME Sea Area, which includes the Persian Gulf, the Sea of Oman, and part of the Arabian Sea. ROPME currently uses satellite technology to monitor sea temperatures, screens for water contamination, and raises public awareness of environmentalism. ROPME is governed by multiple regional treaties that regulate continental shelf exploitation, hazardous waste, and oil pollution.

Watercourses

States also use international law to protect international watercourses, which are shared freshwater resources. This law addresses land-based activities that can harm international watercourses. For example, agricultural and industrial production can release pollution into shared lakes and rivers, poisoning drinking water and limiting fishing and tourism. Customary international law requires that states prevent pollution into international watercourses because states have shared rights to use these resources.[65] A state can use international watercourses for commercial purposes if it does not harm the rights of other states.[66]

Regional treaties also create international watercourse rules. For example, regional agreements govern:

- the Rhine River, which is shared by France, Germany, the Netherlands, and Switzerland;
- the Great Lakes of Canada and the US;

Figure 12.4 ROPME Sea Area and its member states.
Source: Map drawn by author using QGIS. Data from Natural Earth and ROPME.

- the Zambezi Basin in Angola, Botswana, Malawi, Mozambique, Namibia, Tanzania, Zambia, and Zimbabwe; and
- the Mekong River Basin in Cambodia, Laos, Thailand and Vietnam.

Sometimes states disagree about how to interpret and apply these regional treaties. For example, recall the *Pulp Mills* dispute between Argentina and Uruguay described earlier in the chapter. Argentina sued Uruguay at the ICJ for authorizing the construction of two pulp mills along the Uruguay River, which is an international watercourse. This lawsuit was based on a 1975 bilateral agreement for the watercourse. Similar disputes have arisen between: Hungary and Slovakia over the Danube River; India and Pakistan over the Indus Basin; and Costa Rica and Nicaragua over the San Juan River.

Because watercourse disputes are common, the International Law Commission drafted the 1997 International Watercourses Convention to create consistent global rules. This treaty requires its members to use watercourses "in an equitable and reasonable manner."[67] Several factors can affect what is "equitable and reasonable," including:

- "geographic, ... climatic, ecological and other factors of a natural character";
- "the social and economic needs" of states; and

- "conservation, protection, development and economy of use of" watercourses.[68]

The concept of "equitable and reasonable" use reflects the idea that no state has absolute rights over an international watercourse. Rather, state rights must be carefully balanced.

The International Watercourses Convention also reinforces customary international law by requiring members to "take all appropriate measures to prevent the causing of significant harm to other watercourse states."[69] It also requires states to "protect and preserve the ecosystems of international watercourses."[70] Finally, it creates procedures for states to notify and communicate with each other about projects that may affect a watercourse, and to arbitrate disputes over watercourses.

Living Resources

Hundreds of treaties protect living resources, including animals and plants. Table 12.3 shows major living resource agreements. Early living resource agreements were motivated by economic concerns, as well as the recognition that animals are often fugitive resources, which move across the borders of states. By the 1960s and 1970s, states began to believe that living resources should be protected regardless of their economic value. Yet states did not support the protection of all living organisms. Developing states, in particular, wanted to preserve their right to development. As a compromise, states used two approaches in the 1970s to international agreements: site-based and species-based.

Table 12.3 Key Living Resource Agreements

Year	Name	Site-Based Approach	Species-Based Approach	General Approach
1971	Wetlands Convention	X		
1972	World Heritage Convention	X		
1973	Convention on International Trade in Endangered Species		X	
1979	Migratory Species Convention		X	
1982	UN Convention on the Law of the Sea	X		
1992	Biological Diversity Convention*			X
2000	Cartagena Protocol on Biosafety**			X
2010	Nagoya Protocol on Access and Benefit-sharing**			X

* Framework agreement.
** Protocol to the Biological Diversity Convention.

The site-based approach protects all living resources in a specific location. The first site-based treaty is the 1971 Wetlands Convention. After decades of advocacy by bird-watching groups, states pledged to protect selected wetlands, including flood plains, marshes, and swamps. This treaty only applies to sites chosen by states for protection, including wetlands along the San Juan River between Costa Rica and Nicaragua. After a border dispute between these two states, the ICJ ruled in 2015 on legal claims from the Wetlands Convention.[71]

Another site-based treaty is the 1972 World Heritage Convention, which aims to protect sites of "cultural or natural heritage."[72] Such sites include "precisely delineated natural areas of outstanding universal value from the point of view of science, conservation or natural beauty."[73] Environmental conservation is only one value that affects the choice of protected sites. Convention members work together to identify protected sites, which currently include:

- the Ancient Beech Forests of the Carpathians in Eastern Europe;
- the Great Barrier Reef in Australia;
- the Sundarbans mangrove forest in Bangladesh; and
- the Xinjiang Tianshan mountains in China.

States that promise to protect sites within their territory can receive financial assistance, providing a financial incentive to participate.

One final site-based agreement is the 1982 UN Convention on the Law of the Sea. UNCLOS does not create comprehensive rules for marine living resources, but it requires states to cooperate to conserve important fugitive resources, namely, marine mammals (including whales) and "highly migratory species" (including dolphins and swordfish).[74] UNCLOS also allocated property rights over regions that were previously in the high seas, thereby shrinking the global commons—that is, UNCLOS created exclusive economic zones, in which coastal states can regulate economic activities and natural resource conservation.[75]

In contrast, the species-based approach protects specific living resources, regardless of their location. One major species-based treaty is the 1973 Convention on International Trade in Endangered Species (CITES). This treaty—which says that "states are and should be the best protectors of their own wild fauna and flora"— does not contain rules about living resources within states.[76] Instead, it regulates the trade of living resources across states. CITES members periodically meet to decide which species are protected by these rules. Species that are currently protected under CITES include the bald eagle, the giant panda, and various rare orchids.

Another important species-based treaty is the 1979 Migratory Species Convention. This treaty focuses exclusively on fugitive resources—it covers endangered species of wild animals if "a significant portion of [them] cyclically and predictably cross one or more" borders.[77] Once again, treaty members periodically meet to decide which species are protected by these rules. Protected species include the cheetah, which migrates across Africa and central Asia, and the monarch butterfly, which migrates across North America.

After decades of writing site-based and species-based treaties, many states sought a more general approach that emphasized biological diversity. This term lacks a consistent and precise meaning, but biological diversity usually involves a series of linked causal claims:

1. Living resources are part of complex ecosystems.
2. Different interdependent ecosystems make up the earth.
3. Human activities (including habitation and pollution) disrupt ecosystems.
4. Therefore, a variety of sites and species should be protected.

These claims generate a variety of political demands, making international cooperation difficult.

One attempt at a general living resource agreement is the 1992 Biological Diversity Convention, which is a framework agreement. Its main objectives are: "the conservation of biological diversity, the sustainable use of its components and the fair and equitable sharing of the benefits ... of genetic resources."[78] The Convention includes two key principles. First, it says that the right to development includes the use of living resources. Second, it says that states have a "responsibility to ensure that activities within their jurisdiction or control do not cause damage to the environment of other states or of areas beyond the limits of national jurisdiction."[79] This statement is much broader than an obligation to compensate or prevent transboundary harm. The Convention additionally directs states to identify and monitor important biodiversity components. To uphold the Convention, states created an institution that meets regularly with assistance from the UN Environmental Programme.

States have negotiated two subsequent protocols to this framework agreement. First, the 2000 Cartagena Protocol on Biosafety contains rules for "living modified organisms," which it defines as organisms "that [possess] a novel combination of genetic material obtained through the use of modern biotechnology."[80] These include genetically modified crops, which some environmental advocates believe cause harm to biological diversity and human health. The Cartagena Protocol does not prohibit these organisms, but it requires states to follow certain procedures before moving such organisms across borders. While some states (including EU members) believe that these procedures are necessary to protect the environment and human health, other states (including the US) believe that they violate international trade law.

Second, the 2010 Nagoya Protocol on Access and Benefit-Sharing creates procedures to promote fairness and equity when states share genetic resources. For example, states that provide genetic resources can demand payments or intellectual property rights for medicines and vaccines that are developed using those resources. Many public health experts have warned that negotiating benefit-sharing agreements can cause major delays in developing and distributing medicines and vaccines.[81] Because the Nagoya Protocol has complicated implications for intellectual property rights, many states with important biotechnology and pharmaceutical industries—like Israel and the US—refuse to join the Nagoya Protocol.

12.4 Interaction with Other Areas of Law

Other areas of international law also affect the environment. These areas include trade, investment, human rights, and armed conflict law. We discuss each of these areas in turn.

Trade

International trade law promotes the free movement of goods and services across borders. Yet it also allows states to balance free trade against other competing values, including environmental protection. Almost every state now belongs to the World Trade Organization (WTO), whose main rules come from the 1947 General Agreement on Tariffs and Trade (GATT). In some circumstances, Article XX of the GATT allows states to adopt rules that restrict trade if these rules are:

(a) necessary to protect public morals;

(b) necessary to protect human, animal or plant life or health; ...

(g) relating to the conservation of exhaustible natural resources if such measures are made effective in conjunction with restrictions on domestic production or consumption ...

In the GATT's early decades, states usually privileged free trade over competing values. However, this balance changed in the 1990s. States now often restrict trade to protect the environment.

A key transition point was the *US–Shrimps* case. In the 1990s, US law classified all sea turtles as endangered or threatened species. Sea turtles were often killed when they became trapped in the nets used to harvest shrimp from the ocean. To help protect sea turtles, the US government passed laws that required shrimp harvesters to use special nets that allowed turtles to escape. The US government then banned shrimp imports from states that did not adopt similar rules. India, Malaysia, Pakistan, and Thailand sued the US at the WTO, arguing that the US violated international trade law. The US defended itself by invoking Article XX(g) of the GATT. Namely, the US argued that:

• sea turtles are "exhaustible natural resources" if they are endangered or threatened;

- the requirement of special shrimping nets "relat[ed] to the conservation of" sea turtles; and
- the trade restrictions were "made effective in conjunction with restrictions on domestic production" because the US required domestic shrimp harvesters to use the special nets.

The WTO ultimately ruled in this case that animals can be "exhaustible natural resources" and hence can be legitimately protected through trade restrictions.

However, international trade law does not give states the unfettered right to restrict trade under the guise of environmental protection. For example, China was a major producer in the 2010s of rare earth minerals, which are used to make many modern electronics, like laptop computers and cell phones. Rare earth mining can cause immense pollution, so most states had strict environmental regulations that made mining very expensive. In contrast, China had lax regulations that allowed immense environmental damage and low production costs, giving China control over the market for rare earth minerals.

After driving most other mining competitors out of business, China limited the export of rare earth minerals. China hoped that this trade restriction would induce foreign companies to manufacture more electronics in China. Multiple states sued China at the WTO, arguing that China's export restrictions violated the GATT.[82] China crafted a disingenuous defense: it argued that it was restricting exports because of the environmental effects of rare earth mining. However, the WTO ruled against China because it did not restrict "domestic production or consumption" of rare earth minerals, as required by Article XX(g)—that is, the WTO did not believe that Chinese trade restrictions were legitimate attempts to protect the environment. China's export restraints did not improve the environment; they simply forced technology companies to manufacture their goods in China so that they could access the necessary raw materials.

More recently, states have restricted trade to protect the environment by invoking the "public morals" exception in Article XX(a). In 2009, Canada and Norway sued the EU over rules that restricted imported products made from seals. Since seals are not an endangered species, the EU could not argue that its restrictions were "necessary to protect" seals or "relating to the conservation of exhaustible natural resources." Instead, the EU successfully argued that it was responding to "the moral concerns of the EU public with regard to the welfare of seals"[83]—that is, the EU successfully argued that products made from seals should be banned for moral reasons.

Investment

Environmental issues also sometimes arise in investment disputes. International investment law aims to promote capital investment from firms in one state into business activities in another state. To achieve this objective, investment treaties create legal rights for foreign investors. Most investment treaties require that host states provide foreign investors with "fair and equitable treatment." The meaning of this term has changed over time.[84] Yet relevant legal claims include:

- violations of due process in judicial and administrative proceedings;
- non-transparency about government policies and procedures;
- arbitrary, unreasonable, or discriminatory treatment;
- policy changes that violate the legitimate expectations about the regulatory environment; and
- acting in bad faith towards foreign firms.

The fair and equitable treatment standard is sometimes used to challenge environmental rules that harm foreign investors.

For example, the *Metalclad* case famously argued that environmental regulations can violate the rights of foreign investors if they are non-transparent. In this example, Metalclad, a US firm, purchased a site in Mexico for a hazardous waste landfill in 1993. Before making the purchase, Metalclad was told by both the federal and state governments that the previous Mexican owners had obtained all of the necessary permits and authorizations. Shortly after its purchase, Metalclad had problems with the local government, which was concerned about the environmental impact of the landfill. The local government insisted that Metalclad needed an additional construction permit to build the landfill, and then refused to issue this permit on environmental grounds. One major question in the dispute was whether the local government had the legal authority to require and issue such a construction permit.

An investment tribunal ruled that the lack of transparency about government regulations—namely, uncertainty about whether the additional permit was in fact required—violated Metalclad's right to fair and equitable treatment. The tribunal wrote:

> all relevant legal requirements for the purpose of initiating, completing and successfully operating investments ... should be capable of being readily known to all affected investors ... There should be no room for doubt or uncertainty on such matters.[85]

Therefore, the tribunal concluded, Mexico had violated international investment law. The *Metalclad* case was widely denounced by environmental activists, who believed that the US investors should not have been allowed to construct the landfill.

Yet other investment disputes have upheld environmental restrictions. For example, Glamis Gold was a foreign-owned firm that applied for permits in 1994 to dig gold and silver mines in the California desert of the US. Local indigenous groups opposed this mining project because many ceremonial paths and sacred sites were located nearby. While the permit was being reviewed, the California government created new regulations that required mines located near sacred indigenous sites to be refilled with soil after mining was completed. This new regulation reduced Glamis Gold's expected profits, although the mining project was still expected to be highly profitable.[86] Glamis Gold challenged the California regulations under international investment law. An international tribunal ultimately ruled against Glamis Gold, arguing that California had acted to achieve a legitimate government purpose, which was to protect land that had special religious and cultural significance. This ruling suggests that governments can limit foreign investment for environmental reasons if they write transparent regulations.

Human Rights

Different states have different beliefs about what is a human right. Most states agree that individuals have physical integrity rights, which include the prohibition of genocide, torture, and human trafficking. These rights are based on the principle of a right to life.[87] Environmental activists have invoked physical integrity rights to challenge governments at many international institutions.

For example, the American Convention on Human Rights does not explicitly mention the environment. Nonetheless, the Inter-American Commission on Human Rights has decided in numerous disputes that physical integrity rights require environmental protection. It explained:

> There is a direct relationship between the physical environment in which persons live and the rights to life, security, and physical integrity. These rights are directly affected when there are episodes or situations of deforestation, contamination of the water, pollution, or other types of environmental harm.[88]

This logic is common in cases involving indigenous groups.

Similarly, the European Convention on Human Rights includes the civil right that: "Everyone has the right to respect for his private and family life, his home and his correspondence."[89] This text is usually invoked to protect individual privacy. However, the European Court of Human Rights argued that the right to "private and family life" includes a right to well-being, and that states must protect individual well-being by preventing pollution even if individuals cannot prove that pollution is harmful.[90]

Environmental activists have also used international human rights law to challenge governments in domestic courts. For example, an NGO called the Urgenda Foundation sued the Netherlands government in Dutch courts over climate change policies. The Urgenda Foundation invoked the European Convention on Human Rights and numerous international law principles, including sustainable development and the precautionary approach.[91] It ultimately convinced Dutch courts that the government must take more aggressive action to prevent climate change.

Some treaties explicitly define environmental protection as a human right. For example, the African Charter on Human and Peoples' Rights says: "All peoples shall have the right to a general satisfactory environment favourable to their development."[92] Environmental activists used this treaty in numerous lawsuits to challenge oil drilling in the Niger Delta. One such lawsuit was heard by the court of the Economic Community of West African States (ECOWAS). In this case, an NGO argued that Nigeria was responsible for environmental damage caused by oil spills from pipelines, even though these pipelines were operated by foreign-owned businesses and damaged by private individuals. In its defense, Nigeria argued that it had passed extensive laws to regulate the oil industry and created government agencies to enforce these laws. Nonetheless, the ECOWAS court ruled that Nigeria had violated the African Charter. The ECOWAS court first argued that the "right to a general satisfactory environment" was an "obligation of result," meaning that environmental outcomes (rather than policies) mattered.[93] It then concluded that Nigeria had "defaulted in its duties in terms of vigilance and diligence" by failing to prevent oil spills and other environmental damage.[94]

Armed Conflict

The international law of armed conflict also affects the environment by constraining targets, methods, and weapons. One relevant legal principle is military necessity, which posits that force is only lawful if it is necessary to achieve a legitimate military objective. In the 1991 Gulf War, a US-led coalition fought to expel Iraqi troops from Kuwait. As Iraqi troops retreated, they set over 600 Kuwaiti oil wells on fire, causing massive air pollution.[95] Iraqi troops also released four to six million barrels of oil from a Kuwaiti facility into the Persian Gulf.[96] The UN General Assembly denounced these actions, saying: "destruction of the environment, not justified by military necessity and carried out wantonly, is clearly contrary to existing international law."[97] The Gulf War ceasefire held Iraq responsible for environmental damage and required that Iraq pay the cost of extinguishing the fires.[98]

Another relevant legal principle is proportionality, which says that force must be commensurate with a state's objectives. During the 1999 Kosovo intervention, NATO bombed several chemical plants and oil facilities, releasing pollutants. After the conflict, a Review Committee examined the legality of NATO's actions. In its report, the Committee argued that proportionality assessments should include environmental damage. It argued:

> Even when targeting admittedly legitimate military objectives, there is a need to avoid excessive long-term damage to the ... natural environment with a consequential adverse effect on the civilian population ... Military objectives should not be targeted if the attack is likely to cause collateral environmental damage which would be excessive in relation to the direct military advantage which the attack is expected to produce.[99]

Environmental concerns can thus affect the legality of targets and methods.

The environment can also affect the legality of weapons. In 1994, the UN General Assembly asked the ICJ: "Is the threat or use of nuclear weapons in any circumstance permitted under international law?"[100] In an advisory opinion, the ICJ examined many aspects of nuclear weapons, including their environmental impact. The ICJ wrote that "states must take environmental considerations into account when assessing what is necessary and proportionate."[101] It invoked the Rio Declaration, which says: "Warfare is inherently destructive of sustainable development. States shall therefore respect international law providing protection for the environment in times of armed conflict."[102]

Early treaties on armed conflict—including the Hague Conventions (1899/1907) and Geneva Conventions (1949)—do not mention the environment. However, both Hague and Geneva law prohibit pillage during war. The early interpretation of these treaties was that they only prohibited taking moveable property, like art, artifacts, and money. But international law has evolved over time, and pillage now includes taking natural resources, like diamonds, oil, and timber. In the *Armed Activities* case, the Democratic Republic of the Congo (DRC) sued Uganda at the ICJ for pillage during the Great African War of 1996–2003. After reviewing the evidence, the Court concluded that "officers and soldiers of the [Ugandan Army] were involved in the looting, plundering and exploitation of the DRC's natural resources."[103] The Court concluded that Uganda violated international law.[104]

More recent armed conflict treaties explicitly address the environment. For example, AP/I of 1977 included two important provisions on the environment. First, Article 35 says:

> It is prohibited to employ methods or means of warfare which are intended, or
> may be expected, to cause widespread, long-term and severe damage to the natural
> environment.

Second, Article 55 says:

> Care shall be taken in warfare to protect the natural environment against widespread,
> long-term and severe damage. This protection includes a prohibition of the use of
> methods or means of warfare which are intended or may be expected to cause such
> damage to the natural environment and thereby to prejudice the health or survival of
> the population.

While not all states have ratified AP/I, the ICJ argued in its 1996 Advisory Opinion on *Nuclear Weapons* that "these provisions embody a general obligation to protect the natural environment against widespread, long-term and severe environmental damage."[105] Some scholars interpret this statement as evidence that Articles 35 and 55 reflect customary international law, while other scholars argue that these rules only bind states that ratify AP/I.[106]

Additionally, the Environmental Modification Convention prohibits "any technique for changing—through the deliberate manipulation of natural processes—the dynamics, composition or structure of the Earth, including its biota, lithosphere, hydrosphere and atmosphere, or of outer space."[107] Some experts believe that this treaty only prohibits attempts to use natural phenomena—like earthquakes and tornados—as weapons.[108] Yet other experts believe that this Convention also prohibits using herbicides and destroying environmental resources during armed conflict.[109]

An international court has not yet interpreted these laws in a lawsuit. However, the Review Committee that investigated NATO's 1999 Kosovo intervention analyzed whether NATO violated AP/I. It argued that AP/I's standard of "widespread, long-term and severe damage" set a high threshold for legal violations. While NATO bombings increased environmental contamination, the Review Committee did not believe that the damage was significant enough to violate international law.[110]

12.5   Case Study Revisited: What About the Whales?

In our introductory case study, we described Japan's commercial whale hunt in 2019. Recall that Japan initially supported the 1946 International Convention for the Regulation of Whaling, which requires its members to manage whale stocks for their long-term survival. However, the International Whaling Commission banned commercial whaling in 1986 and only allowed whale hunts by indigenous communities and "for purposes of scientific research."[111] Japan continued to hunt whales, claiming that these hunts were "scientific research." However, the ICJ ruled in 2014 that many details of Japan's whaling program suggested that Japan was not hunting "for purposes of scientific research." This ruling prompted Japan to leave the treaty and resume commercial hunts.

This case study connects to each of the following topics:

- *Environment as a common resource*: Whales are a fugitive resource that travel across both national waters and the global commons of the high sea. Japan views whale hunting as a tragedy of the commons and believes that ICRW rules should allow whale hunts to continue for future generations. However, the 1986 ban reflected the changing views of other states about environmental protection. Japan continues to be bound by principles that are part of customary international law.
- *Protecting the environment*: Japan is no longer a member of the ICRW, but Table 12.4 shows that Japan is a member of many treaties that are relevant to whales. These rules may have implications for how Japan conducts whale hunts.

Table 12.4 Treaties Relevant to Whale Hunting			
Year	Treaty Name	Japan Ratification?	Relevance
1973	Convention on International Trade in Endangered Species	Yes	Protects species designated by members
1979	Migratory Species Convention	No	Protects species designated by members
1982	UN Convention on the Law of the Sea	Yes	Contains rules on "highly migratory species" and marine mammals
1992	Biological Diversity Convention	Yes	Urges protection of diverse ecosystems

- *Interaction with other areas of law*: Japan also belongs to trade, investment, human rights, and armed conflict treaties. Most of these rules aren't relevant to whale hunts. However, trade law affects whether other states can restrict imports of Japanese whale meat to deter hunting.

This information allows us to return to the big questions from our case study. First, we asked: do Japan's commercial whale hunts imply that it disdains whale protection? How you answer this question will probably depend on your views about the purpose of environmental law. If environment law exists to solve collaboration problems (like the tragedy of the commons), then whale hunting does not necessarily conflict with environmental protection. Japan carefully monitors whale stocks and limits where, how many, and what type of whales are killed. Perhaps ironically, Japan allowed fewer whales to be killed in the 2019 commercial hunts than it allowed under its ICRW whaling program.[112] However, if you believe that whales have inherent moral value, regardless of their economic value, then you may conclude that commercial whale hunting is fundamentally wrong and should be illegal.

Second, does Japan's exit from the ICRW mean that it can kill an unlimited number of whales, or does international law still constrain Japan? Like all states, Japan is bound by customary international law. Legal experts often debate which environmental principles are part of current customary international law. Most experts agree that transboundary harm is prohibited under customary international law. However, it is unclear whether Japan's commercial whale hunts create transboundary harm. No other state has been materially injured by Japanese whaling, although some states may claim to suffer moral injury. The 2001 draft articles by the International Law Commission define transboundary harm as including harm "to ... the environment."[113] Yet it is unclear whether this broad definition is part of customary international law, and whether Japanese whaling even satisfies this definition of harm.

Additionally, Japan is abiding by principles about balancing development against the environment, regardless of their status under customary international law. Japanese regulations are designed to ensure the long-term survival of whales, thereby ensuring intergenerational equity, the offset of human consumption via natural processes, and the consideration of environmental effects on economic policy-making. The principle of fairness across states might even support Japan's whaling policies. Common but differentiated responsibility was created to protect developing state interests. But Japan often argues that the special cultural and historical significance of whaling in Japan should allow it to behave differently than other states.

Three treaties continue to constrain Japanese whaling. First, Japan is a member of the Convention on International Trade in Endangered Species, which defines many whale species as endangered. However, recall that CITES regulates trade; it does not ban hunting. The CITES definition of "trade" includes "introduction from the sea."[114] CITES members agreed that this definition applies to "marine areas beyond the areas subject to the sovereignty" of members.[115] So hunting whales in the high seas qualifies as "trade" under CITES, but hunting in Japanese waters does not qualify. News coverage of Japan's current whale hunts suggests that Japan moved its hunts from the high seas inwards towards its territorial sea. For example, all of Japan's 2019 commercial whale hunts occurred within Japanese waters.[116]

Second, Japan belongs to the UN Convention on the Law of the Sea. Multiple UNCLOS provisions require states to conserve marine mammals and "highly migratory species," including many whales.[117] However, UNCLOS does not ban whaling. Whale hunts probably do not violate UNCLOS if they are based on careful scientific monitoring aimed at long-term survival.

Finally, Japan joined the 1992 Biological Diversity Convention, a framework agreement whose objectives include "the conservation of biological diversity [and] the sustainable use of its components." This treaty explicitly says that states have "the sovereign right to exploit their own resources pursuant to their own environmental policies."[118] Limited whale hunting is therefore probably allowed under this treaty. Overall, customary international law and treaty law suggest that while Japan cannot kill an unlimited number of whales, its commercial whale hunts probably do not violate international law.

One final question is: what tools can other states use to discourage commercial whale hunts? States that want to discourage Japanese whale hunts can limit whale meat imports under CITES and the GATT. However, trade restrictions would probably not matter because there is little international demand for whale meat.[119] Most Japanese citizens support whaling because of cultural pride; few of them actually eat whale meat.[120] One environmental activist even suggested that international

Figure 12.5 A young Japanese girl eats whale meat as part of her school lunch in 1993. Despite condemnation by environmental groups, whale hunting remains an important part of Japanese cultural heritage and is broadly supported by the Japanese public.

pressure is counterproductive because anti-whaling efforts "actually seem to increase Japanese support for whaling. There's this feeling about them like, 'Here are these Westerners coming to Japan and telling us our culture is wrong.'"[121] Ironically, if the international community stopped pressuring Japan to protect whales, the whales might be better-off.

Endnotes

Note: All URLs cited were accessed at time of writing.

1 COMPETING PERSPECTIVES ON INTERNATIONAL LAW AND POLITICS

1. Paris Climate Agreement (2015), Preamble and Article 3, respectively.
2. Ibid., Article 4(3).
3. Each state's voluntary contributions are available from the UN at https://unfccc.int/process-and-meetings/the-paris-agreement/nationally-determined-contributions-ndcs/nationally-determined-contributions-ndcs. A comparative analysis of contributions is available from Carbon Brief at www.carbonbrief.org/paris-2015-tracking-country-climate-pledges.
4. UN (2016), "The Paris Agreement: Frequently Asked Questions," September 12, available at www.un.org/sustainabledevelopment/blog/2016/09/the-paris-agreement-faqs/.
5. https://unfccc.int/files/meetings/paris_nov_2015/application/pdf/cop21cmp11_leaders_event_australia.pdf.
6. Narendra Modi (2015), "Statement by Prime Minister at COP 21 Plenary," November 30, available at https://unfccc.int/files/meetings/paris_nov_2015/application/pdf/cop21cmp11_leaders_event_india.pdf.
7. David J. Bederman (2001), *International Law in Antiquity*, Cambridge University Press; C.H. Alexandrowicz (2017), *The Law of Nations in a Global History*, edited by David Armitage and Jennifer Pitts, Oxford University Press.
8. Stephen C. Neff (2014), *Justice Among Nations: A History of International Law*, Harvard University Press, pp. 17–25.
9. Ibid., pp. 9–49.
10. Wilhelm G. Grewe (2000), *The Epochs of International Law*, translated by Michael Byers, Walter de Gruyter, p. 90.
11. Ibid., pp. 229–250.
12. Jordan Branch (2014), *The Cartographic State: Maps, Territory, and the Origins of Sovereignty*, Cambridge University Press.
13. Wilhelm G. Grewe (2000), *The Epochs of International Law*, translated by Michael Byers, Walter de Gruyter, pp. 327–332.
14. Stephen C. Neff (2014), *Justice Among Nations: A History of International Law*, Harvard University Press, pp. 179–205.
15. This body of law is also commonly referred to as "positive law." We use the term "voluntary law" because we believe that it more clearly conveys the meaning of the concept.
16. Arthur Nussbaum (1954), *A Concise History of the Law of Nations*, Macmillan, pp. 188–191.

17. Ibid., pp. 181–182, 222–224.
18. Quoted in Anthony Pagden (2013), *The Enlightenment*, Random House, p. 383.
19. John Austin (1832/1998), *The Province of Jurisprudence Determined*, Hackett Publishing, pp. 185–186.
20. Ibid., p. 201.
21. Ibid.
22. Stephen C. Neff (2014), *Justice Among Nations: A History of International Law*, Harvard University Press, pp. 243–249.
23. Martti Koskenniemi (2001), *The Gentle Civilizer of Nations*, Cambridge University Press.
24. Positivist writers include: Bluntschli (Switzerland), Calvo (Argentina), Fiore (Italy), Hall (UK), Heffter (Germany), Martens (Russia), Pradier-Fodéré (France), and Wheaton (US).
25. Edward Keene (2002), *Beyond the Anarchical Society*, Cambridge University Press.
26. Gerrit W. Gong (1984), *The Standard of "Civilization" in International Society*, Clarendon Press.
27. Ibid., pp. 130–163.
28. In contrast, this book focuses on public international law, which regulates interactions that involve at least one state.
29. Detlev F. Vagts (2000), "The Hague Conventions and Arms Control," *American Journal of International Law* 94: 31–41, at 32.
30. Arthur Nussbaum (1954), *A Concise History of the Law of Nations*, Macmillan, pp. 212–218.
31. Wilhelm G. Grewe (2000), *The Epochs of International Law*, translated by Michael Byers, Walter de Gruyter, pp. 517–524.
32. League of Nations Charter (1920), Preamble.
33. Susan Pedersen (2015), *The Guardians: The League of Nations and the Crisis of Empire*, Oxford University Press.
34. Unlike the Permanent Court of Arbitration, the Permanent Court of International Justice had sitting judges who decided disputes based upon legal arguments and provided written explanations for their decisions.
35. Brendan Karch (2013), "A Jewish 'Nature Preserve': League of Nations Minority Protections in Nazi Upper Silesia, 1933–1937," *Central European History* 46: 124–160; Greg Burgess (2016), *The League of Nations and the Refugees from Nazi Germany*, Bloomsbury Academic.
36. UN Charter (1945), Article 1(1).
37. UN Charter (1945), Article 76(b).
38. The scope of its authority to hear disputes is discussed in detail in Chapter 4.
39. Francis Fukuyama (1989), "The End of History?," *The National Interest* 16: 3–18, at 3.
40. See Chapter 5 for a more detailed discussion of this topic.
41. Leslie Johns, Krzysztof Pelc, and Rachel Wellhausen (2019), "How a Retreat from Global Economic Governance May Empower Business Interests," *Journal of Politics* 81: 731–738.
42. Hannah Arendt (1951), *The Origins of Totalitarianism*, Harcourt.
43. Hannah Arendt (1963), *Eichmann in Jerusalem*, Viking Press.
44. John Rawls (1971), *A Theory of Justice*, Harvard University Press.

45. Jürgen Habermas (1996), *Between Facts and Norms: Contributions to a Discourse Theory of Law and Democracy*, translated by W. Rehg, MIT Press.

46. Jürgen Habermas (1998), "Kant's Idea of Perpetual Peace: At Two Hundred Years' Historical Remove," in *Inclusion of the Other: Studies in Political Theory*, edited by Ciaran Cronin and Pablo De Greiff, MIT Press, pp. 165–201.

47. Quoted in Stephen C. Neff (2014), *Justice Among Nations: A History of International Law*, Harvard University Press, p. 368.

48. H.L.A. Hart (1961), *The Concept of Law*, Clarendon Press.

49. Stephen C. Neff (2014), *Justice Among Nations: A History of International Law*, Harvard University Press, pp. 415–422.

50. Arthur Nussbaum (1954), *A Concise History of the Law of Nations*, Macmillan, p. 283.

51. They include: Álvarez (Chile), Cançado Trindade (Brazil), Lauterpacht (Poland/UK), Simma (Germany), and Verdross (Austria). See Stephen C. Neff (2014), *Justice Among Nations: A History of International Law*, Harvard University Press, pp. 373–379, 452–458.

52. Stephen C. Neff (2014), *Justice Among Nations: A History of International Law*, Harvard University Press, p. 379.

53. These arguments are sometimes called liberalism, solidarism, or the sociological school of international law. We use the term "communitarian" because it conveys the influence of an international community.

54. Stephen C. Neff (2014), *Justice Among Nations: A History of International Law*, Harvard University Press, p. 424.

55. Harold D. Lasswell and Myres S. McDougal (1992), *Jurisprudence for a Free Society*, New Haven Press; Thomas M. Franck (1998), *Fairness in International Law and Institutions*, Oxford University Press.

56. Arthur Nussbaum (1954), *A Concise History of the Law of Nations*, Macmillan, p. 281.

57. Montevideo Convention (1933), Article 1.

58. This organization is also sometimes called the Palestinian National Authority.

59. ILC (2011), "Draft Articles on the Responsibility of International Organizations."

60. Rosalyn Higgins (1994), *Problems and Process: International Law and How We Use It*, Clarendon Press, p. 46.

61. ICJ, *Reparation for Injuries*, Advisory Opinion of 11 April 1949, p. 180.

62. Kathryn Bolkovac and Cari Lynn (2011), *The Whistleblower: Sex Trafficking, Military Contractors, and One Woman's Fight for Justice*, St. Martin's Press.

63. UN Document A/59/710.

64. Daphna Shraga (2000), "UN Peacekeeping Operations: Applicability of International Humanitarian Law and Responsibility for Operations-Related Damage," *American Journal of International Law* 94: 406–412.

65. Muna Ndulo (2009), "The United Nations Responses to the Sexual Abuse and Exploitation of Women and Girls by Peacekeepers during Peacekeeping Missions," *Berkeley Journal of International Law* 27: 127–161, at 152–157.

66. Gabrielle Simm (2011), "International Law as a Regulatory Framework for Sexual Crimes Committed by Peacekeepers," *Journal of Conflict & Security Law* 16: 473–506.

67. ICCPR (1966), Article 1(1); ICESCR (1966), Article 1(1).

68. Rosalyn Higgins (1994), *Problems and Process: International Law and How We Use It*, Clarendon Press, p. 113.

69. Ibid., p. 116.

70. Human Rights Committee, *Lubicon Lake Band* v. *Canada*, Communication No. 167/1984 (1990), para. 2.3.

71. Ibid., para. 32.1.

72. African Charter on Human and Peoples' Rights, Article 20(1).

73. Ibid., Article 21(1).

74. Ibid., Article 22(1).

75. Ibid., Article 20(1).

76. ACHPR, C*onstitutional Rights Project* v. *Nigeria*, Communication No. 102/93 (1998), paras. 52–53.

77. ACHPR, *Endorois* v. *Kenya*, Communication No. 276/2003 (2010), para. 3.

78. Ibid., paras. 13–14.

79. African Charter on Human and Peoples' Rights, Articles 21(1) and 22(1).

80. ACHPR, *Endorois* v. *Kenya*, Communication No. 276/2003 (2010), paras. 161, 268, and 298.

81. Rosalyn Higgins (1994), *Problems and Process: International Law and How We Use It*, Clarendon Press, p. 49.

82. Vienna Convention on Consular Relations (1963), Article 36(1)(b).

83. ICJ, *LaGrand*, Judgment of 27 June 2001, para. 76.

84. Ibid., para. 77.

85. Melissa J. Durkee (2017), "Industry Lobbying and 'Interest Blind' Access Norms at International Organizations," *AJIL Unbound* 111: 119–124.

86. Gregory C. Shaffer (2003), *Defending Interests: Public-Private Partnerships in WTO Litigation*, Washington, DC: Brookings Institution, pp. 140–141.

87. Leslie Johns and Krzysztof Pelc (2018), "Free-Riding on Enforcement in the WTO," *Journal of Politics* 80: 873–889.

88. Ryan Brutger (2019), "Litigation for Sale: Private Firms and WTO Dispute Escalation," UC Berkeley Working Paper.

89. Hyeran Jo (2015), *Compliant Rebels: Rebel Groups and International Law in World Politics*, Cambridge University Press; Jessica A. Stanton (2016), *Violence and Restraint in Civil War: Civilian Targeting in the Shadow of International Law*, Cambridge University Press.

90. Louis Henkin (1979), *How Nations Behave: Law and Foreign Policy*, Columbia University Press, p. 47 (emphasis removed).

91. George W. Downs, David M. Rocke, and Peter N. Barsoom (1996), "Is the Good News About Compliance Good News About Cooperation?," *International Organization* 50: 379–406, at 383.

92. Jack L. Goldsmith and Eric A. Posner (1999), "A Theory of Customary International Law," *University of Chicago Law Review* 66: 1113–1177, at 1122–1123.

93. Martti Koskenniemi (2005), *From Apology to Utopia*, Cambridge University Press.

94. Ian Hurd (2017), *How to Do Things with International Law*, Princeton University Press, p. 58.

95. UN Charter (1945), Article 2(4).

96. Jack L. Goldsmith and Eric A. Posner (1999), "A Theory of Customary International Law," *University of Chicago Law Review* 66: 1113–1177, at 1123–1124.

97. Efthymios Papastavridis (2011), "The Right of Visit on the High Seas in a Theoretical Perspective: *Mare Liberum* versus *Mare Clausum* Revisited," *Leiden Journal of International Law* 24: 45–69, at 50–51.

98. Andrew T. Guzman (2008), *How International Law Works*, Oxford University Press.

99. A coordination problem is sometimes called a "battle of the sexes."

100. A coordination problem is sometimes called a "prisoner's dilemma."

101. A commitment problem is sometimes called a "time-inconsistency problem."

102. Cosette D. Creamer and Beth A. Simmons (2020), "The Proof Is in the Process: Self-Reporting Under International Human Rights Treaties," *American Journal of International Law* 114: 1–50.

103. Judith G. Kelley (2017), *Scorecard Diplomacy: Grading States to Influence their Reputation and Behavior*, Cambridge University Press.

104. Judith G. Kelley (2017), "Case Study Supplement: A Closer Look at Outcomes," in *A Companion to Scorecard Diplomacy: Grading States to Influence their Reputation and Behavior*, Cambridge University Press, published online at www.scorecarddiplomacy.org/case-studies/.

105. Margaret E. Keck and Kathryn Sikkink (1998), *Activists beyond Borders: Advocacy Networks in International Politics*, Cornell University Press.

106. Beth A. Simmons (2009), *Mobilizing for Human Rights*, Cambridge University Press.

107. Xinyuan Dai (2007), *International Institutions and National Policies*, Cambridge University Press.

108. Xinyuan Dai (2005), "Why Comply? The Domestic Constituency Mechanism," *International Organization* 59: 363–398, at 378–384.

109. Ibid.

110. Paris Climate Agreement (2015), Preamble.

111. Amanda Kennard (2020), "The Enemy of My Enemy: When Firms Support Climate Change Regulation," *International Organization* 74: 187–221.

112. George W. Downs, David M. Rocke, and Peter N. Barsoom (1996), "Is the Good News About Compliance Good News About Cooperation?," *International Organization* 50: 379–406.

113. Lee Lane and David Montgomery (2009), "Organized Hypocrisy as a Tool of Climate Diplomacy," *American Enterprise Institute: Energy and Environment Outlook*, Report No. 5.

2 MAKING INTERNATIONAL LAW

1. Israel was believed to possess nuclear weapons in 1996, but had neither confirmed nor denied this. India conducted a minor nuclear test in 1974, but was not believed to have nuclear weapons in 1996. For the unilateral declarations, see Jonathan Medalia (2009), "Comprehensive Nuclear-Test-Ban Treaty: Background and Current Developments," *Congressional Research Service Report* #RL33548, pp. 2–8.

2. UNGA Resolution 50/245 (1996).

3. "North Korea Claims First Nuclear Test," *The Guardian*, October 9, 2006, available at www.theguardian.com/world/2006/oct/09/northkorea.

4. Ibid.

5. "N Korea's Nuclear Test Backlash," *Sydney Morning Herald*, October 10, 2006, available at www.smh.com.au/world/n-koreas-nuclear-test-backlash-20061010-gdok7d.html.

6. Preparatory Commission for the CTBT Organization (2017), "The CTBT Verification Regime: Monitoring the Earth for Nuclear Explosions," available at www.ctbto.org/fileadmin/user_upload/public_information/2017/Verification_Regime_final_2017.pdf.

7. Ibid.

8. Jack Moore (2016), "Ban Ki-moon's Full Statement on North Korea's Hydrogen Bomb Test," *Newsweek*, January 6, available at www.newsweek.com/read-transcript-ban-ki-moons-statement-north-koreas-hydrogen-bomb-test-412225.

9. Hugh Thirlway (2014), *The Sources of International Law*, Oxford University Press, p. 3.

10. VCLT (1969), Article 2(1)(a).

11. Prosper Weil (1983), "Towards Relative Normativity in International Law?," *American Journal of International Law* 77: 413–442, at 427.

12. VCLT (1969), Article 26.

13. José E. Alvarez (2005), *International Organizations as Law-Makers*, Oxford University Press, pp. 273–337.

14. UNGA Resolution 260 (1948).

15. VCLT (1969), Article 2(1)(b). We use the term ratification according to its meaning under international law.

16. Rome Statute (1998), Article 126(1).

17. CTBT (1996), Annex 2.

18. Masahiko Asada (2002), "CTBT: Legal Questions Arising from Its Non-Entry-Into-Force," *Journal of Conflict & Security Law* 7: 85–122, at 86.

19. Anthony Aust (2013), "Limping Treaties: Lessons from Multilateral Treaty-Making," *Netherlands International Law Review* 50: 243–266.

20. ICJ, *North Sea*, Judgment of 20 February 1969, para. 27.

21. Ibid.

22. Ibid., at 28.

23. H. Blix (1953), "The Requirement of Ratification," *British Yearbook of International Law* 30: 352–380; Edward T. Swaine (2003), "Unsigning," *Stanford Law Review* 55: 2061–2089.

24. ILC (1966), "Draft Articles on the Law of Treaties with Commentaries" (hereafter "ILC Commentary"), *Yearbook of the International Law Commission, 1966*, vol. II, p. 202.

25. VCLT (1969), Article 18.

26. Ibid.

27. David S. Jonas and Thomas N. Saunders (2010), "The Object and Purpose of a Treaty: Three Interpretive Methods," *Vanderbilt Journal of Transnational Law* 43: 565–609, at 598.

28. David S. Jonas (2007), "The Comprehensive Nuclear Test Ban Treaty: Current Legal Status in the United States and the Implications of a Nuclear Test Explosion," *New York University Journal of International Law and Politics* 39: 1007–1046, at 1039–1040.

29. Jan Klabbers (1997), "Some Problems Regarding the Object and Purpose of Treaties," *Finnish Yearbook of International Law* 8: 138–160, at 142.

30. Joni S. Charme (1991), "The Interim Obligation of Article 18 of the Vienna Convention on the Law of Treaties: Making Sense of an Enigma," *George Washington Journal of International Law and Economics* 25: 71–114, at 104–106.

31. See Jan Klabbers (2001), "How to Defeat a Treaty's Object and Purpose Pending Entry into Force: Toward Manifest Intent," *Vanderbilt Journal of Transnational Law* 34: 283–331.

32. Anthony Aust (2009), "The Comprehensive Nuclear-Test-Ban Treaty: The Problem of Entry into Force," *Japanese Yearbook of International Law* 52: 1–34, at 31.

33. Eric M. Meyer (2005), "International Law: The Compatibility of the Rome Statute of the International Criminal Court with the U.S. Bilateral Immunity Agreements Included in the American Servicemembers' Protection Act," *Oklahoma Law Review* 58: 97–133; Curtis A. Bradley (2009), "The Bush Administration and International Law: Too Much Lawyering and Too Little Diplomacy," *Duke Journal of Constitutional Law & Public Policy* 4: 57–75.

34. David S. Jonas (2007), "The Comprehensive Nuclear Test Ban Treaty: Current Legal Status in the United States and the Implications of a Nuclear Test Explosion," *New York University Journal of International Law and Politics* 39: 1007–1046, at 1044.

35. ICC Office of the Prosecutor (2016), "Report on Preliminary Examination Activities," November 14, paras. 146–191.

36. S.E. Nahlik (1971), "The Grounds of Invalidity and Termination of Treaties," *American Journal of International Law* 65: 736–756, at 744.

37. *The Fables of Phaedrus*, Book I.5.

38. Roozbeh B. Baker (2010), "Customary International Law in the 21st Century: Old Challenges and New Debates," *European Journal of International Law* 21: 173–204; Guilherme Del Negro (2017), "The Validity of Treaties Concluded under Coercion of the State: Sketching a TWAIL Critique," *European Journal of Legal Studies* 10: 39–60, at 48–50.

39. VCLT (1969), Articles 49–52.

40. Ibid., Article 48.

41. Herbert W. Briggs (1967), "Procedures for Establishing the Invalidity or Termination of Treaties under the International Law Commission's 1966 Draft Articles on the Law of Treaties," *American Journal of International Law* 61: 976–989, at 977.

42. Benedetto Conforti and Angelo Labella (1990), "Invalidity and Termination of Treaties: The Role of National Courts," *European Journal of International Law* 1: 44–66, at 51–52.

43. Omar M. Dajani (2012), "Contractualism in the Law of Treaties," *Michigan Journal of International Law* 34: 1–85.

44. Daniel Costelloe (2017), *Legal Consequences of Peremptory Norms in International Law*, Cambridge University Press, pp. 56–62.

45. VCLT (1969), Article 53.

46. Ibid.

47. J.F. Northey (1956), "Constitutional Limitations as Affecting the Validity of Treaties," *University of Toronto Law Journal* 11: 175–201.

48. VCLT (1969), Article 47.

49. Ibid., Article 46(1).

50. Quoted in Catherine J. Redgwell (1997), "Reservations to Treaties and Human Rights Committee General Comment No. 24(52)," *International & Comparative Law Quarterly* 46: 390–412, at 395.

51. VCLT (1969), Article 2(1)(d). Sometimes states also use the term "declaration" or "understanding" for the same purpose.

52. Jean Kyongun Koh (1982), "Reservations to Multilateral Treaties: How International Legal Doctrine Reflects World Vision," *Health Information and Libraries Journal* 23: 71–116.

53. ICJ, *Genocide*, Advisory Opinion of 28 May 1951, p. 24.

54. Ibid., p. 21.

55. Ibid., p. 26.

56. Ibid., p. 23.

57. Ibid.

58. Ibid.

59. UN Document A/66/10/Add.1, pp. 246–249, 391–393.

60. VCLT (1969), Article 19(c).

61. Ibid., Article 20. The historical record suggests that this ambiguity was intentional. See UN Document A/66/10/Add.1, pp. 246–249.

62. The ILC subsequently described the VCLT as "silent on how to deal with invalid reservations." See UN Document A/66/10/Add.1, p. 539.

63. IACHR, *Reservations*, Advisory Opinion of 24 September 1982, para. 29.

64. UN Document CCPR/C/21/Rev.1/Add.6, para. 7.

65. Ibid., para. 11.

66. Ibid., para. 12.

67. Ibid., para. 18.

68. Ibid.

69. Catherine J. Redgwell (1997), "Reservations to Treaties and Human Rights Committee General Comment No. 24(52)," *International & Comparative Law Quarterly* 46: 390–412, at 392.

70. UN Document A/50/40, p. 129.

71. UN Document A/51/40, p. 106.

72. UN Document A/50/40, p. 133.

73. Quoted in ECHR, *Loizidou*, Judgment of 23 March 1995, para. 27.

74. Ibid., para. 96.

75. UN Document A/66/10/Add.1, pp. 248, 256.

76. Other examples include the *Belilos* case at the ECHR and the *Benjamin* and *Constantine* cases at the IACHR.

77. UN Document A/66/10/Add.1, p. 394.

78. Ibid., p. 395.

79. Ibid., p. 26.

80. Ibid., p. 541.

81. Some scholars separate this process into two separate steps: interpretation and application. But we treat these as a unified process to simplify our discussion.

82. Abram Chayes and Antonia Handler Chayes (1995), *The New Sovereignty: Compliance with International Regulatory Agreements*, Harvard University Press, pp. 197–228.

83. Edward Gordon (1965), "The World Court and the Interpretation of Constitutive Treaties," *American Journal of International Law* 59: 794–833.

84. International Convention for the Regulation of Whaling (1946), Article VIII(1).

85. ICJ, *Whaling*, Judgment of 31 March 2014.

86. Itamar Mann (2018), "Maritime Legal Black Holes: Migration and Rightlessness in International Law," *European Journal of International Law* 29: 347–372.

87. Quoted in ICJ, *LaGrand*, Judgment of 27 June 2001, para. 100 (emphasis added).

88. Ibid.

89. Ibid., paras. 104–107.

90. Rome Statute (1998), Article 5(1).

91. Ibid., Article 9(1).

92. Leena Grover (2010), "A Call to Arms: Fundamental Dilemmas Confronting the Interpretation of Crimes in the Rome Statute of the International Criminal Court," *European Journal of International Law* 21: 543–583, at 563.

93. European Convention on Human Rights (1950), Article 4.

94. ECHR, *Rantsev*, Judgment of 7 January 2010. See also George Letsas (2010), "Strasbourg's Interpretive Ethic: Lessons for the International Lawyer," *European Journal of International Law* 21: 509–541.

95. Ian Hurd (2017), *How to Do Things with International Law*, Princeton University Press, pp. 7, 69. See also Anthea Roberts (2010), "Power and Persuasion in Investment Treaty Interpretation: The Dual Role of States," *American Journal of International Law* 104: 179–225, at 199.

96. Statute of the ICJ (1945), Article 38(1)(d).

97. ECHR, *Litwa*, Judgment of 4 April 2000, para. 7.

98. Julian Davis Mortenson (2013), "The *Travaux* of *Travaux*: Is the Vienna Convention Hostile to Drafting History?," *American Journal of International Law* 107: 780–822.

99. Georg Schwarzenberger (1968), "Myths and Realities in Treaty Interpretation," *Virginia Journal of International Law* 9: 1–19, at 13.

100. Edward Gordon (1965), "The World Court and the Interpretation of Constitutive Treaties," *American Journal of International Law* 59: 794–833, at 799.

101. Myers S. McDougal, Harold D. Lasswell, and James C. Miller (1994), *The Interpretation of International Agreements and World Public Order*, New Haven Press, pp. 45–60, 96–97.

102. Ibid., p. 99.

103. H. Lauterpacht (1949), "Restrictive Interpretation and the Principle of Effectiveness in the Interpretation of Treaties," *British Yearbook of International Law* 26: 48–85, at 52.

104. ECHR, *Litwa*, Judgment of 4 April 2000, para. 56.

105. Quoted in ibid., para. 63.

106. Poland prevailed on the interpretation of the word "alcoholic." However, Litwa won the case on other grounds.

107. Richard K. Gardiner (2015), *Treaty Interpretation*, Oxford University Press, p. 25.

108. Joost Pauwelyn and Manfred Elsig (2013), "The Politics of Treaty Interpretation: Variations and Explanations across International Tribunals," in *Interdisciplinary Perspectives*

on International Law and International Relations: The State of the Art, edited by Jeffrey L. Dunoff and Mark A. Pollack, Cambridge University Press, p. 451.

109. Anthony Gottlieb (2016), *The Dream of Reason: A History of Western Philosophy from the Greeks to the Renaissance*, W.W. Norton.

110. The method was not invoked in the *Litwa* judgment.

111. David S. Jonas and Thomas N. Saunders (2010), "The Object and Purpose of a Treaty: Three Interpretive Methods," *Vanderbilt Journal of Transnational Law* 43: 565–609, at 567.

112. ILC Commentary, p. 219.

113. Richard K. Gardiner (2015), *Treaty Interpretation*, Oxford University Press, p. 28.

114. Ibid.

115. ECHR, *Dudgeon*, Judgment of 22 October 1981, para. 60.

116. Christian Djeffal (2016), *Static and Evolutive Treaty Interpretation*, Cambridge University Press, pp. 214–343.

117. George Letsas (2010), "Strasbourg's Interpretive Ethic: Lessons for the International Lawyer," *European Journal of International Law* 21: 509–541, at 513–514, 523.

118. Joost Pauwelyn and Manfred Elsig (2013), "The Politics of Treaty Interpretation: Variations and Explanations across International Tribunals," in *Interdisciplinary Perspectives on International Law and International Relations: The State of the Art*, edited by Jeffrey L. Dunoff and Mark A. Pollack, Cambridge University Press, p. 454.

119. This approach is sometimes described as "restrictive interpretation" since it limits the impact of rules on states. However, in order to avoid confusion, we do not use this term, since a "restrictive interpretation" of rules is one which least restricts a state.

120. Quoted in ECHR, *Golder*, Judgment of 21 February 1975, para. 22.

121. Ibid., para. 35.

122. Luigi Crema (2010), "Disappearance and New Sightings of Restrictive Interpretation(s)," *European Journal of International Law* 21: 681–700, at 684–688.

123. Joost Pauwelyn and Manfred Elsig (2013), "The Politics of Treaty Interpretation: Variations and Explanations across International Tribunals," in *Interdisciplinary Perspectives on International Law and International Relations: The State of the Art*, edited by Jeffrey L. Dunoff and Mark A. Pollack, Cambridge University Press, p. 453.

124. Laurence R. Helfer (2005), "Exiting Treaties," *Virginia Law Review* 91: 1579–1648.

125. VCLT (1969), Part IV, Section 3.

126. Terence Neilan (2001), "Bush Pulls Out of ABM Treaty; Putin Calls Move a Mistake," *New York Times*, December 13, available at www.nytimes.com/2001/12/13/international/bush-pulls-out-of-abm-treaty-putin-calls-move-a-mistake.html.

127. Ibid.

128. VCLT (1969), Article 54.

129. Hugh Thirlway (2014), *The Sources of International Law*, Oxford University Press, pp. 42–44; Bruno Simma (1978), "Termination and Suspension of Treaties," *German Yearbook of International Law* 21: 74–96, at 93.

130. Quoted in Bruno Simma (1978), "Termination and Suspension of Treaties," *German Yearbook of International Law* 21: 74–96, at 92.

131. VCLT (1969), Article 60(3).

132. Ibid., Article 60(5).

133. Daniel Costelloe (2017), *Legal Consequences of Peremptory Norms in International Law*, Cambridge University Press, p. 110.

134. VCLT (1969), Article 61(1).

135. Ibid., Article 61(2).

136. ICJ, *Gabčikovo-Nagymaros*, Judgment of 25 September 1997, para. 102.

137. Quoted in Benedetto Conforti and Angelo Labella (1990), "Invalidity and Termination of Treaties: The Role of National Courts," *European Journal of International Law* 1: 44–66, at 59.

138. Niccolò Machiavelli (1981), *The Prince*, translated by Daniel Donno, Bantam Classic, p. 62.

139. For example, the 1502 Treaty of Perpetual Peace between Scotland and England only lasted until 1513.

140. Quoted in Jeremy Waldron (2006), "The Half-Life of Treaties: Waitangi, *Rebus Sic Stantibus*," *Otago Law Review* 11: 161–181, at 161.

141. Ibid.

142. Detlev F. Vagts (2005), "*Rebus* Revisited: Changed Circumstances in Treaty Law," *Columbia Journal of Transnational Law* 43: 459–476.

143. Albert H. Putney (1927), "The Termination of Unequal Treaties," *ASIL Proceedings* 21: 87–90.

144. Raymond L. Buell (1927), "The Termination of Unequal Treaties," *ASIL Proceedings* 21: 90–93, at 93; John Fischer Williams (1928), "The Permanence of Treaties: The Doctrine of *Rebus Sic Stantibus*, and Article 19 of the Covenant of the League," *American Journal of International Law* 22: 89–104.

145. Herbert W. Briggs (1942), "The Attorney General Invokes *Rebus Sic Stantibus*," *American Journal of International Law* 36: 89–96, at 89.

146. Ibid., p. 90.

147. Quoted in Jeremy Waldron (2006), "The Half-Life of Treaties: Waitangi, *Rebus Sic Stantibus*," *Otago Law Review* 11: 161–181, at 167.

148. VCLT (1969), Article 62.

149. Jeremy Waldron (2006), "The Half-Life of Treaties: Waitangi, *Rebus Sic Stantibus*," *Otago Law Review* 11: 161–181, at 168–169.

150. ECJ, *Racke*, Judgment of 16 June 1998, para. 20.

151. Emily Kadens (2016), "Custom's Past," in *Custom's Future*, edited by Curtis A. Bradley, Cambridge University Press, pp. 11–33.

152. Emily Kadens and Ernest A. Young (2013), "How Customary Is Customary International Law?," *William & Mary Law Review* 54: 885–920.

153. UN Document A/71/10, pp. 76–117.

154. ICJ, *Asylum*, Judgment of 20 November 1950, and *Haya de la Torre*, Judgment of 13 June 1951.

155. The details of how the equidistance method works are not important for our purposes.

156. UN Document A/71/10, p. 83.

157. Ibid., p. 90.

158. UN Document A/71/10, p. 77.

159. Ibid.

160. Ibid.

161. ICJ, *North Sea*, Judgment of 20 February 1969, para. 74 (emphasis added).

162. Emily Kadens and Ernest A. Young (2013), "How Customary Is Customary International Law?," *William & Mary Law Review* 54: 885–920.

163. ICJ, *North Sea*, Judgment of 20 February 1969, para. 74.

164. ICJ, *North Sea*, Dissenting Opinion of Judge Lachs of 20 February 1969, p. 230.

165. Emily Kadens and Ernest A. Young (2013), "How Customary Is Customary International Law?," *William & Mary Law Review* 54: 885–920.

166. ICJ, *North Sea*, Dissenting Opinion of Judge Lachs of 20 February 1969, p. 229.

167. Anthony D'Amato (1971), *The Concept of Custom in International Law*, Cornell University Press.

168. ICJ, *Right of Passage*, Judgment of 12 April 1960, p. 40.

169. Ibid., p. 43.

170. ICJ, *North Sea*, Judgment of 20 February 1969, para. 75.

171. ICJ, *North Sea*, Dissenting Opinion of Judge Lachs of 20 February 1969, p. 229.

172. Ibid., p. 227.

173. UN Document A/71/10, p. 95.

174. Charles de Visscher (1957), *Theory and Reality in Public International Law*, Princeton University Press, p. 149.

175. Ibid.

176. Ibid.

177. Ibid.

178. ICJ, *North Sea*, Judgment of 20 February 1969, para. 74 (emphasis added).

179. ICRC (2005), *Customary International Humanitarian Law*, edited by Jean-Marie Henckaerts and Louise Doswald-Beck, Cambridge University Press.

180. Shelly Aviv Yeini (2018), "The Specially-Affecting States Doctrine," *American Journal of International Law* 112: 244–253, at 246 (emphasis in original).

181. John B. Bellinger, III and William J. Haynes, II (2007), "A U.S. Government Response to the International Committee of the Red Cross Study, Customary International Humanitarian Law," *International Review of the Red Cross* 89: 443–471, at 445–446.

182. George Rodrigo Bandeira Galindo and Cesar Yip (2017), "Customary International Law and the Third World: Do Not Step on the Grass," *Chicago Journal of International Law* 16: 251–270, at 270 (emphasis in original).

183. UN Document A/71/10, pp. 91, 101.

184. Zhiguo Gao and Bing Bing Jia (2013), "The Nine-Dash Line in the South China Sea: History, Status, and Implications," *American Journal of International Law* 107: 98–123.

185. ICJ, *North Sea*, Dissenting Opinion of Judge Lachs of 20 February 1969, p. 229.

186. ICJ, *Nicaragua*, Judgment of 27 June 1986, para. 186.

187. ICJ, *North Sea*, Judgment of 20 February 1969, para. 77.

188. UN Document A/71/10, p. 77.

189. Ibid.

190. Ibid., pp. 77, 100–101.

191. See Chapter 1 for an overview of these perspectives.

192. Martti Koskenniemi (2001), *The Gentle Civilizer of Nations: The Rise and Fall of International Law 1870–1960*, Cambridge University Press.

193. Anthony Anghie (2005), *Imperialism, Sovereignty and the Making of International Law*, Cambridge University Press.

194. Ibid.

195. Arnulf Becker Lorca (2014), *Mestizo International Law: A Global Intellectual History 1842–1933*, Cambridge University Press.

196. Mohammed Bedjaoui (1979), *Towards a New International Economic Order*, Holmes & Meier.

197. ICJ, *Nuclear Disarmament*, Dissenting Opinion of Cançado Trindade of 5 October 2016, para. 304 (emphasis in original).

198. UN Document A/71/10, p. 77.

199. ICJ, *North Sea*, Dissenting Opinion of Judge Lachs of 20 February 1969, p. 231.

200. Anthony D'Amato (1971), *The Concept of Custom in International Law*, Cornell University Press, p. 97.

201. Hugo Grotius (1609/2004), *The Free Sea*, Liberty Fund.

202. Michael P. Scharf (2013), *Customary International Law in Times of Fundamental Change: Recognizing Grotian Moments*, Cambridge University Press, p. 116.

203. UN Document A/71/10, pp. 102–106.

204. Ibid., p. 103.

205. ICJ, *North Sea*, Judgment of 20 February 1969, para. 62.

206. Ibid. According to the International Law Association, "the number of states who had ratified or acceded [to the Geneva Convention at the time of the *North Sea* case] was 39 out of a possible total of over 130, of whom 26 were landlocked." See ILA (2000), p. 53.

207. ICJ, *North Sea*, Judgment of 20 February 1969, para. 76.

208. UN Document A/71/10, p. 98.

209. In theory, this discussion can apply to the acts of other international organizations. However, most legal scholarship has focused on the UN General Assembly because of its relatively long history and near-universal membership.

210. These included the ICJ's 1963 judgment in *Northern Cameroons* and its 1966 judgment in the *South West Africa* cases. See Leslie Johns (2015), *Strengthening International Courts: The Hidden Costs of Legalization*, University of Michigan Press, ch. 4.

211. Mohammed Bedjaoui (1979), *Towards a New International Economic Order*, Holmes & Meier.

212. Jorge Castañeda (1969), *Legal Effects of United Nations Resolutions*, Columbia University Press.

213. For example, see B.S. Chimni (2018), "Customary International Law: A Third World Perspective," *American Journal of International Law* 112: 1–46, at 26, 41.

214. Samuel A. Bleicher (1969), "The Legal Significance of General Assembly Resolutions," *American Journal of International Law* 63(3): 444–478; Jorge Castañeda (1969), *Legal Effects of United Nations Resolutions*, Columbia University Press, p. 171.

215. ILA (2000), p. 58.

216. UN Document A/71/10, p. 78.

217. UN Document A/CN.4/L.869, Draft Conclusion 15, para. 1.

218. James A. Green (2016), *The Persistent Objector Rule in International Law*, Oxford University Press, p. 2.

219. Ibid., pp. 33–56.

220. David A. Colson (1986), "How Persistent Must the Persistent Objector Be?," *Washington Law Review* 61: 957–970.

221. James A. Green (2016), *The Persistent Objector Rule in International Law*, Oxford University Press, pp. 118–120.

222. Patrick Dumberry (2010), "Incoherent and Ineffective: The Concept of Persistent Objector Revisited," *International & Comparative Law Quarterly* 59: 779–802.

223. Ted L. Stein (1985), "The Approach of the Different Drummer: The Principle of the Persistent Objector in International Law," *Health Information and Libraries Journal* 26: 457–482, at 467.

224. Quoted in Bin Cheng (1953), *General Principles of Law*, Stevens & Sons, p. 7.

225. PCIJ Statute, Article 38(3). See also Antony Anghie (2007), *Imperialism, Sovereignty and the Making of International Law*, Cambridge University Press.

226. ICJ, *Corfu Channel*, Judgment of 9 April 1949, p. 22.

227. Ibid.

228. Hersch Lauterpacht (1927), *Private Law Sources and Analogies of International Law*, Longmans, Green and Co.

229. Judge Simma invoked the principle of joint-and-several liability. See ICJ, *Oil Platforms*, Separate Opinion of Judge Simma of 12 December 1996, paras. 65–74.

230. Anthea Roberts (2017), *Is International Law International?*, Oxford University Press.

231. Percy E. Corbett (1961), "The Search for General Principles of Law," *Virginia Law Review* 47: 811–826, at 813.

232. ICJ, *Frontier Dispute*, Judgment of 22 December 1986, para. 150.

233. The ICJ did rule, however, that Uruguay had breached some procedural obligations in the bilateral treaty. See ICJ, *Pulp Mills*, Judgment of 20 April 2010.

234. ICJ, *Pulp Mills*, Separate Opinion of Judge Cançado Trindade of 20 April 2010, para. 52.

235. Ibid., para. 193.

236. M. Cherif Bassiouni (1990), "A Functional Approach to General Principles of International Law," *Michigan Journal of International Law* 11: 768–818.

237. ICJ, *Nuclear Tests*, Order of 22 June 1973.

238. ICJ, *Nuclear Tests*, Judgment of 20 December 1974, para. 43.

239. Recall that under Article 2 of the VCLT (1969), a treaty is "an international agreement concluded *between states* in *written* form and governed by international law" (emphasis added).

240. Hugh Thirlway (2014), *The Sources of International Law*, Oxford University Press, pp. 47–48.

241. Thomas Franck (1975), "Word Made Law: The Decision of the ICJ in the Nuclear Test Cases," *American Journal of International Law* 69: 612–620, at 617.

242. ICJ, *Nuclear Tests*, Judgment of 20 December 1974, para. 44.

243. Ibid., para. 46.

244. Hugh Thirlway (2014), *The Sources of International Law*, Oxford University Press, p. 48.

245. ILC (2006), "Guiding Principles Applicable to Unilateral Declarations of States Capable of Creating Legal Obligations," *Yearbook of the International Law Commission*, vol. II, part 2.

246. A detailed account of the trial is available in UN War Crimes Commission (1949), *Law Reports of Trials of War Criminals*, vol. X, HMSO.

247. United States Military Tribunal, *Krupp*, Ruling of 30 June 1948.

248. Ibid.

249. Emer de Vattel (1758/2008), *The Law of Nations*, translated by Thomas Nugent, Liberty Fund, Preliminaries, section 7 (emphasis removed).

250. Ibid., section 9.

251. Alfred von Verdross (1937), "Forbidden Treaties in International Law," *American Journal of International Law* 31: 571–577, at 574.

252. Alfred Verdross (1966), "*Jus Dispositivum* and *Jus Cogens* in International Law," *American Journal of International Law* 60: 55–63.

253. VCLT (1969), Article 53.

254. International law allows the use of force in self-defense or with UN Security Council authorization.

255. John Tasioulas (2016), "Custom, Jus Cogens, and Human Rights," in *Custom's Future*, edited by Curtis A. Bradley, Cambridge University Press, pp. 95–116.

256. Theodore Meron (1986), "On a Hierarchy of International Human Rights," *American Journal of International Law* 80: 1–23, at 17.

257. Martti Koskenniemi (2005), "International Law in Europe: Between Tradition and Renewal," *European Journal of International Law* 16: 113–124, at 116.

258. Egon Schwelb (1967), "Some Aspects of International *Jus Cogens* as Formulated by the International Law Commission," *American Journal of International Law* 61: 946–975, at 967.

259. In his English language writing, Verdross argued that states had a non-derogable right to protect their citizens abroad, but did not clarify that this entailed shielding them from international prosecution for war crimes. See Alfred von Verdross (1937), "Forbidden Treaties in International Law," *American Journal of International Law* 31: 571–577, at 576.

260. ICTY, *Furundžija*, Judgment of 10 December 1998, para. 153.

261. See Chapter 4.

262. ICJ, *Armed Activities–Rwanda*, Judgment of 3 February 2006.

263. UN Convention on the Law of the Sea (1982), Article 136.

264. Gennady M. Danilenko (1991), "International *Jus Cogens*: Issues of Law-Making," *European Journal of International Law* 2: 42–65, at 58–60.

265. Ibid.

266. Robert Kolb (2015), *Peremptory International Law–Jus Cogens*, Hart, p. 122.

267. Daniel Costelloe (2017), *Legal Consequences of Peremptory Norms in International Law*, Cambridge University Press, p. 16.

268. Jack Moore (2016), "Ban Ki-moon's Full Statement on North Korea's Hydrogen Bomb Test," *Newsweek*, January 6, available at www.newsweek.com/read-transcript-ban-ki-moons-statement-north-koreas-hydrogen-bomb-test-412225.

269. VCLT (1969), Article 53.

270. NPT (1968), Article X(1).

271. Ibid., Article X(2).

272. UN Document NPT/CONF.1995/32 (Part I), Annex.

273. Ryan Chorkey Burke (2011), "Losers Always Whine about their Test: American Nuclear Testing, International Law, and the International Court of Justice," *Georgia Journal of International & Comparative Law* 39: 341–364, at 354.

274. Alan E. Boyle (1990), "State Responsibility and International Liability for Injurious Consequences of Acts not Prohibited by International Law: A Necessary Distinction?," *International & Comparative Law Quarterly* 39(1): 1–26; Daniel Barstow Magraw (1986), "Transboundary Harm: The International Law Commission's Study of 'International Liability'," *American Journal of International Law* 80(2): 305–330.

3 BREAKING INTERNATIONAL LAW

1. Quoted in Ian Traynor (2007), "Russia Accused of Unleashing Cyberwar to Disable Estonia," *The Guardian*, May 16, available at www.theguardian.com/world/2007/may/17/topstories3.russia.
2. Ibid.
3. Michael N. Schmitt (2017), *Tallinn Manual 2.0 on the International Law Applicable to Cyber Operations*, Cambridge University Press, p. 11.
4. UNGA Resolution 56/83 (2001).
5. These critics argue that ILC texts should be considered "teachings of the most highly qualified publicists" under Article 38 of the ICJ Statute, and hence only a "subsidiary means for the determination of rules of law."
6. Malcolm N. Shaw (2014), *International Law*, Cambridge University Press, pp. 569–571.
7. ILC (2001), Draft Articles on the Responsibility of States for Internationally Wrongful Acts (hereafter "ARSIWA (2001)"), Article 4(1).
8. Quoted in ICSID, *Metalclad*, Award of 30 August 2000, para. 73.
9. ARSIWA (2001), Article 5.
10. IACHR, *Velásquez Rodríguez*, Judgment of 29 July 1988, paras. 169–170.
11. ARSIWA (2001), Article 8.
12. ICJ, *Nicaragua*, Judgment of 27 June 1986, para. 75.
13. Ibid., para. 86.
14. Ibid., para. 106.
15. Ibid., para. 115.
16. ICTY, *Tadić*, Judgment of 15 July 1999, para. 117.
17. Ibid., para. 131.
18. ICJ, *Bosnian Genocide*, Judgment of 26 February 2007, para. 406.
19. Antonio Cassese (2007), "The *Nicaragua* and *Tadić* Tests Revisited in Light of the ICJ Judgment on Genocide in Bosnia," *European Journal of International Law* 18: 649–668, at 654.
20. ARSIWA (2001), Article 11.
21. UN Document A/56/10, p. 53.
22. However, the ICJ ruled that Iran broke its obligations under international law by not providing adequate protection to the embassy during the initial attack.
23. ICJ, *Iran Hostages*, Judgment of 24 May 1980, paras. 71, 74.
24. An "excuse" is usually a factor that mitigates responsibility because of the capacity of the violator, while a "justification" is usually an exception to a rule that can be invoked by all persons. For example, murder is usually excused when committed by a child, and justified when committed in self-defense.
25. ARSIWA (2001), Article 20.
26. PCA, *Savarkar*, Award of 24 February 1911.
27. UN Document A/56/10, p. 73.
28. ARSIWA (2001), Article 21.
29. Ibid.
30. Arbitral Tribunal, *Air Services*, Decision of 9 December 1978.
31. Pierre-Hugues Verdier (2002), "International Relations, State Responsibility and the Problem of Custom," *Virginia Journal of International Law* 42: 839–867, at 858.

32. ARSIWA (2001), Article 23.

33. Ian Brownlie (2008), *Principles of Public International Law*, Oxford University Press, pp. 454–455, 466.

34. ARSIWA (2001), Article 24.

35. Emer de Vattel (1758/2008), *The Law of Nations*, translated by Thomas Nugent, Liberty Fund, Book II, Section 123.

36. King James Bible, Mark 2:23–28.

37. Krzysztof J. Pelc (2013), *Making and Bending International Rules: The Design of Exceptions and Escape Clauses in Trade Law*, Cambridge University Press, pp. 63–75.

38. ARSIWA (2001), Article 25.

39. UN Document A/CN.4/318/Add. 5–7, p. 28.

40. Ibid.

41. ICSID, *LG&E*, Decision of 3 October 2006, paras. 251, 257.

42. ICSID, *CMS*, Award of 12 May 2005, para. 355.

43. ARSIWA (2001), Article 30.

44. UN Document A/56/10, p. 89.

45. Dinah Shelton (2002), "Righting Wrongs: Reparations in the Articles on State Responsibility," *American Journal of International Law* 96: 833–856, at 839.

46. ARSIWA (2001), Article 30.

47. UN Document A/56/10, p. 90.

48. Ibid., p. 89.

49. Quoted in ICJ, *LaGrand*, Judgment of 27 June 2001, para. 10.

50. Quoted in ibid., para. 46.

51. Ibid., para. 48.

52. Ibid., para. 124.

53. Ibid.

54. ICJ, *Avena*, Judgment of 31 March 2004, para. 153.

55. PCIJ, *Chorzów*, Judgment of 13 September 1928, p. 29.

56. ARSIWA (2001), Article 31.

57. Dinah Shelton (2002), "Righting Wrongs: Reparations in the Articles on State Responsibility," *American Journal of International Law* 96: 833–856.

58. PCIJ, *Chorzów*, Judgment of 13 September 1928, p. 47.

59. ARSIWA (2001), Article 35.

60. Quoted in ICJ, *Avena*, Judgment of 31 March 2004, para. 117.

61. Ibid., para. 123.

62. Ibid., para. 131.

63. PCIJ, *Chorzów*, Judgment of 13 September 1928, p. 48.

64. Ibid., p. 47.

65. ARSIWA (2001), Article 36(1).

66. Dinah Shelton (2002), "Righting Wrongs: Reparations in the Articles on State Responsibility," *American Journal of International Law* 96: 833–856, at 845.

67. ICJ, *Corfu Channel*, Judgment of 9 April 1949, p. 26.

68. Ibid., p. 35.

69. ARSIWA (2001), Article 37.

70. Ibid. at 37(3).

71. John Austin (1832/1998), *The Province of Jurisprudence Determined*, Hackett, p. 10.

72. Ibid., p. 12 (emphasis in the original).

73. H.L.A. Hart (1961), *The Concept of Law*, Oxford University Press.

74. James H. Lebovic and Erik Voeten (2009), "The Cost of Shame: International Organizations, Foreign Aid, and Human Rights Norms Enforcement," *Journal of Peace Research* 46: 79–97.

75. Andrew T. Guzman (2008), *How International Law Works: A Rational Choice Theory*, Oxford University Press, p. 55.

76. Philip Allott (1988), "State Responsibility and the Unmaking of International Law," *Health Information and Libraries Journal* 29: 1–26, at 14.

77. ARSIWA (2001), Article 8.

78. ICTY, *Tadić*, Judgment of 15 July 1999, para. 131.

79. Ibid., para. 122.

80. Ibid., para. 117.

81. Scott J. Shackelford and Richard B. Andres (2011), "State Responsibility for Cyber Attacks: Competing Standards for a Growing Problem," *Georgetown Journal of International Law* 42: 971–1015, at 984.

82. Robert D. Sloane (2012), "On the Use and Abuse of Necessity in the Law of State Responsibility," *American Journal of International Law* 106: 447–508.

83. ICSID, *LG&E*, Decision of 3 October 2006, paras. 251, 257; ICSID, *CMS*, Award of 12 May 2005, para. 355.

84. Dinah Shelton (2002), "Righting Wrongs: Reparations in the Articles on State Responsibility," *American Journal of International Law* 96: 833–856, at 838.

85. John K. Setear (1997), "Responses to Breach of a Treaty and Rationalist International Relations Theory: The Rules of Release and Remediation in the Law of Treaties and the Law of State Responsibility," *Virginia Law Review* 83(1): 1–126, at 70; Dinah Shelton (2002), "Righting Wrongs: Reparations in the Articles on State Responsibility," *American Journal of International Law* 96: 833–856, at 837; Pierre-Hugues Verdier (2002), "International Relations, State Responsibility and the Problem of Custom," *Virginia Journal of International Law* 42: 839–867.

86. The most developed version of this perspective comes from Abram Chayes and Antonia Handler Chayes (1993), "On Compliance," *International Organization* 47: 175–205; Abram Chayes and Antonia Handler Chayes (1995), *The New Sovereignty: Compliance with International Regulatory Agreements*, Harvard University Press.

87. Louis Henkin (1979), *How Nations Behave: Law and Foreign Policy*, Columbia University Press, p. 47 (emphasis in original).

88. George W. Downs, David M. Rocke, and Peter N. Barsoom (1996), "Is the Good News about Compliance Good News about Cooperation?," *International Organization* 50: 379–406.

89. Thomas M. Franck (1990), *The Power of Legitimacy Among Nations*, Oxford University Press; Thomas M. Franck (1998), *Fairness in International Law and Institutions*, Oxford University Press.

90. A. Burcu Bayram (2017), "Due Deference: Cosmopolitan Social Identity and the Psychology of Legal Obligation in International Politics," *International Organization* 71: S137–S163.

91. UK Ministry of Defence (2004), *The Manual of the Law of Armed Conflict*, Oxford University Press, Preface, p. vii.

92. Ben Westcott (2017), "Reluctant Signatory India Takes Moral High-Ground on Paris Climate Deal," *CNN*, June 2, available at www.cnn.com/2017/06/02/asia/india-paris-agreement-trump/index.html.

93. Natalie P. Stoianoff (2012), "The Influence of the WTO over China's Intellectual Property Regime," *Sydney Law Review* 34: 65–89.

94. Xuan-Thao Nguyen (2011), "The China We Hardly Know: Revealing the New China's Intellectual Property Regime," *Saint Louis University Law Journal* 55: 773–810.

95. Ibid. (emphasis removed).

96. ICJ, *Bosnian Genocide*, Judgment of 26 February 2007, para. 406.

97. Abram Chayes and Antonia Handler Chayes (1995), *The New Sovereignty: Compliance with International Regulatory Agreements*, Harvard University Press, p. 33.

98. B. Peter Rosendorff and Helen V. Milner (2001), "The Optimal Design of International Trade Institutions: Uncertainty and Escape," *International Organization* 55: 829–857; B. Peter Rosendorff (2005), "Stability and Rigidity: Politics and the Design of the WTO's Dispute Resolution Procedure," *American Political Science Review* 99: 389–400.

99. Leslie Johns and B. Peter Rosendorff (2009), "Dispute Settlement, Compliance and Domestic Politics," in *Trade Disputes and the Dispute Settlement Understanding of the WTO: An Interdisciplinary Assessment*, edited by James C. Hartigan, Emerald Group, pp. 139–163.

100. Laurence R. Helfer (2005), "Exiting Treaties," *Virginia Law Review* 91: 1579–1648.

101. Leslie Johns (2015), *Strengthening International Courts: The Hidden Costs of Legalization*, University of Michigan Press.

102. Emilie M. Hafner-Burton, Laurence R. Helfer, and Christopher J. Fariss (2011), "Emergency and Escape: Explaining Derogations from Human Rights Treaties," *International Organization* 65: 673–707.

103. Leslie Johns (2014), "Depth versus Rigidity in the Design of International Trade Agreements," *Journal of Theoretical Politics* 26: 468–495; B. Peter Rosendorff (2005), "Stability and Rigidity: Politics and the Design of the WTO's Dispute Resolution Procedure," *American Political Science Review* 99: 389–400.

104. Warren F. Schwartz and Alan O. Sykes (2002), "The Economic Structure of Renegotiation and Dispute Resolution in the World Trade Organization," *Journal of Legal Studies* 31: S179–S204.

105. Leslie Johns (2019), "The Design of Enforcement: Collective Action and the Enforcement of International Law," *Journal of Theoretical Politics* 31: 543–567.

106. ARSIWA (2001), Article 25(1).

107. Ibid., Article (2)(b).

108. Rachel Brewster (2013), "Pricing Compliance: When Formal Remedies Displace Reputational Sanctions," *Health Information and Libraries Journal* 54: 259–314.

109. Michael N. Schmitt (2017), *Tallinn Manual 2.0 on the International Law Applicable to Cyber Operations*, Cambridge University Press, p. 382.

110. Scott J. Shackelford and Richard B. Andres (2011), "State Responsibility for Cyber Attacks: Competing Standards for a Growing Problem," *Georgetown Journal of International Law* 42: 971–1015, at 975.

111. Michael N. Schmitt (2017), *Tallinn Manual 2.0 on the International Law Applicable to Cyber Operations*, Cambridge University Press, p. 376.

112. Briefing (2010), "Cyberwar: War in the Fifth Domain," *The Economist*, July 3, available at www.economist.com/briefing/2010/07/01/war-in-the-fifth-domain.

113. David E. Sanger (2012), "Obama Ordered Sped Up Wave of Cyberattacks Against Iran," *New York Times*, June 1, available at www.nytimes.com/2012/06/01/world/middleeast/obama-ordered-wave-of-cyberattacks-against-iran.html.

4   UPHOLDING INTERNATIONAL LAW

1. ITLOS, *ARA Libertad*, Ghana Response of 28 November 2012, para. 3.

2. Jacob Goldstein (2012), "Why a Hedge Fund Seized an Argentine Navy Ship in Ghana," *NPR News*, October 22, available at www.npr.org/sections/money/2012/10/22/163384810/why-a-hedge-fund-seized-an-argentine-navy-ship-in-ghana.

3. ITLOS, *ARA Libertad*, Order of 15 December 2012, para. 108.

4. Leslie Johns (2015), *Strengthening International Courts: The Hidden Costs of Legalization*, University of Michigan Press, pp. 93–95.

5. The Court occasionally uses the term "interim measures" or "preliminary measures."

6. ICJ, *Myanmar Genocide*, Order of 23 January 2020, para. 86.

7. Two other stages exist, but are uncommon—the Court can assess reparations, and can reinterpret or revise an earlier judgment.

8. These unilateral declarations are allowed under Article 36(2) of the ICJ Statute, which is sometimes called the "Optional Clause." Such declarations are sometimes described as acceptance of "compulsory jurisdiction" (despite the fact that these declarations are optional). We use the term "unilateral declaration" because we believe that it more clearly and accurately describes how Article 36(2) operates.

9. Leslie Johns (2015), *Strengthening International Courts: The Hidden Costs of Legalization*, University of Michigan Press, pp. 26–27.

10. Quoted in ibid., p. 26.

11. ICJ, *Monetary Gold*, Judgment of 15 June 1954.

12. ICJ, *East Timor*, Judgment of 30 June 1995. An added complication was that East Timor wanted independence, which it ultimately received in 2002.

13. Leslie Johns (2015), *Strengthening International Courts: The Hidden Costs of Legalization*, University of Michigan Press, pp. 27–31.

14. ICJ, *Reparation for Injuries*, Advisory Opinion of 11 April 1949, pp. 181–182.

15. ICJ, *Barcelona Traction*, Judgment of 5 February 1970.

16. CERD, Article 22.

17. ICJ, *South Ossetia and Abkhazia*, Judgment of 1 April 2011.

18. ICJ, *Nuclear Disarmament*, Judgment of 5 October 2016.

19. Leslie Johns, Calvin Thrall, and Rachel Wellhausen (2020), "Judicial Economy and Moving Bars in International Investment Arbitration," *Research Ideas and Outcomes* 15: 923–945.

20. ICJ, *Barcelona Traction*, Judgment of 5 February 1970, para. 64.

21. ICJ, *Northern Cameroons*, Judgment of 2 December 1963, p. 37.

22. PCIJ, *Mavrommatis*, Judgment of 30 August 1924, p. 12.

23. PCA, *Arctic Sunrise*, Award of 14 August 2015, paras. 159–175.

24. ICJ, *Barcelona Traction*, Judgment of 5 February 1970, para. 78.

25. Antônio Augusto Cançado Trindade (2011), *The Access of Individuals to International Justice*, Oxford University Press, p. 6.

26. This territory is now Namibia. For a broader discussion of this dispute, see Leslie Johns (2015), *Strengthening International Courts: The Hidden Costs of Legalization*, University of Michigan Press, pp. 87–92.

27. Ibid., p. 90.

28. ICJ, *South West Africa*, Judgment of 18 July 1966, para. 33.

29. Bruno Simma (1994), "From Bilateralism to Community Interest in International Law," *Recueil des Cours* 250: 217–384.

30. Some treaties refer to *erga omnes partes* obligations, which is a concept that we do not address here.

31. ICJ, *Barcelona Traction*, Judgment of 5 February 1970, paras. 33–34.

32. Some judges have also mentioned the use of force and environment protection.

33. VCLT (1969), Article 53.

34. Bruno Simma (1994), "From Bilateralism to Community Interest in International Law," *Recueil des Cours* 250: 217–384, at 300.

35. See Chapter 2.

36. Christian J. Tams (2005), *Enforcing Obligations Erga Omnes in International Law*, Cambridge University Press, pp. 117–157.

37. Ibid., p. 101.

38. ICJ, *Barcelona Traction*, Judgment of 5 February 1970, para. 33. See also ICJ, *Chagos Archipelago*, Advisory Opinion of 25 February 2019, para. 180.

39. ICJ, *Namibia*, Advisory Opinion of 21 June 1971.

40. ICJ, *Nuclear Weapons*, Advisory Opinion of 8 July 1996, para. 1.

41. ICJ, *Israeli Wall*, Advisory Opinion of 9 July 2004, para. 1.

42. ICJ, *Chagos Archipelago*, Advisory Opinion of 25 February 2019, para. 1.

43. Cedric Ryngaert (2015), *Jurisdiction in International Law*, Oxford University Press.

44. Ibid., pp. 104–110.

45. Ibid., pp. 110–113.

46. Ibid., p. 114.

47. This concept is also discussed in Chapter 11.

48. 28 U.S.C. §1350.

49. Leslie Johns (2018), "The Diverging Theory and Practice of International Law," in *Encyclopedia of Empirical International Relations Theory*, edited by William R. Thompson, Oxford University Press, pp. 513–535.

50. 28 U.S.C. §2333.

51. Naomi Roht-Arrioza (2005), *The Pinochet Effect*, University of Pennsylvania Press.

52. ICJ, *Jurisdictional Immunities*, Judgment of 3 February 2012, para. 57.

53. Ibid.

54. US Supreme Court (1922), *The Sao Vicente*, 260 U.S. 151, 153.

55. Xiaodong Yang (2012), *State Immunity in International Law*, Cambridge University Press, pp. 75–131.

56. Ibid.

57. Some states also do not recognize state immunity for personal injury or property damage.

58. Pierre-Hugues Verdier and Erik Voeten (2015), "How Does Customary International Law Change? The Case of State Immunity," *International Studies Quarterly* 59: 209–222, at 211.

59. Udaibir S. Das, Michael G. Papaioannou, and Christoph Trebesch (2012), "Sovereign Debt Restructurings 1950–2010: Literature Survey, Data, and Stylized Facts," International Monetary Fund Working Paper #WP/12/203.

60. Leslie Johns (2018), "The Diverging Theory and Practice of International Law," in *Encyclopedia of Empirical International Relations Theory*, edited by William R. Thompson, Oxford University Press, pp. 513–535.

61. W. Mark C. Weidemaier (2014), "Sovereign Immunity and Sovereign Debt," *University of Illinois Law Review* 2014: 67–112.

62. Only eight states have ratified the European Convention and twenty-two states have ratified the UN Convention. While the European Convention has entered into force, the UN Convention has not.

63. Xiaodong Yang (2012), *State Immunity in International Law*, Cambridge University Press, pp. 12–13.

64. Neither state had joined the European Convention on State Immunity (1972) or the UN Convention on Jurisdictional Immunities (2004).

65. ICJ, *Jurisdictional Immunities*, Judgment of 3 February 2012, para. 60.

66. ICJ, *Iran Hostages*, Judgment of 24 May 1980, paras. 61, 66.

67. UK Law Lords, *Pinochet*, Judgment of 25 November 1998.

68. ICJ, *Arrest Warrant*, Judgment of 14 February 2002, para. 49.

69. Ibid., paras. 51, 53.

70. Ibid., paras. 54–55.

71. Leslie Johns (2012), "Courts as Coordinators: Endogenous Enforcement and Jurisdiction in International Adjudication," *Journal of Conflict Resolution* 56: 257–289.

72. ICJ, *Iran Hostages*, Judgment of 24 May 1980.

73. Edmund Blair (2016), "Exclusive: EU Takes Aim Where it Hurts Burundi: Peacekeeper Funding," *Reuters*, March 28, available at www.reuters.com/article/us-burundi-security-eu/exclusive-eu-takes-aim-where-it-hurts-burundi-peacekeeper-funding-idUSKCN0WV0BD.

74. ICJ, *Nuclear Tests*, Order of 22 June 1973.

75. See Chapter 3. Some institutions, like the European Union, prohibit countermeasures to uphold their rules.

76. Arbitral Tribunal, *Air Services*, Decision of 9 December 1978.

77. ARSIWA (2001).

78. Ibid., Article 49.

79. Ibid., Article 50(1).

80. Ibid., Article 50(2).

81. Ibid., Article 49.

82. This concept also appears in international law on the use of force and armed conflict.

83. Quoted in David J. Bederman (2001), "Counterintuiting Countermeasures," *American Journal of International Law* 96: 817–832, at 820.

84. Ibid.; ARSIWA (2001), Article 51.

85. *ARSIWA*, Article 52(1)(a).

86. Ibid., Article 52(1)(b).

87. Ibid., Article 52(3)–(4).

88. Other states supported the blockade, but did not participate in it. See Anne Barnard and David D. Kirkpatrick (2017), "Five Arab Nations Move to Isolate Qatar, Putting the U.S. in a Bind," *New York Times*, June 5, available at www.nytimes.com/2017/06/05/world/middleeast/qatar-saudi-arabia-egypt-bahrain-united-arab-emirates.html.

89. Quoted in Patrick Wintour (2017), "Qatar given 10 days to meet 13 sweeping demands by Saudi Arabia," *The Guardian*, June 23, available at www.theguardian.com/world/2017/jun/23/close-al-jazeera-saudi-arabia-issues-qatar-with-13-demands-to-end-blockade.

90. Hugo Grotius (1625/2005), *The Rights of War and Peace*, Book II, p. 1021.

91. Emer de Vattel (1758/2008), *The Law of Nations*, Liberty Fund, p. 462.

92. Prosper Weil (1983), "Towards Relative Normativity in International Law," *American Journal of International Law* 77: 413–442, at 431.

93. ARSIWA (2001), Article 48(1).

94. Ibid., Article 54.

95. Christian J. Tams (2005), *Enforcing Obligations Erga Omnes in International Law*, Cambridge University Press, pp. 90, 217–218.

96. ICJ, *Chagos Archipelago*, Advisory Opinion of 25 February 2019, para. 180.

97. Craig Eggett and Sarah Thin (2019), "Clarification and Conflation: Obligations Erga Omnes in the Chagos Opinion," *EJIL:Talk!*, May 21, available at www.ejiltalk.org/clarification-and-conflation-obligations-erga-omnes-in-the-chagos-opinion/.

98. Edward Keene (2002), *Beyond the Anarchical Society*, Cambridge University Press.

99. Gerrit W. Gong (1984), *The Standard of "Civilization" in International Society*, Oxford University Press.

100. Alastair Ian Johnston (2001), "Treating International Institutions as Social Environments," *International Studies Quarterly* 45: 487–515, at 494.

101. Margaret E. Keck and Kathryn Sikkink (1998), *Activists Beyond Borders: Advocacy Networks in International Politics*, Cornell University Press.

102. Martha Finnemore (1996), "Norms, Culture, and World Politics: Insights from Sociology's Institutionalism," *International Organization* 50: 325–347.

103. Antony Anghie (2005), *Imperialism, Sovereignty and the Making of International Law*, Cambridge University Press.

104. UNGA Resolution 3379 (1975).

105. Scholars sometimes describe these grades as global performance indicators.

106. Kevin E. Davis, Benedict Kingsbury, and Sally Engle Merry (2012), "Indicators as a Technology of Global Governance," *Law & Society Review* 46: 71–104, at 77.

107. See Chapter 8.

108. Cosette D. Creamer and Beth A. Simmons (2018), "The Dynamic Impact of Periodic Review on Women's Rights," *Law & Contemporary Problems* 81: 31–72.

109. Judith G. Kelley (2017), *Scorecard Diplomacy*, Cambridge University Press, pp. 214–218.

110. Rush Doshi, Judith G. Kelley, and Beth A. Simmons (2019), "The Power of Ranking: The Ease of Doing Business Indicator and Global Regulatory Behavior," *International Organization* 73: 611–643.

111. Judith G. Kelley (2017), *Scorecard Diplomacy*, Cambridge University Press, p. 81.

112. Julia C. Morse (2019), "Blacklists, Market Enforcement, and the Global Regime to Combat Terrorist Financing," *International Organization* 73: 511–545.

113. Quoted in Emilie M. Hafner-Burton (2008), "Sticks and Stones: Naming and Shaming the Human Rights Enforcement Problem," *International Organization* 62: 689–716, at 693.

114. UN Charter (1945), Article 24(1).

115. The Council was created in 2006 as the successor to the UN Commission on Human Rights. To avoid confusion, we use this institution's modern name.

116. James H. Lebovic and Erik Voeten (2009), "The Cost of Shame: International Organizations, Foreign Aid, and Human Rights Norms Enforcement," *Journal of Peace Research* 46: 79–97.

117. Timothy M. Peterson, Amanda Murdie, and Victor Asal (2018), "Human Rights NGO Shaming and the Exports of Abusive States," *British Journal for the Philosophy of Science* 48: 767–786; Colin M. Barry, K. Chad Clay, and Michael E. Flynn (2013), "Avoiding the Spotlight: Human Rights Shaming and Foreign Direct Investment," *International Studies Quarterly* 57: 532–544.

118. Rochelle Terman and Erik Voeten (2018), "The Relational Politics of Shame: Evidence from the Universal Periodic Review," *Research Ideas and Outcomes* 13: 1–23.

119. James Meernik, Rosa Aloisi, Marsha Sowell, and Angela Nichols (2012), "The Impact of Human Rights Organizations on Naming and Shaming Campaigns," *Journal of Conflict Resolution* 56: 233–256.

120. Therese O'Donnell (2007), "Naming and Shaming: The Sorry Tale of Security Council Resolution 1530 (2004)," *European Journal of International Law* 17: 945–968.

121. Emilie M. Hafner-Burton (2008), "Sticks and Stones: Naming and Shaming the Human Rights Enforcement Problem," *International Organization* 62: 689–716, at 693.

122. Lora DiBlasio (2020), "From Shame to New Name: How Naming and Shaming Creates Pro-Government Militias," *International Studies Quarterly* 64: 906–918.

123. Doug Bandow (2013), "Supreme Court Moves Us Closer to Holding Deadbeat Argentina Accountable," *Forbes*, October 21, available at www.forbes.com/sites/dougbandow/2013/10/21/supreme-court-moves-us-closer-to-holding-deadbeat-argentina-accountable/?sh=30a66f6b6dce.

124. Alexandra Stevenson (2016), "Judge Deals Setback to Holdouts in Negotiations with Argentina," *New York Times*, February 19, available at www.nytimes.com/2016/02/20/business/dealbook/judge-deals-setback-to-holdouts-in-negotiations-with-argentina.html?_r=0.

125. Some investors filed arbitration cases against Argentina, which are mentioned in other chapters.

126. Leah McGrath Goodman (2014), "After a Decade of Bad Blood with Bondholders, Argentina Faces Default," *Newsweek*, July 30, available at www.newsweek.com/after-decade-bad-blood-bondholders-argentina-faces-default-262072.

5   LAW OF THE SEA

1. Similar disputes over other land masses and maritime areas are ongoing in other parts of the East and South China Seas.

2. Daniel Bishton (2018), "Spratly Islands Military Bases Revealed," *Spatial Source*, March 6, available at www.spatialsource.com.au/gis-data/satellite-images-reveal-completed-military-bases-spratly-islands.

3. Hugo Grotius (1609/2004), *The Free Sea*, Liberty Fund, p. 24.

4. Ibid., pp. 24–25.
5. John Selden (1652/2004), *Mare Clausum*, Lawbook Exchange.
6. Emer de Vattel (1758/2008), *The Law of Nations*, Liberty Fund, p. 257.
7. Jack L. Goldsmith and Eric A. Posner (1999), "A Theory of Customary International Law," *University of Chicago Law Review* 66: 1113–1177, at 1158–1164.
8. Ibid., pp. 1159–1160.
9. See Chapter 12.
10. US Presidential Proclamation 2667, September 28, 1945. See also US Presidential Proclamation 2668.
11. Michael P. Scharf (2013), *Customary International Law in Times of Fundamental Change: Recognizing Grotian Moments*, Cambridge University Press, p. 116.
12. Deep seabed mining became prominent in response to John L. Mero (1965), *The Mineral Resources of the Sea*, Elsevier. This enthusiasm later waned because of decreased commodity prices and improvements in land mining.
13. Agreement Relating to the Implementation of Part XI of UNCLOS (1994).
14. UNCLOS (1982), Article 87(1).
15. Ibid., Article 87(2).
16. This incident occurred in India's exclusive economic zone. UNCLOS rules on the freedom of the high seas extended to this area under Article 58.
17. PCA, *Enrica Lexie*, Award of 21 May 2020, paras. 1017–1043.
18. Ibid., para. 1094.
19. This incident occurred in Russia's exclusive economic zone. UNCLOS rules on the freedom of the high seas extended to this area under Article 58.
20. UNCLOS (1982), Article 87(2).
21. PCA, *Arctic Sunrise*, Award of 14 August 2015.
22. ITLOS, *M/V Saiga (No. 2)*, Judgment of 1 July 1999, para. 106.
23. PCA, *Arctic Sunrise*, Award of 14 August 2015, paras. 159–175.
24. Ibid., para. 171.
25. UNCLOS (1982), Article 192.
26. ITLOS, *Sub-Regional Fisheries Commission*, Advisory Opinion of 2 April 2015.
27. Stephen C. Neff (2014), *Justice Among Nations: A History of International Law*, Harvard University Press, p. 469.
28. Ibid.
29. Ibid.
30. UNCLOS (1982), Article 100.
31. Ibid., Article 101.
32. Ibid., Article 110.
33. Ibid., Article 105.
34. Ibid., Article 99.
35. US Court of Appeals for the Ninth Circuit, *Sea Shepherd*, Opinion of 19 March 2012.
36. Belgian Court of Cassation, *Castle John*, Judgment of 19 December 1986.
37. Tullio Treves (2009), "Piracy, Law of the Sea, and Use of Force: Developments off the Coast of Somalia," *European Journal of International Law* 20: 399–414, at 400.
38. Ibid., pp. 402–404.
39. UNCLOS (1982), Preamble.
40. Ibid.

41. See Chapter 2.
42. UNCLOS (1982), Article 7(1).
43. Ibid., Article 14. Separate rules apply to harbors, reefs, low-tide elevations and archipelagos, which are collections of large islands, like Indonesia and Japan.
44. Ibid., Article 8. Foreign ships sometimes have the right to sail on internal waters. We do not discuss those rules here.
45. Yehuda Z. Blum (1986), "The Gulf of Sidra Incident," *American Journal of International Law* 80: 668–677, at 668–669.
46. Yoshifumi Tanaka (2012), *The International Law of the Sea*, Cambridge University Press, p. 58.
47. All of a state's contiguous zone falls within its EEZ.
48. The legal definition of the "continental shelf" does not match the scientific definition of this term.
49. UNCLOS call this "the Area." We use the term "common seabed" because it more clearly conveys the zone's nature.
50. UNCLOS (1982), Article 121(1).
51. Ibid., Article 121(3).
52. Yoshifumi Tanaka (2012), *The International Law of the Sea*, Cambridge University Press, p. 65.
53. Natalie Klein (2011), *Maritime Security and the Law of the Sea*, Oxford University Press.
54. UNCLOS (1982), Article 87(1).
55. Ibid., Article 58.
56. Ibid., Article 19(1).
57. Ibid., Article 19(2).
58. Ibid., Article 18(2).
59. Ibid., Article 2(1).
60. Ibid., Article 56(1)(a).
61. Ibid., Article 61(2).
62. Ibid., Article 211(5).
63. See Chapter 12.
64. Whitley Saumweber (2020), "Distant-Water Fishing along China's Maritime Silk Road," Stephenson Ocean Security Project Report, July 31, available at https://ocean.csis.org/commentary/distant-water-fishing-along-china-s-maritime-silk-road/.
65. UNCLOS (1982), Article 60.
66. Ibid., Article 60(4).
67. Ibid., Article 60(8).
68. PCA, *Arctic Sunrise*, Award of 14 August 2015, para. 229.
69. UNCLOS (1982), Article 27(2).
70. Ibid., Article 27(1).
71. Ibid., Article 33(1)(a).
72. Ibid., Article 73(2)–(4).
73. Ibid., Articles 220–221.
74. Ibid., Article 221.
75. Ibid., Article 110.
76. Ibid., Article 111.
77. PCA, *Enrica Lexie*, Award of 21 May 2020, para. 874.

78. UNCLOS (1982), Article 77(1).

79. Wil S. Hylton (2020), "History's Largest Mining Operation Is About to Begin," *The Atlantic*, January/February, available at www.theatlantic.com/magazine/archive/2020/01/20000-feet-under-the-sea/603040/.

80. UNCLOS (1982), Article 136.

81. Ibid., Article 137(1).

82. Ibid., Part XI, Section 4, and the 1994 Implementation Agreement.

83. Wil S. Hylton (2020), "History's Largest Mining Operation Is About to Begin," *The Atlantic*, January/February, available at www.theatlantic.com/magazine/archive/2020/01/20000-feet-under-the-sea/603040/.

84. Lisa A. Levin, Diva J. Amon, and Hannah Lily (2020), "Challenges to the Sustainability of Deep-Seabed Mining,"*Nature Sustainability* 3: 784–794.

85. Rakhyun E. Kim (2017), "Should Deep Seabed Mining Be Allowed?," *Marine Policy* 82: 134–137.

86. Delimitation rules vary across water and seabed areas, and across treaties.

87. In theory, states can use different boundaries for water and seabed areas. However, this is extremely rare.

88. Emphasis added.

89. ICJ, *North Sea*, Judgment of 20 February 1969, paras. 47, 88.

90. GCCS (1985), Article 6; GCTSCZ (1958), Article 12; UNCLOS (1982), Articles 74(1) and 83(1).

91. ICJ, *North Sea*, Judgment of 20 February 1969, para. 93.

92. ICJ, *Jan Mayen*, Judgment of 14 June 1993, paras. 57, 58.

93. Law experts often refer to this criterion as "proportionality." We do not use this term because the term "proportionality" has a different meaning for international law on the use of force and armed conflict.

94. ICJ, *North Sea*, Judgment of 20 February 1969, para. 91.

95. ICJ, *Jan Mayen*, Judgment of 14 June 1993, para. 61.

96. Ibid., para. 69.

97. Ibid., para. 76.

98. Ibid., para. 72.

99. Yoshifumi Tanaka (2012), *The International Law of the Sea*, Cambridge University Press, pp. 204–206.

100. Some scholars identify the ICJ's 2008 *Black Sea* ruling as another turning-point in delimitation procedure. See Massimo Lando (2019), *Maritime Delimitation as a Judicial Process*, Cambridge University Press.

6 TRADE

1. Teresa Kuchler (2010), "Nordic Hunters Say EU Seal Ban Wastes Resources," *EU Observer*, April 7, available at https://euobserver.com/news/29803.

2. Associated Press (2009), "In Swipe at Canada, Europe Bans Seal Products," NBC News, May 5, available at www.nbcnews.com/Ibid/wbna30580666.

3. Agence France-Presse (2009), "Seal Hunt Casts Chill over EU–Norway Relations," France 24, April 22, 2009, available at www.france24.com/en/20090422-seal-hunt-casts-chill-over-eu-norway-relations-.

4. See Chapter 1.

5. Krzysztof J. Pelc (2016), *Making and Bending International Rules: The Design of Exceptions and Escape Clauses in Trade Law*, Cambridge University Press.

6. Many legal scholars use the term "escape clause" to refer only to GATT Article XIX. Throughout this chapter, we use the broader meaning of the term, as used in political science. See B. Peter Rosendorff and Helen V. Milner (2001), "The Optimal Design of International Trade Institutions: Uncertainty and Escape," *International Organization* 55: 829–857.

7. B. Peter Rosendorff (2005), "Stability and Rigidity: Politics and Design of the WTO's Dispute Settlement Procedure," *American Political Science Review* 99: 389–400.

8. Krzysztof Pelc (2009), "Seeking Escape: The Use of Escape Clauses in International Trade Agreements," *International Studies Quarterly* 53: 349–368.

9. Congressional Record, April 21, 2010, H2702.

10. EC Regulation No. 1031/2002 of 13 June 2002.

11. "Cold Steel," *The Economist*, November 13, 2003, available at www.economist.com/node/2206255.

12. Warren F. Schwartz and Alan O. Sykes (2002), "The Economic Structure of Renegotiation and Dispute Resolution in the World Trade Organization," *Journal of Legal Studies* 31: S179–S204.

13. Treaty of Amity and Commerce (1778), Article II.

14. Oona A. Hathaway and Scott J. Shapiro (2017), *The Internationalists: How a Radical Plan to Outlaw War Remade the World*, Simon & Schuster, p. 137.

15. Leslie Johns (2015), *Strengthening International Courts: The Hidden Costs of Legalization*, University of Michigan Press, ch. 5.

16. Alfonso S. Bevilaqua, Marcelo Catena, and Ernesto Talvi (2001), "Integration, Interdependence and Regional Goods: An Application to Mercosur," in *Economia*, edited by Andres Velasco, Brookings Institution Press, pp. 153–199.

17. VERs are also commonly called export-restraint agreements, gray-area measures, voluntary restraint arrangements, and orderly marketing arrangements.

18. Julie Michelle Klinger (2015), "A Historical Geography of Rare Earth Elements: From Discovery to the Atomic Age," *The Extractive Industries and Society* 2: 572–580.

19. John H. Jackson (1997), *The World Trading System: Law and Policy of International Economic Relations*, MIT Press, p. 155.

20. American Recovery and Reinvestment Act (2009), Section 1605(a).

21. Stephanie J. Rickard and Daniel Y. Kono (2014), "Think Globally, Buy Locally: International Agreements and Government Procurement," *Research Ideas and Outcomes* 9: 333–352.

22. As described above, the GATT allows preferential trade agreements.

23. GATT (1947), Article III(1).

24. GATT, *EEC–Bananas*, Panel Report of 11 February 1994, para. 143.

25. GATT, *Japan–Alcohol*, Panel Report of 10 November 1987, para. 5.7.

26. GATT (1947), Article XVI(1).

27. Andreas F. Lowenfeld (2008), *International Economic Law*, Oxford University Press, ch. 9.

28. GATT (1947), Article VI(3).

29. Ibid., Article VI(1).

30. Andreas F. Lowenfeld (2008), *International Economic Law*, Oxford University Press, ch. 10.

31. Krzysztof Pelc (2009), "Seeking Escape: The Use of Escape Clauses in International Trade Agreements," *International Studies Quarterly* 53: 349–368.

32. Peter Van den Bossche (2005), *The Law and Policy of the World Trade Organization*, Cambridge University Press, p. 615.

33. This dispute was filed under the General Agreement on Trade in Service (GATS). The US invoked Article XIV(a) of the GATS in its defense, which is nearly identical to Article XX(a) of the GATT.

34. WTO, *US–Gambling*, Panel Report of 10 November 2004, para. 6.461.

35. This argument involves a concept from international environmental law called the precautionary approach.

36. GATT, *Thailand–Cigarettes*, Panel Report of 7 November 1990, para. 73.

37. Ibid., para. 75.

38. WTO, *US–Gasoline*, Appellate Body Report of 29 April 1996, p. 8.

39. WTO, *US–Shrimp*, Appellate Body Report of 12 October 1998, para. 128.

40. Peter Van den Bossche (2005), *The Law and Policy of the World Trade Organization*, Cambridge University Press, pp. 613–614.

41. WTO, *US–Shrimp*, Appellate Body Report of 12 October 1998, paras. 146–184.

42. Krzysztof J. Pelc (2016), *Making and Bending International Rules: The Design of Exceptions and Escape Clauses in Trade Law*, Cambridge University Press, pp. 101–122.

43. GATT, *US–Nicaragua*, Panel Report of 13 October 1986, para. 5.3.

44. Ibid.

45. Tom Miles (2018), "Saudi Cites National Security to Block WTO Case Brought by Qatar," *Reuters*, December 4, available at www.reuters.com/article/us-saudi-qatar-wto-idUSKBN1O31QP.

46. Leslie Johns and Krzysztof Pelc (2016), "Fear of Crowds in World Trade Organization Disputes: Why Don't More Countries Participate?," *Journal of Politics* 78: 88–104.

47. Office of the US Trade Representative (2017), "U.S. Third-Party Submission regarding GATT Article XXI," November 7, available at https://ustr.gov/issue-areas/enforcement/dispute-settlement-proceedings/wto-dispute-settlement/pending-wto-dispute-35.

48. European Union Third Party Written Submission (2017), "Russia–Measures Concerning Traffic in Transit," November 8, available at http://trade.ec.europa.eu/doclib/docs/2018/february/tradoc_156602.pdf.

49. WTO, *Russia–Transit*, Panel Report of 5 April 2019, paras. 7.102–7.104.

50. WTO, *EC–Seals*, Panel Report of 25 November 2013, para. 7.597.

51. Ibid., para. 7.608.

52. WTO, *US–Gambling*, Panel Report of 10 November 2004, para. 6.461.

53. WTO, *EC–Seals*, Panel Report of 25 November 2013, para. 7.274.

54. Pelin Serpin (2016), "The Public Morals Exception after the WTO Seal Products Dispute: Has the Exception Swallowed the Rules?," *Columbia Business Law Review* 2016: 217–251.

55. Leslie Johns and Krzysztof J. Pelc (2014), "Who Gets to Be in the Room? Manipulating Participation in WTO Disputes," *International Organization* 68: 663–699, at 692.

7 INVESTMENT

1. ICSID, *Philip Morris*, Award of 8 July 2016, para. 10.
2. Throughout this chapter, the terms "firm" and "investor" refer to individuals, businesses, partnerships, corporations, and so on that engage in business activities.
3. Purchasing company shares on a foreign stock exchange usually would not qualify as FDI since stockholders are typically not involved in the day-to-day management decisions of companies.
4. See Chapter 1.
5. Leslie Johns and Rachel Wellhausen (2016), "Under One Roof: Supply Chains and the Protection of Foreign Investment," *American Political Science Review* 110: 31–51.
6. See Chapter 1 on collaboration problems generally. See also Andrew Guzman (1998), "Explaining the Popularity of Bilateral Investment Treaties: Why LDCs Sign Treaties that Hurt Them," *Virginia Journal of International Law* 38: 639–688; Beth A. Simmons (2014), "Bargaining over BITs, Arbitrating Awards: The Regime for Protection and Promotion of International Investment," *World Politics* 66:12–46.
7. Andreas F. Lowenfeld (2008), *International Economic Law*, Oxford University Press, pp. 475–476.
8. US State Department (1940), "Note from the US Secretary of State to the Ambassador of Mexico," *Department of State Bulletin* II(42), pp. 380–383.
9. Manuel R. Garcia-Mora (1950), "The Calvo Clause in Latin American Constitutions and International Law," *Marquette Law Review* 33: 205–219.
10. Bolivian Constitution (2009), Article 320.
11. Donald R. Shea (1955), *The Calvo Clause: A Problem of Inter-American and International Law and Diplomacy*, University of Minnesota Press, p. 214.
12. UNGA Resolution 1803 (1962).
13. Ibid.
14. UNGA Resolution 3171 (1973).
15. Ibid.
16. UNGA Resolution 3281 (1974), Chapter II, Article 2(1).
17. Ibid., Article 2(2)(a).
18. Ibid., Article 2(2)(c).
19. Stockholm Chamber of Commerce, *Sedelmayer*, Award of 7 July 1998.
20. ICSID, *Metalclad*, Award of 30 August 2000, para. 103.
21. UNCITRAL, *Pope & Talbot*, Interim Award of 26 June 2000.
22. ICSID, *Cargill*, Award of 29 February 2008.
23. ICSID, *ATA Construction*, Award of 18 May 2010, para. 73.
24. Stephan W. Schill (2009), *The Multilateralization of International Investment Law*, Cambridge University Press.
25. ICSID, *Tidewater*, Award of 13 March 2015.
26. ICSID, *Asian Agricultural Products*, Award of 27 June 1990.
27. ICSID, *Metalclad*, Award of 30 August 2000, para. 76.
28. ICSID, *Micula*, Award of 11 December 2013.
29. Ibid., para. 827.
30. ICSID, *Mobil*, Decision of 22 May 2012, paras. 210–242.
31. For example, ICSID requires the public registration of all investment disputes that it oversees. Yet roughly 40 percent of the ICSID cases from 1972 to 2012 have no public

record of the actual outcome of the dispute. See Emilie M. Hafner-Burton, Zachary C. Steinert-Threlkeld, and David G. Victor (2016), "Predictability versus Flexibility: Secrecy in International Investment Arbitration," *World Politics* 68: 413–453.

32. Rachel Wellhausen (2016), "Recent Trends in Investor–State Dispute Settlement," *Journal of International Dispute Settlement* 7: 117–135; Susan D. Franck (2011), "Rationalizing Costs in Investment Treaty Arbitration," *Washington University Law Review* 88: 769–852.

33. See Chapter 4.

34. PCA, *Saluka*, Award of 7 September 2006.

35. Arbitration tribunals sometimes use the Latin phrase *bona fide* to express this concept.

36. Paul Ames (2015), "ISDS: The Most Toxic Acronym in Europe," *POLITICO*, September 17, available at www.politico.eu/article/isds-the-most-toxic-acronym-in-europe/.

37. "In His Own Words: Lighthizer Lets Loose on Business, Hill Opposition to ISDS, Sunset Clause," *Inside U.S. Trade Daily Report*, October 20, 2017.

38. Jorun Baumgartner (2017), *Treaty Shopping in International Investment Law*, Oxford University Press.

39. Krzysztof Pelc (2017), "What Explains the Low Success Rate of Investor–State Disputes?," *International Organization* 71: 559–583.

40. Kate Kelland (2015), "Gates and Bloomberg Create $4 Million Fund to Fight Big Tobacco," *Reuters News Service*, March 18, available at www.reuters.com/article/us-health-tobacco-fund/gates-and-bloomberg-create-4-million-fund-to-fight-big-tobacco-idUSKBN0ME24C20150318.

41. Carolina Moehlecke (2020), "The Chilling Effect of International Investment Disputes: Limited Challenges to State Sovereignty," *International Studies Quarterly* 64: 1–12.

42. Ibid.

43. ICSID, *Philip Morris*, Award of 8 July 2016, para. 328.

44. Ibid.

8 HUMAN RIGHTS

1. Tracey Eaton (2018), "Would You Let Your Ten-Year-Old Kid Work? It's Perfectly Legal in this Country," *USA Today*, January 9.

2. Mathias Meier (2015), "Embracing Child Labor," *New York Times*, video available at https://nyti.ms/2jXKQdf.

3. For example, see ICCPR (1966), Article 4(1).

4. UN document C.N.703.2015.TREATIES-IV.4.

5. King James Bible, Mark 16:15.

6. Francisco de Vitoria (1539/1991), "On the American Indians (*De Indis*)," in *Political Writings*, edited by Anthony Pagden and Jeremy Lawrance, Cambridge University Press, p. 285 (emphasis removed).

7. Michel de Montaigne (1580/1965), "Of Cannibals," in *The Complete Essays of Montaigne*, translated by Donald M. Frame, Stanford University Press, pp. 150–159.

8. Ibid., p. 152.

9. Jean-Jacques Rousseau (1762/2019), "The Social Contract," in *Rousseau: The Social Contract and Other Later Political Writings*, translated by Victor Gourevitch, Cambridge University Press, p. 43.

10. Executive Board of the American Anthropological Association (1947), "Statement on Human Rights," *American Anthropologist* 49: 539–543, at 540.

11. Ibid., pp. 541, 542.

12. Gerrit W. Gong (1984), *The Standard of "Civilization" in International Society*, Clarendon Press.

13. Susan Pedersen (2015), *The Guardians: The League of Nations and the Crisis of Empire*, Oxford University Press.

14. Fabian Klose (2013), *Human Rights in the Shadow of Colonial Violence*, University of Pennsylvania Press.

15. Roland Burke (2010), *Decolonization and the Evolution of International Human Rights*, University of Pennsylvania Press, pp. 112–144.

16. Jenny S. Martinez (2012), *The Slave Trade and the Origins of International Human Rights Law*, Oxford University Press.

17. Susan Pedersen (2015), *The Guardians: The League of Nations and the Crisis of Empire*, Oxford University Press.

18. Lauren Benton and Lisa Ford (2016), *Rage for Order: The British Empire and the Origins of International Law, 1800–1850*, Harvard University Press, pp. 28–55.

19. A.W. Brian Simpson (2001), *Human Rights and the End of Empire: Britain and the Genesis of the European Convention*, Oxford University Press, p. 108.

20. Ibid., p. 113.

21. Gerrit W. Gong (1984), *The Standard of "Civilization" in International Society*, Clarendon Press.

22. Susan Pedersen (2015), *The Guardians: The League of Nations and the Crisis of Empire*, Oxford University Press, pp. 4–5.

23. Andrew Moravcsik (2000), "The Origins of Human Rights Regimes: Democratic Delegation in Postwar Europe," *International Organization* 54: 217–252.

24. A.W. Brian Simpson (2001), *Human Rights and the End of Empire: Britain and the Genesis of the European Convention*, Oxford University Press, p. 157.

25. Fabian Klose (2013), *Human Rights in the Shadow of Colonial Violence*, University of Pennsylvania Press.

26. UNGA Resolution 217 (III–1948).

27. Emma Stone Mackinnon (2019), "Declaration as Disavowal: The Politics of Race and Empire in the Universal Declaration of Human Rights," *Political Theory* 47: 57–81.

28. ICJ, *Genocide*, Advisory Opinion of 28 May 1951, p. 23 ("the principles underlying the Convention are principles which are recognized by civilized nations as binding on States, even without any conventional obligation").

29. ICERD (1965), Article 1(1).

30. Roland Burke (2010), *Decolonization and the Evolution of International Human Rights*, University of Pennsylvania Press, pp. 74–77.

31. Mohammed Reza Pahlavi (1967), *The White Revolution*, Kayhan Press, p. 171.

32. Cosette D. Creamer and Beth A. Simmons (2015), "Ratification, Reporting, and Rights: Quality of Participation in the Convention against Torture," *Human Rights Quarterly* 37: 579–608.

33. James H. Lebovic and Erik Voeten (2006), "The Politics of Shame: The Condemnation of Country Human Rights Practices in the UNHCR," *International Studies Quarterly*

50: 861–888; James H. Lebovic and Erik Voeten (2009), "The Cost of Shame: International Organizations and Foreign Aid in the Punishing of Human Rights Violators," *Journal of Peace Research* 46: 79–97.

34. Shiyan Sun (2007), "The Understanding and Interpretation of the ICCPR in the Context of China's Possible Ratification," *Chicago Journal of International Law* 6: 17–42.

35. A.W. Brian Simpson (2001), *Human Rights and the End of Empire: Britain and the Genesis of the European Convention*, Oxford University Press, p. 5.

36. Andrew Moravcsik (2000), "The Origins of Human Rights Regimes: Democratic Delegation in Postwar Europe," *International Organization* 54: 217–252, at 233.

37. Ibid.

38. Alexandra Huneeus (2010), "Rejecting the Inter-American Court: Judicialization, National Courts, and Regional Human Rights," in *Cultures of Legality*, edited by Javier A. Couso, Alexandra Huneeus, and Rachel Sieder, Cambridge University Press, pp. 112–138, at 116–117.

39. Individuals may file complaints against states with the Commission. If these complaints have merit and a state does not comply with the Commission's recommendations, the Commission can then file a case against the state at the Court.

40. Francesca Parente (2019), *Past Regret, Future Fear: Compliance with International Law*, unpublished Ph.D. dissertation, UCLA.

41. Simon Zschirnt (2018), "Locking in Human Rights in Africa: Analyzing State Accession to the African Court on Human and Peoples' Rights," *Human Rights Review* 19: 97–119.

42. A.W. Brian Simpson (2001), *Human Rights and the End of Empire: Britain and the Genesis of the European Convention*, Oxford University Press, p. 3.

43. James L. Cavallaro and Stephanie Erin Brewer (2008), "Reevaluating Regional Human Rights Litigation in the Twenty-First Century: The Case of the Inter-American Court," *American Journal of International Law* 102: 768–827, at 773.

44. Ibid., p. 774.

45. Courtney Hillebrecht (2014), *Domestic Politics and International Human Rights Tribunals*, Cambridge University Press, pp. 11, 41–65.

46. ECtHR, *Litwa*, Judgment of 4 April 2000, para. 89.

47. Francesca Parente (2019), *Past Regret, Future Fear: Compliance with International Law*, unpublished Ph.D. dissertation, UCLA.

48. This account is based on Philippe Sands (2016), *East West Street*, Alfred A. Knopf, pp. 143–190.

49. Quoted in ibid., p. 147.

50. Raphael Lemkin (1944), *Axis Rule in Occupied Europe*, Carnegie Endowment for International Peace.

51. Genocide Convention (1948), Article 1.

52. Ibid.

53. William A. Schabas (2009), *Genocide in International Law*, Cambridge University Press, p. 127.

54. Gérard Prunier (1995), *The Rwanda Crisis: History of a Genocide*, Columbia University Press.

55. ICTR, *Kayishema*, Judgment of 21 May 1999, para. 34.

56. William A. Schabas (2009), *Genocide in International Law*, Cambridge University Press, p. 125.

57. ICTR, *Kayishema*, Judgment of 21 May 1999, para. 98.

58. Beth Van Schaack (1997), "The Crime of Political Genocide: Repairing the Genocide Convention's Blind Spot," *Yale Law Journal* 106: 2259–2291.

59. Guatemalan Commission for Historical Clarification (1999), "Guatemala Memory of Silence: Report of the Commission for Historical Clarification Conclusions and Recommendations," para. 116.

60. William A. Schabas (2009), *Genocide in International Law*, Cambridge University Press, pp. 207–221.

61. Catharine A. MacKinnon (1994), "Rape, Genocide, and Women's Human Rights," *Harvard Women's Law Journal* 17: 5–16, at 9.

62. ICTR, *Akayesu*, Judgment of 2 September 1998, para. 731.

63. Lars Berster (2015), "The Alleged Non-Existence of Cultural Genocide," *Journal of International Criminal Justice* 13: 677–692.

64. For an overview of this topic, see William A. Schabas (2009), *Genocide in International Law*, Cambridge University Press, pp. 472–486.

65. As discussed in Chapter 4, this is only possible if states can establish ICJ jurisdiction.

66. See Chapter 3 on attribution.

67. See Chapter 3 on the effective control standard.

68. Genocide Convention (1948), Article I.

69. Ibid., Articles IV and V.

70. Ibid., Article VIII.

71. ICJ, *Bosnian Genocide*, Judgment of 26 February 2007, para. 431.

72. Ibid., para. 438.

73. This topic is also discussed in Chapter 9.

74. See International Commission on Intervention and State Sovereignty (2001), *The Responsibility to Protect*, International Development Research Centre.

75. Samantha Power (2001), "Bystanders to Genocide," *The Atlantic*, September.

76. Payam Akhavan (2016), "Cultural Genocide: Legal Label or Mourning Metaphor," *McGill Law Journal* 62: 243–270.

77. Ian Hurd (2017), *How to Do Things with International Law*, Princeton University Press, pp. 58–81.

78. Jennifer Jackson Preece (1998), "Ethnic Cleansing as an Instrument of Nation-State Creation: Changing State Practices and Evolving Legal Norms," *Human Rights Quarterly* 20: 817–842.

79. This account is based on Michael P. Scharf (1997), *Balkan Justice*, Carolina Academic Press.

80. ICJ, *Bosnian* Genocide, Judgment of 26 February 2007, para. 190 (emphasis in original).

81. For example, see UNGA Resolution 47/121 (1992).

82. See ACHPR (1981), Article 5; ACHR (1969), Article 5(2); ECHR (1950), Article 3.

83. ICCPR (1966), Article 7.

84. CAT (1984), Article 1(1).

85. Committee Against Torture, *GRB* v. *Sweden*, Communication No. 83/1997, para. 2.5.

86. Ibid., para. 6.5.

87. C. Tofan (2011), *Torture in International Criminal Law*, Wolf Legal Publishers.

88. ICCPR (1966), Article 6.

89. Laurence R. Helfer (2002), "Overlegalizing Human Rights: International Relations Theory and the Commonwealth Caribbean Backlash Against Human Rights Regimes," *Columbia Law Review* 7: 1832–1911.

90. For example, CAT (1984), Article 3; HRC, General Comment 20, para. 9.

91. Committee Against Torture, *GRB* v. *Sweden*, Communication No. 83/1997, para. 4.10.

92. Samuel P. Huntington (1993), *The Third Wave: Democratization in the Late Twentieth Century*, University of Oklahoma Press.

93. Melissa Nobles (2010), "The Prosecution of Human Rights Violations," *Annual Review of Political Science* 13: 165–182, at 169.

94. Committee Against Torture, *Kepa Urra Guridi* v. *Spain*, Communication No. 212/2002, paras. 6.6–6.7; HRC, *Hugo Rodríguez* v. *Uruguay*, Communication No. 322/1988, para. 12.4; and IACHR, *Barrios Altos* v. *Peru*, Judgment of 14 March 2001, para. 41.

95. Máximo Langer (2011), "The Diplomacy of Universal Jurisdiction: The Political Branches and the Transnational Prosecution of International Crimes," *American Journal of International Law* 105: 1–49.

96. Máximo Langer and Mackenzie Eason (2019), "The Quiet Expansion of Universal Jurisdiction," *European Journal of International Law* 30: 779–817.

97. A. Mark Weisburd (2001), "Customary International Law and Torture: The Case of India," *Chicago Journal of International Law* 2: 81–99.

98. Ibid., p. 82.

99. Karen J. Greenberg and Joshua L. Dratel (2005), *The Torture Papers: The Road to Abu Ghraib*, Cambridge University Press.

100. Ibid., p. 220.

101. Curtis A. Bradley (2009), "The Bush Administration and International Law: Too Much Lawyering and Too Little Diplomacy," *Duke Journal of Constitutional Law & Public Policy* 4: 57–75, at 71.

102. Louis-Philippe F. Rouillard (2005), "Misinterpreting the Prohibition of Torture under International Law: The Office of Legal Counsel Memorandum," *American University International Law Review* 21: 9–41, at 36–39.

103. Karen J. Greenberg and Joshua L. Dratel (2005), *The Torture Papers: The Road to Abu Ghraib*, Cambridge University Press, pp. 207–213.

104. Michelle Farrell (2014), *The Prohibition of Torture in Exceptional Circumstances*, Cambridge University Press, pp. 83–102.

105. Geoffrey P.R. Wallace (2014), "Martial Law? Military Experience, International Law, and Support for Torture," *International Studies Quarterly* 58: 501–514.

106. Geoffrey P.R. Wallace (2013), "International Law and Public Attitudes Toward Torture: An Experimental Study," *International Organization* 67: 105–140.

107. Details from this account come from Andrea Marie Bertone (2000), "Sexual Trafficking in Women: International Political Economy and the Politics of Sex," *Gender Issues* 18: 4–22.

108. Ibid., p. 12.

109. Asif Efrat (2012), *Governing Guns, Preventing Plunder*, Oxford University Press, p. 181.

110. Judith G. Kelley (2017), *Scorecard Diplomacy: Grading States to Influence their Reputation and Behavior*, Cambridge University Press, p. 73.

111. Anne Gallagher (2001), "Human Rights and the New UN Protocols on Trafficking and Migrant Smuggling: A Preliminary Analysis," *Human Rights Quarterly* 23: 975–1004, at 982.

112. Palermo Protocol (2001), Articles 5 and 6.

113. Beth A. Simmons, Paulette Lloyd, and Brandon M. Stewart (2018), "The Global Diffusion of Law: Transnational Crime and the Case of Human Trafficking," *International Organization* 72: 249–281.

114. Judith G. Kelley (2017), "Case Study Supplement: A Closer Look at Outcomes. A Companion to *Scorecard Diplomacy: Grading States to Influence their Reputation and Behavior*, published by Cambridge University Press, 2017," available at www.scorecarddiplomacy.org/case-studies/, p. 41.

115. Joseph Algazy (2001), "Trafficking in Women Could Threaten U.S. Aid," Haaretz, July 13, available at www.haaretz.com/1.5353983.

116. Judith G. Kelley and Beth A. Simmons (2015), "Politics by Number: Indicators as Social Pressure in International Relations," *American Journal of Political Science* 59: 55–70.

117. Janie Chuang (2006), "Beyond a Snapshot: Preventing Human Trafficking in the Global Economy," *Indiana Journal of Global Legal Studies* 13: 137–163, at 140.

118. Kalen Fredette (2009), "Revisiting the UN Protocol on Human Trafficking: Striking Balances for More Effective Legislation," *Cardozo Journal of International and Comparative Law* 17: 101–134.

119. Janie A. Chuang (2014), "Exploitation Creep and the Unmaking of Human Trafficking Law," *American Journal of International Law* 108: 609–649.

120. ICCPR (1966), Article 2(1).

121. Ibid., Article 18(1).

122. Ibid., Article 19.

123. Ibid., Articles 20–21.

124. Sarah Joseph, Jenny Schultz, and Melissa Castan (2004), *The International Covenant on Civil and Political Rights: Cases, Materials, and Commentary*, Oxford University Press, p. 568.

125. HRC, *Kivenmaa* v. *Finland*, Communication No. 412/1990.

126. Sarah Joseph, Jenny Schultz, and Melissa Castan (2004), *The International Covenant on Civil and Political Rights: Cases, Materials, and Commentary*, Oxford University Press, p. 575.

127. ICCPR (1966), Article 19(3).

128. Ibid., Articles 21 and 22(2).

129. UN Document CCPR/C/GC/34, paras. 35 and 34, respectively.

130. ICCPR (1966), Article 20.

131. Sarah Joseph, Jenny Schultz, and Melissa Castan (2004), *The International Covenant on Civil and Political Rights: Cases, Materials, and Commentary*, Oxford University Press, p. 530.

132. Jamie Frederic Metz (1997), "Rwandan Genocide and the International Law of Radio Jamming," *American Journal of International Law* 91: 628–651, at 630–636.

133. Ibid., p. 631.

134. Wibke Kristin Timmerman (2005), "The Relationship between Hate Propaganda and Incitement to Genocide: A New Trend in International Law Towards Criminalization of Hate Propaganda?," *Leiden Journal of International Law* 18: 257–282.

135. HRC, *JRT* v. *Canada*, Communication No. 104/1981.

136. HRC, *Ross* v. *Canada*, Communication No. 736/1997.

137. HRC, *MA* v. *Italy*, Communication No. 117/1981.

138. ECHR (1950), Articles 10(2) and 11(2).

139. Andrew Moravcsik (2000), "The Origins of Human Rights Regimes: Democratic Delegation in Postwar Europe," *International Organization* 54: 217–252.

140. ECtHR, *Refah Partisi* v. *Turkey*, Judgment of 13 February 2003, para. 99.

141. ECtHR, *Partidul Comunistilor* v. *Romania*, Judgment of 3 February 2005, para. 55.

142. See also ECtHR, *United Communist Party* v. *Turkey*, Judgment of 30 January 1998.

143. RSF News (2020), "How India's Government Tries to Suppress All COVID-19 Reporting," *Reporters without Borders*, April 12, available at https://rsf.org/en/news/how-indias-government-tries-suppress-all-covid-19-reporting.

144. HRC, *Hertzberg* v. *Finland*, Communication No. 61/1979, para. 6.1.

145. Ibid., para. 10.3.

146. Sandra Fredman (2018), *Comparative Human Rights Law*, Oxford University Press, pp. 331–332.

147. Sarah Joseph, Jenny Schultz, and Melissa Castan (2004), *The International Covenant on Civil and Political Rights: Cases, Materials, and Commentary*, Oxford University Press, p. 544.

148. Sandra Fredman (2018), *Comparative Human Rights Law*, Oxford University Press, pp. 341–342.

149. Ibid., pp. 339–348.

150. Quoted in Amy Shepherd (2017), "Extremism, Free Speech and the Rule of Law: Evaluating the Compliance of Legislation Restricting Extremist Expressions with Article 19 ICCPR," *Utrecht Journal of International and European Law* 33: 62–83, at 63.

151. Ibid., p. 63.

152. Alan Travis (2017), "Paralysis at the Heart of UK Counter-Extremism Policy," *The Guardian*, September 17, available at www.theguardian.com/uk-news/2017/sep/17/paralysis-at-the-heart-of-uk-counter-extremism-policy.

153. HRC, *Faurisson* v. *France*, Communication No. 550/1993, para. 7.3.

154. Ibid., para. 10.

155. ECtHR, *Perinçek* v. *Switzerland*, Judgment of 15 October 2015.

156. Paolo Lobba (2014), "A European Halt to Laws Against Genocide Denial," *European Criminal Law Review* 4: 59–77, at 60 (emphasis removed).

157. ACtHPR, *Umuhoza* v. *Rwanda*, Judgment of 24 November 2017, para. 125.

158. Ibid., para. 141.

159. Ibid., para. 147.

160. Ibid., paras. 158–162.

161. Evelyn M. Aswad, Rashad Hussan, and M. Arsalan Suleman (2014), "Why the United States Cannot Agree to Disagree on Blasphemy Laws," *Boston University International Law Journal* 32: 119–146, at 121–124.

162. Ibid., p. 127.

163. Heiner Bielefeldt, Nazila Ghanea, and Michael Wiener (2016), *Freedom of Religion or Belief: An International Law Commentary*, Oxford University Press, p. 11.

164. ICCPR (1966), Article 18(1).

165. ECHR (1950), Article 9; ACHR (1969), Article 12; ACHPR (1981), Article 8.

166. UN Document CCPR/C/GC/22, para. 2.

167. Melissa A. Crouch (2012), "Law and Religion in Indonesia: The Constitutional Court and the Blasphemy Law," *Asian Journal of Comparative Law*, 7: 1–46, at 6–11.

168. UN Document CCPR/C/GC/22, para. 4.

169. Sandra Fredman (2018), *Comparative Human Rights Law*, Oxford University Press, pp. 425–432.

170. ICCPR (1966), Article 18(3).

171. Amos N. Guioar (2013), *Freedom from Religion: Rights and National Security*, Oxford University Press.

172. HRC, *Bhinder* v. *Canada*, Communication No. 208/1986.

173. German Constitutional Court, *Teacher Headscarf*, Judgment of 24 September 2003.

174. ECtHR, *Şahin* v. *Turkey*, Judgment of 10 November 2005, para. 35.

175. ECtHR, *Mann Singh* v. *France*, Judgment of 13 November 2008; HRC, *Mann Singh* v. *France*, Communication No. 1928/2010.

176. Sandra Fredman (2018), *Comparative Human Rights Law*, Oxford University Press, pp. 434–437.

177. Heiner Bielefeldt, Nazila Ghanea, and Michael Wiener (2016), *Freedom of Religion or Belief: An International Law Commentary*, Oxford University Press, pp. 191–203.

178. ECtHR, *Kokkinatis* v. *Greece*, Judgment of 25 May 1993, para. 48.

179. ICCPR (1966), Article 9(1).

180. Ibid., Article (2).

181. Ibid., Article (3).

182. Ibid., Article (4).

183. Sarah Joseph, Jenny Schultz, and Melissa Castan (2004), *The International Covenant on Civil and Political Rights: Cases, Materials, and Commentary*, Oxford University Press, pp. 334–336.

184. Ibid., pp. 312–318.

185. Advocates for Human Rights and Detention Watch Network (2014), "Report to the UN Working Group on Arbitrary Detention: Detention of Migrants in the United States," January 20, paras. 47–57.

186. UN Document A/HRC/36/37/Add.2, para. 26.

187. Some of these rules also extend to civil trials. See Sarah Joseph, Jenny Schultz, and Melissa Castan (2004), *The International Covenant on Civil and Political Rights: Cases, Materials, and Commentary*, Oxford University Press, pp. 388–394.

188. ICCPR (1966), Article 14(1).

189. Sarah Joseph, Jenny Schultz, and Melissa Castan (2004), *The International Covenant on Civil and Political Rights: Cases, Materials, and Commentary*, Oxford University Press, pp. 388–461.

190. Leslie Johns and Frank Wyer (2019), "When Things Fall Apart: The Impact of Global Governance on Civil Conflicts," *Journal of Politics* 81: e80–e84.

191. Rosalyn Higgins (1994), *Problems and Process: International Law and How We Use It*, Clarendon Press, p. 100.

192. Milli Lake (2018), *Strong NGOs and Weak States: Pursuing Gender Justice in the Democratic Republic of Congo and South Africa*, Cambridge University Press.

193. Sultan Mehmood (2019), "Judicial Independence and Development: Evidence from Pakistan," Aix-Marseille School of Economics Working Paper 2041.

194. Krisztina Than (2019), "Hungary Abandons Plan for Administrative Courts, Justice Minister Says," *Reuters*, November 1, available at www.reuters.com/article/us-hungary-courts-idUSKBN1XB3KS; Christian Davies and Jennifer Rankin (2020), "'Declaration of War': Polish Row Over Judicial Independence Escalates," *The Guardian*, January 24, available at www.theguardian.com/world/2020/jan/24/declaration-of-war-polish-row-over-judicial-independence-escalates.

195. Gregory A. Huber and Sanford C. Gordon (2004), "Accountability and Coercion: Is Justice Blind when It Runs for Office?," *American Journal of Political Science* 48: 247–263.

196. Quoted in Sarah Joseph, Jenny Schultz, and Melissa Castan (2004), *The International Covenant on Civil and Political Rights: Cases, Materials, and Commentary*, Oxford University Press, p. 408.

197. ICCPR (1966), Article 7.

198. Ibid., Article 10.

199. UN Document CCPR/C/GC/21, para. 2.

200. UNGA Resolution 70/175.

201. ICCPR (1966), Article 10(3).

202. Ibid., Article 6(1) and 6(4).

203. Ibid., Article 6(5).

204. Ibid., Article 7.

205. Sarah Joseph, Jenny Schultz, and Melissa Castan (2004), *The International Covenant on Civil and Political Rights: Cases, Materials, and Commentary*, Oxford University Press, pp. 223–229.

206. Shiyan Sun (2007), "The Understanding and Interpretation of the ICCPR in the Context of China's Possible Ratification," *Chicago Journal of International Law* 6: 17–42.

207. Laurence R. Helfer (2002), "Overlegalizing Human Rights: International Relations Theory and the Commonwealth Caribbean Backlash Against Human Rights Regimes," *Columbia Law Review* 102: 1832–1911.

208. Manisuli Ssenyonjo (2009), *Economic, Social and Cultural Rights in International Law*, Hart Publishing, pp. 5, 10.

209. ICESCR (1966), Article 2(1).

210. UN Document E/C.12/GC/3, para. 10.

211. ICESCR (1966), Article 2(2).

212. ILO Convention (1919), Preamble.

213. ICESCR (1966), Article 6(1).

214. UN Document E/C.12/GC/18, para. 7.

215. Ibid., para. 31.

216. Ben Saul, David Kinley, and Jacqueline Mowbray (2014), *The International Covenant on Economic, Social, and Cultural Rights: Commentary, Cases, and Materials*, Oxford University Press, p. 287.

217. ICESCR (1966), Article 7.

218. UN Document E/C.12/GC/23, para. 65.

219. ICESCR (1966), Article 8(1).

220. Ben Saul, David Kinley, and Jacqueline Mowbray (2014), *The International Covenant on Economic, Social, and Cultural Rights: Commentary, Cases, and Materials*, Oxford University Press, pp. 506–511.
221. Ibid., pp. 519–530.
222. Cass Sunstein (1993), "Against Positive Rights," *East European Constitutional Review* 2: 35–38, at 36 (emphasis removed).
223. Ibid., p. 317.
224. ICESCR (1966), Article 9.
225. Ben Saul, David Kinley, and Jacqueline Mowbray (2014), *The International Covenant on Economic, Social, and Cultural Rights: Commentary, Cases, and Materials*, Oxford University Press, pp. 609–611.
226. UN Document E/C.12/GC/19, para. 59.
227. Ben Saul, David Kinley, and Jacqueline Mowbray (2014), *The International Covenant on Economic, Social, and Cultural Rights: Commentary, Cases, and Materials*, Oxford University Press, pp. 639–640.
228. UN Document E/C.12/GC/19, para. 24.
229. Ben Saul, David Kinley, and Jacqueline Mowbray (2014), *The International Covenant on Economic, Social, and Cultural Rights: Commentary, Cases, and Materials*, Oxford University Press, p. 654.
230. ICESCR (1966), Article 11.
231. Quoted in Ben Saul, David Kinley, and Jacqueline Mowbray (2014), *The International Covenant on Economic, Social, and Cultural Rights: Commentary, Cases, and Materials*, Oxford University Press, p. 868.
232. The ICESCR does not explicitly mention water. Yet most human rights experts believe that the term "food" includes water, which is needed for human sustenance.
233. Cameron Ballard-Rosa (2020), *Democracies, Dictatorship and Default*, Cambridge University Press.
234. Amartya Sen (1982), *Poverty and Famines*, Oxford University Press, p. 1.
235. Ben Saul, David Kinley, and Jacqueline Mowbray (2014), *The International Covenant on Economic, Social, and Cultural Rights: Commentary, Cases, and Materials*, Oxford University Press, pp. 888–891.
236. IACtHR, *Yakye Axa* v. *Paraguay*, Decision of 17 June 2005.
237. ACmHPR, *SERAC* v. *Nigeria*, Communication No. 155/96, para. 9; ECOWAS, *SERAP* v. *Nigeria*, Judgment of 14 December 2012.
238. ICESCR (1966), Article 11.
239. UN Document E/C.12/GC/4, para. 8.
240. UN Document E/C.12/GC/7, para. 3.
241. Ben Saul, David Kinley, and Jacqueline Mowbray (2014), *The International Covenant on Economic, Social, and Cultural Rights: Commentary, Cases, and Materials*, Oxford University Press, p. 949.
242. ACmHPR, *SERAC* v. *Nigeria*, Communication No. 155/96, para. 61.
243. South African Constitutional Court, *Grootboom*, Judgment of 4 October 2000, para. 4.
244. Ibid., para. 3.
245. Ibid., para. 94.
246. Ibid., para. 95.

247. ICESCR (1966), Article 12.
248. Ben Saul, David Kinley, and Jacqueline Mowbray (2014), *The International Covenant on Economic, Social, and Cultural Rights: Commentary, Cases, and Materials*, Oxford University Press, p. 982.
249. Ibid., p. 985.
250. Ibid., pp. 1013–1016.
251. Ibid., pp. 1009–1013, 1076.
252. South African Constitutional Court, *Minister of Health* v. *Treatment Action Campaign*, Judgment of 5 July 2002.
253. Ben Saul, David Kinley, and Jacqueline Mowbray (2014), *The International Covenant on Economic, Social, and Cultural Rights: Commentary, Cases, and Materials*, Oxford University Press, p. 1025.
254. ICESCR (1966), Article 13(1).
255. Ibid.
256. Ben Saul, David Kinley, and Jacqueline Mowbray (2014), *The International Covenant on Economic, Social, and Cultural Rights: Commentary, Cases, and Materials*, Oxford University Press, p. 1099.
257. Ibid., pp. 1133–1143.
258. Ibid., p. 1117.
259. Ibid., p. 1123.
260. ICESCR (1966), Article 15.
261. ICCPR (1966), Article 27.
262. UN Document E/C.12/GC/21, para. 11.
263. Ibid., para. 13.
264. Ben Saul, David Kinley, and Jacqueline Mowbray (2014), *The International Covenant on Economic, Social, and Cultural Rights: Commentary, Cases, and Materials*, Oxford University Press, pp. 1196–1198.
265. Ibid., p. 1197.
266. ACmHPR, *Endorois* v. *Kenya*, Communication No. 276/2003 (2010), para. 3.
267. Ibid., paras. 13–14.
268. ACHPR, Article 22(1).
269. ACmHPR, *Endorois* v. *Kenya*, Communication No. 276/2003 (2010), paras. 161, 268, 298.
270. Ben Saul, David Kinley, and Jacqueline Mowbray (2014), *The International Covenant on Economic, Social, and Cultural Rights: Commentary, Cases, and Materials*, Oxford University Press, pp. 1199–1200.
271. HRC, *Lovelace* v. *Canada*, Communication No. R.6/24 (1981).
272. Lilian Chenwi and Danwood M. Chirwa (2016), "The Direct Protection of Economic, Social and Cultural Rights in Africa," in *The Protection of Economic, Social and Cultural Rights in Africa*, edited by Danwood M. Chirwa and Lilian Chenwi, Cambridge University Press, pp. 43–44.
273. CEDAW (1979), Article 2.
274. Loveday Hodson (2014), "Women's Rights and the Periphery: CEDAW's Optional Protocol," *European Journal of International Law* 25: 561–578.
275. CRC (1993), Preamble.
276. Ibid., Article 32.

277. ICMW (1990), Article 2(1).

278. Ibid., Article 25.

279. Martin Ruhs and Philip Martin (2008), "Numbers vs. Rights: Trade-Offs and Guest Worker Programs," *International Migration Review* 42: 249–265.

280. CRPD (2007), Article 1.

281. Ibid., Article 9.

282. Rosalyn Higgins (1994), *Problems and Process: International Law and How We Use It*, Clarendon Press, p. 105.

283. Andrea Vilán (2018), *The Domestic Incorporation of Human Rights Treaties*, unpublished Ph.D. dissertation, UCLA.

284. Mathias Meier (2015), "Embracing Child Labor," *New York Times*, December 19, video available at https://nyti.ms/2jXKQdf.

285. Tracey Eaton (2018), "Would You Let your Ten-Year-Old Kid Work? It's Perfectly Legal in this Country," *USA Today*, January 9.

286. Jana Von Stein (2015), "Making Promises, Keeping Promises: Democracy, Ratification and Compliance in International Human Rights Law," *British Journal for the Philosophy of Science* 46: 655–679.

287. Francesca Parente (2019), *Past Regret, Future Fear: Compliance with International Law*, unpublished Ph.D. dissertation, UCLA.

288. This account is based on Laura Martin (2017), "Meet the Children Getting Paid Thousands to Cut Tongues Out of Fish," *Vice*, September 22.

289. Ibid.

9   USE OF FORCE

1. The GCC's members are Bahrain, Kuwait, Oman, Qatar, Saudi Arabia, and the United Arab Emirates.

2. Benjamin Nußberger (2017), "Military Strikes in Yemen in 2015: Intervention by Invitation and Self-Defense in the Course of Yemen's 'Model Transitional Process'," *Journal on the Use and Force of International Law* 4: 110–160, at 114–115.

3. ISIL is also known as Islamic State in Iraq and Syria, Islamic State, and Daesh.

4. UNSC Resolutions 2140 (2014), 2201 (2015), and 2204 (2015).

5. UN Document S/PRST/2015/8.

6. UN Document S/2015/217, p. 4.

7. Ibid., pp. 4–5.

8. Tom Ruys and Luca Ferro (2016), "Weathering the Storm: Legality and Legal Implications of the Saudi-Led Military Intervention in Yemen," *International & Comparative Law Quarterly* 65: 61–98, at 68.

9. UNSC Resolution 2216 (2015).

10. Ian Brownlie (1963), *International Law and the Use of Force by States*, Clarendon Press, pp. 3–4.

11. Ibid., p. 19.

12. Scholars often call this the principle of "necessity," which is the same term used in the law of state responsibility to excuse or justify some legal breaches. Since this principle of jus ad bellum constrains (rather than excuses or justifies) the use of force, we use the term "military necessity" to avoid confusion.

13. Quoted in R.Y. Jennings (1938), "The *Caroline* and *McLeod* Cases," *American Journal of International Law* 32: 82–99, at 89.

14. Ibid., p. 82.

15. Judith Gardam (2004), *Necessity, Proportionality and the Use of Force by States*, Cambridge University Press, p. 149.

16. Ian Brownlie (1963), *International Law and the Use of Force by States*, Clarendon Press, pp. 40–42.

17. Christian Henderson (2018), *The Use of Force and International Law*, Cambridge University Press, p. 230.

18. ICJ, *Nicaragua*, Judgment of 27 June 1986, para. 237.

19. ICJ, *Oil Platforms*, Judgment of 6 November 2003, para. 32.

20. Ibid., para. 76.

21. Judith Gardam (2004), *Necessity, Proportionality and the Use of Force by States*, Cambridge University Press, p. 9.

22. Ian Brownlie (1963), *International Law and the Use of Force by States*, Clarendon Press, p. 261.

23. ICJ, *Oil Platforms*, Judgment of 6 November 2003, para. 77.

24. Ibid.

25. Hague Convention for the Pacific Settlement of International Disputes (1899/1907), Article 1.

26. Hague Convention Relative to the Opening of Hostilities (1907), Article 1.

27. Covenant of the League of Nations (1919), Preamble.

28. Ian Brownlie (1963), *International Law and the Use of Force by States*, Clarendon Press, pp. 55–65.

29. Oona Hathaway and Scott J. Shapiro (2017), *The Internationalists*, Simon & Schuster.

30. Pact of Paris (1928), Article I.

31. Ibid., Article II.

32. Quincy Wright (1933), "The Meaning of the Pact of Paris," *American Journal of International Law* 27: 39–61.

33. Edwin M. Borchard (1929), "The Multilateral Treaty for the Renunciation of War," *American Journal of International Law* 23: 116–120, at 118.

34. Yoram Dinstein (2017), *War, Aggression and Self-Defence*, Cambridge University Press, p. 88.

35. Ian Brownlie (1963), *International Law and the Use of Force by States*, Clarendon Press, p. 95.

36. Ibid., p. 78.

37. Ibid., p. 110.

38. Ibid., p. 109.

39. Tom Ruys (2014), "The Meaning of Force and the Boundaries of the Jus ad Bellum: Are Minimal Uses of Force Excluded from UN Charter Article 2(4)?," *American Journal of International Law* 108: 159–210, at 163.

40. ICJ, *Nicaragua*, Judgment of 27 June 1986, para. 228.

41. Tom Ruys (2014), "Of Arms, Funding and 'Non-lethal Assistance': Issues Surrounding Third-State Intervention in the Syrian Civil War," *Chicago Journal of International Law* 13: 13–53.

42. Olivier Corten (2005), "The Controversies Over the Customary Prohibition on the Use of Force: A Methodological Debate," *European Journal of International Law* 16: 803–822.

43. Tom Ruys (2014), "The Meaning of Force and the Boundaries of the Jus ad Bellum: Are Minimal Uses of Force Excluded from UN Charter Article 2(4)?," *American Journal of International Law* 108: 159–210.

44. Olivier Corten (2010), *The Law Against War*, Hart Publishing, pp. 50–92.

45. Oscar Schachter (1960), "The Enforcement of International Judicial and Arbitral Decisions," *American Journal of International Law* 54: 1–24, at 15.

46. Quoted in Oscar Schachter (1984), "The Right of States to Use Armed Force," *Michigan Law Review* 82: 1620–1646, at 1627.

47. Quoted in Christine Gray (2018), *International Law and the Use of Force*, Oxford University Press, p. 39.

48. W. Michael Reisman (1984), "Coercion and Self-Determination: Construing Charter Article 2(4)," *American Journal of International Law* 78: 642–645, at 642.

49. Thomas M. Franck (1970), "Who Killed Article 2(4)? or: Changing Norms Governing the Use of Force by States," *American Journal of International Law* 64: 809–837, at 810.

50. UNGA Resolutions 290 (1949), 375 (1949), and 2131 (1965).

51. UNGA Resolution 2625 (1970).

52. Ibid.

53. Russell Buchan (2012), "Cyber Attacks: Unlawful Uses of Force or Prohibited Interventions?," *Journal of Conflict and Security Law* 17: 211–227.

54. UN Charter (1945), Article 39.

55. UNSC Resolution 83 (1950).

56. UNSC Resolution 221 (1966).

57. Olivier Corten (2010), *The Law Against War*, Hart Publishing, p. 316.

58. John Quigley (1996), "The Privatization of Security Council Enforcement Action: A Threat to Multilateralism," *Michigan Journal of International Law* 17: 249–283, at 250.

59. Scott Sheeran (2015), "The Use of Force in United Nations Peacekeeping Operations," in *The Oxford Handbook of the Use of Force in International Law*, edited by Marc Weller, Oxford University Press, pp. 347–374.

60. Olivier Corten (2010), *The Law Against War*, Hart Publishing, pp. 311, 314–315; Yoram Dinstein (2017), *War, Aggression and Self-Defence*, Cambridge University Press, p. 353.

61. Christian Henderson (2018), *The Use of Force and International Law*, Cambridge University Press, p. 86.

62. UNSC Resolution 687 (1991).

63. William H. Taft IV and Todd F. Buchwald (2003), "Preemption, Iraq, and International Law," *American Journal of International Law* 97: 557–563.

64. Niels Blokker (2015), "Outsourcing the Use of Force: Towards More Security Council Control of Authorized Operations?," in *The Oxford Handbook of the Use of Force in International Law*, edited by Marc Weller, Oxford University Press, pp. 202–226.

65. Geir Ulfstein and Hege Fosund Christiansen (2013), "The Legality of the NATO Bombing in Libya," *International & Comparative Law Quarterly* 62: 159–171.

66. Christine Gray (2018), *International Law and the Use of Force*, Oxford University Press, pp. 377–378.

67. Jacob Katz Cogan (2015), "Stabilization and the Expanding Scope of the Security Council's Work," *American Journal of International Law* 109: 324–339.

68. UN Charter (1945), Article 24.

69. André Nollkaemper (2015), "'Failures to Protect' in International Law," in *The Oxford Handbook of the Use of Force in International Law*, edited by Marc Weller, Oxford University Press, pp. 437–464.

70. Anne Orford (1996), "The Politics of Collective Security," *Michigan Journal of International Law* 17: 373–409.

71. Songying Fang (2008), "The Informational Role of International Institutions and Domestic Politics," *American Journal of Political Science* 52: 304–321.

72. Alexander Thompson (2005), "Coercion Through IOs: The Security Council and the Logic of Information Transmission," *International Organization* 60: 1–34.

73. Erik Voeten (2005), "The Political Origins of the UN Security Council's Ability to Legitimize the Use of Force," *International Organization* 59: 527–557.

74. Kenneth W. Abbott and Duncan Snidal (2000), "Hard and Soft Law in International Governance," *International Organization* 54: 421–456, at 444–446.

75. Ian Johnstone (2015), "When the Security Council Is Divided: Imprecise Authorizations, Implied Mandates, and the 'Unreasonable Veto'," in *The Oxford Handbook of the Use of Force in International Law*, edited by Marc Weller, Oxford University Press, pp. 227–250.

76. Christine Gray (2018), *International Law and the Use of Force*, Oxford University Press, pp. 385–386.

77. Ian Johnstone (2015), "When the Security Council Is Divided: Imprecise Authorizations, Implied Mandates, and the 'Unreasonable Veto'," in *The Oxford Handbook of the Use of Force in International Law*, edited by Marc Weller, Oxford University Press, pp. 242–243.

78. UNSC Resolutions 1160 (1998), 1199 (1998), and 1203 (1998). As discussed in section 5.2, other states argued that the bombing was justified as humanitarian intervention.

79. Olivier Corten (2010), *The Law Against War*, Hart Publishing, pp. 348–400.

80. Erika de Wet (2014), "The Evolving Role of ECOWAS and the SADC in Peace Operations: A Challenge to the Primacy of the United Nations Security Council in Matters of Peace and Security," *Leiden Journal of International Law* 27: 353–369, at 355.

81. Monica Hakimi (2007), "To Condone or Condemn: Regional Enforcement Actions in the Absence of Security Council Authorization," *Vanderbilt Journal of Transnational Law* 40: 643–685.

82. Recall that Chapter 3 discussed attribution in the *Nicaragua* case.

83. ICJ, *Nicaragua*, Judgment of 27 June 1986, para. 191.

84. Ibid.

85. Olivier Corten (2010), *The Law Against War*, Hart Publishing, p. 404.

86. ICJ, *Nicaragua*, Judgment of 27 June 1986, para. 195.

87. Ibid.

88. Ibid., para. 230.

89. Ibid., para. 231.

90. Christine Gray (2018), *International Law and the Use of Force*, Oxford University Press, pp. 126–129.

91. ICJ, *Nicaragua*, Judgment of 27 June 1986, para. 200.

92. Ibid., para. 235.

93. Ibid.

94. Ibid., para. 195.

95. Ibid., para. 199.

96. ICJ, *Nicaragua*, Dissenting Opinion of Judge Schwebel of 27 June 1986, para. 223.

97. ICJ, *Nicaragua*, Judgment of 27 June 1986, para. 236.

98. Ibid., para. 233.

99. Rosalyn Higgins (1994), *Problems and Process: International Law and How We Use It*, Clarendon Press, pp. 248–251.

100. William H. Taft IV (2004), "Self-Defense and the *Oil Platforms* Decision," *Yale Journal of International Law* 29: 295–306, at 300.

101. Ibid.

102. James A. Green (2017), "The 'Additional' Criteria for Collective Self-Defence: Request but Not Declaration," *Journal on the Use and Force of International Law* 4: 4–13.

103. Christine Gray (2018), *International Law and the Use of Force*, Oxford University Press, p. 125.

104. Experts use a variety of terms to describe such force, including: anticipatory, preventive, and preemptive self-defense.

105. Olivier Corten (2010), *The Law Against War*, Hart Publishing, p. 407.

106. Quoted in John Quigley (2018), "The Six Day War: 1967," in *The Use of Force in International Law*, edited by Tom Ruys and Olivier Corten, Oxford University Press, p. 135.

107. Ibid., pp. 137–141.

108. US White House (2002), "The National Security Strategy of the United States of America," p. 15.

109. Olivier Corten (2010), *The Law Against War*, Hart Publishing, pp. 406–443.

110. Christian Henderson (2018), *The Use of Force and International Law*, Cambridge University Press, pp. 291–292; W. Michael Reisman and Andrea Armstrong (2006), "The Past and Future of the Claim of Preemptive Self-Defense," *American Journal of International Law* 100: 525–550, at 538–546.

111. UN Document, S/PV.2288, para. 85.

112. Anthony Clark Arend and Robert J. Beck (1993), *International Law and the Use of Force*, Routledge, p. 78.

113. Lindsay Moir (2018), "Israeli Airstrikes in Syria: 2003 and 2007," in *The Use of Force in International Law*, edited by Tom Ruys and Olivier Corten, Oxford University Press, p. 663.

114. Ibid., p. 668.

115. Ibid., pp. 666–667.

116. Christian Henderson (2018), *The Use of Force and International Law*, Cambridge University Press, pp. 290–291.

117. Olivier Corten (2010), *The Law Against War*, Hart Publishing, pp. 127–129.

118. See Chapter 3.

119. Anthony Clark Arend and Robert J. Beck (1993), *International Law and the Use of Force*, Routledge, pp. 157–170.

120. UN Document S/PV.2611, p. 65.

121. Ibid., p. 66.

122. Quoted in Enzo Cannizzaro and Aurora Rasi (2018), "The US Strikes in Sudan and Afghanistan: 1998," in *The Use of Force in International Law*, edited by Tom Ruys and Olivier Corten, Oxford University Press, p. 546.

123. Christine Gray (2018), *International Law and the Use of Force*, Oxford University Press, pp. 146–147.

124. UN Document S/PV.4370, pp. 7–8.

125. UN Document S/2001/946.

126. Michael Byers (2018), "The Intervention in Afghanistan: 2001," in *The Use of Force in International Law*, edited by Tom Ruys and Olivier Corten, Oxford University Press, pp. 629–631.

127. Ibid., p. 631.

128. UN Document S/2014/440.

129. UN Document S/2014/695.

130. Laurie O'Connor (2016), "Legality of the Use of Force in Syria Against Islamic State and the Khorasan Group," *Journal on the Use and Force of International Law* 3: 70–96, at 80.

131. Kimberly N. Trapp (2007), "Back to Basics: Necessity, Proportionality and the Right to Self-Defense Against Non-State Terrorist Actors," *International & Comparative Law Quarterly* 56: 141–156.

132. ICJ, *Armed Activities*, Judgment of 19 December 2005, para. 147.

133. Olivier Corten (2010), *The Law Against War*, Hart Publishing, p. 469.

134. ICJ, *Armed Activities*, Separate Opinions of Judges Kooijmans and Simma of 19 December 2005.

135. Olivier Corten (2010), *The Law Against War*, Hart Publishing, p. 173.

136. Antonio Cassese (2001), "Terrorism Is Also Disrupting Some Crucial Legal Categories in International Law," *European Journal of International Law* 12: 993–1001, at 998.

137. David Kretzmer (2005), "Targeted Killing of Suspected Terrorists: Extra-Judicial Executions or Legitimate Means of Defence?," *European Journal of International Law* 16: 171–212; Meagan S. Wong (2012), "Targeted Killings and the International Legal Framework: With Particular Reference to the US Operation Against Osama Bin Laden," *Chicago Journal of International Law* 11: 127–163.

138. Christian Henderson (2018), *The Use of Force and International Law*, Cambridge University Press, p. 246.

139. Emer de Vattel (1758/2008), *The Law of Nations*, translated by Thomas Nugent, Liberty Fund, Book II, Section 71.

140. William H. Wynne (1951), *State Insolvency and Foreign Bondholders: Selected Case Histories of Governmental Foreign Bond Defaults and Debt Readjustments*, Yale University Press.

141. Edwin M. Borchard (1919), *The Diplomatic Protection of Citizens Abroad*, Banks Law Publishing.

142. Arnulf Becker Lorca (2014), *Mestizo International Law: A Global Intellectual History 1842–1933*, Cambridge University Press.

143. Quincy Wright (1933), "The Meaning of the Pact of Paris," *American Journal of International Law* 27: 39–61, at 54–55.

144. Gerald Fitzmaurice (1957), "The General Principles of International Law Considered from the Standpoint of the Rule of Law," *Recueil des Cours* 92: 1–228, at 173.

145. Saul David (2015), *Operation Thunderbolt*, Little, Brown.

146. UN Document S/PV.1939, p. 5.

147. Ibid., p. 13.

148. Ibid., p. 25.

149. UN Document S/PV.1941, p. 8.

150. UN Document S/12138 and S/12139, respectively.

151. Olivier Corten (2010), *The Law Against War*, Hart Publishing, pp. 50–92.

152. Richard B. Lillich (1967), "Forcible Self-Help by States to Protect Human Rights," *Iowa Law Review* 53: 325–351; Natalino Ronzitti (1985), *Rescuing Nationals Through Military Coercion and Intervention on Grounds of Humanity*, Martinus Nijhoff.

153. Natalino Ronzitti (1985), *Rescuing Nationals Through Military Coercion and Intervention on Grounds of Humanity*, Martinus Nijhoff, p. 69.

154. Ibid.

155. Richard Lillich (1992), "Forcible Protection of Nationals Abroad: The Liberian 'Incident' of 1990," *German Yearbook of International Law* 35: 205–223, at 220.

156. Christopher C. Joyner (1984), "Reflections on the Lawfulness of Invasion," *American Journal of International Law* 78: 131–144, at 134.

157. Quoted in Robert Chatham (2011), "Defense of Nationals Abroad: The Legitimacy of Russia's Invasion of Georgia," *Florida Journal of International Law* 23: 75–102, at 76.

158. James A. Green (2014), "The Annexation of Crimea: Russia, Passportization and the Protection of Nationals Revisited," *Journal on the Use and Force of International Law* 1: 3–10.

159. Thomas D. Grant (2015), "Annexation of Crimea," *American Journal of International Law* 109: 68–95, at 80–81.

160. Natalino Ronzitti (1985), *Rescuing Nationals Through Military Coercion and Intervention on Grounds of Humanity*, Martinus Nijhoff, pp. 69–70.

161. Ibid., p. 71.

162. Joseph J. Eldred (2008), "The Use of Force in Hostage Rescue Missions," *Naval Law Review* 56: 251–273, at 270.

163. Natalino Ronzitti (1985), *Rescuing Nationals Through Military Coercion and Intervention on Grounds of Humanity*, Martinus Nijhoff.

164. Ian Brownlie (1963), *International Law and the Use of Force by States*, Clarendon Press, p. 340.

165. Discussions of these examples are available in Natalino Ronzitti (1985), *Rescuing Nationals Through Military Coercion and Intervention on Grounds of Humanity*, Martinus Nijhoff; and Nigel Rodley (2015), "Humanitarian Intervention," in *The Oxford Handbook of the Use of Force in International Law*, edited by Marc Weller, Oxford University Press, pp. 775–796.

166. Gary J. Bass (2013), *The Blood Telegram: Nixon, Kissinger, and a Forgotten Genocide*, Alfred A. Knopf.

167. Kenneth Chan (2018), "The Ugandan-Tanzanian War, 1978–1979," in *The Use of Force in International Law*, edited by Tom Ruys and Olivier Corten, Oxford University Press, p. 256.

168. Ibid., pp. 257–258.

169. Michael J. Levitin (1986), "The Law of Force and the Force of Law: Grenada, the Falklands, and Humanitarian Intervention," *Health Information and Libraries Journal* 27: 621–657.

170. Ved P. Nanda (1992), "Tragedies in Northern Iraq, Liberia, Yugoslavia, and Haiti: Re-visiting the Validity of Humanitarian Intervention under International Law—Part I," *Denver Journal of International Law & Policy* 20: 305–334, at 306; Michael J. Levitin (1986), "The Law of Force and the Force of Law: Grenada, the Falklands, and Human-itarian Intervention," *Health Information and Libraries Journal* 27: 621–657, at 652.

171. W. Michael Reisman (1990), "Sovereignty and Human Rights in Contemporary Inter-national Law," *American Journal of International Law* 84: 866–876, at 875.

172. Ved P. Nanda (1992), "Tragedies in Northern Iraq, Liberia, Yugoslavia, and Haiti: Re-visiting the Validity of Humanitarian Intervention under International Law—Part I," *Denver Journal of International Law & Policy* 20: 305–334, at 306.

173. Quoted in Christian Henderson (2018), *The Use of Force and International Law*, Cambridge University Press, p. 391.

174. Jeremy Levitt (1998), "Humanitarian Intervention by Regional Actors in Internal Conflicts: The Cases of ECOWAS in Liberia and Sierra Leone," *Temple International and Comparative Law Journal* 12: 333–375.

175. Christine Gray (2002), "From Unity to Polarization: International Law and the Use of Force Against Iraq," *European Journal of International Law* 13: 1–19, at 9–10.

176. UNSC Resolutions 1160 (1998), 1199 (1998), and 1203 (1998).

177. Christopher Greenwood (1999), "Humanitarian Intervention: The Case of Kosovo," *Finnish Yearbook of International Law* 10: 141–175, at 151.

178. UNSC Resolution 1244 (1999).

179. UN Document S/PV.3988, p. 12.

180. Ibid., p. 6.

181. Carsten Stahn (2007), "Responsibility to Protect: Political Rhetoric or Emerging Legal Norm?," *American Journal of International Law* 101: 99–120, at 102.

182. International Commission on Intervention and State Sovereignty (2001), *The Respon-sibility to Protect*, International Development Research Centre.

183. Peter Hilpold (2012), "Intervening in the Name of Humanity: R2P and the Power of Ideas," *Journal of Conflict and Security Law* 17: 49–79, at 68.

184. UNGA Resolution 60/1 (2005), paras. 138–140. See also Carlo Focarelli (2008), "The Responsibility to Protect Doctrine and Humanitarian Intervention: Too Many Ambi-guities for a Working Doctrine," *Journal of Conflict and Security Law* 13: 191–213.

185. Fernando R. Tesón (1996), "Collective Humanitarian Intervention," *Michigan Journal of International Law* 17: 323–371; Olivier Corten (2010), *The Law Against War*, Hart Publishing, p. 540.

186. Louis Henkin (1999), "Kosovo and the Law of 'Humanitarian Intervention'," *Ameri-can Journal of International Law* 93: 824–828, at 825.

187. Ruth Wedgwood (1999), "NATO's Campaign in Yugoslavia," *American Journal of International Law* 93: 828–834, at 834.

188. Anne Orford (1999), "Muscular Humanitarianism: Reading the Narratives of the New Interventionism," *European Journal of International Law* 10: 679–711, at 687, 688.

189. Nigel Rodley (2015), "Humanitarian Intervention," in *The Oxford Handbook of the Use of Force in International Law*, edited by Marc Weller, Oxford University Press, p. 787.

190. Anne Orford (1999), "Muscular Humanitarianism: Reading the Narratives of the New Interventionism," *European Journal of International Law* 10: 679–711, at 697.

191. Christopher Greenwood (1999), "Humanitarian Intervention: The Case of Kosovo," *Finnish Yearbook of International Law* 10: 141–175, at 144.

192. UN Document S/PV.4011, p. 12.

193. An excellent overview of the legal issues in this conflict is Tom Ruys (2014), "Of Arms, Funding and 'Non-Lethal Assistance': Issues Surrounding Third-State Intervention in the Syrian Civil War," *Chicago Journal of International Law* 13: 13–53.

194. See Chapter 3.

195. Ademola Abass (2004), "Consent Precluding State Responsibility: A Critical Analysis," *International & Comparative Law Quarterly* 53: 211–225, at 224.

196. James A. Green (2014), "The Annexation of Crimea: Russia, Passportisation and the Protection of Nationals Revisited," *Journal on the Use and Force of International Law* 1: 3–10, at 6.

197. ICJ, *Armed Activities*, Judgment of 19 December 2005, para. 47.

198. ICJ, *Nicaragua*, Judgment of 27 June 1986, para. 246.

199. Tom Ruys (2014), "Of Arms, Funding and 'Non-Lethal Assistance': Issues Surrounding Third-State Intervention in the Syrian Civil War," *Chicago Journal of International Law* 13: 13–53, at 15.

200. Audio recording available in Anne Barnard (2016), "Audio Reveals What John Kerry Told Syrians Behind Closed Doors," *New York Times*, September 30, available at www.nytimes.com/interactive/2016/09/30/world/middleeast/john-kerry-syria-audio.html.

201. UNGA Resolution 2625 (1970).

202. UNGA Resolution 3314 (1974).

203. Louise Doswald-Beck (1985), "The Legal Validity of Military Intervention by Invitation of the Government," *British Yearbook of International Law* 56: 189–252, at 200–207.

204. Ian Brownlie (1963), *International Law and the Use of Force by States*, Clarendon Press, pp. 321–327.

205. Institut de Droit International (1975), "The Principle of Non-Intervention in Civil Wars," *Annuaire de l'Institut de droit international* 56: 545–549, at 545–547.

206. Note that in this context, the phrase "effective control" refers to territory. International law also uses the term "effective control" in the context of attribution for the acts of non-state actors. See Chapter 3.

207. David Wippman (1996), "Military Intervention, Regional Organizations, and Host-State Consent," *Duke Journal of Comparative & International Law* 7: 209–239, at 212.

208. Brad R. Roth (2010), "Secessions, Coups and the International Rule of Law: Assessing the Decline of the Effective Control Doctrine," *Melbourne Journal of International Law* 11: 393–440, at 395.

209. Mohamed S. Helal (2018), "The ECOWAS Intervention in The Gambia, 2016," in *The Use of Force in International Law*, edited by Tom Ruys and Olivier Corten, Oxford University Press, pp. 912–919.

210. Ibid., p. 922.
211. For example, see Nabil Hajjami (2018), "The Intervention of the United States and Other Eastern Caribbean States in Grenada, 1983," in *The Use of Force in International Law*, edited by Tom Ruys and Olivier Corten, Oxford University Press, pp. 393–394.
212. Ian Brownlie (1963), *International Law and the Use of Force by States*, Clarendon Press, pp. 317–319.
213. UN Charter (1945), Article 103.
214. Jean Allain (2004), "The True Challenge to the United Nations System of the Use of Force: The Failures of Kosovo and Iraq and the Emergence of the African Union," *Max Planck Yearbook of United National Law* 8: 237–289; Eliav Lieblich (2011), "Intervention and Consent: Consensual Forcible Interventions in Internal Armed Conflicts as International Agreements," *Boston University International Law Journal* 29: 337–382.
215. ECOWAS Lomé Protocol (1999), Article 10(2)(c).
216. African Union Constitutive Act (2000), Article 4.
217. Ademola Abass (2004), "Consent Precluding State Responsibility: A Critical Analysis," *International & Comparative Law Quarterly* 53: 211–225; Ntombizozuko Dyani-Mhango (2012), "Reflections on the African Union's Right to Intervene," *Brooklyn Journal of International Law* 38: 1–48.
218. UN Document S/PRST/2015/8.
219. Ibid., pp. 4–5.
220. UN Document S/PRST/2015/8 (emphasis added).
221. UNSC Resolution 2216 (2015).
222. UN Document S/2015/217, pp. 4, 5.
223. Luca Ferro and Tom Ruys (2018), "The Military Intervention in Yemen's Civil War, 2015," in *The Use of Force in International Law*, edited by Tom Ruys and Olivier Corten, Oxford University Press, pp. 905–906.
224. UN Document S/2015/217, p. 5.
225. Benjamin Nußberger (2017), "Military Strikes in Yemen in 2015: Intervention by Invitation and Self-Defense in the Course of Yemen's 'Model Transitional Process'," *Journal on the Use and Force of International Law* 4: 110–160, at 114–119.
226. Michael Walzer (1977), *Just and Unjust Wars*, Basic Books, pp. xii, xiii.

10 ARMED CONFLICT

1. ISIL is also known as Islamic State in Iraq and Syria, Islamic State, and Daesh.
2. Tobias Schneider and Theresa Lütkefend (2019), *Nowhere to Hide: The Logic of Chemical Weapons Use in Syria*, Global Public Policy Institute.
3. White House, Office of the Press Secretary (2012), "Remarks by the President to the White House Press Corps," August 20, available at https://obamawhitehouse.archives.gov/the-press-office/2012/08/20/remarks-president-white-house-press-corps.
4. Matt Williams (2013), "John McCain: Obama's 'Red Line' on Syria 'Written in Disappearing Ink'," *The Guardian*, May 5, available at www.theguardian.com/world/2013/may/05/john-mccain-obama-syria-red-line.
5. UK Ministry of Defence (2010), *The Manual of the Law of Armed Conflict*, Oxford University Press, pp. 28–29.

6. ICTY, *Tadić*, Judgment of 2 October 1995, para. 70.

7. AP/I (1977), Article 48.

8. Ibid.

9. ICJ, *Armed Activities*, Judgment of 19 December 2005, para. 211.

10. St. Petersburg Declaration (1868).

11. UNGA Resolution 49/75 (1994), Section K.

12. ICJ, *Nuclear Weapons*, Advisory Opinion of 8 July 1996, para. 78.

13. Ibid., para. 95.

14. Ibid., para. 105(2)E.

15. Scholars often refer to "necessity"—the term used in state responsibility law to excuse or justify some legal breaches. Since necessity under *jus in bello* constrains (rather than excuses or justifies) armed conflict, we use the term "military necessity" to avoid confusion.

16. UK Ministry of Defence (2010), *The Manual of the Law of Armed Conflict*, Oxford University Press, pp. 21–22.

17. UNSC Resolution 678 (1990).

18. Yishai Beer (2015), "Humanity Considerations Cannot Reduce War's Hazards Alone: Revitalizing the Concept of Military Necessity," *European Journal of International Law* 26: 801–828, at 816–818.

19. A.P.V. Rogers (2012), *Law on the Battlefield*, Manchester University Press, pp. 21–27.

20. AP/I (1977), Article 51(5)(b).

21. UK Ministry of Defence (2010), *The Manual of the Law of Armed Conflict*, Oxford University Press, p. 26.

22. A.P.V. Rogers (2012) *Law on the Battlefield*, Manchester University Press, p. 27.

23. US Department of Defense (1992), "Conduct of the Persian Gulf War: Final Report to Congress," Appendix O, p. 613.

24. Burrus M. Carnahan (1998), "Lincoln, Lieber and the Laws of War: The Origins and Limits of the Principle of Military Necessity," *American Journal of International Law* 92: 213–231, at 214.

25. Detlev F. Vagts (2000), "The Hague Conventions and Arms Control," *American Journal of International Law* 94: 31–41, at 32.

26. Hague Convention IV (1907), Preamble.

27. Theodor Meron (2000), "The Martens Clause, Principles of Humanity, and Dictates of Public Conscience," *American Journal of International Law* 94: 78–89, at 89.

28. The Hague Regulations are also known as the Annex to Hague Convention IV (1907).

29. James D. Morrow (2007), "When Do States Follow the Laws of War?," *American Political Science Review* 101: 559–572.

30. Geneva Convention (1929).

31. James D. Morrow (2015), *Order within Anarchy: The Laws of War as an International Institution*, Cambridge University Press, pp. 192–293.

32. Ibid., p. 207.

33. Antonio Cassese (2000), "The Martens Clause: Half a Loaf or Simply Pie in the Sky?," *European Journal of International Law* 11: 187–216, at 204–205.

34. Theodor Meron (2000), "The Humanization of Humanitarian Law," *American Journal of International Law* 94: 239–278, at 247–248.

35. Lawrence Hill-Cawthorne (2017), "Rights under International Humanitarian Law," *European Journal of International Law* 28: 1187–1215.

36. Theodor Meron (2000), "The Humanization of Humanitarian Law," *American Journal of International Law* 94: 239–278, at 247–253.

37. Amanda Alexander (2015), "A Short History of International Humanitarian Law," *European Journal of International Law* 26: 109–138.

38. Hague Regulations (1907), Article 1.

39. Guy B. Roberts (1985), "The New Rules of Waging War: The Case Against Ratification of Additional Protocol I," *Virginia Journal of International Law* 26: 109–170, at 129.

40. Robert Kolb and Richard Hyde (2008), *An Introduction to the International Law of Armed Conflicts*, Hart Publishing, pp. 202–203.

41. AP/I (1977), Article 43.

42. Ibid.

43. AP/I (1977), Article 44(3).

44. Ibid.

45. Guy B. Roberts (1985), "The New Rules of Waging War: The Case Against Ratification of Additional Protocol I," *Virginia Journal of International Law* 26: 109–170, at 128.

46. AP/I (1977), Article 44(2).

47. Emily Crawford (2015), *Identifying the Enemy: Civilian Participation in Armed Conflict*, Oxford University Press, pp. 42–43.

48. Douglas J. Feith (1985), "Law in the Service of Terror: The Strange Case of the Additional Protocol," *National Interest* 1: 36–47.

49. George H. Aldrich (2002), "The Taliban, Al Qaeda, and the Determination of Illegal Combatants," *American Journal of International Law* 96: 891–898, at 891–892.

50. Experts also refer to regular/lawful versus irregular/unlawful combatants. John C. Yoo and James C. Ho (2003), "The Status of Terrorists," *Virginia Journal of International Law* 44: 207–228, at 215–222.

51. Gabor Rona (2005), "Legal Frameworks to Combat Terrorists: An Abundant Inventory of Existing Tools," *Chicago Journal of International Law* 5: 499–509, at 504.

52. Emily Crawford (2015), *Identifying the Enemy: Civilian Participation in Armed Conflict*, Oxford University Press, pp. 60–72.

53. ICRC (2008), "Interpretive Guidance on the Notion of Direct Participation in Hostilities under International Humanitarian Law," *International Review of the Red Cross* 90: 991–1047.

54. Emily Crawford (2015), *Identifying the Enemy: Civilian Participation in Armed Conflict*, Oxford University Press, pp. 126–150.

55. Hague Regulations (1907), Article 25.

56. Richard D. Rosen (2009), "Targeting Enemy Forces in the War on Terror: Preserving Civilian Immunity," *Vanderbilt Journal of Transnational Law* 42: 683–777.

57. Geneva Conventions (1949), Common Article 3(1).

58. Geneva Convention IV (1949), Article 14.

59. Ibid., Article 18.

60. Ibid., Article 15.

61. Ibid., Article 23.

62. Ibid.

63. Ibid., Articles 24 and 25.

64. Ibid., Article 27.

65. Ibid., Article 28.

66. Ryan Goodman (2009), "The Detention of Civilians in Armed Conflict," *American Journal of International Law* 103: 48–74.

67. Richard D. Rosen (2009), "Targeting Enemy Forces in the War on Terror: Preserving Civilian Immunity," *Vanderbilt Journal of Transnational Law* 42: 683–777.

68. AP/I (1977), Article 51(2).

69. Ibid., Article 51(4).

70. Ibid., Article 54.

71. Ibid., Article 57.

72. Richard D. Rosen (2009), "Targeting Enemy Forces in the War on Terror: Preserving Civilian Immunity," *Vanderbilt Journal of Transnational Law* 42: 683–777, at 705.

73. Eric Talbot Jensen (2005), "Combatant Status: It Is Time for Intermediate Levels of Recognition for Partial Compliance," *Virginia Journal of International Law* 46: 209–249.

74. Alexander B. Downes (2006), "Desperate Times, Desperate Measures: The Causes of Civilian Victimization in War," *International Security* 30: 152–195, at 152.

75. Ibid.

76. Anthony Anghie (2005), *Imperialism, Sovereignty and the Making of International Law*, Cambridge University Press.

77. Helen M. Kinsella (2011), *The Image before the Weapon: A Critical History of the Distinction between Combatant and Civilian*, Cornell University Press, pp. 82–103.

78. Tanisha M. Fazal and Brooke C. Greene (2015), "A Particular Difference: European Identity and Civilian Targeting," *British Journal for the Philosophy of Science* 45: 829–851.

79. Alexander B. Downes (2008), *Targeting Civilians in War*, Cornell University Press.

80. Benjamin Valentino, Paul Huth, and Dylan Balch-Lindsay (2004), "'Draining the Sea': Mass Killing and Guerrilla Warfare," *International Organization* 58: 375–407.

81. Benjamin Valentino, Paul Huth, and Sarah Croco (2006), "Covenants without the Sword: International Law and the Protection of Civilians in Times of War," *World Politics* 58: 339–377.

82. Jack M. Beard (2009), "Law and War in the Virtual Era," *American Journal of International Law* 103: 409–445.

83. Leslie Johns and Frank Wyer (2019), "When Things Fall Apart: The Impact of Global Governance on Civil Conflict," *Journal of Politics* 81: e80–e84.

84. R. Charli Carpenter (2005), "'Women, Children and Other Vulnerable Groups': Gender, Strategic Frames and the Protection of Civilians as a Transnational Issue," *International Studies Quarterly* 49: 295–334.

85. Adam Jones (2000), "Gendercide and Genocide," *Journal of Genocide Research* 2: 185–211.

86. R. Charli Carpenter (2003), "'Women and Children First': Gender, Norms and Humanitarian Evacuation in the Balkans 1991–1995," *International Organization* 57: 661–694.

87. Sandesh Sivakumaran (2007), "Sexual Violence Against Men in Armed Conflict," *European Journal of International Law* 18: 253–276.

88. Emily Crawford (2015), *Identifying the Enemy: Civilian Participation in Armed Conflict*, Oxford University Press, p. 2.

89. Eric Talbot Jensen (2005), "Combatant Status: It Is Time for Intermediate Levels of Recognition for Partial Compliance," *Virginia Journal of International Law* 46: 209–249, at 223.

90. Derek Jinks (2004), "The Declining Significance of POW Status," *Health Information and Libraries Journal* 45: 367–442, at 422.

91. Jack M. Beard (2007), "The Geneva Boomerang: The Military Commissions Act of 2006 and US Counterterror Operations," *American Journal of International Law* 101: 56–73.

92. Geneva Conventions I and II (1949), Article 12.

93. Ibid.

94. AP/I (1977), Article 10.

95. Quoted in Geoffrey P.R. Wallace (2015), *Life and Death in Captivity: The Abuse of Prisoners During War*, Cornell University Press, p. 98.

96. Geneva Convention III (1949), Article 4.

97. Ibid., Article 50.

98. Ibid., Article 13.

99. Ibid.

100. AP/I (1977), Article 75.

101. Ibid.

102. For the most egregious incidents, see Karen J. Greenberg and Joshua L. Dratel (2005), *The Torture Papers: The Road to Abu Ghraib*, Cambridge University Press.

103. Robert Cryer (2002), "The Fine Art of Friendship: Jus in Bello in Afghanistan," *Journal of Conflict and Security Law* 7: 37–83, at 76.

104. Ibid., p. 77.

105. Geoffrey P.R. Wallace (2012), "Welcome Guests, or Inescapable Victims? The Causes of Prisoner Abuse in War," *Journal of Conflict Resolution* 56: 955–981.

106. Geoffrey P.R. Wallace (2015), *Life and Death in Captivity: The Abuse of Prisoners During War*, Cornell University Press, pp. 99–128.

107. S.P. MacKenzie (1994), "The Treatment of Prisoners of War in World War II," *Journal of Modern History* 66: 487–520, at 518.

108. Ibid.

109. Geoffrey P.R. Wallace (2012), "Welcome Guests, or Inescapable Victims? The Causes of Prisoner Abuse in War," *Journal of Conflict Resolution* 56: 955–981.

110. James D. Morrow (2015), *Order within Anarchy: The Laws of War as an International Institution*, Cambridge University Press.

111. S.P. MacKenzie (1994), "The Treatment of Prisoners of War in World War II," *Journal of Modern History* 66: 487–520.

112. Hague Regulations (1907), Article 25.

113. AP/I (1977), Article 52(2).

114. Robert Kolb and Richard Hyde (2008), *An Introduction to the International Law of Armed Conflicts*, Hart Publishing, p. 134.

115. Roger O'Keefe (2006), *The Protection of Cultural Property in Armed Conflict*, Cambridge University Press.

116. A.P.V. Rogers (2012), *Law on the Battlefield*, Manchester University Press, p. 112.

117. These statues were not considered protected property because they lacked cultural significance.

118. ICTY, "Final Report to the Prosecutor by the Committee Established to Review the NATO Bombing Campaign Against the Federal Republic of Yugoslavia," para. 17.

119. Quoted in ibid., para. 74.

120. Paolo Benvenuti (2001), "The ICTY Prosecutor and the Review of the NATO Bombing Campaign Against the Federal Republic of Yugoslavia," *European Journal of International Law* 12: 503–529, at 522–524.

121. ICTY, "Final Report to the Prosecutor by the Committee Established to Review the NATO Bombing Campaign Against the Federal Republic of Yugoslavia," para. 78.

122. Peter Beaumont and Rory McCarthy (2003), "British Tanks force Way into Basra and Destroy Ba'ath Party HQ," *The Guardian*, April 6, available at www.theguardian.com/world/2003/apr/07/iraq.rorymccarthy2.

123. Ryan Goodman (2016), "The Obama Administration and Targeting War-Sustaining Objects in Noninternational Armed Conflict," *American Journal of International Law* 110: 663–679, at 666–667.

124. US White House, Office of the Press Secretary (2016), "Remarks by the President on Progress Against ISIL," February 25, available at https://obamawhitehouse.archives.gov/the-press-office/2016/02/25/remarks-president-progress-against-isil.

125. Ryan Goodman (2016), "The Obama Administration and Targeting War-Sustaining Object in Noninternational Armed Conflict," *American Journal of International Law* 110: 663–679, at 665–666.

126. Ibid., pp. 671–676.

127. Hugo Grotius (1603/2006), *Commentary on the Law and Prize of Booty*, Liberty Fund.

128. Paris Declaration (1856), para. 1.

129. Geneva Convention IV (1949), Articles 33 and 34; AP/I (1977), Article 42(1).

130. Sarah L. Wells (2004), "Crimes Against Child Soldiers in Armed Conflict Situations: Application and Limits of International Humanitarian Law," *Tulane Journal of International and Comparative Law* 12: 287–305.

131. Julie McBride (2014), *The War Crime of Child Soldier Recruitment*, Asser Press, p. 2.

132. Bernd Beber and Christopher Blattman (2013), "The Logic of Child Soldiering and Coercion," *International Organization* 67: 65–104, at 68.

133. Mark A. Drumbl (2012), *Reimagining Child Soldiers in International Law and Policy*, Oxford University Press, p. 15.

134. R. Charli Carpenter (2007), "Setting the Advocacy Agenda: Issues and Non-Issues Around Children and Armed Conflict," *International Studies Quarterly* 51: 99–120, at 108–109.

135. Gus Waschefort (2015), *International Law and Child Soldiers*, Hart Publishing, pp. 30–31.

136. Convention on the Rights of the Child (1989), Article 38, paras. 2–3.

137. AP/I (1977), Article 77(2).

138. Rome Statute (1998), Article 8(2)(b)(xxvi).

139. Mark A. Drumbl (2012), *Reimagining Child Soldiers in International Law and Policy*, Oxford University Press, p. 138.

140. Ibid., pp. 102–133.

141. Gus Waschefort (2015), *International Law and Child Soldiers*, Hart Publishing, pp. 9, 10.

142. Mark A. Drumbl (2012), *Reimagining Child Soldiers in International Law and Policy*, Oxford University Press, p. 19.

143. International Institute for Strategic Studies (2018), *Armed Conflict Survey 2018*, IISS, pp. 33–50.

144. International law experts often use the terms "looting," "pillage," and "plunder" interchangeably. A.P.V. Rogers (2012), *Law on the Battlefield*, Manchester University Press, pp. 281–289.

145. Hugo Grotius (1625/2005), *The Rights of War and Peace*, Liberty Fund, Book III, Chapter VI, Section II, para. 1.

146. Hague Regulations (1907), Article 28. See also Articles 46 and 47.

147. Geneva Convention I (1949), Article 15; Geneva Convention II (1949), Article 18; Geneva Convention IV (1949), Articles 16, 33, 53, 147; AP/I (1977), Articles 4(g) and 8.

148. Rome Statute (1998), Article 8(2)(a)(iv), (b)(xvi), and (e)(v).

149. Jean d'Aspremont (2013), "Towards an International Law of Brigandage: Interpretive Engineering for the Regulation of Natural Resources Exploitation," *Asian Journal of International Law* 3: 1–24.

150. Michael A. Lundberg (2008), "The Plunder of Natural Resources During War: A War Crime," *Georgetown Journal of International Law* 39: 495–526, at 497–501.

151. Michael L. Ross (2015), "What Have We Learned about the Resource Curse?," *Annual Review of Political Science* 18: 239–259.

152. John Bellows and Edward Miguel (2009), "War and Local Collective Action in Sierra Leone," *Journal of Public Economics* 93: 1144–1157; Oeindrila Dube and Juan F. Vargas (2013), "Commodity Price Shocks and Civil Conflict: Evidence from Colombia," *Review of Economic Studies* 80: 1384–1421.

153. ICJ, *Armed Activities*, Judgment of 19 December 2005, para. 242.

154. Ibid., paras. 245, 250.

155. Virginia Haufler (2010), "The Kimberley Process Certification Scheme: An Innovation in Global Governance and Conflict Prevention," *Journal of Business Ethics* 89: 403–416.

156. Patrick J. Keenan (2014), "Conflict Minerals and the Law of Pillage," *Chicago Journal of International Law* 14: 524–558, at 539.

157. I use the term "sexual violence" to denote all non-consensual acts that are sexual in nature.

158. Theodor Meron (1993), "Rape as a Crime Under International Humanitarian Law," *American Journal of International Law* 87: 424–428, at 425.

159. Milli Lake (2018), *Strong NGOs and Weak States: Pursuing Gender Justice in the Democratic Republic of Congo and South Africa*, Cambridge University Press.

160. Theodor Meron (1993), "Rape as a Crime Under International Humanitarian Law," *American Journal of International Law* 87: 424–428, at 425.

161. Sandesh Sivakumaran (2007), "Sexual Violence Against Men in Armed Conflict," *European Journal of International Law* 18: 253–276.

162. Christine Chinkin (1994), "Rape and Sexual Abuse of Women in International Law," *European Journal of International Law* 5: 326–341, at 328.

163. Hague Regulations (1907), Article 46.

164. Geneva Convention IV (1949), Article 27.

165. AP/I (1977), Article 76(1).

166. Christine Chinkin (1994), "Rape and Sexual Abuse of Women in International Law," *European Journal of International Law* 5: 326–341, at 334.

167. Karen Engle (2005), "Feminism and its (Dis)contents: Criminalizing Wartime Rape in Bosnia and Herzegovina," *American Journal of International Law* 99: 778–816.

168. Milli Lake (2018), *Strong NGOs and Weak States: Pursuing Gender Justice in the Democratic Republic of Congo and South Africa*, Cambridge University Press.

169. Christine M. Chinkin (2001), "Women's International Tribunal on Japanese Military Sexual Slavery," *American Journal of International Law* 95: 335–340.

170. Rosa Freedman (2018), "UNaccountable: A New Approach to Peacekeepers and Sexual Abuse," *European Journal of International Law* 29: 961–985.

171. Ancient Greeks, Hindus, and Romans all prohibited poisoned weapons. See Adam Roberts and Richard Guelff (2000), *Documents on the Laws of War*, Oxford University Press, p. 53.

172. Lieber Code (1863), Article 70.

173. Hague Regulations (1907), Article 23(a).

174. St. Petersburg Declaration (1868).

175. Hague Declaration III (1899).

176. Kenneth Anderson (2000), "The Ottawa Convention Banning Landmines, the Role of International Non-Governmental Organizations and the Idea of International Civil Society," *European Journal of International Law* 11: 91–120.

177. Mine Ban Treaty (1997), Article 5(1).

178. Conventional Weapons Convention, Protocol II (1980), Article 1.

179. Yoram Dinstein (2016), *The Conduct of Hostilities under the Law of International Armed Conflict*, Cambridge University Press, p. 89.

180. UK Ministry of Defence (2010), *The Manual of the Law of Armed Conflict*, Oxford University Press, p. 112.

181. Conventional Weapons Convention, Protocol IV (1995), Article 1.

182. Associated Press (2019), "China Denies Targeting Australia with Lasers in South China Sea," News Corp Australia Network, May 30, available at www.news.com.au/technology/innovation/military/china-denies-targeting-australia-with-lasers-in-south-china-sea/news-story/4205c1e5b6fce92b25e61f682090dc59.

183. Idrees Ali, Gao Liangping, and Philip Wen (2018), "US Says Chinese Laser Attacks Injured Plane Crews; China Strongly Denies," Reuters News Service, May 4.

184. Conventional Weapons Convention, Protocol V (2003), Article 3.

185. Yoram Dinstein (2016), *The Conduct of Hostilities under the Law of International Armed Conflict*, Cambridge University Press, p. 90.

186. Hague Declaration II (1899).

187. Geneva Gas Protocol (1925).

188. BWC (1972), Article 1.

189. Yoram Dinstein (2016), *The Conduct of Hostilities under the Law of International Armed Conflict*, Cambridge University Press, p. 94.

190. Jack M. Beard (2007), "The Shortcomings of Indeterminacy in Arms Control Regimes: The Case of the Biological Weapons Convention," *American Journal of International Law* 101: 271–321.

191. CWC (1993), Article 1.

192. UNGA Resolution 49/75 (1994), part K.

193. ICJ, *Nuclear Weapons*, Advisory Opinion of 8 July 1996, para. 62.

194. Ibid., para. 63.

195. Ibid., para. 66.

196. Ibid., para. 35.

197. Ibid.

198. Ibid., para. 105(2)(e).

199. Ibid.

200. Jeffrey W. Legro (1995), *Cooperation Under Fire: Anglo-German Restraint During World War II*, Cornell University Press, p. 170.

201. Richard M. Price (1997), *The Chemical Weapons Taboo*, Cornell University Press, p. 28.

202. Jeffrey W. Legro (1995), *Cooperation Under Fire: Anglo-German Restraint During World War II*, Cornell University Press, pp. 152, 153.

203. R. Charli Carpenter (2011), "Vetting the Advocacy Agenda: Networks, Centrality and the Paradox of Weapons Norms," *International Organization* 65: 69–102.

204. Jeffrey W. Legro (1995), *Cooperation Under Fire: Anglo-German Restraint During World War II*, Cornell University Press, pp.193–195.

205. St. Petersburg Declaration (1868).

206. Tanisha M. Fazal and Brooke C. Greene (2015), "A Particular Difference: European Identity and Civilian Targeting," *British Journal for the Philosophy of Science* 45: 829–851.

207. Richard M. Price (1997), *The Chemical Weapons Taboo*, Cornell University Press, pp. 18–30.

208. Organisation for the Prohibition of Chemical Weapons (2021), Report C-25/4, para. 1.2 and Annex 1, available at www.opcw.org/sites/default/files/documents/2021/04/c2504%28e%29.pdf.

209. Ian Hurd (2017), *How to Do Things with International Law*, Princeton University Press, pp. 58–102.

210. Ibid., pp. 91–98.

211. Ryan J. Vogel (2010), "Drone Warfare and the Law of Armed Conflict," *Denver Journal of International Law and Policy* 39: 101–138, at 115–116, 124–129.

212. Ibid., pp. 118–122.

213. Susan Breau and Marie Aronsson (2012), "Drone Attacks, International Law, and the Recording of Civilian Casualties of Armed Conflict," *Suffolk Transnational Law Review* 35: 255–299, at 278–293.

214. Chantal Grut (2013), "The Challenge of Autonomous Lethal Robotics to International Humanitarian Law," *Journal of Conflict and Security Law* 18: 5–23.

215. In contrast, peaceful occupation—in which a territorial state gives consent to another state's authority—is not regulated by the international law of armed conflict.

216. Hague Regulations (1907), Article 42.

217. For example, see Robert Kolb and Richard Hyde (2008), *An Introduction to the International Law of Armed Conflicts*, Hart Publishing, pp. 244–246.

218. ICJ, *Armed Activities*, Judgment of 19 December 2005, para. 168.

219. Ibid., para. 170.

220. See Hague Regulations (1907), Articles 42–56.

221. Ibid., Article 43.

222. A.P.V. Rogers (2012), *Law on the Battlefield*, Manchester University Press, pp. 249–250.

223. Ibid., p. 250.

224. Ibid., p. 249.

225. Hague Regulations (1907), Articles 46–47.

226. Ibid., Article 48.

227. Ibid., Articles 49–50.

228. ICJ, *Armed Activities*, Judgment of 19 December 2005, para. 248.

229. Geneva Convention IV (1949), Articles 47–78; AP/I (1977), Articles 63, 69–79.

230. Geneva Convention IV (1949), Articles 48–49, 51, 53–54, 58; AP/I (1977), Articles 75–76.

231. Geneva Convention IV (1949), Articles 64–77; AP/I (1977), Article 75.

232. Geneva Convention IV (1949), Articles 50, 55–57; AP/I (1977), Article 69.

233. Geneva Convention IV (1949), Articles 59–63; AP/I (1977), Articles 69–71.

234. AP/II (1977), Article 1(2).

235. Jillian Blake and Aqsa Mahmud (2014), "The Arab Spring's Four Seasons: International Protections and the Sovereignty Problem," *Penn State Journal of Law & International Affairs* 3: 161–215.

236. David A. Elder (1979), "The Historical Background of Common Article 3 of the Geneva Convention of 1949," *Case Western Reserve Journal of International Law* 11: 37–69, at 41.

237. Yoram Dinstein (2014), *Non-International Armed Conflicts in International Law*, Cambridge University Press, p. 134.

238. Antonio Cassese (1981), "The Status of Rebels under the 1977 Geneva Protocol on Non-International Armed Conflicts," *International & Comparative Law Quarterly* 30: 416–430, at 418.

239. Yoram Dinstein (2014), *Non-International Armed Conflicts in International Law*, Cambridge University Press, pp. 137–139.

240. AP/II (1977), Article 1(1).

241. William Abresch (2005), "A Human Rights Law of Internal Armed Conflict: The European Court of Human Rights in Chechnya," *European Journal of International Law* 16: 741–767, at 754.

242. Jean-Marie Henckaerts and Louise Doswald-Beck (2005), *Customary International Humanitarian Law: Volumes I and II*, Cambridge University Press.

243. Jean-Marie Henckaerts (2005), "Study on Customary International Humanitarian Law: A Contribution to the Understanding and Respect for the Rule of Law in Armed Conflict," *International Review of the Red Cross* 87: 175–212.

244. ICTY, *Tadić*, Decision of 2 October 1995, para. 119.

245. John B. Bellinger and William J. Haynes (2007), "A US Government Response to the International Committee of the Red Cross Study *Customary International Humanitarian Law*," *International Review of the Red Cross* 89: 443–471.

246. Gabriella Blum (2011), "Re-Envisaging the International Law of Internal Armed Conflict: A Reply to Sandesh Sivakumaran," *European Journal of International Law* 22: 265–271, at 265.

247. See Chapter 1.

248. Quoted in Sandesh Sivakumaran (2012), *The Law of Non-International Armed Conflict*, Oxford University Press, p. 562.

249. Antonio Cassese (1981), "The Status of Rebels under the 1977 Geneva Protocol on Non-International Armed Conflicts," *International & Comparative Law Quarterly* 30: 416–430, at 420.

250. Mohammed Bedjaoui (1961), *Law and the Algerian Revolution*, International Association of Democratic Lawyers.

251. Sandesh Sivakumaran (2011), "Re-Envisaging the International Law of Internal Armed Conflict," *European Journal of International Law* 22: 219–264, at 260–263.

252. Hyeran Jo (2015), *Compliant Rebels: Rebel Groups and International Law in World Politics*, Cambridge University Press; Jessica A. Stanton (2016), *Violence and Restraint in Civil War: Civilian Targeting in the Shadow of International Law*, Cambridge University Press.

253. Idean Salehyan, David Siroky, and Reed M. Wood (2014), "External Rebel Sponsorship and Civilian Abuse: A Principal-Agent Analysis of Wartime Atrocities," *International Organization* 68: 633–661.

254. Anthea Roberts and Sandesh Sivakumaran (2012), "Lawmaking by Nonstate Actors: Engaging Armed Groups in the Creation of International Humanitarian Law," *Yale Journal of International Law* 37: 107–152.

255. Ezequiel Heffes (2015), "Detentions by Armed Opposition Groups in Non-International Armed Conflicts: Towards a New Characterization of International Humanitarian Law," *Journal of Conflict and Security Law* 20: 229–250.

256. Ilana Rothkopf (2019), "International Humanitarian Law and Non-State Practice in Armed Conflict: Combatant's Privilege and Kurdish Fighters in Syria," *Journal of Conflict and Security Law* 24: 1–26.

257. Jean-Marie Henckaerts and Louise Doswald-Beck (2005), *Customary International Humanitarian Law: Volumes I and II*, Cambridge University Press.

258. Tom Ruys (2014), "The Syrian Civil War and the Achilles' Heel of the Law of Non-International Armed Conflict," *Stanford Journal of International Law* 50: 247–280, at 256.

259. Ibid., pp. 251–252.

11 CRIMINAL RESPONSIBILITY

1. Details from Ruth Maclean (2016), "Chad's Hissène Habré Found Guilty of Crimes Against Humanity," *The Guardian*, May 30, available at www.theguardian.com/world/2016/may/30/chad-hissene-habre-guilty-crimes-against-humanity-senegal.

2. Human Rights Watch (2013), "Chad: Habré's Government Committed Systematic Atrocities," December 3, available at www.hrw.org/news/2013/12/03/chad-habre-s-government-committed-systematic-atrocities.

3. Celeste Hicks (2018), *The Trial of Hissène Habré*, Zed Books.

4. Experts debate the exact meaning of the term "international crime." These debates involve complex philosophical disagreements about the nature of law and the relationship between the international and domestic legal systems. We do not delve into this debate, but instead focus on international law that creates and enforces duties for individuals.

5. Special Court for Sierra Leone, *Brima*, Judgment of 20 June 2007, paras. 730–732.

6. Nuremberg Charter (1945), Article 6(a).

7. International Military Tribunal, *The Trial of German Major War Criminals (Nuremberg), Part 22*, Judgment of 30 September–1 October 1946, p. 446.

8.   Ibid.

9.   Ibid., p. 447.

10. Robert K. Woetzel (1960), *The Nuremberg Trials in International Law*, Stevens & Sons, pp. 31–34.

11. Ibid., pp. 96–108.

12. Kirsten Sellars (2013). *"Crimes Against Peace" and International Law*, Cambridge University Press.

13. London Agreement (1945).

14. UNGA Resolution 95 (1946).

15. Yuma Totani (2015), *Justice in Asia and the Pacific Region, 1945–1952*, Cambridge University Press, p. 9.

16. Bosnia's full name is "Bosnia–Herzegovina" or "Bosnia and Herzegovina." Serbia was part of the Federal Republic of Yugoslavia in the early 1990s, which included the Republic of Montenegro. We refer to "Serbia" to keep our discussion clear because Serbia had political and military control over the union.

17. ICTR, *Kayishema*, Judgment of 21 May 1999, para. 34.

18. Oona Hathaway and Scott J. Shapiro (2017), *The Internationalists*, Simon & Schuster.

19. Rome Statute (1998), Article 8-*bis*(1).

20. Ibid., Article 8-*bis*(2).

21. Quoted in M. Cherif Bassiouni (2011), *Crimes Against Humanity*, Cambridge University Press, p. 1.

22. Raphael Lemkin (1947), "Genocide as a Crime Under International Law," *American Journal of International Law* 41: 145–151.

23. Leila Nadya Sadat (2013), "Crimes Against Humanity in the Modern Age," *American Journal of International Law* 107: 334–377.

24. Rome Statute (1998), Article 7(1).

25. Ibid., Article 7(2)(b).

26. Ibid., Article 7(2)(g) and (1)(h).

27. Ibid., Article 7(1)(i)–(j).

28. Leila Nadya Sadat (2013), "Crimes Against Humanity in the Modern Age," *American Journal of International Law* 107: 334–377.

29. Guenael Mettraux (2002), "Crimes Against Humanity in the Jurisprudence of the International Criminal Tribunals for the Former Yugoslavia and for Rwanda," *Health Information and Libraries Journal* 43: 237–316, at 270–282.

30. ICTY, *Kunarac*, Judgment of 12 June 2002, para. 98.

31. M. Cherif Bassiouni (2011), *Crimes Against Humanity*, Cambridge University Press, pp. 40–42.

32. Rome Statute (1998), Article 7(2)(a).

33. ICC, *Gbagbo*, Decision of 16 July 2019, para. 28.

34. Genocide Convention (1948), Article 1.

35. This intent requirement is much stronger than the standard mental element requirement.

36. ICTY, *Jelisić*, Judgment of 14 December 1999, paras. 99–108.

37. Ibid., para. 106.

38. Rome Statute (1998), Article 8(2)(f).

39. ICC (2011), "Elements of Crimes," pp. 13–43.

40. See Chapter 10 for a detailed discussion of these differences.

41. ICTY, *Tadić*, Judgment of 7 May 1997.

42. For example, the ICTY and ICTR wrote extensively about joint criminal enterprises, which does not appear in their statutes. The ICC abandoned this case law because of widespread criticisms. See M. Cherif Bassiouni (2013), *Introduction to International Criminal Law*, Martinus Nijhoff, pp. 373–401.

43. This section is based on Article 25(3)(a) of the Rome Statute. While the Rome Statute does not use the term "perpetrator," its rulings frequently do.

44. Rome Statute (1998), Article 25(3)(a).

45. Because of his confession and cooperation with the ICTY, the prosecutor agreed not to prosecute Erdemović for genocide.

46. Rome Statute (1998), Article 25(3)(a).

47. ICC, *Lubanga*, Judgment of 14 March 2012, para. 1134.

48. Ibid., para. 1222.

49. Rome Statute (1998), Article 25(3)(a).

50. ICC, *Katanga*, Judgment of 7 March 2014, para. 1396 (emphasis removed).

51. Ibid., paras. 1359, 1360.

52. Ibid., para. 1363.

53. Ibid., para. 1396.

54. Rome Statute (1998), Article 25(3)(b).

55. Ibid., Article 3(c).

56. Ibid., Article 3(d).

57. ICC, *Katanga*, Judgment of 7 March 2014, para. 1679.

58. Ibid., para. 1691.

59. ICTR, *Akayesu*, Judgment of 2 September 1998.

60. ICTY, *Krstić*, Judgment of 19 April 2004.

61. ECCC, *Kaing*, Judgment of 26 July 2010.

62. SCSL, *Taylor*, Judgment of 26 September 2013.

63. Guénaël Mettraux (2009), *The Law of Command Responsibility*, Oxford University Press, pp. 37–95.

64. Ibid., p. 7.

65. Rome Statute, Article 28(a).

66. Ibid., Article 28(a)(ii).

67. ICC, *Bemba*, Judgment of 21 March 2016.

68. ICC, *Bemba*, Judgment of 8 June 2018, para. 167.

69. Ibid., para. 169.

70. ICTY, *Čelebići*, Judgment of 16 November 1998, paras. 733–736, 775.

71. ICTR, *Nahimana*, Judgment of 28 November 2007, para. 778.

72. Ibid., para. 795.

73. Rome Statute, Article 28(b).

74. Our use of "defense" thus includes complete defenses—which are grounds for acquittal/exculpation—and mitigating factors—which are grounds for reducing punishment.

75. Failed ICC prosecutions include: *Abu Garda* (Sudan), *Ali* (Kenya), *Kenyatta* (Kenya), *Kosgey* (Kenya), *Mbarushimana* (DRC), and *Muthaura* (Kenya).

76. Rome Statute (1998), Articles 21 and 31(3).

77. Ibid., Article 31(1).

78. SCSL, *Taylor*, Judgment of 31 May 2004, paras. 44–53.
79. Ingrid Wuerth (2012), "Pinochet's Legacy," *American Journal of International Law* 106: 731–768.
80. ICJ, *Arrest Warrant*, Judgment of 14 February 2002.
81. Geoff Dancy (2018), "Deals with the Devil? Conflict Amnesties, Civil War, and Sustainable Peace," *International Organization* 72: 387–421.
82. IACHR, *Barrios Altos* v. *Peru*, Judgment of 14 March 2001.
83. SCSL Statute (2000), Article 10.
84. SCSL, *Kallon*, Judgment of 13 March 2004, para. 86.
85. Rome Statute (1998), Article 17(1).
86. ICC, *Al-Senussi*, Judgment of 11 October 2013, para. 311.
87. Rome Statute (1998), Article 31(1)(d).
88. Ibid.
89. Yoram Dinstein (2012), *The Defense of "Obedience to Superior Orders" in International Law*, Oxford University Press, pp. 38–67.
90. Ibid., pp. 68–75.
91. Rome Statute (1998), Article 33(1).
92. Ibid., Article 33(2).
93. Quoted in ICTY, *Erdemović*, Judgment of 29 November 1996, para. 10.
94. ICTY, *Erdemović*, Judgment of 5 March 1998, para. 17.
95. Ibid.
96. UNSC Resolutions 1593 (2005) and 1970 (2011).
97. "Lithuania and Romania Complicit in CIA Torture—European Court," BBC News, May 31, 2018, available at www.bbc.com/news/world-europe-44313905.
98. Elian Peltier and Fatima Faizi (2020), "I.C.C. Allows Afghanistan War Crimes Inquiry to Proceed, Angering U.S.," *New York Times*, March 5, available at www.nytimes.com/2020/03/05/world/europe/afghanistan-war-crimes-icc.html.
99. Rome Statute (1998), Article 86.
100. Courtney Hillebrecht and Scott Straus (2017), "Who Pursues the Perpetrators: State Cooperation with the ICC," *Human Rights Quarterly* 39: 162–188, at 180–183.
101. David Bosco (2017), "Discretion and State Influence at the International Criminal Court," *American Journal of International Law* 111: 395–414, at 406–408.
102. Paola Gaeta (2009), "Does President Al Bashir Enjoy Immunity from Arrest?," *Journal of International Criminal Justice* 7: 315–332.
103. Dire Tladi (2015), "The Duty on South Africa to Arrest and Surrender President Al-Bashir under South African and International Law," *Journal of International Criminal Justice* 13: 1027–1047.
104. Rome Statute (1998), Article 89(1).
105. Eric M. Meyer (2005), "International Law: The Compatibility of the Rome Statute of the International Criminal Court with the U.S. Bilateral Immunity Agreements Included in the American Servicemembers' Protection Act," *Oklahoma Law Review* 58: 97–133, at 99.
106. This section draws from Leslie Johns, Máximo Langer, and Margaret Peters (2021), "Migration and the Demand for Transnational Justice," unpublished paper available at www.lesliejohns.me/uploads/1/2/4/7/124792770/jlp-lsa.pdf.

107. Máximo Langer (2015), "Universal Jurisdiction Is not Disappearing: The Shift from 'Global Enforcer' to 'No Safe Haven' Universal Jurisdiction," *Journal of International Criminal Justice* 13: 245–256.

108. Stephen C. Neff (2014), *Justice Among Nations: A History of International Law*, Harvard University Press, p. 469.

109. Ibid.

110. Ibid.

111. Raphael Lemkin (1947), "Genocide as a Crime Under International Law," *American Journal of International Law* 41: 145–151, at 146.

112. Máximo Langer and Mackenzie Eason (2019), "The Quiet Expansion of Universal Jurisdiction," *European Journal of International Law* 30: 779–817.

113. Ibid.

114. The UK Law Lords ruled that Pinochet could be extradited to Spain, but the UK Home Secretary refused extradition. See UK Law Lords, *Pinochet*, Judgment of 24 March 1999.

115. Naomi Roht-Arriaza (2005), *The Pinochet Effect: Transnational Justice in the Age of Human Rights*, University of Pennsylvania Press.

116. Charles Chernor Jalloh (2010), "Universal Jurisdiction, Universal Prescriptions?," *Criminal Law Forum* 21: 1–65.

117. Genocide Convention (1948), Article VI.

118. ECtHR, *Jorgić*, Judgment of 12 July 2007, para. 61.

119. Ibid., para. 68.

120. UN Convention against Torture (1984), Article 5(2).

121. Ibid., Article 7(1).

122. ICJ, *Prosecute or Extradite*, Judgment of 20 July 2012.

123. Habré was also convicted of torture as a standalone crime. This crime was included in the jurisdiction of the Extraordinary African Chambers because the case began under the UN Convention against Torture.

124. This charge was overturned on appeal for procedural reasons.

125. The Extraordinary African Chambers used the concept of a joint criminal enterprise.

126. Quoted in Celeste Hicks (2018), *The Trial of Hissène Habré*, Zed Books, p. 111.

127. Human Rights Watch (2016), "Enabling a Dictator," available at www.hrw.org/sites/default/files/report_pdf/ushabre0616web.pdf; Human Rights Watch (2016), "Allié de la France, condamné par l'Afrique," available at www.hrw.org/fr/report/2016/06/28/allie-de-la-france-condamne-par-lafrique/les-relations-entre-la-france-et-le.

128. Antony Anghie and B.S. Chimni (2003), "Third World Approaches to International Law and Individual Responsibility in Internal Conflicts," *Chicago Journal of International Law* 2: 77–104, at 90–92.

129. Celeste Hicks (2018), *The Trial of Hissène Habré*, Zed Books, p. 62.

130. Ibid., p. 69.

CHAPTER 12   ENVIRONMENTAL PROTECTION

1. Quoted in "Japan Resumes Commercial Whaling after Thirty Years," BBC News, July 1, 2019, available at www.bbc.com/news/world-asia-48821797.

2. Ibid.

3. ICRW (1946), Preamble.
4. Ibid.
5. Ian Hurd (2012), "Almost Saving Whales: The Ambiguity of Success at the International Whaling Commission," *Ethics & International Affairs* 26: 103–112.
6. ICRW (1946), Article VIII(1).
7. ICJ, *Whaling*, Judgment of 31 March 2014, para. 226.
8. Kenneth Pomeranz (2001), *The Great Divergence: China, Europe, and the Making of the Modern World Economy*, Princeton University Press.
9. Elinor Ostrom (1990), *Governing the Commons*, Cambridge University Press.
10. Severin Hauenstein, Mrigesh Kshatriya, Julian Blanc, Carsten F. Dormann, and Colin M. Beale (2019), "African Elephant Poaching Rates Correlate with Local Poverty, National Corruption and Global Ivory Price," *Nature Communications* 10: 2242.
11. Xinyuan Dai (2010), "Global Regime and National Change," *Climate Policy* 10: 622–637.
12. Xinyuan Dai (2005), "Why Comply? The Domestic Constituency Mechanism," *International Organization* 59: 363–398.
13. *Bering Sea Fur Seals Fisheries Arbitration* (1893).
14. Ronald B. Mitchell, Liliana B. Andonova, Mark Axelrod, Jörg Balsiger, Thomas Bernauer, Jessica F. Green, James Hollway, Rakhyun E. Kim, and Jean-Frédéric Morin (2020), "What We Know (and Could Know) About International Environmental Agreements," *Global Environmental Politics* 20: 103–121.
15. Kal Raustiala and David G. Victor (2004), "The Regime Complex for Plant Genetic Resources," *International Organization* 58: 277–309.
16. Louis B. Sohn (1973), "The Stockholm Declaration on the Human Environment," *Health Information and Libraries Journal* 14: 423–515, at 427.
17. Ibid.
18. Stockholm Declaration (1972), Principle 13 (emphasis added).
19. Rio Declaration (1992), Principle 11 (emphasis added).
20. Ibid., Principles 10, 15, 16.
21. Ranee Khooshie Lal Panjabi (1993), "From Stockholm to Rio: A Comparison of the Declaratory Principles of International Environmental Law," *Denver Journal of International Law & Policy* 21: 215–287, at 243–247.
22. Alfred P. Rubin (1971), "Pollution by Analogy: The *Trail Smelter* Arbitration," *Oregon Law Review* 50: 259–282, at 264.
23. Stockholm Declaration (1972), Principle 21.
24. Rio Declaration (1992), Principle 6.
25. UN Document A/56/10.
26. ICJ, *Pulp Mills*, Judgment of 20 April 2010, para. 101.
27. ICJ, *Certain Activities*, Judgment of 16 December 2015, paras. 101–105.
28. Ibid., paras. 152–162.
29. For example, compare the Rio Declaration (1992), Principle 15 to the Watercourses Convention (1992), Article 2(5)(a).
30. This policy is sometimes called the "precautionary principle."
31. ICJ, *Certain Activities*, Judgment of 16 December 2015, para. 168.
32. Philippe Sand and Jacqueline Peel (2018), *Principles of International Environmental Law*, Cambridge University Press, pp. 240–244.

33. The obligation to compensate transboundary harm differs from state responsibility rules (discussed in Chapter 3) because it does not rely upon a prior legal violation and state attribution.

34. Statute of the Uruguay River (1975), Article 40.

35. ICJ, *Pulp Mills*, Judgment of 20 April 2010, para. 160.

36. Ibid., paras. 162–164.

37. Ibid., para. 265.

38. Philippe Sand and Jacqueline Peel (2018), *Principles of International Environmental Law*, Cambridge University Press, pp. 217–229.

39. "Countries Violate Rights over Climate Change, Argue Youth Activists in Landmark UN Complaint," UN News, September 29, 2019, available at https://news.un.org/en/story/2019/09/1047292.

40. UN Framework Convention on Climate Change (1992), Article 3(1).

41. Some environmental law texts also include nuclear treaties as atmospheric agreements because of concerns about the impact of nuclear tests on the atmosphere.

42. Jana Von Stein (2008), "The International Law and Politics of Climate Change: Ratification of the United Nations Framework Convention and the Kyoto Protocol," *Journal of Conflict Resolution* 52: 243–268.

43. LRTAP (1979), Article 2.

44. Ibid., Article 6.

45. Ozone Convention (1985), Article 2.

46. Ibid., Annexes I and II.

47. UNFCCC (1992), Article 2.

48. Ibid., Article 3(1)–(4).

49. Ibid., Article 4(2)(b). Some of these states made additional pledges under the UNFCCC to share financial resources and technology with developing states; see Annex II.

50. Paris Climate Agreement (2015), Article 2(1)(a).

51. Ibid., Articles 3 and 2(2).

52. Vegard H. Tørstad (2020), "Participation, Ambition and Compliance: Can the Paris Agreement Solve the Effectiveness Trilemma?," *Environmental Politics* 29: 761–780.

53. International law uses the term "sea" to refer all saltwater bodies, regardless of their name or size.

54. Patricia Birnie, Alan Boyle, and Catherine Redgwell (2009), *International Law and the Environment*, Oxford University Press, p. 468.

55. Dumping Convention (1972), Article 1.

56. Patricia Birnie, Alan Boyle, and Catherine Redgwell (2009), *International Law and the Environment*, Oxford University Press, p. 467.

57. For example, see UNCLOS (1982), Articles 210 and 216.

58. MARPOL stands for "marine pollution." The official name of this treaty is the International Convention for the Prevention of Pollution from Ships (1973), as modified by the Protocol of 1978.

59. Patricia Birnie, Alan Boyle, and Catherine Redgwell (2009), *International Law and the Environment*, Oxford University Press, p. 401.

60. Ronald B. Mitchell (1994), "Regime Design Matters: Intentional Oil Pollution and Treaty Compliance," *International Organization* 48: 425–458, at 444–449.

61. UNCLOS (1982), Articles 194, 199, 204–206, 235.

62. Ibid., Article 198.

63. Ibid., Article 193.

64. Ibid., Article 194(1).

65. PCIJ, *River Oder*, Judgment of 10 September 1929.

66. *Lac Lanoux* Arbitration, Award of 16 November 1957.

67. International Watercourses Convention (1997), Article 5(1).

68. Ibid.

69. Ibid., Article 7(1).

70. Ibid., Article 20.

71. ICJ, *Certain Activities*, Judgment of 16 December 2015.

72. World Heritage Convention (1972), Preamble.

73. Ibid., Article 2.

74. UNCLOS (1982), Articles 64 and 65.

75. Ibid., Article 56(1).

76. CITES (1973), Preamble.

77. Ibid., Article 1(1)(a).

78. Biological Diversity Convention (1992), Article 1.

79. Ibid., Article 3.

80. Cartagena Protocol on Biosafety (2000), Article 3(g).

81. Daniel Cressey (2017), "Treaty to Stop Biopiracy Threatens to Delay Flu Vaccines," *Nature* 542(148), February 8, available at www.nature.com/news/treaty-to-stop-biopiracy-threatens-to-delay-flu-vaccines-1.21438.

82. See the WTO reports in *China—Measures Related to the Exportation of Various Raw Materials*.

83. WTO, *EC—Seals*, Panel Report of 25 November 2013, para. 7.274.

84. Leslie Johns, Calvin Thrall and Rachel Wellhausen (2020), "Judicial Economy and Moving Bars in International Investment Arbitration," *Research Ideas and Outcomes* 15: 923–945.

85. ICSID, *Metalclad*, Award of 30 August 2000, para. 76.

86. Stephan W. Schill (2010), "*Glamis Gold, Ltd.* v. *United States*," *American Journal of International Law* 104: 253–259, at 255.

87. The term "right to life" has a different meaning under international law than in US domestic politics.

88. IACHR, *Kuna*, Report of 30 November 2012, para. 233.

89. ECHR (1950), Article 8.

90. Dinah L. Shelton (2010), "Tatar C. Roumanie," *American Journal of International Law* 104: 247–250.

91. Supreme Court of the Netherlands, *Urgenda*, Judgment of 20 December 2019.

92. African Charter on Human and Peoples' Rights (1981), Article 24.

93. ECOWAS, *SERAP*, Judgment of 14 December 2012, para. 100.

94. Ibid., para. 112.

95. Yoram Dinstein (2001), "Protection of the Environment in International Armed Conflict," *Max Planck Yearbook of United Nations Law* 5: 523–549, at 543.

96. John H. McNeill (1993), "Protection of the Environment in Times of Armed Conflict: Environmental Protection in Military Practice," *Hague Yearbook of International Law* 6: 75–84, at 76.

97. UNGA Resolution 47/37 (1992).

98. UNSC Resolution 687 (1991).

99. ICTY, "Final Report to the Prosecutor by the Committee Established to Review the NATO Bombing Campaign Against the Federal Republic of Yugoslavia," para. 18.

100. UNGA Resolution 49/75 (1994), Section K.

101. ICJ, *Nuclear Weapons*, Advisory Opinion of 8 July 1996, para. 30.

102. Rio Declaration (1972), Principle 24.

103. ICJ, *Armed Activities*, Judgment of 19 December 2005, para. 242.

104. Ibid., paras. 245 and 250.

105. ICJ, *Nuclear Weapons*, Advisory Opinion of 8 July 1996, para. 31.

106. Paolo Benvenuti (2001), "The ICTY Prosecutor and the Review of the NATO Bombing Campaign Against the Federal Republic of Yugoslavia," *European Journal of International Law* 12: 503–529, at 509; Yoram Dinstein (2016), *The Conduct of Hostilities under the Law of International Armed Conflict*, Cambridge University Press, pp. 238–239.

107. Environmental Modification Convention (1977), Article II.

108. UK Ministry of Defence (2010), *The Manual of the Law of Armed Conflict*, Oxford University Press, pp. 74–75.

109. A.P.V. Rogers (2012), *Law on the Battlefield*, Manchester University Press, pp. 214–215.

110. ICTY, "Final Report to the Prosecutor by the Committee Established to Review the NATO Bombing Campaign Against the Federal Republic of Yugoslavia," para. 17.

111. ICRW (1946), Article VIII(1).

112. Associated Press (2019), "Japan Returns to Business of Whale Hunting. But Whales May Be Better Off," *Washington Post*, July 1, available at www.washingtonpost.com/lifestyle/kidspost/japan-returns-to-business-of-whale-hunting-but-whales-may-be-better-off/2019/07/01/fd09c7ee-9c1a-11e9-9ed4-c9089972ad5a_story.html.

113. UN Document A/56/10, Article 2.

114. CITES (1973), Article 1.

115. Quoted in Peter H. Sand (2008), "Japan's 'Research Whaling' in the Antarctic Southern Ocean and the North Pacific Ocean in the Face of the Endangered Species Convention (CITES)," *Review of European Community & International Environmental Law* 17: 56–71, at 62.

116. Associated Press (2019), "Japan Returns to Business of Whale Hunting. But Whales May Be Better Off," *Washington Post*, July 1, available at www.washingtonpost.com/lifestyle/kidspost/japan-returns-to-business-of-whale-hunting-but-whales-may-be-better-off/2019/07/01/fd09c7ee-9c1a-11e9-9ed4-c9089972ad5a_story.html.

117. UNCLOS (1982), Articles 64–65 and Annex I.

118. Biological Diversity Convention (1992), Article 3.

119. Ben Dooley and Hisako Ueno (2019), "Japan Resumes Commercial Whaling. But Is There an Appetite for It?," *New York Times*, July 1, available at www.nytimes.com/2019/07/01/business/japan-commercial-whaling.html.

120. Abigail Leonard (2019), "In Japan, Few People Eat Whale Meat Anymore, but Whaling Remains Popular," *The World: Public Radio International*, April 17, available at www.pri.org/stories/2019-04-17/japan-few-people-eat-whale-meat-anymore-whaling-remains-popular.

121. Ibid.

Glossary

absolute theory of state immunity: doctrine that protects all foreign state acts from domestic courts

accession: process by which a state joins a treaty that it did not sign

accessory liability: a form of criminal liability in which an individual provides material or moral assistance that has a substantial effect on the crime, even though he does not have control over the crime

acknowledgement: attribution standard by which a state adopts responsibility for a non-state actor

acquiescence: tacit support for state practice as reflected by inaction

acta jure gestionis: Latin for "commercial act"; act that can be undertaken by a private company

acta jure imperii: Latin for "sovereign act"; act that can only be undertaken by a state, not a private company

active protest: physical or verbal acts that demonstrate that a state disagrees with a particular asserted rule

ad hoc criminal tribunals: institutions created by the UN Security Council in the 1990s to punish individuals for international crimes committed during the Yugoslavian and Rwandan armed conflicts

Additional Protocol I: 1977 treaty that addresses military conduct and protected people

Additional Protocol II: 1977 treaty that contains rules for NIACs

admissibility: criteria that affect a legal body's willingness to rule, usually based on the specific facts of the case

advisory opinion: a non-binding document that answers legal questions submitted by an international organization

advocacy groups: non-profit groups that promote aspirational collective values

aggression: severe violation of international law on the use of force

amnesty: an agreement not to prosecute individuals for certain offenses, and to pardon individuals already convicted of those offenses

antidumping duty: a duty that protects a domestic industry from harm from dumped imports

arbitration: a process in which one or more individuals decide a dispute based on evidence and arguments

armed opposition groups: non-state actors that fight to achieve political goals

Article 98 agreements: bilateral agreements in which states pledge not to surrender each other's nationals to the ICC

attribution: determining when a legal breach is considered an act of a state

baseline: boundary between a state's territory and international waters

belligerent occupation: when one state has authority over another state's territory without its consent

biological weapon: weapon that uses a living organism—such as a fungus or virus—to wound or kill animals, humans, or plants; examples include anthrax and weaponized measles

Calvo Doctrine: in its narrow form, the claim that foreigners are not entitled to more favorable treatment than domestic nationals; in its broad form, the claim that sovereign equality allows all states to set their own economic policies without interference by other states

Caroline **test:** criteria for evaluating the necessity of force; a threat must be "instant, overwhelming, leaving no choice of means, and no moment of deliberation"

chapeau: French for "hat"; introductory text for a treaty provision

chemical weapon: weapon that uses a toxic chemical—in gas, liquid, or solid form—to wound or kill animals or humans; examples include chlorine, mustard, and tear gases

child soldier: a person below fifteen who is serving in an armed group

chronological paradox: conceptual problem that underlies the creation of customary international law; a belief in law is necessary for customary international law, but how can states hold such beliefs before law exists?

circumstance precluding wrongfulness: a factor that excuses or justifies a legal breach, thus relieving a state of responsibility; CPWs include consent, self-defense, countermeasures, *force majeure*, distress, and necessity

civil remedy: a remedy primarily aimed at making a victim whole

climate change: changes in the earth's climate, including increases in the global average temperature

Cold War: the period of 1945–1989, when US–USSR tensions shaped international law and politics

collaboration problem: a situation in which states jointly benefit from choosing the same action, but each state is tempted to unilaterally deviate to a different action

combatant immunity: legal principle that combatants may not be criminally prosecuted for their legal acts during armed conflict

command responsibility: a form of criminal responsibility in which military commanders are responsible if they fail to prevent or punish crimes committed by the troops under their effective control

commitment problem: a situation in which sequential decision-making ensures that the plan of action that is initially optimal becomes suboptimal as time passes

Common Article 3: a legal provision included in all of the 1949 Geneva Conventions; requires humane treatment and the protection of the wounded and sick during NIACs

common but differentiated responsibility: the claim that while the environment is a common concern, states have different levels of responsibility for protecting the environment

common heritage of mankind: the principle that certain natural resources belong to mankind as a whole and should be protected from exploitation

common seabed: seabed in which no individual state has jurisdiction

communitarian law: rules collectively made by the international community, whose interests and values trump those of individual states

complementarity: the principle that an international criminal tribunal should complement, rather than supplement, other criminal tribunals

compromissory clause: treaty text that gives authority to an international legal body to hear disputes about the treaty's interpretation or application

consular immunity: the principle that protects consular officials from criminal (but not civil) actions in domestic courts of a foreign state

consular jurisdiction: separate legal systems for foreigners that are overseen by consular officials from the foreigners' home state

contiguous zone: sea zone outside of a territorial sea over which the state has limited law enforcement rights; extends up to 12 n.m.

continental shelf: seabed in which a coastal state has exclusive rights over natural resources; extends 200 n.m. or more, depending on topography

contra bono mores: Latin for "against good morals"; reason sometimes provided for the claim that a treaty is invalid because it conflicts with natural law

conventional weapons: weapons with relatively limited and precise effects in combat

coordination problem: a situation in which all states have a shared incentive to use a common rule, but states disagree or are uncertain about what that rule should be

countermeasure: a legal violation taken in response to a prior wrongful act by another state

countervailing duty: a duty that protects a domestic industry from harm from subsidized imports

crime against humanity: a group of criminal acts that are "committed as part of a widespread or systematic attack directed against any civilian population" during peace or armed conflict

criminal remedy: a remedy primarily aimed at punishing a violator

customs union: a trade agreement that requires free trade within member states and common trade policy with outside states

default rules: rules that can be changed by parties to a contract

defense: a legal argument made by a defendant to avoid or minimize punishment

delimitation: the allocation of legal rights when multiple states claim jurisdiction over the same area

derogable right: a right that can be suspended by states during public emergencies

derogation: decision by a pair or group of states to exempt themselves from a norm in their relations with one another

diplomatic immunity: the principle that protects diplomats from civil and criminal actions in domestic courts of a foreign state

diplomatic protection: assertion of legal claims by a state on behalf of private individuals (including ships)

direct expropriation: government actions that deprive a firm of the full value of its investment

distinction: principle that separates civilians and combatants into different groups and limits force against civilians; also sometimes called discrimination or identification

distress: circumstance precluding wrongfulness; a legal breach is not wrongful if "the author of the act in question has no other reasonable way ... of saving the author's life or the lives of other persons entrusted to the author's care"

drones: unmanned aerial vehicles

dumping: selling a good at less than its normal value

duration: criterion for assessing state practice: how long has a state followed a proposed rule?

duress: pressure to perform an illegal act to avoid serious harm

duties: obligations to behave in certain ways

effective control standard: attribution standard under international law; states must have effective control over a non-state actor—including issuing it direct instructions—to be responsible for the non-state actor's conduct

effective control test: principle that a group with control over a piece of territory has authority to represent that territory

Enlightenment: European movement that emphasized individual autonomy, including economic and political rights

entry into force: the point in time at which a treaty becomes legally binding

for states that have fully consented to be bound

environmental impact assessment: a process for evaluating the impact of a policy or project on environmental outcomes

equidistance method: a geographic technique for drawing a line—called the equidistance or median line—that is equally distant from each state

erga omnes **obligation**: an obligation to the international community as a whole

escape clause: a legal provision that allows states to sometimes temporarily break their commitments without severe punishment

ethnic cleansing: the compelled removal of an ethnic group using intimidation or violence

exclusive economic zone: sea zone in which coastal states can regulate economic activities and natural resource conservation; extends up to 200 n.m.

exit clause: a treaty clause that specifies conditions under which a state may exit a treaty

extermination: "the intentional infliction of conditions of life, [including the deprivation of access to food and medicine,] calculated to bring about the destruction of part of a population"

fair and equitable treatment: the requirement that host governments treat foreign investors fairly and equitably

flag state: the state in which a ship is registered

force majeure: Latin for "superior force"; circumstance precluding wrongfulness; "an irresistible force or ... unforeseen event, beyond the control of the state, making it materially impossible ... to perform [an] obligation"

foreign direct investment: the investment of capital from a firm in one state into business activities in another state; requires a long time-horizon and the direct involvement of the investor in the management of the business activities abroad

framework agreement: an agreement that contains objectives and principles, and creates an institution to promote these objectives and principles

free-riding: a situation in which actors provide less cooperation than would be optimal for society as a whole

fugitive resources: resources that move across borders, such as migratory birds, fish, and whales

full protection and security: the requirement that host governments refrain from military attacks against foreign firms and their property

fundamental change in circumstances: modern version of *rebus sic stantibus*; a state can leave a treaty if there is an unexpected change in circumstances of sufficient importance and magnitude

General Agreement on Tariffs and Trade: 1947 treaty that includes broad legal principles to govern international trade and detailed lists of each state's tariff concessions

generality: criterion for assessing state practice; how widespread is a proposed rule across different states?

Geneva Conventions: four 1949 treaties that focus on protected people, including civilians and combatants who are captured, sick, or wounded

genocide: "acts committed with intent to destroy, in whole or in part, a national, ethnical, racial or religious group," including killing; "causing serious bodily or mental harm"; "inflicting on the group conditions of life calculated to bring about its physical destruction"; preventing births; and "forcibly transferring children of the group to another group"

global commons: resources that belong to no specific state

globalization: the increased movement of goods, investment, and people across borders

good faith: the principle that parties to an agreement must act fairly and honestly towards one another

gravity threshold: principle asserted by the ICJ in the *Nicaragua* case; the use of force only qualifies as an "armed attack" (under the law of self-defense) if it is sufficiently severe

greenhouse gases: atmospheric substances—including carbon dioxide and methane—that modify the impact of sunlight on the earth's surface

Group of 77: political coalition of developing states within the United Nations

guerrilla warfare: combat in which armed groups do not distinguish themselves from civilians

Hague law: 1899 and 1907 agreements that regulate military operations and limit weapons

high seas: water in which no state has jurisdiction

hot pursuit: a legal doctrine that allows a state to preserve its law enforcement authority if it follows certain procedures while pursuing crime suspects at sea

Hull Doctrine: claim that states must provide prompt, adequate, and effective compensation if they expropriate property from foreign firms

human trafficking: the use of force, fraud, or coercion to secure labor; includes the recruitment, movement, harboring, or sale of individuals, both domestically and across international borders

humanitarian intervention: using force to protect foreign nationals from mistreatment by their own government

humanitarian law: international laws that address suffering during war

humanity: principle that requires states to avoid unnecessary suffering during war

immobile asset: asset that cannot be easily moved or redeployed for other activities

import substitution industrialization: economic policies that promote manufacturing goods that are sold within the home state (thus reducing imported goods)

indirect expropriation: government actions that violate pre-existing contracts or laws, and substantially reduce the value of a foreign firm's property

indiscriminate attacks: attacks that "are not directed at a specific military objective; ... employ a method or means of combat which cannot be directed at a specific military objective; or ... employ a method or means of combat the effects of which cannot be limited"

individual criminal responsibility: the principle that individuals have duties under international criminal law

individual petition: process that allows individuals to directly complain to an international organization if they believe that their rights have been violated by a state

industrialization: the shift from agrarian production to manufacturing

intergenerational equity: the claim that current generations of humans should leave ample resources for future generations

internal consistency: criterion for assessing state practice; how uniformly has a state followed a proposed rule?

internal waters: water bodies that lie within a state's baseline

International Center for the Settlement of Investment Disputes: international organization created under the World Bank in 1966 to oversee foreign investment disputes

international community: a group of global actors with legal interests and personality, independent of its members

International Court of Justice: an international court created in 1945 as part of the United Nations

International Criminal Court: a permanent court that prosecutes aggression, crimes against humanity, genocide, and war crimes

International Law Commission: international organization created by the UN General Assembly in 1947 to study legal issues and make recommendations about the codification and development of international law

international organization: "an organization established by a treaty or other instrument governed by international law and possessing its own international legal personality"

international watercourses: freshwater resources—including lakes and rivers— that are shared by multiple states

interpretation: the process by which actors understand the meaning of a legal text, and then apply the text's meaning to a factual situation

investor–state dispute settlement: system of legalized dispute settlement that allows foreign investors to directly sue their host states using international arbitration

judicial economy: the principle that a legal body should decline to make a ruling that is not necessary to resolve a dispute

judicial propriety: the principle that a legal body should decline to make a ruling that would not serve a judicial function

jurisdiction: authority of a legal body to rule on a dispute

jus ad bellum: international law that regulates the initiation of armed conflict

jus cogens: Latin for "mandatory law"; rules that cannot be changed by states via treaties

jus dispositivum: Latin for "law adopted by consent"; rules that can be changed by states via treaties

jus in bello: international law that regulates behavior during armed conflicts

League of Nations: an international organization created in 1920 to promote "international peace and security … by the firm establishment of … international law"

Lieber Code: military document issued by US President Abraham Lincoln in 1863 to the northern army during the US Civil War; first modern codification of the laws of war

linkage: the use of conditional economic benefits and punishments to encourage compliance with international agreements

mandatory rules: rules that cannot be changed by parties to a contract

mare clausum: Latin for "closed seas"; the principle that a state can claim exclusive jurisdiction over the sea

mare liberum: Latin for "open seas"; the principle that no state can claim jurisdiction over the sea

margin of appreciation: doctrine that posits that because states have more knowledge about their own social context, a court ought to defer to states when applying legal standards

Martens clause: treaty provision that declares that customary international law also governs armed conflict

material breach: "a repudiation of the treaty not sanctioned by the [VCLT, or] the violation of a provision essential to the accomplishment of the object or purpose of the treaty"

material element: the physical act prohibited by law

material injury: an injury that negatively affects an individual's physical or economic well-being

mental element: individual knowledge of relevant facts and intent to commit a crime

military necessity: principle that force is only lawful if it is necessary to achieve a legitimate military objective; applies to both customary international law on the use of force (*jus ad bellum*) and armed conflict (*jus in bello*)

military objective: "those objects which by their nature, location, purpose or use make an effective contribution to military action and whose total or partial destruction, capture or neutralization, in the circumstances ruling at the time, offers a definite military advantage"

mixed criminal tribunals: institutions that prosecute individuals using a blend of domestic and international law, personnel, and/or procedures

mobile asset: asset that can be easily moved or redeployed for other activities

moral injury: an injury that negatively affects an individual's conscience or mental well-being

most-favored-nation (MFN) treatment: legal standard that requires that any time a GATT member makes a trade concession on a product to a particular state, all other GATT members must receive the same concession

multinational corporations: profit-seeking groups that conduct business in multiple states

naming and shaming: public condemnation of non-compliant states

national treatment: under investment law, the requirement that a foreign investor must receive treatment that is at least as favorable as the treatment received by a similar domestic investor

natural law: a legal theory that claims that universal laws bind all human beings, regardless of their social context or whether they have explicitly consented

necessity: circumstance precluding wrongfulness; a legal breach is not wrongful if it "[i]s the only way for the state to safeguard an essential interest against a grave and imminent peril" and "[d]oes not seriously impair an essential interest of the state or states towards which the obligation exists, or of the international community as a whole"

negative equality doctrine: principle that outside states must remain neutral during civil wars and can only provide assistance to offset outside assistance from other states

New International Economic Order: a set of trade, investment, development, and assistance policies to promote the interests of developing states in the 1970s

non-derogable right: a right that a state must uphold in all circumstances

non-governmental organizations: organizations that operate independently of states to achieve political objectives

non-international armed conflict: the legal term for a civil war or other significant internal violence

non-retroactivity: the principle that: (1) individuals may not be convicted for acts that were not illegal at the time that they were committed; and (2) individuals may not be punished for acts unless law provided for such punishment at the time that the act was committed

non-tariff barrier: a policy that restricts trade, but is not a tariff

nulla poena sine lege: Latin for "no punishment without law"; the principle that punishments cannot be applied retroactively *nullum crimen sine lege*: Latin for "no crime without law"; the principle that law cannot be applied retroactively

obiter dictum: Latin for "something said in passing"; a statement in a judgment that is not necessary to resolve the given legal dispute

object and purpose test: practice under which a treaty reservation is assessed based on whether it is compatible with the object and purpose of the treaty

occupying power: a state whose military has authority over enemy territory

official immunity: the principle that individuals who are official representatives of a state are not subject to another state's jurisdiction

opinio juris: Latin for "acceptance as law"; second component of customary international law—states must accept that a rule is legally binding

overall control standard: attribution standard under international law; states must have only overall control over a non-state actor—including providing financing, equipment, and/or planning—to be responsible for the non-state actor's conduct

ozone layer: the outer layer of the atmosphere that filters dangerous radiation from sunlight

pacta sunt servanda: Latin for "agreements must be kept"; the legal principle that "Every treaty in force is binding upon the parties to it and must be performed by them in good faith"

people: individuals who live in a common cultural, ethnic, national, or racial community

peremptory norm: according to the VCLT, "a norm accepted and recognized by the international community of states as a whole as a norm from which no derogation is permitted and which can be modified only by a subsequent norm of general international law having the same character"

performance requirements: requirements on production and sales

Permanent Court of International Justice: an international court created in 1920 as part of the League of Nations

perpetrator responsibility: a form of criminal responsibility in which an individual has control over whether a crime will occur

persecution: "the intentional and severe deprivation of fundamental rights contrary to international law" of "any identifiable group or collectivity on political, racial, national, ethnic, cultural, religious, gender …, or other grounds that are universally recognized as impermissible under international law"

persistent objector doctrine: the claim that a state that disagrees with a rule before it becomes customary law is not constrained by the rule after it becomes customary law

pillage: the unlawful taking of property during conflict for private ends

police powers doctrine: the principle that a state has an inherent right to protect the public interest

pollution: the release of substances that harm the atmosphere, water, and/or living resources

positivism: modes of knowledge that emphasize observation and direct experience

precedent: the legal principle that current judges should defer to legal rulings made by prior judges in relevant cases

preferential trade agreement: international trade agreement with limited membership

prisoners of war: combatants "who have fallen into the power of the enemy," usually by surrendering or being captured during battle

private international law: law that governs private relationships across states, including business contracts, marriages, and wills

privateering: historical practice in which states gave private actors authority to attack foreign vessels and seize them as prizes during war

proportionality: principle that force and coercion must be commensurate with a state's objectives or injury; applies to countermeasures, use of force (*jus ad bellum*), and armed conflict (*jus in bello*)

protective principle: claim that a state can regulate and punish acts with systematic and important effects on the state's national interests, like its security

protocol: an agreement that contains detailed rules for a specific issue

public good: a good that is non-excludable and non-rivalrous

punishment: any response to a legal breach by states (either individually or collectively) that raises the cost of breaking international law

quantitative restriction: a ban or a quota on a particular good

quota: a limit on the amount of a particular good that can be imported into a state

ratification: under international law, "the international act ... whereby a state establishes on the international plane its consent to be bound by a treaty"

rebus sic stantibus: Latin for "things thus standing"; the claim that a leader can or should break his promises if economic or political circumstances have changed

refoulement: the forced return of migrants to states where they are likely to suffer severe human rights violations, like torture

relativism: a set of ethical, moral, and political theories that argue that human rights must be understood within their social context

repetition: criterion for assessing state practice; how many times has a state followed a proposed rule?

representation: criterion for assessing state practice; are the states that follow a proposed rule diverse with respect to their economic, political, and legal systems?

reservation: "a unilateral statement ... made by a state [that] purports to exclude or to modify the legal effect of certain provisions of the treaty in their application to that state"

resource curse: the claim that states with more natural resource wealth tend to experience worse economic, political, and social outcomes, including more armed conflict

responsibility to protect: principle that (1) every state has responsibility to protect its population from severe violations of human rights and humanitarian law; and (2) failure to meet this responsibility can trigger force by the international community

restitutio in integrum: Latin for "restoration to its whole"; legal principle that an injured state should be made "whole" after a legal violation

restitution: an attempt to make an injured state "whole" by returning it to its *status quo ante*, or the position the injured state was in prior to the breach

restricted theory of state immunity: doctrine that only protects a foreign state's sovereign acts (and not its commercial acts) from domestic courts

retorsion: a lawful act used to punish a state

right to development: the right of a state to create its own policies for exploiting its natural resources

right to diplomatic protection: the doctrine that states have the right to protect their nationals at the international level

right to innocent passage: right of foreign ships to travel through a territorial sea, subject to specified constraints

rights: entitlements to behave or be treated in certain ways

Rio Declaration: a non-binding document from 1992 that includes general principles about development and the environment

safeguard: a trade restriction that protects a domestic industry from an unexpected import surge

satisfaction: a verbal or written statement that acknowledges or apologizes for a legal violation

science: the intellectual claim that natural processes can be understood by human reason based on observation and experimentation

scorecard diplomacy: the public assessment and grading of states to influence behavior

screening problem: a situation in which a state faces difficulty in credibly communicating its preferences to others

severable: able to be cut away; when a reservation is severable, it can be invalidated without affecting a state's ratification of a treaty

signature: process by which a state indicates its support for a treaty and its intent to join the treaty

sink: a system that absorbs more greenhouse gases than it releases

social security: financial assistance to protect individuals from unexpected outcomes that harm their livelihoods, including accidents, disability, illness, involuntary unemployment, and the death of a spouse; sometimes also includes benefits for the elderly and pregnant women

socialization: informal process in which diverse actors internalize social norms through their interactions

soft law: international agreements that are not legally binding

sovereignty: principle that political leaders have both (1) authority over the internal policies of their own territory; and (2) an obligation not to interfere in the internal policies of other territories

special treaty body: an international institution that monitors compliance with a multilateral human rights treaty and assesses individual petitions about possible violations

specially affected states doctrine: the claim that customary international law gives (or should give) more deference to the behavior of states that are more likely to be affected by the formation of a particular rule

standing: admissibility requirement that the actor filing a case must have a legal interest in the dispute

stare decisis: Latin for "let the decision stand"; the legal principle that current judges should defer to legal rulings made by prior judges in relevant cases (same meaning as precedent)

state: an entity with "(a) a permanent population; (b) a defined territory; (c) government; and (d) capacity to enter into relations with the other states"

state immunity: the principle that a domestic court should not rule on a foreign state act without that state's consent

state policy requirement: the requirement that a state must have a common and preconceived plan or policy for committing an attack; relevant to the definition of crimes against humanity

state practice: first component of customary international law; the conduct of states must match the behavior that is required by the proposed rule

state responsibility: area of international law that addresses the attribution, wrongfulness, and consequences of legal breaches

Stockholm Declaration: a non-binding document from 1972 that includes general principles about development and the environment

subsidy: "any form of income or price support" provided by a government

superior responsibility: a form of criminal responsibility in which civilian superiors are responsible if they fail to prevent or punish crimes committed by the subordinates under their effective control

tariff: a tax on a foreign good that is imported into a state

territorial sea: sea zone that lies outside of a state's baseline, but over which the state has exclusive jurisdiction; extends up to 12 n.m.

trade liberalization: a set of policies designed to promote the trade of goods and services between states

tragedy of the commons: a type of collaboration problem in which states jointly benefit from preserving a common resource, but each state is tempted to unilaterally deviate to overconsumption of the resource

transboundary harm: a situation in which an act in one state causes or threatens harm to the persons, property, or environment of another state

travaux préparatoires: French for "preparatory work"; the body of official written documents from a treaty's negotiation

treaty: "an international agreement concluded between states in written form and governed by international law, whether embodied in a single instrument or in two or more related instruments and whatever its particular designation"

ultra vires: Latin for "beyond the powers"; an *ultra vires* act exceeds the legal authority given by a state to the individual/body that commits the act

unilateral declaration: a unilateral statement that creates a legal obligation; must be public and demonstrate a state intention to be bound

United Nations: an international organization created in 1945 "to maintain international peace and security"

universal jurisdiction: use of a state's domestic law and institutions to regulate behavior that occurs outside of its domestic territory, does not involve its nationals, and does not have systematic or important effects on itself

universalism: a set of ethical, moral, and political theories that argue that human rights are inherent to mankind and do not vary across social contexts

voluntary export restraint: an agreement under which an exporter voluntarily limits the amount of a good that it sells in a foreign market

voluntary law: the man-made rules to which political leaders have consented, either explicitly or implicitly, via agreements and state practice

war crimes: serious violations of the law of armed conflict that create individual criminal responsibility

Washington Consensus: a set of economic policies promoted by the International Monetary Fund in the 1980s to prevent economic crises in developing states

World Trade Organization: international organization created in 1995 to promote international trade

wrongful: not excused or justified

Index